...d Superstructuralism

Casting a critical eye upon the position described in his previous book, *Superstructuralism*, Richard Harland claims that structuralist and post-structuralist approaches to language are fatally limited by their focus upon single words. Instead he offers the alternative of a syntagmatic approach, arguing that the nature of meaning is radically transformed in the movement from single words to sentences. The effect of combining words grammatically is seen to be more dramatic than any existing theory – European or Anglo-American – has yet recognized. The wide breadth of coverage in the book takes in post-Chomskyan linguistics, deconstruction, Analytic and speech-act views of language. Harland challenges the very foundation of recent language theory, opening up a range of novel options for literary criticism, linguistics and philosophy.

Richard Harland is a lecturer in the Department of English at the University of Wollongong, Australia. His previous books include the highly influential *Superstructuralism: The Philosophy of Structuralism and Poststructuralism* (1987).

Beyond Superstructuralism

The syntagmatic side of language

Richard Harland

London and New York

First published in 1993
by Routledge
11 New Fetter Lane, London EC4P 4EE

Transferred to Digital Printing 2004

Simultaneously published in the USA and Canada
by Routledge Inc
29 West 35th Street, New York, NY 10001

Typeset by Megaron, Cardiff, Wales

British Library Cataloguing in Publication Data
Harland, Richard
Beyond Superstructuralism
I. Title
410. 1

Library of Congress Cataloging in Publication Data
Harland, Richard
Beyond Superstructuralism/Richard Harland.
p. cm.
1. Structural linguistics. I. Title.
P146.H27 1993
149'.96--dc20
92-31425

ISBN 0 415 06358 2
0 415 06359 0 pbk.

Contents

Preface

This book advances a new theory, a syntagmatic theory, of language. On the one hand, syntagmatic theory differs radically from Structuralist and Poststructuralist ways of thinking about language – what one might call the European perspective. On the other hand, it differs no less radically from Logical Atomist, Logical Positivist, Truth-Conditional, Ordinary-Language and Speech-Act ways of thinking about language – what one might call the Anglo-American perspective. Either of these perspectives could provide an 'opposition' against which to define syntagmatic theory. As it is, I have chosen to expound the new theory initially by reaction against Structuralism and Poststructuralism, invoking Anglo-American language philosophies at a later stage.

To react against Structuralism and Poststructuralism is also to react against my previous book, *Superstructuralism*. There, I tried to describe the rationale, the appeal and the reasons for getting excited about Structuralism and Poststructuralism. Nor do I wish to retract any of the positive claims which I made on behalf of that perspective. But even in the Conclusion to *Superstructuralism*, I suggested that it is one thing to generate a vast range of fascinating insights and illuminations; another, to attain the ultimate insight and final illumination to which Structuralists and Poststructuralists have aspired. Indeed, there was always an ulterior motive behind my attempt to capture that perspective: seeing how much it could encompass, I wanted also to see the limits of its encompassing. What I am now proposing is to look beyond those limits, beyond Superstructuralism. In this respect, my previous book was a kind of springboard for this one. And at the same time, I confess, a kind of Trojan horse.

However, this book does not directly depend upon its predecessor. Certainly, a familiarity with the general tenets of Structuralism and Poststructuralism is presupposed – but not a familiarity with the particular presentation of my previous book. Only one major item calls for recapitulation: the term 'Superstructuralism' itself. One of my purposes in writing *Superstructuralism* was to argue that, in spite of their many disagreements and divisions, there is nonetheless an underlying framework of assumption common to Structuralists, Poststructuralists, (European) Semioticians,

Althusserian Marxists, Lacanians, Foucauldians, *et al.* The term 'Superstructuralism' serves as a convenient coinage to bring them all in under a single umbrella.

Starting from Superstructuralism, then, Part I of this book focusses upon what 'the opposition' has failed to take into account – specifically when theorizing about language. In my previous book, I placed the linguistics of Saussure and the language philosophy of Derrida firmly in the centre of the Superstructuralist enterprise. Now I take Saussure and Derrida as my two main points of reaction. When Superstructuralists theorize about language, I claim, they may sometimes talk about the syntagm, but they never really come to grips with it.

Part II moves on to present the new theory. This is the core argument of the book; and Chapter 2 is the core of that core. The leading ideas of syntagmatic theory are essentially very obvious, and I have tried to present them as such. However, their development soon leads into considerable complexities, as Chapter 4 amply demonstrates. It is indeed one of the lessons of syntagmatic theory that language is not so easily mapped out and schematized as many philosophers of language have wished to believe.

In Part III, the Anglo-American perspective comes to the fore. Here I try to show that Anglo-American philosophers of language also fail to reckon with the syntagmatic side of language, albeit in a totally different way. For whereas the Superstructuralists fall short of syntagmatic theory by their focus upon individual words, Anglo-American philosophers overleap syntagmatic theory by their focus upon sentences as *applied to* or *used in* the world. Still, syntagmatic theory does have a philosophical ancestry of its own – though not in any philosophy of language as such. In Chapter 6, I relate the new theory to the tradition of what I call 'I'-philosophy; and in Chapter 7, I draw a number of interesting analogies to the Phenomenology of Brentano, Husserl and Merleau-Ponty.

Part IV turns to relevant developments in the field of linguistics. The encounter with Generative grammar leads to a clarification of the relationship between rules of syntax and syntagmatic processes of meaning, and thence to certain proposals for sorting out the old vexed issues of 'deep structure' and 'the semantic component'. I also attempt to show how syntagmatic theory can usefully absorb the evidence brought forward by the 'natural grammar' movement of recent years – at least, on one possible interpretation of that evidence.

Part V explores an alternative to current ways of thinking about literature. Here I try to demonstrate that twentieth-century literary criticism derives its concept of the 'literary' from the special characteristics of twentieth-century literature; and that the anti-syntagmatic inclinations of Modernist and Post-modernist writers have encouraged New Critics, Structuralist critics and Poststructuralist critics to proclaim anti-syntagmatic principles for literature in general. Against this, I insist that literature can accentuate – and very often has accentuated – the syntagmatic side of language.

Focussing upon hermeneutics and textual interpretation, Part VI carries obvious implications for literary criticism, and follows on very naturally from Part V. However, it differs from Part V and all the other parts of this book both in the close-up detail of its analyses and the unrelieved hostility of its attack. The objects of this attack are binary-polarization technique and deconstruction, the classical interpretative techniques of Structuralism and Poststructuralism respectively. To my mind, these techniques show Superstructuralism at its very worst and weakest. In my previous book, I applauded the many new perceptions achieved under the general practice of looking at the world as signs or text. But it is a very different story when techniques are developed for turning out Superstructuralist results automatically.

As may be deduced from this outline, *Beyond Superstructuralism* covers an enormous amount of ground. My dealings with existing schools of thought are necessarily brief and, some might complain, simplistic. Typically, I am claiming to grasp the essential rationale behind other people's positions. And, in so far as syntagmatic theory bridges between the before-sentence orientation of Superstructuralism and the after-sentence orientation of Anglo-American language philosophy, I can at least claim to be in a favourable situation for such grasping. (Whereas the Superstructuralists and Anglo-American philosophers have consistently failed to understand one another.) But still there is an obvious danger of misrepresentation when I then proceed to criticize on the basis of my own essentializing grasp. My only defence is that I do not expect to drive the reader out of a prior belief by sheer force of rebuttal; rather, my criticisms represent a kind of 'looking back' from the other side. The reader, I hope, will be prepared to entertain syntagmatic theory as a possibility for its own sake – and will then be interested to see what light this new possibility reflects upon existing schools of thought.

There is another closely related complaint which needs to be headed off: that is, the complaint that I have paid insufficient attention to the most recent and sophisticated versions of the positions I criticize. Indeed, there is in this book a persistent habit of harking back to early and original sources – to Saussure, Frege, Russell, Grice, Standard-Theory Generative grammar, Katz and Fodor, the New Critics, Lévi-Strauss, etc. And although I may deal with more recent versions too, it is nonetheless true that I deal with them very much as extensions and appendices. To many, this harking back may look like a waste of time – have not these early sources been superseded long ago? And is it not a cheap way of scoring points, to attack a position in its most primitive, unimproved and admittedly defective versions? But then I am less concerned with playing fair than with understanding how the syntagmatic position diverges from other positions. And for this purpose, the early and original sources are peculiarly revealing, because they show the most fundamental conceptual choices being made. By modification and adjustment, later versions may succeed in obviating some of the problems resulting from those choices; but in the process of modification and adjustment, the choices themselves tend to get taken for granted. To see how radically syntagmatic theory diverges from other positions, we must dig down to the level of roots.

One thing remains to be said. *Beyond Superstructuralism* is not the kind of book that needs to be read continuously from start to finish. Although Part II is crucial on any reading, the other parts are not strongly interdependent, and it is possible to mix and match according to taste. For readers with a Superstructuralist orientation, the most pertinent chapters are Chapters 1, 6, 13, 14 and 15; whereas readers with an Anglo-American orientation will probably find more of interest in Chapters 6, 8, 9 and 12. In short, the book has a core-and-corollaries structure: from the central theory of Part II, the argument leads off in various directions, responding to the challenge of many different thinkers and schools of thought.

The ideas of *Beyond Superstructuralism* have been a long time a-brewing, and it would be impossible to mention all the many friends and colleagues whose views have helped towards the final concoction. However, I have three particular debts of gratitude to record. Firstly, my thanks to Scott Findlay, who has read each chapter as it was completed, and whose invaluable comments have led to many significant revisions and improvements. Secondly, my thanks to the University of Wollongong, for supporting the writing and typing of this book with successive project grants. And last but not least, my thanks to Jonathan Culler, for launching the whole venture by his wonderful response to *Superstructuralism*, when that precursor to the present book was merely a humble Ph.D. thesis.

Part I

The limits of Superstructuralism

1 The limits of Superstructuralism

SAUSSURE'S PARADIGMATIC PREFERENCE

It is ironic that Saussure provides us with a terminology for what he himself fails to take into account. One of the founding distinctions in Saussurean linguistics is the distinction between 'syntagmatic' relations and 'paradigmatic' relations. For Saussure, it is only by the relations between words that language can sustain itself – since words have no positive substance of their own. But although he proclaims the equal importance of both types of relation, his orientation is entirely towards the paradigmatic. Compared to the new discovery of paradigmatic relations, syntagmatic relations seem very obvious and unexciting.

Paradigmatic relations are the relations holding between one word actually selected for utterance and all the other words which could have been selected but were not. The idea here is that what a word is has significance only by opposition to what it is not. (Just as the *on* position of a switch in a computer has significance only by opposition to the *off* position.) So the uttered word *enseignement* ('teaching') depends for its meaning upon invisible and unuttered semantic neighbours like *éducation* ('education') and *apprentissage* ('apprenticeship'), or *armement* ('armament') and *changement* ('amendment'), etc.[1] In contrast to the horizontal sequence of words uttered one after another, this dependence is as if vertical: the absent words are coeval and simultaneous with the present word.

What's more, these unuttered words are also unthought, at least in the mind of the individual language-user. The dependence of a present word upon absent words is also the dependence of *parole* upon *langue*; and *langue* is a total social system of differentiations, existing before the individual language-user and outside of the language-user's consciousness. Admittedly, Saussure sometimes lapses into a more psychologistic vein, as when he talks of bringing forth absent words by principles of mental association [2] But the overall thrust of his ideas points elsewhere, and subsequent linguists in the Structuralist tradition have discarded all such talk. (They have also substituted the term 'paradigmatic' for Saussure's original term 'associative' – in which substitution I have tacitly followed them.) The kind of vertical dependence to which Saussure draws attention is ultimately logical, not psychological.[3]

There is a certain way of thinking that goes with paradigmatic relations. When we try to understand the relations between *enseignement* and *éducation*, or *enseignement* and *changement*, we immediately find ourselves thinking in terms of likeness and contrast. In some respects, *enseignement* is similar to *éducation*, in other respects different. An opposition is not just any sort of difference, but a difference mounted upon a similarity. Such a way of thinking is appropriate enough when dealing with a taxonomically organized system. But it is not appropriate when dealing with syntagmatic relations.

Syntagmatic relations are the relations holding across the horizontal sequence of words uttered one after another. In the sentence 'If the weather is fine, we will go out', it is obvious that 'the' relates in some way to 'weather', 'weather' to 'is', and 'is' to 'fine'. It is also obvious that these relations are actually thought and present in the minds of utterer and receiver(s). In fact, syntagmatic relations are radically different to paradigmatic relations – not merely as two distinct dimensions of relating, but as two distinct types of relation. Saussure himself recognizes as much when he remarks that they 'correspond to two forms of our mental activity, both indispensable to the life of language'.[4]

But in spite of this recognition, Saussure still tries to bring syntagmatic relations in under the same conceptual framework as paradigmatic relations. 'In the syntagm', he argues, 'a term acquires its value only because it stands in opposition to everything that precedes or follows it, or to both.'[5] But what is the opposition between 'the' and 'weather', between 'weather' and 'is', between 'is' and 'fine'? Such terms are simply different, with no common scale between them. There is not even enough likeness to mount an opposition upon. It may well be true that a term in the syntagm acquires its value only in relation to other terms preceding and following it – I shall be making a claim of this kind myself in Chapter 2. But the nature of syntagmatic relations will never appear to eyes that are looking to perceive likenesses and contrasts.

It is hardly surprising, then, that Saussure never gets around to demonstrating exactly how oppositions work within the syntagm. In fact, his way of dealing with syntagmatic relations is a way of getting rid of them – or rather, two ways of getting rid of them. On the one hand, he relegates them to *parole*; stringing words together in sentences is viewed as a particular, occasional and unpredictable affair. The sentence, he says, 'belongs to speaking, not to language'; and 'speaking is characterized by freedom of combinations'.[6] That is, the choice of what to string together is determined not by language but by personal and psychological factors. Saussure even seems to imply that the sequence of words is merely the sequence of concepts arising in the utterer's mind. As elsewhere, he shows a curious blindness towards the kinds of necessity governing words as parts of speech. By insisting that *langue* and not *parole* is the proper province of linguistic study, he effectively banishes consideration of syntagmatic relations in ordinary sentences.

On the other hand, he is prepared to consider a special type of syntagm which does have its place in *langue*. This is the special type of syntagm where habitual sequences of words have solidified into single blocks. We understand compounds and stock phrases such as 'head-waiter' and 'bury-the-hatchet' all in one go, without ever thinking through their separate components.[7] These single blocks are virtually equivalent to single words, and, like single words, can enter into paradigmatic relations with all the other semantic units in *langue*. But the syntagmatic relations within the blocks are no longer important. When 'head' and 'waiter' were separate components, syntagmatic relations would have been needed to combine them. But now that the combination has become fixed, the real syntagmatic business is over and done with.

It is true that things have changed since Saussure's time. But what Saussure left out of language has never been put back in. The structures which Structuralists pursue are still structures of likeness and contrast, differences played against similarities. And, as we shall see, even Poststructuralists still concentrate upon the vertical dimension of language to the exclusion of the horizontal. The polarization of paradigmatic and syntagmatic continues to work consistently in the interests of one term over the other. Which is, of course, exactly the hidden way of working that Derrida uncovers in so many polarizations other than this one.

BARTHES AND METONYMY

As Structuralism developed, the pursuit of structures of likeness and contrast led from linguistics to anthropology to general semiotics. For there are many kinds of cultural systems where items may be seen as defined by mutual opposition. Thus Barthes, in *Elements of Semiology*, proposes comparing and contrasting the different forms of headgear that women wear (toque or bonnet or hood, etc.); comparing and contrasting the different kinds of entrée on a menu; comparing and contrasting the different styles possible for a single article of furniture.[8] Fashions, foods, furniture, films, architecture, table etiquette – all can be made to respond to the paradigmatic way of thinking.

At the same time, though, semioticians also like to talk of syntagmatic relations amongst cultural phenomena. When Barthes proposes the paradigmatic study of different forms of headgear, he also proposes the syntagmatic study of neighbouring items of clothing – 'juxtaposition in the same type of dress of different elements: skirt–blouse–jacket'; when he proposes the paradigmatic study of different kinds of entrée, he also proposes the syntagmatic study of the 'real sequence of dishes chosen during a meal'; when he proposes the paradigmatic study of possible styles for a single article of furniture, he also proposes the syntagmatic study of the 'juxtaposition of the different pieces of furniture in the same space: bed–wardrobe–table, etc.'.[9] However, these relations are not syntagmatic as relations in language are syntagmatic.

In fact, the neighbouring items that Barthes proposes to study are related by little more than contiguity. The skirt is next to the blouse, the bed is alongside the wardrobe. Clearly, Barthes considers such 'juxtaposition' sufficient to justify the term 'syntagmatic'. But it is not sufficient to justify the term 'syntagmatic' in language, as we can see by translating Barthes' examples into actual strings of words:

> Skirt jacket blouse.
> Hors d'œuvre soup fish entrée main course dessert.
> Wardrobe bed bedside table.

These strings of words do not compose sentences, or anything like sentences. The kind of combination we observe in 'Martha wore her grey skirt to the movies' is entirely absent here.

Of course, this may appear a trivially obvious demonstration. Barthes never supposed that an outfit of clothes was directly equivalent to the string of words in a sentence.[10] But although the demonstration is obvious, it is far from trivial. A skirt, jacket and blouse can not be syntagmatically related for the very same reason that the words 'skirt', 'jacket' and 'blouse' cannot be syntagmatically related: because these items all belong to the same category of being, as entities or as nouns. In such cases, no real interdependence is possible: a noun does not need the support of another noun, and a skirt can exist quite independently of a jacket or blouse. The full implications of this claim will be worked out in Chapter 2.

In fact, when we try to consider the relation that exists between a specific skirt, jacket and blouse, we inevitably fall back upon the play of likenesses and contrasts. The colour of the blouse matches the colour of the jacket, or contrasts against the colour of the jacket, or takes up a similar colour in a different shade . . . How else can we think the juxtaposition? But now we are back with the same kind of relations that appear under a paradigmatic perspective. The contiguity between the garments has served to pick out the items to be related; but it does not condition the relations themselves. So far as the relations themselves are concerned, we could find the same likenesses and contrasts between a jacket modelled in Paris and a blouse displayed in a shop in Buenos Aires.

Admittedly, there may be a reason behind the likenesses and contrasts of a particular person's particular outfit. That is, the blouse might have been deliberately chosen to set off the jacket, and the jacket might have been deliberately chosen to colour-coordinate with the skirt. We can explain why the outfit exists in just this form by referring to a mind which motivates just these relations. But there is no such motivation in the case of sentences. The component parts of 'Martha wore her grey skirt to the movies' are not deliberately chosen – at least, not in the first place – for the sake of likenesses and contrasts. The word 'movies' is not introduced in order to harmonize with the word 'Martha' – even though both are disyllabic and both begin with an 'm'. In language, in the syntagm, there are more pressing concerns to worry about.

To drive home the distinction between Barthes' so-called syntagmatic relations and the true syntagmatic relations of language, we need a distinction of terminology. Happily, there is an alternative term available for what Barthes proposes to study: 'metonymic relations'. The term 'metonymy' comes from Roman Jakobson, and is common in Superstructuralist writings generally. By and large, Superstructuralists talk almost in the same breath of 'metonymic' and 'syntagmatic' relations, recognizing no real difference of principle.[11] But the distinction for which I have argued can be expressed very effectively if we keep the two terms separate. I suggest that we apply the term 'metonymic' to relations of contiguity and juxtaposition such as may occur in a great many cultural systems, whilst reserving the term 'syntagmatic' for the special relations within sentences. As regards the special relations within sentences, contiguity is only the merest beginning of the story.

DERRIDA CLOSES THE BOOK

Whereas general semiotics represents an extension of the Saussurean theory of language, Poststructuralism represents a new twist in the theory of language itself. And yet not so totally new as may at first appear. The Poststructuralist theory still looks from the word actually uttered to the unuttered words on which it depends. The main innovation is that the paradigmatic relations between these words are now set in motion: the single word is no longer held in by the pressure of its invisible coevals, but rather explodes outwards across them. But this innovation will not concern us here.[12]

What concerns us is the continuing focus upon single words, horizontally isolated from their neighbours. When Poststructuralists argue for a subversive working as against a conventional working of language, the syntagm is one aspect of the conventional working which comes under attack. The nature of the attack is plainly visible in Deleuze and Guattari's essay 'Rhizome', where the authors consider the implications of Generative grammar from a Poststructuralist point of view. What they most dislike is that the grammarians' branching tree diagrams are hierarchical. That is, the symbol 'S' ('generate a sentence') dominates over the symbols representing individual words. For Deleuze and Guattari, this is tantamount to political tyranny: 'the categorical symbol S set over all sentences . . . is first of all a power marker'.[13] From a Poststructuralist point of view, the Generative grammarians are seeking to impose the authority of the sentence and deny individual words their rights and freedoms.

Derrida too is in favour of the rights and freedoms of individual words. His opposition to the syntagm is directed specifically against the principle of the book. The principle of the book is here the principle of a totality to which the smaller units of language are hierarchically subordinated. (The sentence is thus a kind of miniature realization of the book.) Derrida challenges this principle: 'what is first of all put in question is the unity of the book and the unity "book" considered as a perfect totality'.[14] He proposes instead a principle of the text. Writing, as Derrida conceives it, represents 'on the one hand the closure of the book, and on the other the opening of the text'.[15]

Yet Derrida does not spend much time arguing for the text as against the book. He is more concerned to argue for writing as against the voice. It is this latter argument which enables him to free words from their traditional connection to an originating mind. For whereas words as voiced may at least appear to be backed up by the presence of their speaker, words as written are quite clearly cut off and orphaned from any such authority.[16] By proclaiming writing as the true condition of language, Derrida accomplishes his main goal, which is to prove the independence of words *from their source*. He seems to assume that the independence of words *from one another* follows almost automatically.

However, the two kinds of independence are really very different. The principle of the book surely associates far more readily with the principle of writing than with the principle of the voice. It is not just that books are, as a matter of fact, written, but that the very large argumentative or narrative coherences which we expect in books are scarcely to be expected in 'live speech'. A unified totality on this sort of scale is far easier to achieve when writing than when speaking.

Indeed, the independence of words from one another might well be seen as inversely proportional to the independence of words from their source. It is in speech that we are most likely to find individual words existing all by themselves – 'Run!' 'You!' 'A boat?' 'Certainly!' – without the support of sentences. In writing, on the other hand, words are almost always combined into sentences. It is as though the absence of a speaker in a real-world context makes it all the more necessary for words to exist in the context of other words.

Derrida, so far as I can see, produces only one argument to justify his assertion that 'the idea of the book, which always refers to a natural totality, is profoundly alien to the sense of writing'.[17] This is the argument of *spacing*. According to Derrida, spacing is 'pause, blank, punctuation, interval in general, etc.'.[18] Following an idea of Mallarmé's, he gives enormous importance to the gaps of whiteness that separate written words from their neighbours on the page. Such spacing 'separates [the written sign] from other elements of the internal contextual chain'; it creates 'horizontal discontinuity'.[19] Indeed, according to Derrida, reading horizontally across the gaps involves a recurrent obliteration of consciousness. 'Spacing as writing is the becoming-absent and becoming-unconscious of the subject.'[20] Between each word, the reader drops into nothingness, into oblivion, into a kind of death.

It should be noted that this argument is only a very incidental one for Derrida. The quotations given above are mere glimpses: Derrida no sooner mentions spacing within the internal contextual chain than he immediately flies off into further applications of the concept in other (non-horizontal) dimensions. Still, if one accepts the argument, it fits the bill perfectly. For the spacing that occurs in writing does not occur in speech. In speech, the words are not separated by any audible gap; according to Jakobson, whom Derrida quotes, 'the stream of oral speech' is 'physically continuous'.[21] Of course, this is a superficial coherence from Derrida's point of view; once again, speech masks the true state of language which writing reveals. But if one accepts Derrida's argument, then it follows that both speech and the book belong on the opposite side of the fence to writing. However, there is no reason to accept Derrida's argument. Does anyone really believe that we drop into oblivion when passing across the gaps of whiteness between the words? Who has ever experienced this recurrent obliteration of consciousness? When has it ever been observed experimentally? Derrida's argument may sound plausible in the abstract, but there is no practical evidence for it whatsoever.

The trouble is that Derrida is not really arguing against the principle of the book but against something much less significant. Just as Barthes reduces the syntagm to mere contiguity, so Derrida reduces it to mere continuity. In spite of his references to 'totality' and 'unity', his conception never seems to rise above the idea of words in a line. 'The end of linear writing is indeed the end of the book.'[22] Of course, if we think in terms of a line of ink or print perceived successively from left to right across the page, then any gaps in the ink or print will appear like absolute holes and voids of perception. But this only proves the inadequacy of such a way of thinking. As will be shown in Chapter 3, the syntagm does not properly exist in linear terms at all. When Derrida defeats this 'rather precious *continuist* prejudice', he defeats no more than a straw opponent.[23]

In the end, Derrida is in the same position as Saussure and Barthes, the same position as the Superstructuralists in general. Although Saussure and Barthes would like to include the syntagm in their account, and Derrida would like to exclude it, yet they can none of them really get to grips with it. It is a classic case of what the Superstructuralists themselves analyse so well in the discourse of other people. Inhabiting a particular paradigmatic way of thinking, they can take in only as much as their way of thinking makes thinkable. Their very approach sets the agenda. And when language comes up on that agenda, the items for discussion are single words, not sentences. To understand how syntagmatic relations work, we must start out from a totally different conceptual framework.

Part II

A theory of the syntagm

2 How words work together

THE CONCEPTUAL CUT OF GRAMMATICAL CATEGORY

Along the horizontal dimension of language, the obvious differences are the differences between different parts of speech. Nouns, verbs, adjectives, adverbs, determiners, prepositions: such categories are different beyond any system of likenesses and contrasts. Yet they are clearly involved in the way that words relate horizontally to one another. To understand the nature of their involvement is the goal of syntagmatic theory.

At first sight, this may not look like a very ambitious goal. Compared to those relations of meaning in which Superstructuralists deal, grammatical relations may seem somewhat incidental to the main business of language. We are not in the habit of placing any great importance upon parts of speech. No doubt every word has to have a grammatical role; there is no known human language in which words are not grammatically categorized. But we tend to think of such categories as tacked on and secondary – certainly not on a par with a word's meaning.

According to syntagmatic theory, however, grammatical category and meaning are profoundly interdependent. To talk of how a word has meaning, one must also talk of its function as a part of speech. Consider the word 'dog'. We cannot learn and know all the cases to which the word ever has applied or ever will apply in the world, yet we can manage to apply the word for ourselves when appropriate cases come within our experience. Some kind of concept seems to be deployed. But to say that the meaning of a word is a concept is to say nothing very much at all. What form does this concept take? and how do we have it in mind?

One thing is clear: the meaning of the word 'dog' does not exist as any sort of image in the mind. Although the word applies to concrete particulars, the concept is not particular or concrete in the manner of an image. Any image necessarily presents a full case: if we picture a dog, it must be a dog of some determinate size and colour, engaged in jumping or sitting or lying down or whatever. But an image of a big black Dobermann jumping is not going to be of much use when we want to find the appropriate word for a small grey poodle lying down. What's needed is a concept somehow shorn of particulars, without the fullness of the real full case.

Of course, this is all very old hat. Philosophers have been seeking to answer these perplexities for over two thousand years. But almost invariably, they have produced their answers without reference to the grammatical categories of the words under consideration. The conjunction of meaning with part of speech has been regarded as a mere accidental cohabitation under the same roof. No one seems to have been particularly surprised about it. No one seems to have suspected that the two sides of a word might have a bearing on each other – might even actually depend upon each other.

Grammatical categories, I suggest, are involved in the conceptual cut of a word's meaning. Far from being merely tacked on, they actually help to divide the world up for meaning in the first place. For it is not enough to divide the world up into entities or portions, as the old noun-dominated, thing-dominated view would have it. Entities and portions are only ever particular parts, and particular parts will never help us to conceptualize the types that are needed for word-meaning. Applying words is not like breaking up a block of cheese into chunks. It is like conceptualizing the cheese under different perspectives, like taking two-dimensional cross-sections across a three-dimensional reality. And what we conceptualize under our noun-perspective or verb-perspective or adjective-perspective is as different as what we conceptualize when we look at the cheese in terms of appearance or in terms of taste or in terms of nourishment. In short, words do not embody *parts*, but *moments* or *aspects* of experience.

Consider again the word 'dog'. The problem is that the relevant concept must not involve any particular size or colour or doing. But then 'dog' is a noun – whereas size and colour are indicated by adjectives like 'small' and 'big', 'grey' and 'black'. And doings are indicated by verbs like 'jumps' and 'sits' and 'lies down'. The noun-perspective disregards content that can be taken care of under the adjective-perspective and verb-perspective. When we look to apply an appropriate noun to a new case, we automatically ignore variations along other conceptual dimensions. The noun-perspective hollows out the fullness of the real full case – as does the adjective-perspective, as does the verb-perspective, each in its own different way.

Grammatical categories are thus integral to the making of meaning, even though they have no kind of meaning in themselves. Meaning is made by an interaction between us and the world: we have to do something to the world in order to get meaning out of it. And one fundamental thing that we do is to impose noun-perspective, adjective-perspective, verb-perspective. The self-same portion of world may be simultaneously 'black' and 'dog' and 'jumps', all together in a single experience. The world itself offers no natural dividing-lines as a basis for distinctions here. The distinctions derive from our ability to attend to the self-same portion of world in different ways. Different grammatical categories are different modes of attention.

Of course, a mode of attention does not remove or eliminate those aspects which are not attended to. The conceptual cut of the noun does not enable us to think some miraculous concept where dogs have no colour and are engaged in no activity (not even standing still!). Rather, our attention holds down one aspect, while other aspects are free to vary. Our concept for the word 'dog' allows dogs to be grey or black or brown or white – any colour within a range of possible colours. (And even the range of possible colours is not so limited as one might suppose; but see the 'On the frontiers' section of this chapter below, and the 'Return of *parole*' section of Chapter 3.) The determination of colour is postponed, left open-ended.

However, this open-endedness also renders the meanings of single words peculiarly elusive. The act of attention which holds down one aspect under a noun-perspective is inherently unstable; there is no postponing other aspects in any permanent way. It is like skating on thin ice, which only supports us so long as we keep moving. We cannot inspect the meaning of the word 'dog' as we can inspect an actual dog, or even as we can study a mental image of a dog. The concept simply refuses to stay steady before the mind's eye. Try to think the meaning of the word 'dog' all by itself, out of the blue. What happens? Do we not find ourselves immediately chasing vanishing phantoms down empty corridors? We may have countless dog-memories and dog-associations, but nothing that will stand firm and central in the place required. The meaning falls away on all sides, opening up and opening out interminably. A most unsatisfactory state of affairs, perhaps: but it is exactly what ought to be expected on the basis of the theory I have been advancing. For an aspect under a noun- or verb- or adjective-perspective is indeed not strictly thinkable on its own. To fix the meaning of a single word in the manner of a dictionary definition or a geometrical diagram would be to falsify the real state of affairs.

Still I have not told the whole story. I have described the imposition of grammatical categories as one fundamental form of imposition which enables us to get meaning out of the world. But clearly there must be other forms of imposition too – if only to distinguish the different ranges of 'dog', 'cat', 'tree', and all the other nouns in the language. However, I shall pursue the issue no further here; and I shall not claim to have wholly answered the traditional philosopher's question of how a single word has meaning. It is enough to have shown how deeply grammatical category is involved in such meaning, involved in the very slice and conceptual cut of such meaning. For now it becomes possible to see how the unstable and precarious meanings of single words are redeemed when words come together syntagmatically.

COMPLEMENTARITY, SYNTHESIS, PROJECTION

When Derrida considers language unsyntagmatically, he reduces words to a condition of ultimate isolation. When he lets meaning spread out around a word like *supplément* or *hymen*, his meditation is akin to the kind of meditation which might be inspired by the word 'ETERNITY' painted up on a rock, a single word in the middle of nowhere. But such a condition is abnormal and leads to an abnormal form of signifying. To deprive a word of all context is to deprive it of the environment that it needs to survive.

ON THE FRONTIERS

When we consider the movement from old meaning to new meaning, the most illuminating syntagmatic combinations are those where the distance from old to new meaning is at a maximum. Such combinations bring together words that are not usually brought together, even words that seem at first glance impossible to bring together. Our previous memories and associations for the word 'dog' will presumably include the action of jumping, and will certainly not preclude the action of jumping out at children in the park. But what happens when we are faced with a sentence like 'A purple dog was sitting at the table serving tea'?

Modern language theorists have typically refused to deal with exceptional syntagmatic combinations. Umberto Eco, a Structuralist and a semiotician, claims that 'the pencil sings' and 'this cat is four feet long' are not proper sentences.[2] According to Eco, the culturally-conventional meaning of the word 'cat' permits only a restricted variation of length, and the word 'pencil' is culturally located under an inanimate categorization quite incompatible with the animate categorization of the word 'sings'. Eco would banish these sentences outside of ordinary language altogether.

It is not difficult to understand Eco's motives. He is trying to maintain a certain conception of the lexicon of a language, a conception which derives ultimately from the Saussurean model of *langue*. In *langue*, the meaning of any individual word depends upon the boundaries which differentiate it from other words.[3] Thus, under the larger category of *feline*, the meaning of the word 'cat' exists by opposition to the meanings of 'panther', 'lion', 'tiger', etc. But clearly one of the crucial criteria for this opposition is the criterion of size. If cats are allowed to extend to four feet in length, the criterion vanishes. Similarly if cats are allowed to dance the fandango, or to be constituted of glass – what boundary then separates them from human beings, or from inanimate objects? Eco's way of thinking cannot permit such infractions of the system.

But so much the worse for Eco's way of thinking. For 'this cat is four feet long' and 'the pencil sings' are perfectly comprehensible sentences. The fact that we have never previously contemplated the possibility of a four-foot-long cat does not in the least prevent us from giving a meaning to a combination of 'cat' and 'four feet long'. Any theory which denies meaning to these sentences is simply wrong.

Nor should we accept any attempt to transfer exceptional syntagmatic combinations into some separate language. Such is Eco's gambit when he claims, elsewhere, that fairy-tales belong to a 'semantically revised universe' in which the meaning of words have undergone 'a complete semantic restructuring'.[4] This way of shuffling aside awkward evidence is altogether too convenient. Of course the meanings of 'the pencil sings' and 'this cat is four feet long' are most likely to occur in fantasy fiction. (At present, that is: though we would surely have no difficulty in understanding a newspaper headline which announced the breeding of a four foot long cat in some scientific laboratory.) But this does not mean that we prepare ourselves for some totally different form of language when we open up a book of fantasy fiction. We may not even know in advance the nature of the book that we are opening up. To suppose that a fairy-tale universe creates the possibility of combining such words as 'pencil' and 'sings' is to put the cart before the horse. It is precisely by combining such words as 'pencil' and 'sings' that we realize we are in a fairy-tale universe.

So what goes wrong with Eco's way of thinking? The problem lies not primarily in his Saussurean model of the lexicon (though I shall have occasion to take issue with that model in the next chapter), but in his equally Saussurean tendency to overestimate the importance of the lexicon in language. As Eco sees it, the meanings of words are determined in the lexicon once and for all. If we can utter and understand 'this cat is four feet long', then the possibility of being four feet long must be somehow written back into the meaning of 'cat' as defined in the lexicon. In which case, the definition will have to forego the apparently obvious criterion for cats as felines that must be of relatively small size.

The problem disappears as soon as we recognize a second level, the syntagmatic level, of meaning in language. For as we have seen, the process of synthesis can change the meanings of single words internally. We don't need to know that cats can be four feet long in order to understand 'this cat is four feet long'. All our previous cat-memories and cat-associations may involve felines of perfectly normal dimensions. It is only the sentence itself which creates for this specific occasion a new and exceptional length of cat. The past meaning of the single word is effectively overridden by the influence of words together. Under the power of syntagmatic synthesis, the meaning of a single word can be shifted around to a truly remarkable degree.

Hence the difficulty of inventing sentences which are grammatically coherent yet absolutely meaningless. Chomsky's famous example succeeds as well as any: 'Colourless green ideas sleep furiously.'[5] But it is only by multiplying exceptional combinations on top of one another that Chomsky succeeds. Taken individually, these combinations are by no means wholly beyond redemption. There are 'ideas' which 'sleep' in Alexander Pope's *Dunciad*; while Andrew Marvell manages something very much like a 'green idea' in his 'green Thought in a green Shade'.[6] And it is surely not difficult to come up with contexts where 'sleeping furiously' becomes a perfectly intelligible phrase. As for 'colourless green', I can think of a certain twilight effect when dark rippling water is haunted by pinpricks of prismatic red, blue and green – a sort of colour that the eye creates out of colourlessness. Admittedly these are 'poetic' applications, straining at the frontiers of language. Yet it is the frontiers of ordinary language which they are straining at. They are still not written in some separate 'semantically revised' language.

Only syntagmatic theory can explain what happens on the frontiers of language. By way of a fresh example, consider the phrase 'billion-ton pebble' – a phrase I have seen used to describe Ayer's Rock in a tourist brochure. In this case, the meaning of 'billion-ton' runs clean against our ordinary understanding of the meaning of 'pebble'. When we synthesize 'big' and 'dog', we merely cut down on the ordinary range of possible dog-sizes. But here we must do more than merely cut down on the ordinary range of possible weights for pebbles. Here we must jettison the ordinary range altogether, totally disregarding the crucial role of weight in the lexical definition of the word 'pebble'. We must subtract from the very heart of the meaning. All that we can take from the word 'pebble' is the sense of a stone of a certain characteristic shape. Only in that very special and off-centre sense is the word 'pebble' capable of combining with the words 'billion-ton'.

Or consider an example from the writings of Derrida: 'primordial supplementation'.[7] This is a conceptual paradox, perhaps even more refractory than our previous concrete examples. In terms of their past meanings, 'primordial' and 'supplementation' simply cancel one another out. Yet a mutual meaning can still be made to pass through. We make it pass through by finding a way to understand 'primordial' as no longer straightforwardly primordial (or primary), and a way to understand 'supplementation' as no longer straightforwardly supplementary (or secondary). Of course, a meaning so finely threaded is a meaning of a peculiarly thin and tenuous kind, a mere glimpse of a meaning. The intersection of 'primordial' with 'supplementation', unlike the intersection of 'big' with 'dog', is very narrow and hard to find. Yet we do manage to find it nonetheless.*

Such a case demonstrates the immense force for unity set up by complementary parts of speech. We are compelled to struggle towards some sort of overall combined meaning almost in spite of the content of the words. If we were merely contemplating the idea of primordial-ness and the idea of supplementary-ness, we should never guess that an overall combined meaning could exist. But the grammar requires us to look for a whole quite over and above the evidence of the parts. We assume the existence of the whole before we ever discover it. Which is also to say that the interpretation of syntagmatic meaning proceeds from the top down as well as from the bottom up.

This is a highly paradoxical state of affairs – but one long recognized in the field of hermeneutics. The traditional problem of the 'hermeneutic circle' is that the meanings of individual words depend upon a surrounding context, while the context comes into being only as a result of combining the meanings of individual words – so how can interpretation ever begin? The circle turns

* Derrida's own actual linguistic practice here provides an ironic counterpoint to his anti-syntagmatic theory of language. In fact, he relies very heavily upon the power of the syntagm to propel us beyond past meanings. His writings are full of such unusual combinations as 'a *sameness* which is not *identical*' and 'the graphic image is not seen; and the acoustic image is not heard'.[8] Of course, he would like us to believe that the paradoxes of his philosophy are achieved within single words, by punning and ambiguity and neologism. When describing the manifold implications of the 'a' in *différance*, for example, he suggests that '*différance* refers to this whole complex of meanings not only when it is supported by a language or interpretative context . . . but it already does so somehow of itself.'[9] However, this is mere wishful thinking. No reader would ever grasp the meanings that Derrida gives to *différance* if the word were presented just by itself. It works as he wants it to work only after its meanings have been explained by words in combination, by the whole sentences of an 'interpretative context'.

particularly vicious with exceptional syntagmatic combinations. In such cases, it is obvious that the interpreter can never get the meaning of one word finalized before going on to the next. There is no possibility of processing the verbal evidence with regular step-by-step or stage-by-stage procedures. Rather, the interpreter must keep the evidence of the parts and the assumption of the whole all up in the air together, juggling between them until everything can be made to slot home simultaneously. This is the art of creative hypothesis, of leaping ahead to hunches and checking back afterwards against the data. In the terminology of C. S. Peirce, it is the art of *abduction* (as distinct from *induction* or *deduction*.).[10]

Exceptional syntagmatic combinations are revealing in another way too. With ordinary combinations, the syntagmatic leap is so rapid as to be subliminal. But with exceptional syntagmatic combinations, there is a momentary delay in getting the words to combine, and this delay gives us the chance to catch ourselves (with a little introspection) in the act of casting around for new syntheses, experimenting with unfamiliar projections. That is, we can actually become aware of trying out possible senses of the words together, trying to get a meaning to fall into place across all of them at once. And when a meaning finally does fall into place, we may well experience a kind of 'click' – the 'click' of successful realization.

Exceptional syntagmatic combinations thus possess a special importance for syntagmatic theory. Certainly, phrases like 'primordial supplementation' and 'billion-ton pebble' are aberrations; and it is true that aberrations can often be discounted as special cases, postponed for later consideration. Such has been the general attitude taken by both Superstructuralists and Anglo-American philosophers of language towards exceptional syntagmatic combinations. But it is also true that an aberration may sometimes be the crack which lets us see through to a deeper truth. The history of science is full of examples where seemingly peripheral phenomena have turned out to be absolutely crucial. (Thus a tiny oddity in the rotation of a single planet undoes the Newtonian system, and opens the way for the Einsteinian.) I suggest that exceptional syntagmatic combinations are aberrations of this latter kind; and theorists of language ignore them at their peril.

3 Saussure and Derrida revisited

THE RETURN OF *PAROLE*

The theory of the syntagm casts a whole new light upon the role of *parole*. Saussure's focus is all upon *langue*, upon the socially shared system that underlies particular utterances. On Saussure's view, particular utterances are little more than the droppings of *langue* – as though speaking a sentence were merely a matter of selecting a small number of verbal items out of a very large catalogue. The social and conventional side of language dominates until it becomes difficult to see how one person can ever communicate something that another person does not already share. But now we can recognize that *parole* has a power of its own. Certainly, the meaning of each single word that goes into an utterance is predetermined by the socially shared system – in which respect, *langue* is larger than *parole*. But in an utterance, the meaning of each single word is itself subjected to the demands of combination with other neighbouring words – and in this respect, *parole* is larger than *langue*. *Parole* has the power of the syntagm.

This power appears most strikingly in exceptional syntagmatic combinations. In the case of an ordinary combination like 'big dog', the power of the syntagm cuts down upon the normal range of meaning socially instituted for the word 'dog' in *langue*. But in the case of 'billion-ton pebble', the power of the syntagm actually pushes 'pebble' out beyond the normal range of its meaning altogether. We can understand such combinations only by giving special attention to some factor of meaning at the expense of others.

Still, this is not to suggest that *parole* ever simply defeats *langue*. The two forms of determination are not alternatives and do not compete upon the same field. There is no source of meaning other than the socially instituted meanings of single words; and no particular utterance can simply leave that source behind. The power of the syntagm does not allow us to set up totally new meanings in *parole*, to give 'primordial' the meaning of 'four feet long', or 'pebble' the meaning of 'cat'. The power of the syntagm is essentially a secondary power: a power to wrench and warp. But on its own field, that power is irresistible.

If *langue* is not all-powerful to the extent that Saussure supposes, then its domination of our thinking is also not a threat to the extent that post-

Saussurean Superstructuralists fear. There is no need for that obsessive Superstructuralist habit of problematizing the meanings of words, eternally seeking to become aware of the restrictions which language imposes upon us. No doubt this move of philosophical self-consciousness is often illuminating. But it is not *necessary*. For we can wrench a word's meaning according to our needs without ever setting ourselves consciously outside or against ordinary language. We can wrench a word's meaning off-centre simply by applying another power which language itself makes available to us.

The possibility of pushing a meaning off-centre is inexplicable on a Saussurean model. For that model allows a word to have meaning only by virtue of the boundaries which separate it from other words: the centre of its meaning is mere emptiness. There can be no flexibility of meaning here, not even in *parole*. Such rigidity is inevitable if we accept the Saussurean view that reality is essentially continuous, and can be classified into separate meanings only by the imposition of arbitrary dividing-lines. If the world offers no natural 'lumpishness' for our words to latch onto, then it is only by artificial dividing-lines that meanings can be prevented from running incontinently into one another. (The Poststructuralists *encourage* incontinence, of course; but they still presuppose the rigid boundaries of an established language-system – precisely in order to transgress them.)

I have already argued against the Saussurean view in *Superstructuralism*.[11] In relation to 'run' and 'walk', for instance, I suggested that these two words do not merely impose an arbitrary dividing-line upon a natural continuum, an arbitrary dividing-line between faster and slower modes of locomotion. True, the distinction between 'run' and 'walk' relates to a difference in speed; but it also relates to a difference in the way that the legs stiffen and bend and make contact with the ground. The arrangement of our bones and muscles is such as to function most efficiently in either a walking action or a running action – rather than anything in between. A certain operation of the limbs *hangs together* with a certain speed of locomotion. Such natural clusterings of features are what our words latch onto.

Similarly with the words 'mountain' and 'hill'. If mountains and hills were distinguished only by their relative altitudes, then it would certainly have to be admitted that Nature has no inclination to produce high or low landforms, rather than anything in between. But the word 'mountain' also typically indicates a peaked shape, while the word 'hill' indicates a more smooth and rounded shape. And the most common cause of a peaked shape is that a landform has been eroded by the gouging action of ice, rather than by the gentle action of water. Since erosion by ice naturally takes place at higher, colder altitudes, it follows that a high landform will tend to be peaked, and a low landform will tend to be rounded. Of course, the world presents many cases which do not fit neatly under these clusterings. But as long as there is a tendency for certain features to hang together, we can justify our classifications by reference to the world's own 'lumpishness'.

Such clusterings of features in the world translate into clusterings of factors in meaning. The normal range of meaning for the word 'mountain' is where the factor of peaked shape overlaps with the factor of high altitude; the normal range for (one sense of) the word 'run' is where the factor of speedy locomotion overlaps with the factor of both feet lifting momentarily off the ground together. (Of course, these are not complete lists of factors, but they will suffice for the purposes of demonstration.) Such areas of overlap give content to the meaning of a word, without ever converging to some single absolute central point – some optimum ideal manner of running, or some perfect Platonic Idea of Mountain. But at the same time, such areas also do not call for absolute circumscribing boundaries. Uncommon and occasional usages are still able to spread out around the normal range of a word's meaning. We may think of a word's meaning as a combination of umbra and penumbra: an area of total shadow fading off into a surround of partial shadow.

As for the way in which uncommon and occasional usages follow out certain factors of meaning at the expense of others – this too is explicable on the model proposed. No need for the word's whole meaning to shift: the uncommon and occasional usages merely move outside the area of total overlap. (In similar fashion, the penumbra of a shadow occurs where the object blocks off some rays from the light source, but not others.) So we might apply the word 'run' to a case of running on the spot – following out the factor of both feet lifting momentarily off the ground together, whilst entirely ignoring the factor of locomotion. Or we might apply the word 'mountain' to a miniature mountain in a sculpted artificial landscape – following out the factor of peaked shape, whilst entirely ignoring the factor of altitude. There are no inalienable factors which can never be set aside from a word's meaning, no quintessential defining properties. In this respect, a word's meaning is amazingly flexible. But it is still not indeterminate – because only *some* factors of meaning can be set aside on any given occasion. We cannot apply the word 'mountain' to something which is neither high, nor peaked, nor possessed of any other property from the normal range of the word's meaning.*

Admittedly, the argument I have been developing is more relevant to nouns or verbs than to adjectives. For adjectives do tend to work by arbitrary

* Since I have introduced the term 'property', this is perhaps the moment to mention that factors of meaning are not limited to 'properties' in the traditional sense of inherent characteristics. The traditional way of thinking about 'properties' may be appropriate enough in the case of a word like 'mountain', but it creates obvious problems in relation to a word like 'desk'. For the meaning of 'desk' cannot be understood merely by reference to the inherent characteristics of desks – after all, there are flat-topped office desks which look exactly like tables. We must take account of a certain typical use that human beings make of desks as distinct from tables. Similarly in the famous case of the word 'weed', which cannot be defined merely by reference to the inherent characteristics of certain plant species. Any plant can be a weed, if in some given environment it interferes with what human beings want to grow. A 'weed' is defined by reference to our concerns and purposes. Even the meaning of a simple concrete noun must be allowed to include considerations of function and place-in-the-world, quite external to the object as such.

dividing-lines set up along a continuum. 'Light' is what 'dark' is not, 'loud' is what 'soft' is not, 'high' is what 'low' is not. There is no natural 'lumpishness' on these continua; and artificial boundaries are crucial in just the way that Saussure claims. We could hardly use the word 'light' without knowing the alternative 'dark': the one meaning is defined against the other. It is no coincidence that Structuralist literary critics and Structuralist anthropologists so often deal in oppositions of the light-versus-dark kind. (Although, as I shall hope to show in Chapter 13, Structuralists typically cast their adjectives into nominalized form: 'lightness', 'darkness', 'loudness', 'softness', etc.) If the different parts of speech slice the world under different perspectives, as proposed in the 'Conceptual cut of grammatical categories' section above, then it seems that there is something peculiarly conducive to boundaries – and to a Saussurean way of thinking – in the adjectival perspective.

A possible explanation for this peculiarity is not difficult to find. For the factor of height which contributes to the meaning of the noun 'mountain' is *all* the meaning of the adjective 'high'; and the factor of speed which contributes to the meaning of the verb 'run' is *all* the meaning of the adjective 'fast'. It seems that adjectives, by their very nature, typically direct us towards simple qualities – and simple qualities do not decompose into clustering or overlapping factors. To the extent that the meaning of a noun or verb is held in place by such clustering, it is hardly surprising that the meaning of an adjective must be held in place by other means.

However, even adjectives are refractory to the Saussurean way of thinking in the end. For not only is the adjective just one part of speech amongst others – it is also an especially dependent part of speech. In the accepted terminology of linguists and philosophers, adjectives are especially likely to function syncategorematically. 'Big dog' makes us think of what is big for a dog but not for a house; 'cold hand' makes us think of what is cold for a hand but not for a metal object; 'slow car' makes us think of what is slow for a car but not for a pedestrian. In each of these cases, it is true that an artificial dividing-line is imposed upon a continuum: dogs have no natural tendency to be big or small rather than anything in between. But the scale for the continuum is determined by the particular noun with which the adjective is syntagmatically combined. Although 'big' and 'small' have meaning by virtue of the boundary which divides them, that boundary is remarkably relative, and cannot be fixed for the language-system in general or in the abstract. The scale for the continuum is established not in *langue* but in *parole*. By a nice irony, the part of speech which most closely agrees with the Saussurean notion of *how* meaning ought to be determined is also the part of speech which most markedly disagrees with the Saussurean notion of *where* meaning ought to be determined.

A MECHANISM FOR CHANGE IN *LANGUE*

So little for *langue* – and there is less to come. I have said that the power of the syntagm is a secondary power; and so it is, in relation to any individual utterance in *parole*. Clearly it makes no difference to the normal range of meaning socially instituted for a word if one particular speaker or writer pushes it off-centre on one particular occasion. As I argued against Eco in the 'On the frontiers' section above, an exceptional combination of 'cat' with 'four feet long' does not need to be written back into the meaning of 'cat' in the lexicon. But the situation looks somewhat different when we survey language over the long term, diachronically.

Consider what would happen if speakers and writers consistently pushed the meaning of a word off its centre in some specific direction. Suppose that a widespread shift in sensibility or interests or lifestyle took place, and a great many people found themselves wanting to express something that people had not wanted to express before. Necessarily, they would put syntagmatic pressure upon an existing word in order to wrench its meaning to their new requirements. But if this happened over a great many utterances, would not the cumulative impact of a million tiny wrenchings have an impact upon the meaning of the word in general? Would not the wrenched meaning gradually become familiar in its own right, until people started to presume upon it, without always creating it syntagmatically on every occasion? And, in the end, would not the word acquire a new socially instituted centre of meaning in *langue*?

Of course, this would be an additional rather than a replacement centre of meaning. Saussure imagines that if *redouter* dropped out of the French language, then *craindre* and *avoir peur* would have to expand to take over the vacant space.[12] But such changes do not seem common in etymological history. The meaning of a particular word may come to be less and less frequently used, but it rarely shrinks in range, and it rarely drops out altogether. Conversely, a particular word may spread into new territories of meaning, but it rarely grows as a simple homogeneous whole. As the dictionary shows, most commonly used words exist in the form of a number of related senses. It is difficult to see how this kind of multiplicatory development could be explained in terms of boundaries and dividing-lines. It is also difficult to see how this kind of development could be compatible with the Saussurean notion of a closed semantic space. On that notion, one word in *langue* is able to acquire new meaning only as another word in *langue* loses it. But surely it is more plausible to think of a word in *langue* acquiring new meaning by capturing it out of the open semantic space of *parole*?

Consider the verb 'catch'. My *Concise Oxford Dictionary* lists twelve senses, including:

> **1.** Capture, ensnare . . . **2.** Surprise, detect, (*at* or *in*, or *doing* . . .) **3.** Hit (Usu. with part specified; *caught him on the nose*) **4.** (Of fire or combustible) ignite, be ignited . . . **7.** Intercept motion of (. . . at cricket, — *ball*, prevent its

touching ground off bat . . . **8.** Check suddenly (— one's *breath* . . .) **9.** Receive, incur, be infected with, (cold, a cold, fever . . .)

Such senses are related in various directions, by various forms of similarity, and with various degrees of proximity. Sense **7** relates to sense **1** in so far as intercepting the movement of a ball suddenly in mid-flight can be seen as a kind of capturing (though hardly an ensnaring!); while sense **9** also relates to sense **1** in so far as being infected by a cold can be seen as another kind of capturing (albeit an involuntary one!). As for sense **4**, catching fire is like an involuntary 'infection' by fire: in this respect, we may recognize a similarity to sense **9**. However, the notion of capturing has now disappeared. As for senses **2**, **3** and **8**, here we may identify three different connections to sense **7**: catching someone doing something involves the sudden discovery or interception of what they are doing in mid-process; catching someone with a blow on the nose involves suddenly making contact with that nose in mid-movement; and catching one's breath involves a sudden arrest or halt in the middle of breathing. But again, senses **2**, **3** and **8** have lost all suggestion of capturing. We are looking at a typically complicated example of what Wittgenstein calls 'family resemblances'.[13] And note the sheer distance between sense **4** and sense **8**: *a halting of activity* when one catches one's breath, as against *an activity starting up* when something catches fire. Developing from common origins, these two senses seem to have arrived at a state of virtual opposition.

Such 'family resemblances' are often explained as the remnants of dead metaphors. Thus 'catch' might once have been used literally to mean 'capture, ensnare', but only figuratively to mean 'receive, incur, be infected with (cold, a cold, fever)'. But although there are doubtless some cases in language where this is the correct explanation, it is hard to believe that figures of speech are sufficiently common to explain so many multiple senses for so many words. Nor does the large jump of a metaphor seem to fit with the typically small size of the displacements involved – especially when etymologists manage to recover smaller and smaller intermediate stages from the past. The syntagmatic mechanism, which works on a much less spectacular scale, is surely more appropriate for a majority of cases. Here the displacements are merely warps or extensions, favouring certain factors of meaning at the expense of others. Looking at the senses of 'catch', it is easy to see the different directions produced by different forms of favouring. And as one sense gives birth to another, which in turn gives birth to another, and another and another, the factors of meaning favoured may keep changing until the furthest senses have nothing visibly in common with the original sense at all.

The syntagmatic mechanism enables us to explain what Saussure is not able to explain: the diachronic evolution of word-meanings. In Saussure's model, *langue* is so self-sufficient that there seems no reason for it ever to change; where change has taken place, we can only suppose that it has occurred suddenly, by a sort of instantaneous reshuffle of the whole system. The consequences of this approach are apparent in Foucault's notion of absolute discontinuity between *epistèmes*. But the syntagmatic mechanism is a mechanism for slow evolution. Slow, because a new sense can enter into *langue* only after having first gone through a thorough apprenticeship in *parole*. Initially the new sense must be always compelled by syntagmatic pressure; then gradually it comes to be taken for granted in a few very clear contexts; and finally it comes to be taken for granted in all contexts. (We may note that Wittgenstein's version of 'family resemblances' stands badly in need of some such restraint, for mere ongoing similarities left to themselves will multiply endlessly and unstoppably.) On any particular occasion, it is *langue* which determines the meanings of single words for *parole*; only over an immense number of occasions does a reverse form of determination start to flow back from *parole* into *langue*.

The interesting thing about the syntagmatic mechanism is that it works quite outside the consciousness of the individual speaker. There is no suggestion that anyone makes a deliberate decision to reshape the meaning of a word in general. The individual speaker merely wrenches a sense for a particular immediate occasion. I shall have more to say in the next section about the place of consciousness in language – but certainly it has no place in the evolution of *langue*. Deliberate decisions about the meanings of words are unlikely to 'take' except in a few specialized areas of scientific and academic usage. The slow historical changes which affect the ordinary words of our ordinary language come about in ways over which we have no control. And this is just as it should be. For how could any individual ever really *know* what is best for words? How could any individual ever rise above and take stock and pass judgements upon *langue*? Trying to make conscious decisions about optimum verbal categories is like trying to lift ourselves up by our own bootstraps.

But this does not mean that *langue* is arbitrary or haphazard. Saussure and the Structuralists see *langue* as a system of purely conventional categories which could just as easily have been laid down to an entirely different pattern. But the syntagmatic mechanism that I have proposed is driven by a motivation of the most valuable kind. For *langue* responds to the pressure of *parole*; and *parole* responds to the pressure of what a great many people find themselves wanting to say. The ordinary words of our ordinary language have been fine-tuned and adjusted over an enormous number of practical applications. *Langue* truly merits the same kind of respect that the Anglo-Saxons accorded to their 'word-hoard'. It is the treasury of a society's most precious tools – its tried and tested verbal categories.

LINEARITY, SPACING, CONSCIOUSNESS

In the 'Derrida closes the book' section of Chapter 1, I claimed that Derrida finds it easy to disprove syntagmatic relations because he never really understands them. Specifically, he can conceive of them only in the form of a line, the meaning of one word linking on to the meaning of the next. I suggested then that this was an inadequate conception. We are now in a position to see just how inadequate.

It is true that the words – and therefore the meanings of the words – between which syntagmatic relations operate are presented to us one after another in vocal utterance, one after another on the page. And the easiest way to distinguish syntagmatic relations from paradigmatic relations is to point to a horizontal dimension of language – as I did myself, following Saussure, at the start of Chapter 1. But still this is only a horizontality of presentation; whereas syntagmatic theory shows that the dimensions of meaning are changed by synthesis and projection. The overall syntagmatic meaning which comes out is not on the same level as the successive individual meanings of the words which went in. We must think of the string of words as merely the site upon which an overall syntagmatic meaning is erected.

Derrida's error is actually a very old one. It is the error of confusing the succession of the words with the structure of the meaning. Listening moment by moment or reading across the page, we may well think the meaning of the word 'dog' before the meaning of the words 'jumped out', and the meaning of the words 'jumped out' before the meaning of the word 'park'. But in the thought of the sentence as a whole, the meaning of the word 'dog' does not come before the meaning of the words 'jumped out', and the meaning of the words 'jumped out' does not come before the meaning of the word 'park'. Such meanings are simultaneous aspects rather than successive segments of the event imagined. After all, the jumping out is 'there' at the same time as the dog; the park is 'there' for just as long as the jumping out. The situation is easily explained when we adopt the syntagmatic notion of words as conceptual cuts or cross-sections.

In fact, it is not even true that we *have to* think the meanings of words successively – at least, not in the case of reading. Proficient readers apparently tend to scan printed words a few at a time, taking them in as small clusters rather than as single items. And readers trained in the technique of speed reading can absorb entire lines simultaneously, without even moving their eyes from left to right. Of course, speed readers must nonetheless move their eyes successively down the page. Our human powers of perceptual recognition are simply not capable of absorbing an entire page of print all in one go. Still, given the variations in what we can absorb, it would seem that our limitations are a matter of practical capacity rather than of necessary principle.

This is not to say that the sequencing of words does not matter. In the English language, sequencing matters for a reason which has nothing to do with any order of thought. Sequencing gives us information about the grammatical roles that words must assume – tells us, for instance, that 'a big dog' and not 'the park' is the Noun Phrase which belongs in Subject position relative to the verb 'jumped out'. Clearly such information relates to syntagmatic processing at the level of what goes in rather than at the level of what comes out. I shall take up this topic again in Chapter 10. For now, it is sufficient to point out that an order of words can be free to express grammatical roles only if it has not been already tied down by some necessary order of thought. The fact that different languages are able to use different conventions of sequencing only confirms the point. So, while English uses a Subject–Verb–Object convention, there are also numerous Subject–Object–Verb languages and Verb–Subject–Object languages. There are even a few cases of Object-Verb-Subject languages (e.g. Hixkaryana), Object–Subject–Verb languages (e.g. Apurina), and Verb–Object–Subject languages (e.g. Malagasy).[14]

Since the principle of the line is irrelevant to the unity of the syntagm, so too is Derrida's counter-principle of 'spacing'. Derrida wields this counter-principle specifically against a notion which he attributes to Husserl, a notion of unity as continuity. And it is true that Husserl does place great stress upon the continuity of consciousness through time. But that is only one side of Husserl: there is another side to which I shall be trying to draw attention in Chapter 7. Derrida fails to observe this other side because of his own fundamentally unsympathetic framework. Derrida sees much of what Husserl is arguing about, but very little of what Husserl is taking for granted.

At any rate, syntagmatic unity is not only not destroyed by the principle of 'spacing', but actually thrives upon it. In syntagmatic unity, 'big' and 'dog' must be superimposed and made to intersect over the same space. But such superimposition would hardly be helped if the words were hooked together like the carriages of a train. We should only have the additional task of unhooking them, before we could begin to make them intersect over the same space. Language cannot reflect the real syntagmatic state of affairs: for that would require us to speak the words of a sentence all at once, or to write the words simultaneously on top of one another. Given the impossibility of such literal superimposition, a discontinuous 'spaced' presentation of words at least manages to avoid getting in the way of the real syntagmatic state of affairs.

A little pictorial representation may be useful at this stage. For the purpose of picturing continuous relations between the meanings of words, Figure 3.1 would suffice.

A ➔ big ➔ dog ➔ jumped ➔ out ➔ at ➔ me ➔ in ➔ the ➔ park

Figure 3.1

Such linkage might indeed be broken by the gaps or 'spacings' between words which Derrida so insists upon. But for the purpose of picturing syntagmatic relations, we must draw Figure 3.2, a diagram of a very different kind:

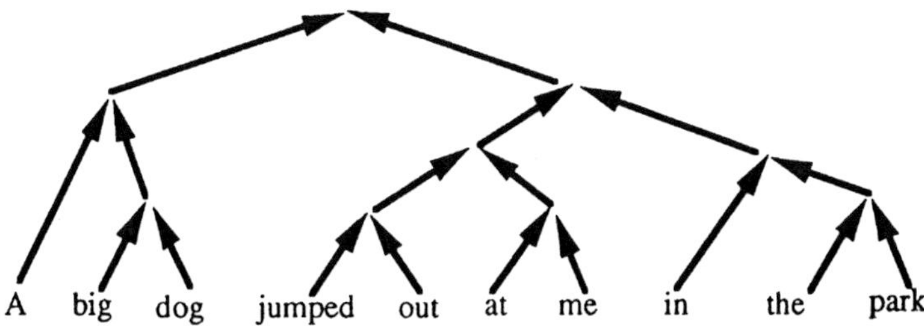

Figure 3.2

Here, syntagmatic relations are not in the least inconvenienced by the gaps between words, but leap up over and above them, rising to meet in another dimension altogether. Of course, any resemblance to the grammarians' branching tree diagrams is entirely deliberate!

This leaping up is also a leaping up of consciousness. For consciousness likewise thrives upon the gaps between words. Again, Derrida could hardly have got it more wrong. According to Derrida, the reader 'blanks out' in reading across the gaps; as we have seen, he suggests that the white spaces on the printed page correspond to periods of obliteration and nothingness. But in fact everything that matters in language occurs in – or, more precisely, over – those spaces. Far from 'blanking out', we are at our most mentally active as we read across the gaps between words. Consciousness comes into play in the very place where Derrida stakes his claim for unconsciousness.

In Chapter 1, I noted that there was no evidence from experience to support Derrida's claim; however, there is evidence to support the opposite claim. Not, admittedly, in cases of ordinary syntagmatic combination, where the processes are so rapid as to be subliminal. But in cases of exceptional syntagmatic combination, we can (with a little introspection) sometimes catch ourselves in the act of *leaping up*. For as I have already suggested, there is often a 'click' of realization when such words as 'primordial' and 'supplementation' finally fall together. And what is this 'click' if not a sudden apprehension, a coming to awareness, a rising onto a higher level of consciousness? Surely this 'click' is the very symptom of the *prise de conscience*?[15]

A strikingly new and different model for language is emerging here. Different, not only in relation to Derrida, but in relation to most other ways of thinking about language too.[16] For the ordinary assumption is that understanding a sentence is a matter of passing from one word-meaning to another, one moment of thought to another – like walking through successive pools of illumination cast by successive streetlights along a street. But in this new model, the thought is not *in* words but *over* words; the meanings of the single words have to be encompassed by a higher, larger cast of illumination. Or to put it another way, the meanings of single words define a thought – and define it uniquely – by laying out that set of elements over which it must fit. Single words are not the containers but the *markers* of thought.

THE RETURN OF INTENTION

It is another ordinary assumption about language that the receiver is passive while the utterer is active. Derrida, of course, inclines even further in the direction of passivity, claiming that the utterer is a mere channel for language, is 'written' by language – and is therefore just as passive as the receiver. But syntagmatic theory claims the reverse: that the receiver is just as active as the utterer. This claim is already implicit in the two key metaphors I have introduced: the metaphor of word-meanings as markers, and the metaphor of word-meanings as superimposed colour-filters. For if word-meanings are like markers over which a thought must be cast, then where does the casting come from? Or if word-meanings are like superimposed colour-filters through which a syntagmatic meaning must pass, then what propels the syntagmatic meaning on its passage? Either way, some source or force outside of the word-meanings themselves is required. And on the receiving side of communication, that source or force can only be located in the mind of the receiver. The listener or reader is necessarily active and creative.

It follows that the two sides of the communicative transaction are not so far apart as the ordinary assumption would suggest. In fact, the receiver's activity is a duplication of that of the utterer. For the receiver must manage to reinvent the sentence in such a way as to mean all of its meanings together. And in this case, it is hardly surprising if the receiver has the sense of stepping into someone else's shoes. Surely it is a natural enough presumption that the position from which all the parts of the sentence can be seen as falling into place is also the position previously occupied by the utterer? Reaching for a thought to fit exactly over the words, projecting beyond our own subjective past experience, are we not entitled to feel that we are striving to match the original intention of the utterer?

Of course, I introduce the word 'intention' as a deliberate challenge. Has not Derrida expelled that old spectre once and for all? But what Derrida has expelled is only one particular version of intention – the version exemplified in Husserl's philosophy of language.[17] According to Husserl, the intention of the utterer serves as the ultimate foundation and support for meaning – even for the meanings of single words. But this is possible only if the intention of the utterer can be somehow apprehended in itself, independently of the verbal medium. Husserl tries to claim just such an apprehension in the case of the direct speech-act, where the speaker's physical presence may convey the impression of an intention directly willed into the mind of the listener. But unless we admit telepathy, that impression is still only an impression, and can hardly be expected to serve as the ultimate foundation and support for meaning. In the end, as Derrida points out, Husserl's ideal case is the case of interior soliloquy, where the receiver has access to the intention of the utterer simply because receiver and utterer are one and the same person.[18] But in this case, the words themselves have become redundant, and there is no real need for language at all.

Husserl's problem is that he can found meaning upon intention only if he can somehow make intention more certain than meaning. But this is contrary to intuition: for we surely feel far more certain about the meaning of a sentence than about the intention behind it. The syntagmatic model agrees with intuition by making intentions essentially conjectural. Just as we hypothesize about the intentions behind other people's behaviour in everyday life, so we may hypothesize about the intentions behind other people's utterances. But this does not involve any kind of access to their private minds. Nor does it matter if our conjectures are sometimes incorrect. A hypothesis about an utterer's intention may enable us to explain something about the meaning of a sentence; but the meaning will not suddenly disappear if we subsequently abandon our hypothesis.

In fact, hypotheses about intentions are probably most useful in explaining *failures* of meaning. Consider the elementary example of a word accidentally omitted in a printed sentence. Unable to make sense of the sentence as it stands, we hypothesize an intention on the part of the author which somehow failed to appear in print. Sometimes, we may even be able to make a guess as to the word actually intended. Here we are bringing the notion of intention into play not in order to understand what someone else utters, but in order to understand why we *don't* understand what someone else utters. And this is much the same as with the intentions that we hypothesize behind behaviour in everyday life. As long as we can assume that other people's intentions are expressed in their behaviour, we simply respond to intentional-behaviour. We recognize intention as a separate area for consideration only when other people's behaviour becomes for some reason problematical.

Syntagmatic theory reintroduces intention into language by altering the terms of the debate. The ordinary assumption has been that, because it is the utterer who forms the intention, therefore it must be the utterer's activity which communicates the intention. But from a syntagmatic point of view, it is the receiver's activity which constructs the intention – simply in so far as the activity of a receiver is analogous to that of an utterer. Intention here appears as an offshoot or side-effect of the synthesis and projection involved in syntagmatic processing. Although intention has a role in language, it is a secondary role; and we will only be able to understand that role if we first understand the primary role of syntagmatic processing. Hence my comments on Derrida's inverted order of priorities, in the 'Derrida closes the book' section of Chapter 1. By concentrating so heavily upon the relation between words and their utterer, Derrida effectively distracts himself from considering the more important relations between one word and another.

4 On the larger scale

HIGHER-ORDER GRAMMATICAL CATEGORIES

So far, so good. A relatively small amount of evidence will suffice to demonstrate the fundamental principle of the syntagm, and reveal the inadequacy of theories which ignore it. And the forms of syntagmatic combination with which I have dealt – adjectives with nouns, nouns with verbs – are undeniably basic. But now it is time to take a backwards step and recognize the sheer size of what still remains to be explained. For there are many further forms of syntagmatic combination, forms which cannot be understood as mere obvious extensions of our existing forms. A way of thinking about synthesis and projection which is appropriate for adjective–noun and noun–verb combinations may be no longer appropriate when other parts of speech combine. We need to develop further ways of thinking in relation to further forms: a daunting task, and one which becomes increasingly difficult as we move up onto higher and higher levels within the sentence.

The main parts of speech in the English language are verbs, nouns, adjectives, adverbs, prepositions, determiners and conjunctions. (No doubt the traditional categorization can be improved upon, but it is familiar and will serve our very limited purposes here.) Adjective–noun and noun–verb combinations bear sufficient similarity to fit under a single way of thinking; though they also differ in one very important respect, to which I shall come shortly. The only other combination to fit under the same way of thinking is the combination between a verb and a verb-modifying adverb. Here the intersection is analogous to the intersection that an adjective makes with a noun. 'Slowly' cuts down on the range of possibilities for 'walked' just as 'big' cuts down on the range of possibilities for 'dog'.

But with other parts of speech the situation is not so straightforward. Consider the case of determiners. When we put an 'a' or a 'the' in front of 'big dog', it is obvious that the determiner combines with the noun phrase not like an adjoined brick but like a simultaneously superimposed colour-filter. However, it is also obvious that an 'a' or a 'the' does not intersect with 'big dog' in anything like the way that 'big' intersects with 'dog'. What the determiner contributes is not a content on the same level at all. Intuitively we recognize that determiners – and conjunctions and prepositions – are somehow more formal than verbs, nouns, adjectives or adverbs. What the determiner contributes is a further definition of the way the meaning is to be projected. To put it crudely, '*a* big dog' asks us to entertain the possibility of a dog which has not been previously projected, whereas '*the* big dog' asks us to identify this present projection with some previous projection. (The distinction may sometimes operate in purely verbal terms, as when the first sentence of a narrative introduces '*a* big dog', and subsequent sentences then go on to refer to '*the* (big) dog'.) Determiners belong to a higher-order grammatical category because they guide and shape a meaning which has been already processed on the basic level of content.

If the function of determiners is difficult to understand, the same is even more true of prepositions. Consider some of the ways in which a 'by' can occur between a verb and related noun:

(a) The tiger was shot by the hunter (i.e. by the agency of the hunter)
(b) Tommy went by the footpath (i.e. by means of or by way of the footpath)
(c) Jenny passed by the tennis court (i.e. by the side of the tennis court)

Intuitively, we would probably say that the 'by' in sentence (a) is formal, a pure grammatical particle; whereas the 'by' in sentence (c) conveys at least something on the level of content. But what about the 'by' in sentence (b)? It seems that a preposition may have both formal and 'contentual' functions, to different degrees in different cases.

Consider the case of sentence (a). As a grammatical particle, the 'by' here serves to give us syntactic instructions, controlling the way in which two *other* words intersect. There is no content in the combination apart from the meanings of 'the hunter' and '[was] shot'; but the 'by' tells us how to bring the hunter and the shooting together. One might draw an analogy with the role of 'to' in 'Mary gave the pipe to John', where the indirect object can be equally well expressed by a sort of dative: 'Mary gave John the pipe.'

The 'by' in sentence (b) is evidently not a grammatical particle; nonetheless, the *by means of* relation seems to bear some sort of a resemblance to the *by the agency of* relation – and certainly more of a resemblance than it bears to the *by the side of* relation. Unlike the 'by' in sentence (c), this 'by' does not specify a spatial relation between separate objects. Indeed, it is very difficult to see exactly what sort of independent content it does specify; much easier to see how it helps towards the intersection of two other contents, how it helps the meaning of 'footpath' to define the manner of Tommy's going. (This kind of 'by' can actually be omitted in certain special phrases like 'They went the long road home'.) We tend to assume that any word which is not a grammatical particle must have content in its own right, just as nouns, verbs and adjectives have content in their own right. But this assumption comes unstuck when we make comparisons with other languages less overwhelmingly addicted to prepositions than English. In Latin, for instance, a whole range of 'by', 'with', 'from' or 'in' relations are taken care of not by a word but a case – by the ablative case of the noun. Clearly, if a mere case can do the work of a preposition, then we need to think about prepositions in a very different way from the way we think about nouns, verbs and adjectives.

The 'by' of sentence (c) is a 'by' of the most contentual kind. A *by the side of* relation between two separate objects is not a part of those objects, but has its own sort of spatial existence. However, this 'by' still does not combine like an adjective with a noun or a verb with an adverb, does not combine its meaning simply with some other single meaning. Consider the possible grammatical analyses for 'Jenny passed by the tennis court'. In the most obvious analysis, 'by' would combine initially with 'tennis court', and 'by the tennis court' would then combine with 'passed'. But it is also very easy for 'by' to combine initially with 'passed'. (In the sentence 'Jenny passed by without a second glance', there is only the possibility of combining 'by' with 'passed' – yet we seem to be dealing with exactly the same sense of the preposition, exactly the same spatial relation.) It is as though this 'by' faces simultaneously in two directions. Either we can refer the sentence to the question of *how or where Jenny passed* – in which case, the answer is 'by the tennis court'; or we can refer the sentence to the question of *what Jenny passed by* – in which case, the answer is just 'the tennis court'. Such elusive behaviour poses problems for the grammarian; but it is perfectly appropriate for a part of speech which serves to mediate a relationship between other parts of speech.

The peculiarities of 'by' are typical of prepositional behaviour generally. And there is one further peculiarity which deserves attention: namely, that a preposition may help to mediate a relationship without ever doing much to narrow down the particular nature of that relationship. This peculiarity is less obvious with prepositions of strong spatial character such as 'underneath', 'towards' or 'within'; but it is impossible to ignore with the more open or non-specific prepositions such as 'with', 'by' and 'for'. Consider the following sentences:

(i) Harry left with a sense of disappointment.
(ii) Harry left with a gold watch and five hundred dollars.
(iii) Harry left with handshakes all around.

Here, the 'with' has to be understood in a different sense in each sentence; and yet we would surely not want to claim that these different applications come from separate lexical senses of the preposition itself. It is not that the 'with' contributes different senses; rather, it takes on different senses. What it contributes is merely a very general schema for some sort of an accompanying relationship. The particular nature of that accompanying is effectively determined by the nature of the other meanings involved. Which is also to say that *we* have to recognize the possibilities for synthesis; *we* have to work out the most plausible relationship. (If this seems to be leaving a great deal up to us, consider just how much more is left up to us by the Latin ablative!) In this respect, the preposition plays what I shall call a *facilitative* role.

The situation with prepositions occurring between two nouns is very roughly analogous. In the phrase 'a man underneath a car', the preposition itself narrows down a fairly definite kind of relationship; but in the phrase 'a man with a smile', the preposition itself provides very little information as to how these two particular items should be combined. Most open of all is the preposition 'of'. For example: 'the intelligence of Mr Jones' (as a simple possessive, i.e. belonging to Mr Jones); 'the idea of Mr Jones' (i.e. on the topic of Mr Jones); 'the peak of his career'; 'ten hours of misery'; 'a story of brave deeds'; 'a person of importance'; 'the disappearance of a diamond necklace'; 'the comfort of a warm bed'. Although there may be some lexically distinguishable senses here, the general schema for 'of' seems to permit virtually any kind of *pertaining to* or *having to do with.* More precise senses can only be worked out from the nature of the nouns involved.

The concept of the facilitative role will reappear in the following section, in relation to conjunctions operating between sentences. But for the present, let us turn from the complications of prepositions to the complications of verbs. So far I have considered only the way in which verbs contribute to a synthesis of meaning with nouns and adverbs. This is their role on the level of content. But verbs also play the part of 'main verbs': they have the unique property that their presence is the defining ingredient which makes a sentence into a sentence. And as 'main verbs', they are involved with the sentence's overall thrust, as interrogative or declarative, negative or affirmative, etc. I shall call this the *assertoric* role of the verb.

The interesting thing about the assertoric role is that it can be separated out in terms of syntax. This is what is done in Generative grammar, under the separate AUX or TENSE or INFL marker. Indeed, Chomsky's account of the behaviour of the AUX was perhaps the single most important revelation of *Syntactic Structures*, and the single revelation most responsible for launching Generative grammar in the first place. What Chomsky showed was that the AUX is tied in with the overall thrust of a sentence, and moves to different sites in the sentence depending on whether that thrust is interrogative or declarative, negative or affirmative, etc. In order to make such movement possible, Chomsky not only separated out the AUX from the verb, but introduced it at the highest level of the branching tree, directly underneath the S of the whole sentence.*

Chomsky's arguments overturned the traditional way of thinking about verbal auxiliaries. Certainly, the AUX marker relates to verbal auxiliaries, to such words as 'was', 'has', 'may' or 'will'. But traditional grammarians had coined the term 'auxiliary' because they saw such words as making only a

* In later Government and Binding Theory, the situation is more complicated. Combining with a VP (or Verb Phrase), the INFL (or Inflection) dominates as the 'head' of the combination; and it is that combination which in turn dominates as the 'head' when combining with the NP (or Noun Phrase) of the sentence-subject. In Government and Binding Theory, a sentence with subject and main verb (though still without Complementizer) is actually termed an IP or Inflection Phrase.[19]

small and secondary contribution to the verb. Verbal auxiliaries were regarded as optional extras, used for shifting a verb into a special tense or mood. Not surprisingly, they were given a fairly lowly site in traditional versions of the branching tree, subordinate and feeding in to the contentual part of the verb. But this could only account for sentences where the parts of the verb occur side by side, as in 'John will wear his new shoes.' There was no way of explaining sentences like 'Will John wear his new shoes?' – where the auxiliary escapes right across to the far side of the noun-phrase subject.

Chomsky's AUX has a different status altogether. It is a grammatical role which is present in every sentence of the English language, but which may or may not be filled by an actual word. In an interrogative, the AUX marker goes to the front of the sentence and is filled by an existing auxiliary if one is available; otherwise, it has to be filled by a dummy form created from the verb 'do' – 'Will/May/Does/Did John wear his new shoes?' In a negative sentence, the AUX marker goes before the 'not', and is filled by an existing auxiliary if one is available; otherwise, it too has to be filled by a dummy form – 'John will/may/does/did not wear his new shoes.' In an affirmative declarative sentence, the AUX marker ordinarily submerges into the content-carrying part of the verb, and is not filled by any separate word at all; if there is no need for an auxiliary to convey a special tense or mood, then we can simply say 'John wears/wore his new shoes.' But still we may sometimes want to drive home an affirmative declarative sentence with special emphasis; and in this case, the assertoric role of the verb again separates out from the content-carrying part of the verb. Countering some contrary assumption, we say: 'John *does/did* wear his new shoes!' The dummy form is called forth to carry the separate weight of a strongly affirmative, strongly declarative thrust.

Chomsky found it necessary to posit the AUX for reasons of syntax; what I am suggesting is that it can also be justified as a category of meaning. And specifically, a higher-order category of meaning, on a level which has nothing to do with meaning as content. This lack of contentual meaning is plainly manifest in the dummy form of a 'does' or a 'did' – the purest realization of the principle of the AUX. Assertoric roles come into play only after meaning has been syntagmatically combined on all contentual and other sub-sentential levels. When we think of a sentence as interrogative or declarative, negative or affirmative, we think of how its meaning as a whole is framed and sent out towards the world. If the determiner guides and shapes certain modes of projection possible for nouns and noun phrases, the verb in its assertoric role guides and shapes certain modes of projection possible for sentences. But whereas the determiner exists as a particular visible word, the assertoric role may not be visible as a particular word at all. Even at best, it will be visible in the *site* rather than in the *sense* of a word.

Recognizing the different ways in which meaning may be sent out towards the world, we are now in a better position to elucidate a claim which I first advanced in Chapter 2. There I proposed that the basic synthesis of 'big' and 'dog' and 'jumps' reconstitutes only the three-dimensionality of reality; it does not bring us any closer to a full perceptual picture of a dog. Such three-dimensionality, I argued, is quite sufficient for reinserting our sentences into the world. Now it is possible to see a sentence's overall assertoric thrust as the very means of that reinsertion. It is also possible to see why basic synthesized meaning not only cannot but must not be realized as a full perceptual picture. For how could one envisage a question or command in the form of a picture? Or how could one un-picture a picture in order to understand the meaning of a negative? The fact is that sentences make *points*, not pictures. We must try to conceive the synthesized content of 'big' and 'dog' and 'jumps' in a form which is equally compatible with an interrogative or declarative, negative or affirmative sentence. And we must distinguish very clearly between the kind of projection which objectifies meaning (as described in the 'Complementarity, synthesis, projection' section of Chapter 2), and the kind of assertoric thrust which makes meaning affirmative and declarative. Meaning simply projected is not yet on the level of being sent out in a particular mode.

Having offered these many suggestions, however, let me admit that they are indeed only suggestions. What I have said about determiners, prepositions and verbs may be in some places totally wrong; certainly it is nowhere totally right. At most, I have opened up a few avenues for further exploration. Considered syntagmatically, language reveals a staggering multitude of radically different levels. And the only consolation is that this is precisely what one ought to expect. Just as meaning is transformed in the passage from single words to basic units of combined content (adjective with noun, noun with verb, verb with adverb), so it is transformed again and again in the passage from basic units of combined content to sentences. Considered syntagmatically, language is not just hierarchical but radically hierarchical, hierarchical with a vengeance.

HOW SENTENCES WORK TOGETHER

Of course, the hierarchy does not stop short at the borders of the sentence. Processes of synthesis and projection are also involved in combining one sentence with another. But, once again, the terms of the processing must be rethought for this higher level. Consider the following pair of sentences:

> A big dog jumped out at me in the park. So Dad's going round to the owners to complain.

Clearly these are not two independent bits of information. There is a point in putting the sentences next to one another; and we take the point when we understand that the dog's jumping out is to be the subject of the complaint, and that the owners are the owners of the dog. Together, the sentences create a meaning which is larger than the aggregate of their parts.

As to the nature of this larger meaning, it is indicated in the word 'so'. It is a 'so'-ness, a sense of consequentiality, which draws the two sentences together. 'So' is the kind of connective that can reach beyond its own sentence and build a bridge across to another sentence. Similarly with 'thus', 'however', 'though', 'on the other hand'; similarly also with conjunctions that can be placed at the heads of sentences, such as 'For . . .' or 'But . . .'; and similarly with phrases that incorporate a reference to the meaning of the previous sentence(s), such as 'This means that . . .' or 'In spite of this . . .'

But the most significant thing about the word 'so' is that we don't actually need it. We can work out the consequentiality simply on the basis of the two sentences themselves:

> A big dog jumped out at me in the park. Dad's going round to the owners to complain.

A 'so' merely guides us towards what is already implicit between the meanings of the sentences. Or if it is not already implicit, then a 'so' on its own does not have the power to create it. There can be no real sense of consequentiality between sentences of unrelated meaning:

> A big dog jumped out at me in the park. So the standard of living rose 2 per cent from January to June.

In the previous section, I referred to the facilitative role of prepositions. In the case of inter-sentence connectives, there is very little to them *except* their facilitative role.

A word like 'so' thus presents a paradox. On the one hand, what it indicates is very important. You miss the whole point if you miss the consequentiality between the dog's jumping out and Dad's going to complain. But the word 'so' itself is quite dispensable. One could even argue that being omitted is its normal condition. Is there not a sense of consequentiality between almost all the successive sentences written in this book? Yet I have only occasionally driven home that sense with a 'so' (or a 'therefore' or a 'This means that . . . '). Words which operate on the higher syntagmatic levels (including conjunctions and auxiliaries) are the words we most readily omit in telegrams. It is not that what they say is trivial, but that the explicit saying of it is more or less optional.

Indeed, not only does a sense of consequentiality between sentences not need saying – in the last analysis, it never really can be said. At least, not in a single word. For the connection between two sentences, between 'A big dog jumped out at me in the park' and 'Dad's going round to the owners to complain', is something quite specific, something peculiar to what the dog has done and what Dad is going to do. No single word could convey this very particular meaning – not unless we had an infinite number of connectives tailor-made for an infinite number of individual cases. A word like 'so' never exactly tells us how to put the meanings of two sentences together: rather, it gives us a push and tells us to try and find a way of doing it for ourselves. How could it be otherwise? For the meanings of sentences are new meanings, unpredictable meanings. Through the processes of syntagmatic synthesis, they have already left behind the old meanings of their constituent single words. So how could the old meaning of a single word now re-encompass them?

What matters between sentences is not so much the connectives which link them as the gaps which divide them. Just as we must leap to a syntagmatic meaning in order to cross the gaps between words, so too with the gaps between sentences. Only the leap between sentences is of course much higher. And we may have to leap yet higher again between clusters of sentences. Points mount up over points, connections mount up over connections – potentially, the hierarchy continues all the way up to the largest overall point of any coherent stretch of discourse.

Given this hierarchy above the level of the sentence, it might seem tempting to continue the grammarian's hierarchical branching tree also above the level of the sentence. In relation to written texts, for example, we might envisage a model with sentences feeding into paragraphs, paragraphs feeding into chapters, and chapters feeding into the ultimate overarching node of the book as a whole. So, if we can represent the structure of a particular sentence as in Figure 4.1,

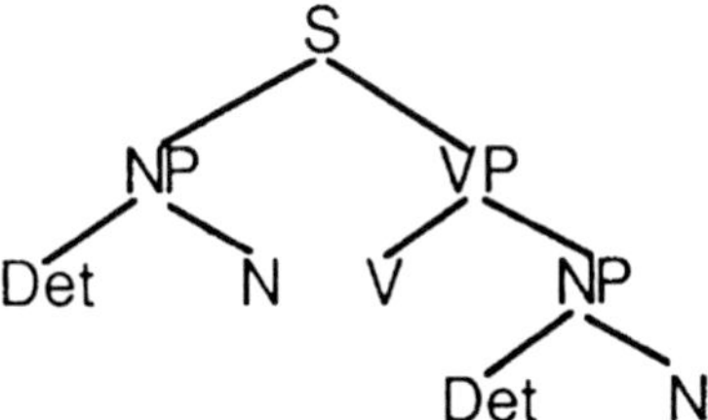

Figure 4.1

then (with P for paragraph, C for chapter, B for book), might we not claim to represent a particular structure above the level of the sentence as in Figure 4.2?

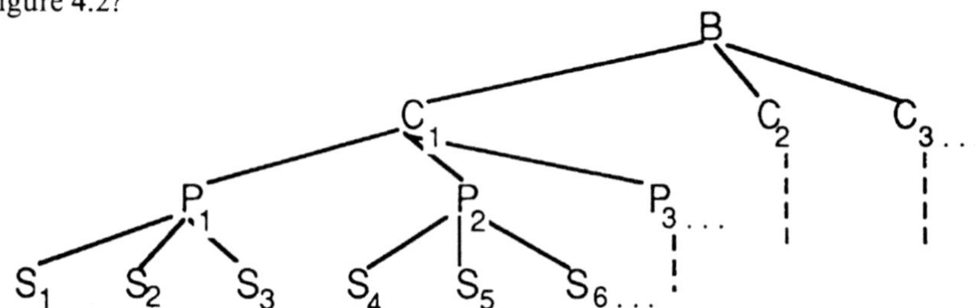

Figure 4.2

But unfortunately for such claims, the latter diagram is almost worthless. For although it shows points continuing to build up, it fails completely as a representation of *how* they build up. It will prove illuminating to examine the reasons for this failure.

In the first place, there is no satisfactory way of defining real units above the level of the sentence. Paragraphs and chapters are units defined by mere punctuation. Admittedly, sentences are punctuated too; but punctuation is secondary to the real unit of the sentence. After all, we cannot make sentences begin and end wherever we choose, simply by throwing in full stops and capital letters. The real unit of a sentence is constituted by internal principles, by the possession of a main verb, etc. Indeed, we can recognize the real unit of a sentence even in the absence of full stops and capital letters. Consider a sample from Molly Bloom's famous soliloquy in *Ulysses*:

> he noticed at once even before he was introduced when I was in the DBC with Poldy laughing and trying to listen I was waggling my foot we both ordered 2 teas and plain bread and butter I saw him looking with his two old maids of sisters when I stood up[20]

On the page, the gap between 'plain' and 'bread' occupies exactly the same space of whiteness as the gap between 'foot' and 'we', yet we have no difficulty in recognizing that the gaps are of different kinds, and require leaps of different heights.

By contrast, there are no internal principles for constituting the real units of paragraphs and chapters. Paragraphs and chapters are not defined by formal rules which we can prescribe in any general way. On this scale, the divisions inserted are essentially optional and stylistic. At best, they may give us a pale and distant reflection of what is really going on; at worst, we can work out what is really going on quite without their assistance. (In narrative fiction, chapter divisions may even be deliberately played against the natural units of the story, as by the consistent use of 'cliff-hanger' endings.) On this scale, syntagmatic meaning has lifted too far away from the page to be strictly correlated with mere on-the-page punctuation.

Furthermore: even if we could somehow define our Ps and Cs, we would still not be able to account for the complementarity by which they are built up. What draws S_3 together with S_1 and S_2, rather than with S_4 and S_5? Within the single sentence, the parts of speech are drawn together by their differences – an adjective with a noun, an adverb with a verb, etc. But our diagram for higher levels represents all sentences indifferently as S, all paragraphs indifferently as P. Nor could it be otherwise. We simply lack the conceptual means for categorizing sentences in such a way as to explain why one depends upon another. The fundamental principle of complementary categories halts once and for all at the level of the sentence.*

* Of course, this is not to claim that the borders of the sentence define the territory for *all* rules of syntax. Some rules may carry across from sentence to sentence – the rules of anaphor would be an obvious case in point. Conversely, there may be words which are relatively unconstrained by rules of syntax even within the sentence – as is the case with many of the connectives mentioned earlier in this section. So we can choose to say 'However, when the demographic data are considered, it becomes obvious that . . .'; or 'When, however, the demographic data are considered, it becomes obvious that . . .'; or 'When the demographic data are considered, however, it becomes obvious that . . .'; or 'When the demographic data are considered, it becomes obvious, however, that . . .'. Similarly with 'thus', 'though' and 'on the other hand'. It seems appropriate that the rules of word-order internal to a sentence should 'thin out' for words which do their work essentially above the sentence level.

Furthermore again: even if we could somehow establish a higher principle of complementarity, we would still not be able to produce the tight and tidy kind of diagram that the grammarian produces. The larger the scale of synthesis, the more the complexities multiply. Any extended stretch of language is likely to present a veritable welter of strong connections and weak connections, detours and incidentals, backward-harkings and cross-references. We understand such complexities as we take in the meanings of the text, but it is quite another matter to understand our own understandings. There seems to be no prospect of ever making a systematic map for all the varieties and subtleties of development from point to point.

But this does not mean that the larger workings of the syntagm are simply indescribable. There are other ways of talking: less comprehensive, less rigorous, but nonetheless viable. What happens above the level of the sentence is too new and unpredictable to be calculated from general principles or laid down in any predetermined pattern of possibilities. But we can still talk in an *ad hoc* way, after the event; and we can still talk about the salient syntagmatic workings of individual texts and discourses. If such an approach seems trivial to the scientifically-minded, it is an approach which the philosophically-minded cannot afford to ignore.

The level of the single sentence thus represents a kind of watershed. Within the sentence, conventional rules of syntax exercise compulsory force. But between sentences and clusters of sentences, the processes of synthesis and projection are largely 'up to us'. Nothing compels us to assume that 'Dad's going round to the owners to complain' connects with 'A big dog jumped out at me in the park.' But if we absolutely refused to go beyond the literal evidence in such cases, no report or argument or narrative could ever amount to more than a list of separate morsels of information. We assume, we have to assume, unity and point; and we must be on the lookout for unity and point wherever possible. On this scale, there are no specific rules other than the general directive to discover as much connection and consequentiality as is compatible with the evidence. If creativity on the part of the receiver is necessary for the understanding of single sentences, the understanding of relations between sentences calls for an even more active degree of creativity.

5 Parts of wholes

SUB-SENTENTIAL UTTERANCES

In arguing for the processes of the syntagm, I have argued for the importance of *parole* as against *langue*. But my *parole* is still an idealized *parole*; it is not a total accumulation of all the raw data, all the verbal utterances which could ever be recorded in the world. For one thing, I have conducted my argument on the basis of full-sentence utterances, cheerfully disregarding the many utterances composed of just a single word or two. 'Forceps!' murmurs the surgeon to the nurse, and perhaps 'Sterilized?' 'Elementary!' says Mr Holmes to Dr Watson; 'A horse! A horse!' cries bad King Richard. Given that full sentences are far less common in oral utterance than in written utterance, and given that the quantity of oral utterance in the world far exceeds the quantity of written utterance, it would not be surprising if, on some ultimate quantificational measure of the raw data, full-sentence utterances actually turned out to be in the minority. In spite of which, I have chosen to take full sentences as my starting-point. How can this be justified?

There is one viewpoint which would reject any kind of idealization – the viewpoint of traditional British Baconian Empiricism. In the current linguistics scene, this viewpoint is well represented by Roy Harris, who ridicules any attempt to hypothesize 'ideal realities . . . accessible to contemplation but immune from observation'.[21] Against Harris, I take the very un-Baconian position that scientific understanding always has involved and always must involve the postulation of underlying abstractions behind the infinite variety of raw data. However, it still behoves me to explain the raw data as an extension or complication of underlying abstractions. Or in this case specifically, to explain sub-sentential utterances as an extension or complication of full sentence utterances.

This is not so difficult as might appear. In many situations, utterances composed of just a single word or two are clearly interpreted as truncated forms of longer utterances. 'Shall we abandon the fight? Never!' cries the orator. Here, the single word 'never' is surrounded by an unspoken reiteration of the previous sentence: '[We shall] never [abandon the fight]!' Similarly if the word 'never' is uttered in response to the orator's question by the audience. 'Shall we abandon the fight?' he asks. 'Never!' comes the reply. In the context of other language, other sentences, it is easy to see the sub-sentential utterance as abbreviated and cut down from a larger implied whole. The fact that individual words may appear on their own in such utterances does not in any way demonstrate that individual words are self-sufficient or foundational. Indirectly, these words still depend upon the syntagmatic support of other words.

But the situation is not so clear when the context is non-linguistic. Consider the following scene in a kitchen:

> *(The chef, busy stirring, addresses the assistant who stands by his side)*
> 'Bowl!'
> *(The assistant picks up a nearby bowl and holds it out for inspection)*
> 'This one?'
> *(The chef glances round and shakes his head)*
> 'Too small!'
> *(Stirring again, the chef flaps an agitated hand)*
> 'In the top cupboard!'
> *(As the assistant pokes vaguely around in the cupboard, the chef raises his voice in annoyance)*
> 'Quickly!!'

The problem here is to say exactly what is being understood. 'Bowl!' might be taken as '[Fetch me a] bowl!' or '[I want a] bowl!' or '[Bring a] bowl [over here]!' The unspoken understandings involved in this scene can hardly be converted into specific sentences.

And yet the understandings are obviously crucial. 'Bowl!' as uttered by the chef is nothing like the word 'bowl' as lifted out of the dictionary. In the latter case, 'bowl' exists in a vacuum, with any and every possibility of its meaning. It unfolds and opens up and reverberates endlessly, like the word 'ETERNITY' carved upon a rock. But 'Bowl!' as uttered by the chef is not thus loosed and liberated. It does not stimulate the assistant to think about the general category of bowlishness, the general state of being bowl. 'Bowl!' is focussed and directed, narrowed down in meaning just as it would be in a syntagmatic sentence. For all their apparent similarity, 'Bowl!' and 'bowl' are separated by a vast difference.

The difference lies in the fact that the utterance of 'Bowl!' in the context described has a point in much the same way that sentences have points. Which is why, in setting the dialogue down on the page, I have had to punctuate single words with the punctuation appropriate to sentences: a capital letter at the beginning, and a full stop, exclamation mark or question mark at the end. The exclamation mark after 'Bowl!' bears witness to a command; the question mark after 'This one?' bears witness to a question. Although the command and question do not exist in the specific words of a full imperative or interrogative sentence, they do exist on the same level of mental operations. Only with the hidden support of a sentence-like point can words on their own be inserted into the world with a communicative value. Only thus does the 'bowl' of *langue* become converted into the 'Bowl!' of *parole*.

Of course, this argument will hardly make sense if we think of words as the containers of meaning. For then there can be no more sentence-point than inheres in the meanings of words actually uttered. But the argument does make sense if we think of words as markers, as serving to delimit a meaning which fits over them. For then it is perfectly conceivable that such meaning might also be launched from a non-verbal source, and at least partially delimited by non-verbal means. In the kitchen scene, for example, the chef and his assistant have many other clues to go by. A mutually understood purpose of food preparation gives point to the meaning of 'Too small!' and 'Quickly!'; while 'Bowl!' and 'In the top cupboard!' are particularized with reference to those objects which are present in the kitchen; and 'This one?' and 'Too small!' may well be further particularized by attention-focussing gestures – by a glance, by a nod, or by holding out the object in question. As for the immediate thrust of intention at the moment of utterance, that is presumably communicated by intonation and body-language. (Is there not some sort of analogy between the intonation-contour of 'Bowl!' and the intonation-contour of the whole imperative sentence 'Bring a bowl over here!'; between the intonation-contour of 'This one?' and the intonation-contour of the whole interrogative sentence 'Is this one the one you want?'? Certainly, the intonation-contours of 'Bowl!' and 'This one?' are nothing like the intonation-contours of 'bowl' and 'this one' when those words occur within sentences.) The contextual clues narrow down a non-verbal impression of purpose and relevance, which intersects to form a more specific point with the actual word(s) uttered.

A child's use of single words in the earliest phase of language acquisition is both similar and different. Similar, to the extent that the child utters a single word with the kind of point which belongs to a whole sentence; different, to the extent that the child does not seem to cognize the single word as a part of a whole, but employs it as if it actually were that whole. For instance, a child may say 'Bring!' for 'Bring me the potty!', or 'Small!' for 'I want the small cup instead of this one!' Since the child has as yet developed very little awareness of the otherness of other people, naturally it can hardly reckon up what a hearer may be expected to know as against what a hearer may not be expected to know. Whereas an adult typically uses a single-word utterance to complement an understanding which can be deduced from non-verbal sources, the child tends to use a single-word utterance as though the single word could create a mutual understanding all on its own. Psycholinguists refer to the child's single-word utterances as 'holophrases', or sometimes 'monoremes', and regard this special kind of language-use as dominant (when language is used to communicate) between the ages of twelve and eighteen months.[22]

The existence of the 'holophrase' enables syntagmatic theory to account for the fact that a child acquires a way of using single words before achieving any mastery of syntagmatic processes as such. For although single words come first, they are by no means self-sufficient or foundational. In using the 'holophrase', the child actually begins from both ends of the linguistic spectrum at once. On the one hand, single words are naturally the simplest and easiest units for the child to learn and reproduce; on the other hand, the child expects those units to be interpreted as though they were equivalent to whole sentences. In adult language, of course, it is the role of syntagmatic processes to bridge between the two ends of the linguistic spectrum. But even in the child's 'holophrase', can we not see the space for syntagmatic processes already marked out? I do not want to make overly dogmatic claims here: the study of early language development is one of the most active areas in psycholinguistics, and the empirical evidence is still coming in. But what I have claimed seems broadly compatible with the evidence so far.

Of course, I am still talking about spoken language. Not only the child's single-word utterances but the adult utterances of my previous examples belong exclusively to 'live' speech situations. After all, it is when utterer and receiver are in one another's presence that attention can be focussed by nods and glances, that objects can be particularized by their immediate presence, that intonations and body-language can be brought into play. However, there are some cases where words occur on their own in writing. 'ENGAGED' we are told by the toilet door; while the application form asks for an answer to the word 'SEX'. In such cases, the clues normally available in a live speech situation are lacking.

What we have instead are specific conventions for interpretation. We have been taught the rules for understanding toilet doors and application forms. Indeed, we should hardly know what to make of a non-conventional case: if the word SOON appeared on a toilet door (meaning: 'I shall be out soon'), or if the word CLEAR appeared on an application form (meaning: 'were you clear as to the sense of the preceding questions?'). In the absence of a particular shared situation, a particular shared convention must take on the role of delimiting meaning. Indeed, this latter kind of delimitation may be often relevant even in live speech situations: thus the surgeon's word 'Forceps!' evidently belongs to a well-grooved routine of utterance and response. But there is no convention involved when the surgeon suddenly asks 'Sterilized?', or King Richard cries out 'A horse! A horse!'. Such spoken utterances are *ad hoc* and genuinely unpredictable, in a way that is rare or impossible for written words.

In the 'Complementarity, synthesis, projection' section of Chapter 2, I suggested that individual words may be supported either by a verbal context of words together in sentences, or by a non-verbal context of shared situation and interactive behaviour. At that stage, I chose to give priority to the former kind of context, as showing language at its fullest stretch, and as demonstrating just how much language can do on its own. Now I have brought the argument around to the non-verbal kind of context – the kind of context upon which Functional Linguists and Speech-Act philosophers (and Roy Harris) concentrate their attention. Logically, there is probably no good reason for giving either kind of context absolute priority over the other. But by starting out with words together in sentences, I have developed a shade of emphasis which will not be found in Functional or Speech-Act discussions of non-verbal contexts. In particular, I have developed a very strong interpretation of 'context', as something much more than a mere surround. For the meanings of words in synthesized sentences are taken up into a new and different kind of meaning, into whole points. And this interpretation of 'context' must inevitably carry over into the interpretation of non-verbal contexts too.

Not that Functional Linguists and Speech-Act philosophers are necessarily disbarred from such an interpretation. In fact, some of them have approached very close to the syntagmatic position.[23] However, it remains true that Functional Linguists and Speech-Act philosophers prefer to think of shared situations and interactive behaviour in a fairly limited way. That is, they prefer to think in terms of observable doings rather than in terms of invisible understandings. Focussing upon the result-producing function of communication, they tend to ignore the sense-making function (including the sense-making function *as a means of* producing results). Their general inclination is to put language behaviour on a par with all other forms of human – or even animal – behaviour.

I suspect that the syntagmatic position probably ties in more readily with the Existentialist position. The 'care-filled' Existentialist world of human concerns and purposes and values is exactly the kind of world required to turn sub-sentential utterances into points. So the chef and his assistant see a bowl not as a mere concrete thing but as an object-to-hand, already pointed towards food preparation. And the whole kitchen scene is riddled with invisible attentions and intentions, ulterior relevances and directives. The Existentialist world is a pre-interpreted world, where observation is always already conditioned by high-level syntheses and projections. But all of this goes beyond the bounds of syntagmatic theory proper, and I shall pursue it no further here. The Existentialist analogy will crop up again briefly in Chapter 6, where I shall be arguing that Existentialism and syntagmatic theory both belong in the same general tradition of philosophy.

PROCESSING ON THE WAY THROUGH

There is another respect in which syntagmatic theory idealizes and abstracts from the raw data: by setting aside the time of syntagmatic processing. To the extent that the unity of a sentence is over and above the linear sequence of its presentation, it is also over and above the time taken to listen or read along the line. And so far I have considered the understanding of such unities as equally timeless – as though all the parts of a sentence were simultaneously available for processing. But although there is an important truth here, it is not the whole truth. When one considers how a particular listener or reader comes to an understanding of a particular utterance, the dimension of time can no longer be set aside. Once again, it behoves me to extend or complicate the ideal of timeless understanding in order to explain the practical facts of *coming to an understanding*.

The ideal of timeless understanding is most easily fitted to those cases where syntagmatic processing only begins after all the elements for processing have already been collected up. This applies in the case of exceptional syntagmatic combinations, where we halt and hover back and forth over the words before any meaning comes to mind. Perhaps it also applies in the case of very short sentences – perhaps we begin to work out the meaning of 'Where's grandad gone?' only after the words have passed by. But it certainly does not apply in the case of very long (yet straightforward) sentences. We certainly do not collect up all the elements of a forty-word sentence as a mere uninterpreted string. With very long sentences, we may actually be unable to recall the opening words by the time we come to the closing words. And even with sentences of more moderate length, we do not normally wait to take in all the evidence before we start moving towards an overall meaning. Listening or reading is not a stop–go affair, drastically changing gear from perceptual intake to conceptual understanding at the conclusion of every sentence.

Similarly on the side of speaking or writing. Of course, the producer of a sentence is likely to be aware of the sentence's overall point in ways that are unavailable to the receiver. But still, the sentence does not fall into words all at once in the producer's mind. With a very long sentence especially, the opening words are spoken or written before the closing words are worked out. Even if the meaning is in some sense simultaneous, the actual production is dynamic. Again, there are developments in time between the opening and closing words of a sentence.

What has to be considered, then, is the murky psychological area of *processing on the way through*. On the side of reception, this is the area of successive states of interpretation developing as we listen or read along the line. What do we know when we know only the initial word 'A—'? or only 'A big dog—'? or only 'A big dog jumped out at me in—'? The problem here is to explain these fragments as something more than individual self-sufficient words. Syntagmatically, these fragments must be understood as parts of larger wholes, just as sub-sentential utterances and holophrases must be understood as parts of larger wholes. But why do we see them *as parts*? And how can the part which is present manage to imply the whole which is not?

Suppose one's hearing or reading of a sentence is somehow suddenly interrupted or blocked off just after the opening words, as shown in Figure 5.1.

A big dog 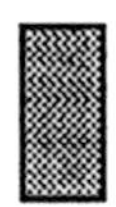 ?

Figure 5.1

Of course, there is no telling what words might have come next. But still this is not like a mere horizontal string chopped off short. There is also the convergence of syntagmatic meaning over and above the string. The situation may be illustrated in Figure 5.2, which borrows from Figure 3.2.

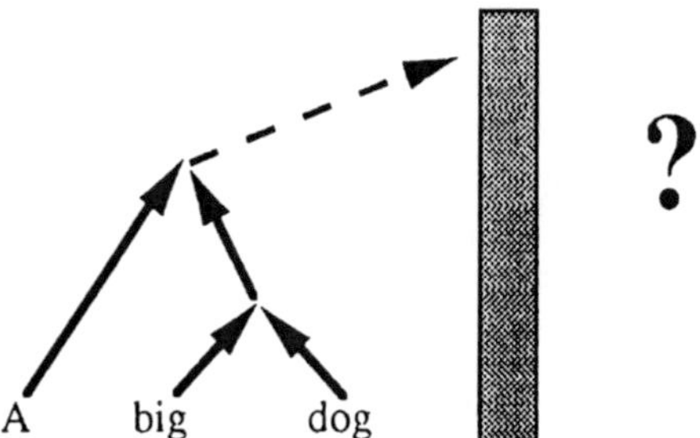

Figure 5.2

The interesting thing here is that the uppermost arrow now has to be left strangely hanging. It rises from a node (in fact, a Noun-Phrase node) on this side of the block: but it cannot be completed on this side of the block. There is as yet no higher node for it to converge upon. As the diagram suggests, it is a part which leans towards a forthcoming whole.

Here it is appropriate to invoke again the syntagmatic notion that words are markers in relation to sentence-meaning. If we think of assembling a sentence-meaning with words in the same way that we build a wall with bricks, then clearly there can be no more meaning than is actually standing as built. But if words are markers, then any presence of markers will indicate that a point of some kind is being defined – even though the first few markers will give almost no specific idea as to what that point may be. After all, there are countless possible points which can still be made to fit over the opening words 'A big dog—'. Perhaps the meaning of 'A big dog' will be negated ('A big dog is not the sort of present to give Jimmy for his birthday'), or perhaps it will be absorbed into a purely abstract assertion ('A big dog is an example of what I shall call an individual entity or particular'). Unfolding sentences have a sort of upwards unpredictability. The opening words can no more define the ultimate point of the sentence than the first few pegs can enclose the ultimate shape of the property to be staked out. In either case, the whole can still expand and 'take off' in any direction.

The situation is different, though, when almost all the words are in: 'A big dog jumped out at me in—'. In this case, we shall probably form a positive expectation as to how the sentence will be completed. Even if the last words are for some reason blocked, we may still be able to make a reasonable guess at them. (Indeed, many of us have the bad habit of breaking in and interrupting before the speaker has finished speaking!) When almost all the pegs around a property are in position, we tend to feel fairly confident about 'filling in' the last remaining gaps; in the same way we tend to feel fairly confident about 'filling in' the last remaining gaps in a sentence. Of course, we sometimes guess wrongly, sometimes have to rethink and readjust in the light of an unexpected late development. Nonetheless, definite anticipations towards the end of a sentence are as much a fact of our psychological processing as are indefinite anticipations near the beginning.

So far, so good. But what has not been specified are the exact levels of anticipation which will be achieved at any given stage of listening or reading along the string. At what moment, for instance, does one first form a positive expectation as to how a sentence will be completed? Such a question admits of no general answer. Anticipations depend upon the receiver's creative input; and that input is highly variable for reasons which have nothing to do with the actual sentence under consideration. One person may guess ahead long before another; or the same person may be more or less active in anticipation on different occasions. No doubt, there are many interesting psychological experiments to be performed here; but there are no determinate standards to be uncovered in relation to language itself. In relation to language itself, it is more useful to talk about the identical understanding which all competent receivers will have attained by the end of a sentence, rather than about the individual variations and degrees of arrival along the way.

On the side of production, the story is both different and similar. As I have already said, the forthcoming point of a sentence is usually known to the producer in ways that are unavailable to the receiver. But as I have also already said, this does not preclude the dynamic aspect of processing: the producer usually has the opening words worked out while the closing words remain quite undecided. Nor should we assume that the producer always knows the forthcoming point in advance. In public interviews, for example, an interviewee may often feel obliged to begin a sentence even before knowing what point it will make: 'In dealing with the question you raise, I think I would have to say that . . . '. Many a politician has made a fine art of thus spinning out words whilst waiting for some plausible answer to come to mind.

The most interesting case, though, is that of a speaker or writer starting off with one point which somehow changes into another point in the process of being uttered. In effect, the sentence ends up saying something very different from the producer's original intention. Nor is this new point merely adventitious, the kind of point that might have arrived at any time in the producer's mind. On the contrary, the new point is dependent upon verbalization, and only arrives because the producer has worked out the earlier words of the sentence. How can syntagmatic theory explain this kind of case?

It is not difficult to guess how Derrida would like to explain it. 'The signifier on its own', he tells us, 'says more than I believe that I meant to say, and in relation to it, my meaning-to-say is submissive rather than active.'[24] On Derrida's view of language, the intentions of a producer are always getting taken over by the independent momentum of words. But is this really what happens here? In the case I have sketched, the earlier words prompt the development of a new overall point which takes over from the first overall point; nonetheless, it is an overall point which does the taking over, and not the words themselves. Or to put it another way, an original intention may be defeated, but the principle of intentionality still survives in a revised intention. Individual words continue to remain under the domination of syntagmatic wholes.

For a syntagmatic explanation, we must turn once again to the notion of words as markers. Whereas Derrida's kind of meaning spreads out around words, the syntagmatic kind of meaning fits over them. And this latter kind of meaning also allows room for change and development, although in a very un-Derridan way. For the earlier words do not plant down a certain quantity of complete and final sentence-meaning; they only begin to mark out that meaning in certain respects. All kinds of overall points may still fit over them. And it is when a meaning has been marked out in certain respects that the speaker or writer may sometimes gain a clearer view of other prospects and possibilities. That is, the speaker or writer may become aware of better and higher points which are equally compatible with the words of the sentence so far. For, in the case I have sketched, the change which happens along the way is very definitely an improvement. The new point rises above the original one. What we are looking at is another version of that upward unpredictability of sentence-meaning which I mentioned a few paragraphs ago.

By way of a final extension, let it be noted that the same murky area between simultaneous syntagmatic meaning and successive reception or production also exists on the scale of much longer stretches of language. In this section, I have restricted discussion to single sentences; but, *mutatis mutandis*, the claims I have been putting forward may be equally well applied to larger syntagmatic wholes. Listening to a speaker in a debate or reading an article in a journal, we soon start to anticipate where the argument is heading. Speaking in a debate or writing an article for a journal, we (sometimes) develop better and higher overall points in the process of articulating our argument into words. On these larger scales, my claims become if anything a little easier to apply, and the murky area becomes if anything a little less murky. At any rate, the same kind of creativity can be recognized in all cases: not a creativity of the words themselves, but a creativity of the subject *through* words.

Part III

Syntagmatic theory and philosophy

6 The place of syntagmatic theory

THREE TRADITIONS OF PHILOSOPHY

In *Superstructuralism*, I argued for the existence of three main traditions in philosophy: an Anglo-Saxon tradition of Empiricism, a European tradition of 'I'-philosophy and another European tradition of Metaphysical philosophy.[1] There are, of course, other possible ways of cutting up the philosophical pie, in the light of other possible interests. But in that previous book, my three-way distinction served to locate the place of Superstructuralism; and in the present book, it may serve to locate the place of syntagmatic theory. First, though, a brief recapitulation.

The Empiricist tradition takes in such figures as Bacon, Locke, Berkeley and Hume. John Stuart Mill can be seen as continuing the tradition into the nineteenth century; Ockham and the Nominalists can be seen as laying the foundations for it in the fourteenth. These philosophers differ widely in their arguments, and even more widely in their conclusions; but they work from a similar set of fundamental principles. Above all, the Empiricists regard *observation* as the most sure and certain ground of knowledge, the basis upon which everything else is to be thought. Observation may here be defined as the contact between outside reality and human experience – but only to the extent that the former imprints itself upon the latter. Observation is essentially a one-way contact, where outside reality is the independent and governing term, human experience the passive and receptive term.

However, observation may be prejudiced if the mind starts influencing experience with its own preconceived ideas. To avoid such distortions, the Empiricists seek to bring experience directly up against outside reality in the closest possible moment of contact. In terms of experience, this leads to the typical Empiricist emphasis upon the pure reception of sensory impressions – the most outwardly facing form of experience. In terms of reality, it leads to the equally typical Empiricist emphasis upon concrete particulars – the most immediately impinging form of reality. As for ideas, they are to be trusted only in so far as they are derived from perceptual impressions by strictly limited processes.

Along with the emphasis on concrete particulars and sensory impressions goes a tendency to atomism. According to Hume, all our perceptions are independent existences. What comes first are the minimal separate sense-data reflecting concrete particulars; relations between these entities are added on afterwards. Inevitably, such relations are external – often mere mental associations rather than real connections. For Empiricists, a complex whole is no more than an agglomeration of simple elements. And the abstract general terms which we use to describe such wholes are only a kind of shorthand. In principle, it is always possible to render them back into their original elements. Everything ultimately belongs on the one same level.

The category of 'I'-philosophy takes in Descartes, Kant, Phenomenologists such as Husserl, and the Existentialists. ('I'-philosophy is not what the Germans call *Ich-Philosophie*, but a convenient coinage of my own.) According to these philosophers, we can never know uninterpreted sense-data, can never live at the level of stimuli on the retina or in the nerve-endings of the skin. It is impossible to bring experience directly up against outside reality, because even the purest observation is always already preconditioned. Nothing can appear to us unless spread out upon a field that the mind has prepared in advance. Sense-data are converted into what we experience as outside reality only by the imposition of innate ideas or Kantian categories or *a priori* schemata.

Such an account casts a new light upon the subject or 'I'. For if mental frames are imposed upon sense-data, then it is the subject which does the imposing. Experience is no longer a matter of passive reception, but of active constitution and creation. Not surprisingly, the 'I'-philosophers all find some sort of a place for free will in their philosophies. And not surprisingly, they all tend to look within the subject for the most sure and certain ground of knowledge, the basis upon which everything else is to be thought. As source and origin of the *a priori*, the individual subject sets the conditions whilst remaining in itself unconditioned.

The 'I'-philosophers' account also casts a new light upon relations and entities. For schemata and categories characteristically impose relations of a unifying synthesizing kind. And such relations are internal rather than external, creating wholes that are something other than the sums of their parts. What's more, such relations are not merely added on afterwards, but go out and meet the evidence, as it were. If concrete particulars still come first in one respect, yet assumptions of relation now come first in another.

Metaphysical philosophers such as Plato, Spinoza and Hegel are even further removed from Empiricism. Like the 'I'-philosophers, these philosophers believe that we can never know uninterpreted sense-data; but they do not locate interpretation inside the subject. In their account, *a priori* ideas exist independently of individual human beings. For Plato, the Forms are fixed in a timeless realm outside the universe; for Spinoza, the Modes and Attributes of God are immanent in every part of the universe; for Hegel, the Categories are embodied in human society, in language and culture and institutions. Such abstract concepts take on a kind of objective status in Metaphysical philosophy – ideas thinking themselves, as it were.

Naturally, this reduces the role of the subject. The subject is no longer a creative source or origin, but a mere nexus through which social ideas and categories pass. The subject is entirely passive, preconditioned and imposed upon. According to Hegel, even the notion of an individual 'I' derives not from our own experience but from the teachings of society. It is indeed a general Metaphysical principle that our own experience is not to be trusted. Anything we may seem to discover inside ourselves has always been planted there from outside. For the Metaphysical philosophers, experience is very definitely not the basis upon which everything else is to be thought – neither the outwardly facing experience of the Empiricists nor the inwardly centred experience of the 'I'-philosophers. Even perception is secondary and suspect – a state most vividly exemplified in Plato's myth of the Cave.

This approach has the effect of putting wholes before parts and relations before entities. Metaphysical philosophers start out from the very largest abstract concepts, which are then made to produce further terms by a process of internal binary fission. According to Plato, Being divides into Identity versus Difference (in the *Sophist*); according to Spinoza, Substance divides into Extension versus Thought; according to Hegel, Being (in one sense) divides into Being (in another sense) versus Nothing. And these divided concepts in turn divide to produce yet further concepts. Logically possible categories fall away on either side of a boundary, defined not by any positive contents but by a kind of mutual interdefinition against other logically possible categories. The Empiricist account is completely inverted: here it is the relations which come first, determining the categories which determine the entities. As for concrete particulars, they no longer come first in any respect. A pebble can be recognized only in so far as it falls under such categories as Hardness, Smallness, Roundness, etc. For the Metaphysical philosophers, outside reality in its own right must be considered as totally formless, almost to the point where it scarcely exists at all. Outside reality is dependent upon ideas, whereas ideas are independent and self-generating.

All three philosophical traditions have had their representatives in the twentieth century. So far I have mentioned only Phenomenology and Existentialism, in the tradition of 'I'-philosophy. But the Metaphysical tradition has also given birth to Superstructuralism, and the Empiricist tradition has given birth to what I shall call 'Analytical philosophy'. The difference, of course, is that Superstructuralism and Analytical philosophy are both primarily philosophies of language: the same cannot be said of Phenomenology and Existentialism. Philosophies of language will be my concern in the following section.

THREE PHILOSOPHIES OF LANGUAGE

What I shall call 'Analytical philosophy' is what I have previously called 'Anglo-American language philosophy'. On this application, 'Analytical philosophy' covers not only the line of thinking which runs from Frege

shall have more to say on this in Chapter 8.) All such expansions are dramatically cut back by syntagmatic theory, which brings out something that is unique to language alone.

To put it bluntly: no sign-system outside of language operates syntagmatically. Other sign-systems may *mean*; but they lack the special capacities for meaning made possible by sentences. (Of course, this is not to exclude the semaphore code, the sign language used by the deaf, or any such sign-system that works *by way of* language.) There is no synthesis of meaning in 'body-language'; nor do traffic lights ever convey messages that are genuinely new. Semioticians may well find interesting and important things to say about what all sign-systems have in common; but they cannot, in the same breath, talk about what is most interesting and important in language itself. The splendid vision of an all-encompassing semiotics looks much less inspiring when we recognize the role of the syntagm.

The very movement which carries human language away from the mechanisms of signalling brings it simultaneously closer to the specifically human activity of *thinking*. Here, too, syntagmatic theory reverses the trend of other twentieth century philosophies of language. Both Superstructuralists and Analytical philosophers have viewed the concept of language as a substitute for older mentalistic concepts of ideas-in-the-mind or subjective representations. Compared to such notoriously elusive concepts, the concept of language apparently offers the prospect of something firm and graspable – as words themselves are firm and graspable. Hence the general eagerness to claim that thought is nothing more than language.

It is the 'nothing more than' to which I take exception. I have no desire to revert to purely mentalistic concepts, to suggest that ideas or representations can subsist all by themselves in the mind. Undeniably language is involved with thought. And twentieth-century philosophers have done well to insist that such involvement is much more than a matter of language merely accompanying or reflecting thought. Language is what makes thinking possible. But, to the extent that language makes thinking possible, it is not firm and graspable as words are firm and graspable.

The paradox is readily explained. I have already begun the explanation at the end of the 'Linearity, spacing, consciousness' section of Chapter 3, where I introduced the metaphor of words as markers. According to this metaphor, the meanings of individual words define a thought – and define it uniquely – by laying out that set of elements over which it must fit. The markers thus keep the thought in position and spread it out in an articulate shape. Take them away and the thought will evaporate.* But the thought – or point, or

* For what experiments in introspection are worth, I find the following experiment illuminating. At some unprepared moment, I catch myself in the middle of a sentence which I am running through in my head; then, even without completing the sentence, I seem to have some sense of what that sentence was going on to express. But this sense is the merest sense-of-a-sense, and immediately begins to slip away; without completing the sentence in words, I simply cannot hold on to it.

syntagmatic meaning – is nonetheless over the words and not in them. The firm and graspable words only serve to define the space of something invisible. In this respect, language must be seen as moving between two poles: the pole of words and the pole of thought. On the one hand, we cannot think without using individual words as markers; on the other hand, the meanings of individual words are unstable unless we use them to think in whole sentences (as I argued in the 'Conceptual cut of grammatical category' section of Chapter 2). The two poles are inseparable. But they are not identical. It is true that thinking involves language and that language involves words, but it is not true that thinking *is* words or that words *are* thinking.

The moral is obvious. Twentieth-century philosophers of language have hoped to discover simple answers to old questions by converting those questions from a mentalistic form to a linguistic form. But such hopes are dispelled by syntagmatic theory. Although the invisibilities of syntagmatic meaning are no doubt more clearly 'placed' than the traditional invisibilities of ideas-in-the-mind, they are still not firm or easily grasped. Syntagmatic theory compels us to reconceive the connection between thought and language. No longer is it the case that thought is nothing more than language; rather, language is nothing less than thought. There are no short cuts. Language is staggeringly complicated and difficult to understand, precisely because it is so much a part of our highest and most human capacities. Far from bringing down the concept of thought, syntagmatic theory effectively raises up the concept of language.

In fact, the reductive view is self-defeating. When Superstructuralists and Analytic philosophers view language as something firm and easily graspable, they rise above it and stand outside it and look down upon it. And yet the medium of this rising above and standing outside and looking down is nonetheless language – the language of their own sentences. The language which they use for describing becomes strangely separated off from the language which is the object of their description. By reducing thought to language, twentieth century philosophers have sought to quell the old subject–object dualism of mind versus matter; but it appears that their efforts have served only to bring forth a new subject–object dualism within language itself.

Hence the recurring myth that there exists a special meta-language which just naturally happens to exist on a level above other language. For many Structuralists and Logical Analytical philosophers, the hypothesis of a meta-language has seemed the only conceivable way to justify their own position. (Poststructuralists are less troubled about their own position because they claim to be deconstructing language from within; while the Ordinary-Language Analytical philosophers allow for a variety of language-games in any case.) The hypothesis of a meta-language evades the consequences of linguistic reduction by getting philosophers 'on top' in a single once-and-for-all jump.

But it is precisely the once-and-for-all character of the jump which leads to absurdities. For surely such a jump should be easy enough to recognize? Yet how do we tell where meta-language begins and ends in a given text – in, say,

Ayer's *Language, Truth and Logic*? Do we argue that only certain passages are written in meta-language? In which case it becomes a matter of empirical testing whether people can actually recognize which passages in the book are meta-linguistic and which are not. Or do we argue that the entire book is written in meta-language? In which case it becomes a matter of empirical testing whether people can actually recognize the meta-linguistic nature of passages extracted at random from the book. The fact that such testing has never been attempted shows that we know only too well the impossibility of obtaining satisfactory results. The hypothesis of a meta-language is motivated by an overwhelming philosophical need, quite regardless of empirical evidence.

Syntagmatic theory removes the philosophical need by explaining ordinary language in a way which enables it to rise up and stand outside and look down. Through synthesis and projection, language has an endless capacity for getting 'on top'. Other language is just one of the things that it can get on top of. No need to set up some special language on a permanently higher level – rising from level to level is what language does all the time anyway. But then if language, even at its most ordinary, possesses such powers, we must treat it very respectfully indeed. No longer can we expect to pin it down in some all-encompassing, all-comprehending explanation. Syntagmatic theory may seem unsatisfyingly vague and open-ended when it leaves language upwardly unpredictable and free 'at the top'. But such is the price to be paid by any theory of language (which is also a theory *in* language) if it wants to allow for the possibility of its own existence.

7 The Phenomenological connection

HUSSERL ON LANGUAGE

At the end of the 'Three traditions of philosophy' section above, I claimed that Phenomenology and Existentialism are not primarily philosophies of language. This may seem something of an over-generalization. After all, two of the most prominent figures in the field, Husserl and Merleau-Ponty, have both had a good deal to say about language. But still there is a very great difference between a philosophy that merely takes in a theory of language and a philosophy that is actually founded upon a theory of language.

Certainly, Merleau-Ponty's theory of language does not arise from a consideration of language in the ordinary sense, the fully developed language that we actually speak and use. Instead he posits the existence of a special kind of ur-language, a primitive childhood medium of rhythm and gesture and bodily movement.[3] It is this highly Romantic form of self-expression which supposedly underlies and gives birth to language in the ordinary sense. Clearly there are similarities here to the pre-social proto-language of the Post-structuralists, to what Kristeva calls 'the black, heterogeneous territory of body/text'.[4] But there are no similarities to syntagmatic theory.

With Husserl, the case is more complicated. He at least considers the fully developed language that we actually speak and use. And at times he seems to be almost on the verge of understanding it syntagmatically. But in the end, his focus is too much upon other matters. The discussion of language in the first Investigation of *Logical Investigations* serves mainly as a stepping-stone to further claims about thinking and perceiving; and the discussion in *Formal and Transcendental Logic* appears only as an appendix to a main argument on the principles of logic. Husserl often sees the forms of language as helping to reveal the forms of thought, but he rarely sees the forms of language as actually determining the forms of thought.

Still, the similarities to syntagmatic theory are undeniably suggestive. Husserl starts off on the right foot by being prepared to talk about meaning *as* meaning. He dismisses the old unworkable notion that the meaning of an expression is a picture in the mind: 'the meaningfulness of an expression – let alone its very meaning – cannot consist in the existence of such images, and cannot be disturbed by their absence'.[5] But in dismissing this version of subjectivity, he does not go to the other extreme of dismissing all subjectivity. Unlike the Logical Analytical philosophers, he does not try to decant the meaning of an expression instantly out onto its real-world referent. (Hence the oddity of the attempt to Fregeanize Husserl in the manner of Follesdal, Mohanty and McIntyre. I share David Bell's view that the reading of Husserl currently fashionable in the Anglo-American world is 'utterly wrong'.[6]) In fact, Husserl proposes a *noematic* conception of meaning: that is, he thinks of meaning as a kind of objectivity projected beyond the subject *by* the subject. Needless to say, an objectivity thus projected is not simply out in the world in the way that objects themselves are out in the world. This is the classical tack of all 'I'-philosophers; and indeed, Husserl's *noemata* (in general) have a good deal in common with Kant's *phenomena*.

As for direct similarities: in the first place, Husserl approaches syntagmatic theory when he recognizes that the member parts of a sentence 'are *non-selfsufficient* under all circumstances; they are what they are in the whole'.[7] And in *Formal and Transcendental Logic*, he speaks of such parts as 'moments', as abstracted aspects. According to his general theory of 'moments', this means that they are in need of supplementation, that they are drawn to a mutual interpenetration by their own mutually 'founded' nature: 'they require no chains or bonds to chain or knit them together'.[8] I have already borrowed the term 'moments' in order to explain the natural complementarity of nouns, verbs, adjectives, etc.

The knitting together is thus grammatical in the way described by syntagmatic theory. Husserl talks readily of 'the *a priori* patterns in which meanings belonging to different semantic categories can be united to form one meaning'.[9] And the one meaning is also a new meaning. For example: 'To any nominal meaning *S*, and any adjectival meaning *p*, there belongs the primitive form *Sp* (e.g. *red house*), the result being a new meaning . . . '[10] In another example, Husserl recognizes a whole hierarchy of such combinations:

> if I judge, *This paper is white*, then . . . the predicate acquires, over and above its own material content, a relation to the subject, *paper*, and engages significantly with the relatedness of the subject to the subject-matter. If I judge *bluish white*, instead of just *white*, the previously simple predicate *white* now has, in itself, a secondary determination, one that concerns the primary subject even more mediately.[11]

Through successive engagements and determinations, meaning builds up into higher and higher forms of unity.

What's more, Husserl is prepared to allow grammatical unities that are certainly not rational unities: ' "wooden iron" ' and ' "All squares have five angles." '[12] Such combinations are very much 'on the frontiers'; yet Husserl insists that such counter-sense ('Widersinn') is still very different from the kind of outright senselessness ('Unsinn') produced by a string of uncombinable grammatical categories: ' "if the or is green" ' or ' "A tree is and" '.[13] Although there are laws of logic which can be brought to bear against counter-sense, they must be brought to bear at a later stage. Unlike Eco and the Analytical philosophers, Husserl recognizes a kind of meaningfulness in even the most bizarre combinations.

But in spite of these many similarities, Husserl never finally manages to understand language syntagmatically. Because his focus is ultimately upon the thinking and perceiving of a single mind, he views language also in terms of a single mind – the utterer's mind. And because his focus is ultimately upon individual thinking and perceiving, he overlooks the crucial role of conventionality in language. This leads him to bring 'intention' into play in far too simplistic a way:

> The articulate sound-complex, the written sign etc., first becomes a spoken word or communicative bit of speech, when a speaker produces it with the intention of 'expressing himself about something' through its means; he must endow it with a sense in certain acts of mind, a sense he desires to share with his auditors.[14]

I have already discussed and endorsed Derrida's critique of this position.[15] If further ammunition is wanted, one might contemplate the extraordinary exclusions to which Husserl finds himself compelled, when he says 'we shall always presume sincerity', or 'we are now excluding mendacious speech . . . which says something other than what is believed'.[16] There is something glaringly wrong with a theory of language that has to prescribe 'honesty' as its first principle.

In truth, Husserl never wholeheartedly identifies his verbal 'moments' with grammatical categories. No doubt he is thinking of nouns and adjectives when he proclaims '*the novel categories of pure grammar: substantivity and adjectivity*'.[17] But how can he then totally ignore the grammatical category of the verb? It seems that he is still mainly interested in the forms of mental act which operate through and behind language. Below the level of the sentence, he really recognizes just one form of act: 'the *ultimate underlying acts* in every complex act . . . must all be *nominal acts*'.[18] Such 'nominal acts' present without judging, as the noun-phrase subject of a sentence presents without judging. Even adjectives are swallowed up under the 'nominal' category of the noun-phrase. To complete a quotation which I previously left unfinished: 'To any nominal meaning *S*, and any adjectival meaning *p*, there belongs the primitive form *Sp* (e.g. *red house*), the result being a new meaning fixed by law in the category of nominal meaning'.[19] For all the novelty of his approach, Husserl ends up by asserting a very traditional '*pre-eminence of the substantival category*'.[20] As James M. Edie has remarked, this is a very disappointing conclusion.[21]

The traditional pre-eminence of the substantival category goes with the traditional assumption that nouns and names can stand meaningfully by themselves. Nor does Husserl escape this assumption. Although he may speak of the member parts of a sentence as being non-self-sufficient, he is very far from considering all types of words as equally non-self-sufficient. A very clear distinction is laid down in *Logical Investigations*: 'A meaning . . . may be called "independent" when it can constitute the *full, entire meaning of a concrete act of meaning,* "non-independent" when this is not the case'.[22] Independent meanings are here the province of such categorematic terms as 'king' and 'redness', while non-independent meanings are the province of such syncategorematic terms as 'equals', 'together with', 'and', 'or'.[23] In *Formal and Transcendental Logic*, the distinction seems to operate more along the lines of a sliding scale. But Husserl still continues to assume that the categorematic terms can stand meaningfully on their own, and continues to apply the concept of 'moments' primarily to the syncategorematic terms. So it is primarily the syncategorematic terms that are given the job of unifying and drawing a sentence together. In the last analysis, Husserl recognizes only two modes of combination: the *conjunctive*, as brought about by linking words like 'and' and 'or'; and the *predicative*, as brought about by the copula 'is'.[24] (Here we can perhaps observe the state to which Husserl has reduced the grammatical category of the verb – the emptied minimal contentless state of the copula.) There is no awareness of the enormous force for combination between categorematic terms themselves, or the crucial role of interdefinition between verbs and nouns, nouns and adjectives, verbs and adverbs.

The fact is that the real similarity between syntagmatic theory and Phenomenology is not a similarity of views about language. To bring out the real similarity, it is necessary to examine the general Phenomenological outlook on matters other than language; and then to envisage the kind of outlook on such matters that syntagmatic theory itself suggests. In the following section, I shall therefore present a version of the general Phenomenological outlook, a version derived from Husserl, Brentano and, to a lesser extent, Merleau-Ponty. But I shall be presenting this version in my own construction and with my own emphases. Whatever may be its weaknesses and limitations, it would be unfair to blame them on any or all of those three philosophers.

THE PHENOMENOLOGICAL PERSPECTIVE

Phenomenology revolves around concepts of mind, experience and consciousness. But not the kind of mind or experience or consciousness which Empiricist philosophers once proposed and which Analytical philosophers now reject. On that very Anglo-American view, mental experience flows through us like a stream – an internal stream of consciousness. The nerves carry messages from the outside world to the brain, where they are realized like images on a screen. To put it crudely, we become armchair observers of a continuous movie show inside our own skulls. The problem here, of course, is that there seems to be no reason for identifying the internal movie show with the outside reality. We are left with two worlds where we only need one.

The problem arises in this form because of the emphasis upon physiological processes of reception through the nerves. On the screen-and-stream model, experience goes only one way, from the outside to the inside. Phenomenology escapes the problem – or at least the worst of the problem – by introducing a reverse direction. Now experience is outward-bound, as volitions through the nerves are outward-bound. Hence the emphasis upon 'intentions' in the special Phenomenological sense of the word. This special sense ties in neatly with the original sense of the Latin word *intendere*, which was apparently applied to the business of drawing and aiming a bow at a target.[25] It is just such outwards-aiming-at-a-target that is proposed in the Phenomenological model. The mind is not a container for images and concepts, but points away to something other than itself. *What* we perceive is entirely different to *where* we perceive it from. The Phenomenologists refuse to think of perception in terms of passive reflection, like taking an imprint on a photographic film; they think of it as an act, like releasing an arrow towards a target.

The general notion of intention may be conveniently illustrated by the specific case of attention. When we turn our attention upon something, we actively focus in such a way as to make that thing stand out. The volitions involved may be normally automatic, but they can often be controllable too. The mind has its own kind of 'muscles'. Consider Figure 7.1.

Figure 7.1

Here it is possible to grasp either a network of white wires and hubs on a shaded background as shown in Figure 7.2,

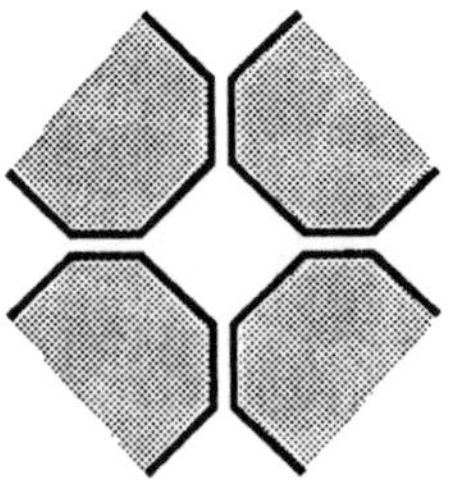

Figure 7.2

or a collection of shaded plate-like forms on a white background as in Figure 7.3.

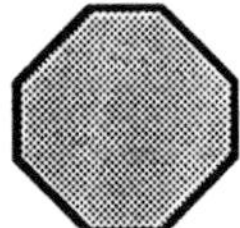

Figure 7.3

Naturally, we cannot apprehend the two versions at the same time; but once we have discovered them both, we can actively and even voluntarily change from one grasp to the other.

Of course, what I have just presented is a Gestalt experiment (an abstract one, to avoid any suggestion that the two versions are determined merely by conventional or familiar images). There is indeed a significant affinity between Gestalt psychology and Phenomenological philosophy – an affinity which was acknowledged by the original Gestalt psychologists, although not by Husserl himself. However, the writings of Aron Gurwitsch more than make up for Husserl's curious aloofness. It may be noted that the Gestaltist Husserl of Gurwitsch's interpretation represents, in the Anglo-American world, the main alternative to the Fregeanized Husserl of Follesdal, Mohanty and McIntyre.

Recognizing the 'muscles of the mind', then, we are led to a bi-polar view of any act of consciousness. On the one hand, the act must have an object-at-which to direct itself. There is no consciousness pure and simple, no consciousness which is not a consciousness *of something*. But on the other hand, the act must also have a place-where-from. The 'intention' always flies towards the target from some particular angle. All consciousness is a position-taking. But this is not to say that the place-where-from presents itself in the same kind of way as the object-at-which. The place-where-from is not known as an object but only experienced as a sense of direction. It is like the barrel of a telescope: we look through it rather than at it. Or if we do occasionally look at it, then we do so in a special act of self-consciousness, in which ordinary consciousness becomes the object and the place-where-from is somewhere else again.[26] The subject-pole is experienced in the act of consciousness, but it is never that which the act is conscious of.

The importance of the place-where-from is very obvious when we consider different modes of apprehension. David Hume, notoriously, put forward the claim that we distinguish between perceived and remembered images because the former are more vivid than the latter. Some such claim is indeed difficult to avoid for any philosopher who accepts the screen-and-stream model of consciousness. For if we experience only a succession of images cast up on an interior screen, then we can 'place' those images only by reference to their own qualities. But of course we do not really distinguish between perceptions and memories in this way. We know without thinking about it the particular kind of mental activity which makes an object appear. The difference between perceiving a tree and remembering a tree is not something about which we can be uncertain, or about which we could make a mistake. The place-where-from is given in the very nature of the experience. When we apprehend a tree, we also know the mode of apprehension by which we got to it.

The place-where-from is no less relevant to differences within a single mode of apprehension. This is especially demonstrable in the case of apprehension by touch. For touch, unlike sight, is not a 'distance' sense. It is unfortunate that epistemological thinking has been so often dominated by the special characteristics of the sense of sight. Indeed, the screen-and-stream model could scarcely have arisen if philosophers had given proper consideration to our more primitive tactile apprehensions. For here it is impossible to ignore the part played by the body at the subject-pole. What we apprehend by touch is not an object as such, but a contact between object and body. If we remained totally passive, we should never experience anything beyond a sensation of pressure on the skin. In order to recognize an object as such, we must assume a more active role. That is, we must shape our fingers around it, or move our hands to touch its surface with varying contacts. We must apply as well as receive pressure. (For a child, the most basic form of encounter is presumably the all-surrounding contact with an object in the mouth.) The object does not exist by one single sensation, but by a simultaneous multiplicity of sensations mapped out in terms of the curve and angle of our fingers; or by a non-simultaneous multiplicity of sensations mapped out in terms of the moving position of our hands. Which is to say that we must know where our fingers and hands 'are at'. We recognize the object as a resistance to our own volitional motor-activity.

The role of the subject-pole is somewhat less obvious in the case of sight – but it is there nonetheless. What we see is continuously correlated with a sense of our own bodily activity. There is a world of difference between an object that presents varying visual profiles because it is rotating on a turntable, and an object that presents varying visual profiles because we are walking around it. In the latter case, we are aware of doing something to the object because we are aware of doing something ourselves. Yet this awareness is still only a subject-sense. We do not need to reflect upon the actual movement of our legs;

nor do we need to fix an actual location for our bodies at any given moment. It is enough that we are aware of a relative and continuous change of place – like someone moving around looking through the viewfinder of a video camera. To look down at our feet in relation to the ground would be to acquire a different, objective grasp of where we 'are at'.

Only by coordinating subject-pole with object-pole can we come to a recognition of things as existing beyond our own moments of contact with them. And only by studying the principles of this coordination can the philosopher escape from the traditional problems of epistemology. For example: looking at a tree, when we close our eyes for a second we give ourselves two separate tree-images. How then do we identify the two images as belonging to one and the same thing? No mere similarity between the images themselves can ever create sameness. The problem is unanswerable until we forget about the images themselves and concentrate upon the gap of blankness between them. The trick is to see the gap as an interruption. For the gap is not on a par with the images, as it would be if cast up on a movie screen, a mere blank-picture between two tree-pictures. Instead, we are aware that the gap exists in a different kind of way. And it exists in a different kind of way because it is *up to us* – just as it is *up to us* when we block out a view by shielding our face with our hands. By voluntary muscular control of the eyelids, we are free to shorten and lengthen the gap, or make it occur exactly when and how often we choose. So it is not too difficult to form an idea of the gap as our own interruption, superimposed upon what could otherwise have been a single continuous tree-image. By coordinating subject-pole and object-pole, we can 'discount for' our own contribution, and recognize something which manages to stay the same in spite of us. And this something, of course, is not the tree as an image but the tree as a thing, existing whether we see it or not.

A related epistemological problem arises when dissimilar images of the same object are involved. Suppose we walk around a tree: then we receive an enormous multitude of visual profiles, of continually varying images of the tree. Naturally, there may not be much difference in what we see from one step to the next; but there is likely to be a great deal of difference in what we see looking at the tree from front and back. How then do we overleap this multitude of profiles and come to a recognition of one single thing to which they all belong? Again, the answer must be sought in a coordination of subject-pole with object-pole. At the subject-pole, we are aware of our own volitional movements as we walk, aware of a relative change of position by means of our own bodily activity. And this awareness can be sufficiently separated out to 'explain' the changes in what we see. (Of course, 'explanation' must here be understood essentially in terms of inarticulate and pre-conscious intuitions.) Again, we can 'discount for' our own subjective contribution and thereby recognize the objective contribution of the tree itself. But we can 'discount for' our own contribution only by being aware of it in the first place. It is our subject-sense of dissimilar places-where-from that enables us to map a multitude of dissimilar visual profiles onto the same object.

The converse holds true too. If dissimilar places-where-from produced no change in profile, we should have to regard our tree-image as a kind of hallucination – or at best, a painted two-dimensional representation of a tree. As for dreams – there seems to be a potentially suggestive connection between the kind of 'perception' experienced in dream and the fact that such experience is unaccompanied by appropriate bodily movements. Lacking the usual subject-sense of volitional effort and activity, the dreamer can hardly be expected to 'place' or 'map out' images in the usual manner. Does this perhaps help to explain the strangeness of shifts and transitions in dreams, the strange ways in which the same thing can be taken as different or different things can be taken as the same? Experience becomes dream-like when place-where-from and object-at-which cannot be consistently correlated.

Returning to ordinary perception, it must be noted that the tree as an object exists on an entirely different level from its profiles. What remains after we have discounted for our own subjective contribution is strictly beyond visualization. Even in imagination, we cannot picture a tree simultaneously from front and back. We cannot take parts from several images – a branch here, a branch there, and so on – and somehow blend and merge them into one single super-image. After all, even the parts of images are still visualized only under a specific angle of observation. Whereas the tree itself allows for all possible angles of observation. What we take from the varying multitudinous images are not parts but abstracted aspects. The tree itself exists not in its visual profiles, but over them and through them.

There is a very general principle emerging here. Objects exist for us as a resistance to our volitions; and we recognize their special kind of existence by a special kind of limitation upon our own freedom. If we walk around a tree, for instance, we are aware of being able to vary what we see in certain respects. We can walk faster or slower, and make the profiles change faster or slower accordingly; or we can walk around in the opposite direction, and make the profiles appear in reverse order. Some of what we see is up to us. But we can never make the profiles appear in a rearranged order. Here we come up against an independent law-like necessity amongst the profiles themselves. And it is the boundary between this necessity and our freedom which marks out the existence of an object – a boundary experienced but invisible, which separates aspects and not parts. There is a principle of inverse proportion between the levels of our subjective freedom and the levels of ontological existence which we are forced to allow outside ourselves.

The principle may perhaps be observed in the behaviour of very young children, when they repeat an action with an object over and over again, sometimes faster and sometimes slower, sometimes forwards and sometimes backwards. Are they not exploring the way in which subject-pole coordinates with object-pole? And, at the opposite extreme of sophistication, the principle may certainly be observed in Husserl's method of 'free variation', which consists of a kind of mental experimentation whereby one tries to discover what can be varied in thought (at any given level) and what cannot . Husserl prescribes this method specifically as a means of making philosophical discriminations and solving philosophical problems – but it obviously ties in with his general epistemological orientation.

The kind of objectivity which exists as a resistance to our freedom of will is not limited to concrete objects. There are also objectivities of thought – ideas which go beyond the subjective moments of our individual thinking just as surely as out-there objects go beyond the subjective moments of our individual perceiving. A mathematical proof no more drops out of existence when we stop thinking about it than does a tree when we stop looking at it. What we think about can still be taken as the same, although we think about it on different occasions. And it can still be taken as the same even when we come at it through quite dissimilar modes of apprehension. So we might read through the proof only half-understandingly in a book; or we might sit down with pencil and paper, and work it out with a feeling of real discovery; or we might repeat it purely by rote in order to impress an examiner; or we might not even think it through, but merely think about it in relation to some further proof. Yet in spite of these differences, we are always aware of directing ourselves towards the same target. A mathematical proof has what Husserl calls an 'ideal' existence. We can approach it, hover around it, consider it from several angles, eventually turn away from it – all such phrasings are perfectly appropriate. It stays; our thinking moves.

One obvious consequence of the Phenomenological perspective, even over the short distance travelled in these pages, is a complicated range of different ontological levels. The Phenomenological perspective runs completely counter to the tradition of Empiricist philosophy. From Ockham to Hume to Russell to Ryle, Anglo-American philosophers have typically sought to bring everything down to a single level of existence. Above all, they have sought to analyse everything 'ulterior' into particular items on a directly observable level. Such is the cut of Ockham's razor, wielded in the interests of ontological simplicity. But ontological simplicity has its price: a spectacular proliferation of particular items on the directly observable level. If we cannot overleap to the tree as a single object, we must live with a truly staggering number of tree-profiles. Or if we cannot understand a single extendable possibility as the meaning of 'vertically opposite angles are equal', we must live with a truly staggering number of occasions on which vertically opposite angles have been or will be equal. Is it really plausible to suppose that we could keep track of such multitudes? Phenomenology is prepared to complicate ontological levels in the interests of a different kind of simplicity. For it is only by 'ulterior' levels of existence that the endless proliferation of particular items can be reduced. No doubt 'ulterior' levels of existence are difficult to conceptualize; but at least they are not made unthinkable by sheer excess of numbers.

Given this range of different levels, it is impossible to think of the mind on the old linear stream-of-consciousness model. We must recognize that a great many different intentional acts are capable of going on simultaneously. We do not have to leave off perceiving tree-profiles in order to apprehend the tree as an object behind them; we do not have to take time out from apprehending the concrete tree in order to realize some idea about it (to think of it as falling under the verbal category of 'tree', for instance). The intentional acts which give us concrete objects and objectivities of thought (to go no further than those two general possibilities) are not of the same ontological status as perceived images, and do not have to find room in the same stream, on the same screen. Let us rather reflect upon the way in which, when watching a movie, we can continue to perceive visual images whilst at the same time getting a grasp on the motivation of a particular character whilst at the same time forming an impression of, say, human society as riddled with deceit and hypocrisy. Which also contradicts any notion of simultaneous processing as merely a matter of simply separate streams or screens – on each of which the images still follow one another one at a time.

This perspective has a further bearing upon the timing of mental processes. For the intentional act which grasps a tree or mathematical proof over and through many perceptual moments can hardly be pinned down as just another moment on the line of perceptual moments. It is not in the least surprising that our higher-order grasps and realizations can never be measured like the length of a shot on a movie screen. At what precise moment did one understand the mathematical proof as a whole? – and at what precise moment did one leave that understanding behind? At what precise moment did one form the impression of human society as riddled with deceit and hypocrisy? – and at what precise moment did one leave that impression behind? For certain Ordinary Language Analytical philosophers, the 'unclockability' of so many mental processes casts doubt upon the very notion of subjective experience and inward consciousness.[27] But from a Phenomenological perspective, it is the nature of questioning itself which is misconceived.

SYNTAGMATIC THEORY AND PHENOMENOLOGY

Discarding Husserl's focus upon the 'intentions' of an utterer, and working from a strictly Phenomenological conception of 'intentional acts', we can soon discover several very interesting analogies to syntagmatic theory. To begin with, there is an analogy between the role of grammatical category in a word and the role of the subject-pole in tactile or visual apprehension. The noun category of the word 'dog' is like a place-where-from; we approach the topic aspectivally, from one side only, leaving out of consideration all adjective-qualities and verb-doings. And grammatical category is bound up with the meaning of a word just as inextricably as the subject-pole is bound up with the content of a perception. Every word-meaning is seen through the 'barrel' of some specific grammatical category. There is always a position-taking, a particular standing-towards.

What's more, the different positions taken in different words are very different indeed. This is where Husserl crucially failed to break away from the traditional view. On the traditional view, a sentence is like a mere stream of words, like a succession of images displacing one another upon a single screen. But the screen-and-stream view can no more account for the unity of a sentence than for the unity of a perceptual object. We recognize an objectively existing tree when the differences of its profiles correlate with the different positions we take towards it. Likewise, we recognize the unified meaning of a sentence not because of any similarities between 'big' and 'dog' and 'jumps', but because the differences of word-meaning correlate with the different grammatical cases. In language as in perception, the trick is to see separate contents as complementary aspects.

Of course, the unified meaning of a sentence enormously reduces the possible contents of individual words. By itself, the word 'dog' can open up an endless proliferation of remembered dogs. But not so when the word becomes part of a sentence: 'A big dog jumped out at me in the park'. The proliferation of dog-possibilities is cut down and collapsed onto a single sentence-meaning, just as the proliferation of tree-profiles is cut down and collapsed onto a single object. Indeed, I have already suggested this very analogy in the 'Complementarity, synthesis, projection' section of Chapter 2. Now it can be seen that syntagmatic theory does for language what Phenomenology does for perception (and what Empiricist philosophers dislike doing in either case): i.e. making an enormous simplification in the number of particulars at the price of a small complication in the levels of existence.

Nor is this the end of the analogy. For in both cases, the move which transcends the sheer quantity of particulars also transcends the personal and subjective quality of those particulars. In the Phenomenological theory of perception, we overleap our own subjective contribution to tree-profiles, and 'discount for' the fact that we happen to be viewing from one particular direction and not another. Similarly in the syntagmatic theory of language, we overleap our own subjective memories of dogs, and 'discount for' the fact that we happen to have made the acquaintance of some particular dogs and not others. The dog in 'A big dog jumped out at me in the park' has to be projected beyond our own personal experience of dogs. Not that such experience is irrelevant, of course; but it serves as a stepping-stone towards the meaning, rather than as the meaning *per se*.

As for the meaning of the sentence as a whole, clearly it has the 'ideal' existence of an objectivity of thought. Although we think it, it is still not our own personal thought. Despite the claims of Derrida and the Post-structuralists, we do not feel entitled to understand it according to our own wish and whim. It offers resistance to our freedom of will. But this resistance is not due to the fact that it is someone else's thought. Our sense that it dwells outside us does not – or not in the first place – involve a sense that it dwells inside someone else. The 'ideal' existence of a sentence-meaning dwells primarily in the syntagmatic nature of language itself.

There are further analogies as regards the non-linear conception of wholes in both Phenomenology and syntagmatic theory. (This is the 'other' side of Husserl mentioned in the 'Linearity, spacing, consciousness' section of

Chapter 3, the side of Husserl that Derrida fails to take into account.) The mere continuous succession of one word after another is like the mere continuous succession of one visual profile after another – the beginning rather than the end of the story. Our processing by synthesis and projection leaps up above the line, whether we are grasping meaning in sentences or objects in the world. And this kind of grasping goes on simultaneously with other perceptual and interpretational activities in the mind. As I argued in the 'Processing on the way through' section of Chapter 5, we can continue taking in one word after another even as we reach towards larger syntagmatic wholes above those words, both retrospectively and in anticipation. (My discussion of anticipation in that section was especially Husserlian, and could well be recast into Husserl's special terminology of 'protention', 'horizons' and 'adumbrations'.[28]) As for the difficulty of pinning down exactly where specific grasps are achieved in the course of reading a sentence or a book, this too has its analogy in the general difficulty of 'clocking' any higher-order grasps or realizations along the line of perceptual moments.

Still, it is necessary to remember that all these analogies remain nothing more than analogies. What they reveal is a common cast of mind, a common manner of approach. But we shall not get very far if we try to make a direct equation between, say, the conventional variety of grammatical categories and the individual variation of profiles produced by walking around a tree. The Phenomenological processes of perception and the syntagmatic processes of language may be related, but there is almost nothing exactly equivalent between them. I shall make a suggestion as to the nature of their relation in the following section.

A POSSIBILITY FROM PIAGET

One obvious way of explaining a relation between Phenomenological and syntagmatic processes is by reference to cognitive development. Can we view the linguistic level as having somehow evolved out of the perceptual level? I think we can. But first we must take on board a theory of cognitive development which credits the growing child with something much more than a mere continuous accretion of knowledge and skills – something much more than the behavioural approach to learning and training will allow. We need a theory of cognitive development which recognizes radical transforming leaps from level to level. And for this, we must turn to Piaget and his 'genetic epistemology'.

The turn to Piaget is a natural enough move for syntagmatic theory. For Piaget also has affiliations to 'I'-philosophy in general and to Phenomenology in particular. We should not be misled by the fact that he calls himself a Structuralist (a terminological accident which I have already discussed in *Superstructuralism*), or by the fact that he argues so strongly against Kant (as often in philosophy, the most visible hostilities are those between neighbours whose positions are at least sufficiently close to make disagreement interesting). If we consider Piaget's position overall, we can recognize the crucial role that he gives to the *a priori*, in the form of successive 'schemata' which the growing child applies to reality. As against Empiricists and Logical Positivists, Piaget claims that it is impossible to observe pure facts.[29] At the same time, he locates this *a priori* in the mind of the individual subject – and not in some abstract or social realm, like the Platonists or Hegelians or Superstructuralists. Hence his typically Phenomenological emphasis upon subjective activity and creativity. And when he insists upon the foundational role of the child's sensori-motor activity, he is even more in tune with that outlook which I described in the 'Phenomenological perspective' section above.

Not that Piaget himself pays much attention to the role of language. Indeed, he has often been criticized on this very point. Like Husserl, he is mainly interested in the logico-mathematical capacities of the human mind. His model for cognitive development incorporates language acquisition as just one element in a general transition from the sensori-motor stage to the pre-concrete operational (or 'intuitive') stage.[30] Although he places great emphasis upon the child's newly evolved power of trying out operations inwardly (without having to carry them through bodily), he places surprisingly little emphasis upon language as the means and medium of such inwardness. Nonetheless, there are certain concepts that he advances in relation to his own logico-mathematical interests which can prove equally serviceable in relation to language.[31] And in particular, the concepts of *accommodation* and *reflective abstraction*.

In *accommodation*, the child constructs a new schema by which to understand experience. In ordinary *assimilation*, the data received are simply absorbed as additional information under an existing schema. But when an existing schema begins to show inadequacies at the object-pole, a change is required at the subject-pole. The process has been compared to the business of adjusting the lens of a camera in order to 'accommodate' objects and bring them into focus. But, in truth, the comparison scarcely does justice to the radical nature of the change required. When one schema replaces another, it is more like introducing an entirely new kind of camera – like exchanging a snapshot camera for a movie camera, or a fixed movie camera for a mobile movie camera. The child must redo and restructure everything that was learnt at the previous stage of development.

The key to *accommodation* is *reflective abstraction*. 'Reflective', in the sense that the child doubles back over its own subjective contribution to experience.[32] The principles of a higher-order cognitive level are not abstracted from objects at the object-pole, but from actions at the subject-pole – or, better still, from actions at the subject-pole as successfully coordinated with objects at the object-pole. As Piaget points out, the child is egocentric precisely to the extent that it does not distinguish between its own doings and those of the world. But when it manages to de-centre itself, it becomes capable of grasping its own grasps. And those grasps are then available for being put to further use. According to Piaget, the child's cognitive development consists of a number of such moves, each one building on top of its predecessor.

How can this be applied to the acquisition of language? As I have said, there is almost nothing exactly equivalent between the perceptual and the syntagmatic processes of synthesis and projection. One very good reason for this is that the end-product of perceptual synthesis and projection is the object, the thing-out-there. But in terms of language, objects and things-out-there fall naturally under the grammatical category of the noun. So the end-product of perceptual synthesis and projection corresponds to just one element of input into syntagmatic synthesis and projection. Clearly, this makes it impossible to lay perceptual and syntagmatic processes side by side, as parallel or cognate forms. But it does suggest the possibility of constructing them one on top of the other, à la Piaget. Can we not regard the grammatical category of the noun as developing out of the particular kind of grasp that yields objects?

If the grammatical category of the noun can be regarded as developing out of the kind of grasp that yields objects, then the grammatical category of the adjective can be regarded as developing out of the kind of grasp that yields qualities. For this latter grasp is evidently a grasp of a more receptive and less effortful kind. A child may react to redness and hardness without as yet recognizing the object, the toy brick, to which those qualities belong.[33] Here we have two entirely different cognitive 'sets' or ways of standing towards the world. And a further different 'set' is involved when the child gets a grip on the unity of an event over time, as by repeatedly knocking a toy brick off the table and watching it fall to the floor. This is a more active and effortful kind of grasp than that which yields objects; indeed, it may subsume multiple objects, just as the grasp of objects may subsume multiple qualities. And does it not correspond to the grammatical category of the verb? If the child can not only learn different kinds of grasp but actually become aware of them *as* different, then we have a natural basis for the major grammatical categories. By grasping its own grasps, the child can come to the principles of categorization on a higher-order cognitive level.

Such an hypothesis would account for the fact that the major grammatical categories are so remarkably consistent from language to language. Since our grammatical categories are not learnt from the world but rather imposed upon it, one might well theorize the possibility of slicing things up quite differently. But the possibility is only theoretical. One cannot even begin to imagine what such alternative ways of slicing might be like in practice. The major grammatical categories seem to be universal – at least, in Chomsky's special sense of the term 'universal'.[34] That is, they may not all appear in every language; some languages manage to get by without adjectives. But no human language deploys any major grammatical categories other than nouns, verbs and adjectives. Which is just what the above hypothesis would lead us to expect.

However, the hypothesis is undoubtedly simplistic as it stands; and two important qualifications are immediately called for. In the first place, this is only the beginning of the story of grammatical categorization in language, and there are a great many further twists and turns. One very obvious twist is that which produces such words as 'squareness', 'stupidity' and 'violence' – grammatical nouns which bear no correspondence to things. If we define nouns *simply* as thing-words, verbs *simply* as action-words and adjectives *simply* as property-words, then this development will seem inexplicable. But the hypothesis I have proposed is not quite so simple. I have not linked nouns to things, but rather to the kind of grasp which (on the level of basic perception) yields things. The distinction is crucial. For the kind of grasp which yields things can not only be put to use as a means of grammatical categorization, but can be put to still further use in the production of still higher levels of abstraction. Thus 'squareness' is not a noun in the same way that 'dog' is a noun: it is the nominalized form of an adjective (or of a predicate 'is square'). Such building of 'operations on operations' is perfectly in accordance with the Piagetian model, which imposes no necessary upper limit.[35] The story of grammatical categorization in language is open-ended. And of course language acquires ever greater flexibility as it distances itself from elementary concrete nouns, verbs and adjectives. Yet it is with elementary concrete nouns, verbs and adjectives that the child begins; and, *pace* Derrida and the Superstructuralists, I believe that these origins are not without significance.

The second qualification has to do with the role of social context in the acquisition of language. In relation to his own logico-mathematical interests, Piaget emphasizes individual cognitive development; and perhaps that emphasis is viable in relation to those interests, at least methodologically. But it is not viable in relation to the acquisition of language. For language can be learnt only by hearing other people speak. It would be ridiculous to suppose that a child could arrive at the system of major grammatical categories entirely on its own. But it would be no less ridiculous to suppose that the system of major grammatical categories could be inculcated entirely by external training. According to Lenneberg's Critical Period Hypothesis, there is only one particular phase in human growth when language can be readily absorbed.[36] A child is incapable of learning language prior to the age of 12–18 months, regardless of how much training it is given; and a human being deprived of exposure to language until the early teens apparently has great difficulty in mastering any linguistic skills at all. One can only conclude that the development of grammatical categories occurs when the child's capacities rise to meet the language that it hears. If these capacities are not brought to appropriate fulfilment, then the system of grammatical categories must remain for ever unrealized.

The Piagetian model thus explains the apparent universality of nouns, verbs and adjectives – and does so without recourse to innatism. This seems to me exactly the right route to steer, avoiding both the Scylla of the *tabula rasa* and the Charybdis of the pre-programmed brain. For although it is not absolutely impossible that the human brain might be wired up to think in terms of nouns, verbs and adjectives, yet it is surely highly implausible. Can we really believe that functions so advanced and so particular could be laid down as mere necessities of synaptic architecture? The Piagetian model allows us to recognize an inevitability about the development of major grammatical categories which is not the inevitability of biological predetermination. Rather, it is an inevitability of the kind which produces a sand-dune in the desert. Given a ripple or hump above a certain critical size, the combination of regularly blowing wind and an infinite number of sand grains will eventually construct a fully grown sand-dune of a perfectly predictable size, shape and alignment. Yet the mighty sand-dune did not exist in kernel form within the tiny ripple. The inevitability here comes from an interreaction between the properties of the ripple and certain standard external conditions of the desert world. Under such conditions, the ripple increases upon itself.

This, I suggest, is how we should think of human cognitive development. No doubt, the brain is wired up for a number of very basic functions. But the more advanced functions, such as those involved in language, emerge only as the mind increases upon itself. The major grammatical categories do not lie ready and waiting within the brain of a new-born child, like some diagram or plan prepared in miniature. They derive from certain earlier operations, certain kinds of grasp interreacting with the standard external conditions of the human world. And these kinds of grasp are not available for further use until they have been built up by ordinary use, until repeated successful application has confirmed them and made them habitual. The *a priori* of the Piagetian model is an evolving *a priori*, not set down all in one go from the start. The major grammatical categories precede our experience in the sense that we impose them as frames upon our experience, but not in the sense that they somehow existed before *any* of our experience. On the contrary, they impose upon one level of experience only after having grown out of another. The *a priori* of the Piagetian model is just a single step ahead at a time.

8 The case against Logical Analytical philosophy

THE PINCER MOVEMENT AGAINST MEANING

Whereas the general Phenomenological framework is highly compatible with syntagmatic theory, the Analytical framework is highly inimical to it. My discussion of Analytical philosophy will therefore be largely negative and uncomplimentary. But Analytical philosophy cannot be criticized on the same grounds as Superstructuralism. For Analytical philosophers, whether Logical Analytical or Ordinary-Language Analytical, have no predilection for single words as against sentences. On the contrary. The Logical Analytical attitude can be traced all the way from Frege – 'only in the context of a sentence does a word have significance' – though to Donald Davidson – 'individual words [may not] have meanings at all, in any sense that transcends the fact that they have a systematic effect on the meanings of the sentences in which they occur.'[37] As for the Ordinary-Language attitude, we need look no further than Searle – 'sentences, not words, are used to say things' – and Austin – 'to say a word or a phrase "has a meaning" is to say that there are sentences in which it occurs which "have meanings"; and to know the meaning which the word or phrase has is to know the meanings of sentences in which it occurs'.[38] Although Analytical philosophers (perhaps especially Russell, and Wittgenstein in both his Logical and Ordinary-Language phases) continue to theorize about the meanings of single words, basically they regard single word-meanings as dependent and unfulfilled. The grounds for criticism lie elsewhere: specifically, in the fact that Logical Analytical philosophers think of sentences in terms of (sentence-sized) *propositions*; while Ordinary-Language Analytical philosophers think of sentences in terms of (sentence-sized) *speech-acts*.

Logical Analytical philosophers will be the subject of this chapter. Under the 'Logical' category, I include Frege, Russell and the early Wittgenstein; Schlick, Carnap and Ayer; and Tarski, Quine, Davidson and Kripke. 'Logical' is an appropriate term here not only because many of these philosophers already belong to the Logical Atomist or Logical Positivist movements, but because it was the advent of the new symbolic logic which gave this whole way of thinking its start. Later I shall be arguing that the more recent developments have also been propelled by developments in logic. But for the time being, I shall follow my usual principle of trying to understand a way of thinking by its roots. The fundamental disagreements with syntagmatic theory are most clearly revealed in the very earliest moves by which Logical Analytical philosophy was first set up.

Symbolic logic seems to give philosophy a new handle on language because it seems to grasp the real inner form of sentences. The predicate calculus, in particular, seems to come closer to the actual grain of language than ever before. Of course, logic is still logic, strictly without meaning, hermetic in a way that language evidently is not. This form still needs a content. But symbolic logic itself suggests an appropriate content. For although logic is not concerned as to what its terms might represent, it does require that they be known as either true or false. Without decided truth-values, logic has nothing to concatenate, nothing to work upon. It is no great step to conclude that the *deciding* must be done by reference to the outside world.

So reference comes into the picture. The expressions of language must be applied to reality in order to be judged true or false; and in the process, they take on a kind of substantiality which logic alone cannot provide. Indeed, this is a substantiality of the most literal kind – the substantiality of real concrete things and states of affairs. Such an orientation is of course very much in line with the general Empiricist inclination to take outside reality as the ultimate court of appeal. And, as an orientation specifically towards reference, it is specifically in line with John Stuart Mill and the old notion of *denotation.*

The Logical Analytical vision of language thus combines the extreme hermeticism of logic with the extreme 'worldliness' of reference. An extraordinary vision! So much so, that only a genuine visionary like Wittgenstein could finally fully launch it. With a logical conception of form on the one side and an out-in-the-world conception of content on the other, the Logical Analytical philosophers propose to account for everything that really matters in language. Meaning as traditionally understood goes down under a double-pronged pincer movement. And so confident are the Logical Analytical philosophers of having seen through to what really matters in language, that they are even prepared to blame ordinary language for falling short of proper standards. Hence the many attempts to set up an ideal alternative language of pure logic and reference – a language capable of doing all the same jobs as ordinary language, but doing them better.

However, certain qualifications are in order here, especially as regards reference. The Logical Analytical understanding of reference is considerably more sophisticated than Mill's notion of denotation. For Mill thought essentially in terms of naming: the meaning of a word was the object or objects that it named. Such a notion collapses in the face of expressions like 'the first woman President of the United States' – expressions which are obviously meaningful but which cannot be attached to any actual bearer in the world. The Logical Analytical philosophers avoid this problem because their approach is based upon propositions rather than single words.

The fact is that a proposition does not name: it asserts. And whereas a name has to attach successfully to the world, a proposition can relate to the world either successfully or unsuccessfully – it is either true or false. As Wittgenstein puts it: 'To understand a proposition means to know what is the case, if it is true. (One can therefore understand it without knowing whether it is true or not.)'[39] The emphasis switches from the goal to the path – to the procedures for testing, the criteria for deciding, the truth-conditions. On the one hand, the truth-conditions of a proposition are not straightforwardly out in the world like an actual state of affairs; but on the other hand, they are also not ensconced in the privacy of the mind like mental images. They are still always aiming at the world, even if they no longer always strike home on their target there.

The propositional approach also comes into play for expressions below the level of sentences. The Logical Analytical philosophers do not think of the meaning of an expression as a bond to some particular named object or objects. Instead, they think of the meaning of an expression as a search for objects. An expression is sent ranging across all possible entities in the world, applying criteria and gathering in the members of a set. This is an altogether more hypothetical way of thinking – very much in line with the hypothetical nature of logic itself. And if it should happen that no entity fulfils the criteria, then of course the set must remain empty. But still the very operation of applying the expression to the world constitutes a kind of meaning.

We can see the propositional approach appearing in the key early texts of Logical Analytical philosophy. Thus Frege in his famous article turns decisively against the old notion of denotation when he observes that, even for proper names, the meaning cannot be simply identified with the bearer.[40] For there is an obvious and important difference between 'the Morning Star' and 'the Evening Star', in spite of the fact that both expressions refer to the same object. Frege pinpoints the difference as a difference in how we pick out the object. 'The Morning Star' gets us there along one path, 'the Evening Star' along another. So Frege arrives at his famous distinction between what he calls *Bedeutung* and what he calls *Sinn*, where *Bedeutung* is the object of reference and *Sinn* is the criterion or public procedure for identifying that object.

Russell carries the propositional approach even further. In his Theory of Descriptions, the kind of propositional assertion that is obvious in sentences is discovered even in definite descriptions – where it is far from obvious.[41] When Russell translates 'The round square is round' into (informally) 'There is one and only one entity *x* which is round and square, and that entity is round', he effectively replaces the reference of a noun phrase ('the round square') with the either-true-or-false options of a mini-proposition ('there is one and only one entity *x* which is round and square'). The variable *x* ranges across every possible entity in the world, testing for roundness and squareness. There is no longer any suggestion, as on the old notion of denotation, that the round square somehow has to exist because it has been named *before* entering into the assertion.

However, it must not be supposed that the new interest in the operation of referring counteracts the old interest in the object of reference. From the Logical Analytical point of view, the operation still serves solely to get to the object; it is not something to be studied for its own sake. Having once covered themselves against the manifest absurdities of denotation, the Logical Analytical philosophers soon drift back to their preferred focus upon out-in-the-world things and states of affairs. If the truth-conditions for a proposition (or mini-proposition) are not realized in the world, then there is nothing further to be done with it – it becomes a write-off. After all, what logic needs to work with is decided truth rather than decided falsehood.

Frege sets the pattern right from the start. Although *Sinn* is the real novelty in his theory, he goes on to say a great deal about *Bedeutung* and relatively little about *Sinn*. Indeed, his very terminology loads the dice, by carrying across to the object of reference the associations of *Bedeutung* as the normal German word for *meaning* (and not *reference* at all). Nor is it without significance that his discussion continues to focus upon the proper names 'Morning Star' and 'Evening Star'. For proper names, even when they require paths of identification, still do not have meaning in the way that 'dog' or 'park' have meaning. Proper names are essentially arbitrary (which is why this particular 'Star' does not have to live up to the common-noun meaning of 'star'). We should pick out Venus in the morning sky by exactly the same criteria even if it went under the name of 'Ferris Major' or 'Zonda's Pride'. It is hardly surprising that Frege finds no place for ideas or representations in his theory of language.

If Frege's terminology of *Sinn* and *Bedeutung* has an ulterior bias, so too does the terminology of *intension* and *extension* which Logical Analytical philosophers have since adopted. In this latter distinction, it is *extension* that covers the things or states of affairs referred to, and *intension* that covers the criteria or means for picking them out. *Intension* thus occupies the same kind of place as what we ordinarily call *meaning*; but whereas *meaning* looks like an independent term and suggests an independent area of study, *intension* looks like a mere parallel or accompaniment to *extension*. In practice, indeed, it is *extension* which typically takes the lead. The situation might well justify an analysis along Derridan lines, where a polarization of terms not only works to delimit the thinkable in a given field, but effectively induces us to allow one term dominance over the other. In what follows, I shall use *intension* specifically to cover that means-of-picking-out to which Logical Analytical philosophers attend – but only on the understanding that *intension* has nothing to do with what we ordinarily call *meaning*.

In fact, the dominance of *extension* is curious even in relation to the Logical Analytical philosophers' own assumptions. If *intension* is what enables us to pick out things and states of affairs, then surely it must exist in some way prior to those things and states of affairs? Just how do these mysterious criteria function, and exactly what form do they take? Such questions, properly pursued, might end up carrying us towards *meaning* after all. But the Logical

Analytical philosophers are not interested in pursuing such questions. They invoke *intension* essentially when *extension* falters – in cases of contrary-to-fact conditionals, opaque contexts, etc. They are strangely happy to ignore *intension* as long as it gets us through to *extension* without difficulties. In their approach, *intension* features only on the rebound, only in second place.

So why this overwhelming urge to avoid what we ordinarily call meaning? As I have already said, the Logical Analytical philosophers advance the claims of language precisely in order to dispose of and substitute for interior mental representations. From their point of view, anything subjectively in the mind is unscientific. Of course, it is especially images and pictures that they regard as being subjectively in the mind – a version of mental representations very different from that proposed by syntagmatic theory. But there is no reason to suppose that they would be mollified by what syntagmatic theory actually does propose. For syntagmatic theory still allows meaning to exist non-publicly and non-observably; still conceives of meaning in a deliberately approximate and 'glimpsing' kind of way; and still invokes the open-endedness of meaning as a matter of principle. This is all inherently unsatisfactory from a Logical Analytical point of view.

What we are looking at is an absolute methodological presupposition as to what may count as a viable theory of meaning. True to Empiricist tradition, the Logical Analytical philosophers consider nothing worth knowing unless it can be laid out clearly and tested. Hence their determination to overleap meaning and tie language on to something firm – as the real outside world is firm. To overleap meaning is the great unspoken drive of all Logical Analytical philosophers. They will take any detours rather than set foot upon the vague and obscure morass of interior mental representations. And they will persist in their attempts no matter how often their routes may block. Needless to say, this is not an attitude susceptible of direct proof or disproof.

In fact, their routes often have blocked. Insuperable difficulties led to the abandonment of Wittgenstein's 'picture theory' and to the abandonment of the Logical Positivists' verificationism. It is very much to the credit of this style of philosophizing that it does at least bring forth and confront its own problems. But the problems still fail to appear in their full size so long as their solutions are sought under the same ultimate methodological presuppositions.[42] It is only when we recognize the possibility of a radically different attitude that we can start to see these problems as symptoms of something profoundly wrong with the whole Logical Analytical enterprise.

A NEED FOR DISENGAGEMENT

Let me then propose a radically different attitude (also probably not susceptible of direct proof or disproof). Language, I suggest, is important not because it ties onto objects and states of affairs in the world, but because it disengages from them. We don't need language in order to know actuality but in order to conceive of possibility. The processes of the syntagm give us the freedom to create meanings independently of reality. To collapse meanings back onto observation or 'direct acquaintance' is to miss the point of language entirely.[43] When Logical Analytical philosophers try to hold language's nose against the grindstone of reality, they are denying its most valuable property.

By way of an opening gambit, consider the role of language in relation to young children. Young children clearly do not make the same sharp distinction of either-true-or-false that adults make. Children learn to understand language long before they learn a critical concept of truth. Typically, the things that are put into a child's mind by language are neither exactly judged as true nor exactly held in abeyance as hypothetical – they are, simply, accepted. And the child's world contains many weird and wonderful semi-beliefs which continue to be accepted even when plainly at odds with what has been learnt through observation. Indeed, for many such beliefs, the child does not even know whether they were actually acquired from observation or from other people's language. In relation to young children, it is *prima facie* implausible to make a proposition's meaning depend upon the ability to judge what would make that proposition true.

To the extent that adult reality is built upon childhood reality, it would seem that a large part of our world never comes to judgement at all. Surely the knowledge that we have by way of language far exceeds the knowledge that we have by way of direct acquaintance? If what we could not directly test for truth had to be left in abeyance as hypothetical, then there would be very little not left in abeyance. The obvious moral to be drawn is that language does not merely reflect but also constitutes our world. That is, language does not merely match up against reality as revealed by perceptual observation: it also functions as an independent and parallel source of knowledge.

The point needs no further labouring as regards ordinary language. But then the Logical Analytical philosophers are not claiming to deal with ordinary language: they are putting forward an ideal language specifically to serve the interests of scientific truth. Still, one may grant the special importance and value of scientific truth, and yet doubt that this ideal language would serve its interests. For the Logical Analytical philosophers, following Empiricist tradition, focus upon one particular aspect of science – the aspect of experiment and observation. This is indeed a characteristic of modern science as distinct from pre-scientific thinking. Scientists are obliged to propose experiments and observations by which their theories may be eventually tested against reality. But it does not follow that language should be co-opted to enforce this obligation, that language should be given the role of tying science back onto the world. Language, I suggest, has another and earlier role – of getting science away from the world in the first place.

If this is a paradox, it is not an unfamiliar one. The mere observation of immediate concrete facts does not produce scientific hypotheses. Only insignificant truths can be drawn from immediate concrete facts. Whereas the spectacular truths of modern science look back at the facts as if from a distance – a strange and extreme theoretical distance. In this respect, the spectacular truths of modern science are not so very different from the spectacular falsehoods of pre-scientific thinking. (I concede the falsehood of pre-scientific thinking only for the sake of argument: in another context, I would want to claim that pre-scientific myths, although erected upon inadequate foundations, are far from lacking in explanatory power; and that modern scientific theories, although wielding enormous explanatory power, may yet turn out to be erected upon inadequate foundations.) Language, as a means of hypothesizing possibilities, is equally at the service of scientific truth or pre-scientific falsehood. There is no way of throwing out gods and ghosts *on a linguistic basis* without also throwing out quantum physics and the theory of continental drift.

What's more, language is crucial to human thinking on the negative as well as the positive side. No doubt the reality-oriented scientist will never need to make positive use of the contrary-to-reality sentence: 'This cat is four feet long.' But the scientist still needs four-foot-long cats as a linguistic possibility. For the scientist needs to recognize that cats *might* have been of a different size. The real characteristics of cats become a matter for scientific explanation only when one recognizes that there is a question as to why they are as they are and not otherwise. The theory of evolution might well be viewed as a response to this kind of question. (In pre-scientific times, presumably, the response would have taken the form of a myth of Creation or a hypothesis about God's design for the Universe.)

It is thus that language opens up the space for our thinking. The Logical Analytical philosophers are gravely mistaken when they try to use language as a means of restricting what we can be permitted to think. Laying down strict limits for the meaningful, they dismiss as nonsense wide tracts of potential discourse. (The sense of circumscription comes through most strongly in Wittgenstein's *Tractatus* and the writings of the Logical Positivists.) But on a syntagmatic view, the interrelationship between thought and language works in a very different fashion. On a syntagmatic view, language has a liberating effect upon thought, creative rather than constrictive. The realm of the potentially meaningful is of vast and indeterminable extent, with possibilities far beyond anything we will ever actually need to use in practice.

The trouble with Logical Analytical philosophy is that it wants to make language always correct – or at least, always readily correctable. Meaning is never to be allowed to stray too far from the observable facts. When Logical Analytical philosophers tie language on to reality, they are adopting a safety-first policy. But trying to keep language safe from error is like trying to live one's life without risk of unhappiness. Language gives us the power of being amazingly right only because it also gives us the power of being amazingly wrong. The use of language involves taking a chance, accepting a risk of error.

This may seem reminiscent of Derrida, who also claims that the use of language involves taking a chance, accepting a risk.[44] And for Derrida too, the element of chance or risk is a necessary consequence of the independence of linguistic meaning. But although the parallel is genuine enough, it cannot be carried very far. For in Derrida's version of meaning, the disengagement from reality is terminal. By processes of 'infinite implication', meaning moves on endlessly from signifier to signifier, pursuing its own courses, self-sufficient and self-sustaining.[45] Truth-to-the-world becomes an irrelevant concept. Whereas in syntagmatic theory, the independent possibilities of meaning created by processes of synthesis and projection are still capable of being brought back round and matched against reality. On a syntagmatic showing, truth-to-the-world appears as problematic but not impossible. That is, it is neither easily and everywhere applicable in the way that Logical Analytical philosophers would have us think, nor simply inapplicable in the way that Derrida would have us think. Here as elsewhere, syntagmatic theory occupies a position between the extremes of Poststructuralism and Logical Analytical philosophy – just as syntagmatic meaning occupies a position between single word-meaning and propositional reference.

LOGICAL RELATIONS VERSUS GRAMMATICAL RELATIONS

If reference fails to encompass language from the one side, so too does logic from the other. Indeed, it is curious how symbolic logic came to get involved with language in the first place. Originally, in the *Begriffsschrift* and the *Principia Mathematica*, symbolic logic was developed with the grand aim of furnishing an ultimate foundation for mathematics (especially arithmetic). But this foundation seemingly went so deep that it ended up founding language too. And yet there is a very important divergence between the way in which symbolic logic claims to found mathematics and the way in which it claims to found language. For while the principles of logic give direct support to the principles of arithmetic, the visible sentences of language must be seen as having somehow shifted away from their proper logical foundations. Hence the Logical Analytical view that the actual sentences of our language are distorted and deceptive. Sentences must be structurally reformulated before they can re-establish contact with their proper foundations. Whereas no one, so far as I know, has ever suggested that mathematical equations are not structurally in order as they are.

On this view, ordinary grammatical relations do the same kind of job as logical relations; only, in the current state of language, they don't do it very well. Hence the invocation of logical syntax, which supposedly represents a superior form of syntax. I shall hope to show that the term 'logical syntax' is a complete misnomer, at least to the extent that we associate syntax with ordinary grammar. Logical syntax is a 'syntax' only to the extent that any system of structural laws might be called a syntax. (Unfortunately, this extended application of the term 'syntax' has become very fashionable – and not only with Logical Analytical philosophers.) On a syntagmatic view, the logical system of structural laws does not do the same kind of job as grammar at all.

Consider the predicate calculus. Logically, the proposition 'The thief tied up all the guards with some rope' translates into a function ('. . . tied up . . . with . . .'), and three arguments ('the thief', 'all the guards', 'some rope'). The odd thing about this is that the three arguments are effectively on a par, distinguished only as being placed first, second or third. There is no recognition that a subject noun and an object noun feed into a verb in different ways, or that a noun in a prepositional phrase feeds in differently again. Totally dissimilar kinds of synthesis are lumped together under the same kind of relation, that of an argument to a function.

But then the predicate calculus does not decompose a proposition in order to bring out the different kinds of relation involved. It decomposes a proposition in order to get at those particular parts which can be quantified – 'the thief', 'all the guards', 'some rope'. For these are parts that the calculus can operate with. Whereas the most interesting feature of Frege's original formulation from a syntagmatic point of view was the notion of an unsaturated function – since *all* parts of speech are ultimately unsaturated from a syntagmatic point of view. But functions in the predicate calculus serve mainly to hold open places for arguments to fit into. What interests the logicians are the arguments – which do the saturating – and the whole propositions – where the saturating has already been done. (For further discussion of a more recent calculus, see the section on 'Montague Grammar' in Chapter 12.)

Turning from arguments and functions to logical connectives, we find that logical connectives embody purely external relations, taking no account of synthesis and projection. A logical 'and', for instance, forms a complex proposition merely by combining the truth-values of elementary propositions. If it is true that 'On Monday the 13th, snow fell heavily across the state', and if it is true that 'Traffic came to a halt on all major roads (on Monday the 13th)', then it is true that 'On Monday the 13th, snow fell heavily across the state, and traffic came to a halt on all major roads.' There is no necessary intersection here between the two elementary propositions, no implication that the halting of the traffic was a consequence of the falling of the snow. Whereas in natural language, we would certainly want to dispute the complex proposition if we happened to know that the traffic came to a halt only because everyone was listening to a vital announcement on their car radios. But such consequentiality does not matter to the logical 'and'. The logical 'and' is perfectly happy to combine totally irrelevant propositions: 'On Monday the 13th, snow fell heavily across the state, and Lisbon is the capital of Portugal.' It is also perfectly happy to combine propositions which natural language would relate by the very different consequentiality of a 'but': 'On Monday the 13th, snow fell heavily across the state, but the traffic kept moving on all major roads.' In logical translation, a natural 'but' ends up exactly the same as a natural 'and'.

Similarly with logical 'or's and 'if . . . then's. The divergences from natural 'or's and 'if . . . then's are obvious, and Logical Analytical philosophy has always recognized them. But it has also sought to minimize them. It has chosen to view the natural way of using connectives as merely a slightly messier and fussier version of the logical way. Frege, for instance, dismissed the special consequentiality of a natural 'but' as a mere colouring, a 'Färbung', an optional extra added on top of the logical 'and'. But syntagmatic theory gives us a new conception of just how much logical connectives leave out of the picture. From a syntagmatic point of view, these supposed optional extras are precisely what matters most about conjunctions in natural language.

The crucial concept here is the concept of the facilitative role. In Chapter 4, I introduced this concept apropos of words such as 'so', which do not simply contribute meaning to a sentence but serve as catalysts to assist the synthesis of other meanings. Similarly with words such as 'and'. Considered purely in itself, an 'and' means no more than a bare plus sign – which is exactly as much meaning as symbolic logic is prepared to allow it. But then the facilitative role of an 'and' can never appear in the world on its own, only in relation to the other meanings that it brings together. (It is hardly surprising that dictionaries do not really define the meanings of such words as 'and', but rather provide sample sentences and clauses to show how they work in context.) For the manner of this bringing together can never be known in advance; it is as unpredictable as the particular nature of the other meanings involved. An 'and' alone cannot tell us how 'On Monday the 13th, snow fell heavily across the state' is going to be relevant to 'traffic came to a halt on all major roads' – it can only tell us that there is a relevance there to be looked for.

Recognizing no synthesis between elementary propositions, the Logical Analytical philosophers arrive at the doctrine of truth-functionality. According to this doctrine, the truth-value of any complex proposition can be calculated, without further reference to reality, from the truth-values of its parts. An extraordinary doctrine! Demonstrating yet again the extraordinary enchantment that logic casts over the eyes of these philosophers. In effect, they are deciding truth-values at the lowest level of elementary propositions, and then merely concatenating decided truth-values for all higher levels. But anyone looking at language with unenchanted eyes can hardly fail to see how meaning continues to combine with meaning above the level of elementary propositions. And it is the truth or falsity of these higher-level combinations that is most likely to concern us, most likely to be the subject of debate. Elementary propositions present little more than elementary observations that something exists. But our human understanding thrives upon interpretations over and above elementary observations, upon consequentialities and connections and relevances such as make their appearance only in whole complex propositions and clusters of propositions.*

* To some extent, a level of deciding may be indicated by an inserted 'It is true that'. A few paragraphs ago, I placed an 'It is true that' in front of 'On Monday the 13th, snow fell heavily across the state, and traffic came to a halt on all major roads.' But the situation looks rather different if we place an 'It is true that' in front of each clause separately: '*It is true that* on Monday the 13th, snow fell heavily across the state, and *it is true that* traffic came to a halt on all major roads.' With insertions on this level, even '*It is true that* on Monday the 13th, snow fell heavily across the state, and *it is true that* Lisbon is the capital of Portugal' does not look quite

The fact is that logical relations can never take over from grammatical relations because they can never actually constitute meanings. Grammatical relations are like an internal supporting skeleton, integral to language. But logical relations come after meaning, fitting over language like a net. Indeed, if logical relations were the only structuring relations in language, there would be no reason to bother with complex propositions at all. Why put an 'and' between elementary propositions if its effect were no more than that of the 'and' in 'On Monday the 13th, snow fell heavily across the state, and Lisbon is the capital of Portugal'? This bizarre combination conveys no point, and there would be no point in making it. Left to their own resources, logical relations are incapable of producing anything worth saying; they are important only as they apply to something which is already worth saying. When complex propositions are discussed in Logical Analytical philosophy, the discussion avoids bombinating in a vacuum only because a certain degree of consequentiality is tacitly taken for granted.

One way of showing how logic 'fits over' language is to consider the size and scale of its application. As I have said, the predicate calculus conveys the impression of getting down to the very grain of language, down to the ultimate atomic propositions and their ultimate sub-atomic components. But the impression is false. The formulae that apply on the tiniest scale can equally well apply on much larger scales. The formula $\forall x(Fx \rightarrow Gx)$ can be fitted to the proposition that if x is human then x is mortal; but it can also be fitted to the proposition that if x is a mortal human being with no genetic defects and living in an appropriate social environment, then x will have mastered the rudiments of a linguistic system by the age of 18 months. We can fill in our constants and variables with content of any size. The only constraint is that, if we want to be able to perform useful logical calculations with them, we shall need to recognize at least some recurrence of the same or substitutable content. But logic as such prescribes no necessary correlative scale of content. Indeed, we can spread our net even more widely. We might dispute the logic of a particular book by showing that the structure of argument in one chapter falls under the form $\forall x(Fx \rightarrow Gx \vee Hx)$, from which the following chapter makes the invalid deduction that $\sim Hx$, therefore $\sim Fx$. Propositions, unlike sentences, are not fixed to any particular measure of language.

The view of logic that is emerging here is the traditional and unspectacular view of logic as a truth-calculus. Logic depends upon language, but language does not depend upon logic. Through the processes of syntagmatic synthesis,

so ridiculous. For Logical Analytical philosophers, of course, there is never any difficulty in translating between a plain proposition and its 'It is true that' equivalent. (Ramsay's 'assertive redundancy theory' claims that we don't need an explicit translation – but only because the 'It is true that' is implicitly present in front of every proposition anyway.[46]) Admittedly, there does not seem to be much difference between 'On Monday the 13th, snow fell heavily across the state' and 'It is true that on Monday the 13th, snow fell heavily across the state.' The difference emerges only when truth-claims on multiple levels are involved; in this case, the placing of an 'It is true that' in front of each and every separate clause makes all the difference in the world. As so often, a seemingly innocuous translation actually effects a shift in our whole frame of thinking. Philosophers, of all people, surely need to be on their guard against such hidden shifts.

language supplies the material for logic to get to work on. Reference alone is incapable of supplying what logic needs. No doubt, this will seem a disappointingly deflationary view. But then logic has long maintained pretensions beyond its proper station. It is time to rein in such imperialistic tendencies.

FORMAL SEMANTICS

Up to now, I have been debating against Logical Analytical philosophy as conceived by the Atomists and Positivists. But there has been a more recent movement of Logical Analytical philosophy, centred largely in America, and influenced especially by Tarski and Quine. This movement has significantly changed some of the parameters of the debate. In this and the following section, I shall be showing how the balance of power between logic and reference has been reconceived by the Formal Semanticists and the Possible-Worlds logicians. In Montague Grammar, the balance of power between logical relations and grammatical relations has also been reconceived; but since Montague Grammar has had its most significant impact upon linguists, I shall reserve that topic for Chapter 12.

As in the time of Frege and Russell, it is logic which mainly initiates the changes. The crucial development this time is the extension of logic from syntax to semantics. Those aspects of meaning which were once studied under a separate theory of reference, complementary to logic, are now brought under the sway of logic itself. Concomitantly, the separate theory of reference has largely fallen by the wayside. The new logic is certainly more referential than the old logic; but the new logical semantics is more hermetic than the old theory of reference. So in the philosophy of language as a whole, the emphasis upon reference has diminished. Although Logical Analytical philosophers have lost none of their interest in truth and truth-conditions, they are no longer concerned to connect language directly onto things and states of affairs in the outside world. Indeed, the outside world now makes much less of an appearance altogether.

From a logical point of view, there are many good reasons for backing away from the old theory of reference. The attempt to connect language directly onto things and states of affairs in the outside world turned out to be a recurring source of difficulty for Logical Atomists and Logical Positivists. Earlier I said that, as logic needs decided truth-values, so reference serves to do the deciding. But although reference is undoubtedly in the right position to do the deciding, it still seems unable to supply the absolutely clear-cut decisions about truth or falsity which logic requires. Consider the proposition 'Oxford is sixty miles from London.' True or false? Apparently we can take it either way, depending on the degree of precision we are looking for. Or what about 'Grass is green'? Again it depends on how we apply the proposition. If we are thinking about ordinary grass under ordinary conditions, we shall judge the proposition true. But we shall judge it false if we want to take account of certain exotic species of grass, or grass under drought conditions in Africa. It is not easy to devise a proposition which is true purely by virtue of what the words say and what the world is like. Nor is it easy to ascribe absolute falsity even to the most implausible proposition. One can imagine an argument under which even 'A human being is not a mammal' might squeeze in as true – an argument accepting all the biological facts, but still insisting that by virtue of their extra-genetic cultural and informational inheritance human beings are as different from (other) mammals as mammals are from reptiles. Certainly, one can imagine a speaker uttering some such attention-grabbing proposition in order to prove it true in some such special sense – without ever changing or seeking to change our general assent to the contrary proposition that a human being is a mammal.

The underlying problem is that the reference of a proposition and a state of affairs in the world are not simple objectivities which can be simply matched up face to face. For the world has to be understood and meanings have to be projected; in both cases, there is the kind of flexibility which goes with any subjective activity. Since we normally assume that a proposition is uttered with the intention of conveying useful information, we normally try to project its meaning and understand the world in a way that will enable us to take it as true. But we still have the option of projecting and understanding in a way that will enable us to take it as false. Indeed, when we contemplate a proposition such as 'Oxford is sixty miles from London', we can actually make it alternate between a true judgement and a false judgement, just as we can make the Gestalt picture alternate between the image of two faces and the image of a vase.[47] A proposition is not like Cinderella's shoe, which either fits or does not fit. But this is small consolation to the logician, who cannot possibly get to work upon such indeterminate material. If logic cannot obtain its clear-cut decisions about truth or falsity from a theory of reference, then it must needs obtain them elsewhere.

Hence the importance of Tarski's 'semantic conception of truth'.[48] This conception still involves correspondence, perhaps more so than ever. But the correspondence no longer takes reality as one of its terms. *The sentence 'Grass is green' is true if and only if grass is green.* Here, the quoted sentence can match perfectly against the unquoted sentence, thereby providing the absolutely clear-cut decision about truth that logic requires. But the perfection of the match depends upon the essential similarity of what is being matched – one linguistic expression against another. (And this holds good even if the quoted sentence appears in a different language, e.g. 'Das Gras ist grün'.) The logician is not concerned as to whether grass is in fact green. It is enough that anyone who asserts or rejects the sentence *grass is green* must be equally prepared to assert or reject the correlated sentence that *The sentence 'Grass is green' is true.*[49] In effect, the logician is claiming to arrive at the extension of the word 'true' without going by way of its meaning. The semantic conception of truth is an operation or function for 'printing out' all the sentences in a language belonging under the word 'true'.

Logic, of course, has its own special needs. But it is a different matter when the Formal Semanticists attempt to carry the semantic conception of truth over into a general philosophy of language. Donald Davidson, for example, sees the Tarskian technique as offering a new means of achieving the old Logical Analytical goal of getting rid of meaning. Like the Logical Analytical philosophers, he believes that to understand a sentence is to understand what it is for that sentence to be true. But the semantic conception of truth enables him to avoid hooking such understandings onto states of affairs in the outside world. 'We don't need the concept of reference', he claims.[50] By defining truth as a relation between linguistic expressions on two different levels, he hopes to achieve 'correspondence without confrontation'.[51]

Clearly, the Formal Semanticists are well named. The formal mathematico-logical half of the original Logical Analytical equation now dominates. Indeed, because this version of correspondence theory puts down no roots into reality, it needs to take on board the claims of a coherence theory too. No longer do the Formal Semanticists seek to connect scientific discourse on to reality at as many separate points as possible. Following Quine (who himself continues the tradition of Peirce), they abandon the atomic propositions of the Logical Atomists and the protocol sentences of the Logical Positivists. Instead, they regard scientific discourse as a largely self-supporting web of mutually confirming sentences. The emphasis has shifted away from separate elementary truths to a total truth-system.

But what exactly are the two different levels on which linguistic expressions exist? It seems that the quoted '*grass is green*' is to be understood as a mere sequence of written letters or spoken sounds. One particular sequence names a particular sentence just as the sequence R,I,O, space, D,E, space, J,A,N,E,I,R,O names a particular city. Thus emptied of meaning, language is evidently ready to be made over into the pure symbols of logic. The unquoted *grass is green*, on the other hand, needs to be understood as a (potential) fact in propositional form. For how can a fact appear except in relation to an articulated proposition? The world does not contain facts in the same way that it contains things, nor are facts directly visible in the same way that things are visible. (This was always a problem for the old Wittgensteinian view which tried to put facts simply out in the world. A fact appears only when reality is seen under the special linguistic form of a proposition.[52]) On this account, the level of the unquoted *grass is green* should be understood as the level of a reality already articulated by language.

But the more we consider this latter level, the more we find it tending to undermine the whole Formal Semanticist enterprise. According to Davidson, truth is the ultimate primitive upon which a general philosophy of language may be founded. But if truth involves the relation between '*grass is green*' and *grass is green*, then it already relies upon what language has done to produce the second term of that relation. Even before the Formal Semanticists begin their explanations, language has somehow gone out and articulated reality into propositional form. Tarski, concerned mainly to establish foundations for logic, can afford to ignore the highly problematic status of the unquoted *grass is green*. But the Formal Semanticists can not.

By following the Formal Semanticists' arguments through to their unintended conclusions, we can actually use them to justify syntagmatic theory or Superstructuralism. For if language in its articulating role is primary, then truth-conditions are clearly secondary, existing only within a framework which is neither true nor false. And if truth-conditions are secondary, then logical relations relying upon decisions of true or false become even more secondary. In the order of dependencies, logical relations stand at the tail of the queue – while grammatical relations stand at the head. For grammatical relations are clearly involved in articulating reality into propositional form in the first place. As I argued in the 'Logical relations versus grammatical relations' section above, the two kinds of relation do not operate over the same kind of ground at all.

In short, the Formal Semanticists have preserved the Logical Analytical way of thinking about language only at the price of ceasing to think about language *in general*. They have retreated to a more rarefied level of correspondence in order to uphold a view of language as essentially reflecting or describing. But in making this retreat, they have allowed a space to open up behind them – a space where language can be seen to function in an altogether earlier and more fundamental mode. And this mode is not a passive mode of reflecting and describing, but a very active mode of articulating and creating and constituting.

POSSIBLE-WORLDS SEMANTICS

Another fairly recent contender in the field of semantics is Possible-Worlds Semantics, as developed by Kripke, Carnap, Kaplan and Montague. Possible-Worlds Semantics is a product of several new 'intensional' forms of logic, especially the logic of possibility or modal logic. In a Possible-Worlds interpretation, something that is possibly true relative to our own actual world is actually true in some possible world(s). Logicians thus refer the proposition 'John may have gone to the movies' to some possible worlds in which he has gone to the movies and others in which he hasn't. Such possible worlds allow reference to terminate short of our actual world in a constructed theoretical space. No longer is it a question of trying to connect expressions onto real things and states of affairs as directly as possible. The earlier Logical Analytical emphasis upon testing and verification is here superseded by a more formal and mathematical way of thinking. To know the meaning of a particular expression is to know – quite in the abstract – the difference between those possible worlds in which the expression is true and those in which it is false.

The Possible-Worlds approach enables logic to get a grip on many previously intractable forms of proposition. By analysing the application of a proposition into a large number of separate applications, the logician can now resolve an indecisive truth-value into some applications that yield a definite 'true' and others that yield a definite 'false'. The Possible-Worlds approach also provides a method for dealing with contrary-to-fact conditionals; turns up elegant solutions to the problem of opaque contexts; and defines a version of (strict) implication which comes much closer to our ordinary understanding than the old paradoxes of material implication. In general, the Possible-Worlds approach facilitates a more subtle, less Procrustean way of translating between natural language and logic.

But although possible worlds are a great help to logic, they are no help at all to a theory of meaning. If the meaning of an expression is the difference between those possible worlds in which it is true and those in which it is false, then we need to be able to think the domain of all possible worlds. But the domain of all possible worlds is the kind of mathematico-logical postulate that is not in any real sense thinkable. For possible worlds must be as many as all the innumerable things in our world which could have been different, multiplied by all the innumerable ways in which they could have been different, further multiplied by all the permutations created by taking such differences in any combination of two or three or a trillion together. To explain the meaning of an expression on the basis of possible worlds is to explain a quality that is admittedly elusive on the basis of a quantity that is demonstrably inconceivable.

Unfortunately, the 'worlds' terminology obscures the size of the difficulty. Thinking of worlds, we tend to think of causally consistent and scientifically coherent worlds, where any particular situation in one place depends upon other particular situations in other places. The number of possible worlds which are 'maximal and complete' in this sense may be ultimately infinite, but at least it is a controllable sort of infinity.[53] David Lewis even suggests that the number of possible worlds is finite, and gives the impression that they can be counted merely in the hundreds or thousands.[54] But Possible-Worlds Semanticists have no right to draw upon consistency in this sense. If I tap a brick with my middle finger, it goes against all causality and scientific plausibility to suppose that the brick will disappear, or cough, or float upwards in the air. But such possibilities are nonetheless expressible and thinkable (and I have just expressed them for thinking about!). As long as semanticists are looking at what can be *said* to be possible, the only consistency they have the right to invoke is pure logical consistency. And pure logical consistency does nothing to control the exploding domain of possible worlds.

The Possible-Worlds Semanticists also encounter a special problem with contrary-to-fact conditionals. Suppose that Joe already has three cars in the actual (or given) world: then we may say 'If Joe had bought the Mercedes, he would have had four cars.' But this consequent does not follow in just any possible world – after all, there are possible worlds where Joe has two cars or twenty-two cars. Stalnaker and Lewis therefore propose a general assumption to the effect that a contrary-to-fact conditional should be understood as holding true for the particular possible world (or worlds) which is (or are) most similar to the actual or given world.[55] Everything has to be kept the same except for the alteration prescribed in the antecedent. But now we must surely begin to wonder whether we really need to invoke a possible world at all. Why does a single alteration need to be backed up by a whole surrounding world of constructed possibility? Why not recognize a single alteration as a single counterfactual possibility projected out against the background of the actual (or given) world? In which case, of course, the possibility goes just as far as and no further than the proposition which supports it.

Here we approach the heart of the issue. The possible worlds of the Possible-Worlds Semanticists are prior to any propositions: they are what the propositions are *about*. This represents a retreat from the traditional Logical Analytical view to the extent that language is now seen as describing and reflecting possible worlds rather than our own actual world. But it is still seen as describing and reflecting. Language is still given the old passive role of corresponding and being true to things and states of affairs, even if those things and states of affairs no longer really exist. To be sure, possible worlds are not out-there in the same solid way as our own actual world – but they are still out-there in a way that enables them to precede language. So the obvious question for the Possible-Worlds Semanticists to answer is: how do such possible worlds come to be out-there in the first place? How do they come to be out-there *except in so far as language itself puts them there*?

Like the Formal Semanticists, the Possible-Worlds Semanticists have drawn logic back from reality, assuming that language will automatically draw back too. But the withdrawal of logic only reveals more clearly than ever the existence of a realm where language operates apart from and prior to logic. Language does not simply describe possible worlds – it constitutes them. As I suggested in the 'Need for disengagement' section above, the role of language is to create possibility. Our peculiarly human ability to look beyond reality is intimately tied in with our ability to project syntagmatic meanings for sentences like 'John may have gone to the movies' and 'If Joe had bought the Mercedes, he would have had four cars.' Logic may depend upon possible worlds, but possible worlds depend upon language – language in its earliest and most fundamental mode. The crucial work of language has already been completed before the Possible-Worlds Semanticists even get started.

Recognizing the syntagmatic creation of possibilities, we must also recognize the subjectivity of that creation. Logic requires possibilities in objective form; and there is no reason why possibilities should not be regarded as objective once we have put them out-there. But the putting out-there is itself a subjective activity; and there is every reason for not forgetting this underlying subjectivity. For the objective perspective alone has no way of limiting the uncontrollable proliferation of possibilities. Absolutely anything can be a possibility. The only way of limiting possibilities is to recognize the subjective effort needed for their creation. Only thus can we allow for possibilities without getting drowned in them. Only thus can we justify the principle of inertia which keeps the rest of the world the same when Joe, counterfactually, buys a Mercedes. The creation of possibilities is a matter of free will – which is to say that, although nothing actually halts it, effort is required to keep it going. This is the exactly the kind of situation which must always bring the Phenomenological perspective into play.

Considering Possible-Worlds Semantics and Formal Semantics together, we can see how both have moved beyond the original Logical Atomists and Logical Positivists – how both have discarded atomism in favour of holism, and concrete reality in favour of formal abstraction. However, such differences do not suffice to carry them outside the overall Logical Analytical framework. For both still adhere to a notion of language as essentially reflective; both still fail to reckon with the syntagmatic side of language. *Plus ça change, plus c'est la même chose.*

9 The case against Ordinary-Language Analytical philosophy

USE, FORCE, BEHAVIOUR

Whereas the various new kinds of Semantics represent a further development of the Atomist and Positivist tradition, Ordinary-Language Analytical philosophy represents a very strong reaction against that tradition. As is often the case, the reaction still shares certain ultimate assumptions with what it reacts against; but the differences are undeniably striking. For Ordinary-Language Analytical philosophers do not regard reflection and description as the primary role of language; they do not translate meaning into truth-conditions; and they do not propose an ideal form of language constructed in the service of science. Instead, they focus upon ordinary natural language and the ways in which it is ordinarily naturally used. 'Back to the rough ground!' as Wittgenstein says in *Philosophical Investigations*.[56] This looks hopeful in relation to syntagmatic theory; and we have already seen how Wittgenstein's 'family-resemblance' approach to single word-meanings converges with the syntagmatic approach.[57] But any hopes of a more general convergence are doomed to disappointment.

We can understand the reasons for the Ordinary-Language reaction by considering those kinds of utterances in ordinary language which are most resistant to a truth-conditional explanation. Scientific language is composed almost entirely of impersonal objectively orientated statements, describing purely for the sake of description. But in everyday speech and conversation, there are relatively few statements of this kind. Far more often we use language to question, to command, to warn, to greet, to request, to announce, to apologize, etc. etc. But a truth-conditional explanation is incapable of accounting for such uses. What truth-conditions can be specified for a command like 'Take out the rubbish!' or a question like 'Where is the dog?'? Neither the real world nor any possible worlds are being described or reflected here. There is nothing already in existence for these utterances to match up against.

The obvious way to explain such uses is by reference to the context in which they are uttered and received – by reference to a speech-act situation. A question is that kind of utterance which calls for an answer from the hearer back to the speaker; a command is that kind of utterance which calls for an action to be performed by the hearer as willed by the speaker. Appropriate roles for speaker and hearer may similarly serve to define a warning, a greeting, and so on. In all such cases, the speaker is trying to do something to the hearer. 'Without language', says the later Wittgenstein, 'we cannot influence other people in such-and-such ways.'[58] It is as though a force runs through the utterance. Following Austin's terminology, we may as well call it an *illocutionary force*.

Especially important to the theory of illocutionary force is the case of the performative. A performative looks like a statement but defies the Logical Analytical mode of explanation. Consider 'I give and bequeath my watch to my brother', or 'I promise to be there by six o'clock.' Such utterances evidently do not match up against anything already existing in the real world, or in any possible world. The promise to be there by six o'clock does not merely describe a future state of affairs: it makes that state of affairs happen. Nor does it merely reflect some inner mental volition on the part of the speaker: the promise is constituted by the very saying of the words, publicly committing the speaker in relation to the hearer. Similarly with the utterance of the words 'I give and bequeath . . . ' And if we follow this line of thinking through, even the phrase 'I'd like a drink' appears less as a description of private feeling and more as a request for public action. Utterances of this kind must be judged by whether they do something successfully, rather than by whether they correspond to something truthfully.

Such claims are not incompatible with syntagmatic theory. Indeed, such claims follow on naturally enough from my arguments about the 'point' of a sentence and the 'assertoric thrust' of interrogatives, imperatives and declaratives (as advanced in the 'Higher-order grammatical categories' section of Chapter 4). But it is vital to appreciate that 'point' is still not the same as 'use', and that interrogatives and imperatives are still not the same as questions and commands. The interrogative thrust may lend itself especially to the asking of questions, but it may also be directed into the issuing of commands ('Will you come in immediately!?') or the declaration of attitudes ('Who'd have thought he could be such a fool!?'). As for performatives, syntagmatic theory can happily accommodate the performative use of 'I'd like a drink.' Being concerned only with the creation of meaning as possibility, syntagmatic theory has no need to prescribe a descriptive use of meaning. But by the same token, it also has no need to prescribe a performative use – and so can allow for those rare but recognizable occasions when 'I'd like a drink' really is uttered as a mere observation, with no hope of a drink actually being brought. What syntagmatic theory proposes is a kind of meaning which takes on a certain thrust through the main verb of a sentence – but which still exists prior to any particular use.

We can appreciate the difference in another way too. An assertoric thrust is tied to the specific linguistic unit of the sentence. Although a sentence may possess several equally-weighted main clauses conjoined by *and*s or *but*s, it can deploy only a single overall thrust, either interrogative or imperative or declarative. (In this respect, the scope of an interrogative or imperative or declarative is co-extensive with what we ordinarily think of as a sentence, i.e. everything between an initial capital letter and a terminal full stop.) But the asking of a question may extend over one or two or many sentences, and so may the giving of a command, the making of a request, the issuing of a warning, etc. In general, Ordinary-Language Analytical philosophers find it convenient to deal with speech-acts only on the scale of the single sentence. But the fact that questions and commands are less tightly tied to specific linguistic units than interrogatives and imperatives is indicative of the fact that they are also less closely related to the syntagmatic meaning which builds up within those units.

A crucial divide has been crossed here. Whereas syntagmatic theory is still concerned with what language means, the Ordinary-Language Analytical philosophers are concerned with what someone means when using language. Certainly, the two senses of 'means' involve one another; and it is a virtue of the concept of 'assertoric thrust' that it leads on to just such an involvement. Nevertheless, from the side of what language means, a sentence has meaning before that meaning is put to a use. Whereas from the side of what someone means, the use of a sentence is primary. And Ordinary-Language Analytical philosophers play up the notion of use precisely in order to dispense with the notion of independent meaning. In Wittgenstein's famous phrase: 'the meaning of a word is its use in the language'.[59]

The ultimate goal of Ordinary-Language Analytical philosophers is plainly visible in some of their favourite linguistic examples. Consider the performative use of 'I give and bequeath . . . ' Syntagmatically, one thinks of the phrase as having a meaning synthesized out of its component parts (just as 'my uncle bequeathed . . . ' has a meaning synthesized out of 'bequeathed' and 'my uncle'). But it is not difficult to imagine how the ritual act of making a bequest might be equally well carried out by uttering a ritual phrase of Latin, say, 'Lego et trado . . . ' And the act would go through exactly the same even if nobody could understand Latin at the scene of the bequest – or even if the phrase had become so mangled and corrupted over time as to be uninterpretable anyway: 'Legeto radeto.' Here language effectively functions without the aid of meaning. Similarly in the case of the single-word sentence 'Hello!', which John Searle adduces as an example.[60] To know how to use 'Hello!' as a greeting is to know everything that can be known about it. No doubt we would normally regard such cases as representing a somewhat specialized and peripheral condition of language: but for Ordinary-Language Analytical philosophers, this is the condition to which all language aspires.

Admittedly, it is not always clear just how far the Ordinary-Language Analytical philosophers want to go. The famous Wittgensteinian phrase which I quoted above appears somewhat differently in its full context: 'For a *large* class of cases – though not for all – in which we employ the word 'meaning' it can be defined thus: the meaning of a word is its use in the language.'[61] And both Austin and Grice allow that some sort of meaning exists before use. Grice labels it 'word-meaning', while Austin locates it as the *rhetic* component of the *locutionary* act.[62] But neither Grice nor Austin attempts to describe what it involves or how it works. The most one can say is that it seems to be an extremely rudimentary sort of meaning, scarcely rising above the level of naming and referring in individual words. Certainly it presents no serious obstacle to the all-conquering advance of the use principle.

In seeking to dispense with independent meaning as far as possible, the Ordinary-Language Analytical philosophers reveal their underlying solidarity with the Logical Analytical philosophers. As I have already argued in the 'Three philosophies of language' section of Chapter 6, the impulse in both cases is to make language connect with something firm, as the real outside world is firm. But whereas in Logical Analytical philosophy utterances are about states of affairs in the world, in Ordinary-Language Analytical philosophy they are doings in the world – ultimately on a par with all other human doings. And such doings are to be studied, as a form of behaviour, from the favourite Analytical standpoint of the third-person observer.

There is here an obvious analogy between Ordinary-Language Analytical philosophy and Behaviourism.[63] But the Ordinary-Language Analytical philosophers are not simple stimulus-and-response Behaviourists of the old school. Austin, for one, is very insistent upon distinguishing *illocutionary force* from *perlocutionary force* – where *perlocutionary force* includes whatever effects an utterance actually causes.[64] Ordinary-Language Analytical philosophers go beyond this kind of causality when they consider illocutionary force in terms of conventions or intentions. For conventions and intentions are both – in their different ways – invisible, and cannot be directly observed on the merely phenomenal level of simple stimulus-and-response Behaviourism.

In the following sections, I shall deal separately with the conventionalist and intentionalist views. This is not to deny that many Ordinary-Language Analytical philosophers think of the two views as complementing one another. Strawson and Searle, for instance, believe that Austin's theory can make good the deficiencies of Grice's theory, and vice versa.[65] (In similar fashion, there are philosophers who believe that Logical Analytical philosophy can make good the deficiencies of Ordinary-Language Analytical philosophy, and vice versa.) But my objective, as usual, will be to show that the deficiencies run much deeper than this – so deep, that they can be remedied only by invoking the radical alternative of a syntagmatic approach.

THE INDEPENDENCE OF MEANING

For the conventionalist view, I shall take Austin as my main point of reference, with side glances towards Wittgenstein (of the *Philosophical Investigations*), Ryle and Searle. (As noted above, Searle also has a foot in the intentionalist camp; and in fact comes to focus more and more strongly upon intention in his later writings.) On this view, linguistic behaviour is a special kind of behaviour governed by rules. In Ryle's formulation:

> Learning to use expressions, like learning to use coins, stamps, cheques and hockey-sticks, involves learning to do certain things with them and not others; when to do certain things with them, and when not to do them.[66]

In the same way that the use of a stamp in certain appropriate conditions produces certain socially established consequences, so too the use of a sentence in certain appropriate conditions produces certain socially established consequences. The convention sets up a non-causal connection between conditions and consequences. As for the stamp, it is nothing in itself, merely a token in a larger game.

It is important to see what is at stake here. No one, presumably, would want to deny that learning to use expressions involves learning to use rules, involves learning what is correct and what is not correct. But the rules of which one most naturally thinks in this case are syntactic rules – rules of the kind that are crucial to syntagmatic theory. Rules of linguistic behaviour are another matter entirely. When philosophers like Austin, Ryle, Searle and Wittgenstein focus upon rules of sentence-using behaviour, they invariably lose sight of the rules operating *within* sentences. The issue, then, is not whether but where language is governed by rules.

Let us start with the claim about appropriate conditions. Certainly, there are certain appropriate conditions laid down by convention for such ritualized speech-acts as bequeathing. 'I give and bequeath my watch to my brother' must be uttered non-jokingly, in the presence of witnesses, while the speaker is of sound mind, free from duress, and so on and so forth. If such conditions are not met, then the act of bequeathing fails to go through, and no consequences follow. In Austin's terminology, the speech-act can only be regarded as a kind of 'infelicity', a 'misfire'.[67]

But it is a different story when we turn to non-ritualized speech-acts, to ordinary warnings or statements or requests or commands. What can we possibly define as the appropriate conditions necessary for an utterance to carry the force of a warning? That the utterer should have some sort of authority-to-warn relative to the person being warned? But suppose one is crossing a field when an unseen voice suddenly shouts 'That bull is dangerous!' Does one need to check up on the status of the utterer before deciding whether to take the utterance as a warning? The obvious answer is that the meaning alone can produce the effect of a warning, quite independently of the right or entitlement of the person behind it.

Similarly with statements. Austin's argument on this topic is particularly unsatisfactory:

> Often there are things you cannot state – have no right to state – are not in a position to state. You *cannot* now state how many people there are in the next room.[68]

On this argument, an utterance can carry the force of a statement only if the utterer is in a position to know the truth of the case. But how can the hearer ever really know what the utterer is in a position to know? There may be all sorts of indirect ways of obtaining information about the number of people in the next room. Whether we ultimately believe or disbelieve will doubtless be influenced by our hypotheses as to the utterer's sources of information; but we take the utterance as a statement simply to the extent that we entertain the possibility of a certain number of people being in the next room.

For ordinary non-ritualized speech-acts, it simply does not seem very important that an utterance should be felicitous by prescribable Austinian standards. Let me therefore suggest a radically different view: that one of language's most crucial powers is the power to generate a meaning which does not depend upon surrounding conditions. Other forms of communication are more limited in this respect. Umpiring signals have significance only if performed by the appropriate person at appropriate moments of the appropriate game; and the signals used by underwater divers will carry no force if used by a policeman at a traffic intersection. But linguistic meaning has an essential independence, and may produce consequences regardless of any particular conditions of utterance. We take in the meaning of a statement before considering whether the utterer is in a position to know the facts; we accept a warning that comes completely out of the blue; we recognize a command even from a person without authority, etc. etc. The rules of language are not broken in such cases; rather, the rules of language – and especially the rules of syntax – are used to break the rules of behaviour. Language is bound by rules in ways that other human social activities are not; but it is not particularly bound by behavioural rules of proper conduct and etiquette.

Independent meaning thus interrupts any direct conventional connection between conditions and consequences. And this applies on the side of consequences too. We can no more define an utterance by its appropriate consequences than by its appropriate conditions. Nor is this merely because the utterance may fail to produce appropriate consequences in practice. Austin allows for this when he distinguishes between the actual causal effect of a perlocutionary force and the potentially proper effect of an illocutionary force. The actual causal effect may come under the influence of numerous extra-linguistic non-conventional factors: which is why the stimulus of a warning does not always produce a response of (or disposition to) caution, and the stimulus of a command does not always produce a response of (or disposition to) obedient action. But from the point of view of illocutionary force, the potentially proper effect is still recognizable. From the point of view of illocutionary force, 'Take out the rubbish!' may be defined in terms of the action by which that command would be satisfied, even if it is not so satisfied in practice.

The trouble with this point of view is that it sets up just two possibilities. A speech-act may be satisfied or not satisfied: but if it is not satisfied, there is only a breakdown of communication. We can notice here a similarity to the truth-conditional view on meaning. As I remarked in the 'Pincer movement against meaning' section of Chapter 8, a proposition may be either true or false: but if it is false, then it becomes a write-off, and there is nothing further to be done with it. Being true is the proposition's whole *raison d'être*. And in the same way, affecting someone successfully is the speech-act's whole *raison d'être*. If the person warned fails to take warning or the person commanded fails to obey, then the warning or command might just as well never have been uttered.

But there is another possibility. Consider some of the more unpredictable replies that a hearer might make on being given the warning, 'There's a lion in that bush near you!' For example: 'That's not a lion, you fool. It's a tawny-coloured gazelle.' Or: 'I saw that lion gorging itself earlier. It's too well fed to be a danger now.' Or: 'So what? Lions almost never attack human beings except in the movies. You've still got a lot to learn about Africa.' In all these cases, the proper effect of warning fails to go through – and yet one would surely not want to speak of a breakdown in linguistic communication.

On the contrary, one might well want to speak of a higher form of linguistic communication. It is not a question of *falling short* but of *rising above*. The hearer does not fail to take the warning as a warning because of any intervening causal influences. Rather, the hearer has discounted the illocutionary force of the utterance on the basis of its meaning. But the hearer could hardly do this if the meaning of the utterance were defined by its illocutionary force, as a 'use' theory would have it. The case is explicable only if, as syntagmatic theory claims, the illocutionary force is in some sense secondary to the meaning.

It is true that this *rising above* kind of reply may occur only in a minority of cases. Perhaps predictable responses are more common than unpredictable ones. But what matters here is that the *rising above* kind of reply is always an option. And this option has a great deal to do with the very special powers of communication through language. Other forms of communication may be able to get people to do things, as when the arm movements of the traffic policeman cause motorists to apply their brakes or step on their accelerators. And certainly, it is advantageous to get other people to do things – to be able to transmit a command and have other people behave accordingly. But it is surely even more advantageous to get them to entertain things as possibilities – to be able to transmit a meaning and have them contribute to it from their own understandings. Again, the independence of meaning is crucial – crucial to our peculiarly human capacity for reformulating situations and coming up with new solutions to them.

It is in this capacity that language serves the purposes of private soliloquy. Of course, Ordinary-Language philosophers prefer to look at language entirely in terms of interpersonal communication. And perhaps one may justifiably claim that private soliloquy is a secondary function of language, which may be left for explanation at a later stage.[69] Nonetheless, it still has to be explained at some stage – and it is difficult to see what explanation could ever be forthcoming on the conventionalist account. Why should we want to impart illocutionary forces to ourselves? Why should the mind need to think out a verbal warning in order to be made warned? Whereas it is very easy to see why the mind might need to use language in order to reformulate situations and come up with new solutions to them.

The conventionalist account also condemns language to an essential conservatism, even in interpersonal communication. For the hearer is always required to respond in terms of the expected social norms of correct communication. Wittgenstein's famous builder-assistant language is exemplary: the builder calls out 'Slab!' or 'Block!', and the assistant obediently fetches him a block or slab-shaped piece of building-stone.[70] For the assistant has been trained to make the correct responses, and his responses can now be tested to find out whether he has learnt the language successfully. This emphasis upon training and testing is everywhere in Ryle, Austin and the later Wittgenstein. It seems that for these philosophers linguistic communication has to be predictable, if only because they see their own task as a matter of making scientific predictions about it. But how one longs for the assistant to show a real mastery of language – and, when given the order 'Slab!', to answer with a contradictory 'Wouldn't you do better to use a block just there?' – or even a gloriously revolutionary 'Fetch it yourself!'

What I am suggesting is that the element of unpredictability is not some additional sophistication which language theory can take on board at a later stage: it is a primitive fact intrinsic to the very nature of linguistic communication. To use language is to surrender control, to hand over certain rights to one's hearers. One may launch a meaning with a specific illocutionary force, but the illocutionary force does not simply predetermine the proper effects of the meaning. Once again, language involves taking a risk. The conventionalist Ordinary-Language Analytical philosophers go astray because, like the Logical Analytical philosophers, they want to make language always safe. And in their determination to prevent it from ever going wrong, they fail to notice how they are also ruling out a higher way in which it may be right.

Since I have reintroduced the notion of taking a risk in language, this seems a suitable moment to reintroduce Derrida too. For Derrida's theory of writing provides a salutary antidote to the Ordinary-Language philosophers' habit of regarding interpersonal communication as the be-all and end-all of language. Of course, Derrida not only questions the conservative, risk-free view of linguistic communication – he even questions whether language exists for the purpose of communication at all.[71] In Derrida's theory, nothing ever carries through from utterer to receiver: there is only the meaning in the middle, the text itself – in relation to which we are all receivers. This is independence of meaning with a vengeance, and it is comprehensible only if we accept Derrida's very special version of meaning. The syntagmatic version of meaning is comparatively traditional, and obviously allows language to be used for the purpose of communication. But communication as conceived along syntagmatic lines is nonetheless uncertain and problematic, not

compatible with a Phenomenological way of thinking. The world which I described at the end of the 'Sub-sentential utterances' section of Chapter 5 is exactly the kind of world he requires, a world riddled with invisible intentions, relevances and directives. Nor do I have any objection to infinitesimal feedback *per se*; after all, some such processes are clearly presupposed in a Phenomenological theory of perception (as described in the 'Phenomenological perspective' section of Chapter 7) or an abductive theory of hermeneutics (as described in the 'On the frontiers' section of Chapter 2). Last but not least, I admit to being impressed by Bennett's Gricean hypothesis as to how the very earliest form of symbolic communication might have begun.[84] In this realm of pure speculation, I find Bennett's hypothesis the most plausible on offer.

But these are general sympathies. It is in relation to the philosophy of language proper that the disagreements appear. For Grice's theory of linguistic communication is not really linguistic at all. This complaint has already been voiced by various critics: and indeed, the theory has been beset by counter-examples right from the start.[85] It is not difficult to find situations where what we think of as linguistic communication clearly diverges from Grice's intentional communication involving language. In what follows, I shall not be concerned to disprove Grice's theory so much as to locate its place and role relative to syntagmatic theory.

Let me hark back here to an earlier argument. In the 'Sub-sentential utterances' section of Chapter 5, I looked at sub-sentence exclamations such as 'Bowl!', 'Too small!', 'In the top cupboard!' In such cases, I admitted, it is necessary to call upon a sense of the utterer's intention based upon extra-linguistic evidence. For the verbal meaning of 'Bowl!' on its own lacks point, which has to be supplied from a sense that the utterer wants something fetched. But the sense of the utterer's intention on its own lacks specificity, which has to be made good by the verbal determination of a bowl as the thing to be fetched. In such cases, verbal meaning and a sense of the utterer's intention complement one another.

But there is another way of looking at the situation. That is, we can think of the utterance as drawing attention to an intention, summoning the receiver to try and understand what the utterer has in mind. Of course, it has to be assumed here that not only the command to fetch but also the thing to be fetched can be read off from the extra-linguistic evidence. In which case, the verbal meaning is ultimately redundant: an attention-drawing grunt would do the job just as well. This is what Grice's view boils down to. In so far as the word 'Bowl!' may be replaced by a grunt, it is essentially without meaning. In fact, it is in much the same condition as the words 'I give and bequeath . . .', in so far as they may be replaced by the phrase 'Legeto radeto'.

The difference between the syntagmatic view and Grice's view becomes crucial when we move from sub-sentential utterances to ordinary full sentences. Grice's view makes nothing of the internal complexity of ordinary full sentences: 'Go and fetch me a bowl!' draws attention to an intention in exactly the same way as 'Bowl!' But a syntagmatic theory sees 'Go and fetch me a bowl!' as itself making a point – a point which no longer needs to be read off from the extra-linguistic evidence. In ordinary full sentences, the syntagmatic dimension of verbal meaning takes over from the sense of an utterer's intention. Or to be more precise, the sense of an utterer's intention now features merely as a by-product or offshoot of the receiver's own effort of syntagmatic understanding. This is the claim already advanced in the 'Return of intention' section of Chapter 3, where I argued against Derrida arguing against Husserl. It is not that the sense of utterer's intention is simply unimportant, but that the syntagmatic meaning and the sense of an utterer's intention are in a relation of inverse proportion: as the former rises to prominence, the latter sinks into the background.

The ultimate bone of contention is the by now familiar one: the issue of independent meaning in language. Grice's theory dispenses with independent meaning in favour of a force which passes directly across between speaker and hearer. It is in this respect that Grice's theory resembles Austin's. And the counter-argument must be, once again, that only the hypothesis of independent meaning can explain the distinctive powers of human language. The overleaping force that Grice envisages is like the direct transmission of belief and feeling in animal communication. One bird in a flock utters cries of danger and panic, and a sense of danger and panic passes immediately across to the rest of the flock. Obviously, this form of communication can be very useful. But it would be even more useful if one member in a community could offer an independent reason for having a sense of danger and panic – thereby allowing the other members to make up their own minds about it. This is where our special human form of communication has the advantage. In using language, we manage to be highly social and yet at the same time individual.

The limitation of Gricean communication can be illustrated by an example which Grice himself provides. As a final and closest analogy to linguistic communication, he takes the situation where Tom communicates a suspicion to Harry by drawing and showing a picture of Harry's wife in a compromising position with the milkman.[86] In this situation, he claims, the communication takes effect only because Harry recognizes the intention behind the drawing and showing. (By contrast, there would be no particular analogy to linguistic communication if Harry were shown a *photo* of his wife in a compromising position with the milkman: the photo would simply prove what actually happened, regardless of anyone's intentions.) The difficulty with Grice's claim is that if the only thing communicated is Tom's intention, then Harry's only reason for believing that his wife is having an affair is that Tom wants him to believe that his wife is having an affair. But why should Harry feel suspicious just because Tom wants him to? Harry may well feel more inclined to question Tom's own motives. In fact, the drawing of Harry's wife with the milkman works as it does only because it sets up an independent possibility. It is not a proof – but it gives Harry something to think about which he has not thought about before. And a cunning Iago who aims to communicate suspicion will do so most effectively by setting up that independent possibility for belief, whilst keeping his own intentions completely in the background.

To the extent that Grice's theory involves directly transmitted belief, he ends up in a very predictable quandary. In his original formula, a statement communicates successfully when it induces belief in the hearer. But then surely a hearer can take in a statement without necessarily believing it? So Grice in later articles changes to a revised version: no longer does the communicative effect require that 'the hearer should believe something', but only that 'the hearer should *think that the utterer believes* something'.[87] Yet if the original formula claims too much, this surely claims too little. Statements do more than merely inform us of the speaker's state of mind. What's needed is the concept of a possibility which lies between the utterer's mind and the receiver's mind, a possibility which can be *offered for belief*. Without such a concept, the intentionalist view must oscillate endlessly between two equally unsatisfactory alternatives.

DISCOVERING MEANINGS THAT AREN'T IN WORDS

More recently, Grice has propounded a theory of 'conversational implicature'. This is an interesting theory in relation to the pragmatics of interpersonal communication; but it is even more interesting when Grice turns to consider the role of connectives like 'or' and 'if . . . then'.[88] For Grice sees that these words 'take on' meaning when used in *parole*; that is, they make us attend to forms of dependence over and above anything which might be attributed to 'or' and 'if . . . then' in their own right. According to Grice, this over-and-above kind of meaning arises out of the cooperative maxims for interpersonal communication – of which the third maxim is 'Be relevant'.[89] (Or, on the receiver's side: 'Prefer to assume that the speaker is conveying something relevant.'[90]) This looks like an opening onto the 'facilitative role' of connectives and the up-to-us understanding of point, as proposed in the 'How sentences work together' section of Chapter 4 and the 'Logical relations versus grammatical relations' section of Chapter 8.

Grice supplies the materials: others have developed them. The question as to whether this over-and-above kind of meaning is internal or external to language has been debated in articles by Cohen and Walker.[91] But the most impressive and subtle discussion, to my mind, comes from Roland Posner.[92] Posner demonstrates that the meanings which rise over and above the connective 'and' far exceed its logical properties, and are far too numerous and incalculable to be fixed in the lexicon. He also recognizes that these meanings may similarly arise over and above a mere semi-colon. Thus

> Annie fell into a deep sleep; her facial colour returned.

has much the same effect as

> Annie fell into a deep sleep and her facial colour returned.[93]

What's more, these over-and-above meanings may always be removed by a further addition to the linguistic context, as in

> Annie fell into a deep sleep and her facial colour returned.
> But I don't know in which sequence that happened.[94]

Such remarkable flexibility is impossible to explain by rules of word meaning or conventions of speech-act behaviour.

It seems that Posner can hardly fail to break through to a fully syntagmatic conception of the facilitative role – and thereby a fully syntagmatic conception of meaning in general. Although he describes the over-and-above kind of meaning as a 'conversational suggestion', he goes beyond Grice with his own preferred term: 'connexity-suggestion'. His orientation is consistently towards the context of language rather than the context of interpersonal communication. Even his claim about semi-colons makes sense only in terms of the written page, not in terms of live speech situations. But the final break-through never comes. In the end, Posner still believes that if a meaning is not in words, then it cannot be in language either – and so must exist outside of language in interpersonal guessings of intention. The notion that 'meaning is somewhere in the air and . . . must be read "between the lines" ' is obviously a possibility that he is unable to take seriously.[95]

However, there is really no way of locating the over-and-above kind of meaning in interpersonal guessings of intention. When Grice first proposed such interpersonal guessings in 'Logic and Conversation', he brought them into play for cases where ordinary meaning fails. Only when two conjoined clauses seem lacking in obvious relevance do we have to suppose that the utterer still has some ulterior form of relevance in mind. But if interpersonal guessings are properly invoked to explain ulterior forms of relevance, they can hardly be invoked to explain obvious relevance too. In 'Annie fell into a deep sleep and her facial colour returned' or in 'On Monday the 13th, snow fell heavily across the state, and traffic came to a halt on all major roads', obvious relevance comes simply from the meanings of the conjoined clauses. We recognize a potential for consequentiality between the two states of affairs described. No particular sense of the utterer's presence is needed (as in the above pair of samples, which I have merely cited, quite out of the blue). An understanding of the over-and-above kind of meaning is indeed up-to-us: but it is up-to-us in our encounter with language, not in our encounter with some person behind language. The distinction is crucial.

There is a further justification for the syntagmatic view in the fact that the syntagmatic sort of up-to-us understanding occurs on every level of language. If it is up-to-us to discover the point between 'Annie fell into a deep sleep' and 'her facial colour returned', it is no less up-to-us to discover the intersection between 'big' and 'dog', or between 'primordial' and 'supplementation'. Even the combination of nouns, verbs and adjectives involves a meaning over and above the individual words. And it is interesting that this issue too has recently surfaced in Ordinary-Language philosophy, quite independently of the debate on 'conversational implicature'. I am thinking of John Searle's arguments in 'The Background of Meaning' and in the chapter on 'The Background' in *Intentionality*.[96]

One of Searle's examples is the meaning of the verb 'cut' in combination with the meanings of various nouns: 'Bill cut the grass'; 'Sally cut the cake'; 'The tailor cut the cloth.' If one thinks of the truth-conditions for these sentences, then 'cut' seems to make a distinctly different contribution in each case. 'The sort of thing that constitutes cutting the grass is quite different from, e.g., the sort of thing that constitutes cutting a cake.'[97] And yet this difference can hardly be carried back into the lexicon, with countless different definitions for countless different senses of 'cut'. For Searle, as for syntagmatic theory, the explanation must be sought in terms of *parole*.

But Searle still does not come to the same explanation as syntagmatic theory. Instead he invokes a background cultural knowledge which we bring to our understanding of particular sentences: a background knowledge of 'practices, institutions, facts of nature, regularities, and ways of doing things'.[98] The problem with this is that the burden shifted from the lexicon now descends upon our store of general knowledge. Can we really be expected to know all the different kinds of cutting appropriate to all the different kinds of things that might be cut? Can we really be expected to have previous knowledge of how haggis-cutting is done? Or of how Peruvians cut the coats of their domesticated llamas? And yet we are able to understand – and understand differently – the meaning that 'cut' contributes to the sentences 'Ian cut the haggis' and 'The coat of the domesticated Peruvian llama has to be cut at least four times a year.' What Searle fails to allow for is the creativity of the language-user. We don't need a previous knowledge of whole practices, corresponding to the combined meaning of 'cut' with 'haggis', or the combined meaning of 'cut' with 'coat of domesticated Peruvian llama'. If we know the meanings of those nouns individually, and if we know the meaning of 'cut' in some general schematic form (e.g. 'to separate physically by means of the pressure of some more or less sharp instrument'), then we can work out for ourselves the most likely manner of their intersection.[99]

Still, the gap between Ordinary-Language Analytical philosophy and syntagmatic theory seems to be narrowing. The Ordinary-Language philosophers have discovered exactly the kind of evidence upon which syntagmatic theory is founded. And in striving to come to terms with that evidence, they have become less and less attached to the attitudes of Behaviourism, more and more willing to entertain concepts of mental representation and subjective intentionality. At the start of this chapter, I said that any hopes of a general convergence between Ordinary-Language Analytical philosophy and syntagmatic theory were doomed to disappointment: and I have since been mainly concerned to demonstrate the divergences. But there is at least some room for hope in the future.

Part IV

Syntagmatic theory and linguistics

10 The Generative approach to syntax

CREATIVITY IN SYNTAX

Syntagmatic theory relates to linguistics especially when linguistics concerns itself with syntax. For the rules of syntax and syntagmatic processing operate over similar territory; and the study of similar territory tends to produce similar results – or, at the very least, mutually illuminating results. In this chapter, I shall be trying to come to grips with Generative grammar, as the dominant movement in linguistics over the past thirty years, and the movement most responsible for bringing syntax forward into the limelight.

One very obvious point of similarity between Generative grammar and syntagmatic theory is that both insist upon the activity and creativity of the individual language-user. When Chomsky argues that language is not acquired by mere imprinting and absorption from the outside, he sets himself decisively apart from Structural Linguists of both the European and the American schools. For the Europeans have typically thought in terms of socially predetermined verbal categories imposed upon individual subjects; while the Americans have typically thought in terms of verbal habits ingrained from outside by repetition and reinforcement. (Ultimately, of course, the Europeans incline towards Metaphysical philosophy and the Americans towards Empiricism: two very different philosophies, but with a common tendency to regard the individual subject as profoundly passive.) In relation to these two schools, Chomsky occupies a third position – a third position of the kind that falls within the general tradition of 'I'-philosophy.

When the American Structural Linguists tried to discuss syntax (mainly in the 1940s and 1950s), they did so under the assumption that syntactic patterns could be learned like single words, by imitating patterns from other people's sentences. But what is plausible in relation to single words is not even remotely plausible in relation to sentences. As Chomsky points out, there are infinitely many possible sentences. 'There is no human language in which it is possible, in fact or in principle, to specify a certain sentence as the longest sentence meaningful in this language.'[1] And even the sentences that we utter and hear every day are in no sense habitual:

> Ordinary linguistic behaviour characteristically involves innovation, formation of new sentences and new patterns in accordance with rules of

> great abstractness and intricacy . . . There are no known principles of association or reinforcement, and no known sense of 'generalization' that can begin to account for this characteristic 'creative' aspect of normal language use.[2]

Whereas the laws of habit enable us to bring forth no more than we have taken in, the rules of syntax are a vehicle, a means to further productivity. Deploying a finite system of rules, we can somehow manage to compose or comprehend syntactic patterns never previously encountered. Chomsky insists upon the as-if-for-the-first-time character of sentence syntax, just as syntagmatic theory insists upon the as-if-for-the-first-time character of sentence-meaning.

As for the European Structural Linguists, it may here be illuminating to re-examine Saussure's famous analogy between language and chess. In *Superstructuralism*, I showed how this analogy brings out the rule-bound nature of language. That is, any single move in a particular game of chess has to be selected from the system of all possible moves; and one cannot even begin to play a particular game until one has absorbed the system of how a pawn is allowed to move, how a bishop is allowed to move, etc., etc. However, there is another totally different dimension to chess – a dimension which encompasses single moves as subordinate parts of larger strategies. A move with a pawn may be part of a plan for bringing a rook into play one move later, or for capturing an opposing knight three moves later, or (always and ultimately) for checkmating the opposing king an indefinite number of moves later. Such strategies involve a kind of creativity over and above anything that can be simply imitated or reproduced from previous experience. It is on this dimension that every game of chess is a new game. Even if the entire sequence of moves should happen to coincide with some other game once played before, this game is still worked out as if for the first time by these players. Nor can we ever play out all possible games of chess – if only because there is no upper limit on the possible number of moves. Considered in terms of whole games, chess is infinitely open-ended.

The analogy between language and chess thus teaches an anti-Saussurean moral on the topic of language acquisition; and it may also tell us something about studying the syntax of a particular sentence. For clearly we cannot reach an overall interpretation of a game of chess merely by building up from local interpretations of individual moves. If one player moves a pawn into a position from which it can take the opponent's knight, then it may be that the move really is just an attempt to take that knight; but on the other hand it may be an attempt to open up a line of attack for a bishop previously blocked by the pawn, or an attempt to distract attention from the vulnerability of the player's own queen on the other side of the board. And even if the pawn is lost, having moved to a position in which it can itself be taken, yet that too may turn out to be a deliberate sacrifice, serving towards the capture of the opponent's queen or an ultimate checkmate. An individual move apparently falling under a certain kind of local interpretation may have to be totally reinterpreted in the light of the game overall.

Similarly in the case of language. We cannot reach an overall interpretation of a sentence's syntax merely by building up from local interpretations of words and parts. Consider the string of words: 'Was the girl inside the house?' Interpreting this string as an interrogative sentence, we can readily specify a grammatical role for each word. But suppose we add another two words, and interpret the string in the light of a larger sentence: 'Was the girl inside the house the murderer?' Although the string itself remains exactly the same, the grammatical roles of its words have changed. And a further change again may be required in the light of an even larger sentence: 'Was the girl inside the house the murderer broke into ever rescued in the end?' It seems that we must determine grammatical roles from the top down as well as from the bottom up.

This is the property of language that Chomsky has called 'structure-dependency'.[3] American Structural Linguists of the 1940s and 1950s believed that they could apply 'discovery procedures' to the atomic evidence of words and attain an interpretation of whole sentences merely by a process of step-by-step assembly of parts. But when the early Generative grammarians turned against the American Structural Linguists, they adopted a resolutely top-down approach. Taking for granted an overarching 'S'-node, they introduced their rules in such a way as to unfold the structure of a sentence downwards, finally ending up with the required string of individual words. Recent Generative grammarians have adopted a more neutral approach, thinking in terms of well-formedness conditions at every level rather than in terms of rules that directly generate sentences. This seems more compatible with what is presumably the real situation of interreactive feedback, cycling between the assumption of a sentence and the evidence of individual words. But such an approach is certainly as far away as ever from any mere assembly of parts.

The real situation reveals once again the lineaments of the hermeneutic circle. In the 'On the frontiers' section of Chapter 2, I examined a general principle of language that emerges with especial clarity in exceptional syntagmatic combinations. That is, we arrive at the syntagmatic meaning of a sentence by keeping the senses of the individual words all up in the air together, juggling between them until we can get a coherent total meaning to slot home simultaneously all along the line. Similarly with the syntactic structure of 'Was the girl inside the house . . . '. We arrive at the structure by keeping the grammatical roles of the individual words all up in the air together, juggling between them until we can get a coherent total structure to slot home simultaneously all along the line. (With more ordinary sentences, of course, we may start settling meaning and structure on the way through, as I argued in the 'Processing on the way through' section of Chapter 5; still, such settling can never be final, and we must always be ready for the possibility of readjustment.) Only by creative *abduction* can we break into the circle – only by trying out guesses as to how the sentence has come to be the way that it is, only by ravelling up structures or meanings until we hit on something which produces the same results.

Nonetheless, it must be said that, although the two kinds of juggling are similar, they are not the same. Everything I have said about syntagmatic processing in Part II could hold good even for a language with an entirely fixed and finite syntax. A language might possess a maximum of two dozen limited-length sentence structures, learned and acquired as passively as you like, and yet users of that language would still be able to combine different words within those structures and produce new meanings as if for the first time. Creativity in the one case does not absolutely necessitate creativity in the other.

But if there is no absolute necessity, there is surely a strong practical probability. It would seem unlikely that the kind of linguistic creativity which produces new meanings could long be 'satisfied' within old structures. If the syntax of a language limited the possible length of sentences, for instance, then the possibilities of new meaning would also be limited in one significant (albeit not the most significant) respect. The two kinds of creativity go naturally hand in hand; and syntagmatic and Generative approaches lend at least a certain persuasive reinforcement to one another. (Indeed, when Chomsky argues that our linguistic behaviour involves innovation, he often seems to be thinking as much about new meanings as about new structures.) As for the exact delineation of the relationship between syntagmatic theory and Generative grammar, that will be my main concern in the next two sections.

THE RULES OF SYNTAX

I have said that syntagmatic processes and the rules of syntax operate over similar territory; yet they are also very different conceptually. As a first step in delineating the relationship between syntagmatic theory and Generative grammar, we need to understand that difference. It appears most clearly, perhaps, when the rules of syntax are not properly obeyed. Consider the following utterance:

> Me go along shop buy cake very sweet. You wanting also cake? Come and I buy you.

These sentences commit errors of morphology, misconstructed word-order and omitted grammatical particles. Nonetheless, we can make perfectly good sense of what is meant. In spite of the imperfections of the syntax, the information offered is still sufficient for us to recognize the syntheses and projections required. Syntagmatic processes may survive even when syntax breaks down.

Generative grammarians have long recognized that correct syntax is not the *sine qua non* of language. In their different ways, Chomsky and Katz have both tried to come to terms with semi-grammatical sentences.[4] But their pre-occupation with the conventional rules of syntax allows them to view such sentences only in terms of permissible degrees of deviation. They have no alternative principles by which to explain *how* meaning can be understood outside the rules. It takes syntagmatic theory to provide such principles. For the real *sine qua non* of language is syntagmatic processing. Syntax serves syntagmatic processing; but since it only serves, we may to some extent dispense with its services. In the last resort, syntagmatic processing is up-to-us. In the 'How sentences work together' section of Chapter 4, I made this claim in relation to synthesis between sentences; within sentences, I suggested, conventional rules of syntax exercise compulsory force. But when conventional rules of syntax break down, then even within the sentence syntagmatic processing is up-to-us. As long as the breakdown is not too severe, we can often manage to work out an appropriate total meaning.

On the level of content-words, syntagmatic theory explains how meaning can be understood outside the rules by invoking the principle of natural complementarity. That is, the different conceptual cuts of nouns, verbs and adjectives need each other and are drawn to each other. Since this process depends upon grammatical categories, it may be described as a process of fundamental grammatical combination. But 'grammatical' here does not refer to compulsory conventional rules. I shall henceforth refer to compulsory conventional rules under the term 'syntax', observing a distinction between what is broadly 'grammatical' and what is specifically 'syntactical'. Needless to say, this distinction has no basis in ordinary usage, where the two terms are employed more or less interchangeably.

But natural complementarity alone is not enough, even on this fundamental level. I have said that nouns and verbs, adjectives and nouns are drawn together. But which noun and which verb? Which adjective and which noun? Here is a whole issue that I have so far ignored. But now it can be raised and answered. For this is precisely where the compulsory conventional rules of syntax come into play. Syntax is a means of giving us the additional instructions that we require, a means of directing natural complementarity into specified channels.

There is one very obvious way of telling us what to combine with what. Given the sentence 'A big dog jumped out at me in the park', how do we know that the adjective 'big' is to be combined with the noun 'dog' and not with the noun 'park'? Obviously because 'big' and 'dog' are contiguous. The principle of contiguity exemplifies Behaghel's First Law, that 'what belongs together mentally is placed close together syntactically'.[5] Indeed, the principle of contiguity seems such an obvious way of telling us what to combine with what that we may easily fall into the error of identifying the form of the instructions with the manner of the processing. A dangerous confusion! For the 'belonging together' of meanings is not at all the same as the 'placing together' of words. As I pointed out long ago, complementarity itself works by superimposition, by absolute coincidence. By their different conceptual cuts, 'big' and 'dog' intersect over the same semantic space. Contiguity may be the closest that we can approach to absolute coincidence in a linear string of words – but it is still only an approach.

The distinction between the form of the instructions and the manner of the processing may be highlighted by looking at an alternative form of instructions. In Latin, for example, instructions within the clause are presented through a system of indexing. An adjective may be separated from the noun to which it belongs, but morphological suffixes on the words tell us what to combine with what. (Of course, Behaghel's First Law still applies to the clause *as a whole*: it would hardly be possible to attach a distinctive morphological feature to every scattered word belonging to a particular clause!) From the perspective of an English-language speaker, the system of indexing may look like a very artificial and burdensome way of giving instructions. But at least there is no temptation to think of indexes as anything other than instructions; and at least it is much easier to think of indexed items as calling for superimposition and absolute coincidence. By its very artificiality, the system of indexing is arguably a more honest reflection of the real state of affairs.

Even in the English language, contiguity will take us only so far. For we may need to be told not only what to combine with what, but also how to do the combining. Consider the case of a transitive verb with a subject and a direct object. Here there are two nouns belonging with the verb, but belonging in very different ways. Since contiguity alone is helpless to express the difference, word-order must be brought into play. In a simple active declarative sentence of the English language, the subject noun is placed before the verb and the object noun after. Thus we can distinguish between 'The hunter shot the tiger' and 'The tiger shot the hunter.' But this rule of ordering does not *reflect* a natural order of meaning.[6] Compared to contiguity, word-order is more purely conventional and compulsory.

Similarly when a main clause and relative clause are headed by the same noun: 'The boy who took the bike was wearing a brown jacket.' Given the rule that verbs follow subject nouns in the English language, 'took the bike' and 'was wearing a brown jacket' both have a claim to follow immediately after 'The boy'. In terms of 'belonging together mentally', it is impossible to say which kind of verb phrase should come first. Only a further rule of ordering can resolve the situation: in the English language, a rule that the relative clause follows immediately after its subject noun, even at the price of separating the verb phrase of the main clause from *its* subject noun. As a result of this rule, 'was wearing a brown jacket' actually ends up coming after 'the bike', a noun phrase to which it bears no direct relation whatsoever. The fundamental-level principle of contiguity is necessarily overridden by higher-level complications of syntax.

There are other higher levels to reckon with too. The situation becomes complicated in a new kind of way when non-contentual levels have to be added over the top of contentual levels. Thus negation and passivization and the declarative–interrogative–imperative modes of assertoric thrust affect the meaning of a sentence – but not in respect of what to combine with what (and how). There is a sense in which what to combine with what (and how) remains constant from 'The hunter shot the tiger' to 'The hunter did not shoot the tiger' to 'Did the hunter shoot the tiger?' to 'The tiger was shot by the hunter.'

Surveying these sentences, we can recognize that something stays the same even while something else changes. What changes, of course, is the manner of projection for the meaning as a whole.

Consider the case of passivization. In an active sentence such as 'The hunter shot the tiger', the subject noun feeds into the verb as agent of the action, and the object noun feeds into the verb as patient of the action. And as prescribed in our previous rule of word-order, subject comes before verb and verb before object. However, there is also another sense of 'subject', the sense of a subject as opposed to a predicate. And although the two kinds of subject will typically tend to coincide (an agent is more likely to serve as topic), there are times when one may wish to treat an object noun as sentence-subject. For example, one may wish to think in terms of what-happened-to-the-tiger, rather than in terms of what-the-hunter-did. But if subject comes before verb and verb before object, then 'the tiger' must come both before and after the verb. Our previous rule of word-order is caught in an impossible clash of interests.

It might seem reasonable that the object noun should continue to come after the verb, while some other means should be found for expressing the sentence-subject. After all, the level of subject and predicate is additional and supervenient; we have to understand how content combines with content before we can think about projecting that combination as a whole. However, the English language finds it easier to transfer rights over word-order to the sentence-subject, while expressing the role of the object noun by other means. Specifically, the English language changes the form of the verb, from 'shot' to 'was shot' – a change which does not alter the verb's essential content, but switches its sockets. This enables us to place the object noun before the verb: 'The tiger was shot.' And if we want to mention the hunter, we can insert the grammatical particle 'by' and place the subject noun after the verb (though not necessarily immediately after): 'was shot by the hunter'. On the other hand, we may choose not to mention or even contemplate the agent responsible for the shooting.

As with passivization, so with negation and the declarative–interrogative–imperative modes of assertoric thrust. All of these higher-order operations affect the projection of the sentence as a whole – albeit along different dimensions. For instance, 'The hunter did not shoot the tiger' combines content with content in the same way as 'The hunter shot the tiger'; the difference lies in the different application of a state of affairs to the world (or a world). Likewise, 'Did the hunter shoot the tiger?' combines content with content in the same way as 'The hunter shot the tiger'; the difference lies in the different situation set up between an utterer and a receiver. The English language expresses such differences not merely by introducing a new element into the sentence (a negative particle, or a WH-element in WH-questions), but by making special use of the AUX (or INFL) as described in the 'Higher-order grammatical categories' section of Chapter 4. In ordinary positive and declarative sentences, the assertoric role of the verb can be taken for granted and conflated with the contentual meaning of the verb – just as the role of the sentence-subject can be taken for granted and conflated with the subject noun in ordinary active sentences. But when it becomes necessary to manipulate the assertoric thrust of a sentence over the top of its content, the AUX (or INFL) takes on an independent status, and provides the necessary information under a further set of syntactical rules.

In a way, it is appropriate that negatives and interrogatives should require expression by more than just a single word; for such modes of assertoric thrust are not merely to be combined on a par with 'hunter', 'tiger' and 'shot'. What concerns the whole sentence is appropriately expressed across the whole sentence, as by the placement of an auxiliary verb. But this leads to a paradox – the same paradox already encountered in the relation between rules of word-order and the principle of contiguity. In that case, our instructions on what to combine with what were overtaken by new instructions on how to do the combining; in the present case, our instructions on how to do the combining are overtaken by further instructions on how to project the combination as a whole. In both cases, higher-level forms of instruction prevail over lower-level forms of instruction – and yet it is only because of the lower-level forms that the higher-level forms have something to operate upon. Syntax, it seems, does not lay down foundations and then build conformably on top of them. Syntax picks up its foundations and moves on.[7]

Of course, we have still touched only the tip of the iceberg. But even this small amount of evidence is sufficient to refute the old style of Immediate Constituent Analysis. For Immediate Constituent Analysis was indeed 'immediate', seeking to exhibit syntactical instructions all at once and on the flat. Not surprisingly, such an approach could hardly advance beyond an account of what to combine with what. In fact, only the final string of words is truly on the flat; behind the words, syntagmatic processing moves up through level upon level upon level. If we fail to attend to these different levels, then inevitably syntactical instructions will seem to crisscross and interfere with one another in the final string. After all, the same means of expression have been used and reused many times over, in the service of different purposes. To escape from this imbroglio, we must unpack syntactic instructions stage by stage, referring them to the successive levels of syntagmatic processing. It was the discovery of the stage-by-stage approach which launched Generative grammar on its triumphant early career.

HOW DO STRUCTURES EXIST IN DEPTH?

Unfortunately for Generative grammar, its triumphant early career led directly to the excesses of the Generative Semanticists. The problem had its source in the original hypothesis of deep structures and transformations. As a means of unpacking syntax stage by stage, deep structures and transformations were responsible for a multitude of revolutionary new insights. But there was something wrong about the way in which the hypothesis was conceived. By the time the excesses of the Generative Semanticists had been curtailed, Generative grammar had lost its innocence for ever. An age of suspicion had begun; and although deep structures and transformations were not easily discarded, they were no longer regarded with favour or trust.

Deep structures as such were originally hypothesized on the basis of our ability to recognize forms of structuring in a sentence not reflected in the surface arrangement of parts of speech. So, on the surface, 'Archibald blew up the house' looks different from 'Archibald blew the house up'; while 'John promised Mary to go' seems much the same as 'John persuaded Mary to go.' Nonetheless, we can recognize that meaning hangs together in exactly the same way in the first pair of sentences; whereas in the second pair, there is a crucial difference as to who will do the going, John or Mary. As for our old example of 'The hunter shot the tiger' and 'The tiger was shot by the hunter', here we can recognize both a similarity and a difference of hanging together – a similarity in respect of agent, verb and patient, but a difference in respect of subject and predicate.

Chomsky and his followers chose to explain such recognitions by reference to invisible sentences underlying visible ones. Seeing that 'Archibald blew the house up' hangs together in the same way as 'Archibald blew up the house', they hypothesized a deeper level on which the first sentence would have the same form as the second. So 'Archibald blew up the house' becomes the deep structure for both sentences, and 'Archibald blew the house up' is derived by a transformation which shifts the position of the particle. (This is the old Generative rule of Particle Movement.) Similarly with 'The tiger was shot by the hunter' and 'The hunter shot the tiger', where the active sentence is viewed as a common deep structure, and the passive is derived by transformation. On the other hand, when two different ways of hanging together can be recognized behind similar surface arrangements, two different deep structures are invoked. Thus 'John promised Mary to go' is traced back to 'John promised Mary – John will go', while 'John persuaded Mary to go' is traced back to 'John persuaded Mary – Mary will go.' In such expanded clausal forms, the difference between the two original sentences is plainly manifest (although compulsory syntactic control between clauses has been abandoned, leaving the connection very much up to us). Such expanded clausal forms are likewise hypothesized as implicit presences behind the strings of words actually uttered.

But there are obvious problems with implicit presences of this kind. In the first place, it is surely very difficult to believe in fully-formed but unuttered sentences hovering around in the backs of our minds. So far as the evidence of psychological testing goes, it notably fails to support any such notion.[8] In the second place, there is the frequent arbitrariness involved in deciding which sentence to count as the underlying one. Why not take 'Archibald blew the house up' as the deep structure, and produce 'Archibald blew up the house' by transformation? And in the third place, the whole hypothesis seems to make surface structures curiously redundant. For if deep structures convey the same information, and convey it more clearly and perspicuously than surface structures, why should we ever bother with surface structures at all? Why burden ourselves with so much additional processing, merely for the sake of introducing unnecessary complications and ambiguities? In *Language and Mind*, Chomsky suggests that the contracted forms of surface structure make smaller demands upon memory; but since, on Chomsky's own showing, these contracted forms must still be processed by way of their deeper expanded forms, this looks like a very expensive method of saving.[9] It would seem much simpler to come right out and speak those invisible sentences hovering around in the backs of our minds.

Syntagmatic theory allows for depths, but it explains them by reference to different levels of syntagmatic processing rather than by reference to different levels of sentences. So, in the case of 'Archibald blew up the house' and 'Archibald blew the house up', the sameness that we recognize is a sameness of what combines with what (and how). But the instructions on what to combine with what (and how) can be given to us in two different ways, by two different forms of code.* In such matters, the English language is less than perfectly tidy and systematic. This very elementary explanation becomes available as soon as one conceives of the arrangements of parts of speech as mere instructions. Explanation by 'deep structure' appears necessary only when the arrangements of parts of speech are confused with the real processes of combining.

The same line of reasoning works in the opposite direction in the case of 'John promised Mary to go' and 'John persuaded Mary to go', where there are two forms of syntagmatic processing but only one form of syntactic instructions. Here, the different forms of syntagmatic processing are determined not by the surface arrangement of parts of speech but by the possibilities for complementarity inherent in the two verbs 'promise' and 'persuade'. This is a more distant kind of complementarity than I have so far considered, spreading the influence of the verb beyond 'John' and 'Mary' to the infinitive 'to go'. Putting it roughly: 'persuade' has to have a someone persuaded as direct object; and its primary complementarity causes it to combine with that direct object first of all. The infinitive then follows on from the direct object as the act to be carried out by the persuadee. With 'promise', on the other hand, the someone promised is essentially in the role of indirect object, as we can see by introducing another noun in a direct-object role: 'John promised Mary a ticket', 'John promised a ticket to Mary.' In these sentences, 'a ticket' is the something promised – just as 'to go' is the something promised in 'John promised Mary to go.' Not surprisingly, then, the primary complementarity of 'promise' causes it to combine with the infinitive first of all, so that 'to go' follows on from the promiser who is the main verb subject, and not from the promisee. In short, the different conceptual cuts of 'promise'

* Both forms of code can be motivated on syntagmatic grounds. On the one hand, there are obvious reasons for putting 'blew' and 'up' together as component parts of the verb. But on the other hand, the combination of 'blew up' and 'the house' is ultimately a matter of syntagmatic superimposition – and it is arguable that such superimposition is most closely expressed by *straddling* the parts of the verb around the object.

and 'persuade' decide what each verb can combine with (and how), even at a distance. And conceptual cuts, according to the terminological distinction established earlier, are a matter of *grammar* but not of *syntax*. Nor should it be supposed that the possibilities of distant complementarity have to be learnt off as arbitrary lexical rules for these two particular verbs (and every other particular verb). We learn a verb's conceptual cut when we learn its meaning; and its possibilities of distant complementarity are a natural consequence of that cut, to be discovered as the occasion arises.

Clearly, the single method of reading back into 'deep structures' does scant justice to the variety of cases involved. And the case of the passive is another case again. With 'The tiger was shot by the hunter', we must recognize not only a difference between instructions and processing, but also a difference between levels of processing. The complexities of the case have already been examined in the previous section, where I suggested that the unpacking of syntactical instructions cannot proceed all at once, but must be carried out stage by stage, referring to the level of agent–verb–patient, and then, separately, to the level of subject–predicate. However, this is not to say that the instructions themselves exist on different levels, or that alternative arrangements of parts of speech actually underlie the surface arrangement. The instructions themselves merely crisscross over one another in the final string of words – which is indeed the *only* string of words. There is no need to suppose that 'The tiger was shot by the hunter' requires the invisible lurking presence of 'The hunter shot the tiger.'

It should now be possible to see just where the original conception of deep structures went wrong. At root, the error is the very same error that was pointed out in the previous section, the error of identifying the form of the instructions with the manner of the processing. When the early Generative grammarians presented their deep structures by means of contiguity and elementary short-clause word-order, they were merely switching between alternative forms of expression. What they sought to display was a kind of hanging together which lies behind the surface arrangement of parts of speech – yet they were still using surface arrangements of parts of speech to display it.

Of course, many of the problems with deep structures have since been recognized. In the days of the old Standard Theory, it seemed that invisible presences could be justified as the simplest and most efficient way of accounting for what *was* visible – a common enough scientific principle, after all. But in this case, the principle failed – and was plainly seen to fail – when abstract syntax 'took off' in the late 1960s and early 1970s. Soon it became apparent that virtually any number of clausal expansions could be claimed as clarifying surface structure, and that simplicity and efficiency alone were helpless to control the proliferation. In the subsequent reaction, Generative grammarians largely renounced the urge to multiply everything into invisible clauses. The D-structures of Government and Binding Theory, for instance, are relatively limited in depth, and the transformations which convert them into S-structures are relatively few in number. What's more, these D-structures no longer exist as fully formed sentences such as one might speak; rather, they are spoken *about*, defined with the aid of such abstract labels as *PRO*, *O*, *e*, etc. An even more abstract version of speaking *about* appears in Relational Grammar and its offshoot, Arc-Pair Grammar, where grammatical relations (subject-of-verb, direct-object-of-verb, etc.) are actually named as such, rather than merely 'read off' from a structural arrangement of parts of speech.[10] And grammarians of the Generalized Phrase Structure and Lexical-Functional schools claim to manage without traditional deep structures altogether.

Especially interesting from a syntagmatic point of view is the growing consensus of opinion directed against *ordered* deep structure. Anti-linear views have been advanced by grammarians of the most diverse approaches.[11] In Relational and Arc-Pair Grammar, for example, grammatical relations are unfolded through successive stages entirely without reference to word-order; as Johnson and Postal put it, 'word order [in this model] . . . is a relatively "superficial" phenomenon . . . compared with its role in standard T[ransformational] G[rammar]'.[12] And, in the current mood of Government and Binding Theory, Chomsky too has contemplated the prospect of eliminating linear sequence from the base component, and has spoken favourably of Lasnik and Kuprin's attempt to define the underlying parts of a sentence in a way which does not involve specifying an order for them.[13] In this respect at least, the more recent versions of Generative grammar appear increasingly compatible with syntagmatic theory.

What remains a problem is the sheer bewildering variety of recent versions. There are many different models for syntax currently on offer, all apparently capable of producing the same surface phenomena, with no obvious reasons for preferring any one particular model over the others. In steering away from the original conception of deep structures, grammarians seem to have headed off in a dozen separate directions. And the cause of their dispersal, I suggest, is that they have still not understood what the old deep structures were really trying to get at. They have sought to avoid the unsatisfactory features of the original conception, without as yet arriving at a more profound conception.

One glaring confusion which has never been properly resolved concerns the different dimensions of depth in language. Consider again the case of 'Archibald blew up the house' and 'Archibald blew the house up', where the identical way in which meaning hangs together is not reflected in the visible strings of words. Here one can make a sort of mental-versus-physical discrimination: a depth of syntagmatic processing underlies a surface arrangement of parts of speech. But another dimension of depth comes into play with 'The tiger was shot by the hunter', where the passive requires two different levels of syntagmatic processing. Here one naturally thinks of the fundamental level (of what goes with what, and how) as being deeper than the higher-order level (of subject *vis-à-vis* predicate). The discrimination in this case has no mental-versus-physical dimension: on either level, syntagmatic processing relies upon visible instructions and involves the synthesis and projection of meaning.

These two dimensions of depth have a bearing upon the original hypothesis of Katz and Postal, that semantic interpretation relates exclusively to deep structures.[14] When applied to structures which are deep in the way that fundamental levels of processing are deep, the hypothesis makes no sense at all. Meaning is shaped by higher-order levels of processing just as much as by fundamental levels of processing. However, the hypothesis does make sense when applied to structures which are deep in the way that syntagmatic processing *per se* is deep. For syntagmatic processing shapes meaning directly, whereas syntactic instructions and surface arrangements of parts of speech shape meaning only by way of syntagmatic processing. The Katz–Postal hypothesis can be justified or refuted, depending on which dimension of depth is under consideration.

Syntagmatic theory thus opens the way for a clearer understanding of what the old deep structures were trying to get at. And no doubt a clearer understanding ought to impact upon the grammarians' models for syntax – perhaps by suggesting modified or revised systems of representation, perhaps by defining general standards against which existing models might be evaluated, perhaps by setting up overarching principles under which existing models might be ultimately reconciled. However, I shall not presume to propose modifications or revisions, or to evaluate or reconcile existing models. In this field, my status is strictly amateur. I claim only that syntagmatic theory offers a kind of independent grounding for Generative grammar to grip onto. Not independent in any directly 'realistic' way, of course: not direct psychological evidence of what actually happens in the minds of language-users. But independent, nonetheless, in the way of an independent theory of meaning, founded upon independent principles. With the aid of syntagmatic theory, it becomes possible to see how considerations of meaning place certain demands upon syntax, and call for certain specifiable kinds of operation to be carried out by compulsory conventional rules.

11 The 'natural grammar' approach to syntax

MOTIVATION AND DIACHRONIC DEVELOPMENT

In claiming that considerations of meaning place certain demands upon syntax, I am also effectively claiming that syntax is not autonomous. In fact, I have already tried to motivate a variety of syntactical phenomena. In the 'Higher-order grammatical categories' section of Chapter 4, I suggested that AUX (or INFL) can be justified as a category of meaning by reference to the assertoric role of a main verb; and in the 'Rules of syntax' section of Chapter 10, I suggested that the way in which an auxiliary verb appears at the front of an interrogative sentence corresponds to the way in which an assertoric role affects the meaning of a sentence as a whole (and not merely the meaning of a verb). Again, in a footnote to the 'How sentences work together' section of Chapter 4, I suggested a natural reason for the highly flexible positioning of such inter-sentence connectives as 'however', 'thus', 'though' and 'on the other hand'; and in a footnote to the last section of the previous chapter, I suggested a possible syntagmatic motivation for what used to be called 'Particle Movement'. Last but not least, in the 'Possibility from Piaget' section of Chapter 7, I suggested that even the categories of noun, verb and adjective may be derived by *reflective abstraction* from pre-linguistic cognitive processes. Behind all of these suggestions lies the assumption that the conventions of syntax are not arbitrary and self-created, but typically owe their form to something outside of syntax.

For methodological reasons, all Generative grammarians study syntax as if it were autonomous. But Chomsky goes further than this, proclaiming the autonomy of syntax in absolute terms. Notoriously, he refers syntax to an innate language faculty, a pattern laid down in the neurological hardware of the human brain. This pattern is only brought into action by experience; it is never affected or shaped by experience. 'The abstract study of states of the language faculty should formulate properties to be explained by the theory of the brain.'[15] Such a view diverges drastically from the syntagmatic view, where the forms of language evolve from more fundamental forms of perception, of which only the earliest are strictly biological. As I have already shown, I prefer a Piagetian version of the *a priori*. But Chomsky has chosen to dismiss all possibility of a dialogue with the Piagetian approach.[16] This divergence is ultimately a reflection of two diverging views within the tradition of 'I'-philosophy: the Cartesian view as against the Phenomenological view.

As syntagmatic theory diverges from Chomsky on this point, so it converges with the 'natural grammar' movement of recent years. I borrow the term 'natural grammar' from Sandra A. Thompson; alternative terms are 'the functional-typological approach', and 'the discourse-pragmatic approach'.[17] The origins of this movement lie with Joseph Greenberg and Dwight Bolinger in the 1960s, and its rise to prominence owes much to the work of Talmy Givón. With current practitioners such as John Haiman, Bernard Comrie, Paul Hopper, Joan Bybee, Bernd Heine and Elizabeth Closs Traugott, 'natural grammar' represents a decisive challenge to all assumptions about the autonomy of syntax.

The 'natural grammarians' seek to motivate syntactic phenomena by general cross-linguistic principles. Joan Bybee, for example, shows how the closeness of morphosyntactic markers to the verb-stem correlates with the closeness of what those markers express to the meaning of the verb.[18] Markers for aspect come closer than markers for tense, because aspect (perfective or imperfective, punctual or completive, etc.) directly affects the action or event described by the verb, whereas tense only affects the situation described by the proposition as a whole. But markers for tense come closer than markers for mood, because mood (indicative or subjunctive, declarative or imperative, etc.) expresses what the speaker *wants to do* with the proposition, over and above the situation actually described.

Another telling example comes from Talmy Givón, who shows how the closeness of syntactical binding between a main clause and a complement clause correlates with the closeness of semantical binding between their respective meanings.[19] So a main verb like 'make' has a very strong, controlling and successful influence upon the event described by the complement verb, which therefore appears in the highly dependent form of a bare infinitive: 'The teacher *made* Jimmy *wipe* his nose.' The influence of a main verb like 'want' is a little less strong, in that the event described by the complement verb may or may not take place: in this case, the infinitive is divided from the main verb by the insertion of a particle: 'The teacher *wanted* Jimmy *to wipe* his nose.' More distant again is the case of a main verb like 'suggest', where suggesting has a comparatively weak and indirect influence upon the event described by the complement verb: 'The teacher *suggested* that Jimmy *wipe* his nose.' Here, the complement clause acquires a complementizer and a finite verb; however, this verb still exists in a restricted tense-less form. The final stage of a fully independent finite verb is achieved only when the event described by the complement verb is essentially independent of the action described by the main verb: 'The teacher *thought* that Jimmy *had wiped / would wipe* his nose.'

There are many other kinds of motivation investigated in 'natural grammar'; but already it should be clear why such motivations are of great interest and importance to syntagmatic theory. The same cannot be said of the hermetic and intra-syntactic 'motivations' which prevail in Government and Binding Theory. In the Government and Binding account of passivization, for example, an NP is said to move from object position to subject position *in order to acquire* case-marking and *thereby avoid* being ruled out of existence by the case-filter. This curiously abstract mode of explanation may have its uses, but it has no relevance to the understanding of real syntagmatic processes. Far more relevant is Givón's account of passivization:

> *Passivization is the process by which a* **nonagent** *is promoted into the role of* **main topic** *of the sentence. And to the extent that the language possesses coding processes which identify main topics as* **subjects** *and distinguishes them from topics, then this promotion may also involve* **subjectivalization.**[20]

It should be noted that this latter account can also be given a much wider application cross-linguistically.

If 'natural grammar' and syntagmatic theory share common interests, this is perhaps because they share common philosophical inclinations. By and large, the 'natural grammarians' have abandoned the old and unavailing attempts to motivate the structure of syntax by reference to the structure of the objective world which we describe in language. Instead, they motivate the structure of syntax by reference to the cognitive structure which *we* impose when doing the describing. Such favourite concerns as presupposition, topic assignment, figure-and-ground typically involve our conceptual strategies for thinking *into* language, our 'perspectives about experience'.[21] Clearly there are Phenomenological inclinations here (and even a direct line to Gestalt psychology in the discussions of figure-and-ground). Particularly suggestive is the final, philosophical chapter of *On Understanding Grammar*, where Givón talks in terms of '*construed* experience' and 'our phenomenological universe', and argues explicitly that 'the seeming irreducible, observable, "objective" element in the meaning of both objects and events is by itself an elaborate *construct*.'[22]

Another side of 'natural grammar' appears in diachronic accounts of the development of syntax. Typically, such accounts propose 'processes by which loose, paratactic, "pragmatic" discourse structures develop – over time – into tight, "grammaticalized" syntactic structures'.[23] Thus Givón suggests that the construction for infinitival complements should be seen as evolving out of constructions in which two finite clauses are merely juxtaposed:

> *I want* ***I****-go* → *I want* ***to****-go*
> *I tell you* ***you****-*go → *I tell you* ***to****-go* [24]

Constructions with juxtaposed clauses, or even juxtaposed verbs, are particularly common in languages which lack subordinating syntax. Heine, Claudi and Hünnemeyer present a similar case of evolution in Faroese, where a shift of reanalysis has changed a concatenated structure into a subordinating structure, and a free interpretation into a compulsory interpretation:

eg sigi tadh: hann kemur → eg sigi at hann kemur
[I say that: he comes] [I say that he comes].[25]

The interpretation of the paratactic construction is 'free' in so far as it is left up to the listener to work out an appropriate connection between the two clauses. But the connection is brought under explicit control when the demonstrative 'tadh' evolves into the specialized grammatical complementizer 'at'.

The new dimension opened up here is highly relevant to syntagmatic theory – albeit in ways that I have not touched upon as yet. For syntagmatic theory does not require that the entire syntax of a language be laid down once and for all *ab ovo*. Syntactical rules may be *a priori* relative to any particular utterance, but they are not *a priori* absolutely, trans-historically. Only an evolving Piagetian version of the *a priori* is compatible with the diachronic development of syntax. And syntagmatic theory actually supplies an enabling mechanism for such development. For syntagmatic theory can explain how '*I say that: he comes*' may be understood with essentially the same meaning as '*I say that he comes*', although nothing in the paratactic construction carries or even guides that meaning. It is up to us to recognize the complementarity involved, just as it is up to us to recognize the complementarity between 'A big dog jumped out at me in the park' and 'Dad's going round to the owners to complain.' Because syntagmatic processing is able to operate beyond the rules, it is also able to move on ahead, to lead the way, to beat a path which formal syntax may later come to codify. As Heine, Claudi and Hünnemeyer put it, 'cognitive restructuring . . . precedes linguistic change'.[26]

Syntagmatic theory not only allows for the general development of syntax from paratax, but also for the specific development of new roles for words like 'that' in the Faroese example. In fact, the study of *grammaticalization* reveals that markers which are used in higher-order syntactical roles have almost always 'risen up' from roles of a lower order. So when Elizabeth Closs Traugott investigates the markers used to express the *if* in conditional constructions, she finds that many such markers have their source in temporal *when*- or *whenever*-words, while others have their source in *maybe*- or *perhaps*-words.[27] Both of these sources, she argues, bear a natural semantic relation to *if*-markers. In the case of *when*- or *whenever*-words, 'when(ever) Bill lies down' establishes a presupposed and framing environment for the assertion 'he falls asleep', just as 'if Bill lies down' establishes a presupposed and framing environment for the claim 'then he will fall asleep'. In the case of *maybe*- or *perhaps*-words, a possible and hypothetical state of affairs is envisaged in 'perhaps Bill will lie down . . .', just as a possible and hypothetical state of affairs is envisaged in 'if Bill lies down . . . '. Neither the sense of presupposition nor the sense of possibility is equivalent to the total sense of the *if*-marker: but they represent at least an aspect of that sense. As Traugott puts it: 'forms that at an earlier stage are signs for one aspect of the meaning of the conditional relation . . . come at a later stage to be signs for the whole protasis relation'.[28] This is surely reminiscent of what was said about the diachronic development of lexical meanings in the 'Mechanism for change in *langue*' section of Chapter

3. There too, a highly constraining context made it possible to extend a word beyond its ordinary range, favouring one factor of meaning at the expense of others; until, with repeated use and habituation, that extension eventually constituted a new centre of meaning on its own. Of course, the development of syntactical roles is not simply parallel to the development of lexical meanings; nonetheless, the similarities remain suggestive.

Adding syntagmatic theory to 'natural grammar', then, we come to the following view of diachronic development: language always involves syntagmatic processing, but there is no permanently fixed dividing-line between those parts of the processing which are under compulsory syntactical control and those parts of the processing which are up to us. Syntax has the power to 'colonize' the up-to-us, to expand into higher-order grammatical categories and encompass higher-level forms of synthesis and projection. This is the dynamism of what Givón calls '*expressive-elaborative* change, motivated by the creative drive to elaborate more complex and subtle nuances of meaning'.[29] It is not that syntax merely rigidifies and formalizes already-existing connections: rather, syntax specializes those connections, and enables us to manipulate them. The loose juxtaposition of 'I say that' and 'he comes' might be interpreted in a variety of ways, according to context; but the tight subordination of 'I say that he comes' compels a specific interpretation, regardless of context. If this precludes 'free' interpretation on the part of the listener, it bestows upon the speaker a freedom of a different kind – the freedom to say something which does not directly depend on – or even flies in the face of – the context surrounding the utterance.

THE 'EMERGENCE OF GRAMMAR' POSTULATE

There are grounds in 'natural grammar' for the reading offered above, but there are grounds for an alternative reading too. The movement enfolds competing tendencies; and while that competition remains submerged in the opposition to Chomsky, it stands sharply revealed when syntagmatic theory is brought into the equation. For example: does the diachronic development of new syntactical forms and roles proceed continuously or by overlapping? 'Natural grammarians' often talk as though overlapping were a kind of continuity; but an overlapping which works by syntagmatic mechanism clearly involves an essential discontinuity. No matter how many or how small the intermediate stages, cognitive restructuring leapfrogs ahead of syntactical change at every stage.[30] Or again: do cognitive processes precede communicative goals or vice versa? 'Natural grammarians' tend to talk of cognitive processes and communicative goals almost in the same breath; but syntagmatic theory insists very definitely that sense-making cognitive processes must be seen as the means of achieving communicative goals. To give priority to communicative goals is to adopt the position of the Ordinary-Language Analytical philosophers.

Perhaps the overarching ambivalence has to do with whether such terms as 'functional' and 'pragmatic' are to be understood as referring to a dimension *of* language or a dimension *outside* language. Either way, imperatives and interrogatives will have to be considered in relation to what the speaker wants to do with an utterance, presuppositions and topics will have to be considered in relation to what the hearer is already supposed to know, etc. Considerations of interpersonal context inevitably come into play on these higher levels of syntax – the very levels which 'natural grammarians' love to explore. But when the functional-pragmatic dimension is seen as a dimension *of* language, such interpersonal contexts are seen as something which language itself creates. That is, the imperative construction actually tells us what the speaker wants to do with an utterance; the presuppositional construction tells us what is to be taken as presupposed. Of course, this is not to deny that further messages may be added on by real-world interpersonal contexts. An imperative uttered by a speaker who has no conceivable right to give orders to the hearer may well be intended as – and may well be received as – a joke. But what the speaker in the real world wants the hearer to do (i.e. laugh) does not supplant what the speaker in language wants the hearer to do (i.e. obey). If the speaker's lack of right to give orders simply removed all possibility of an imperative, then the joke would be removed as well.

It is a very different story when the functional-pragmatic dimension *outside* language is allowed to supplant the functional-pragmatic dimension *of* language. In this case, 'pragmatic' begins to point in the direction of socio-pragmatics, 'functional' begins to reach back to the Functional Linguistics of the post-Firthian school – and the real-world interpersonal context begins to be studied with a view to the causes rather than the consequences of an utterance. No longer is the focus upon language-created relations between speaker and hearer, but upon relations between speaker and hearer already existing prior to language. Naturally, this leads to problems when language is working *against* an existing state of relations: when the speaker deliberately challenges a presupposition which has been always previously shared with the hearer; or when the speaker uses language to implant a presupposition which the hearer might not actually wish to share at all ('Seeing that you'll be going to bed before the movie, Timothy, you're allowed to read with the light on for half an hour . . .'). The more one allows real-world interpersonal contexts to predetermine the possibilities of communication, the less one can allow language to create interpersonal contexts for itself.

When 'natural grammarians' invoke the terms 'functional' and 'pragmatic' in particular analyses, they are most often referring to the functional-pragmatic dimension *of* language; but the dimension *outside* language tends to come to the fore in their larger programmatic claims. Paul Hopper's 'Emergence of Grammar' postulate exemplifies this latter tendency. Hopper explicitly distinguishes his position from the view 'that there are predefined grammatical structures which have discourse-functional correlates'.[31] Like the post-Firthian Functional Linguists, he condemns all versions of the *a priori* in language, evolving or otherwise. 'Structure, or regularity', he claims, 'comes out of discourse and is shaped by discourse as much as it shapes discourse in an on-going process. Grammar is hence not to be understood as a prerequisite for discourse.'[32]* The choice of the term 'regularity' rather than 'rule' is revealing here. Under the Emergence of Grammar postulate, discourse is determined by our natural strategies for achieving communicative goals, and grammar is a mere epiphenomenon of such strategies.

The pivotal claim comes in an article co-authored by Hopper and Sandra A. Thompson, 'The Discourse Basis for Lexical Categories in Universal Grammar'.[33] From a syntagmatic point of view, the creation of new meaning in language requires the synthesis of complementary grammatical categories, and nouns and verbs are the most fundamental of all grammatical categories. But according to Hopper and Thompson, not even nouns and verbs are a prerequisite for discourse. They do not go so far as to claim that there are any existing languages without nouns and verbs, but they do claim that nounhood and verbhood are essentially relative conditions, essentially matters of degree. And what is a matter of degree may also be seen as a matter of *rising* degree, gradually increasing towards a state of full categoriality from a state of zero categoriality. In the conclusion to their article, Hopper and Thompson suggest that 'linguistic forms are in principle to be considered as LACKING CATEGORIALITY completely unless nounhood or verbhood is forced on them by their discourse functions', and that 'far from being "given" to us aprioristically for us to build sentences out of, the categories N and V actually manifest themselves only when the discourse requires it'.[34]

Hopper and Thompson measure degrees of nounhood or verbhood along three scales. The morpho-syntactic scale claims to deal with the 'morphological trappings' characteristic of nouns or verbs.[35] Thus a prototypical noun is able to 'pluralize [and] take modifiers [and] determiners', while a prototypical verb will show 'trappings of tense, aspect [and] person/number agreement'.[36] The semantic-referential scale defines prototypicality in terms of the phenomena which nouns and verbs characteristically describe. So nouns which are high in categoriality refer to 'autonomous, usually quite concrete and individuated entities', while 'the prototypical function of the V is to report an actual event'.[37] As for the salience-and-manipulability scale, the issue here is the degree to which a noun or verb is foregrounded or made prominent, and the degree to which a noun (in particular) may be later redeployed through anaphoric processes. On this scale, prototypical nouns are said to 'introduce participants and "props" and to deploy them', while a prototypical verb 'must

* 'Discourse' is another term which can be interpreted in two ways. Hopper, along with most of the 'natural grammarians', uses it primarily to describe the larger verbal context surrounding a single sentence. But 'discourse' can also be used to describe the interpersonal deployment of language in a practical real-world context. And sometimes the latter use seems to seep into the former – as when Hopper talks of the discourse-context as though it were somehow derived from sources external to the meanings of sentences. But of course the larger verbal context is simply a number of sentences working together, and whatever meaning exists on this scale can only have arisen out of the meanings of those sentences.

ASSERT THE OCCURRENCE OF AN EVENT OF THE DISCOURSE'.[38] Hopper and Thompson deliberately run the last two scales together as much as possible;[39] but we shall get a clearer view of the argument by keeping them distinct.

If these three scales are accepted as measuring degrees of nounhood and verbhood, then it is a foregone conclusion that some nouns and some verbs will take on more morphological trappings than others, will refer to individual entities and actual events more specifically than others, will prove more redeployable and more prominent than others. However, there is no reason why any of these scales should be accepted. For in every case, Hopper and Thompson have missed the dimension on which nouns and verbs really operate, and on which they may be properly defined. They have set their sights upon something other than complementary 'conceptual cuts' at the level of basic content.

The problem with the morpho-syntactic scale appears most glaringly in relation to the claim that prototypical nouns are able to pluralize, while prototypical verbs will show number agreement. For both of these morphologies are a matter of marking for singular or plural. It follows that marking for singular or plural does not characterize nouns as against verbs or verbs as against nouns: the singular–plural opposition is an opposition between nouns of different types, or between verbs of different types.[40] That is, the singular–plural opposition has an additional job to perform, on top of the category of noun or verb. And the same may also be said of Hopper and Thompson's other morphological trappings, even when they do attach peculiarly to one category or the other. A verb may take on contrasts between different tenses or aspects or persons, but such contrasts are not the defining essence of its verbhood; and it does not become more or less of a verb by deploying such contrasts in greater or lesser quantities. The trappings to which Hopper and Thompson point are indeed only trappings.

This is not to deny that these trappings tend to become less relevant precisely when a noun does not refer to an autonomous concrete individuated entity, or a verb does not report an actual event. Imperative verbs, for instance, rarely take on any tense or aspect morphology, and, according to Hopper and Thompson, are signalled in many languages by the verb-stem alone. At the same time, of course, 'it is in the very nature of imperatives to assume that the event named has not yet taken place'.[41] Obviously there will not be much call for a range of tenses if the event is always in the future; nor will there be much call for imperfective aspect (since one cannot command an action to be already going on), or for distinctions of person (since the agent of the action commanded is always essentially a 'you'). Here is a genuine case of iconic correlation between the morpho-syntactic scale and the semantic-referential scale; and Hopper and Thompson are able to bring forward numerous similar cases. They have every right to claim that 'a V presents itself in discourse as fully capable of displaying all the oppositions available for event-coding only if it is reporting an actual event'.[42]

However, they still do not have the right to claim that 'the less a linguistic element is required by the discourse to report an event . . . the less saliently it will be marked *as a member of the category which languages universally designate to carry that function* [my italics]'.[43] The issue of category has been illegitimately imported here. What Hopper and Thompson have proved is simply that the less a linguistic element is required by the discourse to report an event, the less it will be marked *with the morphology appropriate to the specification of events*. The degree to which a verb reports an actual event correlates with the quantity of event-coding oppositions which a verb takes on – but neither of these two measurements correlates with the categoriality of the verb *per se*. To return to the case of the imperative: can anyone seriously believe that the 'go' in 'Go to bed!' is less of a verb than the 'travelled' in 'We travelled from Sweden to France'?

The problem with the semantic-referential scale is that it defines the categories of noun and verb in terms of out-in-the-world phenomena. And this in spite of the fact that Hopper and Thompson themselves challenge Bates and MacWhinney's attempts to tie nouns to visible (tangible, etc.) objects, and verbs to concrete, kinetic, visible, effective actions.[44] Unfortunately, when Hopper and Thompson argue against such 'intrinsic "semantic" features', they refute the 'intrinsic' rather than the 'semantic';[45] and their argument ends up proving only that there are no noun-stems intrinsically tied to objects, and no verb-stems intrinsically tied to actions. (Especially curious is their demonstration that the 'travelling' in 'We know a travelling salesman' is a less than prototypical verb – as though anyone ever supposed that grammatical category could be assigned on the basis of the bare stem '-travel-'.[46]) What they fail to reject conclusively is the appeal to a distinction between different kinds of out-in-the-world phenomena.

So, when they go on to develop their own discourse-functional definitions, they still expect prototypical nouns to refer to autonomous concrete individuated entities, and prototypical verbs to report actual events. If referring and reporting are to be taken as functions here, they add very little to the account – and certainly nothing in the way of a new distinction between nouns and verbs. Could one not talk just as easily of reporting an entity or referring to an event? The essential difference between the two definitions remains the difference between entities and events – which is much the same as the difference between objects and actions. Discourse-functional considerations may alter the application of Bates and MacWhinney's criteria in relation to any given noun or verb, but they scarcely alter the nature of the criteria as such.

In fact, Hopper and Thompson accept 'this broad correlation [of nouns with thing-like entities, and verbs with actions or events] as a starting point'; and although they go on to 'refine it', this starting-point conditions their entire argument.[47] Even the notion of prototypicality and degrees of nounhood or verbhood has its source here. For the attempt to correlate nouns with thing-like entities and verbs with actions or events inevitably reveals that the correlation holds more closely in some cases than in others. One might suppose that, when the correlation itself turns out to be less than adequate, the whole notion of prototypicality would require rejustification. But Hopper and Thompson simply carry prototypicality across from the domain of 'intrinsic "semantic" features' to the domain of discourse-functions.

In conceding so much to out-in-the-world phenomena, Hopper and Thompson are actually harking back to an older version of iconicity, in which syntactical structures are motivated by the structure of the objective world that language describes. Whereas the success of the 'natural grammar' movement, as I suggested earlier, derives largely from a new version of iconicity, in which syntactical structures are motivated by the cognitive structures that we impose when doing the describing. (Thus the 'travelling' in 'We know a travelling salesman' is not a less than prototypical verb, as Hopper and Thompson propose, but a perfectly obvious adjective, under an imposed adjective-perspective.) Instead of concentrating upon 'perspectives about experience', Hopper and Thompson fall back upon the notion of nouns as mere thing-words, verbs as mere action-words – the very notion that I attacked in the 'A Possibility from Piaget' section of Chapter 7. Fundamental grammatical categories, I there claimed, have to be understood as grasps of grasps: for example, the kind of grasp which yields things on the perceptual level is itself grasped and used to create the category of noun on the linguistic level. On this view, fundamental grammatical categories derive from perception only indirectly, only by way of a detour through *reflective abstraction*. But Hopper and Thompson have little time for any sort of abstraction, and 'percepts' feature repeatedly as the bottom line of their argument. In this they reveal their adherence to the traditional assumptions of Anglo-American Empiricism.

As for the salience-and-manipulability scale, here too Hopper and Thompson fail to make contact with the dimension on which nouns and verbs really operate. In relation to nouns, for example, Hopper and Thompson suppose that a noun which is salient and manipulable is more of a noun than one which isn't. So in the sentence 'I went to the library and read a book', the noun 'book' is maximally salient and manipulable, because it introduces a participant for the first time into the discourse, and because that participant can be redeployed anaphorically by means of an 'it'. But in a subsequent sentence, 'At ten o'clock, I put the book down and went out for a coffee', the noun 'book' is 'old information' and therefore backgrounded: in this case, Hopper and Thompson assign only an intermediate degree of categoriality. Lowest in categoriality of all is the incorporated 'book' in 'I went to the library and did some book-reading': here the noun establishes no definite participant in the discourse, and there is no possibility of redeployment by means of an 'it'. Hopper and Thompson also draw on evidence from Modern Hebrew, Bemba, Spanish and Persian to show how, in many languages, a noun which refers to one single object (unlike the 'book' in 'some book-reading') may be nonetheless presented with minimal salience if that object's specific identity is simply not important to the discourse: 'I went to the library and *read book*', as it were.

The answer to all of this must be that the distinctions discussed by Hopper and Thompson are distinctions between different ways of projecting nouns, over and above their actual nounhood. Salience and manipulability do not affect the characteristic 'conceptual cut' of noun-meaning, but only the manner in which that meaning is *sent out*. In fact, what Hopper and Thompson are really talking about is not the function of nouns but the function of determiners. As I argued in the first section of Chapter 4, determiners belong on a higher grammatical level, contentless in themselves, but controlling how we project the content of a noun. Or to be more precise: controlling how we project the content of a noun phrase. For it is the whole synthesized meaning of (adjective)–noun–(adjectival phrase) which we project as presupposed or newly introduced, as specific or non-specific, etc.[48] And it is this whole synthesized meaning which will be taken up in any later anaphoric redeployment.

Higher grammatical levels are also involved in many of the other syntactical forms which Hopper and Thompson draw into their argument. For example: pronouns and nouns within the scope of a negative; gerunds and 'absolute' constructions; irrealis verbs such as conditionals and optatives; verbs in dependent clauses (relative, purpose or bound complement clauses). Certainly these forms do not tie in with simple out-in-the-world phenomena; certainly they tend to involve considerations of larger verbal and non-verbal contexts. But they are all doing something more than mere nouns or verbs alone can do.

In fact, Hopper and Thompson's approach works by a kind of pincer movement. On the one hand, their semantic-referential scale is aimed too low – conceding too much to phenomena as they exist objectively and perceptually, prior to linguistic categorization. Naturally such phenomena cannot be expected to fall into ready-made nouns and verbs. On the other hand, their salience-and-manipulability scale is aimed too high – focussing upon syntactical forms which have already gone beyond categorization on the basic contentual level. And these forms also cannot be expected to fit straightforwardly into the categories of noun and verb. Hopper and Thompson have overleapt the relevant dimension of 'perspectives about experience'. Appealing on the one hand to 'experience', and on the other to 'perspectives about perspectives', they are attempting to depose fundamental grammatical categories in the middle. The Logical Analytical philosophers, it may be remembered, applied a somewhat similar strategy in attempting to depose meaning.

Syntactical forms which have gone beyond basic contentual categorization also create problems in relation to Hopper and Thompson's claim that 'linguistic forms are in principle to be considered as LACKING CATEGORIALITY completely unless nounhood or verbhood is forced on them by their discourse functions'.[49] For it is evident that many of these forms are non-salient: pronouns, for example, and nouns within the scope of a negative; 'absolute' constructions, conditionals, and verbs in dependent clauses. Since they also typically lack morphological trappings (for tense, aspect, pluralization, etc.) and typically fail to refer to thing-like entities or report actual events, Hopper and Thompson have no hesitation in assigning them to a state of low categoriality.[50] But if fully categorial nouns and verbs are to be seen as emerging from a state of zero categoriality, then presumably they must emerge by way of a state of low categoriality – in other words, they must emerge by way of the same state as pronouns, nouns within the scope of a negative, 'absolute' constructions, conditionals, verbs in dependent clauses, etc. It is hard to avoid the impression that advanced and complicated syntactical forms are actually being asked to precede or underlie simple forms.

Hopper and Thompson allow this extraordinary inversion to arise because they are more interested in what these advanced forms are *not* doing (i.e. referring to entities, reporting events) than in what they *are* doing. As soon as we consider what they *are* doing, a natural correlation springs to view – a correlation between the development of higher-level functions and of lower-salience forms. Consider the case of pronouns. The identity of meaning enforced by a pronoun typically helps to bind the unity of a larger many-sided point across several smaller separate points: in this respect, the pronoun serves a higher-level function. But in serving such a function, the pronoun is necessarily a less salient form; for now it has the role of referring back to a previous meaning without standing out individually, without drawing attention to itself. Similarly in the case of dependent clauses. A relative clause, for example, helps us to put meaning together on a larger scale precisely in so far as it contributes meaning to the main clause *without taking over from it*. Different degrees of salience are necessarily involved in all subordinating structures – and subordinating structures are a feature of advanced and complicated states of syntax generally. In relation to the categories of noun and verb, Hopper and Thompson claim that salience emerges out of non-salience; but in relation to many of the categories which actually feature in their argument, it makes more sense to claim that non-salience emerges out of salience.[51]

The irony of the situation is that, in trying to reveal the emergence of nouns and verbs, Hopper and Thompson have effectively obscured the emergence of higher-order categories over and above nouns and verbs. Whereas syntagmatic theory recognizes the emergence of higher-order categories but *not* the emergence of nouns and verbs. According to syntagmatic theory, there never has existed and never could exist a state of discourse prior to all distinctions of grammatical category. Without complementary categories, a string of semantic units would remain just a string – pointless and unproductive. Even before adverbs, even before adjectives, there must always have been at least nouns and verbs (or proto-nouns and proto-verbs). The apparent advance and multiplication of grammatical categories across previously unregulated territory should not lead us to imagine some ultimate origin for the whole process in a state of zero categoriality. Rather, we should think of distinctions building up over distinctions, of categories emerging out of categories – and of nouns and verbs (or proto-nouns and proto-verbs) as constituting the very earliest separation which made discourse in sentences possible.

12 The Generative approach to semantics

THE THEORY OF AMALGAMATED PATHS

Neither the Generative grammarians nor the 'natural grammarians' have been primarily concerned with meaning. However, the Generative grammarians have had high ambitions as regards producing a total theory of language under the Generative banner. And obviously, a total theory of language must find a place for semantics as well as syntax. Unfortunately, semantics under the Generative banner has been limited by the domination of the syntactical model in Generative thinking. Semantics has been expected to fit in around an existing machinery constructed primarily in the interests of syntax. The general attitude is perhaps summed up in Katz and Fodor's famous motto: 'linguistic description minus grammar equals semantics'.[52] Such an attitude does not bode favourably: and the outcome has not been favourable. Or perhaps one should say 'outcomes', given the sheer variety of approaches proposed over the past thirty years. In the present chapter, I shall be looking at some of those approaches in approximate chronological order.

In spite of their motto, the approach proposed by Katz and Fodor has been one of the more promising from a syntagmatic point of view. In the Theory of Amalgamated Paths, meaning combines hierarchically up through the syntactic branching tree – and gets subtracted in the process. Consider: 'The man hits the colourful ball.' Potentially, 'colourful' can have either the sense of *abounding in contrast or variety of bright colours*, or the sense of *having distinctive character, vividness or picturesqueness* (as in 'No novel is less colourful than *Middlemarch*'); while 'ball' can have either the sense of an *object having globular shape*, or the sense of a *social activity* (as in 'The queen danced at the French ambassador's ball').[53] But when we combine the two words to produce 'colourful ball', we can't think of a *globular-shaped* ball as *having distinctive character, vividness or picturesqueness*. This combination therefore blocks, leaving us with the alternatives of a *social-activity* ball *abounding in contrast or variety of bright colours*, a *social-activity* ball *having distinctive character, vividness or picturesqueness*, or a *globular-shaped* ball *abounding in bright colours*.

A further subtraction occurs when we combine '[the] colourful ball' with 'hits'. Potentially, 'hits' can have either the sense of *collide with an impact* (as in

'The rock hit the ground with a thud'), or the sense of *strike with a blow or missile* (as in 'The man hits the ground with a rock'). But in both senses, the direct object of 'hits' must be a physical object: no sort of hitting can be done against a social activity. This rules out the *social activity* sense of ball, leaving us with a *globular-shaped object abounding in contrast or variety of bright colours* as the only viable combined meaning. As for the two senses of 'hits', the *active human agent* status of 'man' combines with 'hits' in the sense of *strike with a blow or missile,* rather than in the sense of *collide with an impact.*

The similarity to syntagmatic theory is plain enough. To be sure, Katz and Fodor are dealing with the various senses of a word, rather than with the range of a single sense. Nonetheless, they clearly recognize an essential principle of syntagmatic synthesis: that words in combination cut down on one another's possibilities of meaning. The overall meaning of 'The man hits the colourful ball' is not the multiplied product of each and every sense of its component parts. What comes through 'colourful' and 'ball' and 'hits' is only so much meaning as can manage to agree with all of them.

But although Katz and Fodor have certainly caught sight of the principle of syntagmatic synthesis, their way of interpreting it is less than satisfactory. In effect, they try to categorize senses under a system of semantic markers and selection restrictions. If the semantic markers of one word's positive features can fit in with the slots of another word's selection restrictions, then the senses are compatible. So, with round brackets for semantic markers ( ), and double angle brackets for selection restrictions ⟨⟨⟩⟩, the sense of 'ball' as an *object having globular shape* is categorized as:

> **Noun concrete → *(Physical Object)* → *[Having globular shape]*,**

while the *abounding in contrast or variety of bright colours* sense of 'colourful' is categorized as:

> **Adjective → *(Colour)* → *[Abounding in contrast or variety of bright colours]* ⟨⟨ *(Physical Object)* or *(Social Activity)*⟩⟩.**

The ***(Physical Object)*** feature of this sense of 'ball' can fit in with the ⟨⟨***(Physical Object)*** **or** ***(Social Activity)***⟩⟩ slots of this sense of 'colourful'. But there are no slots for ***(Physical Object)*** when the *having distinctive character, vividness or picturesqueness* sense of 'colourful' is given the selection restrictions ⟨⟨***(Aesthetic Object)*** **or** ***(Social Activity)***⟩⟩.

The trouble with this system is that it works in terms of hard-and-fast rules, in terms of either–or options. Katz and Fodor present their semantic markers and selection restrictions as following on from pure grammatical categories like **Noun** and **Adjective**; and they certainly think of them as a very natural extension of the kind of marker that needs to be given to a noun in order to determine agreement with a **Human** 'who', or a **Non-human** 'which'. Under such an approach, a particular sense either possesses a feature or it doesn't; it is either compatible with another sense or it isn't. There is no room for probabilities or degrees of likelihood.

Just how far this diverges from the syntagmatic approach may be seen in the case of exceptional syntagmatic combinations. In the 'On the frontiers' section of Chapter 2, I suggested that it is actually quite difficult to invent grammatically coherent sentences that are absolutely meaningless. There is usually some sort of meaning that can be threaded through – even though it may take a great deal of effort and imagination to find it. But the Theory of Amalgamated Paths has no time for anything out of the ordinary. Thus Katz explicitly excludes 'The stick chased the dog' and 'The reflection chased the bandit' – two perfectly viable if unusual sentences.[54] The exclusion is necessary because the system of semantic markers and selection restrictions categorizes the verb 'chase' as requiring a ***(Human)*** or ***(Animal)*** subject noun.

An orientation towards exclusion is doubtless inevitable in a theory which puts the emphasis upon the semantic hurdles to combination, rather than upon the power of combination to overcome them. By contrast, the syntagmatic approach helps us to see how a particular combination of senses may be ignored without being absolutely ruled out. Given the *active human agent* status of 'man', the most obviously compatible sense of 'hits' is certainly the *strike with a blow or missile* sense; and the *collide with an impact* sense therefore takes a back seat. But it is still perfectly possible to think of a man colliding with a colourful ball. Indeed, a further development of the context may even make this the preferred reading.

Once we admit degrees of probability, we soon begin to see how all sorts of subtle semantic factors may influence a preferred reading. Thus, 'the French ambassador's ball' is more likely to involve the *social-activity* sense of 'ball'; whereas 'little Jimmie's ball' is more likely to involve the *object having globular shape* sense. But what possible semantic markers can capture this influence? Are we seriously going to assign a selection restriction for ⟨⟨(***Noble***)⟩⟩ to the *social-activity* sense of 'ball', so that it will be especially compatible with a possessive that has (***Noble***) as a marker? Or a selection restriction for ⟨⟨(***Young***)⟩⟩ to the *object having globular shape* sense, so that it will be especially compatible with a possessive that has (***Young***) as a marker? Or again, how do we explain the fact that 'Mr Godolphin went to the ball' is more likely to involve the *social-activity* sense, whereas 'Mr Godolphin went across to the ball' is more likely to involve the *object having globular shape* sense? Clearly there is a bottomless pit yawning here. The problem was pointed out by Dwight Bolinger in an article published very soon after Katz and Fodor's original article.[55]

If the system of semantic markers and selection restrictions is inadequate to the facts of combination, it is no less inadequate to the facts of individual word-meaning. Thus Katz and Fodor assign the selection restriction ⟨⟨***(Aesthetic Object)*** **or** ***(Social Activity)***⟩⟩ to 'colourful' in the sense of *having distinctive character, vividness or picturesqueness*, thereby offering no slots for the feature ***(Physical Object)***. But 'colourful clothes' may be taken in this sense, as well as in the sense of *abounding in contrast or variety of bright* *colours*; think, for instance, of a picturesque peasant costume. (What makes it so difficult for a globular ball to have distinctive character is that this is a peculiarly simple and elementary kind of physical object!) More importantly, it may not even be necessary to take 'colourful clothes' in one of these senses *as against* the other. In many contexts, the phrase 'colourful clothes' will make us think of bright colours *and* distinctive character or vividness; and similarly with 'colourful ball', in the *social-activity* sense of 'ball'. After all, 'colourful' in the *abounding in contrast or variety of bright colours* sense is not a colour adjective like 'red' or 'blue', even though Katz and Fodor assign it the marker ***(Colour)***. The concept of a *contrast* or a *variety* is already partly an abstract concept – and a concept not very far removed from the concept of *vividness*, which Katz and Fodor locate under the alternative sense. Here one can see a kind of bridge between the two senses, the kind of bridge by which one sense evolves into another under the theory proposed in 'A mechanism for change in *langue*'. Katz and Fodor wish to enforce an absolute division into separate senses; nonetheless, it is still possible to stand on that bridge and look both ways at once.

The selection restrictions assigned to 'colourful' in the *having distinctive character, vividness or picturesqueness* sense present problems in what they allow as well as what they disallow. Indeed, the slots of ⟨⟨***(Aesthetic Object)* or *(Social Activity)***⟩⟩ are scarcely even honest. On the one hand, ⟨⟨***. . . (Social Activity)***⟩⟩ is oddly specific in a way that obviously lines up ready to combine with the *social-activity* sense of 'ball'; on the other hand, ⟨⟨***(Aesthetic Object)* . . .**⟩⟩ takes care of the rest of the sense only by being so open as to include almost anything. For clearly we cannot put any weight upon the ***Object*** part of the term: we must think not of an ***Aesthetic*** thing but of an ***Aesthetic*** something. (Rightly so, since the most usual nouns to combine with 'colourful' in this sense are nouns like 'personality', 'language', 'behaviour'.) But then what weight can we put upon ***Aesthetic***? Surely anything whatsoever can be regarded as aesthetic? It all depends upon *our* way of looking and thinking and talking; and in talking, we make something aesthetic precisely by applying such adjectives as 'distinctive', 'picturesque' and 'colourful'.

If the appropriate approach to syntagmatic synthesis eludes Katz and Fodor, yet it is not difficult to see how their own approach has been carried across from the study of syntax. For syntax does indeed work with either–or options and hard-and-fast rules. A sentence is either syntactically well formed or it isn't; a word either falls under the category of transitive verb or it doesn't. Nor is there anything wishy-washy about markers of the kind which govern agreement with a 'who' or a 'which'. As I suggested earlier, syntax works by rules and conventions when it gives us our instructions for syntagmatic processing. But syntagmatic processing itself works in a different kind of way, and requires a different kind of thinking. To understand how meaning combines with meaning, we need to recognize (amongst other things) the degrees and varieties of creative effort involved. Unfortunately, when Katz and Fodor try to bring meaning into the picture, they inevitably follow the methodology already established for the study of syntax.

THE LOGICAL ANALYTICAL INFLUENCE

Because of its fairly obvious deficiencies, the Theory of Amalgamated Paths did not hold sway for very long. But from a syntagmatic point of view, the moral of its deficiencies was never properly drawn. For Katz and Fodor were indeed looking in the right place, where grammatical relations determine the processing of meaning; only they tried to explain such relations and processing under a rule-oriented either–or approach. It is therefore somewhat ironic that subsequent Generative grammarians have sought semantics in other places precisely in order to be able to maintain a rule-oriented either–or approach. In fact, subsequent Generative grammarians have turned increasingly to logical relations, where either–or rules are naturally quite at home. And here they have come under the influence of Logical Analytical philosophy.

Considering the environment in which Generative grammar grew up, the Logical Analytical influence was probably inevitable. When Generative grammarians looked around for a way of thinking about meaning, there was not only no Phenomenological theory of language available, but no tradition of 'I'-philosophy at all. The American philosophical scene was dominated – as it continues to be dominated – by the Logical strand of Analytical philosophy. (The Ordinary-Language strand has played a smaller role in America than in England, and has had a correspondingly smaller influence upon Generative grammar.) Given the arguments of Chapter 8, it will come as no surprise that I regard the Logical Analytical influence as almost entirely unfortunate.

At the same time, this influence was also encouraged by certain apparent analogies, especially prominent in the early development of Generative grammar. In the first place, both Generative grammar and Logical Analytical philosophy analysed sentences into structures in depth. That is, both supposed that the true structure of a sentence lay hidden behind its visible surface structure. And in the second place, both had a habit of deriving phrasal structures on the surface from underlying main-verb clauses. So Russell derived 'the round square' from (roughly) 'there is one and only one entity *x* which is round and square'; while Chomsky derived 'the shooting of the hunters' from either 'the hunters shoot' or 'they shoot the hunters'. Chomsky also suggested – to take a simple non-ambiguous example – that the surface structure of 'the tall boy' might be traced back to a deep structure in the form of 'the boy is tall'.[56] Naturally it began to look as though Generative grammar and Logical Analytical philosophy could lend each other some useful mutual support.

The notion of an affinity between syntactic deep structures and underlying logical structures grew increasingly upon Generative grammarians in the latter part of the 1960s. Lakoff, Bach, and especially McCawley strove to identify sentences, noun phrases and verbs ever more closely with propositions, arguments and predicates.[57] And with the arrival of Generative Semantics proper, the affinity became an identity. Deep structures were pushed so far back that they could now be regarded as a kind of 'natural logic' – a truer-to-language version of what symbolic logic had long been trying to capture.[58] From this remarkable self-confidence followed many remarkable claims.

For example: the Generative Semanticists claimed that one and the same deep structure must underlie 'John bought a car from Harry' and 'Harry sold a car to John', on the grounds that these two sentences are logically equivalent. Conversely, they claimed that two different deep structures must underlie 'Bill wants to marry a girl with blue eyes', on the grounds that this sentence is logically ambiguous – i.e. it may either imply that whoever Bill marries will have to have blue eyes (though he has no specific girl in mind), or that there is a specific girl (with blue eyes) whom Bill wants to marry. Such claims might look like a natural enough development from Chomsky's claims in *Syntactic Structures*, e.g. that one and the same deep structure underlies the active and passive forms of a sentence, or that two different deep structures underlie 'They are flying planes.' But in fact a crucial watershed has been crossed.

Consider 'John bought a car from Harry' and 'Harry sold a car to John'. The equivalence here is not essentially a matter of meaning but of truth-conditions. That is, the two sentences end up referring to exactly the same state of affairs in all possible worlds. And if we think of structure as the structure of a state of affairs, as a concatenation of objects and events, then evidently there is only a single concatenated structure for both sentences. Out in the world, we find ourselves looking at John and Harry occupying the same positions relative to the same transaction. Such is the nature of logical structure. But grammatical structure is something else again. Grammatical relations do not hold between objects and events, but only between grammatical slices of world. And such slices, as I argued long ago, are a product of *our* activity: they are not purely objective, but a fusion of objective with subjective. Linguistics cannot afford to leap too quickly to an out-in-the-world perspective. Grammatically structured meanings have to be thought in their own way – which is *not* the way of logically structured objects and events. Certainly, 'John bought a car from Harry' and 'Harry sold a car to John' end up at the same referential goal, the same objective state of affairs. But the two sentences start out from quite different meanings, which have to be thought in quite different ways.

Similarly in the case of 'Bill wants to marry a girl with blue eyes.' Only when we try to collect up the extension for 'a girl with blue eyes' do we discover that the sentence is capable of picking out either one single girl or any one of a whole set of girls. Out in the world, we find ourselves looking at two quite different states of affairs, with two quite different concatenations of objects and events. The ambiguity here is not an ambiguity of meaning but an ambiguity of reference. Specifically, it is an ambiguity as to whether the indefinite article in 'a girl with blue eyes' is a matter of Bill's reference as well as our reference. For Bill, from his own point of view, might refer either to 'a' girl or 'the' girl, depending on whether he has or has not picked out the object of his affections. But this distinction gets submerged under overriding considerations which determine the use of the definite or indefinite article relative to an addressee. If we – who are listening to the sentence – cannot be assumed to know 'the' girl with blue eyes, then the speaker will have to convert 'the' girl (as she appears to Bill) into 'a' girl (as she will appear to us). Considered in relation to *our* subjective apprehension of the sentence, there is no separation of meanings: either way, we are thinking of an 'indefinite' girl. But there *is* a separation of references, which appears as soon as one moves to an out-in-the-world perspective, and considers the objective states of affairs to which the sentence may apply.

Of course, there are many more claims of the Generative Semanticists which could be discussed. In the heyday of Generative Semantics, their claims proliferated so wondrously and so uncontrollably that it soon became impossible to take them seriously. By the mid-1970s, the movement had drowned in its own excesses. Like the semantics of Katz and Fodor, the semantics of the Generative Semanticists is now largely forgotten. But again, from a syntagmatic point of view, the lesson of that failure has never been properly drawn. For Generative grammarians have continued to believe that the business of semantics is above all logical business.

So instead of separating semantics from logic, Generative grammarians have ended up separating logico-semantics from syntax. Indeed, the rationale for a merger between logico-semantics and syntax has gradually disappeared with the development of new ways of conceiving and representing deep structures. No longer do deep structures resemble the mini-propositions of symbolic logic; no longer do they take the form of multiple expanded clauses. On this issue, the arguments of the Interpretive Semanticists have carried the day. Logico-semantics now comes after syntax, merely interpreting what syntax has produced.

What is especially interesting from a syntagmatic point of view is that logico-semantics now comes after syntax in another respect too. For, in the progress from Standard Theory to Extended Standard Theory to Revised Extended Standard Theory to Government and Binding Theory, the semantic component has been gradually relegated to a later and later stage of sentence generation. No longer does logico-semantics interpret what syntax has produced at the level of deep structure, or even what syntax has produced at a variety of levels from deep structure to surface structure. In Government and Binding Theory, logico-semantics only comes to interpret what syntax has produced at the level of S-structure. The new situation may be appreciated by looking at the location of the Logical Form and Semantic Representation components in Figure 12.1, a diagram for the so-called 'T-model'.

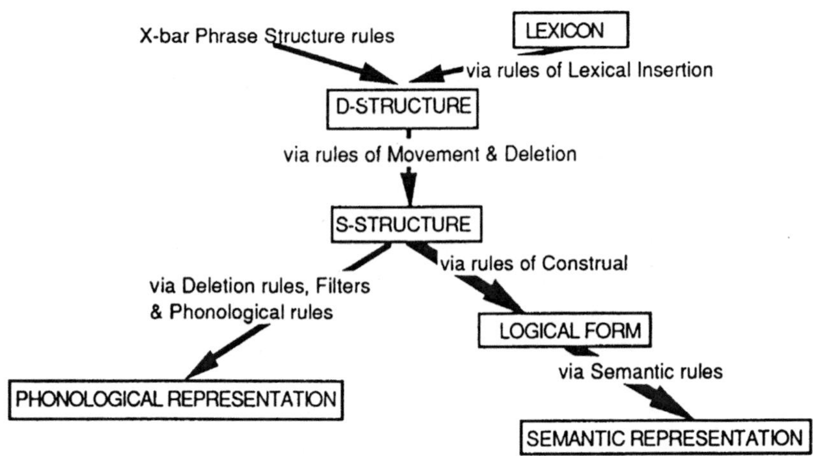

Figure 12.1

Here, S-structure is only fractionally deeper than the old surface structure (which would have to be placed somewhere after the application of Deletion rules and Filters, but before the application of Phonological rules).

In so far as logico-semantics has to do with logic, this appendix-like location is perfectly appropriate. For, as I argued in the 'Logical relations versus grammatical relations' section of Chapter 8, logic applies to sentences only after they have become fully formed in other respects. Logical relations do not constitute sentence-meaning, and are not integral to the sentence as grammatical relations are. A logical calculus only interprets what has already been generated by the action of syntactic instructions and grammatical relations upon meaning. So when the Logical Form and Semantic Representation components are made subsequent to all considerations of syntax and grammar, logico-semantics has finally gravitated to its proper place from a syntagmatic point of view.

But, by the same token, logico-semantics can no longer claim to be dealing with *meaning*. For meaning must be involved in sentence generation from the most fundamental levels – not merely tacked on after a sentence has already been developed to its highest syntactical and grammatical form. How could sentences ever evolve on the basis of syntax and grammar alone? It is not just that the notion of syntax and grammar coming before meaning is implausible here: the notion of syntax and grammar interreacting with meaning at just a single interface would be implausible regardless of whichever component came first. The real interreaction of syntax and grammar with meaning must take place on every level of syntagmatic processing: it can never be represented in the kind of diagram which deals only in simple 'block' components.

MONTAGUE GRAMMAR

It has to be said that what Government and Binding Theory puts into the Logical Form component is only a very pale shadow of what Generative Semantics once sought to incorporate into 'natural logic'. Logical Form deals with the old issue of the logical scope of quantifiers – but not a great deal more. In fact, Logical Form incorporates only so much of logico-semantics as can be made accountable to rules and principles already invoked for the D-structure and S-structure levels of syntax – the projection principle and Empty-Category Principle, for example.[59] As for the Semantic Representation component, its potential contents are still highly uncertain (although Chomsky has gestured towards some development of the predicate calculus). Nor is there even any general agreement that a Semantic Representation component is needed in the model at all. Although grammarians of the Government and Binding school continue to believe that the business of semantics is logical business, they no longer believe that it is particularly *their* business. In a sense, the Government and Binding approach is essentially a clearing operation, setting semantics aside for the sake of an uninterrupted view of syntax.

However, another school of Generative grammar brings semantics right to the front of the stage again – in the new form of Montague Grammar. Montague Grammar *per se* is a further development of the logics discussed in Chapter 8, and might well have been dealt with after the section on Possible-Worlds Semantics. But Montague Grammar seems to possess an especial relevance for linguists; and Partee, Dowty, Gazdar, Pullum and others have taken it up most eagerly. For these linguists (mainly of the Generalized Phrase-Structure school), Montague has opened the way to a new understanding of semantics particularly compatible with Generative grammar.

Semantics comes to the front of the stage because of Montague's view that every syntactical move ties in with a parallel move of semantics. Rules of syntax and rules of meaning implicate one another at every smallest step of the way. Indeed, there is here no possibility of separating out semantics as a 'block' component, or of relating it to some part of the syntax at just a single interface. In this respect at least, the Montague-orientated linguists seem to be coming a little closer to syntagmatic theory.

There are other promising concurrences too. For example, the logical types in Montague Grammar correspond to the separate parts of speech in natural language, unlike the functions and arguments of standard predicate calculus. In the 'Logical relations versus grammatical relations' section of Chapter 8, I particularly criticized the way in which quite different grammatical items are all reduced to the same status of arguments, distinguishable only as occupying first place, second place, third place, etc. But this kind of criticism cannot be levelled against Montague. In Montague Grammar, there are different logical types set up for common nouns, noun phrases, intransitive verbs, transitive verbs, verb-modifying adverbs, sentence-modifying adverbs, prepositions, determiners – in short, all the major grammatical categories as recognized in traditional grammar, Generative grammar and syntagmatic theory.[60]

Along with the recognition of many different types goes a recognition of many different modes of combination between those types. Montague is interested not merely in how quantification and logical constants affect truth-values, but in how complex expressions are built up out of simple expressions in language generally. So in Montague Grammar, a determiner may combine with a common noun to produce a noun phrase, a preposition may combine with a noun phrase to produce a prepositional phrase, and a noun phrase and a verb phrase may combine to produce a sentence. It is scarcely surprising that the analysis trees of Montague Grammar bear a strong resemblance to the branching trees in the phrase structure component of Generative grammar. Figure 12.2 is an example.[61]

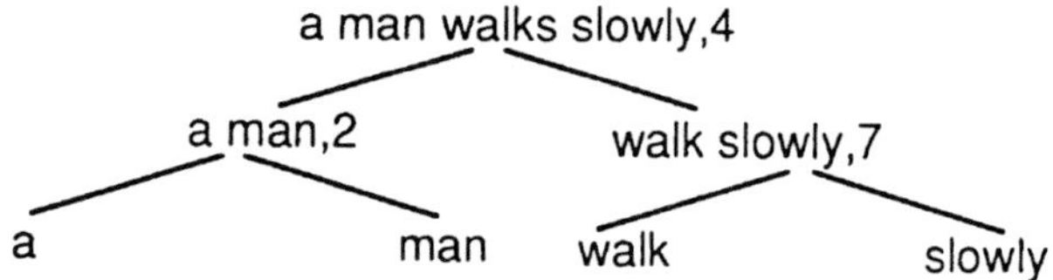

Figure 12.2

Whereas the only potentially syntagmatic relation in standard predicate calculus is the relation of function to argument, in Figure 12.2 we have a whole stage-by-stage hierarchy of potentially syntagmatic relations.

What's more, these potentially syntagmatic relations involve intensions and not just extensions. In the 'Pincer movement against meaning' section of Chapter 8, I claimed that Logical Analytical philosophers typically invoke intensions only in second place, only when extensions falter. But this complaint cannot be brought against Montague – at least, not in the same way. For Montague does not treat opaque contexts, *de dicto* constructions, etc., as mere intensional addenda to an extensional theory of language; on the contrary, he treats the extensional cases as a special sub-class within an overarching intensional theory. In Montague Grammar, for instance, the phrase 'is red' refers us to the *property* of being red, rather than to the extensional set of all the things in the world that are red.[62] This certainly looks much closer to an ordinary understanding – which is also the syntagmatic understanding – of such meanings.

The intensional approach overcomes one very obvious hurdle that must be faced by any logic trying to come to terms with grammatical relations. Consider the simple adjective-to-noun combination: 'a short basketball player'.[63] On an extensional approach, this would have to be seen as picking out in the world an intersection or overlap between the set of all the things which are short and the set of all the things which are basketball players. But how can we possibly pick out a general set of all the things which are short? And even if we tried, we should never be able to draw the boundaries of that set in such a way as to overlap onto the set of basketball players (who are all, by any general standard, tall). This is the sort of combination upon which syntagmatic theory thrives, where a meaning for the whole has to be projected beyond the meanings of the parts. To the extent that Montague allows for the intersection of intensional properties rather than extensional sets, he seems to be heading in the same direction.

But these similarities are all more apparent than real. Although Montague advances beyond standard predicate logic, he continues to build upon identical foundations. In particular, he continues to build upon the same *substantial* elements of meaning. As I showed in the 'Pincer movement against meaning' section of Chapter 8, Logical Analytical philosophers give meaning substance by referring it to solid reality. And there are just two possible points where language makes contact with solid reality: in propositions which can be either true or false to real states of affairs; and in arguments which can collect up real entities or individuals under an extensional set. Montague adds nothing new to this account. The only substantial elements of meaning in Montague Grammar are the two traditional forms of denotation: denoted truth-values and denoted entities.[64]

What's new is the complication of functions. In standard predicate logic, a single non-substantial function carries us from the level of arguments to the level of propositions. But Montague breaks this single function up into a great many functions – into functions upon functions upon functions. This makes it possible to identify different parts of speech with different functions at specific stages in the overall movement from entities to truth-values. In Montague Grammar, everything that is done is done with the aid of functions. But still it is the same overall movement as in standard predicate logic, defined by the same beginning and the same ending.

To study Montague's strategy in more detail, let us adopt the conventional notation of e for the type of an expression denoting entities, and t for the type of an expression denoting truth-values. Then, in the sentence 'Mary runs', the denotation of 'Mary' is an $\langle e \rangle$ for entity, the denotation of 'Mary runs' is a $\langle t \rangle$ for truth-value; and the denotation of 'runs' is that function which carries us from an entity to a truth-value – or in other words, $\langle e, t. \rangle$ Similarly in the sentence 'Mary chases John': the denotation of the verb phrase 'chases John' is that function which carries us from 'Mary' as an entity to 'Mary chases John' as a truth-value – or, again, $\langle e, t. \rangle$ As for the denotation of the transitive verb 'chases', this is the function which carries us from 'John' as an $\langle e \rangle$ to 'chases John' as an $\langle e, t \rangle$ – or in other words, $\langle e, \langle e, t \rangle \rangle$.

Another move of the same logic comes into play with a verb-modifying adverb like 'furiously'. Evidently this is the function which carries us from the unmodified to the modified state of a verb phrase like 'chases John'. Since the denotation of the verb phrase is $\langle e, t \rangle$ in either state, the denotation of the adverb is a function from $\langle e, t \rangle$ to $\langle e, t \rangle$ – or in other words, $\langle \langle e, t \rangle, \langle e, t \rangle \rangle$.

Similarly with a sentence-modifying adverb like 'probably', which carries us from a sentence like 'Mary chases John furiously' to a modified state of the same sentence, 'Probably Mary chases John furiously.' It follows that the denotation of 'probably' is a function from $\langle t \rangle$ to $\langle t \rangle$ – or in other words, $\langle t, t \rangle$.[65]

As regards the different kinds of grammatical category, clearly this approach has almost nothing in common with syntagmatic theory. In syntagmatic theory, we understand the different kinds of category in terms of different ways of standing towards the world, different 'conceptual cuts' taken across reality. Such different ways of standing are fundamental and primitive: they are the specific possibilities available to our subjective psychological apparatus. In a sense, they could not be otherwise than as they are. Not so in Montague's system. Behind the different categories defined by Montague lie always the same elements, the same *e*'s and *t*'s out of which they are all composed. Nor is there any necessity which makes them the way they are. On the contrary, Montague Grammar actually generates any number of usable categories, as many as there are ways of stringing together unlimited *e*'s and *t*'s. Montague Grammar only furnishes a range of sites, and the actual categories of a particular language take up residence wherever seems appropriate. Indeed, it may sometimes happen that two or more categories end up inhabiting the same site: thus verb-modifying adverbs, prepositional phrases and infinitive-complement verbs (like 'try' or 'wish') are all cast as $\langle\langle e, t\rangle, \langle e, t\rangle\rangle$. (In a somewhat different notation for categories of the English language proper, Montague Grammar recognizes such distinctions with a mere convention of punctuation: thus a verb-modifying adverb appears as *IV/IV* with a single solidus, while an infinitive-complement verb appears as *IV//IV* with a double solidus.) Such an approach is clearly indifferent to the nature of grammatical categories in themselves.

As regards the combination of categories, here too Montague Grammar has little in common with syntagmatic theory. To arrive at the sentence 'Probably Mary chases John furiously', we need the analysis tree of Figure 12.3.

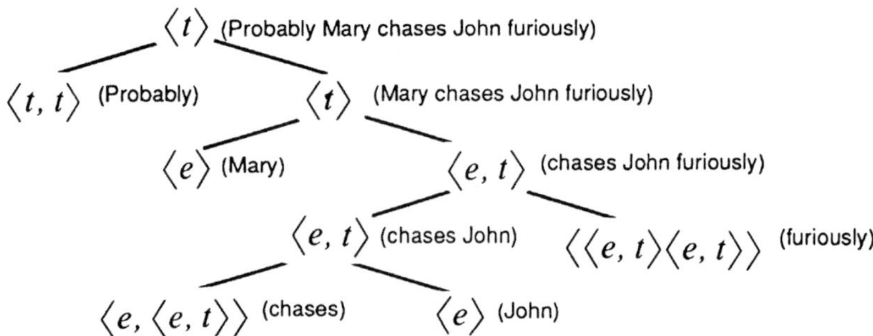

Figure 12.3

An $\langle e\rangle$ with an $\langle e, \langle e, t\rangle\rangle$ yields an $\langle e, t\rangle$; an $\langle e, t\rangle$ with an $\langle\langle e, t\rangle \langle e, t\rangle\rangle$yields an $\langle e, t\rangle$; and an $\langle e\rangle$ with an $\langle e, t\rangle$ yields a $\langle t\rangle$. Or to put it another way, an expression of type $\langle e\rangle$ combines with another expression by 'knocking out' one of its *e*'s; and an expression of type $\langle e, t\rangle$ combines with another expression by 'knocking out' one of its $\langle e, t\rangle$'s. Mathematically, we subtract the same term from both sides. This kind of *cancellation operation* is the most common form of combination under Montague Grammar.[66]

To the extent that cancellation operations produce a successive convergence and narrowing down, it might seem that there is some analogy here to the processes of syntagmatic synthesis. But if this is a version of synthesis, it is a synthesis entirely without projection. The syntagmatic version of synthesis leaps from the old meanings of individual words to the genuinely new kind of meaning in a sentence. But in Montague Grammar, the kind of meaning in a sentence is *precontained*, as it were, within the individual words. If the category of truth-values always emerges as the sentence's ultimate kind of meaning, this is because it has always already been introduced as the *t* within an $\langle e, t\rangle$, an $\langle e, \langle e, t\rangle\rangle$, an $\langle\langle e, t\rangle,\langle\langle e, t\rangle, t\rangle\rangle$, etc. In the 'Complementarity, synthesis, projection' section of Chapter 2, I inveighed against the traditional error of fixating so strongly upon meaning at the level of individual words that one fails to allow for a new kind of meaning at the level of sentences. Montague's error is the exact converse: of fixating so strongly upon meaning at the level of sentences that there is no truly independent definition of meanings at the level of individual words. The impressive way in which successive cancellations bring us to a desired outcome is largely due to the fact that the desired outcome has been built into the input. So, in order to produce the desired result for the sentence 'John loves his horse', the verb 'loves' will have to be given a denotation of type $\langle e, \langle e, t\rangle\rangle$; but in order to produce the desired result for the sentence 'John loves to ride his horse', the same verb will have to be given a denotation of type $\langle\langle e, t\rangle,\langle e, t\rangle\rangle$. A curious foreknowledge haunts the whole system.

So far, so disappointing. Nor does the situation improve when intensions are incorporated into the picture. For intensions are also conceived as a kind of function – a function which imposes intensionality on top of entities or on top of functions composed of entities and truth-values. In the notation, this function is represented by an *s* (a mnemonic for 'sense'); and one forms the intension of an *e* or a *t* simply by adding an *s* in front: $\langle s, e\rangle$, or $\langle s, t\rangle$. For derived expressions composed of *e*'s and *t*'s, this involves the incorporation of intensions internally: so an intransitive verb, previously described as a function from entities to truth-values, $\langle e, t\rangle$, now appears as a function from an *intension* of entities to truth-values, $\langle\langle s, e\rangle,t\rangle$. As a whole, however, this expression remains an extension; if we want to intensionalize it as a whole, we must add a further *s* in front: $\langle s,\langle\langle s, e\rangle,t\rangle\rangle$. Such complications (which are still highly simplified) will come into play later on. For now, the thing to notice is that no *s* can ever occur on its own; unlike an *e* or a *t*, an *s* is not a substantial element of meaning.* Earlier I noted that intensions in Montague Grammar are not secondary in the traditional way of Logical Analytical philosophy: that is, they are invoked for all contexts, and not merely for those special contexts where extensions alone run into logical trouble. Yet they are still secondary in so far as they have no moment of independent existence prior to extensions. They are still not meanings such as we might hold in mind without yet knowing the sum total of what they will pick out.

Hence the very specialized sense which Montague gives to *property*, a term which I have so far allowed to flourish in its more usual sense. For Montague is not interested in the sort of qualitative concept which might enable us to apply an expression like 'is red' to cases never previously encountered. An intension is not defined in itself, but only by its results – by the sum total of what it will pick out (or will have picked out) under all possible indices in all possible worlds at all possible times. As Dowty, Wall and Peters put it, an intension in Montague Grammar is nothing more than all the varying extensions of an expression 'organized' into a function.[67] It is essentially irrelevant whether our applications of 'is red' have anything in common at all.

This is very much a Proper Name way of thinking. As I have noted long ago, Logical Analytical philosophers make no particular investment in proper names as such; and Montague even rarefies them into *properties of properties* – a function far removed from any simple reference to bearers.[68] Nonetheless, Montague's way of thinking about expressions in general resembles the way in which we ordinarily think about proper names. For it is obviously irrelevant to look for something shared in common by all bearers of the name 'Marion' (streets and boats, as well as human individuals); and it is obviously impossible to apply the name for ourselves in cases never previously encountered. We can only know the cases where it has been applied. Or, more abstractly, we can only hypothesize the cases where it has been applied even if we don't know about them.

It is here that the concept of the 'model' becomes crucial, not only in Montague Grammar, but in model-theoretic semantics generally. For the model is a constructed domain where all extensions of all expressions have been already settled. As an overall hypothesis, the model reaches into the unknown; but within that model, everything is hypothesized as being finally and completely *known*. The dimension of possibility and potentiality in language is thus dealt with once and for all, cleared out of the way in a single opening stroke. After which, there is no problem as to how we can manage to

* In fact, the *e* also does not occur on its own, though for a different reason. I have deliberately glossed (and shall continue to gloss) the full story by allowing expressions such as 'Mary' and 'John' to denote entities. In Montague Grammar, no actual grammatical category of the English language directly denotes entities. The only category which is truly simple is the *t* of the final sentence: below this, there is a strong tendency for subordinate categories to lift off into ever-increasing states of abstraction. As a logic, Montague Grammar relies upon *e*'s independently defined by reference to extensional sets of entities; but in the analysis of language, it starts out from a point already further down the track.

apply expressions in cases never previously encountered; under the terms of the hypotheses, the situation simply does not arise.[69]

Montague's intensions are not only limited in themselves, but limited in the way that they feature in the cancellation operation. Consider the combination of 'chases' and 'John'. Allowing for internal intensions, the extension of 'chases' will be represented as $\langle\langle s,e\rangle\langle\langle s,e\rangle,t\rangle\rangle$, and the extension of 'John' as $\langle e\rangle$. But if the $\langle e\rangle$ only 'knocks out' the initial *e* of $\langle\langle s,e\rangle\langle\langle s,e\rangle,t\rangle\rangle$, then evidently the initial *s* of that expression will be left hanging. Montague therefore prescribes that, in any such combination, we take the extension of the function-term (i.e. the longer term) together with the intension of the argument-term (i.e. the shorter term). This gives us $\langle s,e\rangle$ for 'John', and enables us to subtract an $\langle s,e\rangle$ from both terms, leaving $\langle\langle s,e\rangle,t\rangle$ as the expression corresponding to 'chases John'. In effect, we have had to introduce an *s* in order to remove an *s*. And this same process is repeated for cancellation operations at every level.

This is all very different from syntagmatic theory. When we combine individual words syntagmatically, we progress towards new meaning, towards a mentally conceivable possibility beyond all cases previously encountered. Putting it very loosely, one might say that the results of syntagmatic combination are increasingly intensional. Whereas Montague's kind of combination always comes back to extensions. The *s* is introduced into the argument-term only to disappear again, winking in and out of existence at every level. The end-product of any cancellation operation is an extension – as the $\langle\langle s,e\rangle,t\rangle$ of 'chases John' is an extension. And the terminus of all combinations, the invariable category for whole sentences, is the simple extensional $\langle t\rangle$. By repeatedly invoking intensions, Montague avoids that premature rush into reference which creates so many problems for standard predicate logic. But still he invokes intensions only on the way through, only as a means to a non-intensional end.

Underlying all these many differences is Montague's mathematically derived concept of a function. As I suggested earlier, everything that is done in Montague Grammar is done with the aid of functions. Indeed, the concept of a function is a multi-purpose one, which we have already seen adapted to several distinct roles in several distinct fields. But this very adaptability should give us pause. Functions can be used to cover all sorts of correlation between one set of terms and another; but by the same token, they will not explain the why and wherefore of any *particular* correlation. So in Montague Grammar, there is a type of function which correlates the expression 'is red' with all the cases to which it will have applied under all possible indices in all possible worlds at all possible times. But such a function does not tell us what brings those specific cases together under that expression. Or again, there is a type of function which carries us from one state of a truth-value to another, the $\langle t,t\rangle$ function identified with sentence-modifying adverbs like 'probably'. But to know that a sentence-modifying adverb carries us from a $\langle t\rangle$ to a $\langle t\rangle$ hardly tells us much about the manner of the modification. Montague Grammar 'takes care' of numerous natural-language features ignored in standard predicate logic – but it does so in a way which leaps clean over the problems standing most in need of explanation. Just what do such functions really represent? In Montague Grammar, mathematical processes are made to 'model' or 'shadow' the grammatical processes of natural language more closely than ever before; but in the end, this ultimate imitation still only serves to reveal an ultimate disparity. There is an unbridgeable difference in kind between the way in which mathematical processes work and the way in which grammatical processes work.

JACKENDOFF IN THE 1980s

So far, I have presented the semantics of Generative grammar fairly negatively, with a sense of wasted opportunity. But let me end on an upbeat note, with the case of Ray Jackendoff. In his writings of the 1980s, Jackendoff has cast off the influence of Logical Analytical philosophy, and has adopted a new influence, the influence of Gestalt psychology. This links him specifically to the Phenomenological perspective; he has also associated himself in a more general way with the tradition of 'I'-philosophy, invoking Kant and describing himself as a 'constructivist'.[70] Admittedly, this new side is not the only side to his thinking. Still, it produces some striking parallels to syntagmatic theory.

As regards the Logical Analytical philosophers, Jackendoff's criticisms bring out the same fundamental divergence as the criticisms presented in Chapter 8 of this book. Above all, he 'part[s] company with the enterprise of semantics as it is generally conceived' by refusing to provide 'an account of how the language maps into the world'.[71] Insisting that truth and reference are secondary, he claims that expressions do not directly tie onto the real world, but on to a construed world. Construed worlds are of course typical of philosophy in the 'I'-tradition, where their projection is explained in terms of mental activity. Nor does Jackendoff shrink from the currently unfashionable idea 'that a meaning is a sort of mental representation'.[72] As for the purpose of language, he denies that language serves primarily to designate or point to the real world; on the contrary, 'the purpose of language is to make one's internal structures projectable to others . . . i.e., to express thought'.[73]

Jackendoff also opposes the characteristic Logical Analytical mania for reducing mental or abstract states of being to a foundational level of 'things' or 'co-occurrences of things'. Ontological parsimony for its own sake is given short shrift:

> The existence of a particular ontological category is not a matter of physics or metaphysical speculation or formal parsimony, but an empirical psychological issue, to be determined on the basis of its value in explaining the experience and behaviour of humans and other organisms.[74]

Following a Phenomenological line, Jackendoff is prepared to accept the value of 'a rich range of ontological categories'.[75] And as regards the categories of language, he specifically disputes the traditional logical reduction of all categories to that mere pair of ultimate elements, argument-terms and predicates. 'The underlying problem with first-order logic is that it does not have enough categories to go around'.[76]

The parallels to syntagmatic theory emerge especially in relation to single words. Jackendoff too demands an explanation for the way in which we manage to apply words in cases never previously encountered:

> For example, consider the concept expressed by the word *dog*. Someone who knows this concept, upon encountering an indefinitely large variety of objects, will be able to judge whether or not they are dogs. Thus the concept cannot be encoded as a list of the dogs one has previously encountered; nor, because the brain is finite, can it be a list of all dogs there ever have been and will be, or of all possible dogs. Rather, it must be some sort of finite schema.[77]

This argument he calls 'the argument from creativity'; and his emphasis upon the as-if-for-the-first-time activity of the language-user goes not only against Logical Analytical philosophy but against Superstructuralist philosophy as well. Indeed, he even suggests that we can generate for ourselves new conceptual 'Types' of the kind that our existing words express.[78] Whereas Generative grammarians have generally concentrated upon the creativity of syntax whilst ignoring the creativity of semantics, Jackendoff now explicitly rejects such 'syntactocentrism', and discovers an equal creativity in semantics.[79]

If the language-user creatively assimilates new cases to a schema, it is impossible to draw objective once-and-for-all boundaries around the range of a word's meaning. Again in opposition to the Logical Analytical philosophers, Jackendoff argues that a word's meaning is not sharply circumscribed by either–or rules, by necessary-and-sufficient conditions for membership of a set. Rather, a word's meaning has wide and fuzzy margins, permitting a multitude of more or less assimilable instances. (The Gestalt influence is particularly strong here.) In such circumstances, the only workable rules are what Jackendoff calls 'preference rules', specifying graded degrees of centrality or marginality.[80]

By way of a practical example, he puts forward four sentences involving the verb 'climb': (a) 'Bill climbed up the mountain'; (b) 'Bill climbed down the mountain'; (c) 'The snake climbed up the tree'; (d) 'The snake climbed down the tree.'[81] Here, (a), (b) and (c) are all acceptable, but (d) is very odd. Jackendoff suggests that 'climb' has two main conceptual conditions: travelling upwards, and moving with grasping, clambering motions. These conditions do not merely cohabit in the form of 'a standard Boolean conjunction or disjunction', but have a natural tendency to hang together.[82] However, they can be separated out, as in sentence (b), which satisfies only the condition of moving with grasping, clambering motions; or as in sentence (c), which satisfies only the condition of travelling upwards. Such cases are less central than sentence (a), which satisfies both conditions, but they are still perfectly acceptable. Only sentence (d) fails to come in under either condition. This is all very similar to the view advanced in the 'Return of *parole*' section of Chapter 3. Indeed, Jackendoff's more detailed analysis, especially in *Semantics and Cognition*, should be read as an invaluable supplement to that section.[83]

With this kind of flexibility to call upon, Jackendoff can avoid the usual premature appeal to ambiguity of meaning. For instance, the word 'see' may be used as in (i) 'I must have been looking at it but I never actually saw it', or as in (ii) 'I must have seen it, but I never actually noticed it.'[84] From the extensional perspective, 'see' is here picking out two quite separate sets of cases; therefore the word must be given two quite separate definitions, and its ordinary use must be regarded as ambiguous. But Jackendoff, far more plausibly, recognizes related senses in the word, neither simply the same nor simply separate. In effect, the schema for 'see' can be followed out along the notion of 'cast one's gaze upon', or followed out along the notion of 'become aware of what one's gaze is cast upon'. As I argued in the 'Mechanism for change in *langue*' section of Chapter 3, this is the mechanism primarily responsible for the 'family resemblance' character of all our common words.[85]

Given so many similarities in relation to single words, it is perhaps disappointing that Jackendoff's interests diverge from those of syntagmatic theory at the level of words in combination. Pondering the combination of a fuzzy-edged concept of 'foolish' with a fuzzy-edged concept of 'boy', he concludes: 'my assessment is that at the moment we have too few actual analyses in terms of preference rules to be able to attack the combinatorial problem intelligently'.[86] At this level, he does not concern himself with how such ordinary combinations work, but with the very different question of what combinations are possible. What categories of words are compatible or incompatible in this or that structure? Here, his studies certainly have more to do with underlying grammatical relations than with the rules of syntax. But still he is studying the conditions necessary and sufficient for such relations to operate, rather than the consequences of their operation upon meaning. It is hardly surprising that the 'conceptual indeterminacies' so crucial for single words play only a minor role in these studies, which can function quite happily on the basis of 'those aspects of conceptual structure that are more or less discrete and digital'.[87]

However, there is one significant case where Jackendoff comes very close to a syntagmatic theory of combination, when he examines the difference of meaning between (a) 'The light flashed', and (b) 'The light flashed until dawn.'[88] Here sentence (a) is naturally understood in terms of a single flash, whereas sentence (b) requires us to imagine repeated flashing. Yet as Jackendoff points out, the sense of repetition cannot be located in the phrase 'until dawn', which contributes no such sense to the sentence 'Bill slept until dawn.' The sense of repetition evidently arises not from the parts but from the whole. Jackendoff's explanation runs as follows. The phrase 'until dawn' places a temporal boundary upon an event; but the single-event sense of 'flash' sets its own terminus and already has a boundary. We are therefore compelled to find another sense, an unbounded sense, for 'flash' – in this case, the sense of a repeating event which can continue over an indefinite period of time. The phrase supplies what the verb lacks: and the verb *has to* lack it before the two expressions can be combined. This is the syntagmatic principle of complementarity; and Jackendoff gives as neat a demonstration of it as one could wish.

In his writings of the 1980s, then, Jackendoff finally points semantics in the direction most natural and appropriate for Generative grammar. In fact, he goes all the way with the Chomskyan orientation towards 'I-language' as against 'E-language'. Chomsky himself is mainly concerned to attack the methodology of the American Structural Linguists: on Chomsky's interpretation, 'E-language' is language understood e-xternally, in terms of observable behavioural data, whereas 'I-language' is language understood i-nternally, within the mind or brain of the language-user.[89] But on Jackendoff's interpretation, 'E-language' is also language understood e-xtensionally, as a matter of impersonal reference and truth-conditions, whereas 'I-language' is language understood i-ntensionally, in terms of mental schemata.[90] The attack is thus turned against the whole Logical Analytical approach to semantics. In Jackendoff's hands, the grammarians' 'I-language' meets up with the perspective of 'I'-philosophy – a happy typographical coincidence, marking a true affinity.

Part V

Syntagmatic theory and literature

13 Syntagmatic theory and literature

THE SYNTAGMATIC SIDE OF POETRY

Modern poetry begins with the French Symbolists: and the French Symbolists discovered how to do something new with language. That is, they discovered how to drop a word (or cluster of words) like a pebble into a pond, letting ripples of meaning spread out all around. As Mallarmé explains:

> I say: a flower! and, out of the forgetfulness where my voice banishes any contour, inasmuch as it is something other than known calyxes, musically arises, an idea itself and fragrant, the one absent from all bouquets.[1]

Left to its own devices, the word possesses a power of suggestion which far exceeds any simple dictionary definition. Meaning, if not channelled syntagmatically, will open out into further and further evocations and implications. (I use these two terms to approximate the concrete and abstract forms of suggestion, respectively.) 'A flower!', uttered all by itself and out of the blue, is in much the same condition as the word ETERNITY carved upon a rock.

Another way of thinking this condition is to regard the word as a sort of verbal mantra. In *Superstructuralism*, I related Derrida's theory of writing both to the Symbolist poets and to the practice of meditation.[2] Now it is appropriate to link those two latter terms in a direct comparison. For a mantra-word also sends out ripples of meaning, evocations and implications, further and further afield. But such evocations and implications are not located within the mantra-word itself, not in the way that an ordinary word has traditionally been thought to contain its meaning. The mantra-word is only surrounded by meaning; in itself, we may think of it as perfectly solid and impenetrable. (So, in meditation, a verbal mantra may be a word with no signified at all, a pure signifier like the famous 'OM!') As I pointed out in *Superstructuralism*, an interest in this special kind of meaning is by no means incompatible with an interest in the physical body of a word.[3] On the contrary: the Symbolist poets and their successors are orientated both towards the material features of language and towards ideas of a particularly far-flung and insubstantial type.

Using Mallarmé as our guide, let us think through some further effects of the Symbolists' discovery. 'The poet', says Mallarmé, 'abandons the initiative to words . . . they light one another up with mutual reflections like a virtual trail of fire upon precious stones.'[4] Language takes over. The poet cannot directly communicate this special kind of meaning, cannot actively compel the spread of ripples. Nor is this the kind of meaning that the reader can actively grasp. Evocations and implications arise in an essentially passive state of mind. The power of suggestion must be left up to the words themselves.

This special kind of meaning is not under the control of syntax either. In Mallarmé's ideal form of poetry, '[the mind] perceives [words] independently of the ordinary sequence, projected like the walls of a cavern'.[5] Ripples of meaning spread out in the space around a word; they flourish most freely when words can be taken in isolation. The ordinary continuity and connectedness of a sentence restricts them. It is hardly surprising that poets ever since the time of the Symbolists have regarded the connections of grammar as so many fetters and chains. Syntax has come to be associated with those forms of discourse against which poetry must define itself – the logical, the rational, the scientific, the prosaic.

It follows that a poem should not be expected to present the overall coherence of an argument or line of thinking. According to Mallarmé, the Symbolist poem 'refuses the natural materials and, as if it were brutal, an exact thought ordering them'.[6] The Symbolist poem aims 'to keep nothing but the suggestion . . . [to] institute an exact relationship between the images, and let there stand out from it a third aspect, bright and easily absorbed, offered to divination'.[7] Between different words or clusters of words, the relationships are essentially musical, juxtapositional, paradigmatic: 'Everything becomes suspense, a fragmentary arrangement with alternation and opposition at the white spaces combining in the total rhythm, which the silent poem would form.'[8] Instead of a meaning that converges syntagmatically, here we have evocations and implications suspended all across a poem in a state of balance.

The Symbolists' discovery sets the agenda for poetry, and subsequently other forms of literature, right down to the present day. What we are looking at is not merely a peculiar characteristic of French Symbolist poetry, but a general principle which has gone on to dominate Modernist literature, Surrealist literature and even Postmodernist literature. For we should not think of this as merely the 'symbolism' taught in schools, where the spread of implication reaches only so far as one single neat abstraction ('The image of the moth symbolizes Death . . . etc.'). We are looking at a kind of meaning that can be made to open out as far as we like. So in Postmodern literature (and its ever-present companion, Postmodern theory), the spread of implication is limitless, the balance of implications becomes an irresolvable oscillation, and writers lose the capacity not only to compel but even to calculate or be conscious of the implications of their own writing. Of course, there are real and important differences between French Symbolists, Modernists, Surrealists and the Postmodernists. But they all adhere to one or another version of the pebble-and-ripples principle; they all regard this special kind of meaning as peculiarly poetic, or literary, or 'writerly'. And they are all profoundly opposed to the syntagmatic kind of meaning.

Still, the syntagmatic kind of meaning should not be dismissed too easily. For there is one way of using syntagmatic meaning which surely has a natural affinity with poetry – the way described in the 'On the frontiers' section of Chapter 2. As I pointed out there, the exceptional syntagmatic combination of 'ideas' and 'sleeping' is most likely to occur in poetry – in Pope's *Dunciad*, for instance; while the exceptional syntagmatic combination of 'green' and 'thought' is to be found in Andrew Marvell's 'green Thought in a green Shade'. I also suggested that 'colourless green' might be understood in terms of a certain twilight effect when dark rippling water is haunted by pinpricks of prismatic red, blue and green – when the eye creates a kind of colour out of colourlessness. And is this not the very type of perception that poetry so often seeks to communicate? As for 'billion-ton pebble', such a phrase would seem most at home in poetic language, while 'the pencil sings' evidently belongs in literary fantasy or whimsy. With these examples in mind, one may well wonder whether poetry might have room not only for a special kind of meaning which arises out of a deliberate weakening of syntagmatic combination, but also for a special kind of meaning which arises out of a deliberate intensifying of syntagmatic combination.

Let us take a few examples. Consider Keats' famous phrase in *Ode to a Nightingale*: 'tender is the night'. In the ordinary range of its meaning, 'tender' has the sense of soft and yielding to the touch, or the sense of soft-hearted, loving, kindly. But a night is not the sort of thing that can be touched, nor does it have the sort of personal sensibility which can feel soft-hearted, loving or kindly. We can manage to thread through a meaning only by cutting down drastically on associations derived from the ordinary use of 'tender', only by thinking of 'night' in a very special way. And the meaning thus threaded through will be a meaning of a very tenuous and exiguous kind, a bare glimpse of a meaning. A mere conventional personification of 'the night' will not suffice: 'the night is loving and kindly' would not have the same effect at all. 'Tender' as we must understand it here takes in some quality of both its ordinary senses. Perhaps we could come closer with 'the night is soft'. But still this combination is not so extreme as 'tender is the night' – presumably because the ordinary range of meaning instituted for the word 'soft' is wider and more flexible than that instituted for the word 'tender'. With 'tender is the night', Keats draws very near to the edge of sheer meaninglessness.

Or consider a more complex case from Milton's *Samson Agonistes*:

> The Sun to me is dark
> And silent as the Moon,
> When she deserts the night
> Hid in her vacant interlunar cave.
>
> (lines 86–9)

There is a progression of increasingly unusual syntagmatic combinations here. In the first place, the adjective 'dark' cancels out all our usual associations for the word 'sun', all the usual cultural evocations and implications. Still, the intersection itself can be envisaged in concrete terms. But the combination of 'sun' with 'silent' is more difficult: not because the sun is noisy, of course, but because it doesn't even make sense to think of it as anything other than silent. The sun is just not the kind of thing that we weigh on the scales of silence versus noisiness. To make sense of the combination, we have to take 'silent' with a specially abstract and absolute meaning, so that the sun is *incommunicado*, beyond any kind of contact. (This is more the kind of silence involved when one speaks of a 'silent phone number' or a 'silent partner'.) And an even greater effort is required to incorporate the moon. For this is a moon which is dark and silent to the extent of not being there in the sky at all. In effect, the moon is presented only to be effaced. Meditating upon the possibilities of meaning suggested by the word 'moon' will not help us to this kind of meaning: quite the contrary. By syntagmatically whittling away the usual concrete properties of 'moon' and 'sun', Milton compels us to project far beyond our ordinary experience – as the state of blindness is far beyond our ordinary experience. Indeed, the state of blindness virtually defies the usual meanings of words – especially our sight-oriented visually objectified concrete nouns.

There is a further effect of the same kind in the phrase: 'her vacant interlunar cave'. (T. S. Eliot actually faulted this line for failing to convey any single strong impression!) 'Cave' is a concrete noun, and having the moon go into a cave is a concrete way – the old mythological way – of making it disappear from view. But in this case, the concretion of 'cave' must be combined with the very abstract adjective 'interlunar'; while 'vacant' certainly does not have here the usual meaning that it would have in an expression such as 'They found a vacant cave.' To fit 'vacant' in with 'Hid in her . . . interlunar cave', we must take it with a meaning more akin to 'null' or 'devoid' or 'blanked out'. We must identify the cave with utter absence, a period of non-being.

For another example, consider one of Emily Dickinson's striking opening lines:

I felt a Funeral, in my Brain.

Ordinarily, a funeral is not the sort of thing that can be *felt* – it is not an object but an activity, and an activity in the non-physical form of a social institution. Nor, of course, is it the sort of activity that belongs in the brain. Yet it will not do to explain the word 'funeral' as a mere metaphor for something else which can be ordinarily felt and in the brain – a pounding headache or whatever. And it will not do to explain the word 'felt' as a mere figure of speech for some more obviously compatible meaning – like the meaning of the word 'imagined'. To escape from the literal assertion of the line by converting it into metaphor and figure of speech would be to reduce something remarkable into something relatively mundane. For this funeral really is felt and really is in the brain –

albeit in a special kind of way; and what is felt and in the brain really is a funeral – albeit in a special kind of way. We can reach a coherent unified meaning only by straining and stretching beyond the everyday senses of the words, only by discarding much of their habitual central content. It is the grammar of subject noun, verb, object noun and prepositional phrase which compels us to this effort of synthesis and projection; and it is this effort of synthesis and projection which brings us to the *vision* of the poem. The vision of the poem will scarcely appear to a reader who disregards coherent unified meaning and allows the word 'funeral' to evoke or imply any and every funeral, general principles of funereality, etc. etc. (Of course, the vision is only set up in the opening line: the full nature of the vision emerges through many further syntagmatic combinations in the rest of the poem.)

By way of a final example, let me indulge a personal preference and take a few lines from my favourite poet: Rainer Maria Rilke.* In *Turning-Point* (where the 'he' is emotionally and contextually equivalent to an 'I'), we are told:

> Towers he would gaze at so
> That they were terrified:
> Building them up again, suddenly, in an instant![9]

Once again, this doesn't make much sense to an ordinary way of thinking. How can one combine the noun 'towers' with the adjective 'terrified'? ('Towers' is the term that Rilke typically uses for tall city buildings.) How can one combine the phrase 'building [the towers] up' with the phrase 'in an instant'? To arrive at a meaning for these lines, we must step outside the ordinary way of thinking and into a Rilkean way of thinking. That is, we must imagine a *gaze* as an act of outward appropriation (although not in the manner of current feminist theory); and we must imagine *seeing* as an act of inward reconstitution. Rilke's special apprehension transcends the usual categorizations of animate and inanimate, physical and mental – the usual categorizations embodied in the words of *langue*. In reading such lines as these, we find ourselves shifting position, leaping across to a new and unfamiliar perspective. (Needless to say, the perspective is further reinforced by many other lines in the poem as a whole.) If Mallarmé's kind of meaning calls for an unusual passivity on the part of the reader, this kind of meaning calls for an unusual activity. And once again, it is the power of the syntagm which enforces this activity.

* It may seem odd that I am countering the influence of the French Symbolists with a poet who is himself commonly and appropriately classed as a Symbolist. But the historical development of Symbolism shows two aspects: a mystical apprehension of hidden significances and implications in the world, and an artistic creation of hidden significances and implications in the poem. Rilke is very much a Symbolist of the first aspect (the same could be said for those other non-French Symbolists, Blok and Jiminez), but not of the second. Indeed, it is difficult to see how Mallarmé's kind of meaning could ever serve to communicate Rilke's extraordinary *langue*-defying apprehensions.

Looking back over my four examples, I trust it will be agreed that there is something distinctively poetic about them. This is not to suggest that their special kind of meaning is necessarily present in every possible poem, a defining criterion of Poetry in general; but rather that their special kind of meaning is something which poets, of all people, are peculiarly likely to use. Confronting my examples as sentences out of context, even with the typographical clues removed, one would still feel fairly confident about assigning them to the discourse of poetry. The principle of syntagmatic synthesis and projection is a principle of language at large: but only poets make a habit of carrying it to this extreme, this degree of intensity.

My four examples may also serve to show – along with my examples in the 'On the frontiers' section – that grammar and syntax have no intrinsic connection to logical, rational, scientific or prosaic ways of thinking. Certainly those ways of thinking depend upon grammar and syntax: but grammar and syntax do not belong exclusively to those ways of thinking. The point has already been argued in another context, in the 'Logical relations versus grammatical relations' section of Chapter 8. There I tried to demonstrate that Logical Analytical philosophers can never successfully identify logical relations with grammatical relations, because logical relations are not creative or constitutive in themselves. Logic may be applied to a grammatically generated sentence meaning, yielding a judgement of logicality: but logic itself is incapable of generating sentence-meanings. Turning to the present context, this suggests that illogical or trans-logical meanings depend upon grammar no less than logical meanings. Grammar not only fails to rule out illogical or trans-logical meanings, but actually brings them into existence. Without grammar, there could be no green thoughts, no silent suns, no terrified towers, etc. Since the time of the French Symbolists, poets have tended to regard grammar as restrictive, as a burden and an enemy; but there are equally good reasons for regarding it as empowering, as a tool and a friend. It is grammar and grammar alone which makes possible the distinctively poetic effects illustrated in my four examples.

In fact, a very cursory glance at poetry from before the twentieth century reveals that poets have not always thought of grammar as a burden and an enemy. Even leaving aside the special kind of meaning I have so far discussed, there have clearly been periods when poets devoted a great deal of effort and energy to the syntactical construction of their sentences. Consider, for example, the drawn-out and highly-connected sentences of Spenser; or the varying subordinations and long complex developments used by Wordsworth. Indeed, it is arguable that one of the characteristics of the Renaissance revolution in poetry was a new interest in elaborate sentence construction for its own sake, while the Romantics undoubtedly reacted against the short-breathed play of oppositional and contrastive effects in Restoration/Augustan poetry. It seems that the syntactic shape of a sentence may be a source of aesthetic satisfaction in itself, no less than an abstract shape in sculpture, no less than a rhythmical movement in music.

What we are coming to is a view of poetry as exploring different linguistic possibilities in different periods. The only thing that is consistently poetic is the fact of exploration. For I am not claiming that the special kind of meaning I have discussed is more valuable or more important or more poetic than Mallarmé's special kind of meaning. I am not even claiming that these two possibilities exhaust the field (although it has naturally been convenient to set up my argument in polar terms). Nor, for that matter, am I claiming that the Renaissance and Romantic interest in extended sentence construction is more valuable or more important or more poetic than the Restoration/Augustan interest in oppositional and contrastive effects. Poetry, I suggest, cannot be characterized by any single typical way of using language. And those who have imagined otherwise have generalized falsely from the special orientation of their own particular period.

But even the relativity of historical periods is still too monolithic. For although a certain interest or focus may become dominant in a particular period, other tendencies are not thereby excluded. There are many earlier poets who achieve effects of symbolic evocation and implication, even if they do not wield them with quite the conscious deliberation of twentieth-century poets. And many twentieth-century poets continue to create syntagmatic effects, even if they do not think about them as such. The dominant manner of a particular period is essentially a matter of what is attended to, what is conceptualized. And in this respect, although the poets initiate a new manner, it is the critics (including poets-as-critics) who confirm and reinforce it.

THE LIMITS OF TWENTIETH-CENTURY LITERARY CRITICISM

In the twentieth century, literary criticism has tended to claim a more impartial and objective stance than ever before – sometimes even a scientific stance. This can be seen as reflecting the explosive growth of professional university criticism, and the arrival of a whole new class of critics no longer tied by any direct involvement in the contemporary writing scene, no longer needing to clear a space for their own kind of writing. And yet twentieth-century literary critics have generally remained just as partial and limited as their predecessors, still taking for granted the framework of their own particular historical period. No matter how objective their subsequent procedures, they still see only so much as that initial framework allows to appear.

What's more, the framework has remained fairly constant across even the most dramatic revolutions in critical thinking. Certainly, Structuralist literary criticism differs significantly from the New Criticism; and Poststructuralist literary criticism differs at least as much again. Yet in relation to the two special kinds of meaning which I described in the previous section, literary critics in the twentieth century are almost all on the same side – Mallarmé's side – of the fence. On a long view, Poststructuralist criticism continues to develop from the same fundamental premisses as the New Criticism. Of course, a long view has to be paid for with a certain amount of simplification; and I admit that I shall be simplifying drastically in what follows. My justification for such simplification, here as elsewhere, is that only on a long view can the deepest sorts of difference emerge.

The New Critics use the pebble-and-ripples principle to interpret individual texts. (I take 'New Critics' in a very comprehensive sense, including not only Brooks, Tate and Penn Warren but also such American affiliates as Wimsatt, Beardsley and Wellek, and even the more distantly related British figures, Richards and Empson.) Consider Cleanth Brooks' account of the 'babe' imagery in *Macbeth*. 'The babe signifies the future', he claims; also 'it symbolizes all those enlarging purposes which make life meaningful, and it symbolizes, furthermore, all those emotional and . . . irrational ties which make man more than a machine – which render him human'.[10] This is a further movement of signifying on top of the ordinary movement. Just as the marks on the page or sounds in the air call up a meaning for the word 'babe', so that meaning in turn calls up ideas of 'the unpredictable future' and 'human compassion'.[11] And such signifying moves typically from the concrete to the abstract, the particular to the general. Hence the sixth and seventh articles of Brooks' critical faith:

> *That literature is ultimately metaphorical and symbolical.*
> *That the general and the universal are not seized upon by abstraction, but got at through the concrete and the particular.*[12]

Interpretation as practised by the New Critics is above all a matter of drawing out hidden generalities and ulterior universals.

The New Critical focus upon the signifying of the symbol goes hand in hand with the New Critical focus upon imagery. In one respect, this latter focus can be seen as exemplifying the traditional Anglo-American liking for the language of physical description and sensory impression – a liking which is peculiar to the Anglo-American scene, and of no further interest to us here. What is of interest is that the notion of an image suggests not just any impression or physical description, but an impression of a particularly brief, vivid, instantaneous kind. This is the emphasis in Pound's original definition: 'an "Image" is that which presents an intellectual and emotional complex in an instant of time'.[13] Hardy's description of Egdon Heath in the first chapter of *The Return of the Native* is not an image, or even a moment-by-moment succession of images. An image is like a slide flashed up suddenly on a screen; and like a slide, it exists essentially on its own, appearing out of the blue, not directly subsumed as part of some larger integrated whole. Which is also to say that an image is in that isolated and disconnected condition most appropriate for the release of evocations and implications. As I have already noted, it is when there is space around a word (or cluster of words) that the ripples of Mallarmé's kind of meaning can spread out.

If the notion of an image fits in on one side of the signifying of the symbol, so the notion of a theme fits in on the other. For the implications that emerge from such signifying are not ideas in a suitable form for making arguments or assertions. They are ideas merely touched upon, summoned forth, essentially old ideas. Whereas assertion depends upon a syntagmatic narrowing down, these ideas open out as generalities and universals (Life, Death, Art, History, Nature, etc.). And in this opened-out state, they can be seen as being played off one against the other, after the manner of 'themes' in music. In a typical New Critical interpretation, ideas as implications are juxtaposed, contrasted, balanced, harmonized all across a poem. But they remain for ever separate, never losing themselves in the constitution of a new idea. To quote Brooks again:

> the principle of unity which informs [poetic structure] seems to be one of balancing and harmonizing connotations, attitudes and meanings . . . [it does not] reduce the contradictory attitudes to harmony by a process of subtraction . . . It is a positive unity, not a negative; it represents not a residue but an achieved harmony.[14]

Of course, the subtraction which Brooks dismisses is the very subtraction upon which syntagmatic theory insists. But then Brooks never recognizes subtraction as the necessary means to projection. 'Subtraction' on its own sounds highly undesirable, but 'projection' has an entirely different ring.

The terminology of 'image'–'symbol'–'theme' thus constitutes a kind of mutually-reinforcing, self-supporting system. The apparently innocuous notion of the image quietly directs our thinking along a particular track: the signifying of the symbol would not appear nearly so quickly if our expectations were geared to physical description of the continuous and connected kind. Similarly, when we approach a poem with the notion of theme in mind, we are already on the lookout for implications produced by symbolic signifying, already tending to overlook argument and assertion. In fact, the terminology of the New Critics is a *discourse* in the sense made famous by Foucault. It divides up the field in what seems to be a comprehensive way; but the nature and placing of the divisions is such as to encourage certain phenomena to appear, whilst leaving others invisible and excluded.

Compared to the Anglo-American New Critics, the European literary critics are more theoretically and philosophically inclined. They do not insist that a text should start out from concrete particulars: the term 'image' has no special importance in their vocabulary. Nor are they interested in the New Critical version of 'themes', where ideas are typically associated with moral values and attitudes. In European eyes, the ideas implied by a text are of a more strictly Platonic kind, pure categories and abstractions. As for the movement of this implication, it too undergoes a sea-change. For whereas the New Critics attribute implication to the text itself (though not of course to the writer's intention), the Europeans are more likely to attribute it to literary discourse at large, or to language at large. 'Symbol' can no longer be used in quite the Anglo-American sense here.

But still the focus is upon the pebble-and-ripples kind of meaning, at the expense of syntagmatic meaning. In *Writing Degree Zero*, for example, Barthes gives us another dose of Mallarmé's prescription: 'Each poetic word is thus an unexpected object, a Pandora's box from which fly out all the potentialities of language.'[15] We can see what this leads to in *On Racine*, where Barthes discovers general categories of Light and Shade, Desire and Authority, Power and Weakness, etc., played one against another all across Racine's tragedies.[16] The resemblance to the New Critics is obvious, as is the line of descent from Mallarmé's 'fragmentary arrangement with alternation and opposition . . . combining in a total rhythm'.

Jakobson takes a similar view when he claims that the paradigmatic kind of relation dominates over the syntagmatic kind of relation in poetry: '*The poetic function projects the principle of equivalence from the axis of selection into the axis of combination.*'[17] This assertion has become famous as a characterization of all aspects of poetry; yet it actually follows from a discussion of equivalence in the very limited context of rhyming words. Jakobson brings forward no evidence to justify an extension from rhyming words in particular to poetry in general. The determination of a single simple 'poetic' tilt here appears in all its blind partiality. What it leads to can be seen in the analysis of Baudelaire's 'Les Chats' by Jakobson and Lévi-Strauss, where the poem turns into an endlessly intricate interplay of animate versus inanimate, sensual versus intellectual, lover versus knower, singular versus plural, numbered days versus eternity, spatio-temporal limits versus removal of boundaries, passivity versus activity, dark versus light, extrinsic versus intrinsic, empirical versus mythological, metaphorical versus metonymical.[18]

Jakobson's statements on poetry represent a bridge between Russian Formalism and Structuralism, while *On Racine* comes from a time when Structuralism is still establishing its foothold. In its most ambitious phase, of course, Structuralist literary criticism abandons the description of individual texts for the explication of literature as a total system. Yet still there is the same anti-syntagmatic isolation of disconnected textual items: in Todorov's words, 'every text can be decomposed into minimal units'.[19] And still those items are typically interpreted in forms of increasing generality and abstraction.

Poststructuralist literary criticism turns away from the systematic approach of the Structuralists. For Poststructuralists, a literary mode of reading becomes especially valuable and important, over and above all other uses of language – just as literature itself was especially valuable and important for the New Critics. Specifically, a literary mode of reading brings to the fore the true condition of language which all other uses repress. And once again, this true condition is a condition of paradigmatic movement, of the pebble-and-ripples kind of meaning.

The key notion here is Derrida's notion of *dissemination* (along with Barthes' and Kristeva's *signifiance*, and other such congeners). Dissemination is a signifying that spreads out in all directions around the material signifier. Needless to say, this is most likely to occur when the signifier – as word or cluster of words – is separated out from any syntagmatic connection. Surrounded instead by open empty space, the signifier can be made to yield implications endlessly and indefinitely. Barthes, now moving into his Poststructuralist phase, offers the following description:

> what [criticism] reveals cannot be a signified . . . but only chains of symbols, homologies, of relations; the 'meaning' which it is entitled to attribute to the work is finally nothing but a new flowering of the symbols which constitute the work. When a critic draws from the bird and fan of Mallarmé a common 'meaning', that of *coming and going*, of *vitality*, he is not designating a final truth about the image but simply a new image, itself suspended . . . the critic can only continue the metaphors of the work.[20]

It should be noticed that terms like '*coming and going*' and '*vitality*' exist on a more general, abstract level than terms like 'bird' or 'fan'.

This is a radicalized version of New Critical practice. For the New Critics, the spread of ripples was always limited by a commonsensical size of pond. Nor were they so eager to allow ripples in every direction. Even Empsonian ambiguities, even of the sixth and seventh types, never came close to the sheer multiplication of meanings in Poststructuralist dissemination. 'We know now', says the Poststructuralist Barthes, 'that a text is not a line of words releasing a single "theological" meaning . . . but a multi-dimensional space in which a variety of writings, none of them original, blend and clash.'[21] And the word 'clash' is important here too. For these meanings are in an essentially negative state: not so much enriching one another as cancelling and contradicting one another. Dissemination scatters meaning abroad in a way that becomes almost unthinkable, mind-boggling. Barthes again: 'writing ceaselessly posits meaning ceaselessly to evaporate it'.[22] For the New Critics, the open empty space around a word disappears as soon as it has done its work; but for the Poststructuralists, it remains like a perpetual abyss, underlying and undermining all positive meaning.[23]

However, such differences are still only differences within the same general perspective. And this is also true of the difference between the unity of the text which New Critics emphasize and the disunity of the text which Poststructuralists emphasize. In Poststructuralist mythology, this difference has been elevated to the status of a fundamental divergence. But one only needs to introduce syntagmatic theory into the picture to recognize a far deeper divergence. Certainly, the New Critics insist upon gathering the ripples of meaning into some overall pattern, some 'organic' interdependence. (I use the term 'organic' because it has become so firmly established in this context, not because there is anything genuinely in common between the New Critical kind of unity and the unity of an organism.) But they have already chosen to ignore the crucial kind of unity which works by synthesis and projection in ordinary language. Theirs is a secondary kind of unity, a play of harmonies and balances cast over the top of independent units of meaning. And in the last analysis, relations of harmony and balance are not so very different from relations of clash and contradiction. The fundamental divergence lies not between unity and disunity, but between the primary unity of syntagmatic theory and the secondary harmonies and balances of the New Critics.

As for the deconstructive technique of the Poststructuralists, I shall be examining its *modus operandi* in Chapter 15. In particular, I shall be trying to show how it can be made to apply always and everywhere, regardless of the kind of meaning actually present in the text under consideration. Similarly with the binary-polarization technique of the Structuralists, which I shall be examining in Chapter 14. Whereas the old poet-critics simply devalued other ways of writing from alien historical periods, the Structuralists and Poststructuralists now have the power to convert other ways of writing into their own favoured form. A particularly insidious form of imperialism is at work here. But I shall take the argument no further for the present.

THE SEPARABILITY OF FORM AND CONTENT

Twentieth-century critics have erected a number of principles for literature and poetry on the basis of general arguments – principles which seem to have a certain general plausibility, and are not obviously derived from Mallarmé's special kind of meaning. And yet, it is Mallarmé's special kind of meaning which most obviously lives up to them in practice. There is the sense that they ought to be true for all meaning in poetry and literature; but they *are* true, simply and uncontroversially, for Mallarmé's kind of meaning. Could it be that the general arguments have sprung to mind because critics were already thinking in terms of Mallarmé's kind of meaning? Syntagmatic theory furnishes alternative terms and makes the twentieth century principles look much less plausible.

Consider the principle that the content of poetry is or should be impossible to disengage from the form. Cleanth Brooks, on behalf of the New Critics, argues that '*in a successful work, form and content cannot be separated*' and that '*form is meaning*'.[24] He particularly attacks

> the common error [which] conceives of the 'form' as the transparent pane of glass through which the stuff of poetry is reflected, directly or immediately . . . of form as a kind of box, neat or capacious, chastely engraved or gaudily decorated, into which the valuable and essentially poetic 'content' of the poem is packed.[25]

The same sort of notion comes under attack from the Poststructuralist Barthes:

> If until now we have regarded the text as a species of fruit with a kernel (an apricot, for example), the flesh being the form and the stone the content, it would be better to see it as an onion, a construction of layers (or levels, or systems) whose body contains finally no heart, no kernel, no secret, no irreducible principle, nothing except the infinity of its own envelopes – which envelop nothing other than the unity of its own surfaces.[26]

The difference between Brooks and Barthes is that Barthes tends to regard the impossibility of separable content not as a distinctive feature of literature, but as the true condition of all language. From a Poststructuralist standpoint, it is the special role of a literary mode of reading to keep making us aware of the illusion of content, to keep drawing our attention to the fact that signifiers are the only true reality.

In either version, the principle of inseparable content favours the pebble-and-ripples kind of meaning. For this kind of meaning really does keep content tied down to form, in two main senses of the term 'form'. If we think of 'form' as the physical body of a poem, then, as has been shown, this kind of meaning works directly from the body of the signifier. Metaphorically, the signifier is like a solid pebble, not like a window. We do not look through to a meaning; here there are only evocations and implications surrounding the body of the signifier. Or on the other hand, if we think of 'form' as the structure of a poem, then, as has been shown, this kind of meaning produces a paradigmatic play of balance and harmonization – or clash and contradiction – between all the different words and clusters of words across a poem. There is no content which rises above the structure of words and clusters of words, no meaning synthesized and projected beyond the configuration of the parts. The paradigmatic play is itself structural: if we view it as a sort of 'content', it is also undeniably a 'form'.

But none of this applies when poetry accentuates the syntagmatic side of language. Consider again my example from Milton:

> The Sun to me is dark
> And silent as the Moon,
> When she deserts the night
> Hid in her vacant interlunar cave.

Here the meaning of the whole stretches even further than usual away from the individual words. It is irrelevant to follow up the evocations and implications surrounding each word, or played across between different words. (For one thing, the normal contrast between sun and moon is simply short-circuited.) This is not the sort of poetry where the critic can find – as New Critics love to find – an overall attitude reflected in the microcosm of an individual word or cluster of words. Here one has the sense that Samson's experience of blindness is almost beyond words, that is only just manages to get expressed in words at all.

And yet this *stretch* away from individual words is still due to the combining of words and not to something outside of words altogether. There is no question of setting up content and form like two separate things on the table. This is where the similes of Brooks and Barthes are so misleading. For we *can* extract the contents from the box and set them out side by side on the table; and we *can* extract the kernel from the flesh and hold them up one in either hand. The contents and box, or kernel and flesh, are separate as entities, but very much akin in their nature (being both physical matter). Whereas content and form are not separate entities at all on the syntagmatic view: the differences between them are differences of nature within a single entity.

Nor does the syntagmatic view have any sympathy with similes which represent form as an *outside* and content as an *inside*. Rather, the appropriate simile is the one developed in the 'Linearity, spacing, consciousness' section of Chapter 3, where I talked about words as the markers of thought. On this view, words uniquely define a thought by laying out that set of elements over which it must fit. Instead of wrapping a thought up, words demarcate the shape of its passage. Here, the content of the thought is not *in* the words, or spreading out *around* the words – it is pinned down *over* the words. And in this simile too, the content of the thought exists in a totally different way, has a totally different nature, from the form of the words (in either sense of the term 'form').

We can also see how a thought may become especially dependent upon words in a particular combination, even as it moves further away from words individually. With an ordinary prose sentence, we feel that much the same thought might have been expressed otherwise. But when a thought barely manages to get expressed at all, there are unlikely to be alternative ways of expressing it. Try to paraphrase Milton's sentence, and you will hardly find another form of words capable of marking out the extremity of Samson's blindness. The syntagmatically stretched kind of meaning is almost impossible to reduce to a plain prose sense. In which respect, of course, it falls in with Brooks' general claims about the heresy of paraphrasing poetry. But it does not defy paraphrase because of any inseparability of form and content. With Mallarmé's kind of meaning, the words cannot be changed without changing the fullness of evocations and implications peculiar to each individual particular word. But with the syntagmatically stretched kind of meaning, the words cannot be changed without changing the *subtraction* of meaning peculiar to this particular combination of words. Only these very words will cut down to the exact narrowness of space required for this exact meaning to squeeze through.

The syntagmatic argument in favour of separable form and content is not, then, a return to the way of thinking which New Critics and Poststructuralists condemn. It is a rethinking of the very terms in which the debate is conducted. Specifically, it is a rethinking in Phenomenological terms – where discriminations are made on the basis of different degrees of effort and activity in *our* input. We must stop thinking of the form-and-content distinction as a distinction between objects, and start thinking of it as a distinction between levels of objectification.

WHY MULTIPLY MEANINGS?

Another general principle of twentieth-century literary criticism has to do with quantity of meaning. To put it baldly, this is the principle that more is better. The New Critics admire complexity and multiplicity of meaning as a *richness*, with all the usual positive associations of that term. In Cleanth Brooks' value-scale for poetry, the lowest-ranking poems are composed of similar elements and a simple attitude, while the highest-ranking poems enfold a complex of attitudes and a maximum 'variety and clash among the elements to be comprehended'.[27] As for the Poststructuralists, they also glorify multiplicity of meaning, though not as a matter of richness. From their point of view, dissemination represents a liberation from the tyranny of the 'single "theological" meaning'. As Barthes puts it:

> The Text is plural. This does not mean only that it has several meanings but that it fulfills the very plurality of meaning: an *irreducible* (and not just acceptable) plurality. The Text is not coexistence of meaning, but passage, traversal; hence, it depends not on an interpretation, however liberal, but on an explosion, on dissemination.[28]

To appreciate the value-system here, we must recognize positive political associations for the notions of explosion, overthrow, radical breaking away – the further the better.

A very different emphasis emerges from my four examples of syntagmatic effects in poetry. As I argued in relation to 'tender is the night', the meaning threaded through is a meaning of a very tenuous and exiguous kind. This is not a case of multiple meanings, but a case of barely even a single meaning. Similarly with Rilke's lines: 'Towers he would gaze at so / That they were terrified.' If we value these lines, it will not be because of any great variety or clash of meanings opening out around the words, but because the meaning that the words do let through is especially rare and remarkable. Above all, these lines express something new, something at a far stretch of the imagination, something that we would be most unlikely ever to discover by ourselves. Whereas the ideas summoned up by Mallarmé's kind of meaning are, as I have suggested, essentially old ideas, our own ideas.

Of course, even the New Critics are not prepared to claim outright that quantity matters more than quality. Thus Empson recognizes the danger of an approach which 'ignores the fact that the selection of meanings is more important to the poet than their multitude, and harder to understand'.[29] However, this does not prevent him from going on to ignore the fact himself. Unfortunately, quantities can be laid out and totted up in a way that qualities can't; and a measure – any measure – by which to evaluate meanings is naturally very tempting to critics who want to make criticism objective (and perhaps even scientific). But if we accept that some meanings are more rare and remarkable than others, then it is hard to see how sheer quantity can ever make up for a difference in quality. Can one rare and remarkable meaning really be outweighed by two or ten or fifty more obvious and ordinary meanings – even if those two or ten or fifty are expressed in an equivalent number of words?

In fact, syntagmatic theory casts a whole new light upon the relation between number of words and quantity of meaning. If we think of words as the bearers of meaning, then naturally it seems a most admirable feat to get a small number of words to incorporate a vast quantity of meaning – a sort of loaves-and-fishes miracle. But things appear very differently when we think of words as the markers of meaning. On the syntagmatic view, the meanings of individual words are wide open with possibilities compared to the meaning of a sentence. We use words as markers precisely in order to delimit and narrow and specify our meaning. The fewer the markers, the less the delimitation; and the less the delimitation, the greater the spread of possible meaning. There is nothing miraculous in getting a small number of words to call up a vast quantity of meaning – on the contrary, this is just what we should expect from language.

The desire for a maximum quantity of meaning in a minimum number of words leads to a characteristic depreciation of connectives and facilitative words. According to Empson, 'logical connectives . . . are usually unnecessary and often misleading, because too simple'.[30] In fact, facilitative words go against the maximum–minimum equation in a double respect. On the one hand, since they only guide syntagmatic synthesis, we can often arrive at the same synthesized meaning by ourselves (as I have already argued in Chapter 4). To this extent they are superfluous or, in Empson's terms, 'unnecessary': poetry can save on the number of words by omitting them. On the other hand, since they do guide syntagmatic synthesis, they also delimit the relations possible between the words which they connect. To this extent they are restrictive or, in Empson's terms, 'too simple': poetry can multiply relations and meanings by omitting them.

But consider again the lines from Rilke's *Turning-Point*. Obviously the 'so that' ('so . . . daß' in German) could be omitted:

> Towers he would gaze at.
> They were terrified.

But something has been lost here. For what gives us the strange Rilkean vision is the idea of the gaze directly and actively making the towers terrified. It is the consequentiality between the two clauses which is at once so very difficult and yet so very necessary to grasp. Rilke's 'so that' *compels* us to a leap of imagination beyond our habitual ways of thinking. To the extent that facilitative words control the higher levels of syntagmatic synthesis, they take on a particular importance whenever higher-level meanings exist at a stretch from lower-level meanings. And these considerations apply to a great deal of poetry – especially from before the twentieth century, especially Renaissance, Baroque and Romantic poetry. It is simply not the case that poets have a general tendency to omit connectives and facilitative words. Surveying the evidence with an unbiased eye, we must surely observe that, while some poets in some periods play down connectives and facilitative words, other poets in other periods play them up, employing them with special intensity and more than ordinary emphasis.

The Poststructuralist view also comes under challenge from the syntagmatic approach, though not in quite the same way. For the Poststructuralist literary critics are not interested in richness as such, or in the feat of getting a minimum number of words to incorporate a maximum quantity of meaning. In the end, the particular collection of meanings produced by Poststructuralist dissemination scarcely matters – since dissemination is literally interminable, the collection can never be finalized anyway. What matters is to see how language escapes from a single 'theological' meaning, and to come to a consciousness of the principle of dissemination itself. The revelation of multiplying meaning is more important than the actual content of meaning multiplied. (Exactly how this vertical move of consciousness occurs will be more fully explained in Chapter 15.) Poststructuralist literary criticism encourages us to rise to a position from which the paradoxes of clash and traversal and multiplying meaning appear as necessary. Recognizing their necessity, we discover the true state of language in general – and therefore of reality in general. This is a discovery so important that we need not only to make it but to keep on making it, again and again. Indeed, on a Poststructuralist perspective, our consciousness of dissemination is always under threat from opposing social forces, always in danger of being obscured by the persistent myths of univocity and logocentricity.

The syntagmatic answer is short and simple: this is not the true state of language, and there is no reason why we should keep on having to discover it. At best, the possibility of multiplying meaning is a partial revelation – interesting in itself, and interesting in a way that literature can make use of (as Postmodernist writers characteristically make use of it). But it is not the ultimate recognition of recognitions, and we do not need to have our noses repeatedly rubbed in it. Indeed, after so many readings have brought it to our attention, one might well wonder just how much longer it will be able to remain even interesting. Of course, anything paradoxical can be made to sound exciting, and Poststructuralist literary critics have certainly made a fine art of beating up the sense of excitement. But after so many risings to the same revelation, is it not perhaps time to start exploring other possibilities?

CONSIDERING AUTHORIAL INTENTIONS

Another general principle of twentieth-century literary criticism may be summed up under the New Critical slogan of 'the intentionalist fallacy' and the Poststructuralist slogan of 'the death of the author'. On behalf of the New Critics, Wimsatt and Beardsley argue that 'the poem . . . is not the author's (it is detached from the author at birth and goes about the world beyond his power to intend about it or control it)'.[31] The same view appears in Wellek and Warren's claim that 'the meaning of a work of art is not exhausted by, or even equivalent to, its intention'.[32] And as usual the Poststructuralists go even further. From their point of view, the concept of authorial intention is a crucial form of control which has to be removed in order that the text may disseminate freely. 'To assign an Author to a text', says Barthes, 'is to impose a brake on it, to furnish it with a final signified, to close writing'.[33] But writing 'is the destruction of every voice, every origin'.[34] And even the consciousness of dissemination should not be seen as a consciousness on the part of the author: as de Man puts it, 'the cognitive function resides in the language and not in the subject'.[35]

The groundwork for a counter-argument has already been laid in the 'Return of intention' section of Chapter 3 and the 'Grice on intention' section of Chapter 9. The real intention of an utterer as deduced from the real context of an utterance is indeed inessential. In this respect, Husserl and Grice are wrong, and Derrida is right. The case of writing helps to demonstrate more clearly the true situation of all language; and the particular form of writing known as literature carries the demonstration even further. For we cannot connect a poem onto a real context even to the extent that we can with ordinary practical utterances. Even if we had the evidence to deduce how a certain poet felt about his mistress, we could never be sure that a poem about her would be consistent with those feelings. The poem might express totally fictional feelings; or might express unacceptable feelings that the poet totally excluded from his real-world behaviour. Similarly, even if we knew exactly what stance a certain poet held on a particular moral issue, we could never be sure that the poet might not be 'trying out' some totally different stance in a poem. With literature, the kind of real intention that can be deduced from a real-world context is liable to be downright misleading.

But this is not the only kind of intention. As I have argued apropos of Grice, the intention that we can deduce outside of language from a real context may be needed to deliver the point of a truncated utterance ('Bowl!' 'Too small!', etc.), but it ceases to matter as language rises to whole sentences and clusters of sentences. With whole sentences and clusters of sentences, the points are made syntagmatically, through language itself. At the same time, though, another kind of intention emerges: the impression of utterer's intention that is produced as a side-effect of the receiver's own syntagmatic processing. Making shift to find a position from which we can make sense of all the words together, we naturally tend to assume that this position is, or has been, the utterer's position too. Of course, an impression of intention does not have the same status as an intention known or deduced outside of language. But if the latter kind of intention is peculiarly unimportant in literature, the former may be more than usually important.

The impression of intention is more than usually important when we have to project with more than usual effort beyond our personal past experience. Such is the case with my four examples of syntagmatic effects in poetry. It takes a great deal of effort to grasp (or glimpse) the extraordinary vision behind Dickinson's line and the strange way of thinking behind Rilke's sentence. As we struggle to achieve that grasp (or glimpse), naturally we seem to be striving to step into someone else's shoes. Wimsatt and Beardsley ignore this dimension of effort:

> If the poet succeeded in doing it, then the poem itself shows what he was trying to do. And if the poet did not succeed, then the poem is not adequate evidence, and the critic must go outside the poem – for evidence of an intention that did not become effective in the poem.[36]

For Wimsatt and Beardsley, it's a simple case of either-there-or-not-there. But the case is not so simple when one admits the role of the reader's creative contribution. We have surely all had the experience of making sense of a poem without really getting through to the vision of it; then rereading the same poem on another occasion, and suddenly realizing the extraordinary place-from-where-it-comes. Nor can this creative contribution be standardized merely by reference to what Beardsley calls 'public conventions of usage that are tied up with habit patterns in the whole speaking community'.[37] For the rules of syntax only impel us to synthesize 'I felt a funeral in my brain': they do not tell us how to perform the synthesis, and they do not specify the unconventional projection required. To invoke an impression of authorial intention is one way, at least, of making discriminations along this dimension of struggle and effort.

Similar considerations apply when we turn from intentional meaning to the intention-to-produce-a-response. Of course, it is possible to think of our response as simply *following on* from the meaning: how we feel is how we feel, and that's all there is to it. But this ignores the effort involved in responding – or at least, the directed activity. We have surely all had the experience of reading a text and trying to take it in one way – seriously, for example; until we realize that it is actually intended to be taken in a very different way – say, comically. When we then try to take it comically, we discover that it is indeed hilarious. What we think the text is aiming to do directs our attention, and the direction of our attention helps to determine what we see. And in the case of literature, the question of what a text is aiming to do may often prove especially demanding, especially subtle and complicated. If someone in ordinary circumstances asks 'Can anyone lend me a dollar?', it is easy enough to guess the response that the utterance is intended to produce. But if a line of poetry asks 'Can anyone lend me a dollar?', the practical kind of response is irrelevant, and we must contemplate a more rarefied order of intentions altogether. Perhaps the poet is seeking to evoke pathos? To challenge a conventional social attitude? To present a realistic portrait of a certain lifestyle? With literature, there is never any obvious reason for saying anything at all.

The absence of authorial intention, then, is not a necessary condition for poetry or literature in general. But it is a necessary condition for Mallarmé's special kind of meaning. As I pointed out earlier, this kind of meaning does require the poet to abandon the initiative to words. Evocations and implications cannot be compelled; they can only be allowed to spread out by themselves. Here there is no thrust of syntagmatic meaning projected by the reader as if from the place of the writer. Like the principle of inseparable form and content, and like the principle of multiple meaning, the principle of 'the intentional fallacy' or 'the death of the author' effectively promotes one special kind of poetic meaning at the expense of others.

TRUTH IN LITERATURE

Syntagmatic theory also has a bearing upon the issue of whether literature can make assertions and state truths. The usual twentieth-century attitude has been to say that it can't. According to the New Critics, the power to state truths is the exclusive prerogative of science. Literature should not 'march out of its context to compete with the scientific and philosophical generalizations which dominate our world'.[38] This leads the New Critics to divide language into two quite separate modes; and the literary mode is saved from ever being false by never really making assertions in the first place. So Brooks regards it as 'positively misleading' to suppose that 'the poem constitutes a "statement" of some sort, the statement being true or false'.[39] The same attitude carries through to Frye, who also recognizes two modes of language, and insists that there is 'no clear line of connection between literature and life'.[40] Even in defending literature, the Anglo-American critics display a typical and traditional Anglo-American reverence towards science.

Poststructuralism presents a very different picture overall, though it comes to much the same in relation to literature. For the Poststructuralists too, a literary text tells us nothing about the world. The difference is that the Poststructuralists do not believe in the world as a simple objective *given* anyway, and have no respect for the science which claims to tell us about it. Here the concept of truth is under challenge in every context (as I have already noted at the end of the 'Need for disengagement' section of Chapter 8). The Poststructuralists recognize only one ultimate mode of language; and the literary mode of reading is distinctive and valuable mainly to the extent that it unmasks the referential illusions under which language ordinarily labours. De Man exemplifies this attitude when he doubts 'that literature is a reliable source of information about anything but its own language'.[41]*

Once again, syntagmatic theory suggests a counter-argument. In this case, though, we need to look beyond my previous examples. Strange and special poetic visions are less relevant here than generalizing commentary and

* Admittedly, there is one wing of Poststructuralism which disagrees with this all-encompassing textuality, and insists upon a relation to something outside of language. This is the wing especially influenced by Foucault; in the field of literary criticism, it includes such critics as Said, Eagleton, Belsey, MacCabe, Greenblatt and Dollimore. At times, the sheer violence of the exchanges between Foucauldians and Derridans, between socio-political critics and linguistico-philosophical critics, might lead one to suppose that their views have absolutely nothing in common. But as so often, the deepest difference lies elsewhere. Compared to the view that literature has something to say about the world, it is obvious that the Foucauldian view is just as indifferent to the possibility of real assertion as is the Derridan view. For the socio-political critics do not consider what in the world a text may point at, but only where in the world it has come from. And although they relate a text to something outside of language, the relation still proceeds in the usual Poststructuralist direction – that is, back up through the text by a reading of implications.

statements about the world at large. Such statements – think of La Rochefoucauld, think of La Bruyère – are at least as likely to appear in prose as poetry. And such statements, I shall argue, not only look like assertions of truth: they really are assertions of truth. But not, of course, scientific truth. To account for such statements in literature, we must expand our notion of truth until scientific truth occupies just one end of the spectrum. For although scientific truth is undeniably impressive, it is not the only kind of truth we need to live by.

The argument for an expanded notion of truth has already been broached in relation to Logical Analytical philosophy, especially in the 'Formal Semantics' section of Chapter 8. In that section I pointed out the difficulty of explaining truth as a purely objective match between language and reality. The proposition that 'Oxford is sixty miles from London' may be judged true or false depending on whether or not we are prepared to allow for a large measure of approximation; the proposition that 'grass is green' may be judged true or false depending on whether or not we want to include certain exotic species of grass and exceptional conditions of drought. Normally we try to project the meaning and understand the world in a way which will enable us to take the proposition as true. But there is always projection and understanding involved, always a flexible element of subjective effort and activity. It is this that makes truth problematical.

The element of subjective effort and activity becomes especially important in the practical assertions of ordinary language. Typically we rely upon our hearers to find the appropriate way of taking our assertions. Science, on the other hand, typically minimizes the element of subjective effort and activity – spelling out all relevant conditions and circumstances, deploying predefined terms the scope of which has been fixed with special boundaries. Of course, the very definition of special terms still rests in the end upon ordinary language; nonetheless, science certainly tries to specify the application of its assertions as inflexibly as possible. But there is no reason why all language, or even all truth-oriented language, should aspire to this condition. As Wittgenstein argues in *Philosophical Investigations*: 'we can draw a boundary – for a special purpose. Does it take that to make a concept usable? Not at all! . . . No more than it took the definition: 1 pace = 75 cm. to make the measure of length "one pace" usable.'[42] If we *can* rely upon our hearer's subjective effort and activity, then why should we not do so?

The generalizing statements that we find in literature lie at the subjective end of the spectrum. They are especially similar to the 'commonplaces' of ordinary language ('You can never trust a German Shepherd', 'Tourists always head for the big cities', etc.). However, the literary generalizations we most value are not common: they are striking new insights and *aperçus*. Consider the Conclusion to Part II of Coleridge's *Christabel*:

A little child, a limber elf,
Singing, dancing to itself,
A fairy thing with red round cheeks,

That always finds, and never seeks,
Makes such a vision to the sight
As fills a father's eyes with light;
And pleasures flow in so thick and fast
Upon his heart, that he at last
Must needs express his love's excess
With words of unmeant bitterness.
Perhaps 'tis pretty to force together
Thoughts so all unlike each other;
To mutter and mock a broken charm,
To dally with wrong that does no harm.
Perhaps 'tis tender too and pretty
At each wild word to feel within
A sweet recoil of love and pity.
And what if, in a world of sin
(O sorrow and shame should this be true!)
Such giddiness of heart and brain
Comes seldom save from rage and pain,
So talks as it's most used to do.

These lines, I suggest, are impressive not because of any overwhelming linguistic or stylistic felicity, but because of the penetrating insight that they convey.[43] From them, we learn something about the real world, about real human nature. But not about a certain definite number of human beings at definite times and places. This insight is not a scientific prediction: it will not tell us in what circumstances and under what conditions we may expect to observe 'words of unmeant bitterness'. We cannot say that Coleridge's statements apply to all fathers; or even, ultimately, that they apply only to fathers. No doubt it would be an excellent thing if we could lay down an exact and total extension for the set of relevant cases. But for that, we should require absolute omniscience. As it is, we must make do with a less comprehensive, less systematic kind of knowledge. What Coleridge gives us is a principle of understanding, a principle to bear in mind and apply whenever and wherever appropriate. This is the kind of truth that is up-to-us.

Similarly with the generalizations which appear in novels of authorial commentary. In George Eliot's *Daniel Deronda*, for example, we find the following analysis of hatred and fear:

> The embitterment of hatred is often as unaccountable to onlookers as the growth of devoted love, and it not only seems but is really out of direct relation with any outward causes to be alleged. Passion is of the nature of seed, and finds nourishment within, tending to a predominance which determines all currents towards itself, and makes the whole life its tributary. And the intensest form of hatred is that rooted in fear, which compels to silence and drives vehemence into a constructive vindictiveness, an imaginary annihilation of the detested object, something like the hidden

> rites of vengeance with which the persecuted have made a dark vent for their rage, and soothed their suffering into dumbness.[44]

Or consider the following reflection upon sleep and awakening in *A la recherche du temps perdu*:

> The great modification which the act of awakening effects in us is not so much that of introducing us to the clear life of consciousness, as that of making us lose all memory of that other, rather more diffused light in which our mind has been resting, as in the opaline depths of the sea. The tide of thought, half veiled from our perception, over which we were drifting still a moment ago, kept us in a state of motion perfectly sufficient to enable us to refer to it by the name of wakefulness. But then our actual awakenings produce an interruption of memory. A little later we describe these states as sleep because we no longer remember them. And when shines that bright star which at the moment of waking illuminates behind the sleeper the whole expanse of his sleep, it makes him imagine for a few moments that this was not a sleeping but a waking state; a shooting star, it must be added, which blots out with the fading of its light not only the false existence but the very appearance of our dream, and merely enables him who has awoken to say to himself: 'I was asleep.'[45]

In both cases, a relation to particular characters and events supports the generalization in a way which is characteristic of fictional narrative. George Eliot's analysis draws upon our sympathetic identification with the hatred and fear that Gwendolen feels towards her husband; while Proust's reflections upon sleep and awakening come immediately after a particular confusion experienced by 'Marcel' as to whether he has or has not been asleep. (I might add that Coleridge's generalization also purportedly relates to particular characters and events, to Sir Leoline and his harsh words to Christabel; only in this case, the relation seems rather strained – hardly an overall plus for the poem.) A particular central sample helps to get us into the right position for appreciating the general statement. Sympathizing with Gwendolen's hatred and fear, understanding 'Marcel's' confusion, we can see how the same kind of principle might apply more widely too. This is an understanding that works from the inside outwards; and again, there are no decisive boundaries where the principle becomes suddenly inapplicable. All sorts of unforeseeable conditions and circumstances may have to be allowed for. But then it scarcely matters if these generalizations do not apply to every instance of hatred and awakening – or even to most instances of hatred and awakening. What matters is that we acquire a power of explanation merely by understanding how such generalizations *might* be true. Such is the beauty of provisional truth.[46]

Thinking in terms of provisional truth, we can steer between the Scylla of total referentiality and the Charybdis of total hermeticism. On the one hand, these literary generalizations are possibilities to be borne in mind, relying upon what I have previously described as the independence of linguistic meaning. They cannot be turned out instantly upon the world in the manner favoured by Logical Analytical philosophers. On the other hand, they can also not be simply divorced from the world in the manner favoured by twentieth-century literary critics. Indeed, it is interesting to consider what might happen to Proust's insight under the New Critical and Poststructuralist approaches. The New Critic, presumably, would follow up the associations and implications of Proust's words and arrive at an overall opposition of Sleep versus Wakefulness – which is precisely the conventional and obvious opposition that Proust is trying to overthrow. (In similar fashion, Coleridge is trying to overthrow the conventional and obvious opposition of Love versus Harshness, Pity versus Rage.) As for the Poststructuralist critic – well, certainly, deconstruction is the avowed enemy of all conventional oppositions. But deconstruction overthrows conventional oppositions only to the extent of setting up an oscillation or undecidability between opposing poles of language. Whereas what Proust demonstrates is not an oscillation but a complicated relationship – and a relationship of the kind which exists not in language but in the causal processes of the world. The language-bound methods of twentieth-century literary criticism must inevitably lead us away from the real value of Proust's insight.

Admittedly, generalizing insights are only occasionally encountered in literature; while the kind of poetic vision discussed in earlier sections, although more widely encountered, is still only one of many moves that literature can choose to make. But then I have not wished to suggest that all 'literary' qualities and characteristics should be attributed to the syntagmatic side of language. On the other hand, I have also not got around to describing many further qualities and characteristics which *do* belong on the syntagmatic side. Mainstream twentieth-century literary criticism has ignored a whole range of literary strategies that syntagmatic theory can bring to light. But the description of such strategies is too large a task for the present book. I hope to attempt that task in a sequel to *Beyond Superstructuralism*.

PART VI

Syntagmatic theory and textual interpretation

14 Binary-polarization technique

HOW BINARY POLARIZATION WORKS

I have suggested that the reader whose perspective is orientated towards Mallarmé's special kind of meaning will fail to see syntagmatic effects when they are present in literature. Such blindness is doubtless unfortunate. But far more unfortunate is the case of a reader managing to see Mallarméan effects even when they are not present. This is the danger with certain techniques of textual interpretation. As I remarked at the end of the 'Limits of twentieth-century literary criticism' section above, the deconstruction technique of the Poststructuralists can convert any kind of text into a Poststructuralist text. And similarly with the binary-polarization technique of the Structuralists. (As for the New Critics, their interpretative methods may reasonably be regarded as an earlier and less systematic version of binary-polarization technique.) These techniques are not to be condemned merely for blindness – but for false vision.

In this and the following chapter, I shall be trying to show how such false vision manages to impose itself. However, I do not want to restrict discussion to literary texts: the issues at stake here are issues of general hermeneutics. For this reason, I have deliberately chosen my examples from non-literary areas. In the present chapter, my main example of binary-polarization technique comes from an interpretation of American Indian mythology by Lévi-Strauss; in the next chapter, my main example of deconstruction comes from Derrida's interpretation of a philosophical text by Plato. But in both chapters, it is the form rather than the content of the interpretation which matters; and I trust that my negative analysis will be found to apply wherever the same form rears its head, in literary or in non-literary areas.

Lévi-Strauss' approach to mythology follows on from his approach to primitive systems of classification, as described in Chapter 2 of *Superstructuralism*. According to Lévi-Strauss, narrative myths are essentially attempts to 'rationalize' classification-systems. Suppose that the classification-system of a particular tribe sets up an opposition between snakes and eagles, and an affinity between snakes and running water. Such classifications, which may be embodied in totemic taxonomy, clan organization, and rituals and taboos, constitute a formal conceptual system for the tribe, both necessary and arbitrary. But the tribe does not understand the real reasons for a formal conceptual system. So it accommodates to the arbitrary necessity of its own classifications by making them emerge out of a story. The opposition between snakes and eagles, and the affinity between snakes and running water, can be explained as the consequences of certain long-ago events involving an ancestral snake and ancestral stream and ancestral eagle. Lévi-Strauss is here following up a suggestion first broached by Durkheim and Mauss, that 'every mythology is fundamentally a classification'.[1] To interpret a myth, it is necessary to uncover the classificatory 'problem' which lies at its source.

So far so good. But what happens in practice is not so good. Consider Lévi-Strauss' interpretation of an episode in a myth (M9) told by the Apinaye Indians. Here the boy-hero returns to his village after being given some advice by the jaguar who has adopted him:

> [the jaguar] explained to him how to return to his village by following along the creek. But he was to be on his guard: if a rock or the aroeira tree called him, he should answer; but was to keep still if he heard 'the gentle call of a rotten tree'.
>
> The hero moved along the brook, replied to the first two calls and, forgetting the jaguar's warnings, to the third as well. That is why men are short-lived: if the boy had answered only the first two, they would enjoy as long life as the rock and the aroeira tree.[2]

Lévi-Strauss sets to work as follows:

> The myth lists three calls to which the hero must reply or keep still. In order of diminishing loudness, these are the calls of the rock, the hardwood aroeira tree, and the rotten tree. We have some information about the symbolic value of rotten wood in Ge mythology; it is a vegetable antifood, the only food eaten by men before the introduction of agricultural techniques . . . Formerly men used to eat their meat accompanied by rotten wood instead of vegetables . . . It can be concluded from this that, in the nature versus culture context, rotten wood represents the reverse of cultivated plants.[3]

Lévi-Strauss next draws upon a later episode of the same myth, in which the boy-hero is captured by an ogre and put into a basket, but eventually manages to escape and disguises his escape by weighting the basket with a heavy stone:

> Now the episode of the ogre shows how the hero tricked his abductor by leaving him a stone to eat instead of a body. Stone, or rock, appears then, as the symmetrical opposite of human flesh. By filling in the empty space with the only culinary term still available, animal flesh, we arrive at the following table:

	rock	human flesh		
wood	hard wood	animal flesh		*meat*
	rotten wood	cultivated plants		

> What does this mean? The series of three 'calls' corresponds, in reverse, to a division of the sources of food into three categories: agriculture, hunting, and cannibalism.[4]

The episode is thus explained as the product of three binary oppositions: rock versus human flesh, hard wood versus animal flesh, and rotten wood versus cultivated plants.

But Lévi-Strauss has not finished yet. He now proceeds to polarize the above table vertically as well as horizontally: rock versus rotten wood and cultivated plants versus human flesh. (The middle terms, hard wood and animal flesh, drop out of the analysis.) This new axis of polarization gives birth to some new kinds of opposition:

> Furthermore, these three categories [human flesh, animal flesh, cultivated plants], which could be called 'gustatory', are coded in terms of a different sensory system: that of hearing. Finally, the auditory symbols used have the remarkable property of immediately suggesting two other sensory coding systems – one olfactory, the other tactile – as can be seen from the following table:

Code:	*auditory*	*gustatory*	*olfactory*	*tactile*
Rock	loud call	cultivated plants	imputrescible	loud
Hardwood		animal flesh		
Rotten wood	faint call	human flesh	putrid	soft

> We can now understand the very precise meaning that must be attributed to the calls uttered by the rock and the wood: the things that emit sounds must be chosen in such a way that they also possess other sensory connotations. They are operators, which make it possible to convey the isomorphic character of all binary systems of contrasts connected with the senses, and therefore to express, as a totality, a set of equivalences connecting life and death, vegetable foods and cannibalism, putrefaction and imputrescibility, softness and hardness, silence and noise.[5]

According to Lévi-Strauss, such oppositions are what the episode of the three calls is ultimately about. Such oppositions represent a problem which mythological thinking tries to 'understand'.

However, Lévi-Strauss does not suppose that this kind of 'understanding' can reach any conclusive solution. After all, the classificatory oppositions are as arbitrary as they are necessary. Mythological thinking can create only temporary harmonizations. It may, for instance, soften the contradictory nature of an opposition by introducing an intermediate term: by introducing sickness as that which mediates between life and death, or rain as that which mediates between sky and earth, or cooking as that which mediates between nature and culture (raw meat being cooked to produce human food). Or it may transpose the opposition into alternative terms where the degree of contradiction is less sharply felt: thus Lévi-Strauss sees a developing progression of oppositions in the successive episodes of the myth of Asdiwal, as shown in Figure 14.1.[6]

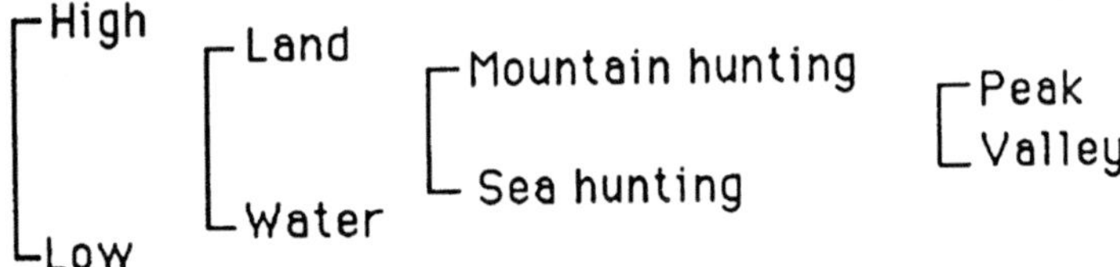

Figure 14.1

Here it is as though two debaters are striving to move towards a consensus of opinion. But the oppositions laid to rest in one myth inevitably break out again elsewhere. Although 'mythological thought always progresses from the awareness of oppositions towards their resolution', it never finally arrives.[7] In this respect, it is a 'mixture of powerlessness and persistence'.[8]

Hence the endless recurrence of the same oppositions in all mythological thinking. Nature versus culture, life versus death, silence versus noise – these oppositions are not peculiar to Apinaye myth M9. Lévi-Strauss discovers them over and over again in other myths of the Apinaye, and in the myths of other South American Indian tribes. Similarly with the oppositions of fire versus water, the sky versus the earth, the inside versus the outside, the full versus the empty, the high versus the low. It looks as though such binary polarizations can explain an enormous number of separate cases. It looks as though Lévi-Strauss has achieved the goal of all scientists: to reduce the incalculable multiplicity of appearances to a very few underlying principles.

And yet . . . somehow, somewhere along the line, the character of Lévi-Strauss' mythological project has changed. For the binary oppositions in which he is now dealing are on an entirely different scale from the particular systems of classification which he analysed so effectively in the early chapters of *The Savage Mind.* No longer is he interested in the difference between the system of one tribe which classes bees with pythons and the system of another tribe which classes honey with canoes – differences produced by different habitats and preoccupations and demographic histories.[9] Binary oppositions between life and death, the high and the low, the inside and the outside, etc., are not only not peculiar to one particular South American Indian tribe as distinct from other South American Indian tribes – they are not even peculiar to all South American Indian tribes as distinct from any other primitive culture; and in the end, they are not even peculiar to all primitive cultures as distinct from modern Western culture. What Lévi-Strauss is now proposing to capture is nothing less than the universal classification-system of the human mind in general – which cannot be compared or contrasted with any alternative classification system at all.

UNLIKELIHOOD AND FALSIFIABILITY

Non-Structuralist anthropologists have often had doubts over Lévi-Strauss' brand of mythological analysis, and have sought to refute his claims by adducing evidence about the American Indians and their myths which he ignores. But such refutations only chip away at the edifice. The real challenge to Lévi-Strauss must be a challenge to binary-polarization technique itself, and must be posed not on the anthropological but on the philosophical level.

Lévi-Strauss' analysis looks scientific because it seems to be confirmed in so many separate cases. Mere coincidence might account for the possibility of applying binary oppositions to one particular episode of one particular myth; but when binary oppositions are successfully applied to episode after episode of myth after myth, it seems too much for mere coincidence. It seems that the sheer unlikelihood of a consistent match between theory and evidence proves the real existence of binary oppositions in mythological thinking, just as the sheer unlikelihood of a consistent match between theory and evidence proves the real existence of the (unobservable) forces of friction and momentum in the physical world.

But in the case of binary-polarization technique, this unlikelihood is not all it seems. Binary oppositions can always be made to match up with even the most random concatenations of meaning. What we need here is a *reductio ad absurdum*. Suppose I write down the first noun on every hundredth page of the novel I am currently reading, *Midnight's Children* by Salman Rushdie.[10] I arrive at the following list: '*web*' (p. 100), '*(seven) seconds*' (p. 200), '*victims*' (p. 300) and '*the future*' (p. 400). By calling upon binary-polarization technique, I can at once recognize an opposition between '*seconds*' and '*the future*' as representing two different kinds of Time; for Time in *seconds* is instantaneous and immediate and experienced moment by moment, whereas Time as *the future* involves prevision and prediction. I can also draw out from the metonymic relation between a *web* and its *victims* an opposition between the encircling and the encircled, the encompassing and the encompassed, the hunter and the prey.

Suppose I now record the first noun on every intervening fiftieth page. I thus add to my list '*protection*' (p. 50), '*the image*' (p.150), '*head*' (p. 250), '*body*' (p. 350) and '*fear*' (p. 450). Here I can claim a classic opposition between the *head* and the *body*, between the thinking mind and the physical instincts. And this opposition ties in with the previous opposition between different kinds of Time, since it is the thinking mind that plans ahead for *the future*, while the physical instincts live rather from moment to moment. There is a further tie-in with the *web-and-victim* opposition too, since it is a *web* created by planning and forethought which traps the unthinking *victims*.

I can also claim an opposition between *fear* and *protection*, since the state of feeling afraid is clearly the contrary of the state of feeling protected. This opposition ties in with all the previous oppositions, whilst significantly transposing their terms. On the one hand, *fear* naturally belongs to the *victims*; but since *fear* involves a mental *image* of the future, the *victims* are no longer to be regarded as simply unthinking. On the other hand, *protection* encircles and encompasses and requires prevision; but such activities are now to be seen as benevolent and not (as in the case of the *web*-spinner) malevolent. With this transposition of terms, it even begins to look as though the play of oppositions is turning into a kind of debate.

Convincing? Certainly, there appears to be considerable unlikelihood in the way the evidence systematically locks and meshes together. Certainly, it seems too much for mere coincidence that the same oppositions can keep on being successfully applied to more and more evidence. And yet, as we know very well, the nature of the first noun on every fiftieth and hundredth page of Salman Rushdie's novel is not in fact determined by any such debate or play of oppositions. The nature of the first noun of every fiftieth and hundredth page is motivated by other considerations entirely. The impression of unlikelihood is a false impression.

The trouble with binary-polarization technique is that it can too easily digest and incorporate whatever is fed to it. It is not that binary oppositions fail to match up with the evidence – but that they never fail to match up with the evidence. One does not need to be a Logical Positivist to recognize here a disturbing lack of what Karl Popper calls *falsifiability*. And in this case, the issue is not truth but meaningfulness. If binary oppositions never fail to match up with the evidence, then by the same token they cannot be telling us anything very much about the particular evidence that they *do* match up with.

This point of view casts a different light over Lévi-Strauss' success in extending his mythological interpretations. Is there not something suspiciously easy about the way in which he can keep on finding more and more of the same oppositions the more widely he looks? In 'The Story of Asdiwal', for instance, he originally ignored an alternative version of the myth; but when he gets around to examining the alternative version in a later postscript, he manages to find in it exactly the same oppositions as in his original interpretation.[11] From his own point of view, this triumphantly proves the truth of his original interpretation. But from our new point of view, it may equally prove the non-falsifiability of his original interpretation.

Binary-polarization technique, then, is not just one more scientific technique like any other. It is a very special type of technique, and raises a very special type of problem. Above all, it raises the problem of what is actually inherent in reality and what is merely cast over the top of it. The old correspondence criterion of truth is simply inadequate to the kind of situation presented in my analysis of *Midnight's Children*, the kind of situation where a system of binary oppositions can manage to correspond to the facts without ever really being true to them. What's needed is a further criterion such as that proposed by Jean Piaget:

> understanding or explaining is not just a matter of applying our operations to the real and finding 'that it can be done' . . . Causal explanation requires that the operations that 'fit' the real 'belong' to it.[12]

Binary-polarization technique has a way of allowing the explanation to come unstuck from the reality, whilst still maintaining a perfect 'fit' between them.

Lévi-Strauss himself recognizes the distinction between what 'fits' and what 'belongs' when he defines *form* as against *structure*:

> *Form* is defined by opposition to material other than itself. But *structure* has no distinct content; it is content itself, apprehended in a logical organization conceived as a property of the real.[13]

Unfortunately, he recognizes this distinction only in order to claim that his own analyses are entirely structural; he never contemplates the possibility that they might sometimes degenerate into the merely formal. He is prepared to contemplate such a possibility only when binary-polarization technique is applied in fields of study other than his own. Thus he arraigns the Structuralist literary critics on the grounds that

> the work studied and the analyst's thought reflect each other, and we are deprived of any means of sorting out what is simply received from the one and what the other puts into it.[14]

Structural Anthropology is supposedly immune to this unhappy condition – but not for any good reasons ever brought forward by Lévi-Strauss.

THE SECRET MOVE

Where then does binary-polarization technique come unstuck from reality? The crucial step, I suggest, takes place very early, even before the stage of polarization into oppositions. As with all great conjuring tricks, we are dazzled and distracted by a show of 'business' while the real sleight of hand is executed elsewhere. Only in this case, of course, the conjurer is no less dazzled and distracted than his audience.

Let me draw an analogy with my own not-so-great discovery of Universal Triangulation. Once when lying sick in bed, in the hazy pattern-forming state of mind that sometimes accompanies sickness, I began to trace out mental lines between the things in the room around me: from the corner of a window-pane to the top of a mirror, from the tip of the light-switch to an intersection of the shapes in the wallpaper, and so on. And wonder of wonders! I discovered that the things in the room could be everywhere and unfailingly linked up in triangles! Just as in the case of binary-polarization technique, the more I looked for triangles the more I found them. I felt as though I had discovered the ultimate explanation for the nature of the universe! Alas, later and healthier reflection dissipated the illusion. Just as in the case of binary polarization technique, there was really no unlikelihood about the way my triangles matched up with the evidence. Triangular relations could indeed be cast everywhere and unfailingly over the top of the things in my room; but the things in my room were not as they were *for the sake of* triangular relations.

The trouble with my Universal Triangulation was that I never took hold of the full substance of things at all. I linked together only corners and intersections and extremities – I saw things only in terms of points. And this was the crucial step in the whole process, long before the actual linking up into triangles. Because it is obvious that points – whether located on things or summoned up in mid-air or posited in theoretical space – can always be linked up in sets of three to construe plane-figure triangles. (Whereas the linking up of four or more points will not construe a plane figure.) Triangulation became universally possible the moment I abstracted the world into isolated desubstantialized points.

Similarly when Lévi-Strauss applies binary-polarization technique to Apinaye myth M9. Consider again his interpretation of the episode where the boy-hero escapes from the ogre's basket and disguises his escape by weighting the basket with a heavy stone:

> Now the episode of the ogre shows how the hero tricked his abductor by leaving him a stone to eat instead of a body. Stone, or rock, appears, then, as the symmetrical opposite of human flesh.[15]

Such an interpretation would hardly occur to anyone looking at the narrative syntagmatically. It is, after all, natural enough that the boy-hero should not want to be eaten (such being the nature of human sensitivity); natural enough that he should seek to disguise his escape (such being the nature of human intelligence and forethought); and natural enough that he should find a stone the handiest and most portable object with which to replace his own weight in the basket (such being the nature of the environment in which the story is set). Lévi-Strauss discovers a binary opposition between the two things that are in-a-basket only because he has first disregarded the obvious consequentiality of events connecting the two in-a-basket situations. He has lifted two isolated moments out of the full substance of the narrative: the moment when the boy is in the basket and the moment when the stone is in the basket. And since his interpretation needs no more than these two moments, it could be equally well derived from an entirely different narrative – a narrative, for instance, in which the boy-hero took a stone out of the ogre's basket and jumped in himself to replace it!

What's more, something happens to the boy and the stone in the process of being thus lifted out. We can see it happening in the passage quoted above. In one sentence, Lévi-Strauss is talking about 'a stone' and 'a body'; in the next he is suddenly talking about 'stone, or rock' and 'human flesh'. There is a crucial change in conceptual level here. For a stone and a body are single things; as specified syntagmatically in the narrative, the body is not just any body but the particular body of our particular boy-hero, and the stone is a particular stone in a particular place and of the particular appropriate weight. But Lévi-Strauss disregards all this as he disregards the full substance of the narrative. When he talks about 'stone, or rock' and 'human flesh', he is talking about kinds of thing. He has leapt up onto the level of stone in general, of human flesh (i.e. any human body) in general.

This is a shift away from the concrete, a shift of abstraction. And there is a further shift of the same type when Lévi-Strauss goes on to his second table. Here, a general kind of thing is seen as representing its own general properties. Because stone in general is hard and imputrescible, Lévi-Strauss sees the stone that the boy puts into the basket as representing the general properties of hardness and imputrescibility. And these are the terms which enter into his final list of large-scale polarized oppositions: 'putrefaction and imputrescibility, softness and hardness, silence and noise'.[16]

Of course, binary polarization becomes very simple as soon as the conceptual level of general properties has been attained. A single particular stone is just one thing amongst a million other things; and, being different from a million other things, is not defined in obvious opposition to any specific other thing. But stone or rock as a general kind of thing occupies a much larger segment of the universe; and the general property of hardness applies more widely yet again. 'Hardness', in fact, draws a dividing-line half way across the universe, and inevitably summons up, on the other side of that line, its mutually defining polar opposite, softness. There is very little that cannot be described as being in some way hard or soft. So it is hardly surprising that, if one item in a myth seems to represent hardness, other items – in this case, human flesh and rotten wood – will immediately seem to represent softness. And similarly with such other universe-dividing oppositions as imputrescibility (the inorganic) versus putrefaction (the organic), silence versus noise, the high versus the low. A relatively small number of binary oppositions will always be able to digest any number of single particular things – provided that those things have first been abstracted into kinds of thing and general properties of themselves.

TWO VERSIONS OF ABSTRACTION

The mere fact that binary polarization 'can be done' to American Indian myths does not therefore prove that binary polarization 'belongs to' those myths. What we need to know is whether the conversion to kinds of thing and general properties itself 'belongs to' those myths. We need to take a good look at exactly what is being claimed for this conversion, and exactly where it is supposed to take place. Unfortunately, a good look is very difficult to take – not only because Lévi-Strauss shifts into abstractions almost without noticing, but also because of the nature of abstraction itself.

Let us begin by drawing Roland Barthes into the discussion. Compared to Lévi-Strauss, Barthes is less concerned with the business of polarizing and more aware of the business of abstracting. In his semiotics of contemporary culture, he sees the need to account for the relation between concrete particulars and general social concepts. And he accounts for it as a relation of signifying. Thus a particular photographic image of tomatoes, capsicums, mushrooms, onions and pasta stands for or represents the general principle of 'Italianicity'.[17] The famous diagram (see Figure 14.2) makes it all very explicit.[18]

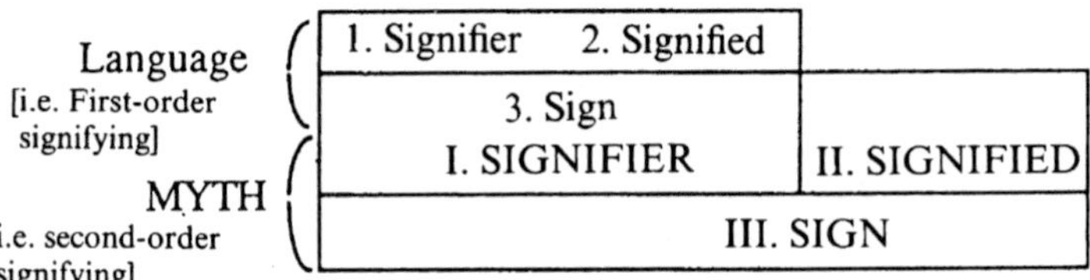

Figure 14.2

Behind the ordinary level of signifying lies a further and more esoteric level of signifying. Just as two-dimensional shapes on flat paper represent real tomatoes, capsicums, mushrooms, onions and pasta, so tomatoes, capsicums, mushrooms, onions and pasta represent 'Italianicity'.

This helps to clarify the situation with Lévi-Strauss. Here too, the general principles of 'imputrescibility', 'hardness', etc. are meanings, meanings created on a further level of signifying. Just as the phonetic sounds [*a s t ou n*] stand for the concept of a stone, so now, by a further leap of the same kind, the concept of a stone stands for such general stone-ish properties as 'imputrescibility' and 'hardness'.

But we must recognize another side to the shift of abstraction. Once again, Barthes spells it out. There is 'a highly sensible proportional rule' by which an adjective can always be made to yield an abstraction.[19] In the case of 'Italianicity', it is simply a matter of 'the suffix *-icity* deriving an abstract noun from the adjective'.[20] So we derive 'Basquity' from 'Basque', 'Imperiality' from 'imperial', 'governmentality' from 'governmental', 'grammaticality' from 'grammatical'. The '-ity' suffix in English here corresponds to the '-ité' suffix in French. Such abstractions can also be rendered with a '-ness' suffix, which is perhaps the more common and more flexible derivation in English. So Barthes' English translator gives us 'sininess' and 'goodness, kindness, wholeness, humaneness'. As Barthes recognizes, semioticians need words of this special type in order to name general social concepts.[21] And he finds no difficulty in coining his own words over and above the dictionary's limited stock. The resulting neologisms, though sometimes barbarous, are always perfectly comprehensible. In this respect at least, language is remarkably open-ended, spilling easily over the fixed borders of the Saussurean lexicon.

Lévi-Strauss' key words belong to the same logical type. Although they appear in various forms, they can all be translated into abstract nouns ending in '-ity' or '-ness'. Taking the '-ness' form as more flexible and common in the English language, we can see that 'imputrescibility' and 'putrefaction' are essentially equivalent to 'imputrescibleness' and 'putrefyingness', 'silence' and 'noise' to 'silentness' and 'noisiness'. As for '*the* high' and '*the* low', '*the* full' and '*the* empty', these are the general principles behind things that are high and low and full and empty, the principles of 'highness' and 'lowness', 'fullness' and 'emptiness'. And even such kinds of thing as 'stone' and 'flesh' and 'fire' and 'water' have a '-ness' quality about them; ultimately, what Lévi-Strauss is talking about are the general principles of 'stoniness' and 'fleshiness', 'fire-iness' and 'wateriness'.

The shift of abstraction thus has two totally different aspects. On the one hand, abstractions can be produced by a purely verbal process. By changing to words of the '-ness' and '-ity' type, we can change the conceptual level of our own thinking. On the other hand, abstractions may exist as signified meaning in someone else's thinking. In this latter case, the abstract level is not produced but discovered in the object under study. And while Lévi-Strauss and Barthes necessarily derive their abstract words by verbal process, they also claim that those words correspond to real abstractions discovered in the thinking of the South American Indians or contemporary Western culture. Lévi-Strauss clearly assumes some sort of human agency when, in the quotation given earlier, he asserts that 'the things that emit sounds *must be chosen* in such a way that they also possess other sensory connotations'; and that 'they . . . *make it possible to convey* the isomorphic character of all binary systems of contrasts connected with the senses [my italics]'. In effect, the category of 'hardness' determines the presence of the stone in Apinaye myth M9. Similarly for Barthes, 'Italianicity' actually precedes the photograph of tomatoes, capsicums, mushrooms, onions and pasta; it is 'the motivation which causes the myth to be uttered'.[22] The level of general social concepts is underlying and foundational, just as Barthes represents it in his famous diagram.

The difficulty here is that the signifying relation and the verbal process of abstraction are both peculiarly elusive. The signifying relation is elusive because the jump from signifier to signified is so automatic and unthinking. In ordinary linguistic understanding, for example, the concept of a stone just coincides absolutely with the phonetic sounds [*a s t ou n*]. In the case of a causal relation, we can look to the cause and look to the effect, and give reasons for passing from one to the other. But there are no *reasons* for passing from signifier to signified.

As for the verbal process of abstraction, this relation is elusive because we do not ordinarily apprehend shifts in the conceptual level of our own thinking *as such*. What we apprehend is the object under study, which is not ordinarily affected by such shifts. Anything that can be described as 'hard' can also be described as possessing 'hardness'. The use of abstract nouns may be little more than a matter of style – especially in French, a language well known for its effortless abstract drift. But a problem certainly arises when the object under study is simultaneously shifted, from a something that is 'hard' to a real motivating principle of 'hardness'.

Unfortunately, it is all too easy to confound rather than to correlate the two kinds of relation. In particular, it is all too easy to operate the verbal process on its own, as though the possibility of producing abstractions somehow proved the real existence of abstractions in the object under study. But the verbal process on its own merely generates words available for use – and an unlimited reserve of such words. Since any adjective yields an abstract noun, then for any given concrete particular we can produce as many abstract nouns as we can apply adjectives. Thus the stone in the ogre's basket might be described as possessing not only the general properties of 'hardness' and 'imputrescibility', but also the general properties of 'weightiness', 'minerality', 'solidity', 'immobility', 'inanimacy', 'density', and so on and so forth. Clearly it would be ridiculous to suggest that the stone in the ogre's basket actually signifies all of these abstractions. The verbal process on its own proliferates abstractions endlessly and uncontrollably.

OF SCIENCE AND METAPHYSICS

The full size of the problem now appears. The fact that we can polarize abstractions in binary patterns proves nothing about the world, but follows merely from the nature of abstractions. And the fact that we can produce abstractions from concrete particulars proves nothing about the world, but follows merely from the nature of language. What we need is some independent evidence for the real existence of abstractions – which is to say, some independent evidence for the real existence of a signifying relation to support such abstractions. But what independent evidence can guarantee the real existence of a signifying relation?

In the case of ordinary linguistic signifying, there is of course no difficulty. Here we can rely upon the elicited responses of language-users themselves. Although the passage from sounds to meanings is unthinking in the moment of communication, language-users are quite capable of explaining in a general way that, when they hear such-and-such sounds, they do indeed understand such-and-such meanings. Similarly with any conventionally instituted signifying system: everyone knows that black is worn in token of mourning.

The difficulty arises only when the signifying relation retreats into the unknown, into the Unconscious. The vision of signifying; the hypothesis of the Unconscious; the shift of abstraction – such are the three mutually supporting principles of Structuralism (and indeed, of Poststructuralism too). When Lévi-Strauss claims that the meaning of the stone in the ogre's basket exists in a kind of cultural Unconscious, he denies all possibility of evidence gleaned from elicited responses. The Apinaye Indians do not and cannot know the system of signifying which operates in their myths. But without such evidence, how can we be sure that Lévi-Strauss is not merely rediscovering his own mind as though it were somebody else's?

There is obviously a very great danger here. But the danger does not trouble Lévi-Strauss. Supremely confident of his scientific credentials, he walks straight into it:

> it is in the last resort immaterial whether . . . the thought processes of the South American Indians take shape through the medium of my thought, or whether mine take place through the medium of theirs.[23]

Although Lévi-Strauss has somewhat qualified the *hubris* of this assertion elsewhere, hostile commentators have rightly seized upon it as symptomatic. Lévi-Strauss recognizes no difference between his own thinking and that of the South American Indians, since both may stand as examples of the human mind in general. But there is a difference. Let us grant that the capacity to see everything in terms of polarized pairs does indeed demonstrate an *a priori* capacity of the human mind in general. The very fact that one can always do it proves as much. For that matter, the capacity to turn space into points and points into triangles also demonstrates an *a priori* capacity of the human mind. But such *a priori* capacities are not everywhere and equally applied. What always can be done is not the same as what always is done. So in the case of Apinaye myth M9, the *a priori* capacities that Lévi-Strauss chooses to exercise may be quite different from those exercised by the Apinaye Indians. There are other *a priori* capacities of the human mind which may be far more relevant to the narrative of the boy-hero.

Roland Barthes is less prone to this kind of *hubris*, at least in 'Rhetoric of the Image' and 'The Photographic Message', and in the essays of *Mythologies* and *The Eiffel Tower*. For although the meanings that Barthes studies are essentially unconscious, still it is our modern Western Unconscious that they are unconscious in – and we can to some extent draw them out and get a glimpse of them. This is what Barthes is tacitly encouraging when he speaks of 'imperiality' as 'a purposeful mixture of Frenchness and militariness', or when he speaks of 'sininess' (Chinese-i-ness) as a 'peculiar mixture of bells, rickshaws, and opium dens'.[24] Clearly, the abstract nouns alone will not in themselves suffice; the word 'imperiality' will not give us the particular quality of *glamour* invoked by the photo of a Negro in French military uniform saluting under the French flag. On the contrary, the abstract nouns are mere indicators, pointing towards the reality in a very distant and approximate way. To know the reality, we must summon it up in ourselves. In effect, Barthes is asking us to elicit our own responses, to realize that, yes, there is a special sort of 'Italian' aura associated with a picture of tomatoes, capsicums, onions, mushrooms and pasta. If our own intuitions fail to match up to Barthes's abstractions, then his line of argument comes to a halt.

This, of course, is the method of the novelist, the method of imaginative cooperation. But Barthes also proposes to make his semiotics into a science. And the appeal to imaginative cooperation is unacceptable in a science. As

Barthes says in *The Fashion System*: 'it is no longer possible to rely on immediate evidence shared by the mass of users of the system'.[25] Data and results cannot be allowed to depend upon the *ad hoc* efforts of individuals, striving to realize what they have never realized before. Science needs regular discovery procedures.

Unfortunately, Barthes fails to set up such procedures. *The Fashion System* is a disappointing book, arbitrary in its abstractions, impressive only when Barthes reverts to *ad hoc* insights in his last three chapters. In practice, the scientific programme of Structuralist semiotics has remained at the level of mere aspiration; the grand vision of *Elements of Semiology* has never come to fruition. And of course Barthes himself eventually abandoned the 'euphoric dream of scientificity'.[26]

Barthes's failure to set up satisfactory discovery procedures is a failure to see the peculiar nature of the problem he is facing. Ordinarily, discovery procedures are concerned with how to discover; but the major problem here is how to stop discovering. When Barthes uses the novelist's method, he works against the implicit resistance of his readers' experience; naturally he must always push and persuade to extend the number of 'myths' and glamours. But when such resistance drops out of the equation, it becomes necessary to have criteria for limiting the number of discoverable 'myths' and glamours. For, as we have seen, abstractions can always be made to proliferate by mere verbal process from any object we care to consider, endlessly and everywhere. Structuralist semiotics fails as a science because it lacks clear and explicit criteria for not discovering what doesn't exist.

The problem arises in this peculiar form because Barthes, like Lévi-Strauss, is trying to erect a science upon the foundation of a Metaphysical philosophy. Not that the Metaphysical position is intrinsically unscientific. Far from it: there is an element of Metaphysics in the setting up of any science. One does not set up a science merely by observing the concrete appearances of the world, but by positing the existence of forces behind those concrete appearances (like inertia, like electro-magnetism). And such forces, which can never be directly observed or described in concrete words, must necessarily be conceived and named in the abstract. This is the Platonic gambit in science, an opening gambit all too often forgotten by Anglo-American Empiricists. When Althusser insists that a scientific practice 'has to be set on correct theoretical bases so that it corresponds to a *real* object', it is precisely this that he has in mind.[27]

But the Platonic gambit, left to its own devices, can easily run out of control. In the realm of the unknowable, anything might exist. By opening up a space beyond observation, the Platonic gambit opens up a vacuum where mere names – and the ghost-entities deriving from them – can multiply interminably. Herein lies the danger of Metaphysics. It is the very danger against which Empiricists have always warned – and in this case they are surely right. Metaphysical philosophies have a propensity for generating entities far beyond the call of nature, and Metaphysically-based 'sciences' clearly share the same propensity.

Is there any escape from this dilemma? So far as I can see, there is only one possible objective criterion for discriminating between genuine cases of second-order signifying and the limitless proliferation of ghost-entities. Let us look once again at the process of first-order signifying. Why does a string of words appear as a sign? Is it not that these particular sounds seem somehow distinct and different from the natural noises of the world? And similarly with other signs, whether written or painted or whatever – do they not somehow stand out from the natural consequentiality of things and events? *Standing-out* and *standing-for* are curiously correlative conditions.

We can transfer this correlation to second-order signifying. Consider again Apinaye myth M9. The myth does contain one genuine case of an underlying abstract meaning – a case so obvious that Lévi-Strauss scarcely bothers to pay attention to it. Why is it that human beings are condemned to a brief life-span because the boy-hero answered the call of the rotten tree? Why is it that human beings 'would enjoy as long life as the rock and the aroeira tree' if he had answered only the first two calls? Plainly, the hardwood and the rock have here been selected in order to represent the general principle of durability or 'long-lived-ness', while the rotten tree has been selected in order to represent the opposing general principle of decay or 'putrescibility'. It is, after all, the general principle of decay which dooms human beings to their brief life-span.

What counts in this case is that there is no way of accounting for the connection between human mortality and the answering of the calls in terms of ordinary narrative consequentiality. The connection stands out from the things and events of the boy-hero's world, just as a string of words stands out from the things and events of the natural world. Whereas the connection which Lévi-Strauss seeks to draw between the boy in the basket and the stone in the basket does *not* stand out. As I argued earlier, the successive presence of two different things in the basket is perfectly explicable in terms of ordinary narrative consequentiality. In this latter case, the processes of syntagmatic synthesis produce a level of 'reality' which effectively closes off the movement of first-order signifying. Hence the crucial need for interpreters of myth – or any such cultural phenomena – to be aware of the processes of syntagmatic synthesis. Only a further standing-out can justify a further standing-for. Unaware of the processes of syntagmatic synthesis, Lévi-Strauss fails to see how the energy of first-order signifying can be absorbed or 'naturalized'. From a Structuralist perspective (and also from a Poststructuralist perspective), there is no reason why a sign should ever cease signifying, over and over again.*

* Hence Barthes's predilection for erecting second-order signifying only upon a ground of first-order signifying. It is indeed curious that in his famous diagram he launches second-order signifying only from the movement of the first-order sign *as a whole*. Curious, too, that, in *The Fashion System*, he discusses fashion only as represented in the *words* of fashion magazines.[28] After all, is it not possible to discover the meanings of fashion in clothes as actually worn? To discover the meaning of Imperiality in a live performance of saluting under the French flag by a Negro in French military uniform? To discover the meaning of Italianicity in a shop-window display of real tomatoes, capsicums, mushrooms, onions and pasta? No doubt *glamours* and cultural concepts flourish most readily upon texts, photographs and similar significations; but

Syntagmatic theory thus enables us to set up some sort of a criterion for the presence of second-order signifying, some possibility of debate when personal experiences differ. But a possibility of debate is still not a possibility of scientific proof; and this criterion will not furnish us with anything like a hard and fast rule. For our sense of syntagmatic 'naturalization' hardly rises above the level of common sense; it is as *ad hoc* and unpredictable as our sense of the syntagm itself. In the end, perhaps, we can do no more than own up honestly to our limitations, and at least avoid a premature rush into a fallacious form of 'scientificity'.

they surely have no essential need for such a foundation. If Barthes believes that he can circumscribe the spread of second-order signifying by erecting it only upon a ground of first-order signifying, he is seriously mistaken.

15 The art of deconstruction

HOW DECONSTRUCTION WORKS

As binary-polarization technique is the favourite technique of Structuralism, so deconstruction is the favourite technique of Poststructuralism. Deep down, the two techniques have a great deal in common; but we must first reckon with their more obvious difference. Above all, we must observe that deconstruction does not claim for its interpretations the same ontological status as binary-polarization technique. The interpretations of Lévi-Strauss and Barthes supposedly correspond to something that actually exists in the object under study: a taxonomic system in the tribal Unconscious or a myth in the mind of the modern Western consumer. Like all scientists, Lévi-Strauss and Barthes claim to unearth the motivating realities which lie behind surface phenomena. But the deconstructors are Poststructuralists who have cast aside the scientific role. They are not looking for what actually exists in the object of study – but for what that object can be made to produce under the general influence of language. Their interpretations develop onwards and outwards, deliberately leaving behind the original evidence. This is the logical consummation of the Superstructuralist position; and it renders irrelevant that form of objection which I levelled against Lévi-Strauss and Barthes. The deconstructors are not likely to be troubled over complaints that they lose contact with 'the facts' or that their technique is 'mere' verbal process. As Poststructuralists, they propose for themselves a different kind of goal, beyond objectivist notions of truth altogether.

I shall take my example of deconstruction from Derrida's essay on 'Plato's Pharmacy'. Here Derrida rebuts the condemnation of writing put forward in Plato's *Phaedrus*. Central to Plato's presentation is an originary myth of writing, in which Theuth, the inventor of writing, offers his invention as a useful and helpful tool to the God-King of Egypt. The King, however, rejects the invention as dangerous and superfluous. From Derrida's point of view, this condemnation of writing represents a conceptual misdirection which has held Western thinking captive ever since.[29]*

* Plato's condemnation of writing is consistent with his condemnation of painting, poetry and storytelling. By the general principles of Platonic philosophy, the natural world which we

The technique of deconstruction makes its appearance to the extent that Derrida's rebuttal of Plato also involves a subversion of Plato's word *pharmakon*. The word features in the myth when Theuth praises writing as a *pharmakon* – i.e. a remedy. However, the sense of 'remedy' is only one side of the word's full meaning, and Derrida lists a number of other possible translations: ' "recipe", "poison", "drug", "philter" '.[30] In stressing the worth of his invention, Theuth '*turns* the word on its strange and invisible pivot, presenting it from a single one, the most reassuring, of its *poles*.'[30] When the King replies that Theuth 'has exhibited the reverse of the true effects of writing', he evidently sees writing from the very opposite pole, not as a remedy but as a poison, an insidiously destructive drug.[32] From the King's point of view, that which is additional to nature – like the *pharmakon*, like writing – appears suspect and life-threatening.

It is important to grasp the drift of Derrida's argument here. Naturally he does not favour the King's rejection of writing. But neither does he favour Theuth's simple advocacy. For Theuth tries to present writing as an unambiguous benefit for mankind, a controllable technological tool. Whereas the King at least recognizes the real power of what he rejects – 'the magic virtues of a force whose effects are hard to master, a dynamics that constantly surprises the one who tries to manipulate it as master and as subject'.[33] From Derrida's point of view, the two poles of the *pharmakon* are inextricably linked: a dangerous benefit and a beneficial danger. One cannot ultimately distinguish 'the medicine from the poison, the good from the evil, the true from the false, the inside from the outside, the vital from the mortal, the first from the second, etc.'.[34] That which is additional to nature – like the *pharmakon*, like writing – both heals and threatens, gains and loses, produces and takes away.

What Derrida holds against Plato, then, is not simply that he condemns writing through the King's mouth, but rather that, through the mouths of Theuth and the King together, he 'attempts to master [the ambiguity of the *pharmakon*] by inserting its definition into simple, clear-cut oppositions'.[35] Plato uses only one sense of the word at a time. Elsewhere in the *Phaedrus*, the negative sense is to the fore, as in the reference to Pharmacia.[36] Similarly in the *Timaeus*, where the *pharmakon* appears as a drug to avoid.[37] On the other

observe with our senses is secondary to an ideal realm of Forms or Ideas. Retaining the normal assumption that paintings, poems and stories copy from the natural world (as writing copies from speech), Plato concludes that all such artificial or fictional constructs are secondary in a double respect, mere copies of copies. But he could have taken a very different tack. After all, our normal assumptions as to what's secondary and what's primary are *already* under challenge from the general principles of Platonic philosophy. If the natural world is itself only a copy, how can we continue to trust the natural at the expense of the artificial? Perhaps artificial and fictional constructs may even recover a paradoxical primacy of their own, overleaping the 'real' world to establish contact with the realm of Forms? Such has been the claim of many later Platonists, especially during the Platonic revival of the Renaissance. Derrida himself clearly follows the Renaissance Platonists in his argument on *mimesis* in Section 6 of 'Plato's Pharmacy'. As I suggested in the 'Three philosophies of language' section of Chapter 6, Derrida's disagreement with Plato is very much an internal disagreement within the Metaphysical family.

hand, the *Critias*, the *Charmides* and *The Republic* invoke the *pharmakon* as a medicine; and it is allowed an essentially beneficent effect in the *Protagoras* and the *Philebus*.[38] Everywhere, 'Plato decides in favor of a logic that does not tolerate . . . passages between opposing senses of the same word.'[39] But everywhere, on Derrida's showing, language defies such repression with a logic of its own. In spite of 'the intentions of an author who goes by the name of Plato', the ambiguity keeps creeping in, the meaning keeps crossing over.[40]

What Derrida is doing here obviously differs from what Lévi-Strauss does with the myths of the South American Indians. Whereas binary-polarization technique strings oppositions between separate terms, deconstruction technique locates oppositions within a single term. It is true that Derrida shares with Lévi-Strauss a tendency to spread his net more and more widely – reaching from one Platonic text to another, reaching from *pharmakon* to *Pharmacia* to *pharmakeus* to *pharmakos*, even reaching as far as the actual (poisonous/liberating) hemlock which Socrates drinks in the *Phaedo*.[41] But always the oppositions exist over the same spot, 'remain within the unity of the same signifier'.[42] And because of this identity and this unity, Derrida is able to proclaim that what is opposed is also identical.

But this is not to deny the intensity of the opposition. Derrida is not suggesting that good and evil, true and false, inside and outside, vital and mortal, first and second are really much more similar than we usually suppose. Nor is he interested in 'mediating' between opposing poles, or bringing them (temporarily) closer together in the manner of Lévi-Strauss. For Derrida, the difference is as inescapable as the identity. Hence the peculiarly elusive meaning of the word *pharmakon*. 'We will watch it', says Derrida, 'infinitely promise itself and endlessly vanish through concealed doorways that shine like mirrors and open onto a labyrinth.'[43] This is meaning in a state of paradox, meaning oscillating perpetually between poles, impossible to pin down as any kind of fixed entity or substance. 'The "essence" of the *pharmakon* lies in the way in which, having no stable essence, no "proper" characteristics, it is not, in any sense . . . of the word, a substance.'[44]

For Derrida, this state of meaning is the state of all meaning. In the long run, he is concerned not merely with a particular case of paradox involving the particular content of the word 'pharmakon', but with the general form or principle of that paradox, potentially capable of infinite extension. We have already seen the beginnings of such extension in the way he multiplies his list from 'the good' and 'the evil' to 'the true' and 'the false', 'the inside' and 'the outside', 'the vital' and 'the mortal', 'the first' and 'the second', 'etc.' It is obvious that the last opposition in the list is far less directly relevant to the *pharmakon* than the first; and the 'etc.' holds promise of yet further multiplication. What deconstruction produces is a single ultimate paradox of identity and difference. Thus Plato's *pharmakon* takes on a general representative status in Derrida's philosophy – like Rousseau's *supplément* or Mallarmé's *hymen* or Kant's *parergon*.[45] In the long run, all such deconstructed terms become equivalent to Derrida's own term *différance*. Which is to say, they all express a philosophical message – Derrida's message.

But there is surely something very suspicious here. For deconstruction began by liberating language from 'the intentions of an author who goes by the name of Plato'. Language, as it seemed, was to be opened up to its own logic, to its own ongoing freewheeling centrifugal movement – in short, to *dissemination*. But it is one thing for language to behave according to its own true condition – and quite another for it to inform us about that condition. Why should dissemination speak the *philosophy* of dissemination?

The fact is that Derrida is able to suggest a special sort of validity for his philosophy by getting language to make his claims for him. Although he eschews the traditional role of the scientist, in this respect he lays claim to the traditional scientific virtue of letting the evidence speak for itself. His approach has a 'hands-off' look about it: as though the views of one philosopher are being disproved not merely by another philosopher, but by the language which is bigger than both of them. But is it really plausible that language should preach the views of Poststructuralism? That language, in spite of the centrifugal movement of dissemination, should keep coming back to the expression of Derrida's own central paradox? Or could it be that language is somehow being made to obey the intentions of an author who goes by the name of Derrida?

REPRESSING OR SPECIFYING?

The first thing to notice is that Derrida, like Lévi-Strauss, picks out only single isolated terms. The argument of Plato's text as a whole is outweighed by the 'message' of a single word. Of course, many writers seize upon some particular word in an opponent's vocabulary and try to turn it against its user. But this is essentially a debating ploy. Not so for Derrida. For Derrida, the 'message' of a single word is intrinsically more important than any syntagmatically created argument.

Hence Derrida's view that to focus upon just one aspect of the meaning of *pharmakon* constitutes a repression of other aspects. The tacit assumption is that a word ought to possess all its aspects. And so it does – in the abstract, in potential, in *langue*. For Derrida, this state is evidently the true state of language. When he sees the limited meaning of *pharmakon* in the *Phaedrus*, he imagines that Plato has somehow imposed his will upon the word, compelled it to submit to extra-linguistic force. But the only force in the case is the perfectly linguistic force of words together in *parole*. A word becomes fully functional only with the help of other words in a sentence; and sentences belong to language just as much as potential word-meanings in *langue*.

What Derrida regards as repression is in fact the narrowing, delimiting process which necessarily occurs whenever a word combines with other words. As I emphasized earlier, the role of the syntagm is precisely to subtract from the full range of a word's meaning. Language would be of very little use if it couldn't specify something more particular than the meanings of individual words. The child who tells us that 'a big dog jumped out at me in the park' is simply not interested in the general meaning of the word 'dog'. The sentence deliberately cuts away the possibility of any dog that is small or standing still. But it would be ridiculous to claim that being small and standing still have been *repressed.* Or to claim that the speaker is trying to deny the very possibility of littleness and stasis.

Similarly if a word has developed several sub-centres of meaning, like the word *pharmakon.* Suppose that one wants to talk about the particular case of a drug which is simply medicinal and not at all poisonous. If one's vocabulary offers only a single word for drugs in general, then how can one manage to speak in such a way as to exclude the irrelevant sub-centres? Under Derrida's approach, the general implications of a word are inescapable, and the pattern of thinking implicit in the potential meaning of a word is called into play every time that word is uttered in *parole.*

The trouble with deconstruction technique is that it translates a useful insight into an absolute prescription. Certainly, it is true that a society's pattern of thinking is influenced by its *langue*; but there are many habitual social discriminations which are not laid down in *langue.* Although the English language offers us a variety of words in place of the Greek *pharmakon* – not only 'medicine', 'remedy', 'poison', 'philtre', but also 'hallucinogen', 'tonic', etc. – we can still make do in practice with the single word 'drug'. The word 'philter' is probably not even familiar to most speakers of English. But then most speakers of English operate with a working vocabulary of fewer than 3,000 words, completely ignoring the millions of discriminations available in *langue.* This is perhaps unfortunate; but it certainly does not show that the thinking of most speakers of English is relatively lacking in discriminations. It shows that the discriminations are being made syntagmatically, at the level of *parole* rather than at the level of *langue.*

So it is not in the least surprising that Plato uses *pharmakon* now in one sense and now in another. We all make words assume different senses in different sentences. For example, in that very sentence I have just written ('We all make words assume different senses in different sentences'), the sense of 'make' is not the same as in the penultimate paragraph of the 'Higher-order grammatical categories' section of Chapter 4 ('sentences make points, not pictures'); and nor is the sense of 'assume' ('why should we assume that declarative sentences ever came first...?'); and nor is the sense of 'sense' ('we are now in a position to make better sense of a claim . . .'). Generally one tries to avoid the clash of different senses in neighbouring sentences – often by opting for a synonym. But otherwise, it is the most natural thing in the world to let the senses vary according to the context.

In sum, the technique of deconstruction seeks to make language run backwards, reversing the process of specification and particularization which takes place when the words of *langue* enter into the sentences of *parole.* Derrida opens words up to their most general possibilities of meaning, propelling them into the curious and abnormal state described at the beginning of the 'Complementarity, synthesis, projection' section of Chapter 2. For Derrida, this state is a veritable revelation. The *pharmakon*, he proclaims, is unthinkable as an entity, it is 'not in any sense . . . a substance', but is 'antisubstance itself'.[46] But a more cynical interpretation would suggest that the word is insubstantial only because Derrida himself has desubstantialized it. The word has lost its determinate sense only because Derrida has refused to allow it to be specified in the context of other words.

THE SHIFT OF ABSTRACTION AGAIN

Still, one may feel that there is a 'message' in a word like *pharmakon*, quite regardless of what Plato is or is not entitled to do with it. For it is not as though the word has merely a wider range of meaning that gets cut down in *parole*; in the abstract, in potential, *pharmakon* appears to exist in a state of remarkable paradox, impossibly strung between the sense of 'remedy' and the sense of 'poison'. How could a single word ever arise upon two such incompatible poles? Does this not tell us something about language in general?

But the incompatibility seems much less obvious when we take all the senses of *pharmakon* into account: not only 'remedy' and 'poison', but also 'drug', 'philtre' and 'recipe'. The sense of 'drug', in particular, functions as a kind of middle term, extending to both remedies and poisons, yet being in itself neither demonstrably medicinal nor demonstrably noxious. The meaning of *pharmakon* may look like a remarkable identity of opposites when we foreground the senses of 'remedy' and 'poison', but not when we foreground the sense of 'drug'.

Taking all senses of *pharmakon* into account, it is possible to envisage a very unparadoxical evolution for the word, along the lines proposed in the 'Mechanism for change in *langue*' section of Chapter 3. Suppose, for example, that *pharmakon* originally had the overall sense of 'drug', as referring to any kind of potion. However, in the human world, such potions are most likely to be concocted for certain purposes: in particular, for the purpose of restoring life and health, and for the purpose of destroying life and health. Would it not naturally follow that, under syntagmatic pressure from what people consistently wanted to say, the word should come to develop distinct sub-centres of sense around the idea of 'remedy' and the idea of 'poison'? Similarly with the sense of 'philtre', which could be seen as forming a focus upon another common group of potions, inspired by (what used to be) another common human purpose. As for the sense of 'recipe', might not that sub-centre derive from the extension of an altogether different aspect of the original meaning – the aspect of concocting and mixing together?

To be sure, this is all uninformed guesswork, and a philological investigation might unearth a totally different sequence of development. For example, it could be that the word originally started out with a narrower focus as 'remedy'; subsequently expanded into the sense of 'drug'; and then eventually took on another narrower focus as 'poison'. But this too is compatible with my overall claim. What I want to deny – and what Derrida has to maintain – is that the word could have been born into the simultaneous senses of 'remedy' and 'poison', *with nothing in between.*

However, there is more to deconstruction than the selection of these two senses: the senses also have to be conceived in a special kind of way. As long as we think of remedies and poisons as actual potions, it is to their similarity as substances that we attend. Between a potion which has a remedial effect and a potion which has a poisonous effect, there is difference but hardly opposition. To bring the opposition to the fore, the substances have to be displaced in favour of their effects – and especially the *principles* of their effects. From 'drug which has a remedial effect', we need to draw off the general principle of Remedy or remedial-ness; from 'drug which has a poisonous effect', we need to draw off the general principle of poisonousness. But of course poisonousness is no longer limited to drugs as such – snakes too can be said to possess poisonousness. And the principle of remedial-ness can be invoked for massage, healing words, anything which has a remedial effect. As with binary-polarization technique, we have made a shift of abstraction and arrived at a new conceptual level. And on this level, it is very easy to see how poisonousness and remedial-ness can be opposed as restoration versus destruction, gain versus loss, Good versus Evil, etc., etc.[47]

An interlude of parody may be appropriate here. Let us take two other senses listed for the word *pharmakon* : the sense of 'philtre' (i.e. 'love-potion') and the sense of 'recipe'. Perhaps these two other senses did not seem particularly oppositional when first listed above? But suppose we attend to effects and principles. Since 'philtre' has to do with illicit sexual desire, we may immediately draw off from it the general principle of 'debauchery'. And since the 'recipe' has to do with cookery, we may immediately draw off from it the general principle of 'domesticity'. 'Debauchery' versus 'domesticity': is there not already a contrast looming here? Another small step, and we have discovered the ultimate oppositions of sin versus duty, danger versus safety, the intense versus the mundane, the forbidden versus the conventional. (Or, translating into a standard '-ness' form, the ultimate oppositions of sinful-ness versus dutiful-ness, dangerous-ness versus safe-ness, intense-ness versus mundane-ness, forbidden-ness versus conventional-ness.) As with Lévi-Strauss' polarization of terms in Apinaye myth M9, as with my own polarization of terms in *Midnight's Children*, abstractions can always be made to meet up in oppositions if developed on a large enough scale.

The danger of this shift of abstraction, in deconstruction as in binary-polarization technique, is that it can be executed almost unnoticeably. In fact, I tried to execute it unnoticeably myself when, in the third paragraph of the previous section, I slipped from 'small' to 'littleness' and from 'standing still' to 'stasis'. After all, anything that is small can be said to represent the category of 'littleness'; and anything that is standing still can be said to represent the category of 'stasis'. As a matter of style, the new conceptual level may seem to make relatively little difference; but as a matter of objective meaning, it changes everything.

By way of a supporting example, consider the most celebrated of all Derrida's deconstructions: the deconstruction of Rousseau's word *supplément*. Derrida looks up the word (which is very close to the English 'supplement') in *Littré*, and discovers the definition: 'To add what is missing, to supply a necessary surplus'.[48] Here there is scarcely a separation of senses, let alone a paradox: what could be more natural than to add on in order to make up for a lack? The paradox arises only when Derrida draws off from 'add' and 'surplus' a principle of pure incrementality. And on this level of purity, what's added appears as entirely supererogatory and superfluous to something which already exists perfectly well by itself. But according to the definition, the something supplemented does not already exist perfectly well by itself; and the principle of pure incrementality contradicts a principle of original insufficiency which Derrida draws off from 'what is missing' and 'necessary'. Hence the ultimate paradox, the incompatibility within the same word, the undecidable oscillation between concepts of first-ness and second-ness, inside-ness and outside-ness, and so on. But this state of meaning has been achieved by leaving behind the very particular complication of meaning which properly belongs to *supplément*. Derrida refines pure principles from the component parts of the dictionary definition; but if we look at that definition syntagmatically, we shall see that 'add' and 'what is missing' are synthesized in such a way as to narrow down to a meaning far more specific than any general sense of 'add' or any general sense of 'what is missing'. This is not 'adding' as pure incrementality, but a special sort of adding, a mixed sort of adding – as when one takes a vitamin supplement in order to make up for a lack in one's body. There is nothing very spectacular about the co-occurrence of adding and lacking in the case of a vitamin supplement. Thinking of such practical cases, we find it perfectly obvious that such aspects should cohere in one and the same meaning.

The fact is that deconstruction, like binary polarization, can always be made to work. For the particular complications and specificities of our world never fit simply under large general categories of abstraction. And the larger and more general those categories, the more likely it becomes that we will have to invoke something on both sides of a boundary. So the meaning of *supplément* comes in partly under first-ness and partly under second-ness, and the meaning of *pharmakon* comes in partly under 'restoration' and partly under 'destruction'. In Beckett's *Endgame*, Clov at first describes the outside world as 'grey'; then, faced by Hamm's apparent disbelief, proposes an alternative: 'light black'.[49] On the scale of ultimate abstractions, the meaning of 'grey' must indeed be categorized under both 'lightness' and 'blackness'. But that should hardly lead us to view the meaning of 'grey' as some sort of paradox, oscillating undecidably between opposing poles!

The interesting thing about all of this is that the movement of meaning which takes place in deconstruction diverges so markedly from the movement of meaning which is supposed to take place in dissemination. When a signifier is left to its own devices in dissemination, it implies another signifier, and another and another, spilling endlessly onwards and outwards across language. In deconstruction, on the other hand, the movement is not onwards and outwards, but very definitely upwards. Potions with poisonous effects imply the principle of poisonousness; particular forms of addition imply the principle of incrementality – in short, every meaning implies the larger and more general categories under which it exists. This is no simple spread of signifying, but a spiralling up onto higher and higher levels of abstraction. Derrida seems strangely unmindful of this dimension of his deconstructive activity.

What's more, whereas the movement of dissemination is supposedly centrifugal, the movement of deconstruction is very definitely convergent. On higher and higher levels of abstraction, the categories automatically become more and more encompassing. Of course, they are still always organized oppositionally: but the oppositions are original and ultimate oppositions. Even though Derrida sets himself against historical origins and psychological origins, he moves persistently in the direction of categorial origins. There is a logic in deconstruction which impels him towards the most fundamental boundary lines, where the indeterminate whole of everything first separates out into distinct categories. And no matter what word he may take as his starting-point, he always manages to work back up to the same ultimate paradoxes of inside versus outside, presence versus absence, first-ness versus second-ness, etc.

In deconstructing, Derrida sees himself as liberating language and allowing words to follow their own free trajectories. And admittedly we shall not see him *pushing* the movement of categorial implication by personal thought-associations. But still it is not language alone which refutes the philosophy of Plato and promulgates the philosophy of Derrida. For the movement of categorial implication depends upon a kind of abstracting space or vacuum around a word.[50] By setting this vacuum up in advance, and by setting it up in an appropriate manner, Derrida can have words *pulled* exactly where he wants them to go, consistently in the direction of certain recurring abstractions. In spite of appearances, deconstruction is not a 'hands-off' technique after all. Like many Superstructuralists, Derrida is fond of showing how those who lay claim to an impartial view are typically trapped by presuppositions hidden in their very way of framing the evidence. Now it can be seen that Derrida's own results are also predetermined by his very way of framing the evidence.

DECONSTRUCTION AND THE MOVE OF THE CRITIQUE

Of course, I have been unfair to Derrida. Derrida not only deconstructs; he also argues as one philosopher against another. And in arguing against Plato, he tries to discover the unrecognized assumptions underlying the whole way of thinking which Plato represents. Just as the King reveals what Theuth has failed to take into account, so Derrida tries to reveal what both the King and Theuth together have failed to take into account. He is not responding directly to the assertions in the text, but getting round behind them, showing where they come from. This is the classical philosopher's move, the move of the critique. And Derrida certainly makes us question Plato's (and our) typically Western fear of the artificial and unnatural; and makes us reconsider Plato's (and our) typically Western belief that anything is ever other than artificial and unnatural. I have already paid my respects to Derrida's capacities as a philosopher in *Superstructuralism*.

The move of the critique is a peculiarly powerful one. It does not work by superior facts or logic, but by superior consciousness – by *out-conscious-ing*. By bringing forth unrecognized assumptions, one sees what an opponent has failed to see, one rises to a higher level of awareness, and one *gets the look-down* upon everything that an opponent has said or will be able to say. But the difficulty of this move is in direct proportion to its power. For it is not easy to bring forth unrecognized assumptions, whether they be one's own or someone else's. And it is not easy to encompass any kind of thinking under a genuinely higher perspective. Philosophers have always struggled to achieve a superior consciousness; but the history of philosophy is more notable for the struggle than for the achievement.

This is where deconstruction comes in. Like the philosopher, the deconstructor apparently sees what an opponent has failed to see, rises to a higher level of awareness, and gets the look-down upon everything that an opponent has said or will be able to say. And yet deconstruction requires no special effort of insight or understanding. On the deconstructor's own view, it is language itself which is responsible for the critique, and the deconstructor merely shares in the higher perspective which language itself opens up. On the view that I have argued above, this higher perspective is actually the automatic consequence of a certain standard technique which causes language to behave in a certain standard manner. But on either view, deconstruction gives the impression of producing a successful critique without having to go through any of the difficulty.

Of course, this impression is only an impression. What deconstruction produces is the *glamour* of the critique, the aura of *critique-icity*. For deconstruction does not encompass and rise above a whole argument; it encompasses and rises above only the meaning of a single word. The assumption is that the single word is always mightier than the argument. But one may manage to look down from a very lofty vantage upon the way in which an opponent uses a particular word, yet still be very far from looking down upon the opponent's argument as a whole. For the points of an argument leap up between words – and between sentences, and clusters of sentences. This is the upward movement of consciousness which was explored in the 'Linearity, spacing, consciousness' section of Chapter 3, and it generates a very different vantage to anything that can be erected over and above a single word. In relation to this higher perspective, the deconstructor's higher perspective may be quite irrelevant.

Herein lies the danger of deconstruction: the danger of never really taking in an opponent's argument at all. Getting round behind an opponent's assertions may serve to produce a critique, but it may also serve as a means of avoiding confrontation. Deconstruction can become a tactic for infallible victory without risks. Why bother to grasp an alien perspective, why struggle to step into someone else's shoes, when language itself can always be made to pass a verdict in one's favour? By limiting other people to the old meanings of their single words, the deconstructor can avoid ever having to learn anything new.

Even Derrida is sometimes seduced by the temptations of sheer deconstruction, particularly in his later writings. In *Of Grammatology*, his deconstruction of Rousseau's word *supplément* is inextricably bound up with a full philosophical critique of Rousseau's overall perspective. No one, I think, would claim that Derrida fails to confront his opponent here. But there is less critique and more *critique-icity* in 'Plato's Pharmacy'. After all, the King in the *Phaedrus* does not even reject the invention of writing by explicitly describing it as a *pharmakon*. It is Derrida who decides that writing, at this crucial juncture, is being viewed as a kind of poison. One might start to suspect that any occurrence of the word *pharmakon* anywhere in the text could be used to launch essentially the same deconstruction. And such suspicions grow even stronger by the time of 'Limited Inc a b c', where Derrida's deconstruction of Searle's words (in sections (d) to (k)) clearly precedes any response to Searle's arguments (in sections (l) to (z)).[51] In fact, Derrida manages to convey an impression of getting the look-down upon Searle without seriously attempting to grasp his opponent's position at all.

Still, Derrida is at least genuinely capable of making the move of the critique. The same cannot be said for many of his followers. It is unfortunate that Derrida's technique of deconstruction is much easier to reproduce than his capacities as a philosopher. In the hands of Derrida's followers, deconstruction has all too often become a means of warding off any real encounter with alternative perspectives. All possible non-Poststructuralist arguments are defeated before they even get started, defeated by an effortless out-conscious-ing. Thus does an apparently liberating height of awareness turn into a very great closer of minds.

THE MOVE OF THE CRITIQUE AS A POSTSTRUCTURALIST STRATEGY

In the opening paragraph of this chapter, I noted that Poststructuralists aim to pass beyond objectivist notions of truth. So far as 'real' facts are concerned, all discourses are seen as relative: no discourse can lay claim to superiority. And yet Poststructuralists obviously regard their own discourse as being in some way superior – superior to the discourses of philosophers oriented towards Existentialism, for example, or literary critics oriented towards Realism, or social scientists oriented towards Behaviourism. From where, then, does such superiority arise, if not from a more accurate reflection of the facts?

The arguments of the previous section will help us to an answer. But first let us spread the net more widely, beyond the particular form of Post-structuralism represented by Derrida and the deconstructors. Michel Foucault is a Poststructuralist of a different stripe, yet equally vehement in opposing all objectivist notions of truth. In his archaeological phase, he claims to show how discourses are entirely relative to the epistemic framework within which they have been composed. However, this leaves him with no visible way of explaining the superior status of his own discourse.[52] Nor is the explanation forthcoming when, in his genealogical phase, he claims to show how discourses are an outgrowth of social power and political interest. In this phase, he seems to think of himself as engaging in some almost physical kind of struggle. 'Knowledge', he tells us, 'is not made for understanding; it is made for cutting'; and 'one's point of reference should not be to the great model of language and signs, but to that of war and battle . . . relations of power, not relations of meaning'.[53] But it is difficult to find a satisfactory interpretation for such metaphors. What power can a discourse possess that does not depend upon meaning? And how can knowledge act like a physical blade?

Two possible interpretations must be dismissed as unsatisfactory. In the first place, the power of Foucault's discourse cannot be equated with its possible physical consequences. Foucault proclaims the virtues of political intervention as against conceptual understanding, and of struggling with bodies rather than arguing with propositions. But his own discourse only incites to intervention and struggling with bodies: in itself, it remains purely conceptual and propositional. It is not by any physical form of superiority that Foucault's propositions conquer other propositions.

The other unsatisfactory interpretation looks to a certain kind of power-struggle involving words and ways of using words. This is the kind of struggle which is waged unconsciously through usage, rather than consciously through understanding. Such a struggle took place between the language of the subjugated Anglo-Saxon majority and the language of the French-speaking conquerors in the centuries after 1066. But so slow and circumstantial a combat will not serve Foucault's purposes. His discourse is aiming at an altogether more immediate and deliberate victory. If Foucault's own characteristic words and ways of using words have been so widely taken up in recent years, this is certainly not because of any ordinary unconscious percolation into *langue*.

In fact, Foucault's discourse triumphs not by unconscious but by conscious means – by a strategy of *higher* consciousness. Foucault's discourse looks down upon and gets round behind other discourses. He relies upon the principle that a discourse which claims to reflect the facts more accurately can always be undermined by a discourse which claims to discover the assumptions behind that reflection. And he is extremely good at encompassing previous conceptual frameworks, extremely good at showing what other people take for granted. He can afford to discard the principle of objectivist truth because he has an alternative principle of superiority. He wins his battles by out-conscious-ing.

This is evidently another version of the same move which we have seen Derrida execute. With or without deconstruction, out-conscious-ing is the favourite strategy of Poststructuralists generally. Not that they talk or think about it as such – after all, the practice sits somewhat oddly with their professed materialist principles (although there was always a large measure of idealism folded in with that materialism, as I tried to show in *Superstructuralism*). Nonetheless, their insistence upon problematizing and challenging existing assumptions is a perpetual summons to the move of the critique. 'Theory', in the special Poststructuralist sense of that term, has become not merely desirable but absolutely compulsory. Thinkers with 'Theory' habitually look down upon their less aware, less sophisticated brethren, upon those benighted souls who remain trapped in a 'natural' or 'obvious' perspective. It is hardly surprising that, under Poststructuralist influence, a great many intellectual disciplines have taken a strongly philosophical turn.

This sort of boost to philosophy has always tended to follow from a Metaphysical way of thinking. In Hegel's scheme of things, philosophy is as far superior to science as science is superior to common thought. Even the supreme form of Absolute Spirit is ultimately a form of philosophy (the Hegelian form, as it so happens!). And Plato's claims are no less overweening. According to Plato, only philosophers are able to pierce through the illusory world of obvious, natural appearances – therefore only philosophers are fit to rule and make laws for the state. This bizarre conclusion is not so very far removed from the attitude implied in the work of certain politically-minded Poststructuralists.

Of course, there is a rationale for making 'Theory' compulsory. For if what we observe is conditioned by our assumptions, then inadequate assumptions will inevitably produce false observations. So, in an ultimate sense, we ought to begin by making sure of our assumptions before we start trying to observe objective facts. But unfortunately for that rationale, it seems that we can never really make sure of our assumptions, no matter how conscientiously we subject them to critique. Human knowledge is condemned to begin *in medias res*. In the history of the sciences, the most drastic revolutions of conceptual framework have typically occurred only as scientists have improved their relation to objective facts. For better or worse, we must feel for our footing as we go along. It is pointless to be always wanting to make the move of the critique, quite in advance of actually needing to make it.

However, a taste for the critique may easily develop its own momentum. For there is something gloriously breathtaking and exhilarating about rising to a higher level and getting the look-down. And in any particular debate, the move of the critique offers a means to a peculiarly crushing kind of victory. After all, what answer can be made by someone who has less grasp of their own position than you do? Opponents are left floundering and helpless, unable to speak. By encompassing their assumptions, you not only argue against what they have said, but pre-empt anything they will be able to say. It is very tempting to reach for the move of the critique when it holds out the promise of this special kind of superiority. And the Poststructuralists are often tempted.

Foucault and Derrida themselves fall into temptation when quarrelling with one another. In their internecine strife, these two thinkers – responsible, between them, for so many of Superstructuralism's best insights – display an unedifying readiness to resort to the critique as a mere blunt instrument. When Derrida, in 'Cogito and the History of Madness', seeks to criticize Foucault's views on Descartes, he does so by presenting Foucault as circumscribed within a limited set of assumptions, as capable of only a '*naive* reading of the *Meditations* [my italics]'.[54] And when Foucault, who is naturally averse to being looked down upon in this manner, responds with a counter-critique in 'Mon corps, ce papier, ce feu', he in turn presents Derrida as naively incapable of questioning the assumptions of his old-fashioned bourgeois conditioning.[55] Either way, there is a mighty overthrowing, one perspective utterly out-conscious-ing the other. One can hardly help but conclude that the habit of the critique has blown out of all proportion what is really a relatively small difference of opinion.

Even more passionately devoted to the critique is Jean Baudrillard, who claims to be aware of assumptions by which both Foucault and Derrida are unconsciously trapped. In *Oublier Foucault*, he treats Foucault like any poor outdated thinker from an earlier era.[56] And in *Simulations* and *In the Shadow of the Silent Majorities . . . Or, The End of the Social and Other Essays*, his desire for earth-shattering inversions goes far beyond the limits of genuine analysis.[57] Relentlessly upping the ante, transcending at a million miles an hour, he indulges in a veritable frenzy of out-conscious-ing. He seems determined to keep on leaving and leaving behind every perspective that ever existed – his own included. In his later writings, Baudrillard ends up at a supreme height of almost total vacuity.

The moral, evidently, is that we cannot expect to be forever encompassing existing assumptions, or forever outleaping previous frameworks. No doubt, successful critiques are enormously important whenever they occur. And whenever they occur, they take precedence over simple objectivist notions of truth. But it is in the nature of things that they do not occur very often. When Poststructuralists reach for the move of the critique as a regular means of superiority, they all too often reproduce the gesture without the substance. An ordinary orientation towards 'real' facts may not be the only principle to be observed, but we cannot afford to leave it totally out of account either. The accurate reflection of facts is our daily bread and butter; an exclusive diet of pure critique is far too rich.

Conclusion

It is appropriate that syntagmatic theory should place so much emphasis upon the sympathetic creative activity of the reader in general, because I have certainly made very heavy demands upon the sympathetic creative activity of the reader in this particular book. Again and again, I have started hares running without hunting them down. There are suggestions about a facilitative role for higher-order grammatical categories; suggestions about a general epistemology of perception; suggestions about a possible convergence between syntagmatic theory and Generative grammar; suggestions about various applications of syntagmatic theory to literature. But in all of these areas (and many more besides), most of the hard work still remains to be done.

It follows that such a book does not lend itself to a tidy and comprehensive wrap-up. So, by way of an alternative conclusion, let me draw attention to what I consider the three most important ideas to have emerged overall. Given the multitude of different debates going on in different sections and chapters, these ideas often wove their way through several scattered appearances, were often invoked mainly in relation to other lines of argument. Let me then reinvoke them, bringing them forward with all due prominence.

The first idea is the subtractive idea of meaning: that what comes out of the syntagm is a lot less than what goes in. Grammatically combined words allow us to think only so much meaning as can manage to pass through all of them. In the 'Complementarity, synthesis, projection' section of Chapter 2, I illustrated this idea with the metaphor of superimposed colour-filters. Such subtraction depends upon a complementarity of conceptual cut in the different meanings of component words; and leads to a projection of meaning for the syntagm as a whole. In projection, we squeeze a meaning together by squeezing it out beyond the old meanings of component words. This is an exercise of active subjectivity in the 'I'-philosophers' sense, enabling an individual to transcend the passive subjectivity of that which is merely personal.

The second idea is the idea of words as the markers of thought. This idea first surfaced in the 'Linearity, spacing, consciousness' section of Chapter 3, and subsequently resurfaced in Chapter 5, in the 'Language and thinking' section of Chapter 6, in Chapter 13, and elsewhere. As markers, words do not contain our thinking, but hold it in place by laying out that set of meanings over which it must, uniquely, fit. Thinking in language is not *in* words, but across the gaps *between* words. On this idea, the relation between language and thought needs to be radically reconceived.

The third idea is an idea which emerges from my presentation of the general Phenomenological position in philosophy. In Chapter 7, I showed how our acts of mind necessarily involve a subject-sense of where those acts are from; on an *intentional* view, we can come to a recognition of objectivities by discounting for our own subjective contribution to experience. This is all very true to the spirit of Brentano and Husserl and Merleau-Ponty. But what has especially emerged from my presentation, and what does not exactly appear in any of those thinkers, is the manner in which objectivities announce themselves specifically as resistances to our powers of free variation, resistances to our sense of what we can or could do, bodily or with the 'muscles of the mind'. The third idea, then, is that there is a relation of inverse proportion between the levels of our freedom and the levels of ontological existence which we are compelled to construe outside ourselves. This seems to me a philosophical principle of far-reaching significance.

If these ideas are acceptable, then we have already moved decisively *beyond Superstructuralism* – and beyond Analytical philosophy too. Not 'beyond' in the sense of simple progress: as I said long ago, there is a certain recurring inevitability about all three approaches. Nor would I wish to devalue the numerous insights and illuminations thrown off by Superstructuralism and Analytical philosophy in the course of their careers. But their careers have faltered somewhat in recent years. Ordinary-Language philosophy languishes in the doldrums, while Formal Semantics appears to have shot its bolt. And Superstructuralism, although surviving on political energy, seems to have lost its conceptual momentum (at least in France, its conceptual heartland). The time is ripe for a new way of thinking about language: and syntagmatic theory is that new way.

Notes

PART I THE LIMITS OF SUPERSTRUCTURALISM

1 See Ferdinand de Saussure, 1966, *Course in General Linguistics*, ed. Charles Bally, Albert Sechehaye and Albert Riedlinger, trans. Wade Baskin (New York: McGraw-Hill), 123, 126.
2 See ibid., 123, 125–7.
3 For a fuller exposition, see Richard Harland, 1987, *Superstructuralism* (London: Methuen), 6–13.
4 *Course in General Linguistics*, 123.
5 ibid.
6 ibid., 124.
7 ibid., 124–5.
8 Roland Barthes, 1967, *Elements of Semiology*, trans. Annette Lavers and Colin Smith (New York: Hill & Wang), 63.
9 ibid.
10 See for example p. 68 of *Elements of Semiology*, where Barthes expressly states that 'the units of both syntagms do not necessarily coincide'.
11 Thus Barthes slides very freely between the two terms on pp. 60–1 of *Elements of Semiology*.
12 For a full account of this new twist, see *Superstructuralism*, 123–54.
13 Gillès Deleuze and Félix Guattari, 1981, 'Rhizome', trans. Paul Foss and Paul Patton, *Ideology and Consciousness*, VIII, 53. Of course, the symbols have changed in more recent versions of Generative grammar; in Government and Binding Theory, for example, the overarching marker is now CP (for Complementizer Phrase) or C″. But the hierarchical principle remains the same.
14 Jacques Derrida, 1981, *Positions*, trans. Alan Bass (London: Athlone Press), 3.
15 Jacques Derrida, 1978, *Writing and Difference*, trans. Alan Bass (London: Routledge & Kegan Paul), 294.
16 See *Superstructuralism*, 125–40.
17 Jacques Derrida, 1974, *Of Grammatology*, trans. Gayatri Chakravorty Spivak (Baltimore: Johns Hopkins University Press), 18.
18 ibid., 68.
19 Jacques Derrida, 1982, *Margins of Philosophy*, trans. Alan Bass (Chicago: University of Chicago Press), 317; *Writing and Difference*, 225.
20 *Of Grammatology*, 69.
21 ibid.
22 ibid., 86.
23 ibid., 69.

PART II A THEORY OF THE SYNTAGM

1 For an account of Derrida's argument here, see Richard Harland, 1987, *Superstructuralism* (London: Methuen), 127–31.
2 Umberto Eco, 1976, *A Theory of Semiotics* (Bloomington: Indiana University Press), 169.
3 See the 'Saussure's paradigmatic preference' section of Chapter 1; and *Superstructuralism*, 15–16.
4 *A Theory of Semiotics*, 110.
5 This example made its first appearance in Noam Chomsky, 1957, *Syntactic Structures* (The Hague: Mouton), 15.
6 See line 48 of 'The Garden'.
7 Jacques Derrida, 1973, *Speech and Phenomena: and Other Essays on Husserl's Theory of Signs*, trans. David B. Allison (Evanston: Northwestern University Press), 88.
8 *Speech and Phenomena*, 129; *Of Grammatology*, trans. Gayatri Chakravorty Spivak (Baltimore: Johns Hopkins University Press), 65.
9 *Speech and Phenomena*, 137.
10 See for example C. S. Peirce, 1934, *Collected Papers of Charles Sanders Peirce*, ed. Charles Hartshorne and Paul Weiss, V (Cambridge, Mass.: Belknap Press), paragraphs 144–5, 171–3, 602–3.
11 See *Superstructuralism*, 88–91.
12 Ferdinand de Saussure, 1966, *Course in General Linguistics*, ed. Charles Bally, Albert Sechehaye and Albert Riedlinger, trans. Wade Baskin (New York: McGraw-Hill), 116.
13 Ludwig Wittgenstein, 1967, *Philosophical Investigations*, trans. G. E. M. Anscombe (Oxford: Basil Blackwell), 32e, paragraph 67.
14 I borrow these examples from Neil Smith and Deirdre Wilson, 1979, *Modern Linguistics: The Results of Chomsky's Revolution* (Bloomington: Indiana University Press), 204. However, the evidence for Object–Subject–Verb languages is apparently somewhat equivocal.
15 *Prise de conscience* was a favourite term of the later Phenomenologists such as von Hildebrand. In more recent times, the term has appeared mainly in the arguments of anti-Phenomenologists. Lacan, for example, has claimed that language has no real need for the *prise de conscience* at all. See Jacques Lacan, 1968, *The Language of the Self*, trans. Anthony Wilden (New York: Delta Books), 16.
16 The nearest approach, perhaps, is to be found in certain proposals from the Form–Content school of linguists. Thus Robert Kirsner suggests that 'meanings . . . are not *concrete building blocks* of messages', and that 'messages are not *signaled* by meanings but are instead *inferred from* them'. (See Robert S. Kirsner, 1985, 'Iconicity and Grammatical Meaning', in *Iconicity in Syntax*, ed. John Haiman (Amsterdam: John Benjamins), 259, 256.) However, Kirsner and the other members of the school develop their proposals in a Functional rather than a syntagmatic direction, leading to a position which is if anything even more extreme than the Emergence of Grammar position discussed in the second section of Chapter 11.
17 Derrida also argues against Searle's Gricean version of intention, using much the same arguments as he employs against Husserl. See Jacques Derrida and John Searle, 1988, *Limited Inc*, ed. Gerald Graff (Evanston: Northwestern University Press).
18 For a fuller exposition, see *Superstructuralism*, 125–7. In fact, although Husserl deals with interior soliloquy, he does not himself think of it as the ideal case for his philosophy of language. See Section 8 of Investigation I in Edmund Husserl, 1970, *Logical Investigations*, trans. J. N. Findlay (London: Routledge & Kegan Paul).

19 My information on Government and Binding Theory is derived, I must confess, from secondary sources – especially from the lucid and illuminating account in Liliane Haegeman, 1991, *Introduction to Government and Binding Theory* (Oxford: Basil Blackwell).

20 James Joyce, 1960, *Ulysses* (London: The Bodley Head), 880–1.

21 Roy Harris, 1981, *The Language Myth* (London: Duckworth), 74. Harris also ridicules 'the scientific role of idealisation' in his parody of Saussure's ideal speaker-hearers. See Harris, 1987, *The Language Machine* (Ithaca: Cornell University Press), 165ff.

22 There are important discussions of the 'holophrase' in Grace de Laguna, 1927, *Speech: Its Functions and Development* (New Haven: Yale University Press); Heinz Werner and Bernard Kaplan, 1963, *Symbol Formation* (New York: John Wiley); David McNeill, 1970, *The Acquisition of Language: The Study of Developmental Psycholinguistics* (New York: Harper & Row); Lois Bloom, 1973, *One Word at a Time* (The Hague: Mouton); and Maris Monitz Rodgon, 1976, *Single-Word Usage, Cognitive Development, and the Beginnings of Combinatorial Speech* (Cambridge: Cambridge University Press). A somewhat different perspective is proposed by Greenfield and Smith, who claim that the child *does* cognize the single word as part of a whole, and, like the adult, deliberately uses single-word utterances to complement what may be undersood from contextual sources. See Patricia Marks Greenfield and Joshua H. Smith, 1976, *The Structure of Communication in Early Language Development* (New York: Academic Press).

23 H. P. Grice, for example, approaches the syntagmatic position when he stresses the as-if-for-the-first-time character of language communication, while Roy Harris approaches the syntagmatic position when he stresses the role of creativity in non-verbal contexts. But of course this *rapprochement* does not extend to the discussion of verbal contexts – Harris has no time for grammatically combined sentences, and Grice tries to explain full-sentence utterances in exactly the same way that he explains sub-sentential utterances. I shall pursue the debate with Grice in the 'Grice on intention' section of Chapter 9.

24 *Writing and Difference*, trans. Alan Bass (London: Routledge & Kegan Paul), 178.

PART III SYNTAGMATIC THEORY AND PHILOSOPHY

1 Richard Harland, 1987, *Superstructuralism* (London: Methuen), 70–6.

2 Jacques Derrida, 1978, *Writing and Difference*, trans. Alan Bass (London: Routledge & Kegan Paul), 224.

3 See especially Maurice Merleau-Ponty, 1973, *Consciousness and the Acquisition of Language*, trans. Hugh Silverman (Evanston: Northwestern University Press).

4 Julia Kristeva, 1980, *Desire in Language*, trans. Thomas Gora, Alice Jardine and Leon S. Roudiez (Oxford: Basil Blackwell), 163.

5 Edmund Husserl, *Logical Investigations*, trans. J. N. Findlay (London: Routledge & Kegan Paul), 299. See also 328.

6 David Bell, 1990, *Husserl* (London: Routledge), 130.

7 Edmund Husserl, 1969, *Formal and Transcendental Logic*, trans. Dorion Cairns (The Hague: Martinus Nijhoff), 295.

8 *Logical Investigations*, 477. For the general theory of 'moments', see Investigation III, especially sections 17, 21, 22, 23.

9 ibid., 493.

10 ibid., 520.

11 *Formal and Transcendental Logic*, 299.

12 ibid., 517.

13 ibid., 512.

14 ibid., 276–7.

15 See *Speech and Phenomena: and Other Essays on Husserl's Theory of Signs*, trans. David B. Allison (Evanston: Northwestern University Press). The essential drift of Derrida's argument is presented in *Superstructuralism*, 125–36.

16 *Logical Investigations*, 284, and *Formal and Transcendental Logic*, 22. There is an interesting parallel here to the 'sincerity'-condition which Austin proposes for performatives. See J. L. Austin, 1971, 'Performative-Constative', in *The Philosophy of Language*, ed. John Searle (London: Oxford University Press), 14; and 1962, *How to Do Things with Words* (Oxford: Clarendon Press), 39–43.

17 *Formal and Transcendental Logic*, 308.

18 *Logical Investigations*, 650.

19 ibid., 520.

20 *Formal and Transcendental Logic*, 310.

21 See James M. Edie, 1987, *Edmund Husserl's Phenomenology: A Critical Commentary* (Bloomington: Indiana University Press), 55.

22 *Logical Investigations*, 506.

23 ibid., 508.

24 See *Formal and Transcendental Logic*, 300.

25 I borrow this information from Seppo Sajama and Matti Kamppinen, 1987, *A Historical Introduction to Phenomenology* (London: Croom Helm), 11.

26 There is, it is true, a kind of self-consciousness in Brentano's conception of the subject-pole; but Husserl disagrees most strongly with his mentor on this point. See particularly Investigation V of *Logical Investigations*.

27 Especially Ryle and the later Wittgenstein. See Gilbert Ryle, 1963, *The Concept of Mind* (Harmondsworth: Penguin/Peregrine); and Ludwig Wittgenstein, 1967, *Philosophical Investigations*, trans. G. E. M. Anscombe (Oxford: Basil Blackwell).

28 For an excellent brief exposition of Husserl's thinking on this topic, see Izchak Miller, 1982, 'Husserl's Account of Our Temporal Awareness', in *Husserl, Intentionality and Cognitive Science*, ed. Hubert L. Dreyfus (Cambridge, Mass.: MIT Press).

29 See Jean Piaget, 1929, *The Child's Conception of the World*, trans. Joan and Andrew Tomlinson (London: Routledge & Kegan Paul), 23. For arguments specifically against the Logical Positivists, see Chapter 4 of Jean Piaget, 1971, *Psychology and Epistemology*, trans. A. Rosin (New York: Viking); Jean Piaget, 1971, *Insights and Illusions of Philosophy*, trans. W. Mays (New York: Meridian Books); and Jean Piaget and Barbel Inhelder, 1969, 'The Gaps in Empiricism', in *Beyond Reductionism*, ed. A. Koestler and J. R. Smythies (Boston: Beacon Press).

30 See especially Jean Piaget and Barbel Inhelder, 1966, *The Psychology of the Child*, trans. H. Weaver (New York: Harper). The authors here discuss the role of the semiotic function in detaching thought from action, but they include language as only one aspect of that function.

31 In recent years, a number of American child psychologists have sought to understand language acquisition within a Piagetian framework. Their data and hypotheses are most illuminating. However, they seem to have lowered their sights from a 'strong cognitive hypothesis' to a 'weak cognitive hypothesis' to a 'correlational hypothesis'. From a syntagmatic perspective, I would suggest that they have tended to look for too direct a dependence of linguistic capacities upon sensori-motor capacities; what's more, they have expected to find this dependence continuing through into later language learning, as though linguistic development were incapable of ever taking on a momentum and logic of its own. For the 'strong cognitive hypothesis', see John MacNamara, 1972, 'The Cognitive Basis of Language Learning in Infants' in *Psychological Review*, LXXIX. For the 'weak cognitive hypothesis', see Richard F. Cromer, 1974, 'The Development of Language and Cognition: The Cognition Hypothesis', in *New Perspectives in Child Development*, ed. Brian Foss (Harmondsworth: Penguin). For the 'correlational

hypothesis', see J. Miller, R. Chapman, M. Branston and J. Reichle, 1980, 'Language Comprehension in Sensorimotor Stages V and VI', *Journal of Speech and Hearing Research*, XXIII; also Elizabeth Bates, *et al.*, 1979, *The Emergence of Symbols: Cognition and Communication in Infancy* (New York: Academic Press).

32 A similar notion is expressed by Bartlett, who, in a memorable phrase, speaks of the organism's 'ability to turn round upon its own "schemata" and to construct them afresh'. See Frederic C. Bartlett, 1932, *Remembering* (Cambridge: Cambridge University Press), 302.

33 Of course, this is not to suggest that language acquisition will follow the same order of development, adjectives before nouns. On the contrary: the child has learnt to live in a world of objects long before language comes upon the scene.

34 Specifically, Chomsky's sense of a 'substantive universal': 'A theory of substantive universals claims that items of a particular kind in any language must be drawn from a fixed class of items.' Noam Chomsky, 1965, *Aspects of the Theory of Syntax* (Cambridge, Mass.: MIT Press), 28.

35 I borrow the phrase 'operations on operations' from Evert W. Beth and Jean Piaget, 1966, *Mathematical Epistemology and Psychology*, trans. W. Mays (Dordrecht: D. Reidel), 242.

36 See Eric Lenneberg, 1967, *Biological Foundations of Language* (New York: John Wiley). For a Piagetian translation of the hypothesis, see Sacha W. Felix, 1978, 'Some Differences between First and Second Language Acquisition', in *The Development of Communication*, ed. N. Waterson and C. Snow (New York: John Wiley).

37 Gottlob Frege, 1953, *The Foundations of Arithmetic*, trans. J. L. Austin (Oxford: Basil Blackwell), Section 62; Donald Davidson, 1984, *Inquiries into Truth and Interpretation* (Oxford: Clarendon Press), 18.

38 John Searle, 1969, *Speech Acts: An Essay in the Philosophy of Language* (Cambridge: Cambridge University Press), 25; J. L. Austin, 1974, 'The Meaning of a Word', in *Readings in Semantics*, ed. Farhang Zabeeh, E. D. Klemke and Arthur Jacobson (Urbana: University of Illinois Press), 422.

39 Ludwig Wittgenstein, 1981, *Tractatus Logico-Philosophicus*, trans. C. K. Ogden (London: Routledge & Kegan Paul), 67, paragraph 4.024.

40 Gottlob Frege, 1960, 'On Sense and Reference', in *Philosophical Writings of Gottlob Frege*, trans. Peter Geach and Max Black (Oxford: Basil Blackwell), 56–78.

41 Bertrand Russell, 'On Denoting', in *Readings in Semantics*, 156.

42 This applies even to the profound criticisms raised by Urmson (as an Analytical philosopher of the Ordinary-Language persuasion) and Chisholm (as an Analytical philosopher with strong Phenomenological leanings). See J. O. Urmson, 1956, *Philosophical Analysis* (Oxford: Clarendon Press); and Roderick M. Chisholm, 1952, 'Intentionality and the Theory of Signs', *Philosophical Studies*, III; 1957, *Perceiving: A Philosophical Study* (Ithaca: Cornell University Press); 1965, 'The Problem of Empiricism', in *Perceiving, Sensing, and Knowing*, ed. Robert Swartz (New York: Doubleday); and 1966, *Theory of Knowledge* (Englewood Cliffs: Prentice-Hall). Chisholm's criticisms are forcefully re-presented in Michael Corrado, 1975, *The Analytic Tradition in Philosophy: Background and Issues* (Chicago: American Library Association).

43 The claim about 'direct acquaintance' comes specifically from Bertrand Russell. See, for instance, Russell, 1946, *The Problems of Philosophy* (London: Oxford University Press), Chapter 5.

44 See especially the essay 'From Restricted to General Economy: A Hegelianism Without Reserve', in Jacques Derrida, *Writing and Difference*, trans. Alan Bass (London: Routledge & Kegan Paul).

45 I have attempted to characterize Derrida's version of meaning in Chapter 10, Section (ii) of *Superstructuralism*.

46 See F. P. Ramsay, 1964, 'Facts and Propositions', in *Truth*, ed. George Pitcher (Englewood Cliffs: Prentice-Hall).

47 The Oxford example is borrowed from J. L. Austin. See 'Performative-Constative', 21. But my interpretation of the example is somewhat different. According to Austin, the proposition that 'Oxford is sixty miles from London' is valid or invalid according to the implicit conventions of a speech-act situation in a given context. But in this case, if the context calls only for an approximation to the nearest five miles, then the answer 'Sixty two and a quarter miles' must be judged as actually invalid. This is surely not very plausible. One is always entitled to be more precise than one has to be. (Wearing a digital watch, I now find it easier to answer a query about the time by reading off the exact display of minutes, regardless of what the situation calls for.) A fixed level of approximation prescribed for a given context is hardly more appropriate than absolute truth prescribed universally. What Austin fails to recognize is the extent to which the level of approximation is up-to-us.

48 See Alfred Tarski, 1944, 'The Semantic Conception of Truth and the Foundation of Semantics', in *Philosophy and Phenomenological Research*, IV, *Symposium on Meaning and Truth*. See also the papers on 'The Concept of Truth in Formalized Languages' and 'The Establishment of Scientific Semantics' in Tarski, 1956, *Logic, Semantics, Metamathematics: Papers from 1923 to 1938*, trans. J. H. Woodger (Oxford: Clarendon Press).

49 'The Semantic Conception of Truth and the Foundation of Semantics', 71.

50 *Inquiries into Truth and Interpretation*, 224.

51 Donald Davidson, 1986, 'A Coherence Theory of Truth and Knowledge', in *Truth and Interpretation*, ed. E. LePore (Oxford: Basil Blackwell), 307.

52 P. F. Strawson argues along these lines in 1950, 'Symposium on Truth' (with J. L. Austin), *Proceedings of the Aristotelian Society*, Supplementary Volume 24; and in 1965, 'Truth: A Reconsideration of Austin's Views', *Philosophical Quarterly*, XV, 289–301.

53 The phrase 'maximal and complete' comes from Alvin Plantinga, 1974, *The Nature of Necessity* (Oxford: Clarendon Press), 45.

54 David Lewis, 1973, *Counterfactuals* (Oxford: Basil Blackwell), 84–9.

55 See Robert Stalnaker, 1968, 'A Theory of Conditionals', in *Studies in Logical Theory*, ed. N. Rescher (Oxford: Basil Blackwell), 98–112; and Lewis, *Counterfactuals*.

56 *Philosophical Investigations*, 46e, paragraph 107.

57 Austin's notion of 'paronymity' similarly points towards the syntagmatic approach. By 'paronymity', a single word over time evolves various centres of sense running off in various directions of analogy, until there may be no single element common to the final spread of its meaning at all. See 'The Meaning of a Word', in *Readings in Semantics*, 435–44. Austin also comes particularly close to the syntagmatic conception of a 'word-hoard', as argued at the end of the 'Mechanism for change in *langue*' section of Chapter 3. 'Our common stock of words', says Austin, 'embodies all the distinctions men have found worth drawing, and the connections they have found worth making, in the lifetime of many generations.' See J. L. Austin, 1964, 'A Plea For Excuses', in *Ordinary Language: Essays in Philosophical Method*, ed. V. C. Chappell (Englewood Cliffs: Prentice-Hall), 46.

58 *Philosophical Investigations*, 137e, paragraph 491.

59 ibid., 20e, paragraph 43.

60 *Speech Acts*, 46–9.

61 *Philosophical Investigations*, 20e, paragraph 43.

62 For Grice on 'word-meaning', see H. P. Grice, 1971, 'Utterer's Meaning, Sentence Meaning and Word-Meaning', in *The Philosophy of Language*, ed. Searle; for Austin on the *rhetic* component of the *locutionary* act, see *How to Do Things with Words*, Lectures VIII and IX. Roy Harris takes a more dogmatic stand than

Austin, when he laments that 'Austin's instrumentalism . . . was not sufficiently thoroughgoing to make do without the support of a surrogationalist foundation, in the form of what Austin designated "locutionary" . . . acts.' See Roy Harris, 1980, *The Language-Makers* (London: Duckworth), 91. In his own war against 'surrogationalism', Harris has no time for the notion that an utterance may possess meaning or sense or reference in itself.

63 The inclination towards Behaviourism is especially strong in Ryle, Wittgenstein and Bennett.

64 See *How to Do Things with Words*, 101–31.

65 For Strawson's views, see P. F. Strawson, 'Intention and Convention in Speech Acts', in *The Philosophy of Language*, ed. Searle; for Searle's views, see *Speech Acts*, especially 42–50.

66 Gilbert Ryle, 'Ordinary Language', in *Readings in Semantics*, 463.

67 See *How to Do Things with Words*, 14–16.

68 *How to Do Things with Words*, 137.

69 Chomsky is even more violently anti-Ordinary Language on this issue. Discussing philosophers such as Searle, Strawson and Grice, he asserts point-blank that the primary purpose of language is not communication but expression – including expression in private thought. See Noam Chomsky, 1976, *Reflections on Language* (London: Temple Smith), 68ff.

70 *Philosophical Investigations*, 3e–10e, paragraphs 2, 6, 8, 9, 10, 19, 20.

71 See, for example, Jacques Derrida, 1982, 'Signature. Event. Context', in *Margins of Philosophy*, trans. Alan Bass (Chicago: University Press), especially 309–11. 'The concept of writing', says Derrida, 'could no longer, henceforth, be included in the category of communication, at least if communication is understood in the restricted sense of transmission of meaning' (p. 310). For an account of Derrida's own special version of meaning, see *Superstructuralism*, Chapter 10.

72 *Philosophical Investigations*, 11e–12e, paragraph 23.

73 *How to Do Things with Words*, 137.

74 See *Speech Acts*, 70–1.

75 Austin's legalistic way of thinking is noted by Max Black, 1970, *The Margins of Precision: Essays in Language and Literature* (Ithaca: Cornell University Press), 217.

76 *How to Do Things with Words*, footnote on p. 115. The account of explicit performatives occurs in Lectures VI and VII. See especially p. 69.

77 Following Austin, certain linguists of the Generative Semantics school have introduced performative verbs into generative deep structures. So, a surface structure of the form 'Go home!' is supposedly derived from '[I order you to] go home', and a surface structure of the form 'There's a lion in that bush near you!' is supposedly derived from '[I warn you that] there's a lion in that bush near you!' See John R. Ross, 1970, 'On Declarative Sentences', in *Readings in English Transformational Grammar*, ed. R. A. Jacobs and P. S. Rosenbaum (Waltham: Ginn); also George Lakoff, 1972, 'Linguistics and Natural Logic', in *Semantics of Natural Language*, ed. D. Davidson and G. Harman (Dordrecht: Reidel), and 1975, 'Pragmatics in Natural Logic', in *Formal Semantics of Natural Language*, ed. E. L. Keenan (Cambridge: Cambridge University Press).

78 *How to Do Things with Words*, 149.

79 For a more comprehensive argument against the drawing forth of performatives, I recommend Manfred Bierwisch, 1980, 'Semantic Structure and Illocutionary Force', in *Speech Act Theory and Pragmatics*, ed. John Searle, Ferenc Kiefer and Manfred Bierwisch (Dordrecht: D. Reidel), 1–36.

80 See *How to Do Things with Words*, Lecture XII; and John Searle, 1979, *Expression and Meaning* (Cambridge: Cambridge University Press), Chapter 1.

81 See H. P. Grice, 'Meaning', in *Readings in Semantics*, 509, 508. This article, first published in 1957, is the source and origin of the intentionalist view; and, as usual,

sources and origins are especially useful for understanding the fundamental divergences between different ways of thinking. The modifications that Grice later made to his formulae will be discussed – albeit in passing – below.

82 Jonathan Bennett, 1976, *Linguistic Behaviour* (Cambridge: Cambridge University Press), 183.

83 Strawson, for example, is prepared to accept a regression without terminus, but recognizes that this will create enormous difficulties for analysis. See 'Intention and Convention in Speech Acts', 33–4.

84 See *Linguistic Behaviour*, 137–41.

85 See, for example, Strawson in 'Intention and Convention in Speech Acts', 28–30, and Searle in *Speech Acts*, 44–8.

86 See 'Meaning', 507–8. I have substituted somewhat more memorable names for Grice's Mr X, Mr Y, etc.

87 'Utterer's Meaning, Sentence-Meaning, and Word-Meaning', 59.

88 See Paul Grice, 1989, *Studies in the Way of Words* (Cambridge, Mass.: Harvard University Press). The general theory is presented in 'Logic and Conversation' and 'Further Notes on Logic and Conversation'; the analysis of connectives appears in 'Further Notes on Logic and Conversation' and 'Indicative Conditionals'.

89 ibid., 27.

90 This translation on the receiver's side comes from Kent Bach and Robert M. Harnish, 1979, *Linguistic Communication and Speech Acts* (Cambridge, Mass.: MIT Press).

91 L. Jonathan Cohen, 1971, 'Some Remarks on Grice's Views about the Logical Particles of Natural Language', in *Pragmatics of Natural Languages*, ed. Yehoshua Bar-Hillel (Dordrecht: D. Reidel), 50–68; Ralph Walker, 1975, 'Conversational Implicatures', in *Meaning, Reference and Necessity*, ed. Simon Blackburn (Cambridge: Cambridge University Press), 133–81.

92 Roland Posner, 1980, 'Semantics and Pragmatics of Sentence Connectives in Natural Language', in *Speech Act Theory and Pragmatics*, 169–204.

93 See ibid., 187, 186.

94 See ibid., 183. Posner is here applying Grice's principle of 'cancelability', as expounded in 'Further Notes on Logic and Conversation'.

95 ibid., 187.

96 John Searle, 1980, 'The Background of Meaning', in *Speech Act Theory and Pragmatics*, 221–32; and 1983, *Intentionality: An Essay in the Philosophy of Mind* (Cambridge: Cambridge University Press). See also the chapter on 'Literal Meaning' in *Expression and Meaning*.

97 'The Background of Meaning', 223.

98 ibid., 227.

99 I have borrowed this general schematic definition of 'cut' from Searle, ibid., 224.

PART IV SYNTAGMATIC THEORY AND LINGUISTICS

1 Noam Chomsky, 1972, *Language and Mind* (enlarged edition) (New York: Harcourt Brace Jovanovich), 118.

2 Noam Chomsky, 1966, 'Linguistic Theory', in *Language Teaching: Broader Contexts*, ed. Robert G. Mead, Jr (Northeast Conference Reports), 44.

3 See, e.g., Noam Chomsky, 1976, *Reflections on Language* (London: Temple Smith), 30–3. Chomsky's reasons for claiming 'structure-dependence' are actually much broader than anything I have been able to suggest by my simple illustration here.

4 Noam Chomsky, 1961, 'Some Methodological Remarks on Generative Grammar', *Word*, XVII, 219–39; Noam Chomsky and George Miller, 1963, 'Introduction to the Formal Analysis of Natural Languages', in *Handbook of Mathematical Psychology*, ed. P. Luce, R. Bush and E. Galanter (New York: John Wiley); Jerrold

J. Katz, 1976, 'Semi-sentences', in *The Structure of Language: Readings in the Philosophy of Language*, ed. Jerry A. Fodor and Jerrold J. Katz (Englewood Cliffs: Prentice-Hall). Unfortunately, Chomsky and Katz confuse the issue by discussing both syntactic and semantic irregularities in the same breath.

5 I have borrowed Slobin's translation of the original German: 'das geistig eng Zusammengehörige auch eng zusammengestellt wird'. See Dan I. Slobin, 1985, 'The Child as Linguistic Icon-Maker', in *Iconicity in Syntax*, ed. John Haiman (Amsterdam/Philadelphia: John Benjamins), 228.

6 To say that a rule of ordering does not reflect a natural order of meaning is not to deny that it may follow an optimal strategy for processing. Different languages place the verb before, between, or after the subject and object; but very few languages actually place the object ahead of the subject overall.

7 The paradox here is very much in the Derridan mould. Although I have been critical of Derrida's theory of language, and shall be critical of Derrida's technique of deconstruction, it may be noted that I have twice adopted his logic of supplementarity: apropos of the relation between lower-level and higher-level syntactical instructions, and apropos of the relation between spoken language and written language, sub-sentential utterances and full-sentence utterances.

8 See Jerry A. Fodor, Thomas Bever and M. F. Garrett, 1974, *The Psychology of Language* (New York: McGraw-Hill).

9 *Language and Mind*, 156.

10 On the subject of Relational Grammar, see David Perlmutter, 1982, 'Syntactic Representation, Syntactic Levels, and the Notion of Subject', in *The Nature of Syntactic Representation*, ed. Pauline Jacobson and Geoffrey K. Pullum (Dordrecht: D. Reidel); Peter Cole and Jerrold Sadock (eds), 1977, *Syntax and Semantics 8: Grammatical Relations* (New York: Academic Press); and Jerry Morgan *et al.*, 1976, 'Topics in Relational Grammar', *Studies in the Linguistic Sciences*, 6.1, 47–248. A useful overall survey is to be found in Barry J. Blake, 1990, *Relational Grammar* (London: Routledge). On the subject of Arc-Pair Grammar, see David Johnson and Paul Postal, 1979, *Arc Pair Grammar* (Princeton: Princeton University Press).

11 See, for instance, G. Hudson, 1972, 'Is Deep Structure Linear?', *UCLA Papers in Syntax*, II, 51–77; T. Peterson, 1971, 'Multi-ordered Base Structures in Generative Grammar', in *Papers from the 7th Regional Meeting of the Chicago Linguistic Society*, 181–92; Gerald Sanders, 1970, 'Constraints on Constituent Ordering', *Papers in Linguistics*, II, 406–52; Geoffrey Pullum, 1979, *Rule Interaction and the Organization of a Grammar* (New York: Garland); along with the writings of the Relational and Arc-Pair Grammarians cited above.

12 *Arc Pair Grammar*, 1976.

13 See Noam Chomsky, 1982, *The Generative Enterprise* (Dordrecht: Foris), 85, 103–4; Howard Lasnik and J. Kuprin, 'A Restrictive Theory of Transformational Grammar', *Theoretical Linguistics*, IV, iii, 173–96.

14 See Jerrold J. Katz and Paul Postal, 1964, *An Integrated Theory of Linguistic Descriptions* (Cambridge, Mass.: MIT Press).

15 Noam Chomsky, 1986, *Knowledge of Language: Its Nature, Origin and Use* (New York: Praeger), 39.

16 See especially Noam Chomsky, 1980, 'On Cognitive Structures and their Development', in *Language and Learning: The Debate between Jean Piaget and Noam Chomsky*, ed. M. Piattelli-Palmarini (London: Routledge & Kegan Paul).

17 Sandra A. Thompson, 1988, 'A Discourse Approach to the Cross-Linguistic Category "Adjective" ', in *Explaining Language Universals*, ed. John A. Hawkins (Oxford: Basil Blackwell), 167. My reasons for avoiding terms like 'functional', 'pragmatic' and 'discourse' will appear in the following section.

18 Joan L. Bybee, 1985, 'Diagrammatic Iconicity in Stem-Inflection Relations', in *Iconicity in Syntax*. Needless to say, I have presented only a skimming from Bybee's

precise and detailed argument; similarly with Givón's argument in the following example.

19 Talmy Givón, 1980, 'The Binding Hierarchy and the Typology of Complement', *Studies in Language*, IV, 333–77.

20 Talmy Givón, 1979, *On Understanding Grammar* (New York: Academic Press), 186.

21 The phrase 'perspectives about experience' comes from Talmy Givón, 1985, 'Iconicity, Isomorphism and Non-Arbitrary Coding in Syntax', in *Iconicity in Syntax*, 191. On the same page, Givón proclaims his adherence to a 'prudent Kantian approach'.

22 *On Understanding Grammar*, 324, 333, 313.

23 ibid., 208. See also Talmy Givón, 1979, 'From Discourse to Syntax: Grammar as a Processing Strategy', in *Syntax and Semantics*, XII: *Discourse and Syntax*, ed. Talmy Givón (New York: Academic Press), 82–3.

24 See *On Understanding Grammar*, 214; 'From Discourse to Syntax', 89.

25 See Bernd Heine, Ulrike Claudi and Friederike Hünnemeyer, 1991, *Grammaticalization: A Conceptual Framework* (Chicago: University of Chicago Press), 180, 216.

26 ibid., 224.

27 Elizabeth Closs Traugott, 1985, 'Conditional Markers', in *Iconicity in Syntax*. Three other sources for *if*-markers are investigated by Traugott: interrogatives, copula constructions, and words expressing a sense of 'givenness'. As usual, I have presented only a skimming from the full argument.

28 ibid., 302.

29 *On Understanding Grammar*, 121.

30 Heine, Claudi and Hünnemeyer take the discontinuous view when they announce: 'Instead of the term "continuum", we shall use here the label "grammaticalization chain" . . . since there is always some kind of overlapping of both conceptual and morphological structures involved.' See *Grammaticalization: A Conceptual Framework*, 221. It may be noted that many small intermediate stages also feature in the account of discontinuously extended lexical meanings put forward in the 'Mechanism for change in *langue*' section of Chapter 3.

31 Paul J. Hopper, 1988, 'Emergent Grammar and the A Priori Grammar Postulate', in *Linguistics in Context: Connecting Observation and Understanding*, ed. Deborah Tannen (New Jersey: Ablex), 121.

32 Paul J. Hopper, 1987, 'Emergent Grammar', *Berkeley Linguistics Society*, XIII, 77.

33 Paul J. Hopper and Sandra A. Thompson, 1984, 'The Discourse Basis for Lexical Categories in Universal Grammar', *Language*, LX, No. 3. A variant of the same article appears as 'The Iconicity of the Universal Categories "Noun" and "Verb" ', in *Iconicity in Syntax*.

34 'The Discourse Basis for Lexical Categories in Universal Grammar', 747.

35 See ibid. The phrase 'morphological trappings' first appears on p. 709.

36 ibid., 710.

37 ibid., 718, 732.

38 ibid., 710, 708.

39 For example, the statement that nouns of high categoriality 'stand for autonomous, usually quite concrete and individuated entities' is immediately followed by the claim that these entities 'act as participants and props in the discourse'; and the statement that prototypical nouns function to 'introduce participants and "props" and to deploy them' is followed two sentences later by the claim that non-prototypical nouns are 'forms which fail in some way to *refer to concrete*, deployable *entities*' [my italics]. See ibid., 718, 710–11.

40 Or an opposition between sentences of different types. John Haiman calls attention to a potential 'fluidity' in plural marking, and adduces the example of Tagalog, a

language where plurality may be marked on either subject or predicate – or both. What matters, apparently, is that 'plurality is marked *somewhere* in the sentence'. John Haiman, 1985, *Natural Syntax: Iconicity and Erosion* (Cambridge: Cambridge University Press), 186.

41 'The Discourse Basis for Lexical Categories in Universal Grammar', 732.
42 ibid., 744.
43 ibid., 747.
44 See ibid., 707.
45 ibid., 710.
46 'The Iconicity of the Universal Categories "Noun" and "Verb" ', 156.
47 'The Discourse Basis for Lexical Categories in Universal Grammar', 705.
48 In the case of relative clauses, it is at least arguable that the distinction between 'The young man who came from Newcastle stepped forward' and 'The young man, who came from Newcastle, stepped forward' is precisely a distinction as to the scope of the determiner. That is, the definite article controls 'who came from Newcastle' in the first sentence, but not in the second.
49 'The Discourse Basis for Lexical Categories in Universal Grammar', 705.
50 Apropos of nouns, Hopper and Thompson also assign non-salient forms to the 'unmarked' class, while maximally salient forms are assigned to the 'marked' class. See ibid., 723.
51 In the long run, it probably makes even more sense to claim that *distinctions of salience* emerge out of an undifferentiated average foregrounding. For presumably the emergence of non-salient forms must also work changes in the nature of salience itself.
52 Jerrold J. Katz and Jerry Fodor, 1964, 'The Structure of a Semantic Theory', in *The Structure of Language: Readings in the Philosophy of Language*, 483.
53 See ibid, 505–13. The italicized meaning definitions are precisely as given by Katz and Fodor. Of course, there are several other senses of 'colourful' and 'ball'; but Katz and Fodor simplify their exposition by ignoring most of them, and I have simplified further by ignoring the sense of 'ball' as *solid-missile-for-projection-by-engine-of-war*.
54 Jerrold J. Katz, 1972, *Semantic Theory* (New York: Harper & Row), 106.
55 Dwight Bolinger, 1967, 'The Atomization of Meaning', in *Readings in the Psychology of Language*, ed. Leon Jakobovits and Murray Miron (Englewood Cliffs: Prentice-Hall).
56 Noam Chomsky, 1957, *Syntactic Structures* (The Hague: Mouton), 72.
57 See especially James McCawley, 1976, 'Where do Noun Phrases Come from?' and 'Semantic Representation', in *Grammar and Meaning* (New York: Academic Press), 133–54, 240–56.
58 For a good overall account of these developments, see Frederick J. Newmeyer, 1980, *Linguistic Theory in America* (New York: Academic Press).
59 I draw my account of Logical Form mainly from Chapter 9 of Liliane Haegeman, *Introduction to Government and Binding Theory*, and from Chapter 11 of Henk Van Riemsdijk and Edwin Williams, 1986, *Introduction to the Theory of Grammar* (Cambridge, Mass.: MIT Press).
60 For a typical list of the categories employed in Montague Grammar, see Richard Montague, 1974, *Formal Philosophy*, ed. Richmond Thomason (New Haven: Yale University Press), 249–50. Although I find it convenient to use the familiar terminology, it should be noted that Montague himself employs a slightly different terminology, in which a noun phrase appears as a 'term phrase', an intransitive verb as a 'one-place verb', an adverb modifying a sentence as an 'ad-formula', etc.
61 The numbers alongside the linguistic expressions are the numbers of the rules used in their production.
62 See *Formal Philosophy*, 152, 155.

63 I borrow this example from p. 21 of Thomason's introduction to *Formal Philosophy*. In fact, there are various kinds of adjective-to-noun combination which defy the extensional approach. For a good comprehensive presentation, see George L. Dillon, 1977, *An Introduction to Contemporary Semantics* (Englewood Cliffs: Prentice-Hall), 57–61.

64 Oddly enough, the entities and truth-values of Montague Grammar also derive from Husserl's division of linguistic meaning into either judgemental meaning or 'nominal' meaning – that is, either the kind of meaning to be found in whole sentences or the kind of meaning to be found in noun phrases. Husserl's influence descends to Montague by way of the two Polish logicians who first developed Categorial Grammar, Ajdukiewicz and Lesniewski. It is ironic that this division of meanings is precisely the aspect of Husserl's language theory which I criticized in the opening section of Chapter 7. From a syntagmatic point of view, Husserl missed his way to a truly phenomenological theory of language when he failed to recognize other non-'nominal' kinds of meaning below the level of the whole sentence.

65 This brief exposition is inevitably inadequate. One deliberate simplification and one deliberate misrepresentation will be corrected later. Even so, there are many further intricacies about which I shall remain silent – and doubtless more again about which I have remained ignorant. (It does not help matters that Montague developed his system through successive changing versions, and produced no final comprehensive formulation before his untimely death.)

66 I borrow the term *cancellation operation* from David Dowty, Robert Wall and Stanley Peters, 1981, *Introduction to Montague Semantics* (Dordrecht: D. Reidel), 85.

67 ibid., 145.

68 *Formal Philosophy*, 61–2.

69 Bernard Harrison is one philosopher who regards this problem as central, and insists that Analytical philosophy ought to provide an answer to it. Harrison's own answer relies upon the Wittgensteinian notion of 'family resemblances'. Unfortunately, he fails to temper this notion with any restraining principle (such as I have suggested in the 'Mechanism for change in *langue*' section of Chapter 3), thereby leaving resemblances to multiply endlessly and everywhere. See Bernard Harrison, 1979, *An Introduction to the Philosophy of Language* (London: Macmillan).

70 See Ray Jackendoff, 1985, *Semantics and Cognition* (Cambridge, Mass.: MIT Press), 29; and 1990, 'The Problem of Reality' (paper presented at the Max Planck Institute for Psycholinguistics, Nijmegen), 5, 30–2.

71 Ray Jackendoff, 1987, *Consciousness and the Computational Mind* (Cambridge, Mass.: MIT Press), 128.

72 Ray Jackendoff, 1990, *Semantic Structures* (Cambridge, Mass.: MIT Press), 11.

73 *Semantics and Cognition*, 94.

74 ibid., 52.

75 ibid., 56.

76 ibid., 63.

77 *Semantic Structures*, 9.

78 See *Semantics and Cognition*, 82–3.

79 *Semantic Structures*, 19.

80 The fullest discussion of preference rules is to be found in *Semantics and Cognition*, Chapter 8.

81 See *Semantic Structures*, 35–6.

82 ibid., 35.

83 Particularly important is the breakdown into necessary conditions, centrality conditions, and typicality conditions; and the discussion of default values. See *Semantics and Cognition*, Part III.

84 ibid., 150–1.

85 Recognizing related senses in a word, Jackendoff also avoids the usual premature appeal to metaphor whenever a word appears out of its ordinary context. In a review article written with David Aaron, he criticizes Lakoff and Turner for their readiness to discover metaphor everywhere. Under Jackendoff's approach, the verb 'move' requires no sudden figurative leap to appear in the expression 'Time moves', but only a perfectly natural extension along one arm of its meaning. See Ray Jackendoff and David Aaron, Review of *More than Cool Reason* by G. Lakoff and M. Turner, *Language* (forthcoming). Section 4.2 is especially relevant. See also *Semantics and Cognition*, 209–10.

86 *Consciousness and the Computational Mind*, 148.

87 *Semantic Structures*, 284.

88 See Ray Jackendoff, 1989, 'What is a Concept, that a Person may grasp it?', *Mind & Language*, IV, Nos 1–2, 87–8; and 'Parts and Boundaries', to appear in *Cognition* (see especially Sections 3 and 8.4). The relevant paragraphs of 'What is a Concept. . .?' are also reproduced in *Semantic Structures*, 28–9. In these writings, Jackendoff adduces a whole range of related examples.

89 See *Knowledge of Language: Its Nature, Origin and Use*, especially Chapter 2. Of course, the grounds for this distinction were built into Generative grammar from the very beginning.

90 See 'What is a Concept, that a Person may grasp it?', 69–75. The argument is repeated in *Semantic Structures*, 7–13.

PART V SYNTAGMATIC THEORY AND LITERATURE

1 Stéphane Mallarmé, 1965, 'Crisis In Verse', in *Mallarmé*, trans. Anthony Hartley (Harmondsworth: Penguin), 174–5. I have chosen to draw my quotations from Hartley's translation because it keeps very close to the original; but in this particular case, it may be useful to look also at a looser version from Bradford Cook:

> When I say: 'a flower!' then from that forgetfulness to which my voice consigns all floral form, something different from the usual calyces arises, something all music, essence, and softness: the flower which is absent from all bouquets.

See Stéphane Mallarmé, 1956, *Mallarmé: Selected Prose Poems, Essays & Letters*, trans. Bradford Cook (Baltimore: the Johns Hopkins University Press), 42.

2 See Richard Harland, 1987, *Superstructuralism* (London: Methuen), 150–3.

3 ibid., 152–3.

4 'Crisis in Verse', 171.

5 'Mystery in the Art of Letters', in *Mallarmé*, 203.

6 'Crisis in Verse', 169.

7 ibid.

8 ibid., 172.

9 Rainer Maria Rilke, 1987, *The Selected Poetry of Rainer Maria Rilke*, trans. Stephen Mitchell (London: Picador/Pan), 133. In the original German, these particular lines read:

> Türme schaute er so,
> daß sie erschraken:
> wieder sie bauend, hinan, plötzlich, in Einem!

So far as I can judge, the excellence of *Turning-Point* in translation is very much a reflection of the excellence of *Wendung* in German. Still, if anyone believes on principle that poetry is untranslatable, I am quite happy to claim that the English-language poem *Turning-Point* measures up with the best of Donne, Keats, Yeats, etc. In which case, my admiration for Rilke should simply be read as an admiration for Stephen Mitchell, the 'creator' of the poem in the English language.

10 Cleanth Brooks, 1949, *The Well Wrought Urn* (London: Dennis Dobson), 42, 42–3. I choose this as a particularly famous example, not as a particularly implausible one.
11 ibid., 42.
12 Cleanth Brooks, 1951, 'The Formalist Critic', *Kenyon Review*, XII, 72.
13 Ezra Pound, 1954, *Literary Essays of Ezra Pound*, ed. T. S. Eliot (London: Faber & Faber), 4.
14 *The Well Wrought Urn*, 178–9.
15 Roland Barthes, 1967, *Writing Degree Zero*, trans. Annette Lavers and Colin Smith (London: Jonathan Cape), 48.
16 See Roland Barthes, 1963, *On Racine*, trans. Richard Howard (New York: Hill & Wang).
17 Roman Jakobson, 1960, 'Linguistics and Poetics', in *Style in Language*, ed. Thomas A. Sebeok (Cambridge, Mass.: MIT Press), 358.
18 Roman Jakobson and Claude Lévi-Strauss, 1972, 'Charles Baudelaire's "Les Chats" ', in *The Structuralists: From Marx to Lévi-Strauss*, ed. Richard T. De George and Fernande M. De George (New York: Anchor Doubleday), 124–146.
19 Tzvetan Todorov, 1981, *Introduction to Poetics*, trans. Richard Howard (Minneapolis: University of Minnesota Press), 41.
20 Roland Barthes, 1987, *Criticism and Truth*, trans. Katrine Pilcher Keuneman (London: Athlone Press), 86–7.
21 Roland Barthes, 1986, 'The Death of the Author', in *The Rustle of Language*, trans. Richard Howard (Oxford: Basil Blackwell), 52–3.
22 ibid., 54.
23 For a further account of the relation between New Criticism and dissemination, see Chapter 10, Section (ii) of *Superstructuralism*.
24 'The Formalist Critic', 72.
25 *The Well Wrought Urn*, 203.
26 Roland Barthes, 1971, 'Style and its Image', in *Literary Style: A Symposium*, ed. Seymour Chatman (London: Oxford University Press), 10.
27 *The Well Wrought Urn*, 230.
28 'From Work to Text' in *The Rustle of Language*, 59.
29 William Empson, 1984, *Seven Types of Ambiguity* (London: Hogarth Press), 7.
30 ibid., 234.
31 W. K. Wimsatt and Monroe C. Beardsley, 1967, 'The Intentional Fallacy', in W. K. Wimsatt, *The Verbal Icon: Studies in the Meaning of Poetry* (Lexington: University of Kentucky Press), 5.
32 René Wellek and Austin Warren, 1963, *Theory of Literature* (Harmondsworth: Penguin), 42.
33 'The Death of the Author', in *The Rustle of Language*, 53.
34 ibid., 49.
35 Paul de Man, 1983, *Blindness and Insight* (Minneapolis: University of Minnesota Press), 137.
36 'The Intentional Fallacy', 4.
37 Monroe C. Beardsley, 1958, *Aesthetics: Problems in the Philosophy of Criticism* (New York: Harcourt, Brace & World), 25.
38 *The Well Wrought Urn*, 151.
39 ibid., 179.
40 Northrop Frye, 1964, *The Educated Imagination* (Bloomington: Indiana University Press), 93.
41 Paul de Man, 1986, *The Resistance to Theory* (Minneapolis: University of Minnesota Press), 11.

42 Ludwig Wittgenstein, 1967, *Philosophical Investigations*, trans. G. E. M. Anscombe (Oxford: Basil Blackwell), 33e, paragraph 69.

43 A Poststructuralist account of these same lines has been put forward by Richard A. Rand. See Richard A. Rand, 1981, 'Geraldine', in *Untying the Text: A Post-Structuralist Reader*, ed. Robert Young (London: Routledge & Kegan Paul). Predictably, Rand passes over everything that makes Coleridge's statements uncommon and striking, and discovers only the usual Poststructuralist 'meditation on the sign-structure' (pp. 288–9).

44 George Eliot, 1967, *Daniel Deronda* (Harmondsworth: Penguin), 736–7.

45 Marcel Proust, 1967, *Remembrance of Things Past*, trans. C. K. Scott Moncrieff (London: Chatto & Windus), VI, 34.

46 A somewhat similar line of argument is to be found in Chapter 6 of David Novitz's book, *Knowledge, Fiction and Imagination*. The similarity is evidently due to the fact that Novitz starts out from a version of the Romantic theory of the imagination – thus, his general philosophical position lies within the same tradition as the general philosophical position embraced in this book. See David Novitz, 1987, *Knowledge, Fiction and Imagination* (Philadelphia: Temple University Press).

PART VI SYNTAGMATIC THEORY AND TEXTUAL INTERPRETATION

1 Emile Durkheim and Marcel Mauss, 1963, *Primitive Classification*, trans. Rodney Needham (Chicago: University of Chicago Press), 77.

2 Claude Lévi-Strauss, 1970, *The Raw and the Cooked: Introduction to a Science of Mythology*, trans. John and Doreen Weightman (London: Jonathan Cape), 69.

3 ibid., 152.

4 ibid.

5 ibid., 152–3.

6 Claude Lévi-Strauss, 1978, *Structural Anthropology 2*, trans. Monique Layton (Harmondsworth: Penguin), 163.

7 Claude Lévi-Strauss, 1963, *Structural Anthropology*, trans. C. Jakobson and B. Grundfest Schoepf (New York: Basic Books), 224.

8 *The Raw and the Cooked*, 6.

9 Claude Lévi-Strauss, 1966, *The Savage Mind* (London: Weidenfeld & Nicolson), 56.

10 Salman Rushdie, 1982, *Midnight's Children* (London: Pan/Picador).

11 *Structural Anthropology 2*, 185–94.

12 Jean Piaget, 1971, *Structuralism*, trans. Chaninah Maschler (London: Routledge & Kegan Paul), 40.

13 *Structural Anthropology 2*, 115.

14 ibid., 275.

15 *The Raw and the Cooked*, 152.

16 ibid., 153.

17 See Roland Barthes, 1977, 'Rhetoric of the Image', in *Image–Music–Text*, trans. Stephen Heath (Glasgow: Fontana/Collins), 32–51.

18 Roland Barthes, 1973, *Mythologies*, trans. Annette Lavers (St Albans: Paladin), 115.

19 ibid., 121.

20 *Image–Music–Text*, 48.

21 *Mythologies*, 121.

22 ibid., 118.

23 *The Raw and the Cooked*, 13.

24 *Mythologies*, 119, 121.

25 Roland Barthes, 1983, *The Fashion System*, trans. Matthew Ward and Richard Howard (New York: Hill & Wang), 231.

26 Roland Barthes, 1971, 'Réponses', *Tel Quel*, XLVII, 97.
27 Louis Althusser, 1977, *For Marx*, trans. Ben Brewster (London: New Left Books), 168.
28 His attempts to rationalize this restriction occur especially on pp. x–xi of *The Fashion System*.
29 It is interesting that writers associated with the 'orality movement' also regard Plato as a crucial figure – but for reasons which are exactly the opposite of Derrida's. Walter Ong, for example, recognizes that Plato 'expresses serious reservations in the *Phaedrus* and his *Seventh Letter* about writing', but asserts nonetheless that 'the philosophical thinking Plato fought for depended entirely upon writing'. From Ong's point of view, Plato 'lived at the time when the alphabet had first become sufficiently interiorized to affect Greek thought . . . the time when patiently analytic, lengthily sequential thought processes were first coming into existence because of the ways in which literacy enabled the mind to process data'; paradoxically, 'Plato could formulate . . . his preference for orality over writing . . . only because he could write.' Walter J. Ong, 1982, *Orality and Literacy: The Technologizing of the Word* (London: Methuen), 24, 168. See also Eric Havelock, 1963, *Preface to Plato* (Cambridge, Mass.: Belknap Press).
30 Jacques Derrida, 1981, *Dissemination*, trans. Barbara Johnson (London: Athlone Press), 71.
31 ibid., 97.
32 ibid.
33 ibid.
34 ibid., 169.
35 ibid., 103. In fact, Derrida also blames Plato's French translators for narrowing and polarizing the meaning of the word; but since this second level of attack does not affect the form of Derrida's argument, I have chosen to ignore it here.
36 ibid., 69–70.
37 ibid., 71–2, 100–2.
38 ibid., 124, 124–5, 137, 99, 103.
39 ibid., 98–9.
40 ibid., 95.
41 For *pharmakeus*, see ibid., 117–19; for *pharmakos*, 130–4; for Socrates and the hemlock, 126–7.
42 ibid., 98.
43 ibid., 128.
44 ibid., 125–6.
45 For Derrida's discussion of Rousseau's *supplément*, see especially Part II of *Of Grammatology*, trans. Gayatri Chakravorty Spivak (Baltimore: Johns Hopkins University Press); for Mallarmé's *hymen*, see 'The Double Session', in *Dissemination*; for Kant's *parergon*, see 'Parergon' in Jacques Derrida, 1987, *The Truth in Painting*, trans. Geoff Bennington and Ian McLeod (Chicago: University of Chicago Press). It says something about Derrida's philosophical affiliations that Hegel uncovers a very similar paradoxicality in his favourite term *aufgehoben*. Normally translated as 'to cancel' or 'to supersede', this word signifies, according to Hegel, 'at once a *negating* and a *preserving*': and he uses the word as a kind of linguistic warrant for that special double movement which is characteristic of his whole system. G. W. F Hegel, 1977, *Phenomenology of Spirit*, trans. A. V. Miller (Oxford: Clarendon Press), 68.
46 *Dissemination*, 125–6, 70.
47 It may be remembered that I performed a somewhat similar trick with the verb 'catch', when, in order to emphasize oppositionality, I converted the sense of catching one's breath into the general principle of *halting an activity*, and the sense of something catching fire into the general principle of *an activity starting up*.

48 Jacques Derrida, *Writing and Difference*, trans. Alan Bass (London: Routledge & Kegan Paul), 178.

49 Samuel Beckett, 1964, *Endgame* (London: Faber & Faber), 26.

50 See Richard Harland, 1987, *Superstructuralism* (London: Methuen), 152. In the present book, the notion of a surrounding space or vacuum has appeared in the 'Syntagmatic side of poetry' section of Chapter 13, where I invoked the analogy of empty mental space created around the mantra in meditation.

51 See 'Limited Inc a b c', in Jacques Derrida and John Searle, 1988, *Limited Inc*, ed. Gerald Graff (Evanston: Northwestern University Press).

52 See *Superstructuralism*, Section (iv) of Chapter 9, especially the discussion of the closing pages of *The Archaeology of Knowledge*.

53 Michel Foucault, 1977, *Language, Counter-Memory, Practice*, ed. Donald F. Bouchard (New York: Cornell University Press), 154; and 1980, *Power/Knowledge*, ed. Colin Gordon (Brighton: Harvester Press), 114.

54 *Writing and Difference*, 61.

55 'Mon corps, ce papier, ce feu' is published as an appendix in the second French edition of Michel Foucault, 1972, *Folie et Déraison* (Paris: Gallimard).

56 Jean Baudrillard, 1982, 'Oublier Foucault', *Local Consumption*, Theoretical Strategies Issue (Sydney).

57 Jean Baudrillard, 1983, *Simulations*, trans. Paul Foss, Paul Patton and Philip Beitchman (New York: Semiotext(e)); and 1983, *In the Shadow of the Silent Majorities . . . Or, The End of the Social and Other Essays*, trans. Paul Foss, Paul Patton and John Johnston (New York: Semiotext(e)).

Bibliography

The following list contains all the titles cited in the notes, along with a selection of other relevant works.

Almeder, Robert, 1980, *The Philosophy of Charles S. Peirce: A Critical Introduction* (Oxford: Basil Blackwell).
Alston, William P., 1964, *The Philosophy of Language* (Englewood Cliffs: Prentice-Hall).
Althusser, Louis, 1977, *For Marx*, trans. Ben Brewster (London: New Left Books).
Angelelli, Ignacio, 1967, *Studies on Gottlob Frege and Traditional Philosophy* (Dordrecht: D. Reidel).
Austin, J. L., 1962, *How to Do Things with Words* (Oxford: Clarendon Press).
Ayer, A. J., 1982, *Philosophy in the Twentieth Century* (London: Weidenfeld & Nicolson).
Bach, Kent, and Harnish, Robert M., 1979, *Linguistic Communication and Speech Acts* (Cambridge, Mass.: MIT Press).
Bachelard, Suzanne, 1968, *A Study of Husserl's 'Formal and Transcendental Logic'*, trans. Lester E. Embree (Evanston: Northwestern University Press).
Barry, Peter (ed.), 1987, *Issues in Contemporary Critical Theory* (London: Macmillan).
Barthes, Roland, 1963, *On Racine*, trans. Richard Howard (New York: Hill & Wang).
—— 1967, *Elements of Semiology*, trans. Annette Lavers and Colin Smith (New York: Hill & Wang).
—— 1967, *Writing Degree Zero*, trans. Annette Lavers and Colin Smith (London: Jonathan Cape).
—— 1971, 'Réponses', *Tel Quel*, 47.
—— 1971, 'Style and its Image', in *Literary Style: A Symposium*, ed. Seymour Chatman (London: Oxford University Press).
—— 1972, *Critical Essays*, trans. Richard Howard (Evanston: Northwestern University Press).
—— 1973, *Mythologies*, trans. Annette Lavers (St Albans: Paladin).
—— 1975, *S/Z*, trans. Richard Miller (London: Jonathan Cape).
—— 1977, *Image–Music–Text*, trans. Stephen Heath (Glasgow: Fontana/Collins).
—— 1983, *The Fashion System*, trans. Matthew Ward and Richard Howard (New York: Hill & Wang).
—— 1986, *The Rustle of Language*, trans. Richard Howard (Oxford: Basil Blackwell).
—— 1987, *Criticism and Truth*, trans. Katrine Pilcher Keuneman (London: Athlone Press).
Bartlett, Frederic C., 1932, *Remembering* (Cambridge: Cambridge University Press).
Bates, Elizabeth, *et al.*, 1979, *The Emergence of Symbols: Cognition and Communication in Infancy* (New York: Academic Press).
Baudrillard, Jean, 1982, 'Oublier Foucault', *Local Consumption*, Theoretical Strategies Issue (Sydney).

—— 1983, *In the Shadow of the Silent Majorities . . . Or, The End of the Social and Other Essays*, trans. Paul Foss, Paul Patton and John Johnston (New York: Semiotext(e)).
—— 1983, *Simulations*, trans. Paul Foss, Paul Patton and Philip Beitchman (New York: Semiotext(e)).
Beardsley, Monroe C., 1958, *Aesthetics: Problems in the Philosophy of Criticism* (New York: Harcourt, Brace & World).
—— 1970, *The Possibility of Criticism* (Detroit: Wayne State University Press).
Beckett, Samuel, 1964, *Endgame* (London: Faber & Faber).
Bell, David, 1990, *Husserl* (London: Routledge).
Belsey, Catherine, 1980, *Critical Practice* (London: Methuen).
Bennett, Jonathan, 1976, *Linguistic Behaviour* (Cambridge: Cambridge University Press).
Berman, Art, 1988, *From the New Criticism to Deconstruction* (Chicago: University of Illinois Press).
Beth, Evert W., and Piaget, Jean, 1966, *Mathematical Epistemology and Psychology*, trans. W. Mays (Dordrecht: D. Reidel).
Black, Max, 1970, *The Margins of Precision: Essays in Language and Literature* (Ithaca: Cornell University Press).
—— 1972, *The Labyrinth of Language* (Harmondsworth: Penguin).
Blackburn, Simon, 1984, *Spreading the Word* (Oxford: Clarendon Press).
Blake, Barry J., 1990, *Relational Grammar* (London: Routledge).
Bloom, Harold, *et al.*, 1979, *Deconstruction and Criticism* (London: Routledge & Kegan Paul).
Bloom, Lois, 1973, *One Word at a Time* (The Hague: Mouton).
Bolinger, Dwight, 1967, 'The Atomization of Meaning', in *Readings in the Psychology of Language*, ed. Leon Jakobovits and Murray Miron (Englewood Cliffs: Prentice-Hall).
Brooks, Cleanth, 1949, *The Well Wrought Urn* (London: Dennis Dobson).
—— 1951, 'The Formalist Critic', *Kenyon Review*, XII.
—— 1967, *Modern Poetry and the Tradition* (Chapel Hill: University of North Carolina Press).
—— 1987, 'Irony as a Principle of Structure', in *Debating Texts*, ed. Rick Rylance (Milton Keynes: Open University Press).
Bruns, Gerald L., 1974, *Modern Poetry and the Idea of Language* (New Haven: Yale University Press).
Carnap, Rudolf, 1956, *Meaning and Necessity* (Chicago: University of Chicago Press).
Chappell, V. C., 1964, *Ordinary Language: Essays in Philosophical Method* (Englewood Cliffs: Prentice-Hall).
Chisholm, Roderick M., 1952, 'Intentionality and the Theory of Signs', *Philosophical Studies*, III.
—— 1957, *Perceiving: A Philosophical Study* (Ithaca: Cornell University Press).
—— 1965, 'The Problem of Empiricism', in *Perceiving, Sensing, and Knowing*, ed. Robert Swartz (New York: Doubleday).
—— 1966, *Theory of Knowledge* (Englewood Cliffs: Prentice-Hall).
Chomsky, Noam, 1957, *Syntactic Structures* (The Hague: Mouton).
—— 1961, 'Some Methodological Remarks on Generative Grammar', *Word*, XVII, 219–39.
—— 1965, *Aspects of the Theory of Syntax* (Cambridge, Mass.: MIT Press).
—— 1966, 'Linguistic Theory', in *Language Teaching: Broader Contexts*, ed. Robert G. Mead, Jr (Northeast Conference Reports).
—— 1972, *Language and Mind* (enlarged edition) (New York: Harcourt Brace Jovanovich).
—— 1976, *Reflections on Language* (London: Temple Smith).

—— 1980, 'On Cognitive Structures and their Development', in *Language and Learning: The Debate between Jean Piaget and Noam Chomsky*, ed. M. Piattelli-Palmarini (London: Routledge & Kegan Paul).
—— 1981, *Lectures on Government and Binding* (Dordrecht: Foris).
—— 1982, *The Generative Enterprise* (Dordrecht: Foris).
—— 1986, *Knowledge of Language: Its Nature, Origin and Use* (New York: Praeger).
Chomsky, Noam, and Miller, George, 1963, 'Introduction to the Formal Analysis of Natural Languages', in *Handbook of Mathematical Psychology*, ed. P. Luce, R. Bush and E. Galanter (New York: John Wiley).
Cohen, Jonathan L., 1971, 'Some Remarks on Grice's Views about the Logical Particles of Natural Language', in *Pragmatics of Natural Languages*, ed. Yehoshua Bar-Hillel (Dordrecht: D. Reidel).
Cole, Peter, and Sadock, Jerrold (eds), 1977, *Syntax and Semantics 8: Grammatical Relations* (New York: Academic Press).
Cook, V. J., 1988, *Chomsky's Universal Grammar* (Oxford: Basil Blackwell).
Cooper, David E., 1973, *Philosophy and the Nature of Language* (London: Longman).
Corrado, Michael, 1975, *The Analytic Tradition in Philosophy: Background and Issues* (Chicago: American Library Association).
Creswell, M. J., 1988, *Semantical Essays: Possible Worlds and their Rivals* (Dordrecht: Kluwer Academic Publishers).
Croft, William, 1990, *Typology and Universals* (Cambridge: Cambridge University Press).
Cromer, Richard F., 1974, 'The Development of Language and Cognition: The Cognition Hypothesis', in *New Perspectives in Child Development*, ed. Brian Foss (Harmondsworth: Penguin).
Culler, Jonathan, 1975, *Structuralist Poetics: Structuralism, Linguistics and the Study of Literature* (London: Routledge & Kegan Paul).
—— 1981, *The Pursuit of Signs: Semiotics, Literature, Deconstruction* (London: Routledge & Kegan Paul).
—— 1982, *On Deconstruction: Theory and Criticism after Structuralism* (Ithaca: Cornell University Press).
Dasenbrock, Reed Way (ed.), 1989, *Redrawing the Lines: Analytic Philosophy, Deconstruction and Literary Theory* (Minneapolis: University of Minnesota Press).
Davidson, Donald, 1984, *Inquiries into Truth and Interpretation* (Oxford: Clarendon Press).
—— 1986, 'A Coherence Theory of Truth and Knowledge', in *Truth and Interpretation*, ed. E. LePore (Oxford: Basil Blackwell).
Davis, Robert Con, and Schleifer, Robert (eds), 1989, *Contemporary Literary Criticism: Literary and Cultural Studies* (London: Longman).
Davis, Steven, 1976, *Philosophy and Language* (Indianapolis: Bobbs-Merrill).
de Laguna, Grace, 1927, *Speech: Its Functions and Development* (New Haven: Yale University Press).
de Man, Paul, 1979, *Allegories of Reading: Figural Language in Rousseau, Nietzsche, Rilke, and Proust* (New Haven: Yale University Press).
—— 1983, *Blindness and Insight* (Minneapolis: University of Minnesota Press).
—— 1986, *The Resistance to Theory* (Minneapolis: University of Minnesota Press).
Deleuze, Gillès and Guattari, Félix, 1981, 'Rhizome', trans. Paul Foss and Paul Patton, *Ideology and Consciousness*, VIII.
Derrida, Jacques, 1973, *Speech and Phenomena: and Other Essays on Husserl's Theory of Signs*, trans. David B. Allison (Evanston: Northwestern University Press).
—— 1974, *Of Grammatology*, trans. Gayatri Chakravorty Spivak (Baltimore: Johns Hopkins University Press).
—— 1978, *Writing and Difference*, trans. Alan Bass (London: Routledge & Kegan Paul).

—— 1981, *Dissemination*, trans. Barbara Johnson (London: Athlone Press).
—— 1981, *Positions*, trans. Alan Bass (London: Athlone Press).
—— 1982, *Margins of Philosophy*, trans. Alan Bass (Chicago: University of Chicago Press).
—— 1987, *The Truth in Painting*, trans. Geoff Bennington and Ian McLeod (Chicago: University of Chicago Press).
Derrida, Jacques, and Searle, John, 1988, *Limited Inc*, ed. Gerald Graff (Evanston: Northwestern University Press).
Dillon, George L., 1977, *An Introduction to Contemporary Semantics* (Englewood Cliffs: Prentice-Hall).
Dowty, David, Wall, Robert and Peters, Stanley, 1981, *Introduction to Montague Semantics* (Dordrecht: D. Reidel).
Dreyfus, Hubert L. (ed.), 1982, *Husserl, Intentionality and Cognitive Science* (Cambridge, Mass.: MIT Press).
Durkheim, Emile, and Mauss, Marcel, 1963, *Primitive Classification*, trans. Rodney Needham (Chicago: University of Chicago Press).
Eco, Umberto, 1976, *A Theory of Semiotics* (Bloomington: Indiana University Press).
Edie, James M., 1976, *Speaking and Meaning: The Phenomenology of Language* (Bloomington: Indiana University Press).
—— 1987, *Edmund Husserl's Phenomenology: A Critical Commentary* (Bloomington: Indiana University Press).
Eliot, George, 1967, *Daniel Deronda* (Harmondsworth: Penguin).
Ellis, John M., 1989, *Against Deconstruction* (Princeton: Princeton University Press).
Ellis, Willis D. (ed.), 1938, *A Source Book of Gestalt Psychology* (London: Routledge & Kegan Paul).
Empson, William, 1952, *The Structure of Complex Words* (London: Chatto & Windus).
—— 1984, *Seven Types of Ambiguity* (London: Hogarth Press).
Felix, Sacha W., 1978, 'Some Differences between First and Second Language Acquisition', in *The Development of Communication*, ed. N. Waterson and C. Snow (New York: John Wiley).
Fodor, Janet Dean, 1977, *Semantics: Theories of Meaning in Generative Grammar* (Hassocks, Sussex: Harvester Press).
Fodor, Jerry A., Bever, Thomas and Garrett, M. F., 1974, *The Psychology of Language* (New York: McGraw-Hill).
Fodor, Jerry A. and Katz, Jerrold J. (eds), 1967, *The Structure of Language: Readings in the Philosophy of Language* (Englewood Cliffs: Prentice-Hall).
Foucault, Michel, 1972, 'Mon corps, ce papier, ce feu', in the second French edition of *Folie et Déraison* (Paris: Gallimard).
—— 1977, *Language, Counter-Memory, Practice*, ed. Donald F. Bouchard (New York: Cornell University Press).
——— 1980, *Power/Knowledge*, ed. Colin Gordon (Brighton: Harvester Press).
Frege, Gottlob, 1953, *The Foundations of Arithmetic*, trans. J. L. Austin (Oxford: Basil Blackwell).
—— 1960, *Philosophical Writings of Gottlob Frege*, trans. Peter Geach and Max Black (Oxford: Basil Blackwell).
Frye, Northrop, 1957, *Anatomy of Criticism: Four Essays* (Princeton: Princeton University Press).
—— 1964, *The Educated Imagination* (Bloomington: Indiana University Press).
Gazdar, Gerald, 1979, *Pragmatics: Implicature, Presupposition and Logical Form* (New York: Academic Press).
Givón, Talmy, 1979, *On Understanding Grammar* (New York: Academic Press).
—— (ed.), 1979, *Syntax and Semantics, XII: Discourse and Syntax* (New York: Academic Press).

—— 1980, 'The Binding Hierarchy and the Typology of Complement', *Studies in Language*, IV.
Graff, Gerald, 1979, *Literature Against Itself: Literary Ideas in Modern Society* (Chicago: University of Chicago Press).
Greenfield, Patricia Marks, and Smith, Joshua H., 1976, *The Structure of Communication in Early Language Development* (New York: Academic Press).
Grice, Paul, 1989, *Studies in the Way of Words* (Cambridge, Mass.: Harvard University Press).
Gurwitsch, Aron, 1964, *The Field of Consciousness* (Pittsburgh: Duquesne University Press).
—— 1974, *Phenomenology and the Theory of Science* (Evanston: Northwestern University Press).
Haegeman, Liliane, 1991, *Introduction to Government and Binding Theory* (Oxford: Basil Blackwell).
Haiman, John, 1985, *Natural Syntax: Iconicity and Erosion* (Cambridge: Cambridge University Press).
—— (ed.), 1985, *Iconicity in Syntax* (Amsterdam/Philadelphia: John Benjamins).
Hammond, Michael, Moravcsik, Edith and Wirth, Jessica (eds), 1988, *Studies in Syntactic Typology* (Amsterdam: John Benjamins).
Harland, Richard, 1987, *Superstructuralism* (London: Methuen).
Harrari, Josué V. (ed.), 1980, *Textual Strategies: Perspectives in Post-Structuralist Criticism* (London: Methuen).
Harris, Roy, 1980, *The Language-Makers* (London: Duckworth).
—— 1981, *The Language Myth* (London: Duckworth).
—— (ed.), 1983, *Approaches to Language* (Oxford: Pergamon Press).
—— 1987, *The Language Machine* (Ithaca: Cornell University Press).
—— 1988, *Language, Saussure and Wittgenstein: How to Play Games with Words* (London: Routledge).
Harrison, Bernard, 1979, *An Introduction to the Philosophy of Language* (London: Macmillan).
Havelock, Eric, 1963, *Preface to Plato* (Cambridge, Mass.: Belknap Press).
Hawkins, John A. (ed.), 1988, *Explaining Language Universals* (Oxford: Basil Blackwell).
Hegel, G. W. F., 1977, *Phenomenology of Spirit*, trans. A. V. Miller (Oxford: Clarendon Press).
Heine, Bernd, Claudi, Ulrike and Hünnemeyer, Friederike, 1991, *Grammaticalization: A Conceptual Framework* (Chicago: University of Chicago Press).
Hintikka, K. J. J., Moravcsik, J. M. E., and Supes, P., 1973, *Approaches to Natural Language* (Dordrecht: D. Reidel).
Hirsch, E. D., 1967, *Validity in Interpretation* (New Haven: Yale University Press).
——— 1976, *The Aims of Interpretation* (Chicago: University of Chicago Press).
Hopper Paul J. (ed.), 1982, *Tense-Aspect: Between Semantics and Pragmatics* (Amsterdam: John Benjamins).
—— 1987, 'Emergent Grammar', *Berkeley Linguistics Society*, XIII.
—— 1988, 'Emergent Grammar and the A Priori Grammar Postulate', in *Linguistics in Context: Connecting Observation and Understanding*, ed. Deborah Tannen (New Jersey: Ablex).
Hopper, Paul J., and Thompson, Sandra A., 1984, 'The Discourse Basis for Lexical Categories in Universal Grammar', *Language*, LX, No. 3.
Horrocks, Geoffrey, 1987, *Generative Grammar* (London: Longman).
Hudson, G., 1972, 'Is Deep Structure Linear?', *UCLA Papers in Syntax*, II, 51–77.
Hudson, Richard A., 1976, *Arguments for a Non-Transformational Grammar* (Chicago: University of Chicago Press).
Husserl, Edmund, 1969, *Formal and Transcendental Logic*, trans. Dorion Cairns (The Hague: Martinus Nijhoff).

—— 1970, *Logical Investigations*, trans. J. N. Findlay (London: Routledge & Kegan Paul).
Ingarden, Roman, 1985, *Selected Papers in Aesthetics* (Washington: The Catholic University of America Press).
Iser, Wolfgang, 1974, *The Implied Reader* (Baltimore: Johns Hopkins University Press).
Jackendoff, Ray, 1972, *Semantic Interpretation in Generative Grammar* (Cambridge, Mass.: MIT Press).
—— 1977, *X̄-Syntax: A Study of Phrase Structure* (Cambridge, Mass.: MIT Press).
—— 1985, *Semantics and Cognition* (Cambridge, Mass.: MIT Press).
—— 1987, *Consciousness and the Computational Mind* (Cambridge, Mass.: MIT Press).
—— 1989, 'What is a Concept, that a person may Grasp it?', *Mind & Language*, IV, Nos. 1–2.
—— 1990, *Semantic Structures* (Cambridge, Mass.: MIT Press).
—— 1990, 'The Problem of Reality' (paper presented at the Max Planck Institute for Psycholinguistics, Nijmegen).
—— 'Parts and Boundaries', *Cognition* (forthcoming).
Jackendoff, Ray, and Aaron, David, Review of *More than Cool Reason*, by G. Lakoff and M. Turner, *Language* (forthcoming).
Jakobson, Roman, 1960, 'Linguistics and Poetics', in *Style in Language*, ed. Thomas A. Sebeok (Cambridge, Mass.: MIT Press).
Jakobson, Roman, and Lévi-Strauss, Claude, 1972, 'Charles Baudelaire's "Les Chats" ', in *The Structuralists: From Marx to Lévi-Strauss*, ed. Richard T. De George and Fernande M. De George (New York: Anchor Doubleday).
Johnson, Barbara, 1980, *The Critical Difference: Essays in the Contemporary Rhetoric of Reading* (Baltimore: Johns Hopkins University Press).
Johnson, David, and Postal, Paul, 1979, *Arc Pair Grammar* (Princeton: Princeton University Press).
Joyce, James, 1960, *Ulysses* (London: The Bodley Head).
Juhl, P. D., 1980, *Interpretation: An Essay in the Philosophy of Literary Criticism* (Princeton: Princeton University Press).
Katz, David, 1951, *Gestalt Psychology: Its Nature and Significance*, trans. Robert Tyson (London: Methuen).
Katz, Jerrold J., 1972, *Linguistic Philosophy: The Underlying Reality of Language and its Philosophical Importance* (London: Allen & Unwin).
—— 1972, *Semantic Theory* (New York: Harper & Row).
Katz, Jerrold J., and Postal, Paul, 1964, *An Integrated Theory of Linguistic Descriptions* (Cambridge, Mass.: MIT Press).
Kempson, Ruth, 1977, *Semantic Theory* (Cambridge: Cambridge University Press).
Klein-Andreu, Flora, 1983, *Discourse Perspectives on Syntax* (New York: Academic Press).
Kockelmans, Joseph K. (ed.), 1967, *Phenomenology* (New York: Doubleday Anchor).
Kraft, Victor, 1969, *The Vienna Circle: The Origin of Neo-Positivism* (New York: Greenwood Press).
Kripke, Saul A., 1980, *Naming and Necessity* (Oxford: Basil Blackwell).
Kristeva, Julia, 1980, *Desire In Language*, trans. Thomas Gora, Alice Jardine and Leon S. Roudiez (Oxford: Basil Blackwell).
Lacan, Jacques, 1968, *The Language of the Self*, trans. Anthony Wilden (New York: Delta Books).
Lakoff, George, 1972, 'Linguistics and Natural Logic', in *Semantics of Natural Language*, ed. Donald Davidson and Gilbert Harman (Dordrecht: D. Reidel).
—— 1975, 'Pragmatics in Natural Logic', in *Formal Semantics of Natural Language*, ed. E. L. Keenan (Cambridge: Cambridge University Press).

Lasnik, Howard, and Kuprin, J., 'A Restrictive Theory of Transformational Grammar', *Theoretical Linguistics*, IV, iii, 173–96.

Leitch, Vincent B., 1983, *Deconstructive Criticism: An Advanced Introduction* (New York: Columbia University Press).

Lenneberg, Eric, 1967, *Biological Foundations of Language* (New York: John Wiley).

Lévi-Strauss, Claude, 1963, *Structural Anthropology*, trans. C. Jakobson and B. Grundfest Schoepf (New York: Basic Books).

—— 1966, *The Savage Mind* (London: Weidenfeld & Nicolson).

—— 1970, *The Raw and the Cooked: Introduction to a Science of Mythology*, trans. John and Doreen Weightman (London: Jonathan Cape).

—— 1978, *Structural Anthropology 2*, trans. Monique Layton (Harmondsworth: Penguin).

Lewis, David, 1973, *Counterfactuals* (Oxford: Basil Blackwell).

Lodge, David (ed.), 1972, *20th Century Literary Criticism: A Reader* (London: Longman).

—— (ed.), 1988, *Modern Criticism and Theory: A Reader* (London: Longman).

McCawley, James, 1976, *Grammar and Meaning* (New York: Academic Press).

McGinn, Colin, 1984, *Wittgenstein on Meaning: An Interpretation and Evaluation* (Oxford: Basil Blackwell).

MacNamara, John, 1972, 'The Cognitive Basis of Language Learning in Infants', *Psychological Review*, LXXIX.

McNeill, David, 1970, *The Acquisition of Language: The Study of Developmental Psycholinguistics* (New York: Harper & Row).

Mallarmé, Stéphane, 1956, *Mallarmé: Selected Prose Poems, Essays & Letters*, trans. Bradford Cook (Baltimore: Johns Hopkins Press).

—— 1965, *Mallarmé*, trans. Anthony Hartley (Harmondsworth: Penguin).

Martinich, A. P. (ed.), 1985, *The Philosophy of Language* (Oxford: Oxford University Press).

Merleau-Ponty, Maurice, 1973, *Consciousness and the Acquisition of Language*, trans. Hugh Silverman (Evanston: Northwestern University Press).

—— 1976, *Phenomenology of Perception*, trans. Colin Smith (London: Routledge & Kegan Paul).

Miller, J., Chapman, R., Branston, M., and Reichle, J., 1980, 'Language Comprehension in Sensorimotor Stages V and VI', *Journal of Speech and Hearing Research*, XXIII.

Miller, J. Hillis, 1982, *Fiction and Repetition: Seven English Novels* (Cambridge, Mass.: Harvard University Press).

Mitchell, Sollace, and Rosen, Michael, 1983, *The Need For Interpretation* (London: Athlone Press).

Montague, Richard, 1974, *Formal Philosophy*, ed. Richmond Thomason (New Haven: Yale University Press).

Morgan, Jerry, *et al.*, 1976, 'Topics in Relational Grammar', *Studies in the Linguistic Sciences*, 6.1, 47–248.

Mundle, C. K. W., 1970, *A Critique of Linguistic Philosophy* (Oxford: Clarendon Press).

Munitz, Milton K., 1981, *Contemporary Analytic Philosophy* (London: Macmillan).

Naremore, Rita C. (ed.), 1984, *Language Science* (San Diego: College-Hill Press).

Natanson, Maurice, 1973, *Edmund Husserl: Philosopher of Infinite Tasks* (Evanston: Northwestern University Press).

Neisser, Ulric, 1967, *Cognitive Psychology* (New York: Appleton-Century-Crofts).

Newmeyer, Frederick J., 1980, *Linguistic Theory in America* (New York: Academic Press).

Newton, K. M. (ed.), 1988, *Twentieth-Century Literary Theory* (London: Macmillan Education).

—— 1990, *Interpreting the Text* (London: Harvester Wheatsheaf).

Norris, Christopher, 1985, *The Contest of Faculties* (London: Methuen).

Novitz, David, 1987, *Knowledge, Fiction and Imagination* (Philadelphia: Temple University Press).

Ong, Walter J., 1982, *Orality and Literacy: The Technologizing of the Word* (London: Methuen).

Pap, Arthur, 1972, *The Elements of Analytic Philosophy* (New York: Hefner Publishing).

Parkinson, G. H. R. (ed.), 1968, *The Theory of Meaning* (London: Oxford University Press).

Partee, Barbara (ed.), 1975, 'Montague Grammar and Transformational Grammar', *Linguistic Inquiry*, VI.

—— 1976, *Montague Grammar* (New York: Academic Press).

Peirce, C. S., 1934, *Collected Papers of Charles Sanders Peirce*, ed. Charles Hartshorne and Paul Weiss (Cambridge, Mass.: Belknap Press).

Perlmutter, David, 1982, 'Syntactic Representation, Syntactic Levels, and the Notion of Subject', in *The Nature of Syntactic Representation*, ed. Pauline Jacobson and Geoffrey K. Pullum (Dordrecht: D. Reidel).

Peterson, T., 1971, 'Multi-ordered Base Structures in Generative Grammer', in *Papers from the 7th Regional Meeting of the Chicago Linguistic Society*, 181–92.

Peursen, Cornelius A. Van, 1972, *Phenomenology and Analytical Philosophy* (Pittsburgh: Duquesne University Press).

Piaget, Jean, 1929, *The Child's Conception of the World*, trans. Joan and Andrew Tomlinson (London: Routledge & Kegan Paul).

—— 1971, *Insights and Illusions of Philosophy*, trans. W. Mays (New York: Meridian Books).

—— 1971, *Psychology and Epistemology*, trans. A. Rosin (New York: Viking)

—— 1971, *Structuralism*, trans. Chaninah Maschler (London: Routledge & Kegan Paul).

Piaget, Jean, and Inhelder, Barbel, 1966, *The Psychology of the Child*, trans. H. Weaver (New York: Harper).

—— 1969, 'The Gaps in Empiricism', in *Beyond Reductionism*, ed. A. Koestler and J. R. Smythies (Boston: Beacon Press).

Plantinga, Alvin, 1974, *The Nature of Necessity* (Oxford: Clarendon Press).

Pound, Ezra, 1954, *Literary Essays of Ezra Pound*, ed. T. S. Eliot (London: Faber & Faber).

Pratt, Mary Louise, 1977, *Towards a Speech Act Theory of Literary Discourse* (Bloomington: Indiana University Press).

Proust, Marcel, 1967, *Remembrance of Things Past*, trans. C. K. Scott Moncrieff (London: Chatto & Windus).

Pullum, Geoffrey, 1979, *Rule Interaction and the Organization of a Grammar* (New York: Garland).

Putnam, Hilary, 1975, *Philosophical Papers, II: Mind, Language and Reality* (Cambridge: Cambridge University Press).

Quine, Willard Van Orman, 1960, *Word and Object* (Cambridge, Mass.: MIT Press).

—— 1964, *From a Logical Point of View* (Cambridge, Mass.: Harvard University Press).

Ramberg, Bjorn T., 1989, *Donald Davidson's Philosophy of Language: An Introduction* (Oxford: Basil Blackwell).

Ramsay, F. P., 1964, 'Facts and Propositions', in *Truth*, ed. George Pitcher (Englewood Cliffs: Prentice-Hall).

Ray, William, 1984, *Literary Meaning: From Phenomenology to Deconstruction* (Oxford: Basil Blackwell).

Rice, Phillip, and Waugh, Patricia (eds), 1989, *Modern Literary Theory: A Reader* (London: Edward Arnold).

Riemsdijk, Henk, and Williams, Edwin, 1986, *Introduction to the Theory of Grammar* (Cambridge, Mass.: MIT Press).

Rilke, Rainer Maria, 1987, *The Selected Poetry of Rainer Maria Rilke*, trans. Stephen Mitchell (London: Picador/Pan).

Roche, Maurice, 1973, *Phenomenology, Language and the Social Sciences* (London: Routledge & Kegan Paul).

Rodgon, Maris Monitz, 1976, *Single-Word Usage, Cognitive Development, and the Beginnings of Combinatorial Speech* (Cambridge: Cambridge University Press).

Ross, John R., 1970, 'On Declarative Sentences', in *Readings in English Transformational Grammar*, ed. R. A. Jacobs and P. S. Rosenbaum (Waltham: Ginn).

Rushdie, Salman, 1982, *Midnight's Children* (London: Pan/Picador).

Russell, Bertrand, 1946, *The Problems of Philosophy* (London: Oxford University Press).

Ryle, Gilbert, 1957, 'The Theory of Meaning', in *British Philosophy in the Mid-Century: A Cambridge Symposium*, ed. C. A. Mace (London: Allen & Unwin).

—— 1963, *The Concept of Mind* (Harmondsworth: Penguin/Peregrine).

Sajama, Seppo and Kamppinen, Matti, 1987, *A Historical Introduction to Phenomenology* (London: Croom Helm).

Saussure (de), Ferdinand, 1966, *Course in General Linguistics*, ed. Charles Bally, Albert Sechehaye and Albert Riedlinger, trans. Wade Baskin (New York: McGraw-Hill).

Searle, John, 1969, *Speech Acts: An Essay in the Philosophy of Language* (Cambridge: Cambridge University Press).

—— (ed.), 1971, *The Philosophy of Language* (London: Oxford University Press).

—— 1979, *Expression and Meaning* (Cambridge: Cambridge University Press).

—— 1983, *Intentionality: An Essay in the Philosophy of Mind* (Cambridge: Cambridge University Press).

Searle, John, Kiefer, Ferenc and Bierwisch, Manfred (eds),1980, *Speech Act Theory and Pragmatics* (Dordrecht: D. Reidel).

Seung, T. K., 1982, *Semiotics and Thematics in Hermeneutics* (New York: Columbia University Press).

Sluga, Hans, 1980, *Gottlob Frege* (London: Routledge & Kegan Paul).

Smith, Neil, and Wilson, Deirdre, 1979, *Modern Linguistics: The Results of Chomsky's Revolution* (Bloomington: Indiana University Press).

Sokolkowski, Robert, 1974, *Husserlian Meditations: How Words Present Things* (Evanston: Northwestern University Press).

Stalnaker, Robert, 1968, 'A Theory of Conditionals', in *Studies in Logical Theory*, ed. N. Rescher (Oxford: Basil Blackwell).

Strawson, P. F., 1952, *Introduction to Logical Theory* (London: Methuen).

—— 1965, 'Truth: A Reconsideration of Austin's Views', *Philosophical Quarterly*, XV, 289–301.

Strawson, P. F., and Austin, J. L., 1950, 'Symposium on Truth', *Proceedings of the Aristotelian Society*, Supplementary Volume 24.

Tarski, Alfred, 1944, 'The Semantic Conception of Truth and the Foundation of Semantics', *Philosophy and Phenomenological Research, IV: Symposium on Meaning and Truth.*

—— 1956, *Logic, Semantics, Metamathematics: Papers from 1923 to 1938*, trans. J. H. Woodger (Oxford: Clarendon Press).

Thurley, Geoffrey, 1983, *Counter-Modernism in Current Critical Theory* (London: Macmillan).

Todorov, Tzvetan, 1981, *Introduction to Poetics*, trans. Richard Howard (Minneapolis: University of Minnesota Press).

Tugendhat, Ernst, 1982, *Traditional and Analytical Philosophy*, trans. P. A. Gomer (Cambridge: Cambridge University Press).

Urmson, J. O., 1956, *Philosophical Analysis* (Oxford: Clarendon Press).

Verhaar, John W. M., 1973, 'Phenomenology and Present-Day Linguistics', in *Phenomenology and the Social Sciences*, I, ed. Maurice Natanson (Evanston: Northwestern University Press).

Walker, Ralph, 1975, 'Conversational Implicatures', in *Meaning, Reference and Necessity*, ed. Simon Blackburn (Cambridge: Cambridge University Press).

Wellek, René, and Warren, Austin, 1963, *Theory of Literature* (Harmondsworth: Penguin).

Werner, Heinz, and Kaplan, Bernard, 1963, *Symbol Formation* (New York: John Wiley).

Wimsatt, W. K., 1967, *The Verbal Icon: Studies in the Meaning of Poetry* (Lexington: University of Kentucky Press).

Wittgenstein, Ludwig, 1967, *Philosophical Investigations*, trans. G. E. M. Anscombe (Oxford: Basil Blackwell).

—— 1981, *Tractatus Logico-Philosophicus*, trans. C. K. Ogden (London: Routledge & Kegan Paul).

Young, Robert (ed.), 1981, *Untying the Text: A Post-Structuralist Reader* (London: Routledge & Kegan Paul).

Zabeeh, Farhang, Klemke, E. D. and Jacobson, Arthur (eds), 1974, *Readings in Semantics* (Urbana: University of Illinois Press).

Zaner, Richard M., 1970, *The Way of Phenomenology: Criticism as a Philosophical Discipline* (New York: Pegasus).

Index

Printed in the United Kingdom
by Lightning Source UK Ltd.
135790UK00003B/171/A

9 780415 063593

Expanding Nursing and
Health Care Practice

Series Editor: Lynne Wigens

Management of Pain

A practical approach for health care professionals

Kathleen Mac Lellan

Published in 2006 by:
Nelson Thornes Ltd
Delta Place
27 Bath Road
CHELTENHAM
GL53 7TH
United Kingdom

06 07 08 09 10 / 10 9 8 7 6 5 4 3 2 1

A catalogue record for this book is available from the British Library

ISBN 0-7487-9621-5

Cover photograph by Stockbyte RF (NT)
Illustrations by Florence Production Ltd, Stoodleigh, Devon
Page make-up by Florence Production Ltd, Stoodleigh, Devon

Printed and bound by UniPrint Hungary Kft, Székesfehérvár

Contents

Important Notice

The various methods of management of pain both pharmacological and others are subjects of on-going research and debate. As such evidence changes rapidly, all health professionals should continuously update and review new evidence as it emerges. Pain management should be based on the best available evidence. Good evidence is likely to come from good systematic reviews of good clinical trials. Whilst every effort has been made in this book to ensure that best evidence is presented, health care professionals should always consult drug company literature, local and national protocols and other sources of evidence before utilising pain interventions detailed. The accuracy, currency or completeness of the information on the websites and information sources listed cannot be guaranteed and no legal liability or responsibility is assumed.

Introduction

This book aims to support health professionals during their undergraduate education and as they start out as qualified health professionals to understand and provide appropriate, effective pain management. All health professionals are in the privileged position to ensure that the patients they care for, whether in the community or in hospital, receive care that ensures that their pain is minimised and that both functional activity and quality of life are maximised. Modern health care supports the concept that patients receive better care when health professionals work as a team and provide evidence-based care. There are no benefits for patients to endure pain and indeed, as this book outlines, the prevalence of pain is the cause of many adverse effects from reduced quality of life to decreased lung volumes, myocardial ischaemia, decreased gastric and bowel motility and anxiety. Planned, strategic approaches to pain management are emphasised in the book. The evidence suggests that it is not always new approaches that are needed, that the key to effective pain management is often good and systematic use of current methods of pain management.

Chapter 1 provides the foundation for this book outlining contemporary definitions of pain and associated terms. Pain management as part of health and social policy is detailed in **Chapter 2**, which outlines socio-economic and quality-of-life issues. The management of pain has evolved over time with the introduction of specialist pain services and new therapeutic interventions including new medicines. These are described in **Chapter 3**. **Chapter 4** provides an overview of the physiology of pain including illustrations of the nervous system linking these with the processes of pain management techniques. Many factors from anxiety to culture are thought to influence the pain experience as described in **Chapter 5**. **Chapter 6** reviews the common pain assessment techniques and tools. The array of pain interventions including medications, transcutaneous electrical nerve stimulation (TENs) and behavioural therapy are detailed in **Chapter 7**. **Chapter 8** reviews complementary therapies and their role in pain management. Management of acute pain including chest pain, postoperative pain and pain in the emergency department are outlined in **Chapter 9**.

Chapter 10 provides a review of chronic pain including back pain and arthritis. The principles of palliative care are outlined in **Chapter 11**. **Chapter 12** is the concluding chapter and highlights the role of nurses and health professionals in pain management.

The most important message for you, as a health professional, emerging from this book is the **critical role of evidence-based practice**. Evidence for pain management is the subject of ongoing research and debate. As such evidence changes rapidly, all health professionals should continuously update and review developments. Good evidence is likely to come from sound systematic reviews of well-planned clinical trials. This means that you as a health professional must be able to access, understand and interpret research in order to provide evidence-based care.

1 Definitions of pain and associated terms

Learning outcomes

By the end of this chapter you should be able to:

- ★ Detail contemporary definitions of pain and associated terms
- ★ Understand the difficulties in defining pain
- ★ Appreciate the main ways of classifying pain
- ★ Outline the main components of a pain care service.

Introduction

This chapter provides an overview of the definitions of pain and associated terms. These definitions provide the foundation for the chapters that follow where more detail is provided on the particular subject areas. Numerous definitions of pain are available, all attempting to provide meaning to a complex phenomenon that has been debated and researched over time. This chapter will look at the more common definitions of pain as well as how pain is classified. These classifications can be based on a number of factors, such as intensity and duration and whether it is acute or chronic in nature. Key resources for research and information on pain are provided throughout.

Defining pain – a contemporary debate

Within the field of health care you will come across people experiencing pain in almost all clinical settings, both within acute clinical specialties and in the community. The pain experience of the older adult with arthritis in a nursing home differs from the pain of a 20-year-old who has undergone surgery for a sports injury to the knee. The sting of a wasp will cause severe pain for one adult and minimal pain in another. It is these contradictions that create the debate, difficulties and interest in defining and understanding pain.

Everyone has experienced pain at some time thus each individual has an innate sense of what pain is, based on their personal experiences. The experience of the person is influenced by past encounters with pain, physical and mental wellbeing, culture and coping mechanisms.

It is therefore reasonable to state that while much is known about the physiology of pain, the sensory and emotive aspects of pain can be difficult to interpret, separate and describe. The interactions of the mind and body in the production and perception of pain therefore are ongoing subjects for research and debate.

Defining pain is a difficult task and the definitions provided try to encompass a phenomenon with many facets. It is in the context of these considerations that this chapter provides an overview of the more common definitions of pain.

Keywords

Nociception
A neurophysiologic term which denotes activity in the nerve pathways

Pain and **nociception** can be considered two different terms. Pain is a subjective experience that accompanies nociception, but can also arise without any physiological stimuli, such as due to an emotional response. Pain can be present in the absence of tissue damage or inflammation, for instance a person can experience a headache but not necessarily have a nociceptive stimulus or tissue damage.

Background to defining pain

In order to contextualise and interpret pain definitions, a brief overview of the process of the pain experience is provided here. Chapter 4 discusses this further and provides a detailed account of the physiology of pain.

Pain is part of the functioning of the nervous system – both central and peripheral. At the peripheral nervous level, free nerve endings called nociceptors send pain messages via a series of nerve fibres or neurones (this is called nociception) to the central nervous system entering it at the spinal cord. **Synapses** occur at the dorsal horn of the grey matter of the spinal cord which comprises layers or laminae of cells.

Keywords

Synapse
Nerve impulses are conducted from one neuron to another across a synapse – a junction between two neurons

The signal then reaches the sensory cortex of the brain via the ascending pain pathways where it can be distributed to other centres in the brain for analysis and the attribution of meaning, linking it with emotions and motor activity. Pain is a key component of the body's defence system. It is part of the rapid warning system. For example, if a person accidentally touches a hot barbeque grill and burns his/her hand the nerve endings in the skin will send messages to the brain via stimulation of the nerve endings (nociceptors). These messages are relayed, via the dorsal horn of the spinal cord and the ascending pain pathways, to the brain. The response may be emotional such as crying or motor such as moving the affected area, i.e. removing the hand from the grill. The individual therefore experiences the pain in a subjective manner. The extent of the pain is directly related to the size and depth of the burn and the individual's personal emotional response to the pain.

Reflective activity

Pain is a common experience yet defining it is elusive.
Consider this statement; can you define pain in a way that will allow you to manage your patients' pain?
What are the pros and cons of this statement?

Definitions of pain

Pain refers to a category of complex experiences, not to a specific sensation that varies only along a single-intensity dimension. There are numerous aspects to pain. Pain can be described as a private and internal sensation that cannot be directly observed or measured. A person's experience of pain is influenced by past experience, family attitudes, culture, meaning of the situation, attention, anxiety, suggestion and other factors unique to the individual. Pain appears to have three main dimensions: **sensory**, **emotional** and **intensity**. So, it is understandable that people suffering a similar pain experience that pain differently.

Keywords

Pain dimensions:

Sensory
The nature of the pain, e.g. ache, sharp, burning

Emotional
Pain feelings, e.g. frustration, anger, fed up, depression, annoyance

Intensity
Strength or severity of the pain, e.g. on a scale of 1–10 with 1 being no pain and 10 severe pain

One of the more common definitions of pain that has emerged is McCaffrey's: 'Pain is whatever the experiencing patient says it is, existing whenever he says it does'. This 1972 definition is a 'catch all' that could describe pain in any setting of any severity. The difficulty with this definition is that it is almost an approach or philosophy to pain management. It does, however, provide a strong foundation for the need for individual pain assessment and management. A weakness is that McCaffrey's 1972 definition relies on the person being able to describe his/her own pain. Many people are unable to or have difficulty describing their own pain for example patients receiving assisted respiratory ventilation or confused patients.

Another well-known definition is supplied by the International Association for the Study of Pain (1994):

> Pain is an unpleasant sensory and emotional experience associated with actual or potential tissue damage, or described in terms of such damage.
>
> Notes accompanying definition:
>
> Note 1: The inability to communicate verbally does not negate the possibility that an individual is experiencing pain and is in need of appropriate pain-relieving treatment.
>
> Note 2: Pain is always subjective. Each individual learns the application of the word through experiences related to injury in early life. Biologists recognise that those stimuli which cause pain are liable to damage tissue. Accordingly, pain is the experience we associate with actual or potential tissue damage. It is unquestionably a sensation in a part of the body, but it is also always unpleasant, and therefore is also an emotional experience.
>
> Experiences which resemble pain but are not unpleasant e.g. pricking should not be called pain. Unpleasant abnormal

> experiences (dysesthesias) may also be pain but not necessarily so because, subjectively, they may not have the usual qualities of pain.
>
> Many people report pain in the absence of tissue damage or any likely pathological cause and usually this happens for psychological reasons. There is usually no way to distinguish this experience from that due to tissue damage. If a person regards their experience as pain caused by tissue damage, it should be accepted as pain. This definition avoids tying pain to a physiological stimulus. Activity induced in the nociceptor and nociceptive pathways by a noxious stimulus is not pain, which is always a psychologic state, even though we may well appreciate that pain most often has a proximate physical cause.

This definition given by the International Association for the Study of Pain, although lengthy, is quite helpful in teasing out the complex nature of pain. It attempts to draw together the many facets of the pain experience, and it encompasses both the nociception and the emotional aspects of pain.

Crombie *et al.* (1999) provide the following definition:

> Pain is an unpleasant sensory and emotional experience associated with actual or potential tissue damage or described in terms of such damage. Acute pain is associated with acute injury or disease. Chronic pain is defined as pain that has persisted for longer than three months or past the expected time of healing following injury or disease. Patients with cancer may suffer from both acute and chronic pain. Epidemiological studies have revealed widespread unrelieved pain throughout society.

This definition is quite practical in that it describes the pain sensation and also gives a sense of the meaning of the much utilised categories of pain: acute and chronic.

Dame Cicely Saunders is responsible for coining the term 'total pain' which captures not only the physical but also the psychological, social and spiritual components of suffering, as developed and illustrated by Robert Twycross (2003). Embracing the concept of total pain helps to remind health care professionals that the personal experience of pain is far deeper than just the physical pain.

The true sense of what pain is begins to emerge as we read the variety of available definitions. Each definition, on its own, adds to an understanding of the phenomenon of pain. It is clear that pain is not a simple phenomenon.

> **Over to you**
>
> At your next journal club, clinical supervisory session, or in-service session review your management of the last patient you dealt with who presented with pain. Present to your colleagues how you assessed that pain, how you managed it and how you communicated this to the patient and others involved in the care. Detail two of the definitions of pain outlined above and discuss whether they supported your decision making.

Classification of pain

The definitions of pain previously discussed give a sense of the broadness of the term pain which can be used to encompass many facets of the same phenomena. Pain is classified in a number of ways according to the type of pain, source of pain, speed of transmission of nerve signals or associated problems/pains. These classifications are detailed further in Chapter 4. Figure 1.1 illustrates these classifications.

Category of pain

Pain is described as having two main categories: acute and chronic.

Acute pain subsides as healing takes place, i.e. it has a predictable end and it is of brief duration, usually less than six months. Acute pain often means sudden severe pain. An example would be postoperative pain felt after surgery.

Chronic pain is prolonged. It is pain that persists beyond the usual healing phase of the disease process. An example is low back pain that persists beyond 3–6 months.

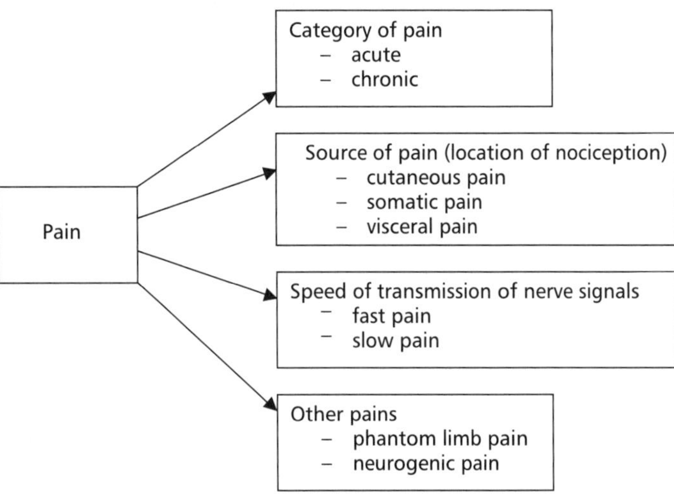

Figure 1.1 Classification of pain

Source of pain

The source or site of pain provides another classification of pain. The source of the pain influences a number of the reactions of the body to the pain.

Cutaneous pain is produced by stimulation of the pain receptors in the skin. It can be accurately localised due to the large number of receptors in the skin. An example would be the pain from a first-degree burn injury.

Somatic pain is produced by stimulation of pain receptors in the deep structures, i.e. muscles, bones, joints, tendons, ligaments. Unlike cutaneous pain, somatic pain is dull, intense and prolonged. An example could be the pain caused by an ankle fracture.

Visceral pain is that produced by stimulation of pain receptors in the viscera. Visceral nociceptors are located within body organs and internal cavities. It is poorly localised and often radiates to other sites. An example of this type of pain is myocardial ischaemia which is often felt in the left upper arm or shoulder.

Speed of transmission of nerve signals

Two types of nerve transmit pain signals from the peripheral nervous system to the central nervous system: A-delta and C fibres. See Figure 1.2.

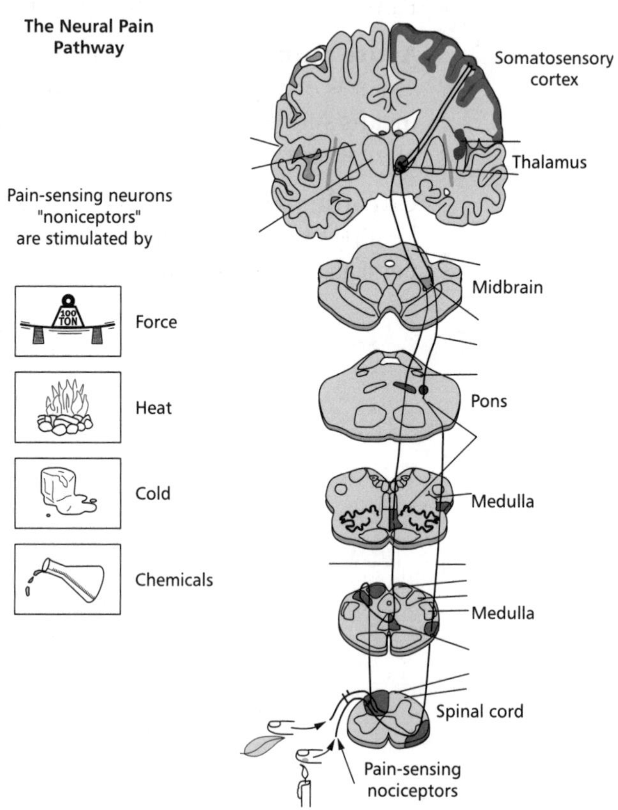

Figure 1.2 Line diagram of pain pathways

Fast pain is transmitted by A-delta fibres. It occurs very rapidly, usually within 0.1 seconds after the stimulus is applied, and is not felt in the deeper tissues of the body. This type of pain is also known as sharp, fast and pricking pain. An example is pain felt from a needle puncture or a knife cut into the skin.

Slow pain is transmitted by C fibres. C fibres take slightly longer than A-delta fibres to transmit pain and terminate over a wide area of the brain stem and thalamus. These slow pain signals are not relayed to the somatosensory cortex and are difficult to localise. An example of this type of pain is a toothache.

Other pains

There are other pains or associated problems that do not fit neatly into the above classifications yet are important to understand. Some examples are given here.

Phantom limb pain is the sensation of pain from an absent or inert limb – an experience sometimes discussed by amputees or quadriplegics.

Neuropathic pain or neuralgia can occur as a result of injury or disease to the nerve tissue itself. An example this might be trigeminal neuralgia.

Mr Jones is a 69-year-old with peripheral vascular disease. He returns from theatre with a right below-knee amputation. During the night he complains of a tingling sensation and pain in his right toe.

Consider how you would explain to Mr Jones why he has such a pain.

Pain management

Pain management is an overall term used to describe the care provided for those in pain. Pain management encompasses pain assessment, pain treatment, pain interventions, pain therapies, pain audit, staff and patient education and any other activities involved in providing care and services for those with pain. Pain management approaches are tailored to the clinical situations involved. Aspects of pain management are discussed throughout this book, with pain audit detailed in Chapter 2 and pain interventions examined in Chapter 7.

How would you define pain management for your clinical setting?

Keywords

Intensity
The strength of the pain, e.g. how severe the pain is

Quality
The character of the pain, e.g. throbbing, aching

Location
The site of the pain, e.g. right upper arm

Pain assessment

Pain assessment can be defined as the determination of the **intensity**, **quality**, **location** and duration of pain. In relation to pain assessment a number of terms are used to describe the methods and tools. The following is a brief overview of the terms. Chapter 6 provides more detail on these.

Pain assessment tools tend to be either single or multidimensional (see Figures 1.3 and 1.4).

VRS: comprises four to five words descriptive of pain, of which the patient picks the word which best describes their pain. Each word has a score and the patient's intensity score is the number associated with the word they choose as most descriptive of their pain level. For example, words like mild, moderate or severe pain could be used with each word getting a score.

VAS: consists of a straight line, the ends of which are defined in terms of the extreme limits of the pain experience. The number corresponding to the patient's mark on the line is their pain intensity score.

NRS: this is a variation of the VAS and consists of asking the patient to rate their pain on a numerical scale 0–10. The number on the scale that the patient chooses is their pain intensity score.

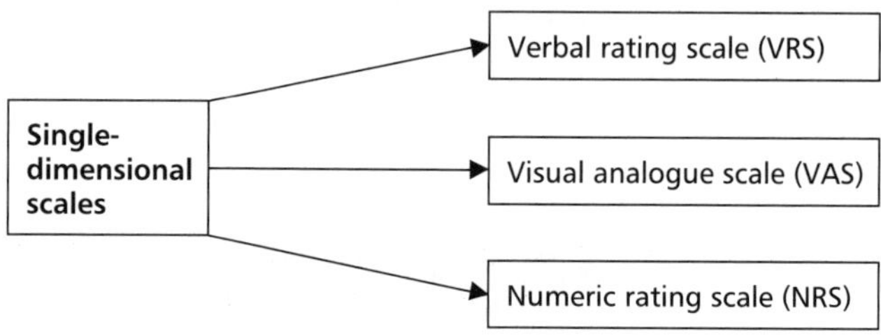

Figure 1.3 Examples of single-dimensional scales

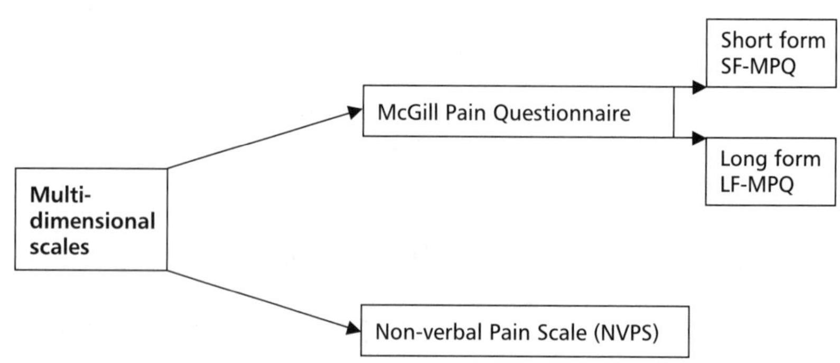

Figure 1.4 Examples of multidimensional scales

MPQ: The McGill Pain Questionnaire (MPQ) both long (LF-MPQ) and short (SF-MPQ) forms are multidimensional scales involving subscales, which represent different aspects of pain.

NVPS: attempts to capture all aspects of pain multidimensional scales for those patients who cannot verbalise their pain experience.

Pain services

The breadth of care required to manage pain has provided numerous challenges to health care professionals. In the early 1980s, it began to emerge that the need to have dedicated staff to support pain management was critical if progress was to be made in the everyday management of pain. It was evident that pain could be targeted better by recognising that particular areas of pain practice were becoming too specialised for generalist practitioners to manage effectively. A number of terms began to emerge under the broad term 'pain service' such as pain teams, acute pain services, pain clinics, chronic pain services, pain management programmes and palliative care services. A **pain service** is an umbrella term to encompass the various services that have emerged such as pain teams, pain clinics etc.

A number of desirable characteristics emerge which help in defining pain services.

It should be noted that various expert organisations have standards and detailed requirements for such services. Specialised services in acute pain, chronic pain and palliative care have emerged. Even within the specific area of pain care, sub-specialties have developed, e.g. neuropathic pain, migraine. The critical issue was the need to focus specialised knowledge and skills towards this important aspect of patient care, and the speciality in question. These developments allow for dedicated time and resources from health professionals to support and develop more effective processes for pain management. Chapter 3 discusses the evidence base for acute pain services and the key components of chronic pain services.

Keywords

Pain service
A dedicated facility for specific classifications of pain that provides diagnosis, treatments and interventions as appropriate. The facility is staffed by a multidisciplinary team with committed time and resources. The pain service has a philosophy of continuous quality improvement and education and empowerment of other health care staff

Palliative care services

The World Health Organization describes palliative care as an approach that improves the quality of life of patients and their families facing the problems associated with life-threatening illness, through the prevention and relief of suffering by means of early identification and impeccable assessment and treatment of pain and other problems, physical, psychosocial and spiritual (Sepulveda *et al.*, 2002). Implicit in palliative care is the provision of relief from pain and other distressing symptoms.

Everyone facing a life-threatening illness will need some degree of supportive care in addition to treatment for their condition. The National Institute for Clinical Excellence (NICE, 2004: 18) describes supportive care for people with cancer as follows: 'Supportive care helps the patient and their family to cope with their condition and treatment of it – from pre-diagnosis, through the process of diagnosis and treatment, to cure, continuing illness or death and into bereavement. It helps the patient to maximise the benefits of treatment and to live as well as possible with the effects of the disease. It is given equal priority alongside diagnosis and treatment.'

Supportive care should be fully integrated with diagnosis and treatment. The elements it encompasses are shown in Figure 1.5.

Chapter 11 provides in-depth material in relation to palliative care.

A number of qualities emerge as defining characteristics of pain services as shown in Figure 1.6.

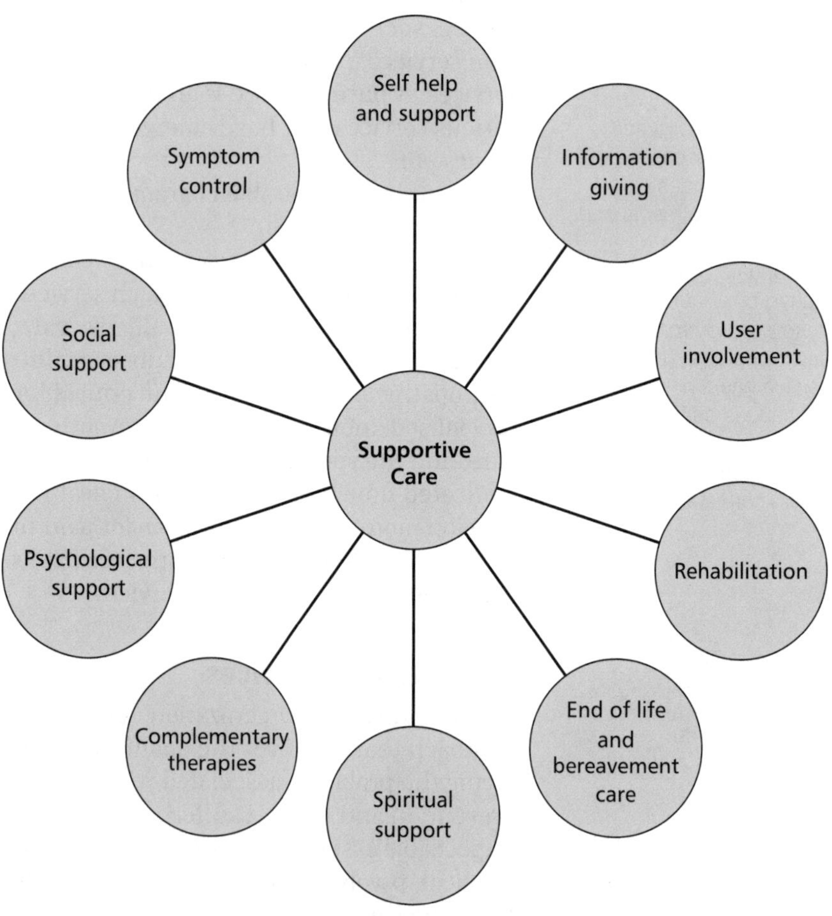

Figure 1.5 The elements of supportive care required in palliative services

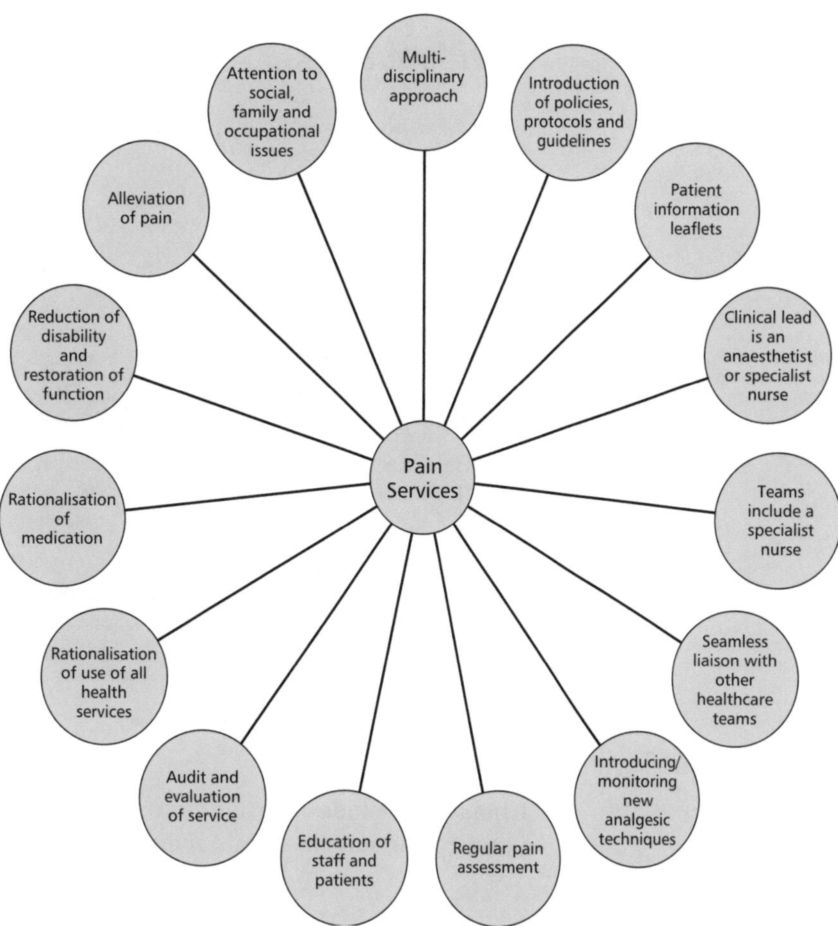

Figure 1.6 Essential requirements of pain services

Evidence base

Go to this website: www.iasp-pain.org and review International Association for the Study of Pain: desirable characteristics for pain treatment facilities (1990).

When you are reviewing the characteristics of pain treatment facilities consider how you treat pain in your clinical setting. Is there anything that could enhance how this pain is managed?

Evidence-based resources for pain and its management

The management of pain and its associated definitions are the subject of ongoing intense research and debate. As such evidence changes rapidly, all health professionals should continuously update and review developments.

Evidence base

The following are some key resource websites and journals that you should look at.

Key resources

- The Royal College of Anaesthetists, 48/49 Russell Square, London WC1B 4JY. www.rcoa.ac.uk
- The Pain Society, 21 Portland Place, London W1B 1PY. www.britishpainsociety.org
- International Association for the Study of Pain (IASP), 909 NE 43rd St., Suite 306, Seattle, WA 98105–6020, USA. www.iasp-pain.org
- Bandolier Internet site which accompanies *Bandolier's Little Book of Pain* (Moore *et al.*, 2004). www.ebandolier.com
- *Journal of Pain Medicine and Palliative Care*
- *Pain* (the journal)
- *Journal of Pain and Symptom Management*
- *Clinical Journal of Pain*

Chapter 2 includes further discussion in relation to evidence-based practice and its role in pain management.

Key points Top tips

- Pain is a complex phenomenon and, therefore, difficult to define
- Pain is classified in a number of ways: according to type of pain, source of pain, speed of transmission of nerve signals or other pains
- Specialised services in acute pain, chronic pain and palliative care have emerged
- Pain management encompasses pain assessment, pain treatment, pain interventions, pain therapies, pain audit, staff and patient education and any other activities involved in providing care and services for those with pain.
- A pain service is a dedicated facility for a specific classification of pain which provides diagnosis, treatment and intervention as appropriate. The facility is staffed by a multidisciplinary team with committed time and resources. The pain service has a philosophy of continuous quality improvement and education and empowerment of other health care staff
- Evidence for pain changes rapidly – health professionals need access to quality evidence-based journals and websites

Pain affecting quality of life

Liz is a housewife who has two children, aged 11 and 16. The children are very sporty and the 11-year-old is an excellent hockey player. They usually play in the local grounds but also have to travel to neighbouring counties for matches. Her partner is a builder and labourer who travels with a building contractor all over the country. He is generally only home at weekends. Liz is very active in the local community and has been very involved in running a number of fundraising events for the school. She used to spend two mornings a week on voluntary duty in the local older persons' home. Liz has always been very popular in the community and, with a good sense of fun, has been a welcome addition to local events. Two years ago a car travelling at high speed ran into the back of Liz's car. She suffered a severe whiplash neck injury and had to have intensive physiotherapy for more than a year. She was on nonsteroidal anti-inflammatory medications for 12 months.

After the accident, Liz had to give up her voluntary work. She is unable to be as involved in community events as she would have liked. Her children are getting older and becoming more independent. Liz's neck has improved a lot although she continues to have chronic aches and pains in her neck. Liz's doctor has advised her not to go back to work in the older persons' home as this could exacerbate her neck pain. Liz has started to become less outgoing and has begun to avoid the local social events. If she is feeling stressed the neck pain becomes more acute and she has started to get regular headaches. Her doctor can't find any cause for the headaches. Liz's quality of life is much poorer than it was two years ago.

- What are the main features of Liz's pain?
- How would you define her pain?
- What is the source of Liz's pain?

Rapid recap

1. What are main dimensions of pain?
2. What is the main message for health care professionals coming from the more common definitions of pain?
3. Which parts of the nervous system are concerned with the transmission of pain?
4. List five desirable characteristics of a pain care service.

References

Crombie I.K., Croft P.R., Lindon S.J., Resche L. and Von Korff M. (eds.). (1999) *Epidemiology of Pain*. IASP Press, Seattle.

IASP Task Force on Taxonomy (1994) *Classification of Chronic Pain*, 2nd edn, (eds. Merskey H. and Bogduk N.) IASP Press, Seattle.

McCaffrey M. (1972) Pain in the context of nursing care. In: *Nursing Management of the Patient with Pain.* J.B. Lippincott Company, Toronto p. 8.

The National Institute for Clinical Excellence (2004) *Guidance on Cancer Services. Improving Supportive and Palliative Care for Adults with Cancer: The Manual* (available at www.nice.org.uk/pdf/csgspmanual.pdf).

Sepulveda C., Marlin A., Yoshida T. and Ulrich A. (2002) Palliative Care: The World Health Organization's Global Perspective. *Journal of Pain Symptom Management.* **24**(2): 91–96.

Twycross, R. (2003) *Introducing palliative care*, 4th edn. Radcliffe Medical Press, Oxon.

2 Health and social policy issues in pain management

Learning outcomes

By the end of this chapter you should be able to:

- ★ Understand why pain should form part of health and social policy
- ★ Detail the prevalence of pain
- ★ Discuss integrated approaches to pain management
- ★ Explain how evidence-based practice and clinical auditing are involved in effective pain management.

Introduction

This chapter will help you to consider the broader context of pain. By taking into account the implications of national and international collaboration on standards and guidelines, pain as a public health issue is addressed. Evidence-based approaches and processes are provided as the foundation for all health professionals to ensure best practice. The concepts of quality and integrated approaches to pain management are also considered.

Pain as a public health issue

Pain has become a world public health issue. Both acute and chronic pain are often poorly managed, for many reasons, including culture, attitude, education and logistics. The gap between an increasingly sophisticated knowledge of pain and its treatment and the effective application of knowledge is large and widening (Brennan and Cousins 2004). Under-treated severe pain is associated with a number of harmful effects including decreased lung volumes, myocardial ischaemia, decreased gastric and bowel motility and anxiety (Macintyre and Ready, 2002). The economic and social cost of pain is high.

The economic burden of pain may be evaluated by considering the following:

- direct costs (medical expenditure, such as the cost of prevention, detection, treatment, rehabilitation, long-term care and ongoing, medical and private expenditure)
- indirect costs (lost work output attributable to a reduced capacity for activity, lost productivity, lost earnings, lost opportunities for family members, lost earnings of family members and lost tax revenue)
- intangible costs (psychosocial burden resulting in reduced quality of life, such as job stress, economic stress, family stress and suffering).

Pain management is of proven benefit in improving the quality of life of patients. When untreated, pain can cause helplessness, depression, isolation, family breakdown and inappropriate disability (CSAG, 2000). For example, one study of chronic pain demonstrated that lower levels of quality of life were associated with loss of efficiency in the workplace and eventual absenteeism (Lamers *et al.*, 2005). Annual costs of chronic pain in Canada are in excess of $10 billion based on direct care costs. This does not include the less quantifiable costs of quality of life and productivity (Chronic Pain Association of Canada, 2004). Pain is clearly an issue that should form part of health and social policy.

Enhancing quality of life

Mary is 42 and has had rheumatoid arthritis for 10 years. She suffers constant pain and has considerable reduced mobility. She has had to reduce her working hours in the local library to 15 hours per week and attends her general practitioner monthly.

Mary is admitted to the local hospital emergency department with acute pain in her right knee.

- How has Mary's quality of life been affected?
- As a health professional, what could you do to enhance Mary's quality of life?

International collaboration is an expanding feature of public health. Increasingly, it is recognised that public health issues transcend national boundaries, and The International Association for the Study of Pain and the World Health Organization (WHO) have led the way on raising global awareness of poorly relieved acute pain as a major factor contributing to the delayed recovery of health and function after surgery and trauma. They have also highlighted the immense burden of chronic pain unrelated to cancer. The WHO's influence on governments worldwide and on national health care programmes and policies is seen to lay the ground work for better management of acute and chronic pain and improved health-related quality of life in a number of major diseases and conditions that involve pain (Bond and Breivik, 2004).

The WHO has had immense impact on health care policies and in changing the culture of pain relief for cancer pain and symptom control (Bond and Breivik, 2004). The WHO analgesic ladder was a major landmark in the management of pain (see Chapter 7 for further information on the analgesic ladder). It recommended cheap, widely available and effective analgesics. It was a strong simple message that changed the culture of cancer pain management. It can be seen from the World Cancer Report that worldwide medical use of morphine is increasing significantly (Stewart and Kleihues, 2003).

The core purposes of public health centre around:

- health promotion including the wider public health
- improving quality of clinical standards and
- protection of public health and management of risk (Hunter, 2003).

The common understanding of public health and the implications of pain and its management place pain as a broad public health issue worldwide. This understanding increases the imperative for health care providers to review current processes and management techniques for pain.

Clinical Caseload

You need to be constantly reviewing the way you undertake pain care. For instance, we have recently changed our way of managing the administration of oral morphine solution. Previously the Trust had treated all concentrations of Oramorph as controlled drugs even though there was no legal requirements to treat low concentrations like 10mg in 5ml in this way. Information obtained from the Department of Health, the Royal Pharmaceutical Society and the Nursing and Midwifery Council helped the pain care team to convince the Trust that deregulating Oramorph would be acceptable. We worked with the pharmacists, doctors and nurses to get policies in place that were acceptable to everyone. The acute pain team introduced a local education programme delivered through individual face-to-face sessions (doctor to doctor, nurse to nurse) rather than through seminars. This ensured that the process had minimal impact on clinical commitments, and that the tutorials were designed to reflect the likely concerns and anxieties of professionals. This now means that pain relief when required is given more speedily as there is no delay due to the controlled drug procedures, and what was great was that this change in pain care management has been reflected in improved patient satisfaction with their pain care treatment.

The right to pain relief and the consideration that poor management of pain constitutes negligence have led to a vibrant debate among key stakeholders. Indeed Haugh (2005) describes case studies where patients and families sue health care providers for inadequate pain management. The International Association for the Study of Pain suggests that there is no single 'right' to pain relief; instead there is a constellation of 'rights', each with a variable degree of legal enforceability. Reform in current pain management will depend on a combination of approaches including education for health care undergraduates, adoption of universal pain management standards by professional bodies, the promotion of legislative reform, liberalisation of national policies on opioid availability, reduction of cost of analgesics, domestic pain treatment forums and continued lobbying of the major stakeholders (Brennan and Cousins, 2004).

Prevalence of pain

It will be obvious, anecdotally, how prevalent pain is in most health care and community settings. This prevalence is not always measured; however, there are some studies which detail the statistics in various care

Keywords

Prevalence of pain
The proportion of individuals in a population who have pain at a specific instant (Prevalence = number of individuals with pain/total population at a given point in time)

Incidence of pain
The proportion of individuals in a population who get pain during a specified period of time (Incidence = number of new individuals with pain/total population at risk of pain)

settings. Comparisons of **prevalence** and **incidence** can be difficult due to differing definitions, methods of measurement and reporting.

Over to you

Consider the patient profile within your current clinical setting.Is pain prevalence audited? If not complete this simple quick task:

- Estimate the prevalence of pain in your clinical area.
- Take a simple numeric rating scale and do a point prevalence for 10 patients (this will take about five minutes).

Are the pain levels what you expected? How do they compare to national and international statistics?

Pain in hospitals

Various surveys have measured the extent and prevalence of pain in hospital settings. In 1994 a survey of 5150 hospital patients found that 61% suffered pain, 87% of whom had severe or moderate pain (Bruster *et al.*, 1994). In another survey 80–89% of patients surveyed were experiencing pain with 45.8–57.2% of patients reporting moderate to severe pain, yet 90% of patients were satisfied or very satisfied with the pain management provided. These were hospital patients from both medical and surgical areas (Comley and DeMeyer, 2001).

Postoperative pain studies demonstrate that patients still suffer moderate to severe pain after their surgery (Weis *et al.*, 1983; Donovan *et al.*, 1987; Melzack *et al,*. 1987; Kuhn *et al.*, 1990; Owen *et al.*, 1990; Wilder-Smith and Schuler L., 1992; Watt-Watson *et al.*, 2001; Mac Lellan, 2004). The issue of persistent acute pain following tissue damage after surgery or chronicity of acute pain is relevant. For example, Bay-Nielson (2001) highlight that, one year after inguinal hernia repair, pain is common (28.7%) and is associated with functional impairment in more than half of those with pain.

Pain is cited as the number one reason for attending emergency departments. Cordell *et al.* (2002) on reviewing patients' charts over one week (n = 1665) found a prevalence of 52.2% of pain as the chief complaint for visits to emergency departments (United States). Chest pain accounted for 2–4% of all new attendances at emergency departments per year in the UK (Herren and Mackway-Jones, 2001).

Palliative care – prevalence of pain

Pain in palliative care includes both cancer pain and non-malignant pain.

Cancer pain

More than 11 million people are diagnosed with cancer every year. It is estimated that there will be 16 million new cases every year by 2020. Cancer causes 7 million deaths every year – or 12.5% of deaths worldwide (World Health Organization, 2002).

Ross (2004) claims that, in the United States, cancer pain occurs in one-quarter of all patients at time of diagnosis, and two-thirds of patients receiving anti-cancer therapy report pain. As the stage of the disease advances the number of patients experiencing pain increases. Three quarters of patients hospitalised with advanced cancer report unrelieved pain. However, it is still important to note that cancer and pain are not synonymous (Twycross, 2003).

Non-malignant pain

The prevalence of pain in non-malignant conditions is often underestimated. Approximately 60% of patients with advanced diseases suffer troublesome pain and this figure is similar for cardiac disease, neurological disorders and AIDS. Unfortunately, the chances of patients being treated for pain due to non-malignant conditions is reduced (Regnard and Kindlen, 2004).

Over to you

Brian is 70 and he has been retired for 10 years. He has suffered from angina over the past five years and if he walks for more than 25 minutes he gets tightness in his chest and a dull pain. He finds this very frightening and has started to stay in the house rather than do his usual walk to the shops in the morning. His general practitioner in consultation with the local hospital cardiologist agrees that his heart disease does not warrant major intervention and is ideally controlled with medication.

Do you think that there are many others in the community like Brian with pain and reduced qualify of life? Go to the internet/Medline or CINAHL and search for 'prevalence of angina in the community'.

Chronic pain prevalence

Chronic pain tends to be considered as pain without apparent biological value that has persisted beyond the normal tissue healing time (usually taken to be three months).

Common conditions that cause chronic pain include: low back pain, headache, arthritis and peripheral neuropathy. Chronic pain has a significant effect on the lives of sufferers and their families, as it will effect patients' mood, social relationships and quality of life (Veillette *et al.*, 2005).

Ferrell (1995) reports that 62% of nursing home residents have pain. A study by the American Geriatrics Society (AGS) Panel found that 25–50% of those living in the community suffer significant pain problems (AGS Panel on Chronic Pain in Older Persons, 1998). Elliot *et al.* (1999) in a UK survey of 29 general practices (5036 patients, 72% response rate) report that 50.4% of patients self report chronic pain. Back pain and arthritis were the most common complaints. Unsurprisingly, with ongoing pain, increased pain intensity is associated with decreased quality of life (Laursen *et al.*, 2005).

Palmer *et al.*, (2000) report on two prevalence surveys of back pain at an interval of 10 years. Measurements included low back pain and low back pain making it impossible to put on hosiery. Over a 10-year interval the one-year prevalence of back pain, standarised for the age and sex distribution, rose from 36.4% to 49.1%. There was no increase in the prevalence of symptoms sufficient to prevent people putting on hosiery. A recent Canadian study (Veillette *et al.*, 2005) identified that between 18% and 29% of Canadians experience chronic pain.

The challenges of reviewing studies on measuring prevalence of chronic pain are numerous due to variations in population sampled, methods used to collect data and criteria used to define chronic pain. Standard definitions for chronic pain are not available. Harstall and Ospina (2003) call for a research agenda to conduct concurrent, prospective, epidemiological studies to estimate the chronic pain prevalence using clear, standardised definitions and well-validated and reliable collection tools.

Table 2.1 presents data from nine studies which are part of a systematic review by Harstall and Ospina (2003) highlighting the prevalence of pain and also some of the issues in measuring chronic pain.

Table 2.1 The prevalance of pain

Definition used	Number of studies	Population	% pooled prevalence
International Association for Study of Pain definition (chronic pain)	5 studies (1993–2001)	Adults	11% among adults
American College of Rheumatology definition (chronic widespread pain)	3 studies (1993–2000)	Adults	11.8% among adults (7.2% male and 14.7% female)
International Association for Study of Pain definition (chronic pain)	1 study (1997)	Elderly general population aged 65 years and older	50.2%

Recommendations and guidelines

A number of key agencies have emerged as leaders in providing resources, guidelines and standards in relation to pain management. The common theme emerging from these statements is that pain is a common and often under-treated phenomenon. Management of pain should become a key objective of health providers with an evidence-based, high-quality service provided. Multidisciplinary and multi-modal methods of pain management should be utilised. Key to this is robust undergraduate education on pain and continuing professional development for all health professionals.

Evidence base

The following timeline details some of the key position statements that have emerged over time.

Timeline

- **2003** The Royal College of Anaesthetists and The Pain Society, the British Chapter of the International Association for the Study of Pain, *Pain Management Services – Good Practice.*
- **2000** Services for Patients with Pain, *Clinical Standards Advisory Group (CSAG).* London, Department of Health.
- **2000** American Pain Society, *Pain assessment and treatment in the managed care environment. A position statement from the American Pain Society.*
- **1999** National Health and Medical Research Council, Australia. *Acute Pain Management: The Scientific Evidence.*
- **1995** American Pain Society. Quality Improvement Guidelines for the Treatment of Acute Pain and Cancer Pain (American Pain Society Quality of Care Committee). *JAMA.* **274**(23): 1874–80.
- **1992** Acute Pain Management Guideline Panel. *Acute Pain Management: Operative or Medical Procedures and Trauma. Clinical Practice Guideline.* AHCPR Pub. No. 92–0032. Rockville, MD: Agency for Health Care Policy and Research, Public Health Service, U.S. Department of Health and Human Services. Feb. 1992.
- **1991** International Associations for the Study of Pain, Task Force on Acute Pain. (Ready and Edwards, 1992): *Clinical Practice Guideline for Acute Pain Management.* IASP.
- **1990** Royal College of Surgeons and Anaesthetists, Commission on the Provision of Surgical Services, *Report on the Working Party on Pain after Surgery.*

In 2000, the clinical standards advisory group (CSAG) published a report on services for patients with pain. This group, which is now disbanded, was set up under statute as an independent source of expert advice to the UK health ministers and to the NHS on standards of clinical care for, and access to and availability of services to, NHS patients with acute and chronic pain. Key recommendations in relation to various types of adult pain are summarised in Table 2.2 below.

The common thread in the recommendations is effective communications, rapid access to appropriate services, dedicated staff and services and education for staff.

The Royal College of Anaesthetists and The Pain Society, the British Chapter of the International Association for the Study of Pain (2003) suggest that integration with primary care teams is essential for maximum patient benefit. They further state that pain management provides outstanding potential for fruitful working across the boundaries between primary and secondary care. They recommended that new and innovative models for supporting care should be supported and developed. For instance, Hewlett *et al.* (2000), in a randomised controlled trial with two years of follow up, describe a shared care system of hospital follow-up for patients with rheumatoid arthritis. Patient and general practitioner initiated shared care was compared to traditional rheumatologist initiation hospital care in patients with established rheumatoid arthritis. The study concluded that a shared system of hospital follow-up reduced both pain and use of health care resources.

Table 2.2 Key recommendations of the CSAG on the management of pain in adults (Source: CSAG, 2000)

Chronic pain	Postoperative and other acute pain	Accident and Emergency (A&E) departments
Objective of pain management services should include prevention of the development of chronicity and the disability that follows. GPs should have early access to appropriate investigations and specialist secondary care services when needed.	All patients undergoing potentially painful procedures should have access to the services of an acute pain team if necessary. The components of an acute pain team are described.	There should be greater emphasis on effective pain management in patients attending A&E departments. Actions to achieve this are described.

Community physiotherapist

Integrated care between the hospital and community means that the patient can get rapid access to care or treatments needed without delays and bureaucracy. For example, I had a young lad last week who was attending for a sports injury to the knee. After two treatments I decided he would benefit from a visit to the pain clinic in the local hospital. This was easily arranged though the shared care processes set up between my services, the entire community services and the local hospital. It involved a brief phone call to the nurse co-ordinating the clinic and an electronic appointment was sent for the next week. Such rapid access meant that the patient was able to continue my treatments and also benefit from a specialised service provided at the hospital.

The American Pain Society (1995) advised key processes for improving acute pain management which include:

- recognition and timely, prompt treatment
- making information about analgesics readily available
- developing policies for advanced analgesic techniques
- the goal of continuous improvement examining the process and outcomes of pain management.

Audit and quality of pain management practices

In order to improve the quality of care, ongoing monitoring of practice utilising clinical audit tools is required. Audit is concerned with the monitoring of current practice against standards. Clinical audit is at the heart of clinical governance. It is there to improve the quality of patient care and clinical practice.

Clinical audit of pain will establish the baseline performance for a clinical area/service. Once this is completed, the data can be reviewed and the process of identification of opportunities for improvement of practice can begin. Practice can be monitored over time. The pain service can be benchmarked with national and international standards. All of this supports proactive planned service-planning processes. This is a continuous cycle supporting continuous quality improvement (see Figure 2.1).

What should be included in the clinical audit?

Clinical audit is used to improve all aspects of patient care. Table 2.3 identifies examples of these areas for pain management.

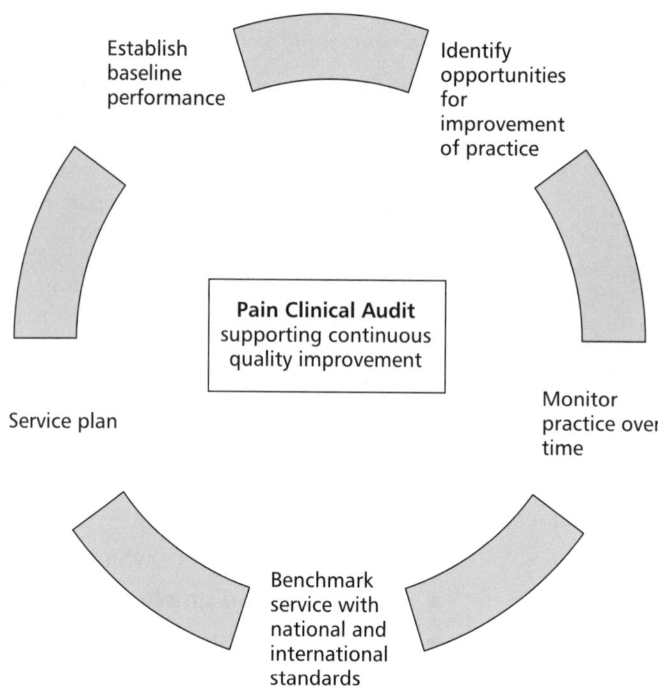

Figure 2.1 Example of clinical audit cycle for pain

Table 2.3 Clinical audit: areas for pain management

• Patient outcomes	o pain scores o mobility o function o quality of life
• Compliance with national and international standards	
• Knowledge of staff	
• Patient preferences	
• Protocols, policies and guidelines in place	
• Trends in service	o medication usage o pain assessment tools o quality of documentation

Keywords

Systematic review
A widely used method to synthesise the literature; it includes a comprehensive search, critical appraisal of the quality of selected studies and pooled analysis either qualitative or quantitative, of the results

Evidence-based approaches to pain management

Pain management, like any aspect of patient care, should be based on the best available evidence. Moore *et al.* (2004) are clear that good evidence is likely to come from robust **systematic reviews** of sound clinical trials. This means that health professionals must be able to access, understand and interpret research in order to provide evidence-based practice. As technology, skills and knowledge grow, nurses and health care professionals need to develop systems to ensure they are accessing, interpreting and utilising the best available evidence. Health care organisations need to consider multiple strategies to facilitate and promote evidence-based practice. Managerial support, facilitation and a culture that is receptive to change are essential (Gerrish, 2004).

Evidence base

Table 2.4 details current sources of research evidence.

Table 2.4 Sources of research evidence

Source	Research category	Quality checked – Pre-appraised	Sources
Evidence-based journals	**Systematic reviews** Randomised controlled trials Case control studies Cohort studies Qualitative research	Yes	Evidence-based nursing (http://ebn.bmjjournals.com/) Evidence-based medicine (http://ebm.bmjjournals.com/)
Cochrane database	Systematic reviews	Yes	www.cochrane.org/index0.htm
Medline CINAHL	– Research – Opinions – Discussions – Literature reviews	No	Check your local library

View the following websites for evidence on pain management

www.jr2.ox.ac.uk/bandolier/booth/painpag/index2.html
www.jr2.ox.ac.uk/bandolier/painres/MApain.html – systematic reviews with pain as an outcome
www.cochrane.org
www.jr2.ox.ac.uk/cochrane/

Go to one of the above websites and search for a systematic review on pain prevalence in the community.

Organisational reponsibility

Organisations have responsibility in a number of areas to support improvement of pain management practices. National and international standards and guidance form the platform for organisational responsibility (see Figure 2.2).

Figure 2.2 Example of components necessary for organisational responsibility for pain

Key points Top tips

- Pain is a public health issue
- The economic and social cost of pain is high
- The prevalence of pain is high in both the hospital and the community
- A number of key agencies such as The Royal College of Anaesthetists and The Pain Society have issued recommendations, standards and guidelines in relation to pain
- Clinical audit of pain supports high-quality pain services
- Evidence-based approaches should be used to manage pain

Pain as an indicator of quality of care

St Margaret's is a small general hospital with 200 beds. It has two surgical and four medical wards. There is a critical care area that manages acutely ill patients from both medicine and surgery. There is a minor injuries unit, but the hospital does not operate an accident and emergency department. The hospital performs routine surgery such as appendectomies and cholecystectomies. It has a day unit for endoscopies.

St Margaret's has just appointed a new clinical director and a new director of nursing. Both are keen to prove their worth and make St Margaret's a centre of excellence. They realise that, while the staff all work hard and provide excellent care, there has been little investment in new technologies, equipment or professional development of staff. They decide to do an audit of some of the main indicators of quality of care including pain in order to benchmark care.

A three-day audit of pain in the hospital is shown in Table 2.5.

The clinical director and director of nursing sit down to review their entire audit. Their eyes fall on the pain prevalence. It strikes them both that pain prevalence in the surgical ward is rather high.

- Why is pain a good indicator of the quality of patient care?
- What do you interpret from the table of pain prevalence?
- Why do you think there is more pain at night in the minor injuries unit than during the day?

Table 2.5 St Margaret's three-day audit of pain

Location	Mean pain prevalence (using visual analogue scale)
Medical wards	Daytime: 4.5 Night-time: 3.8
Surgical wards	Daytime: 7.6 Night-time: 7.8
Day unit	Daytime: 2.1
Minor injuries unit	Daytime: 4.5 Night-time: 5.3

Rapid recap

1. How do you define prevalence of pain?
2. How would you describe the economic burden of pain?
3. What are the sources of research evidence?

References

AGS Panel on Chronic Pain in Older Persons (1998) The management of chronic pain in older persons: AGS Panel on Chronic Pain in Older Persons. American Geriatrics Society. *Journal of American Geriatric Society*, **46**: 635–512.

American Pain Society Quality of Care Committee (1995) Quality improvement guidelines for the treatment of acute and cancer pain. *JAMA*, **274**(23): 1871–1880.

Bay-Nielson M., Perkins F.M. and Kehlet H. (2001) Pain and functional impairment 1 year after inguinal herniorrhaphy: A Nationwide Questionnaire Study. *Annals of Surgery*, **233**(1): 1–7.

Bond M. and Breivik H. (2004) Why pain control matters in a world of killer diseases. *Pain Clinical Updates*, XII(4).

Brennan F. and Cousins M.J. (2004) Pain relief as a human right. *Pain Clinical Updates*, XII(5).

Bruster S., Jarman B., Bosanquet N., Weston D., Erens R. and Delbanco T.L. (1994) National survey of hospital patients. *BMJ*. **309**(6968): 1542–1546.

Chronic Pain Association of Canada (2004) Pain Facts. www.chronicpaincanada.com

Clinical Standards Advisory Group(CSAG) (2000) Services for Patients with Pain. London, Department of Health.

Comley A.L. and DeMeyer E. (2001) Assessing patient satisfaction with pain management through a continuous quality improvement effort. *Journal of Pain and Symptom Management*, **21**(1): 27–40.

Cordell W.H., Keene K.K., Giles B.K., Jones J.B., Jones J.H. and Brizendine E.J. (2002) The high prevalence of pain in emergency medical care. *American Journal of Emergency Medicine*, **20**(3): 165–169.

Donovan M, Dillon P. and McGuire L. (1987) Incidence and characteristics of pain in a sample of medical-surgical inpatients. *Pain*, **30**: 69–78.

Elliot A.M., Smith B.H., Penny K.I., Cairns Smith W. and Chambers W.A. (1999) Epidemiology of chronic pain in the community. *Lancet*, **354**: 1248–1252.

Ferrell B.A. (1995) Pain evaluation and management in a nursing home. *Annals Internal Medicine*, **123**: 681–687.

Gerrish K. (2004) Promoting evidence-based practice: an organizational approach. *Journal of Nursing Management*, **12**: 114–123.

Harstall C. and Ospina M. (2003) How prevalent is chronic pin? *Pain Clinical Updates*, XI(2).

Haugh R. (2005) Hospitals and clinicians confront a new imperative: Pain management. *Hospitals and Health Networks*, **79**(4): 51–56.

Herren K.R., and Mackway-Jones K. (2001) Emergency management of cardiac chest pain: a Review. *Emergency Medical Journal*, **18**: 6–10.

Hewlett S, Mitchell K., Haynes J., Paine T., Korendowych E. and Kirwan J.R. (2000) Patient-initiated hospital follow-up for rheumatoid arthritis. *Rheumatology*, **39**: 990–997.

Hunter D.J. (2003) Public Health Policy. In *Public Health for the 21st Century. New Perspectives on Policy, Participation and Practice* (eds. Orme J., Powell J., Taylor P.) Open University Press, McGraw-Hill Education, Berkshire.

Kuhn S., Cooke K., Collins M,. Jones M. and Mucklow J.C. (1990) Perceptions of pain relief after surgery. *BMJ*, **300**: 1687–1690.

Lamers L.M., Meerding W.J., Severens J.L. and Brouwer W.B.F. (2005) The relationship between productivity and health-related quality of life: An empirical exploration in persons with low back pain. *Quality of Life Research*, **14**: 805–813.

Laursen B.S., Bajaj P., Olesen A.S., Delmar C. and Arendt-Nielsen L. (2005) Health related quality of life and quantitative pain measurement in females with chronic non-malignant pain. *European Journal of Pain*, **9**: 267–275.

Mac Lellan K. (2004) Postoperative pain: Strategy for improving patient experiences. *Journal of Advanced Nursing*, **46**: 179–185.

Macintyre P.E. and Ready L.B. (2002) *Acute Pain Management, A Practical Guide*, 2nd edn. W.B. Saunders, Philadelphia.

Melzack R, Abbott F.V., Zackson W., Mulder D.S. and Davis M.W.L. (1987) Pain on a surgical ward: a survey of the duration and intensity of pain and the effectiveness of medication. *Pain*, **29**: 67–72.

Moore A., Edwards J., Barden J. and McQuay H. (2004) *Bandolier's Little Book of Pain*. Oxford University Press, Oxford.

Owen H., McMillan V. and Rogowski D. (1990) Postoperative pain therapy: a survey of patients' expectations and their experiences. *Pain*, **41**: 303–307.

Palmer K.T., Walsh K., Bendall H., Cooper C. and Coggon D. (2000) Back pain in Britain: Comparison of two prevalence surveys at an interval of 10 years. *BMJ*, **320**: 1577–1578.

Regnard C. and Kindlen, M. (2004) What is pain? In *Helping the Patient with Advanced Disease* (ed. Regnard C.). Radcliffe Medical Press, Oxford.

Ross E. (2004) *Pain Management*. Hanley & Belfus, Philadelphia.

Royal College of Anaesthetists and The Pain Society, the British Chapter of the International Association for the Study of Pain (2003) *Pain Management Services – Good Practice*. The Royal College of Anaesthetists and The Pain Society, London.

Spranger M.A.G., de Regt E.B., Andries F., van Agt H.M., Bijl R.V., de Boer J.B. *et al.* (2000) Which chronic conditions are associated with a better or poorer quality of life? *Journal of Clinical Epidemiology*,. **53**: 895–907.

Stewart B.W. and Kleihues P. (eds) (2003) World Cancer Report. IARC Press, Lyon.

Twycross R. (2003) *Introducing Palliative Care,* 4th edn. Radcliffe Medical Press, Oxford.

Veillette Y., Dion D., Altier N. and Choiniere M. (2005) The treatment of chronic pain in Quebec: a study of hospital-based services offered within anesthesia departments. *Canadian Journal Anesthesia*, **52**(6): 600–606.

Watt-Watson J.H., Stevens B., Garfinkel P., Streiner D. and Gallop R. (2001) Relationships between nurses' pain knowledge and pain management outcomes for their postoperative cardiac patients. *Journal of Advanced Nursing*, **36**: 535–545.

Weis O.F., Sriwatanakul K., Alloza J.L., Weintraub M. and Lasagna L. (1983) Attitudes of patients, housestaff and nurses toward postoperative analgesic care. *Anesthesia and Analgesia*, **62**: 70–74.

Wilder-Smith C.H. and Schuler L. (1992) Postoperative analgesia: pain by choice? The influence of patient attitudes and patient education. *Pain*, **50**: 257–262.

World Health Organization (2002) *National Cancer Control Programmes: Policies and Managerial Guidelines,* 2nd edn. WHO, Geneva.

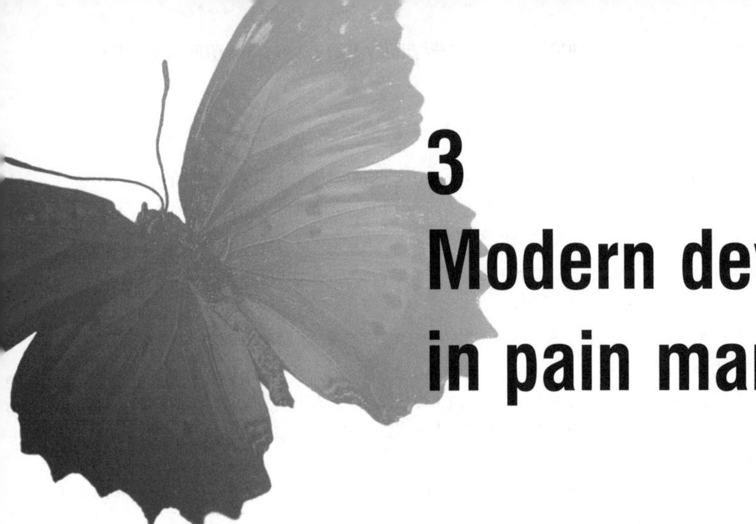

3 Modern developments in pain management

Learning outcomes

By the end of this chapter you should be able to:

- ★ Describe developments in the approaches to pain management
- ★ Outline modern, contemporary approaches to pain management
- ★ Understand how service improvements in pain management link to evidence-based care.

Introduction

This chapter begins by describing the developments in pain management over the past few decades. The major landmarks in the history of pain management are highlighted including the development of new advanced medications. Technology has had a major impact on pain interventions, and technologies such as patient-controlled analgesia are detailed. Future developments that are currently being researched are referred to. The importance of pain services and the evidence base for their development are outlined.

History

The nature of pain has puzzled society for centuries. Pain has been and remains the subject of medicine, philosophy, religion and politics. As an age-old problem it is interesting and challenging that society and, indeed, health professionals continue to struggle with its understanding, physiological basis and subsequent management. The past 20 years have seen new drugs being developed, many of which are refinements of the traditional approaches to pain. The development of more refined nonsteroidal anti-inflammatories such as the new COX-2 inhibitors or research currently being conducted on the use of intravenous paracetamol are examples. New methods of delivery of medications have emerged, such as patient-controlled analgesia and epidural analgesia. Pain physiology is better understood, but many questions still remain.

Pain relief has been used since the late 1600s, with new developments emerging over time. Here are some of the key developments in pain management over time (source: Meldrum, 2003).

- In 1680 laudanum, a mix of opium and sherry, was introduced by Thomas Sydenham
- In 1868 W.T.G. Morton demonstrated anaesthesia
- Throughout the 19th century opiates were standard treatment for acute pain. There was much concern about addiction
- During World War I, Rene Leriche introduced the concept of nerve blocks
- In 1953 John Bonica published *The Management of Pain* bringing together available information on pain treatments
- In the 1950s and 1960s nerve block clinics were set up
- 1950s Dame Cecily Saunder's concept of palliative care and 'total pain' was founded
- 1965 Melzack and Wall published the *Gate Control Theory of Pain*
- In the 1970s the concept of endogenous neurochemical reactions to pain was debated and researched
- 1972 Formation of International Association of Pain
- 1982 Development of the World Health Organization *analgesic ladder*
- 1980–2006 Clinical drug research
- 1980–2006 Dedicated acute and chronic pain services emerged
- 1990–2006 Multidisciplinary multi-modal approaches to pain. Pain management standards emerging from interest groups
- 2001 Patients and families sue health care provider for inadequate pain management (source: Haugh, 2005).

Impact of technology on pain management

Technology has revolutionised modes of analgesic administration allowing for smaller, more regular amounts of analgesia to be administered in a safe and efficient manner. Patients have been enabled to take more control over pain relief. It is suggested that refinements in systemic opioid administration and epidural analgesia have by far the greatest impact on the quality of acute pain care (Carr *et al.* 2005). Patient-controlled analgesia (PCA) using traditional intravenous opioids, the newer concept of the fentanyl hyrdrochloride patient-controlled transdermal system (PCTS) and epidural analgesia are reviewed below.

Patient-controlled analgesia (PCA)

Active involvement of the patient in the management of postoperative pain by the use of PCA is now a well-established part of clinical practice. The PCA system consists of a syringe pump and a timing device. The patient activates the system by pressing a button, which causes a small dose of analgesia to be delivered into the venous circulation. Simultaneously, a lockout device is activated, ensuring another dose cannot be delivered until a pre-set time. PCA is now over 30 years old and is in widespread use.

PCA systems have the following features: bolus demand dose, lockout interval, background infusion and maximum dose. The bolus demand dose is a predetermined dose which is delivered by the machine when the patient presses the button. Drugs commonly used in PCA systems include morphine, pethidine and fentanyl.

The literature details numerous studies on the effects, advantages and disadvantages of PCA systems. Advantages such as ease of use, time saving and patient control are all cited. Ballantyne *et al.* (1993) published a **meta-analysis** of initial randomised controlled trials of postoperative patient-controlled analgesia compared with conventional intramuscular analgesia. They included 15 randomised controlled trials. Their conclusions were that:

- Patient preference strongly favours PCA over conventional analgesia
- Patients using PCA obtain better pain relief than those with conventional analgesia, without an increase in side effects
- Favourable effects of PCA upon analgesic usage and length of hospital stay did not attain statistical significance (the authors suggest that this may be due to the low numbers involved in the randomised controlled trials).

Keywords

Meta-analysis

A meta-analysis uses *statistical methods* to combine the results from a number of previous experiments or studies examining the same question, in an attempt to summarise the totality of evidence relating to a particular issue. Meta-analysis includes a qualitative component (applies predetermined criteria of study quality) and a quantitative component (integration of numerical information) (Cochrane Collaboration, 2001).

The debate with regard to the efficacy of PCA continues in the literature with conflicting evidence emerging (Passchier *et al.*, 1993; Thomas *et al.*, 1995; Williams, 1996; Snell *et al.*, 1997). The overall incidence of potentially life-threatening complications with PCA is reported as low (Fleming and Coombes, 1992; Sidebotham and Schug, 1997). However, Choiniere *et al.* (1998) reported PCA costs as higher and found no clinical advantages with its use.

The main advantage of a patient-controlled analgesia is that it is a system that is designed to accommodate the wide range of analgesic requirements that can be anticipated when managing acute pain. Control over pain relief is cited in a number of studies as an advantage (Chumbley *et al.*, 1998).

Macintyre (2001), in a review of the literature, suggests that PCA can be a very effective and safe method of pain relief and may allow easier individualisation of therapy compared to conventional methods of opioid analgesia. The success lies in how well it is used. He suggests that if similar attention was given to other methods of opioid administration, conventional methods of analgesia could be as effective as PCA in many patients. Larijani *et al.* (2005) suggest that successful postoperative pain management using PCA is difficult to achieve on a consistent basis unless treatment is individualised.

Clinical Caseload . . .

If successful pain management utilising PCA is difficult to achieve on a consistent basis unless treatment is individualised, think about what you can do to support individualised treatment on a busy surgical ward.

Patient-controlled transdermal analgesia (PCTS)

A fentanyl hyrdrochloride patient-controlled transdermal system (PCTS) is under development as an alternative to PCA. It delivers small doses of fentanlyl by iontoporesis with electro transport delivery platform technology. The system uses a low intensity direct current to move fentanyl from a hydrogel reservoir into the skin, where it then diffuses into the local circulation and is transported to the central nervous system. The self-adhesive unit, which is about the size of a credit card, is worn on the patient's upper arm or chest (unlike PCA it does not have intravenous tubing or pump etc.) (Viscusi *et al.*, 2004). A patient-controlled transdermal analgesic delivery system provides the patient with a locus of control akin to the PCA. It is suggested that PCTS does not require the personnel and resource requirements of a conventional intravenous PCA and is as effective (Carr *et al.*, 2005).

In a randomised controlled trial Chelly *et al.*, (2004) demonstrated that fentanyl hydrochloride 40 μg was superior to placebo for the management of acute postoperative pain after surgery. Viscusi *et al.* (2004) assessed whether the transdermal PCTS system is equivalent to a standard morphine IV PCA regimen in postoperative pain management. The authors conclude that the pain control is equivalent and that the incidence of opioid-related side-effects similar.

Studies comparing PCTS with conventional postoperative treatments are needed.

Further research and development is required to evaluate the efficacy and feasibility of PCTS for potential widespread use.

Over to you

Research on patient-controlled transdermal systems is in its infancy. Go to Medline and CINAHL and see if you can access any new research on such systems.

Epidural analgesia

The spinal epidural space extends from the sacral hiatus to the base of the skull. Drugs injected into the epidural space can block or modulate afferent impulses and cord processing of those impulses. Both epidural local anaesthetics and epidural opioids can produce analgesia (McQuay, 1994).

Epidural analgesia is indicated for the provision of postoperative analgesia (Mallet and Bailey, 1996). Block *et al.* (2003) conducted a meta-analysis of efficacy of postoperative epidural analgesia including 100 studies (1966–2002). They concluded that epidural analgesia, regardless of analgesic agent, location of catheter, and type and time of pain assessment, provided better postoperative analgesia compared with parenteral opioids.

Keywords

Presurgical nociceptive blockage
This is the blockage of pain nerve fibre transmission prior to surgery

Wheatley *et al.* (2001) consider the efficacy and safety of epidural analgesia in patients recovering from major surgery, based on a computerised search of the literature from 1976 to 2000. The authors conclude that continuous thoracic epidural analgesia with a low-dose local anaesthetic-opioid combination has the potential to provide effective dynamic pain relief for many patients, even those undergoing major upper abdominal or thoracic procedures. However, there are major factors to consider in the safe and effective ward-based use of epidural analgesia including the need for staff training and regular monitoring of vital signs. Furthermore, the authors say that it is not uncommon for epidurals to be ineffective in terms of dynamic pain relief on a surgical ward for these reasons.

Pre-emptive analgesia

The concept of pre-emptive analgesia prior to surgery to reduce analgesic consumption and post surgical pain has been under discussion, review and research for a number of decades. The principle behind pre-emptive analgesia is that giving an intervention prior to surgery prevents or decreases surgical pain by preventing central sensitisation by administering a **presurgical nociceptive blockage**. This means that before surgery an analgesia is given in order to try to prevent nerve sensitisation once surgery commences.

Keywords

Randomised controlled trials
RCTs are quantitative, comparative, controlled experiments in which investigators allocate at random two or more interventions to a series of individuals and measure specified outcomes. In a double-blind trial neither the researchers nor the patients know whether they are receiving the control or the intervention

To date, however, research reports have shown modest or disappointing results in showing reduced surgical pain (Ochroch *et al.*, 2003; Wnek *et al.*, 2004). However, it is suggested that nonsteroidal anti-inflammatories will have an increasing role in pre-emptive analgesia. Aida (2005) states that pre-emptive analgesia is challenging and that to be successful it must be deep enough to block all nociception, wide enough to cover the entire surgical area and prolonged enough to last throughout surgery and even into the postoperative period.

Moiniche *et al.* (2002) report on a systematic review of 80 double-blind **randomised controlled trials** (RCTs) designed to compare the role of timing of analgesia, i.e. preoperative versus intraoperative or postoperative initiation of analgesia. They conclude that the current evidence available reveals a lack of evidence for any important effect (rather than evidence for lack of effect) with pre-emptive analgesia.

Further research and development in this area will demonstrate whether there is a clinical justification for widespread use of pre-emptive analgesia.

Role of intravenous paracetamol and nitroxparacetamol

The use of paracetamol in the management of postoperative pain has been a source of interest for some time. Power (2005) discusses its use and proposes the introduction of an intravenous preparation. He reports that the analgesic and anti-inflammatory properties and safety advantages of a nitric oxide (NO)-releasing form may represent significant advances in the use of oral paracetamol. It is suggested that the intravenous formulation may have a safety advantage over the oral form by producing more predictable plasma paracetamol concentrations in the immediate postoperative period. Further research will demonstrate whether this will have any clinical advantage.

Over to you

Speak to your local pain care service team, and find out their views on any recent or future development in pain care and its associated technological advances.

Pain services

The need to have dedicated staff to support pain management has emerged over the past three decades. It was becoming evident that pain management was complex, required specialised staff and dedicated education and training. Each particular pain area was creating its own evidence base and process for pain management. Pain management could be better targeted by recognising that there is a need to view particular pain areas as specialisms. Acute pain, chronic pain and palliative care are now viewed as specialist areas of pain care and within these areas sub-specialties have emerged, e.g. neuropathic pain, migraine. The need for pain treatment facilities has emerged and there are a number of terms utilised to describe the types of pain services developed. This section details the development of acute pain services, chronic pain services and palliative care services.

Acute pain services

Worldwide acute pain services are developing in response to increasing recognition that the solution to the problem of inadequate postoperative pain relief lies not so much in development of new techniques but in the development of a formal organisation for better use of existing techniques (Rawal and Berggren, 1994). In 1988, Ready *et al.* drew attention to the potential role of an acute pain service by developing an anaesthesiology-based postoperative pain management service. They said, 'just as chronic pain management has become a special area of medical practice, treatment of acute pain deserves a similar commitment by practitioners with special expertise.' Following systematic review of acute pain teams McDonnell *et al.* 2003a describe them as multidisciplinary teams who assume day-to-day responsibility for the management of postoperative pain. Team members generally include specialist nurses, anaesthetists and pharmacists. Acute pain services and acute pain teams are in the main providing similar services. It appears that significant investment has been put into these approaches by some services and that it takes time and organisational commitment to set up a good service.

Windsor (1996) reported that 42.7% of UK hospitals had a multidisciplinary acute pain service in place by 1994. In 1995, 44% of UK hospitals reported having some form of acute pain service (Harmer *et al.*, 1995). Of these, 28% employed a dedicated pain nurse and 16% had specific 'fixed' consultant sessions allocated to acute pain. By 2003, this number had almost doubled, with 84% of acute English hospitals performing inpatient surgery for adult patients, having an acute pain team (McDonnell *et al.*, 2003a). Warfield surveyed 300 US hospitals in 1995. She found that 42% of hospitals had acute pain management programmes and that an additional 13% had plans to establish an acute pain management programme. A survey of acute pain services in Canada showed that 53% of hospitals were operating such a service in 1993. (Zimmermann and Stewart, 1993).

Key points Top tips

Acute pain teams/acute pain services usually encompass the following elements:

- introduction of policies, protocols and guidelines
- education of staff and patients
- audit and evaluation of service
- development of patient information leaflets
- introduction of regular pain assessment

- introduction and monitoring of new analgesic techniques
- clinical lead is an anaesthetist or specialist nurse
- services/teams include a specialist nurse
- seamless liaison with other health care teams

Evidence base

Benefits of acute pain service/acute pain team

Many benefits are ascribed to acute pain services and acute pain teams. There are numerous published studies, using both research and audit techniques, which report the benefits of such services. The following presents a sample of published work.

Timeline

- **1991** Wheatley *et al.* describe the benefits, risk and resource implications of providing an acute pain service indicating that their daily audit of the service and feedback to the anaesthetic and surgical colleagues had led to the delivery of a more consistent standard of postoperative care.
- **1992** Gould *et al.* outline the effect of sequential changes in a policy for controlling pain after surgery. Their objective was to observe the effects of introducing an acute pain service to the general surgical wards of a large teaching hospital. Main results showed a reduction in median visual analogue pain scores 24 hours after surgery for pain during relaxation, pain on movement and pain on deep inspiration.
- **1993** Schug and Torrie, in relation to the safety of acute pain services, reported no serious complications in morbidity and mortality in a study of 3016 patients receiving care from an acute pain service.
- **1997** Mackintosh and Bowles evaluated the impact of a nurse-led acute pain service. The evaluation focused on three areas of concern: preoperative information, patients' self-reported levels of pain and analgesics prescribed. The results of evaluation indicate significant reductions in reported levels of pain and patterns of analgesic prescribing.
- **1997** Pesut and Johnson evaluated the effectiveness of an acute pain service in Canada. No significant differences in mean pain scores were noted following the introduction of the pain service.
- **1997** Tsui *et al.* audited 2509 patients under the care of an acute pain service. They documented all side-effects and complications. They concluded that a standard monitoring and management protocol, an experienced nursing team and a reliable acute pain service coverage is mandatory for the safe use of modern analgesic techniques.
- **1998** Tighe *et al.*, following the introduction of an acute pain service whose emphasis was on multimodal pain therapy, reported that the service significantly improved inpatient perception of pain relief upon return of consciousness after anaesthesia and for two days postoperatively. They report

no changes in the incidence of emetic sequelae. They found a significant improvement in patient satisfaction and sleep pattern in hospital.

- **1998** Harmer reported on the effect of education, assessment and a standardised prescription on postoperative pain management following a clinical audit of 15 hospitals in the United Kingdom. He reported that following the introduction of the above there was an overall reduction in the percentage of patients who experienced moderate to severe pain at rest from 32% to 12%. The incidence of severe pain on movement decreased from 37% to 13% and moderate to severe pain on deep inspiration from 41% to 22%. He also noted decreases in the incidence of nausea and vomiting.
- **2003** McDonnell *et al.* report a systematic review and meta-analysis of 15 studies. The research team reported that the difference in quality between the studies made meta-analysis difficult. They conclude that there is insufficient robust research to assess the impact of acute pain teams (APTs) on postoperative outcomes of adult patients or on the processes of postoperative pain relief.

Reflective activity

Consider the timeline of evidence presented above. Read McDonnell *et al.* (2003b) and contemplate how future evaluations of acute pain services/acute pain teams should be undertaken.

Chronic-pain services

Many patients with chronic pain continue to have symptoms and may develop psychological distress, overall disability and increased dependency on family members and social services even though there are many advances in pain-relieving techniques. Pain management programmes have been developed to enhance the patient's physical performance and help them cope more effectively with their pain (Nurmikko *et al.*, 1998). Flor *et al.* (1992), following meta-analysis evaluating the efficacy of multidisciplinary treatments for chronic pain, suggest that patients treated in multidisciplinary pain clinics show improvements in pain and psychological functioning compared to conventional treatments. Guzman *et al.* (2001) conducted a systematic review of 10 trials in relation to multidisciplinary rehabilitation for chronic low back pain. The authors suggest that there was strong evidence that intensive multidisciplinary biopsychosocial rehabilitation with functional restoration improves function when compared with inpatient or outpatient non-multidisciplinary treatments and moderate evidence that such rehabilitation reduces pain. Ospina and Harstall (2003) support this through analysis of the literature, concluding that the evidence for the effectiveness of multidisciplinary pain programmes is strong for chronic low back pain. However, they state the evidence is inconclusive for widespread pain, neck and shoulder pain. Good practice in chronic-pain management suggests the provision of core services for chronic-pain in all district general hospitals and most specialist hospitals (The Royal College of Anaesthetists and The Pain Society 2003).

Veillette *et al.* (2005) report on a Canadian survey of the availability of hospital-based anaesthesia departments with chronic non-cancer pain services. The survey indicates that 73% of anaesthesia departments offer chronic non-cancer pain services, with 26% providing some form of multidisciplinary assessment and treatment. However, 4500 patients were waiting for their first appointment to see a pain consultant, with 67% of these waiting for nine months or more.

There is limited published empirical work on the prevalence or effectiveness of chronic-pain services. It emerges, however, that chronic pain services should include the following as detailed below.

Key points Top tips

Chronic-pain services usually encompass the following elements:

- introduction of policies, protocols and guidelines
- education of staff and patients
- audit and evaluation of service
- alleviation of pain
- reduction of disability and restoration of function
- rationalisation of medication
- rationalisation of use of all health services
- attention to social, family and occupational issues
- multidisciplinary approach

Palliative care

The history of palliative care spans a number of centuries. From the beginning of the nineteenth century, charitable endeavours led to the creation of 'hospices', meaning a place of rest and recovery for pilgrims. In 1842, Jeanne Garnier formed 'L'Association des Dames du Calvaire' in Lyon, France and her influence led to six other 'Calvaire' hospices in Paris and New York by the end of the century.

In 1879, Our Lady's Hospice for the Dying in Harold's Cross, Dublin, Ireland, opened thanks to the ambition of Mother Mary Aikenhead, the Superior of a religious Order – the Irish Sisters of Charity. Here, religious Sisters offered care, shelter, comfort and warmth to the destitute, chronically frail and to those whose condition was beyond cure. Many consider this to be the first institutional provision of its kind beyond the mainland of Europe (O'Brien and Clark, 2005). Healy (2004) reports that consequently the Irish Sisters of Charity founded London's first hospice, St Joseph's Hospice in Hackney. It was in this very London hospice in the 1950s that modern palliative care was born.

Dame Cicely Saunders was responsible for establishing the discipline and the culture of palliative care. During her lifetime, she worked as a nurse, medical social worker, volunteer and, eventually, as a physician. In 1967, Dame Cicely Saunders founded the first modern hospice, St Christopher's Hospice in London. Here, she promoted an integrated approach that recognised all of the difficulties that the dying have to face and helped them in meeting these challenges, but without pain. Since then, palliative care has developed and evolved worldwide. In the UK, Palliative care is provided by two distinct categories of health and social-care professionals:

- Those providing the day-to-day care to patients and carers in their homes and in hospitals
- Those who specialise in palliative care (consultants in palliative medicine and clinical nurse specialists in palliative care, for example) supported by a multidisciplinary palliative care team.

The National Council for Palliative Care's website indicates the recent provision of specialist palliative care services in England, Wales and Northern Ireland. As at January 2004, there were:

- 196 specialist inpatient units providing 2730 beds, of which 19.9% were NHS beds.
- 341 home care services – this figure includes both primarily advisory services delivered by hospice and NHS-based community palliative care teams as well as other more sustained care provided in the patient's home. Some 17% of referrals were at time of diagnosis.
- 324 hospital-based services.
- 237 day-care services.
- 273 bereavement support services.

(Source: The National Council for Palliative Care, 2004)

Key points Top tips

Palliative care aims to:

- affirm life and regard dying as a normal process
- provide relief from pain and other distressing symptoms
- integrate the psychological and spiritual aspects of patient care
- offer a support system to help patients live as actively as possible until death
- offer a support system to help the family cope during the patient's illness and in their bereavement

Integrated approaches to pain management

This chapter title hints at a panacea of modern developments that will revolutionise the way all types of pain are managed. Yet many of the modern developments are messages highlighting the importance of listening to the patient, assessing pain regularly, and using multidisciplinary, multimodal approaches. Above all, the modern message is to take pain seriously, seriously enough to have dedicated services, protocols and guidelines, and have staff and patient education in place.

Organisational approaches to pain management should be co-ordinated, planned, audited and firmly rooted in an evidence-based process utilising policies and guidelines. It would appear that improvement in one part of the pain process will have greater impact if an integrated, multidisciplinary approach is taken. This means that there should be a dependent interrelationship between pain assessment, pain history, pain management, knowledge of patients and staff and clinical audit. It is only by adopting this modern approach that the quality of pain will improve for patients.

The knowledge and attitudes of patients and health care staff has become a subject of increasing interest in pain management. The context of pain, culture, past experiences and family all influence patient perception of pain. Figure 3.1 illustrates this.

Figure 3.1 Influences on the quality of pain management

Increasingly, nurses have taken on more specialist and advanced practice roles in pain management. They are seen as the lead in some pain teams (Mackintosh, 1997). Titles such as pain resource nurses (Holley *et al.*, 2005), nurse specialists, pain nurse consultants have all emerged. Nurses are seen are key members of the multidisciplinary team in managing pain (CSAG 2000). The Pain Society (The British Chapter of the IASP) (2002) has produced recommendations for nursing practice in pain management. These guidelines support a career pathway for nurses in pain management and outline competencies for novice, intermediate and higher levels of practice. They were developed in response to the development of nursing at a range of levels in pain management across acute and chronic settings. They can be accessed at www.britishpainsociety.org.

The US agency for health care policy and research (AHCPR, 1992) recommends an integrated approach to pain management and states that pain control options should include:

- cognitive-behavioural interventions, relaxation, distraction and imagery: these can be taught preoperatively and can reduce pain, anxiety and the amount of drugs needed for pain control
- systematic administration of nonsteroidal anti-inflammatory drugs (NSAIDs) or opioids using the traditional 'as needed' schedule or round-the-clock administration
- patient-controlled analgesia (PCA) usually means self-medication with intravenous doses of an opioid; this can include other classes of drugs administered orally or by other routes
- spinal analgesia, usually by means of an epidural opioid and/ or local anaesthetic injected intermittently or infused continuously
- intermittent or continuous local neural blockade (examples of the former include intercostal nerve blockade with local anaesthetic or cryoprobe; the latter includes infusion of local anaesthetic through an interpleural catheter)
- other forms of analgesia – such as transcutaneous electrical nerve stimulation.

Key points Top tips

- Pain management has developed significantly over time
- Pain management has developed into various specialisms: acute, chronic and palliative care
- Multidisciplinary teams and multimodal approaches support quality patient care
- New technologies continue to develop which will support the development of analgesic management in clinical areas

An audit of pain prevalence to inform practice development

Derek is the clinical nurse manager in one of St Margaret's two surgical wards (see case study in Chapter 2). The ward manages patients post routine surgery such as appendectomies and cholecystectomies. St Margaret's new clinical director and director of nursing have just completed a pain audit as part of an overall quality of care audit in the hospital. They are keen to benchmark care and are very aware that St Margaret's has not invested in new technologies, equipment or professional development of staff.

Derek reviews the data for his ward: daytime mean pain prevalence is 7.6 and night-time mean pain prevalence is 7.8 using a visual analogue scale. Derek decides to call a ward meeting to discuss it. He quickly realises from feedback from his staff that the mean pain prevalence presented to him is so crude that it is not indicative of the true picture. He decides to investigate further and take a sample of 10 patients and measures their pain score every six hours after surgery for three days. Table 3.1 details the results.

When Derek and his staff review the results, they see they have a pain prevalence peak at 12 hours post surgery. One of the staff nurses suggests that, at this stage, the patients have recovered from their anaesthetic, and analgesia given in theatre has worn off. After this, patients are given intramuscular analgesia on an as-needed basis or if there is a patient-controlled analgesia pump available they will be given that. There are only five PCA pumps for the surgical wards so not all patients will get a PCA pump.

- Do you think that the pain scores in Table 3 compare favourably to the national average post routine surgery?
- What do you think is the issue with the analgesic regime utilised on the ward?
- If you were in Derek's shoes what would you do next?

Table 3.1 Record of pain scores taken six-hourly for three days

Day	Time post surgery	Mean pain score
Day 1	6 hrs	3.4
	12 hrs	8.2
	18 hrs	6.5
	24 hrs	7.6
Day 2	30 hrs	6.6
	36 hrs	6.8
	42 hrs	5.4
	48 hrs	5.6
Day 3	54 hrs	4.7
	60 hrs	3.2
	66 hrs	4.6
	72 hrs	4.1

Rapid recap

1 Name two new technologies that have emerged in relation to analgesic administration in the last 30 years.
2 What are the main elements of a pain service?
3 What new roles in pain management are emerging for nurses?

References

Agency for Health Care Policy and Research, Public Health Service (AHCPR) Acute Pain Management Guideline Panel (1992) *Acute Pain Management: Operative or Medical Procedures and Trauma. Clinical Practice Guideline.* AHCPR Pub. No. 92–0032. Department of Health and Human Services, Rockville, Maryland.

Aida S. (2005) The challenge of pre-emptive analgesia. *Pain Clinical Updates IASP,* XIII(2).

Ballantyne J.C., Carr D.B., Chalmers T.C., Keith B.G., Angelillo I.F. and Mosteller F. (1993) Postoperative patient-controlled analgesia: Meta-analyses of initial randomised control trials. *Journal of Clinical Anethesia*, **5**: 182–193.

Bennett R.L., Batenhorst R.L., Bivins B.A., Bell R.M., Bauman T., Graves D.A. *et al.* (1982) Drug use patterns in patient controlled analgesia. *Anaesthesiology,* **57**(3): A210.

Block B.M., Liu S.S., Rowlingson A.J., Cowan A.R. and Wu C.L. (2003) Efficacy of postoperative epidural analgesia. *JAMA*, **290**(18): 2455–2463.

Carr D.B., Reines D., Schaffer J., Polomano R.C. and Lande S. (2005) The impact of technology on the analgesic gap and quality of acute pain management. *Regional Anesthesia and Pain Medicine*, **30**(3): 286–291.

Chelly J.E., Grass J., Houseman T.W., Minkowitz H. and Pue A. (2004) The safety and efficacy of a fentanyl patient-controlled transdermal system for acute postoperative analgesia: A multicenter, placebo-controlled trial. *Anesthesia and Analgesia*, **98**: 427–433.

Choiniere M., Rittenhouse B.E., Perreault S., Chartrand D., Rousseau P., Smith B. and Pepler C. (1998) Efficacy and costs of patient-controlled analgesia versus regularly administered intramuscular opioid therapy. *Anesthesiology*, **89**: 1377–1388.

Chumbley G.M., Hall G.M. and Salmon P. (1998) Patient controlled analgesia: an assessment of 200 patients. *Anaesthesia*, **53**: 216–221.

Clinical Standards Advisory Group (CSAG) (2000) *Services for Patients with Pain*, Department of Health, London.

Cochrane Collaboration (2001) Definitions www.vichealth.vic.gov.au/cochrane/overview/definitions.htm.

Fleming B.M. and Coombes D.W. (1992) A survey of complications documented in a quality control analysis of patient controlled analgesia in the postoperative patient. *Journal of Pain and Symptom Management*, **7**(8): 463–469.

Flor H., Fydrich T. and Turk D.C. (1992) Efficacy of multidisciplinary pain treatment centres: a meta-analytic review. *Pain,* **49**: 221–230.

Gould T.H., Crosby D.L., Harmer M., Lloyd S.M., Lunn J.N., Rees G.A.D. *et al.* (1992) Policy for controlling pain after surgery: effects of sequential changes in management. *BMJ*, **305**: 1187–1193.

Guzman J., Esmail R., Karjalainen K., Malmivaara A., Irvin E. and Bombardier C. (2001) Multidisciplinary rehabilitation for chronic low back pain: systematic review. *BMJ*, **322**:1511–1516.

Harmer M. and Davies K.A. (1998) The effect of education, assessment and a standardised prescription on postoperative pain management. *Anaesthesia,* **53**: 424–430.

Harmer M., Davies K.A. and Lunn J.N. (1995) A survey of acute pain services in the United Kingdom. *BMJ*, **311**: 360–361.

Haugh R. (2005) Hospitals and clinicians confront a new imperative: Pain management. *Hospitals and Health Networks*, **79**(4): 51–56.

Healy, T. (2004) *Our Lady's Hospice: 125 Years of Caring in Ireland.* A. & A. Farma, Dublin.

Holley S., McMillan S.C., Hagan S.J., Palacios P. and Rosenberg D. (2005) Training pain resource nurses: Changes in their knowledge and attitudes. *Oncology Nursing Forum*, **32**(4): 843–848.

Larijani G.E., Sharaf I., Warshal D.P., Marr A., Gratz I. and Goldberg M.E. (2005) Pain evaluation in patients receiving intravenous patient controlled analgesia after surgery. *Pharmacotherapy*, **25**: 1168–1173.

Macintyre P.E. (2001) Safety and efficacy of patient-controlled analgesia. *British Journal of Anaesthesia*, **87**(1): 36–46.

Mackintosh B.A. and Bowles S. (1997) Evaluation of a nurse-led acute pain service. Can clinical nurse specialists make a difference? *Journal of Advanced Nursing*, **25**: 30–37.

Mallett J. and Bailey C. (1996) Epidural Analgesia in *The Royal Marsden NHS Trust Manual of Clinical Nursing Procedures*, 4th edn. Blackwell Science, Oxford, p.259.

McDonnell A., Nicholl J. and Reid S.M. (2003a) Acute pain teams in England: current provision and their role in postoperative pain management. *Journal of Clinical Nursing,* **12**: 387–393.

McDonnell A., Nicholl J. and Reid S.M. (2003b) Acute pain teams in England: a systematic review and meta-analysis. *Journal of Advanced Nursing*, **41**(3): 261–273.

McQuay H.J. (1994) Epidural Analgesics. In Melzack R. and Wall P. *The Textbook of Pain.* Churchill Livingston, Edinburgh, pp.1025–1033.

Meldrum M.L. (2003) A capsule history of pain management. *JAMA*, **290**(18): 2479–2475.

Moiniche S., Kehlet H. and Berg Dahl J. (2002) A qualitative and quantitative systematic review of preemptive analgesia for postoperative pain relief: the role of timing of analgesia. *Anesthesiology*, **96**(3): 725–741.

National Council for Palliative Care. (2004) Palliative care explained. Availaible at: www.ncpc.org.uk/palliative_care.html.

Nurmikko T.J., Nash T.P. and Wiles J.R. (1998) Recent advances: control of chronic pain. *BMJ*, **317**: 1438–1441.

O'Brien, T. and Clark, D. (2005) A national plan for palliative care – the Irish experience. In: *Palliative Care in Ireland* (eds. Ling J. and O'Siorain, L.). Open University Press, Berkshire.

Ochroch E.A., Mardini I.A. and Gottschalk A. (2003) What is the role of NSAIDs in pre-emptive analgesia? *Drugs*, **63**(24): 2709–2723.

Ospina M. and Harstall C. (2003) Multidisciplinary pain programmes for chronic pain: Evidence from systematic reviews. Alberta Heritage Foundation for Medical Research, *Health Technology Assessment*, HTA 30 (Series A): 1–48.

Pain Society, The British Chapter of the International Association for the Study of Pain (2002) *Recommendations for Nursing Practice in Pain Management*. The Pain Society, London.

Passchier J., Rupreht J., Koenders M.E.F., Olree M., Luitweiler R.L. and Bonke B. (1993) Patient controlled analgesia leads to more postoperative pain relief, but also to more fatigue and less vigour. *Acta Anaesthesiology Scandinavia*, **37**: 659–663.

Pesut B. and Johnson J. (1997) Evaluation of an acute pain service. *Canadian Journal of Nursing Administration*, Nov–Dec: 86–107.

Power I. (2005) Recent advances in postoperative pain therapy. *British Journal of Anaesthesia*, **95**(1): 43–51.

Rawal N. and Berggren L. (1994) Organisation of acute pain services: a low cost model. *Pain*, **57**:117–123.

Ready B.L., Oden R., Chadwick H.S., Benedetti C., Rooke G.A., Caplan R *et al*. (1988) Development of an anaestiology-based postoperative pain management service. *Anaesthesiology*, **68**(1): 100–106.

Royal College of Anaesthetists and The Pain Society, the British Chapter of the International Association for the Study of Pain (2003) *Pain Management Services – Good Practice.* Royal College of Anaesthetists and The Pain Society, London.

Schug S.A. and Torrie J.J. (1993) Safety assessment of postoperative pain management by an acute pain service. *Pain*, **55**: 387–391.

Sidebotham D. and Schug S.A. (1997) The safety and utilisation of patient controlled analgesia. *Journal of Pain and Symptom Management*, **14**(4): 202–209.

Snell C.C., Fothergill-Bourvonnais F. and Durocher-Henriks S. (1997) Patient controlled analgesia and intramuscular injections: a comparison of patient pain experiences and postoperative outcomes. *Journal of Advanced Nursing*, **25**: 681–690.

Thomas V., Heath M., Rose D. and Flory P. (1995) Psychological characteristics and the effectiveness of patient controlled analgesia. *British Journal of Anaesthesia*, **74**: 271–276.

Tighe S.Q.M., Bie J.A., Nelson R.A. and Skues M.A. (1998) The acute pain service: effective or expensive care? *Anaesthesia*, **53**: 382–403.

Tsui S.L., Irwin M.G., Wong C.M.L., Fung S.K.Y., Hui T.W.C., Ng K.F. *et al*. (1997) An audit of the safety of an acute pain service. *Anaesthesia*, **52**: 1042–1047.

Veillette Y., Dion D., Altier N. and Choiniere M. (2005) The treatment of chronic pain in Quebec: a study of hospital-based services offered within anesthesia departments. *Canadian Journal of Anesthesia*, **52**(6): 600–606.

Viscusi E.R., Reynolds L., Chung F., Atkinson L.E. and Khanna S. (2004) Patient-controlled transdermal fentanyl hydrochloride vs intravenous morphine pump for postoperative pain. *JAMA*, **291**(11): 1333–1341.

Warfield C.A. and Kahn C.H. (1995) Acute pain management programs in U.S. hospitals and experiences and attitudes among U.S. adults. *Anaesthesiology*, **83**: 1090–1094.

Wheatley R.G., Madjel T.H., Jackson I.J.B. and Hunter D. (1991) The first year's experience of an acute pain service. *British Journal of Anaesthesia*, **67**: 353–359.

Wheatley R.G., Schug S.A. and Watson D. (2001) Safety and efficacy of postoperative epidural analgesia. *British Journal of Anaesthesia*, **87**(1): 47–61.

Williams C. (1996) Patient controlled analgesia: a review of the literature. *Journal of Clinical Nursing*, **5**: 139–147.

Windsor A.M., Glynn C.J. and Mason D.G. (1996) National provision of acute pain services. *Anaesthesia*, **51**: 228–231.

Wnek W., Zajaczkowska R., Wordliczek J., Dobrogowski J.and Korbut R. (2004) Influence of pre-operative ketoprofen administration (preemptive analgesia) on analgesic requirement and the level of prostaglandins in the early postoperative period. *Polish Journal of Pharmacology*, **56**: 547–552.

Zimmermann D.L. and Stewart J. (1993) Postoperative pain management and acute pain service activity in Canada. *Canadian Journal of Anaesthesia*, **40**(6): 568–575.

4 Pain physiology

Learning outcomes

By the end of this chapter you should be able to:

- ★ Describe the functions of the nervous system relative to pain
- ★ Detail the pain pathways
- ★ Explain the importance of the pain pathway for modulating pain
- ★ Appreciate the link between pain classification and the physiology of pain.

Introduction

In order to manage pain effectively health professionals should have a firm understanding of the physiology of pain including the concept that each individual perceives their pain uniquely. This provides the basis for management and modulation of pain. This chapter provides an overview of the central and peripheral nervous system as they relate to pain. The important structures in understanding the physiological mechanisms of pain are provided. As each of these is described, possibilities for modulation of pain at this stage of the pain process will be presented.

Pain pathways

Traditionally, the pain pathway is viewed as consisting of a three-neuron chain that transmits pain signals from the periphery to the cerebral cortex (Cross, 1994). This is the peripheral nociceptor, the spinal cord and the supra-spinal (brain) levels.

At the level of the peripheral nervous system, free nerve endings called nociceptors send pain messages via a series of nerve fibres (neurones) to the central nervous system entering it at the spinal cord. Neurones are highly complex cells sensitive to changes in the environment. They consist of nerve endings, axons (the long fibre of a nerve cell that carries messages) and dendrites (short arm-like protuberances that are branced like a tree from the axon). The speed at which a nerve impulse travels is determined by the diameter of the axon and the presence of myelin. Myelin is a sheath around the axons and dendrites of peripheral neurons. The greater the diameter and the presence of myelin the faster the nerve impulse travels. Synapses (specialised junctions between nerve cells that are bridged by neurotransmitters) occur at the dorsal horn of the grey matter of the spinal cord. These comprise layers or laminae of cells.

The nerve signal then reaches the sensory cortex of the brain via the reticular formation. The reticular formation is a massive neural area of white and grey matter that has a role in the control of body posture, musculoskeletal reflex activity and general behavioural states. It is here that the brain analyses the pain, attributes meaning and links this with emotions and motor activity. The ascending pain pathways comprise:

- neospinothalamic tract (fast ascending fibres)
- paleospinothalamic tract (slow ascending fibres) (also called spino-reticulo-diencephalic tract)
- other ascending pain pathways.

The descending pathway consists of descending fibres passing from brainstem to spinal cord, inhibiting incoming sensations of pain. See Figure 4.1.

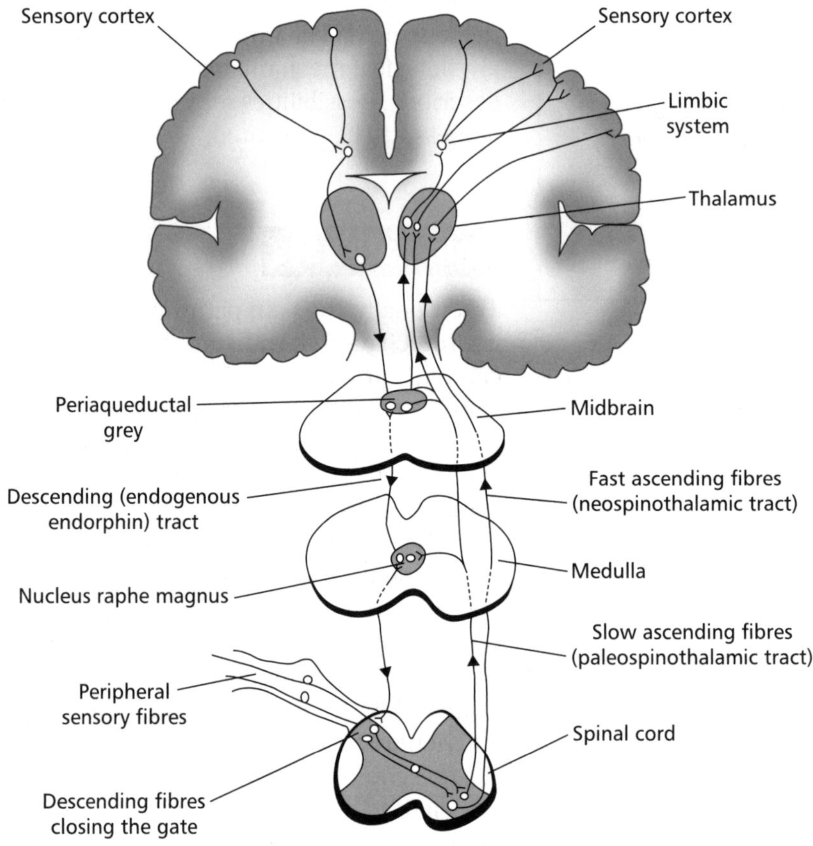

Figure 4.1 Pain pathways. Reproduced with permission from Davis B.D. (2002) Caring for people in pain *p. 37. London, Routledge, part of the Taylor & Francis Group.*

The nervous system

The physiology of pain is a function of the nervous system. It is therefore necessary to understand its anatomy and physiology in order to comprehend the physiological mechanisms of pain. The nervous system consists of two major components:

- the central nervous system (CNS) and
- the peripheral nervous system (PNS).

(See Figure 4.2)

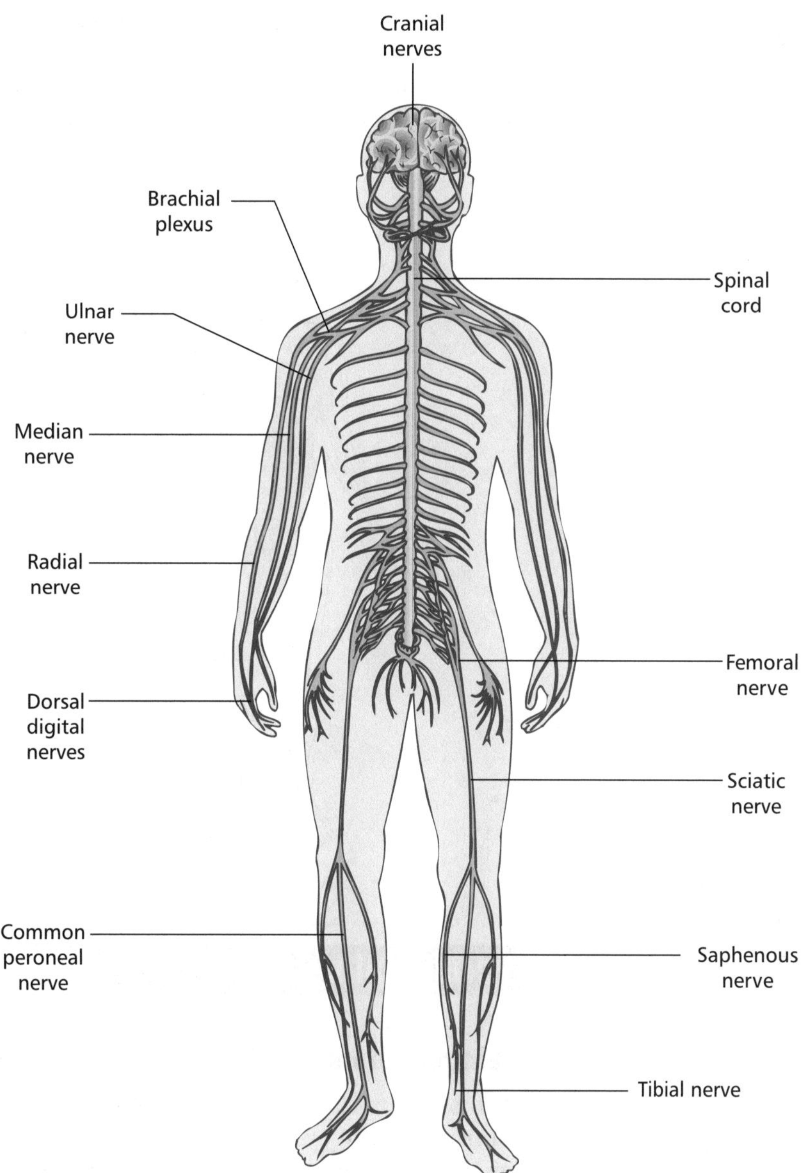

Figure 4.2 The central and peripheral nervous sytem

The CNS, which consists of the brain and spinal cord, receives and processes information.

The PNS consists of 12 pairs of cranial nerves arising from the brain and 31 pairs of nerves arising from the spinal cord. Two types of nerves, afferent and efferent, service the PNS. Afferent nerves form the sensory division of the PNS and carry sensory data including pain data from receptors in the skin, muscles, joints and internal organs to the CNS. Efferent nerves carry nerve impulses from the CNS to the rest of the body making up the motor division of the PNS. Voluntary movement of the body occurs in response to efferent nerves which serve the musculoskeletal system. Involuntary responses occur in response to the autonomic nervous system which supplies the glands, blood vessels, gastrointestinal, respiratory system and other internal organs.

The skin is innervated (stimulation of a muscle or an organ by nerves) by particular nerves and these skin areas are called dermatomes – see Figure 4.3.

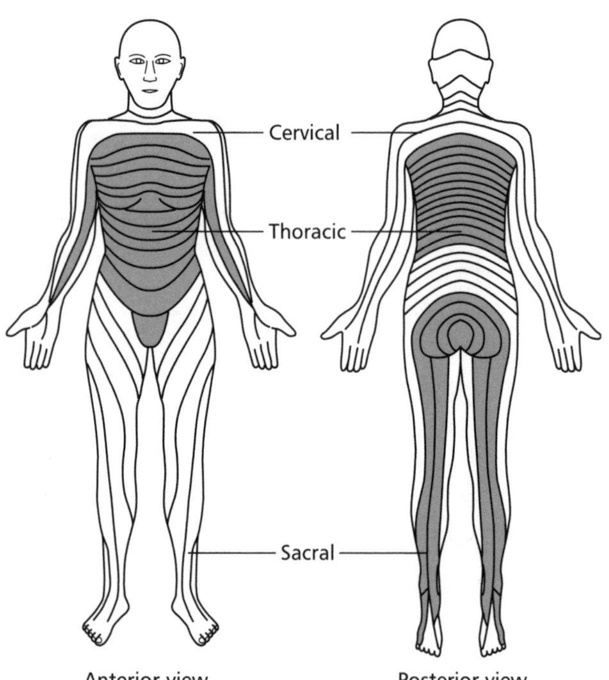

Figure 4.3 Dermatomes

Peripheral nervous system

Pain receptors

Pain receptors are called nociceptors. These are free nerve endings found in almost every tissue of the body including the skin, synovium of joints, artery walls and internal organs. Synovium is a thin layer of tissue which lines the joint space. Nociceptors respond to any type of stimulus if it is strong enough to cause tissue damage. Excessive stimulation of a sense organ causes pain. When stimuli for sensations such as touch, heat and cold reach a certain threshold they stimulate the sensation of pain. Additional stimuli for pain receptors include excessive distension or dilation of a structure, prolonged muscular contractions, muscle spasms, inadequate blood flow to an organ, or the presence of certain chemical substances.

Nociceptors are specific for painful stimuli, responding to damaging or potentially damaging mechanical, chemical and thermal stimuli. Although the actual stimulus for nociceptors is not known, it is assumed that chemicals released from cells damaged by the pain stimulus, such as histamine or bradykinin, activate the nociceptors. Pain receptors perform a protective function by identifying changes that may endanger the body.

Nociceptors are located at the distal end of sensory neurones (see Figure 4.4). They transmit messages to the spinal cord's dorsal horn via nerve fibres.

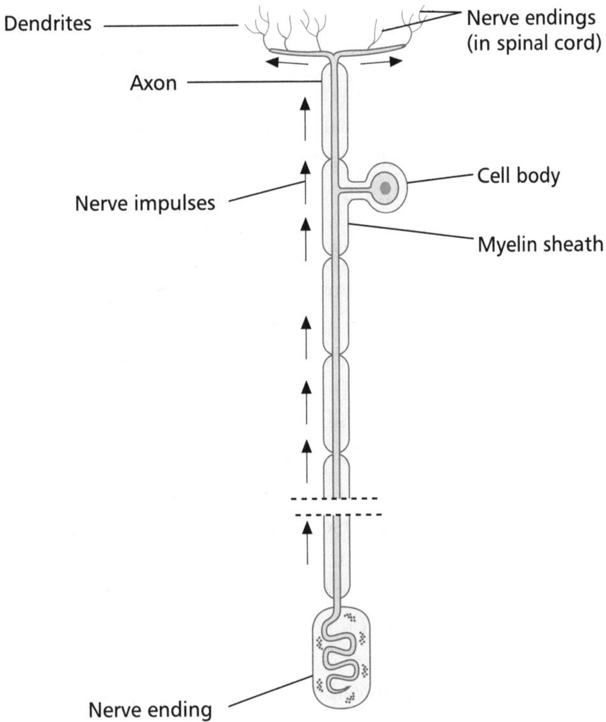

Figure 4.4 A sensory neurone

Nerve fibres are classified by size and according to whether they originate in skin or muscle.

There are two main types of nerve fibre involved in the transmission of pain (nociceptors): A-delta fibres and C-polymodal fibres. Large-diameter fibres (A-beta) are found in the skin and muscle and respond to touch. A-beta fibres are not directly involved in the transmission but are important when discussing the Gate Control Theory (see page 55).

A-delta nociceptors (nerve fibres)

A-delta nociceptors are small-diameter fibres which are myelinated and conduct the transmission of pain rapidly. The myelin sheath speeds up the process of nerve transmission. A-delta nociceptors are found mainly in and just under the skin with some present in muscle. They are activated by noxious stimuli such as pressure, surgery and ischaemia. They are known as high-threshold mechanoreceptors. Some respond to heat and are known as mechanothermal nociceptors. Fast pain occurs very rapidly, usually within 0.1 second after the stimulus is applied, and is not felt in the deeper tissues of the body. This type of pain is also known as sharp, fast and pricking pain. Fast pain is a well-localised, pinprick sensation that results from activating the nociceptors on the A-delta fibres.

C-polymodal nociceptors (nerve fibres)

C-polymodal fibres are small-diameter fibres which are not myelinated and conduct the transmission of pain slower. They are called polymodal because of their ability to respond to mechanical, chemical or thermal stimulus. Slow pain begins after a second or more and then gradually increases in intensity after a period of several seconds or more. It is referred to as burning, aching, throbbing and slow pain. An example is the pain associated with toothache. Slow or delayed pain is a poorly localised, dull, burning sensation that results from activating the nociceptors on the C fibres. This activation is due to the effects of substances released and triggered by damaged cells (see below).

The two types of pain sensation elicit different reflexes. Fast pain evokes a withdrawal reflex and a sympathetic response including an increase in blood pressure and a mobilisation of body energy supplies. Slow pain produces nausea, profuse sweating, a lowering of blood pressure and generalised reduction in skeletal muscle tone (Wang, 1991).

Chemicals at the site of pain

Prostaglandins, histamine, bradykinin and serotonin are chemicals found at the site of pain and thought to excite nociceptors thus increasing the pain sensation (see Table 4.1).

Table 4.1 Chemicals found at the site of pain

Chemical	Action
Prostaglandins	Very specialised fatty acids. They are found at the site of pain/injury. They can cause vasodilation or vasoconstriction, muscle contraction or relaxation, and increase intensity of pain.
Histamine	Released at the site of injury and causes vasodilation and oedema.
Bradykinin	Released upon tissue injury and is present in inflammatory exudates. It evokes a response in nociceptors.
Serotonin	Found at site of pain-activating nociceptors.

Hyperalgesia

Nociceptors can be sensitised so that they continue to send pain messages long after the stimulus is removed. Hyperalgesia is the phenomenon of increased sensitivity of damaged areas to painful stimuli and is categorised as follows:

- primary hyperalgesia occurs within the damaged areas
- secondary hyperalgesia occurs in undamaged tissues surrounding the area.

Modulation of pain at the nociceptor

The aim of modulating pain at the nociceptor is to prevent transmission of the pain signal at the site of pain. Pain at the site is exacerbated by the presence of certain chemicals, such as prostoglandins or bradykinin which is released naturally by the body as part of the inflammatory response. Pain perception is diminished by the reduction or eradication of these chemicals. The drug class of nonsteroidal anti-inflammatory drugs (NSAIDs) act at the site of pain reducing the presence of prostaglandins. NSAIDs have the ability to inhibit prostaglandins, one of the sensitisers of nociceptors. This is why it is clinically indicated in certain circumstances to use NSAIDs early to prevent sensitisation and the consequent augmentation of pain. NSAIDs have numerous side-effects however. COX-2 inhibitors (which are specific NSAIDs selectively inhibiting the cyclo-oxygenase enzyme COX-2) have fewer side-effects than traditional non-selective NSAIDs. NSAIDs (such as Nimesulide (Aulin/Mesulid), which are COX-2 inhibitors, are particularly useful for inflammatory pains such as rheumatoid arthritis.

Peripheral effects of opioids are now being explored. The use of opioid drugs, whose function is to bind with specialised opioid receptors, reduces excitability of nociceptors, and inflammatory peptide release from nerve endings (Power, 2005).

Modulation of pain at the nerve fibre

The aim of modulating pain at the nerve fibre is to prevent the transmission of pain signals along the nerve cell. Nerve conduction depends on sodium ion channels in the axon. Sodium channels help to maintain a neuron's resting state (when sodium channels are closed) and its activation (when sodium channels open). Local anaesthetic agents are absorbed across the membrane of the neurone and block the sodium channels. This means that the electrical impulse cannot be transmitted. For example, a local anaesthetic agent such as lignocaine injected prior to inserting sutures for a traumatic wound in the emergency department is very useful for preventing pain.

Central nervous system

The CNS consists of the brain and spinal cord. A number of neurotransmitters are found in both the brain and spinal cord that are thought to stimulate or modulate the perception of pain. Neurotransmitters facilitate, excite or inhibit post-synaptic neurons. They establish the lines of contact between brain cells (see Table 4.2).

In addition, neuropeptides are present within the brain and spinal cord. They are chemical messengers in the brain. Most act primarily to modulate the response of or the response to a neurotransmitter. (see Table 4.3).

Table 4.2 Neurotransmitters involved in the sensation of pain

Neurotransmitters	Action
Substance P	Found in sensory nerves, spinal cord pathways and parts of the brain associated with pain: stimulates perception of pain. Endorphins may exert their pain-inhibiting properties by suppressing release of substance P.
5-hydroxytryptamine (serotonin)	Modulates pain when acting in the CNS
Glutamine	Likely to be major transmitter in afferent A and C fibres – this occurs in the spinal cord after nerve injury. Glutamine is likely to be a key transmitter in central sensitisation. NMDA (N-methyl-D-aspartine) is a receptor for glutamine. It is found in the dorsal horn. Ketamine is an NMDA antagonist.

Table 4.3 Neuropeptides

Neuropeptide	Action
Enkephalins	Concentrated in the thalamus, hypothalamus, parts of the limbic system and spinal cord pathways that relay pain impulses. They inhibit pain impulses by suppressing substance P. It is suggested that enkephalins are the body's natural painkillers. They act by inhibiting impulses in the pain pathway and by binding to the same receptors in the brain as morphine.
Endorphins	Concentrated in the pituitary gland. They also function by inhibiting substance P. Like enkephalins they have morphine-like properties that suppress pain.
Dymorphin	Found in the posterior pituitary gland, hypothalamus and small intestine. May be related to controlling pain.

Spinal cord and brain

Once pain receptors are stimulated the impulse they discharge travels to the spinal cord and on to the brain via the pain pathways. In the spinal cord the grey matter is divided into 10 laminae. The dorsal part is divided into five laminae (i–v), components of which deal with most incoming pain fibres. A-delta and C fibres enter laminae i and ii. A-beta fibres enter laminae iii and iv. A mixture of A-beta and A-delta enter lamina v. Links between laminae are achieved and maintained through chemical neurotransmitters (Melzack and Wall, 1982). It is in laminae i and ii that the Gate Control Theory mechanism is observed.

In the spinal cord, information on pain is received by cells in the dorsal horn and is passed on to higher centres in the brain along tracts in the spinal cord.

Pain fibres ascending into the cerebrum from the spinal cord may end in a number of sites, particularly the reticular formation, the thalamus and the cerebral cortex. In the reticular formation, the pain stimuli may evoke arousal, changes in heart rate, blood pressure, respiration and other activities. The appreciation or conscious awareness of pain is found in the thalamus and cerebral cortex.

Gate Control Theory

This theory was proposed in 1965 by Melzack and Wall to describe the transmission of pain through the dorsal horn in the spinal cord. Pain impulses must pass through the substantia gelantosia cells, which are present in the dorsal horn of grey matter, in order to travel to the brain and here there is some integration of sensory stimuli. The theory proposes that a neural mechanism in the dorsal horns of the spinal cord acts like a gate which can increase or decrease the flow of nerve impulses from the peripheral fibres to the central nervous system – see Figure 4.5.

This theory is of critical importance because it describes the mechanisms of transmission and modulation of nociceptive signals and it recognises pain as a psycho-physiological phenomenon resulting from the interaction between physiological and psychological events. The Gate Control Theory provided a framework for examining the interactions between local and distant excitatory and inhibitory systems in the dorsal horn and has generated much debate and discussion leading to many research studies. Melzack and Wall expanded the conceptualisation of pain from a purely sensory phenomenon to a multidimensional model that integrates the motivational-affective and cognitive-evaluative components with the sensory-physiological one (Turk and Melzack 2001). Dickenson (2002) suggests that the Gate Control Theory was a leap of faith but that it was right. The concepts of convergence and modulation reduced the emphasis on destruction of pathways and led to the idea that pain could be controlled by modulation. The capacity of pain signalling and modulating systems to alter in different circumstances has changed thinking about pain control.

The Gate Control Theory is a very important milestone in understanding the physiology of pain. The fact that it is relatively recent (1965) emphasises the newness of our understanding of pain physiology.

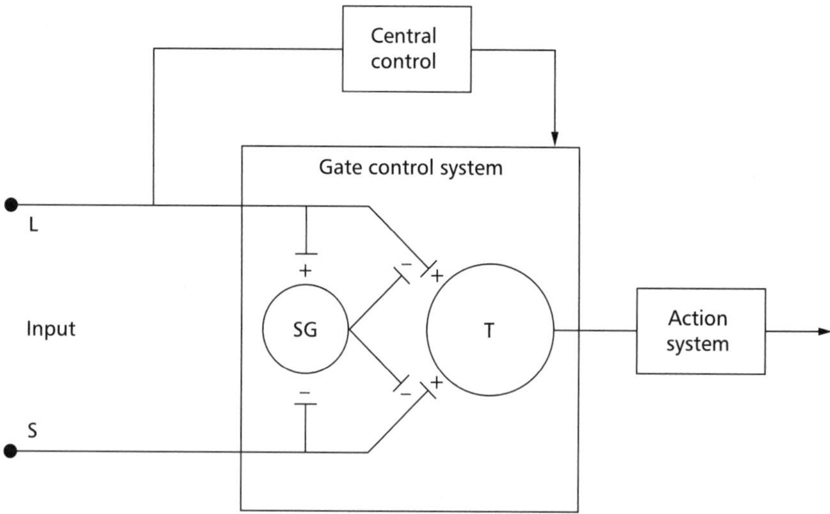

Figure 4.5 Gate Control Theory (adapted from Melzack and Wall, 1965).

Modulation of pain using the Gate Control Theory

The degree to which the gate increases or decreases sensory transmission is determined by the relative activity in large-diameter (A-beta) and small-diameter (A-delta and C) fibres and by descending influences from the brain. Entry into the CNS can be visualised as a gate, which is opened by pain-generated impulses and closed by low-intensity stimuli such as rubbing or electrical stimulation (TENS). Furthermore, it can be closed by endogenous opioid mechanisms which can be activated from the brain or peripherally by acupuncture or by gentle rubbing, massage, electrical stimulation and hot or cold therapies. The theory suggests that descending influences consist of attention, anxiety, anticipation and past experience – all of which may exert control over sensory input (Melzack and Wall, 1982).

Modulation of pain within the spinal cord and brain

The aim of modulating pain within the spinal cord is to prevent the transmission of pain signals to the brain. The Gate Control Theory, as described above, suggests processes for such modulation.

These include the inhibition of the release of chemical transmitters at the various synapses within the dorsal horn of the spinal cord and brain as a result of the uptake of naturally occurring morphine-like substances by specialised receptors on relevant neurones. The use of opioid drugs whose function is to bind with these specialised receptors will reduce pain perception. There are three main types of opioid receptor (mu μ, delta δ and kappa κ). For example, the use of morphine in a patient-controlled analgesia pump (PCA) post surgery is extremely effective for pain relief. The morphine acts as an **agonist** for the opioid receptor. Naloxone is an **antagonist**.

Keywords

Agonists
Drugs that bind to and stimulate opioid receptors

Antagonists
Drugs that bind to but do not stimulate opioid receptors and may reverse the effect of opioid agonist

Classification of pain

Pain can be classified in a number of ways according to type of pain, source of pain, speed of transmission of nerve signals or other pains (see Figure 4.6).

Categories of pain

Pain is usually classified into two major categories, i.e. acute and chronic, based on speed of onset, quality and duration of the sensation.

Acute pain

A distinguishing characteristic of acute pain is that it subsides as healing takes place, i.e. it has a predictable end and it is of brief duration, usually less than six months. Acute pain usually means sudden severe pain. Postoperative pain is an example. Acute pain is characterised by a

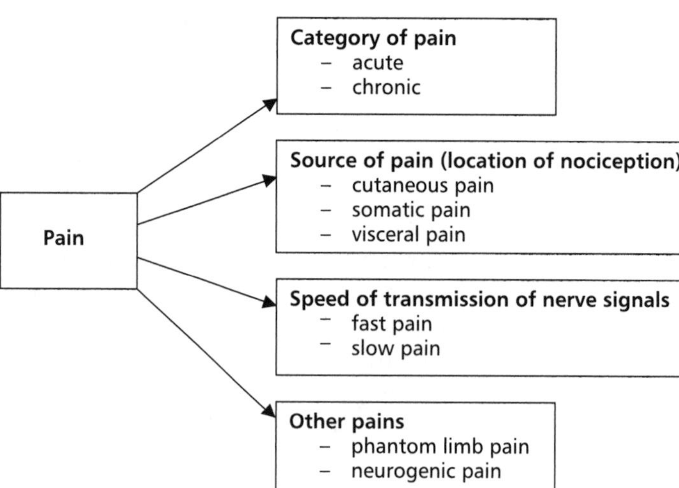

Figure 4.6 Classification of pain

well-defined time of onset and is associated with both subjective and objective signs indicating activation of the autonomic nervous system.

Chronic pain

Chronic pain is prolonged. It is pain that persists beyond the usual healing phase of the disease process. Chronic pain is characterised by patient distress rather than pain (Hardy, 1997).

Pain types

Pain can be classified into cutaneous, deep somatic or visceral pain according to the site of stimulation.

Cutaneous pain is produced by stimulation of the pain receptors in the skin. It can be accurately localised due to the large number of receptors in the skin. Touch and vision greatly increase localisation of cutaneous pain.

Somatic pain is produced by stimulation of pain receptors in the deep structures, i.e. muscles, bones, joints, tendons, ligaments. Unlike cutaneous pain, deep somatic pain is dull, intense and prolonged. It is usually associated with autonomic stimulation, e.g. sweating, vomiting and changes in heart rate and blood pressure. Pain from deeper structures can also initiate reflex contraction of nearby muscles, e.g. muscle spasm associated with bone fractures. The adequate stimuli for deep somatic pain include:

- mechanical forces, e.g. severe pressure on a bone, traction of muscle or ligament
- chemicals such as venom, acids or alkalis
- ischaemia, e.g. muscle ischaemia such as angina.

Visceral pain is produced by stimulation of pain receptors in the viscera. Visceral nociceptors are located within body organs and internal cavities. Visceral pain is caused by disorders of internal organs such as the stomach, kidney, gallbladder, urinary bladder, intestines and others. These disorders include distension from impaction or tumours, ischaemia and inflammation (Al-Chaer and Traub, 2002).

In contrast to the skin, which is richly innervated by sensory neurons, the visceral receptors of the abdominal and thoracic viscera are sparsely innervated. This means that they have fewer sensory neurons than other areas such as the skin. Therefore, severe visceral pain indicates diffuse stimulation of pain receptors from a wide area of the viscus. Visceral pain:

- is poorly localised
- is often referred or radiates to other sites, e.g. pain of a myocardial infarction is classically felt centrally just behind the sternum, radiating down the left arm and up the root of the neck into the jaw – see Figure 4.7
- is often associated with autonomic disturbances, e.g. vomiting, sweating, tachycardia
- can be associated with rigidity and tenderness of nearby skeletal muscles.

Neurogenic/neuropathic pain is described as burning, electric, tingling or shooting in nature. It may be continuous or paroxysmal in

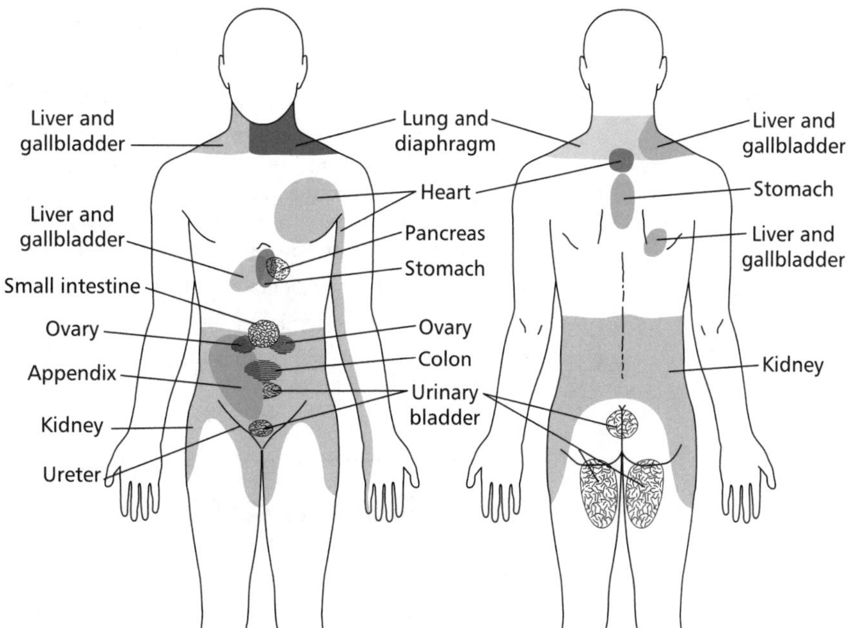

Figure 4.7 Referred pain

presentation. Neuropathic pain is produced by damage to or pathological changes to the nerve itself. Neuropathic pain, thus, does not always respond to traditional analgesic therapies of NSAIDS or opioids. It responds to co-analgesics such as tricyclics.

Key points Top tips

- Pain is a function of the nervous system, both central and peripheral
- Pain is classified in a number of ways: according to type of pain, source of pain, speed of transmission of nerve signals or other pains
- Gate Control Theory can help in understanding how some pain care treatments work
- Pain can be modulated at the site of pain, in the spinal cord and brain

Referred pain

Sue presents to her general practitioner (GP) with pain in her right side. Sue is a 42-year-old accountant. She is fit – running 45–60 minutes on the treadmill five days a week. She is slim and eats sensibly. She is studying part time for a law degree and seems to be very busy with a full life. She has had the pain for some time and is now getting anxious. The general practitioner suspects gallstones and refers Sue to the local hospital. Three weeks later, Sue is reviewed by the general surgeon who elicits a full history and performs a physical examination. Agreeing with the GP, he suspects gall stones and orders an ultrasound to confirm diagnosis. Sue is subsequently diagnosed with gall stones despite being an atypical profile. The ultrasound identified three rather large stones in the gallbladder and one in the biliary tract. She is scheduled for a laparoscopic cholecystectomy the next month.

Sue continues to have pain at home while she waits for her surgery. In addition to the pain in her side, she is also suffering from a darting pain in her right shoulder. She describes her pain as a sharp biting kind of pain, which is very acute.

Sue goes back to the general practitioner. He reassures her by telling her that her pain including that in her shoulder is classic gallstones. He prescribes her a nonsteroidal anti-inflammatory for her pain while she is waiting to go into hospital.

- Can you explain what is meant by referred pain?
- How will the nonsteroidal anti-inflammatory medication help alleviate Sue's pain?
- How would the Gate Control Theory help you manage Sue's pain?

RRRRRRapid recap

1 What are the main ascending pain pathways?
2 How do the various chemicals at the site of pain work?
3 What is the Gate Control Theory of Pain?

References

Al-Chaer E.D. and Traub R.J. (2002) Biological basis of visceral pain: Recent developments. *Pain*, **96**: 221–225.

Cross S.A. (1994) Symposium on pain management – Part 1 pathophysiology of pain. *Mayo Clinical Proceedings*, **69**: 375–383.

Dickenson A.H. (2002) Gate Control Theory of Pain stands the test of time. Editorial *British Journal of Anaesthesia*, **88**(6): 755–757.

Hardy P.A.J. (1997) The Essentials. In *Chronic Pain Management: The Essentials.* Oxford University Press, Oxford, p. 8.

Melzack R. and Wall P. (1982) The Gate Control Theory of Pain. In: *The Challenge of Pain.* 2nd edn. Penguin books, London, pp. 222–231.

Power I. (2005) Recent advances in postoperative pain therapy. *British Journal of Anaesthesia*, **95**(1): 43–51.

Turk D.C. and Melzack R. (2001*) Handbook of Pain Assessment*, 2nd edn. The Guilford Press, New York.

Wang M.B. (1991) Neurophysiology. In: *Physiology,* 2nd edn. (eds. Bullock J., Boyle J. and Wang M.B). Williams and Wilkins, Baltimore, pp. 43–44.

5 Influencing factors for the pain experience

Learning outcomes

By the end of this chapter you should be able to:

- ★ Understand the factors that influence the pain experience for the patient
- ★ Be able to discuss the emotional aspect of pain
- ★ Understand the importance of the role of the patient in their pain experience

Introduction

This chapter will help in understanding the factors that influence the pain experience. Pain is a personal and unique experience for the individual. While much is known about the physiology of pain the emotive and contextual aspects of pain continue to challenge our understanding. The meaning of pain to an individual and the importance of culture and knowledge of patients will be discussed. Influences on pain experiences will be described at a macro level (pain as a public health issue), meso level (organisational responses to pain) and a micro level (how the individual experiences their pain).

Meaning of pain

The cause of an individual's pain will strongly relate to how that pain is experienced by any individual, i.e. the extent of pain will relate to the level of nociception involved (see Chapter 4 for more detail on nociception). However, the context of that pain will shape the experience and subsequent management of that pain. The patients' knowledge of pain and analgesia, their expectations of pain, past experiences of pain, fear of addiction, anxiety, culture, age, lack of information and the influence of public and organisational policy and health professional responsible for care all form part of the pain experience. For those attending health services the overall service philosophy and approach to pain will be instrumental in the way pain is perceived and managed. Figure 5.1 highlights these issues.

Epidemiological studies examine pain as it occurs in groups of people or even whole populations attempting to discern the populations who suffer pain. This chapter, while attempting to review the evidence of the influences on pain, highlights the lack of empirical evidence available on the influences on pain and the need for further research in this area. Crombie (1999) supports this and details the difficulty with accessing the many studies on the epidemiology of pain due to their being published in a diverse array of journals. He stresses

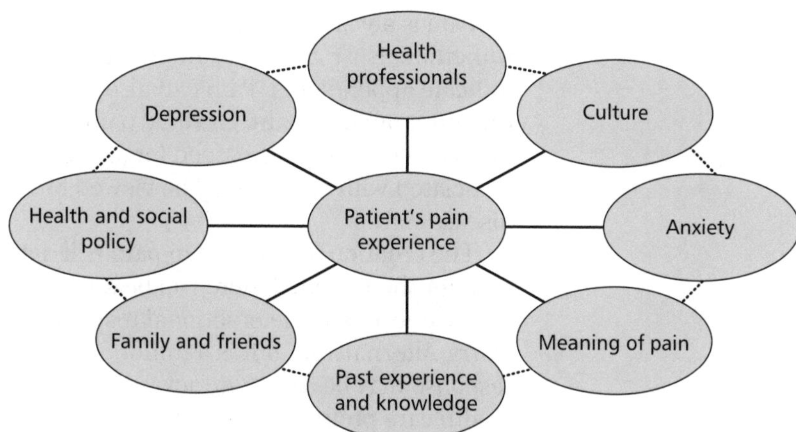

Figure 5.1 Factors that influence the pain experience

the importance of the need for more systematic reviews to grade the quality of these studies. There is great potential for the epidemiology of pain to help decide what kind and what level of health service provision should be provided and to influence health promotion. The International Association for the Study of Pain (IASP) (1999) bring together a number of high-quality research studies on the epidemiology of pain which are summarised in Table 5.1.

Table 5.1 Research studies on the epidemiology of pain. (Source: ISAP, 1999)

Factors	Key messages
Role of Psychological Factors	• Psychology contributes to the understanding of individuals' pain perception and behaviour • A psychological view enhances a holistic conception of pain • A psychological perspective may explain a patient's reactions in specific contexts
Gender Considerations in the Epidemiology of Chronic Pain	• No simple relationship in gender consideration of the epidemiology of chronic pain • Patterns differ from condition to condition • Gender-specific prevalence for most conditions varies across the life cycle
Cross-cultural Investigations of Pain	• Coping style and disability/dysfunction reflect the most variance in pain experiences across cultures
Pain in Older People	• The well-documented increase in pathological load, particularly degenerative joint and spine disease and leg and foot disorders may help explain the increased frequency of pain report in surveys of older persons • Age-related increases in overall pain prevalence does not continue beyond the seventh decade of life

Pain is a warning of danger and is often the first indication that something is wrong, for example right-sided lower abdominal pain may indicate appendicitis. Pain can also be seen as life threatening, such as the onset of chest pain. Chronic pain may indicate a potential reduction in quality of life and the need for subsequent lifestyle changes. Pain associated with cancer may be viewed by the patient as deterioration in disease status.

The emotional response to pain will depend on the meaning of the pain for the patient. There will be an emotional response. If there is severe chest pain the emotional response may be intense anxiety and worry. Alternatively, if it is a minor, superficial burn the emotional response may be that of annoyance. It is therefore important for the health care professional to be aware of the likely responses of patients and how they might affect decisions in relation to developing pain management regimes.

Various models of pain perception have evolved over the years. Linton and Skevington (1999) provide a model which demonstrates a cross-sectional view of the psychological processes involved in pain perception including attributions, coping and behaviour (Figure 5.2). The first step in the model is the noxious stimulus. The model stresses the role of appraisal and beliefs, which compliment those of coping and learning. The authors state that these may not be conscious processes. The consequences of the behaviour affect the emotional, cognitive and behavioural aspects.

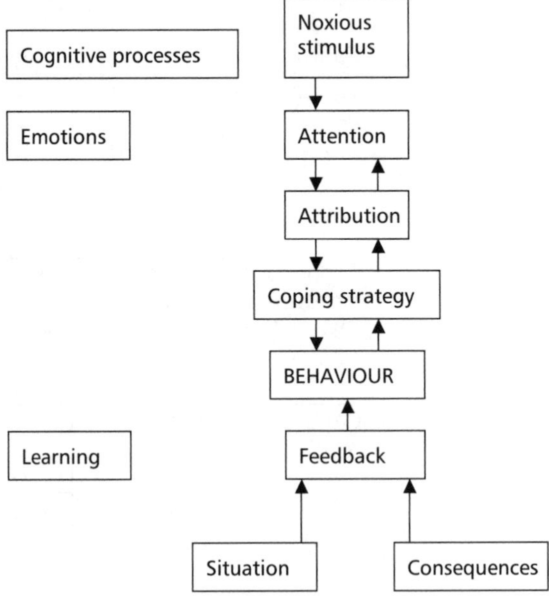

Figure 5.2 Cross-sectional view of the psychological processes involved in pain perception. Reproduced with permission from IASP Press. Originally published in Epidemiology of Pain. *Steven J Linton and Suzanne M Skevington. Editors Crombie, I.K., Croft, P.R., Linton S.J., Le Resche, L., and von Korff, M. IASP Press, Seattle.*

Linton and Skevington (1999) suggest that a psychological approach may help explain the relationship between physiological, behavioural and cognitive and emotional aspects of pain. They emphasise the reciprocal nature of the relationship, showing that pain may influence mood but mood may also affect pain perception.

Pain as a public health issue

At a macro level pain is a public health issue with international collaboration as an expanding feature of public health (further detail in Chapter 2). The influence and need for such influence from organisations such as the World Health Organization (WHO) and the IASP is critical in ensuring that pain is viewed as a public health issue and as such a global problem. The WHO's influence on governments worldwide and on national health care programmes and policies is seen to lay the ground work for better management of acute, chronic and cancer pain.

The seriousness with which governments and health service providers consider pain a health issue has considerable influence on how individuals will experience their pain. Where national protocols and guidelines exist to set templates for service providers, the more likely it is that the recipients of care will receive an adequate pain management plan.

Pain initiatives have staff and resource implications, but economic justification can be found in the reduced morbidity, faster convalescence, increased quality of life and work days, and improved satisfaction in patients who receive adequate relief from pain (Clinical Standards Advisory Group (CSAG), 2000; Macintyre and Ready, 2002). Service providers should use quality assurance procedures periodically to ensure that best practice in pain management is being carried out. The use of clinical audit described in Chapter 2 could be viewed in conjunction with evidence-based guidelines as significant influencers of change and as factors that impact on how pain is experienced.

Culture and ethnicity

Worldwide mobility has raised the profile of culture, race and ethnicity in health care in general and in pain management specifically. Culture can be defined as the beliefs, customs and behaviours of a group of individuals due to ethnicity, religion, origin or current residence (Green, 2004). Dimsdale (2000) identifies that ethnicity affects the type of illness suffered. Cultural factors related to the pain experience include pain expression, pain language, lay remedies for pain, social roles and expectations, and perceptions of the medical care system

(Lasch, 2002). Globally migration patterns challenge traditional homogeneous views of the universal problem of pain management with little research reported about pain management related to culture (Sherwood *et al.*, 2005).

Green *et al.* (2003) undertook a literature review and conclude that there are racial and ethnic disparities in pain perception, assessment and treatment across all types of pain (acute, cancer, chronic non-malignant and experimental). Sources of pain disparities are complex involving patient (e.g. patient/health care provider communication, attitudes), health care provider (e.g. decision making) and health care system (access to pain medication) factors. Blanchard *et al.* (2003) outline a number of factors that contribute to racial disparities in emergency and acute medicine care:

- poverty and access to care
- differences due to health insurance levels
- differences in the delivery of care
- physician characteristics and factors within the doctor–patient relationship.

The literature, however, reports mixed views highlighting the important need for further research in this area. Choi (2000) conducted a chart review of long-bone fractures in a UK hospital accident and emergency department with attendees from a number of ethnic backgrounds. The authors found no difference between those who received analgesia. Tamayo-Sarver *et al.* (2003) in a US study utilising vignettes (hypothetical clinical cases) identified no effect of patient race or ethnicity on physician prescription of opioids at discharge for African American, Hispanic and white patients. Tan *et al.* (2005) suggest that attitudes, beliefs, coping mechanisms and adjustments to chronic pain are comparable among non-Hispanic black and white patients comparing self reports of 128 non-Hispanic black Americans and 354 non-Hispanic white Americans. However, Bonham (2001), following a literature review on disparities in treatment of pain based on race and ethnicity, suggests that patients coming from racial and ethnic minority groups are at more risk of ineffective treatment of pain.

Over to you

Read the article by Bonham (2001): Bonham V.L. (2001) Race, Ethnicity, and Pain Treatment: Striving to Understand the Causes and Solution to the Disparities in Pain Treatment. *Journal of Law, Medicine and Ethics*, 29: 52–68.

Identify three key points from the article and bring them for discussion to your next journal club meeting or mentor/supervisor meeting.

Jones (2005), on reviewing 119 qualitative studies on end-of-life and ethnicity/race/diversity issues, stressed that a common theme emerging is a need for sensitivity to the varying expectations and the mix of involvement of patients, practitioners and families and the need for information sharing in end-of-life care. Jones also cautioned against 'cookbook' solutions to ethnicity, highlighting that there is diversity within ethnic groups themselves. Choi (2000) supports this suggesting that factors such as ethnicity, pain threshold, communication of pain to health care staff and relationships between patients and staff all influence determination of prescription of analgesia.

While it emerges that access to care, expression of pain and usage of interventions can vary among various cultures, for the nurse or health care professional managing a pain situation some common guidelines apply:

- sensitivity to individual needs of patient and their family
- utilising a comprehensive pain history and assessment appropriate to classification of pain
- constant attention to communications
- underlying philosophy of pain management 'pain is what the patient says it is'.

Reflective activity

Are there a number of different cultures represented in your patient caseload? How many of the following four principles do you use when considering pain management for your patients?

1 Sensitivity to individual needs of patient and their family
2 Utilising a comprehensive pain history and assessment appropriate to classification of pain
3 Constant attention to communications
4 Underlying philosophy of pain management 'pain is what the patient says it is'

The future may partly lie in genetic research. Kim and Dionne (2005) describe how genetic research in pain is just beginning, but that in the future it may be possible to determine treatments based on each individual's genetic profile. It may be possible to identify genes involved in the mediation of pain and genes that contribute to experimental painful stimuli.

Key points Top tips

- Understand that the pain experience is unique to each individual patient regardless of culture or ethnicity or age
- Be sensitive to individual needs
- Obtain a comprehensive pain history
- Utilise appropriate pain assessment techniques
- Ensure communication of pain assessment and management is understood by patient, family and health professionals

Team approaches

At a meso/organisational level pain is a multidimensional phenomenon which requires team approaches to its management. It requires professionals working together involving the input of doctors, anaesthetists, nurses, physiotherapists, occupational therapists and psychologists. The combined expertise of individual practitioners provides a more effective service to patients and their families. Pain management is an interactive and collaborative process involving the patient and family, nurse, doctor and other providers, as appropriate to the care setting.

The knowledge and attitudes of patients and health care staff have become an increasing subject of interest in pain management. Erroneous knowledge with regard to pain, analgesics and pain management contribute to patients not receiving best possible pain interventions. In the early 1980s it began to emerge that the need to have dedicated staff with specialised knowledge to support pain management was critical in order to improve the day-to-day management of pain. Professional standards for treatment facilities for pain set out definitions and standards for pain clinics and pain centres. There is a strong commitment to a multidisciplinary approach to diagnosis and treatment of pain. A number of statements and standards have emerged in relation to pain facilities. Chapter 3 discusses types of pain services in more detail.

Evidence-based approaches are critical to ensure that patients receive tested pain management approaches which are up to date and in line with international standards.

Modern approaches are about taking pain seriously, seriously enough to have dedicated services, protocols, guidelines, staff and patient education in place. The importance of listening to the patient, assessing pain regularly, and using multidisciplinary, multimodal approaches is advocated.

Organisational approaches to pain management should be evidence-based, planned, co-ordinated and audited utilising policies and guidelines as appropriate. Central to integration of care is a focus on the client with the most important objective being to improve continuity of care within the organisation and across providers and settings. Models of service delivery which place the client at the centre of the care continuum can help providers to reduce gaps, avoid unnecessary duplication, and ensure that clients are well supported in navigating 'the health system'. Such integration requires organisations to develop the simplest and most accessible pathways for clients. This means that there is a dependent interrelationship between pain assessment, pain history, pain management, knowledge of patients and staff, and clinical audit. By utilising this modern approach, the pain experience for patients will improve. Figure 5.3 highlights these interactions.

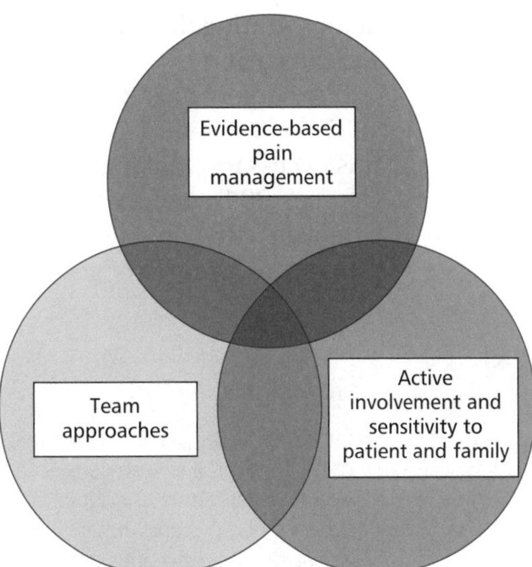

Figure 5.3 Example of interactions necessary for a modern approach to pain management

Clinical Nurse Specialist Pain Management

It is not enough any more to concentrate on looking after your patient in isolation, nurses and all the members of the health care team . . . the doctors, physiotherapists, anaesthetists must actively work together, sharing information and discussing and reviewing best case management through care pathways and audit. In addition bridges must be put in place between hospital and community to ensure that when your patient is discharged from hospital there is continuity and a smoothness in the transition of care in the community.

Patient knowledge and attitudes

At a micro level the influence that the patients themselves have on their pain management has become an increasing subject for research. It is reasonable to assume that while the patient is a recipient of care, they then have an influence on how their pain is managed. The consideration that patient expectations will influence how they communicate their pain and when they will request pain interventions has emerged. Patients expecting to have pain may make fewer demands and less reports of pain, making it a more difficult task to control. Patients believing that it is possible to become addicted to strong pain-killers while in hospital may compound these expectations (Winefield, 1990; Lavies 1992).

Many patients wait until they have severe pain before asking for medication (Owen, 1990; Winefield 1990). Juhl (1993) supports this demonstrating that only 64% of patients would always complain if they were in pain.

Pre surgery most patients anticipate a high amount of pain (Carr, 1997; Pellino 1997). Many patients believe that pain following surgery was necessary thinking they would 'just have to put up with it' (Hume,1994), and that 'you should put up with a bit of pain rather than complain' (Brydon, 1996; Scott & Hodson, 1997). Patients do not always rate the importance of good pain relief to their recovery (Laing, 1993).

Staff Nurse surgical ward

I find that older patients don't talk about pain. . . they talk about some soreness or discomfort. It is easy to ignore this and not consider it as pain and I have to explain to students and junior nurses that this is the terminology these older patients use . . . and that it is as important to manage that 'soreness' as actively as we manage the patient who complains of severe pain or that older patient will not be able to mobilise or cough which will slow his/her recovery and may mean a longer length of stay and more complications such as chest infections.

Interestingly in 2004 Fosnocht *et al.* reported that the expectations of patients attending the accident and emergency department may differ from that of other clinical settings. Their study showed that patients with pain reported a mean expectation for pain relief of 72% with 18% expecting complete relief of their pain. Expectation did not vary based on age or gender.

Patients, however, continue to have a high degree of confidence in the ability of doctors and nurses to treat pain (Scott and Hodson, 1997).

Interestingly many studies agree that patients continue to report high satisfaction with pain management in spite of high levels of pain (Miaskowski *et al.*, 1994; Jamison *et al.*, 1997; McNeill *et al.*, 1998) perhaps because they do not have sufficient knowledge of pain relief and may judge the kindness of staff rather than their way of treating pain (Bostrom *et al.*, 1997).

Increasing patients' knowledge and engaging them more actively in their own care can be the beginning of a process to improve pain management. Patients expecting to have pain make fewer demands and less reports of pain, making it a more difficult task to control. Stoic attitudes with regard to pain and fear of addiction all contribute to how patients view themselves within the health care system. It is only in the last 20 years that the need to provide appropriate information to patients has become routine. It has become evident that pain will not be managed well if the patient is not an active participant in the process. Pain standards recommend that it is part of all health professionals' history taking and assessment of pain to review patient knowledge with regard to any pain and pain relief and ensure that patients are given accurate, appropriate information in a timely manner.

Reflective activity

Consider your patient profile. How much do your patients know about pain and pain relief? Ask three patients: (a) do they think suffering pain is bad for them? (b) what painkillers are they on? and (c) are there any side effects from the painkillers?

Anxiety and depression

The role of anxiety and depression in the experience of both acute and chronic pain has been the subject of debate for some time. Anxiety, depression and pain are often linked together in the literature. However, Symreng and Fishman (2004) suggest that rigorous studies on the interactions between anxiety and pain are still in their infancy. There is increasing evidence that psychological disorders such as depression (Tsai, 2005) often coexist with or are exacerbated by chronic pain. For example, Kenefick (2004) conducted a study to examine the relationships among cognitive impairment, communication and pain in elderly nursing residents (n = 111). Results identified that cognitive impairment is significantly associated with depression, and pain increases the strength of the relationship between cognitive impairment and depression.

Carr *et al.* (2005) explored the impact of anxiety and depression on women's pain experience over time following surgery. Preoperative anxiety was found to be predictive of postoperative anxiety, with patients who experienced high levels of anxiety before surgery continuing to feel anxious afterwards. Anxiety and depression scores increased as pain increased.

Evidence base

The role of patient information and knowledge on pain perception and anxiety has been the subject of considerable research over time. It is intuitive that if patients were more knowledgeable they would be less anxious, more informed and take more control of their pain management. The research studies of Hayward (1971)and Boore (1978) are considered seminal in terms of examining the role of patient information and its effect on anxiety post surgery. One of the first studies in relation to patient information came from Hayward in 1971. He hypothesised that those patients who were given information appertaining to their illness and recovery would, when compared with an appropriate control group, report less anxiety and pain during the postoperative period. He studied two hospitals and had an informed group and a control group in each hospital. In the first hospital, although the informed group consistently had lower pain scores the only significant differences were for day five post surgery when informed patients were recording significantly less pain. In the second hospital the differences in pain between the informed group and the control group reached significance on both day four and day five post surgery. Hayward concluded that the results gave strong support to the idea that informed patients became relatively pain free more rapidly than usual. Patients in both hospitals in the informed group consistently received less analgesic medications. However, this did not reach statistical significance on all postoperative days.

Following on from this Boore (1978) tested the hypothesis that giving information about prospective treatment and care preoperatively, and teaching exercises to be performed postoperatively, would minimise the rise in biochemical indicators of stress. Pain scores were measured. There was very little difference to be seen between experimental and control groups and no significant results were obtained. Much other work has been completed since then measuring narcotic use, pain and anxiety following information given to patients. However, experimental studies on information given pre surgery do not demonstrate significant differences in level of pain experienced postoperatively (Hawkins and Price,1993; Schwartz-Barcott *et al.*, 1994; Hawkins, 1997).

More recently Lin and Wang (2005) suggest that preoperative nursing intervention for pain has positive effects for patients undergoing surgery. This experimental study provided patients with preoperative education. The study reports decreased anxiety and pain levels with a preoperative nursing intervention.

The role of anxiety, depression and patient information in the reporting and management of pain will remain topical for some time. Due to their inevitable interaction, when pain and anxiety are both present, it may be difficult to identify which one is the predisposing factor. Rigourous scientific research with larger sample sizes and more diverse patient groups is required.

Key points Top tips

- Patients' knowledge and attitudes influence how their pain is managed
- Culture, race and ethnicity are important considerations
- Education of staff is critical
- Multidisciplinary teams and multimodal approaches support quality patient care
- Governments and service managers have significant roles in ensuring quality pain management approaches

The importance of a comprehensive pain assessment

Michael is a 75-year-old farmer living in a very rural area. He runs a 150 acre farm with his wife Kate, looking after livestock, growing wheat and selling a number of market garden vegetables. They have two farm labourers who help three days a week. Michael is very 'hands on' and likes to spend about six to eight hours on the farm a day. He is very fit, although he has some arthritis but it is not so severe as to hamper his work. Michael is also very sociable and leads on the local whist games in the community hall and enjoys a few pints of beer at the weekends.

Kate has been getting a bit worried that in the last few weeks Michael doesn't seem to have much energy and falls asleep most evenings around seven o'clock which is very unlike him. He has also stopped going out to his whist games. She persuades him to visit the general practitioner. The general practitioner discusses Michael's tiredness with him. They talk about how busy the farm is. She is not unduly concerned as she perceives he is not getting any younger and maybe needs to slow down a bit. Michael leaves the general practitioner satisfied that he knew all along nothing was wrong and that Kate was worrying unnecessarily.

Michael and Kate's daughter Fiona comes to visit the next weekend. She is alarmed at how her Dad seems to be deteriorating and goes out with him for a walk. Fiona notices that every now and again her Dad puts his right hand behind him and rubs his back. She asks him if there is a problem. He says no but Fiona insists on looking at his back. She is astonished to see large fading bruises and asks him what happened. It turns out a gate had fallen on his back a few weeks beforehand. He admits to it being a bit sore saying he is not sleeping well.

Fiona immediately brings him back to the general practitioner for a full examination. Following an X-ray at the local hospital it turns out that Michael has no serious damage but has soft tissue injury. He is started on nonsteroidal anti-inflammatories and over the course of a week starts to sleep again and in three weeks has his usual energy levels back.

Kate asks him why he didn't say anything. He said that it was only a bit of pain which you should be able to put with. He knew it was going to get better anyway so why worry anyone. He said he thought he was just wasting the general practitioner's time.

1 By taking the approach that Michael's age was slowing him down meant that the general practitioner missed Michael's real diagnosis. What other questions could she have asked him?

2 How did Michael's stoic attitude affect his quality of life?

Rapid recap

1 Name three factors which form the context of patients' pain.
2 Define what is meant by culture.
3 Name two organisations who view pain as a public health issue.

References

Blanchard J.C. (2003) Racial and ethnic disparities in health: An emergency medicine perspective. *Academic Emergency Medicine*, **10**(11): 1289–1293.

Bonham V.L. (2001) Race, ethnicity, and pain treatment: striving to understand the causes and solution to the disparities in pain treatment. *Journal of Law, Medicine and Ethics*, **29**: 52–68.

Boore J. (1978) *Prescription for Recovery*. London, RCN Publication, pp. 50–56.

Bostrom B.M., Ramberg T., Davis B.D. and Fridlund B. (1997) Survey of post-operative patients' pain management. *Journal of Nursing Management*, **5**: 341–349.

Brydon C.W. and Asbury A.J. (1996) Attitudes to pain and pain relief in adult surgical patients. *Anaesthesia*, **51**: 279–281.

Carr E.C.J. (1990) Postoperative pain: patient's expectations and experiences. *Journal of Advanced Nursing*, **15**: 89–100.

Carr E.C.J. and Thomas V.J. (1997) Anticipating and experiencing post-operative pain: the patient's perspective. *Journal of Clinical Nursing*, **6**: 191–201.

Carr E.C.J., Thomas V.N.T. and Wilson-Barnet J. (2005) Patient experiences of anxiety, depression and acute pain after surgery: a longitudinal perspective. *International Journal of Nursing Studies*, **42**: 521–530.

Choi M., Yate P., Coats T., Kalinda P. and Paul E.A. (2000) Ethnicity and prescription of analgesia in an accident and emergency department: Cross-sectional study. *BMJ*, **320**: 980–981.

Clinical Standards Advisory Group (CSAG) (2000) Services for Patients with Pain. Department of Health, London.

Crombie I.K. (1999) In *Epidemiology of Pain* (eds. Crombie I.K., Croft P.R., Linton S.J., LeResche L. and Von Korff M.). IASP Press, Seattle, p. xi.

Dimsdale J.E. (2000) Stalked by the past: The influence of ethnicity on health. Presidential address. *Psychosomatic Medicine*, **62**: 161–170.

Fosnocht D.E., Heaps N.D. and Swanson E.R. (2004) Patient expectations of pain relief in the *American Journal of Emergency Medicine*, **22**(4): 286–288.

Green C.R., Anderson K.O., Baker T.A., Campbell L.C., Decker S., Fillingim R.B. *et al.* (2003) The unequal burden of pain: Confronting racial and ethnic disparities in pain. *Pain Medicine*, **4**(3): 227–294.

Green R.G. (2004) Racial Disparities in Access to Pain Treatment. *Pain Clinical Updates,* XII(6).

Hawkins R. and Price K. (1993) The effects of an education video on patients' requests for postoperative pain relief. *Australian Journal of Advanced Nursing*, **10**(4): 32–40.

Hawkins R.M.F. (1997) The role of the patient in the management of post surgical pain. *Psychology and Health*, **12**: 565–577.

Hayward J. (1971) *Information – A Prescription Against Pain*. RCN Publication, London. Series 2 Number **5**: 67–112.

Hume A. (1994) Patient knowledge of anaesthesia and peri-operative care. *Anaesthesia*, **49**: 715–718.

International Association for the Study of Pain (1999) *Epidemiology of Pain* (eds. Crombie I.K., Croft P.R., Linton S.J., LeResche L. and Von Korff M.). IASP Press, Seattle.

Jamison R.N., Ross M.J., Hoopman P., Griffen F., Levy J., Daly M. and Schaffer J.L. (1997) Assessment of postoperative pain management: patient satisfaction and perceived helpfulness. *The Clinical Journal of Pain*, **13**(3): 229–236.

Jones K. (2005) Diversities in approach to end-of-life: A view from qualitative literature. *Journal of Research in Nursing*, **10**(4): 431–454.

Juhl I.U. (1993) Postoperative pain relief, from the patients' and the nurses' point of view. *Acta Anaesthesiololgy Scandinavia*, **37**: 404–409.

Kenefick A.L. (2004) Pain treatment and quality of life. *Journal of Gerontological Nursing*, **30**(5): 22–29.

Kim H. and Dionne R.A. (2005) Genetics, pain, and analgesia. *Pain Clinical Updates*, XIII(3).

Kuhn S., Cooke K., Collins M., Jones M. and Mucklow J.C. (1990) Perceptions of pain relief after surgery. *British Medical Journal*, **300**: 1687–1690.

Laing R., Lam M., Owen H. and Plummer J.L. (1993) Perceived risks of postoperative analgesia. *Australian and New Zealand Journal of Surgery*, **63**: 760–765.

Lasch K.E. (2002) Culture and pain. *Pain Clinical Updates.* X(5).

Lavies N., Hart L., Rounsefell B. and Runciman W. (1992) Identification of patient, medical and nursing staff attitudes to postoperative analgesia: stage 1 of a longitudinal study of postoperative analgesia. *Pain*, **48**: 313–319.

Lin L.Y., Wang, R.H., (2005) Abdominal surgery, pain and anxiety: preoperative nursing intervention. *Journal of Advanced Nursing*, **51**(3): 252–260.

Lindon S.J. and Skevington S.M.(1999) In *Epidemiology of Pain* (eds. Crombie I.K., Croft P.R., Linton S.J., LeResche L. and Von Korff M.). IASP Press, Seattle, p. 27.

Macintyre P.E. and Ready L.B. (2002) *Acute Pain Management, A Practical Guide,* 2nd edn. W.B. Saunders, Elsevier Science, Philidelphia.

McNeill J.A., Sherwood G.D., Starck P.L. and Thompson C.J. (1998) Assessing Clinical Outcomes: Patient Satisfaction with Pain Management. *Journal of Pain and Symptom Management*, **16**(1): 29–40.

Miaskowski C., Nichols R., Brody R. and Synold T. (1994) Assessment of patient satisfaction utilising the American Pain Society's quality assurance standards on acute and cancer related pain. *Journal of Pain and Symptom Management*, **9**(1): 5–11.

Owen H., McMillan V. and Rogowski D. (1990) Postoperative pain therapy: a survey of patients' expectations and their experiences. *Pain*, **41**: 303–307.

Pellino T.A. (1997) Relationships between patient attitudes, subjective norms, perceived control and analgesic use following elective orthopaedic surgery. *Research in Nursing and Health*, **20**: 97–105.

Schwartz-Barcott D., Fortin J.D. and Kim H.S. (1994) Client–Nurse interaction: testing for its impact in preoperative instruction. *International Journal of Nursing Studies*, **31**(1): 23–35.

Scott N.B. and Hodson M. (1997) Public perceptions of postoperative pain and its relief. *Anaesthesia*, **52**:438–422.

Sherwood G., McNeill J.A., Hernandez L., Penarrieta I. and Peterson J.M. (2005) A multinational study of pain management among Hispanics. *Journal of Research in Nursing*, **10**(4): 403–423.

Symreng I. and Fishman S.M. (2004) Anxiety and Pain. *Pain Clinical Updates*, XII(7).

Tamayo-Sarver J.H., Hinze S.W., Cydulka R.K., Baker D.W. (2003) Racial and ethnic disparities in emergency department analgesic prescription. *American Journal of Public Health*, **93**(12): 2067–2073.

Tan G., Henson M.P., Thornby J. and Anderson K.O. (2005) Ethnicity, control appraisal, coping and adjustment to chronic pain among black and white Americans. *Pain Medicine*, **6**(1): 18–28.

Tsai P.F. (2005) Predictors of distress and depression in elders with arthritic pain. *Journal of Advanced Nursing*, **51**(2): 158–165.

Winefield H.R., Katsikitis M., Hart L.M. and Rounsefell B.F. (1990) Postoperative pain experiences: relevant patient and staff attitudes. *Journal of Psychosomatic Research*, **34**(5): 543–552.

Zinn C. (2003) Doctors told to use positive language in managing pain. *BMJ*, **326**: 301.

6 Assessment of pain and the effect of pain interventions

Learning outcomes

By the end of this chapter you should be able to:

★ Discuss the importance of pain assessment

★ Describe various approaches to assessment of pain

★ Detail pain assessment tools.

Introduction

This chapter looks at how the effective assessment of pain contributes towards the development of an appropriate pain management plan. Pain assessment is not a choice; it is a necessary component of the management of patients' pain in all health care settings. It is the key to decision making in relation to pain management interventions and provides evidence as to whether such interventions are effective.

Pain assessment

The key to accurate pain assessment lies in a consistent scientific approach. Appropriate assessment and management is essential in light of the many disabling effects of pain which are referred to in this and other chapters. A freshness of thinking and modern approaches are needed. Health professionals should be confident in their pain assessments and patients empowered to contribute to this approach. It should be remembered that much of the physical, psychological and social assessment of patient symptoms is highly dependent on careful, accurate health-professional skills and on patient reporting. Pain assessment should be approached with considered, reliable and valid processes. The accurate recording of patients' reported pain will provide sensitive and consistent results for the majority of the patient population (Moore *et al.* 2004).

Traditional debates continue to highlight the difficulty of assessing pain in the absence of quantitative definitive pain assessment tools in the form of physiological measures. The literature is replete with evidence of underassessment and poor documentation of pain. Little wonder then that health professionals, patients and families approach pain assessment with hesitation and a sense of suspicion. Societal anecdotes only compound the thinking by promoting the consideration that a little pain never harmed anyone. Who wants to be labelled a complainer?

A team approach

Evidence supports the concept that patient interactions linked to pain assessment should not be left to one person and that the patient benefits more from a multidisciplinary team approach utilising an integrated pathway process. An organisational system's approach to pain assessment will ensure a culture of regular appropriate pain assessment and ensure that pain assessment is part of an overall pain policy linked to organisational and national targets and guidelines.

Organisations should take pain assessment seriously and ensure that pain policies/protocols and guidelines are comprehensive enough to encompass modern approaches to pain assessment.

Nursing Practice Development Co-ordinator

We as an organisation decided to take an overall approach to pain management. We developed a hospital policy which adopted a definition of pain aligned to 'pain is what the patient says it is'; all patients now receive regular pain assessment . . . we use a Visual Analogue Scale (VAS) for surgical patients and a longer scale for chronic and cancer pain. Additionally we introduced short pain courses for all staff . . . these are multidisciplinary . . . they are provided by doctors, nurses, pharmacists, anaesthetists and physiotherapists and attended by the same groups. These are now part of induction programmes for new staff.

The individuals providing care at particular points in the patient episode have a responsibility to assess and document pain appropriately. However, approaches to deciding which methods are appropriate for assessment of pain should be based on relevant timely information and audit. This will allow for planning of necessary training and education for staff and ensure that pain assessment approaches are relevant to patient groups and case mix.

Pain assessment is an interactive and collaborative process involving the patient and family, nurse, doctor, anaesthetist, physiotherapist and other health carers as appropriate to the care setting (see Figure 6.1 below, which highlights the interactions). Such assessment will provide the basis for selecting and monitoring interventions.

A considered approach in the form of service guideline is key to successful and valid pain assessment.

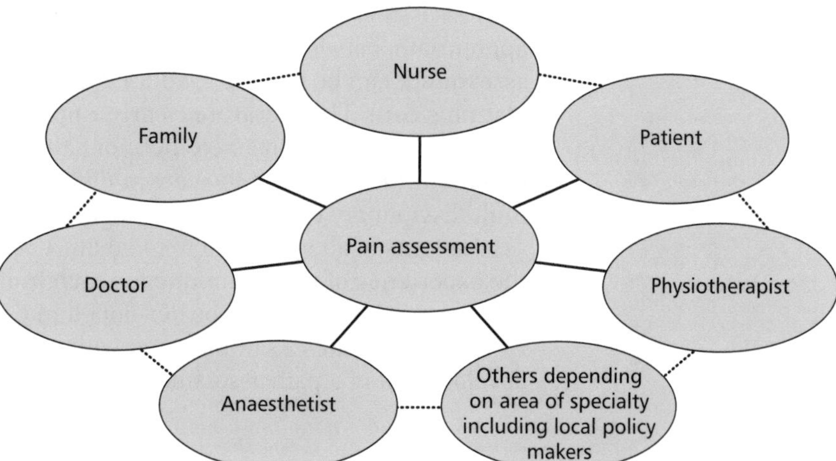

Figure 6.1 Multidisciplinary team involved in pain assessment

Reflective activity

You have just moved to a new general surgical ward in a medium-sized district hospital – there are no processes in place to record pain assessments on this ward (although you are aware that some of the other wards do undertake some pain assessment). There is no work that you are aware of to standardise pain assessment and management. Your clinical experience informs your thinking that this as hoc approach is not in the patients' best interests.

Consider how you, as one health care professional, can approach making a service guideline happen.

Top tip: Are there guidelines in the service for other activities? How were these developed? Who else is interested in pain management? View the following website: www.whocancerpain.wisc.edu/eng/14_2/resources.html to support your arguments to introduce pain assessment processes.

Key points

- Pain remains the most common symptom associated with acute, chronic and palliative care
- Pain assessment provides the only way to ensure that methods to manage pain are appropriate and effective
- Pain impacts on an individual's physical and psychological wellbeing and is an important challenge to functional ability
- Pain is a determinant of quality of life
- Pain is a key indicator of effectiveness of services and interventions
- Pain assessment identifies patterns of pain occurrence
- Pain assessment is complex and subjective
- Many pain assessment tools exist – which to choose?

Pain assessment at clinical service level, regardless of setting, should be appropriate, consistent and documented. This means that the assessment can be reviewed, audited and taken into consideration when planning care. The literature clearly emphasises the role of the nurse, as the continued carer, in assessment of pain. It must be recognised that different nurses provide the care at different times as part of a multidisciplinary team. The challenge lies in combining the varied assessments of all contributors to create a cohesive patient plan. While the experience of pain is unique for each individual, a process for monitoring this pain must be developed in a collaborative manner.

Table 6.1 details a sample audit with results which could support the development of a pain assessment strategy.

Table 6.1 A sample audit

Steps	Actions	Sample results
STEP 1	Audit of patient caseload: 1. How many patients go through the service per week? 2. What is the case mix of patients? 3. What is the average length of stay? 4. How many on average have pain?	A general surgical ward with mixed age group performs on average 10 bowel resections and 10 transurethral prostatectomies per week. Average length of stay is five days. Fifty per cent of patients have moderate pain on day two experienced on movement.
STEP 2	Audit of pain experiences: 1. What types of pain? 2. What levels of pain? 3. What is the average age group?	Maximum pain score is 8 on a 1–10 scale and minimum 2. Pain peaks on day one post surgery and generally decreases.
STEP 3	Current methods of pain assessment: 1. Regular? 2. Single or multidimensional scales? 3. Is this documented?	Pain is assessed in an ad hoc manner depending on nurse on duty.
STEP 4	How many health professionals have responsibility for the patient's pain management? 1. Identify who and when the various health professionals interact with the patients. 2. How often are decisions made with regard to pain management?	A surgical patient will on average have at least six different health professionals evaluate and monitor their progress, i.e. nurse(s) × 3 from each shift, doctor(s), anaesthetist, physiotherapist.
STEP 5	Now there is a baseline of pain and the patterns of pain on the clinical area are identified.	

Over to you

What information can you gain from the above audit to support your thinking on developing pain assessment processes for the above surgical ward?

Pain assessment – moving forward

Pain assessment techniques determine the intensity, quality, location and duration of pain; they aid diagnosis and provide a process to evaluate the relative effectiveness of different therapies. The language of pain frequently provides the key to diagnosis and may even suggest the course of therapy (Melzack and Katz, 1994).

Two decades ago, McCaffrey said that the 'assessment of pain and its relief is no simple matter' (McCaffrey 1983). There is little since then to suggest that assessment of pain has become less complex. Indeed there is much research to indicate that pain continues to be under-assessed. Current assessment and the recording of pain by nurses has been shown to be incomplete, inaccurate (often underestimated) and descriptive of location rather than severity of pain (Harrison, 1993; Bowman, 1994; Field, 1996; Idvall *et al.,* 2002; Sloman *et al.*, 2005).

The patient's self report of pain remains the single most reliable indicator of pain and should be recorded in the patient's record as the pain assessment (Acute Pain Management Guideline Panel, 1992; McCaffery and Ferrell, 1994; Moore *et al.,* 2004). It is pleasing to note that new approaches for assessment of pain have emerged and a number of policy and guidance documents give clear direction that assessment of pain in a consistent manner is key to successful pain management.

The nurse's possession of adequate knowledge is critical to effective pain management. The nurse spends the most time with the patient in pain, assesses the patient's pain level, evaluates the information based on assessment and communicates patient progress to the multidisciplinary team. Therefore, nurses, in particular, have a direct responsibility for the provision of measures to relieve pain. Regardless of clinical speciality, pain is a common clinical situation encountered by nurses. Nurses are with patients during their care episodes, when patients report the presence of pain, and monitoring pain control depends on the expertise of the individual nurse. Yet formal pain assessment, such as the use of a pain score or pain chart, does not appear to be regular practice for nurses (Hastings, 1995; Francke, 1996; Taylor, 1997).

Key points Top tips

- The assessment of pain is integral to the planning and implementation of nursing care to relieve pain (Zalon, 1993)
- Assessment of pain should be included in the regular recording of vital signs (Black, 1991)
- Accurate pain assessment is essential for good nursing and medical care, for judging the status and progress of patients, the impact and efficacy of treatments and even for reaching a proper diagnosis (Choiniere *et al.*, 1990)
- The patient's self report is the most reliable indicator of pain

Pain charts and tools have been developed to assist in the accurate measurement and documentation of patients' subjective pain.

Benefits of using such pain assessment charts and tools can be summarised as follows:

- information obtained helps to establish the pattern of pain
- recording when pain intervention occurs and relating the level of pain with the timing and the type of medication/pain intervention provides evaluation of the effects of such intervention
- including the patient in monitoring their pain involves them in their plan of care and supports objective thinking about their pain
- the care provider and the patient can be more specific setting targets for pain relief.

Reflective activity

Assessment of pain requires the recognition that patients' self report of pain is the single most reliable indicator. Consider a time when you found the above statement challenging and felt that your own clinical experience was more relevant.

Difficulties in communicating pain

Pain assessment tools utilised must conform to the communication capabilities of the patient. Some patients will not be able to verbalise their pain or may not be able to describe their pain in the manner requested by the health care professional.

Existing pain charts and tools support the measurement of various aspects of pain. However, not all patients can communicate their pain. One of the biggest challenges in pain assessment is capturing the non-verbal aspects of pain. This is of particular interest to nurses working in clinical areas such as critical care.

Challenges to pain assessment approaches

- There are differences reported in patients' and nurses' assessment of pain.
- Patients depend on health professionals to recognise their pain.
- Some patients are cognitively impaired and therefore cannot express their pain, e.g. confused, unconscious or elderly.
- Patients may have low expectations of pain relief and therefore underestimate pain.

- Patients may not report pain as they may not understand the importance of pain assessment and documentation in reducing pain.
- Pain assessment may not be documented.
- Lack of a consistent approach from the health care team.
- Health professionals consider they know best.
- Lack of a systematic approach to pain assessment.

Evidence base

Key position statements regarding pain assessment and documentation

Timeline

- **2005** National Cancer Institute: *'Failure to assess pain is a critical factor leading to undertreatment. Assessment involves both the clinician and the patient. Assessment should occur: At regular intervals after initiation of treatment, at each new report of pain and at a suitable interval after pharmacologic or nonpharmacologic intervention, e.g., 15 to 30 minutes after parenteral drug therapy and 1 hour after oral administration.'*
- **2003** The Royal College of Anaesthetists and The Pain Society, the British Chapter of the International Association for the Study of Pain: *'Pain and its relief must be assessed and documented on a regular basis. Pain intensity should be regarded as a vital sign and along with the response to treatment and side effects should be recorded as regularly as other vital signs such as pulse or blood pressure.'*
- **2001** The Joint Commission on Accreditation of Healthcare Organisations (JCAHO) implemented pain assessment and management standards and began to assess compliance. *'In the initial assessment, the organisation identifies patients with pain. When pain is identified, the patient can be treated within the organisation or referred for treatment. The scope of treatment is based on the care setting and services provided. A more comprehensive assessment is performed when warranted by the patient's condition. This assessment and a measure of pain intensity and quality (e.g., pain character, frequency, location, duration) appropriate to the patient's age, are recorded in a way that facilitates regular reassessment and follow up according to the criteria developed by the organisation.'*
- **2000** American Pain Society provides a statement on pain assessment and treatment in the managed care environment highlighting timely and effective assessment of pain: *'all patients benefit from timely and effective assessment and treatment by their primary care providers.'*
- **1990** The report of the Royal College of Surgeons and Anaesthetists Working Party on Pain after Surgery: *'postoperative intervention can be assessed and improved only if some form of measurement of effect is made. The report suggests that the routine use of a simple pain assessment system, with treatment based on assessment is essential, if progress is to be made.'*

Advance Nurse Practitioner

Finding an approach to pain assessment that is used consistently to support all the clinical team to make appropriate decisions regarding pain management requires consideration and . . . hard work! Firstly, I would recommend identifying key interested parties such as the anaesthetist, ward nurses, practice development etc. Gather up some evidence examples to share and, if possible, some exemplars of charts/tools from other organisations.

The pain experience

Pain is not a single sensory experience. It has many dimensions and facets. These must be considered and understood before approaches to pain assessment can be decided upon. Pain appears to have three main dimensions: sensory, emotional and an intensity aspect. Clinical pain measures consist of behavioural measurements, observational data, self-reported behaviours and subjective pain reports.

Pain is an individual experience which will be influenced by many factors including culture, coping strategies, fear, anxiety, cause of pain and previous experiences.

The box below details the pain aspects to be considered when assessing pain.

- Location
- Onset
- Duration
- Quality or characteristics (neuropathic or nerve, nociceptive, visceral)
- Aggravating factors
- Interventions/relieving factors
- Associated symptoms, e.g. dizziness, headache, nausea, sweating, palpitations, shortness of breath, vomiting
- Pain and sleep
- Pain caused by physical activity such as coughing, deep breathing or movement

A pain history, as outlined in Table 6.2, can be utilised. Some pain histories will be quite short and others will be longer depending on your patient case mix. You should choose which aspects suit your patients' needs, e.g. a patient having a simple surgical procedure may need questions with regard to pain intensity on a regular timescale while a patient diagnosed with cancer metastasis may require a multidimensional comprehensive pain history.

Table 6.2 Elements to be considered when taking a pain history

Domain	Process
Circumstances associated with pain onset	For example coughing, exercise
Primary site of pain	Consider utilisation of a body chart (see Figure 6.2)
Radiation of pain	Consider utilisation of a body chart (see Figure 6.2)
Character of pain	A multidimensional pain measurement tool as described later in this chapter will support this description, e.g. is pain throbbing, sharp, aching etc.?
Intensity of pain	A single-dimensional pain measurement tool as described later in this chapter will support this description, e.g. use of a visual analogue scale or verbal rating scale. It is important also to assess intensity of pain in certain circumstances such as at rest and on movement. Utilise time periods to support this such as: – at present – during last week Ask questions such as lowest and highest rating experienced by patients
Factors altering pain	Ask what makes it worse and what makes it better, e.g. is the pain aggravated on movement?
Associated symptoms	Does the pain bring on other symptoms such as nausea, dizziness, vomiting?
Temporal factors	Is pain present continuously or otherwise?
Effect of pain on activities	Is pain preventing the patient carrying out their daily activities?
Effect of pain on sleep	Is pain interrupting sleep? It is important to ask whether pain wakes the patient up or if it prevents the patient from sleeping
Medications taken for pain	Is the patient taking any medications for pain at time of history taking? List these medications, how often they are taken and which the patient rates as being helpful. How long has the patient been on these medications? Are there any unwanted side effects from the medication?
Other interventions used for pain Health professionals consulted for pain treatment	Is the patient using any other interventions such as physiotherapy, acupuncture etc.? (See chapter 8.) Encourage the patient to think about this. Has the patient been treated for this pain before? Are they currently attending anyone?

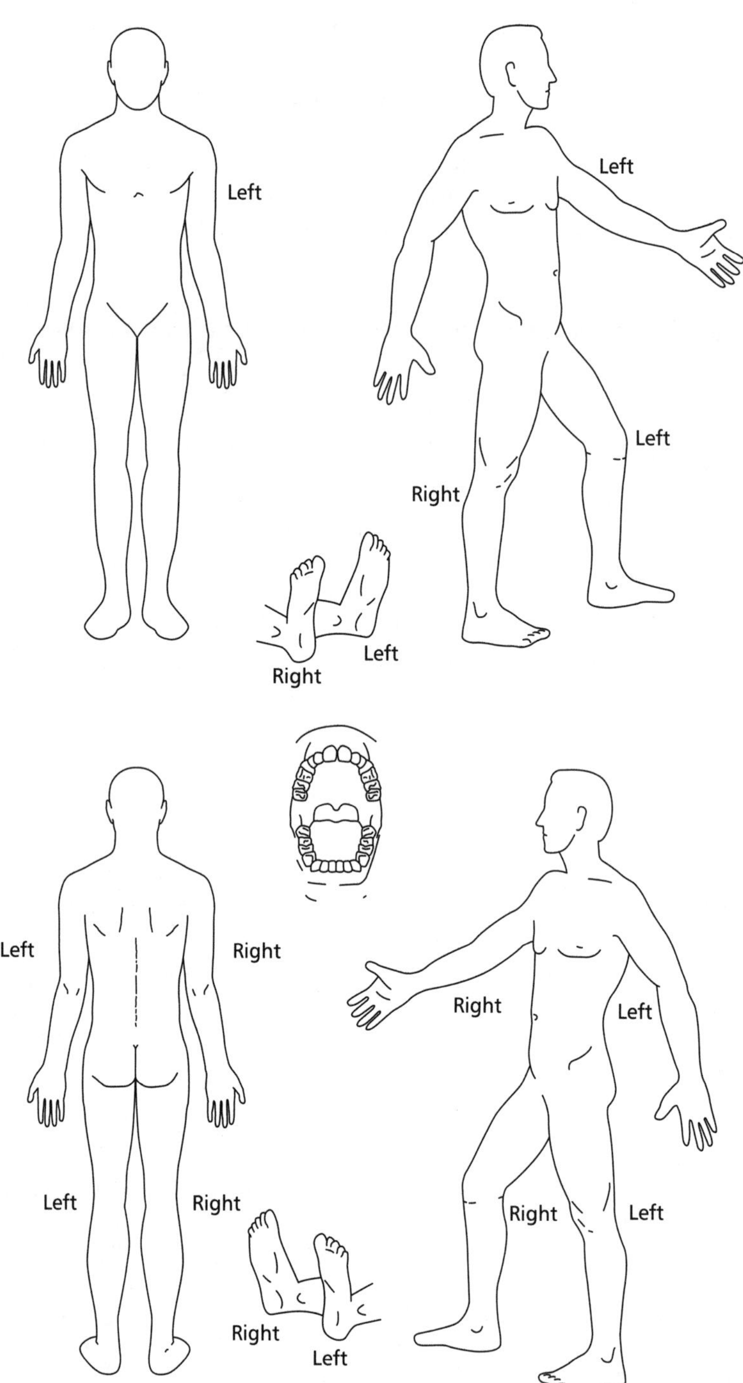

Figure 6.2 Body chart

The box below highlights other information that is useful to gather when obtaining a pain history.

- Expectations of outcome of pain treatment
- Patient's belief concerning the causes of pain (are there cultural issues?)
- Reduction in pain required to resume 'reasonable activities'
- Patient's typical coping response for stress or pain, including presence of anxiety
- Psychiatric disorders (e.g. depression or psychosis)
- Family expectations and beliefs about pain, stress and postoperative course
- Ways the patient describes or shows pain
- Patient's knowledge, expectations and preferences for pain management

The pain history list above has been adapted from the National Health and Medical Research Council, Australia Acute Pain Management Scientific Evidence of 1999 and 2005 (www.nhmrc.gov.au).

Clinical pain measurement tools

The pain history should involve the use of pain assessment tools. There are numerous tools described in the literature and the following qualities should be considered when choosing the tool best suited for your patient case mix – see the box below.

Validity of tool. *This is an expression of the degree to which a measurement measures what it proposes to measure.*
Reliability of tool. *Reliability is defined as determining that the instrument is measuring something in a reproducible and consistent fashion. A reliable instrument is stable, i.e. repetition of that measurement gives the same result.*
Ease of use for both patients and health care professionals. *If the tool is very lengthy or complex to use it may not be suitable for particular patient groups. Depending on the patient case mix there will be different dimensions of pain to capture.*

Pain tools are generally categorised as single and multidimensional with single-dimensional capturing the intensity aspect of pain.

Single-dimensional tools

The three most commonly used single-dimensional tools are the Visual Analogue Scale (VAS), the Numeric Rating Scale (NRS) and the Verbal

Keywords

Pain intensity

This is a measure of the strength of the pain, i.e. how bad the pain is. Pain intensity is usually relative to previous pain experienced. It does not take into account quality of pain, e.g. burning, shooting

Rating Scale (VRS) (see Figure 6.3). **Pain intensity** only is measured. Such tools are suitable for patient groups such as postoperative patients or those with minor injuries. This type of measurement is often included as part of a multidimensional scale.

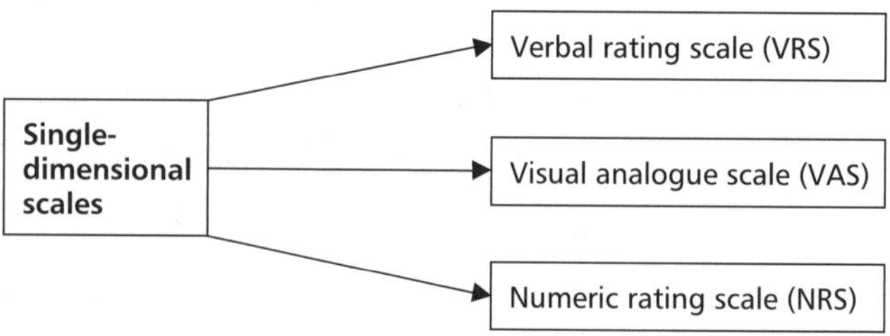

Figure 6.3 Single-dimensional scales

Evidence base

Much of the seminal research on the reliability, validity and sensitivity of these scales was completed in the 1970s and 1980s. However, new research compares these scales with various groups of patients. In 1974 Huskisson described the VAS as sensitive in measuring pain and pain relief. Early comparisons of the VAS and the VRS suggest that the VAS gives a closer assessment of patient experience (Ohnhaus, 1975; Scott and Huskisson, 1976; Sriwatanakul, 1983).

More recently, Cork *et al.* (2004) surveyed 85 chronic pain patients to determine if the simple VRS could be substituted for the VAS to measure pain intensity in chronic pain patients. Pearson correlation coefficient ($r = 0.906$) and p value (< 0.0001) showed excellent correlation between the two, although VRS showed a tendency to be higher than VAS ($p = 0.068$). The authors proposed that the VRS provides a useful alternative to the VAS scores in assessment of chronic pain. Breivik *et al.* (2000) suggest that a four-point VRS was less sensitive than the 100 mm VAS in acute pain but that the 11-point Numeric Rating Scale (NRS) compares well to the VAS and that choice should be based on subjective preferences.

Coll *et al.* (2004), following an integrated literature review, found the VAS to be methodologically sound, conceptually simple, easy to administer and unobtrusive to the patient.

Verbal Rating Scale (VRS) and Verbal/Graphic Rating Scale

See Figures 6.4 and 6.5.

Verbal Rating Scale (VRS)

- No pain
- Mild pain
- Severe pain
- Very severe pain

Figure 6.4 Four-point verbal rating scale

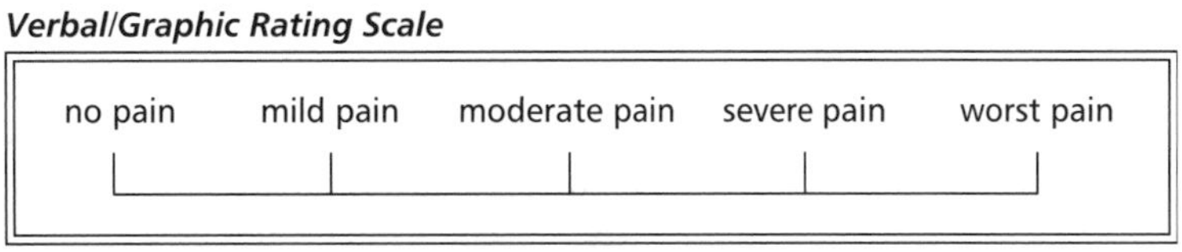

Verbal/Graphic Rating Scale

no pain | mild pain | moderate pain | severe pain | worst pain

Figure 6.5 Five-point verbal/ graphic rating scale

Descriptive rating scales consist of a list of adjectives which describe different levels of pain.These types of scale generally comprise 4–5 word categories. These word categories consist of descriptive pain words. The patient is asked to pick the word which best describes their pain. These words are then given a score. The least intense descriptor is given a score of zero, the next a score of one and so on. The descriptive rating scale can be given in verbal or written form. The patient's intensity score is the number associated with the word they choose as most descriptive of their pain level.

Visual Analogue Scale (VAS)

See Figures 6.6 and 6.7.

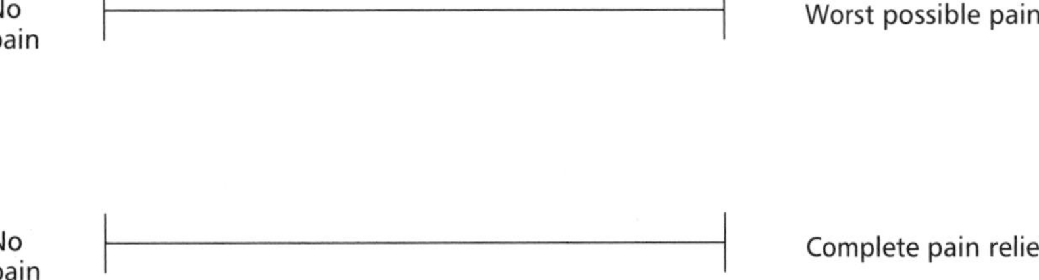

Figure 6.6 The VAS for pain severity measurement

Figure 6.7 The VAS for treatment effect

A Visual Analogue Scale (VAS) is a method of providing a simple way of recording subjective estimates of pain. It can be used to measure severity or improvement.

A VAS provides a continuous scale for estimation of the magnitude of pain. It consists of a straight line, the ends of which are defined in terms of the extreme limits of the pain experience. The scale, conventionally a 10 cm long straight line, may be printed either horizontally or vertically. Each end of the scale is marked with labels that indicate the range being considered. Phrases such as 'pain as bad as it could be' and 'no pain' can be used. The patient is asked to place a mark on the line at a point representing the severity of his pain. Measuring the distance of a patient's mark from zero scores the scale. The scale requires only about 30 seconds to complete. A comparison of 5 cm, 10 cm, 15 cm and 25 cm lines suggested that the 10 cm and 15 cm lengths have the least measurement error and that the 5 cm line provides the greatest error (Seymour, 1985). A number of steps are involved in the construction of the VAS.

The sensation or response and the extremes of that response must be clearly defined. End phrases and descriptive words should be short, readily understood and not so extreme that they will never be employed. Definite cut-off points must be made for the line, which should be of a length that can be interpreted as a unit. Although verbal labels define end points of the VAS it is recommended that neither numbers nor verbal labels be used to define intermediate points, as this may cause a clustering of scores around a preferred digit. As the scale is continuous, the restriction of a 3- or 5-point rating scale is overcome. McDowell and Newell (1996) conclude that the VAS is a more sensitive and precise measurement than descriptive pain scales and that, for the VAS, horizontal lines, are preferred to vertical.

Numeric Rating Scale (NRS)

See Figure 6.8.

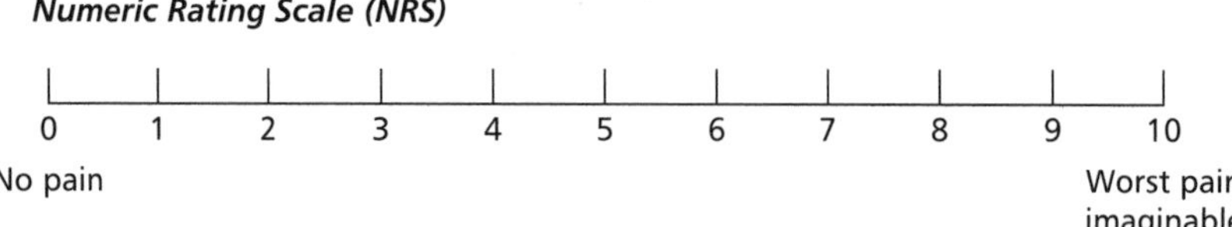

Figure 6.8 Numeric Rating Scale

This is a variation of the VAS and consists of asking the patient to rate their pain on a numerical scale 0–10 with 0 equalling no pain and 10 equalling worst pain imaginable. It has been described as sensitive to change and may be preferred for statistical purposes. The NRS, like the VAS, can be of varying lengths. The 101 cm length appears to have some advantages. It has 101 response categories, which may overcome the limitations in response categories found in other scales.

Pros and cons of single-dimensional scales

Pros:

- Can be used quickly.
- Only minimal instruction to patients is required, i.e. easy to administer.
- Are easily scored.
- Very sick patients are not taxed.
- Have been tested as reliable and valid pain intensity measures.
- Can be incorporated easily into current patient documentation, e.g. as part of vital signs chart.

Cons:

- Most assume that patients are either literate or numerical.
- Pain is treated as a single dimension only.

- *VRS*. With the VRS there is reliance on the use of words, i.e. it is necessary for the patient to translate a feeling into specific words which may not express exactly what the person is experiencing. Words can be ambiguous and the same word does not necessarily mean the same thing to each patient. It limits choices and improvements in pain relief. Effect of analgesic cannot always be measured due to the word restrictions.
- *VAS*. The estimation of pain intensity with the VAS requires an ability to transform a pain experience into a visual display, which involves perceptual judgement and accuracy. This perceptual ability is likely to influence the results, therefore the use of the VAS may not be possible in the elderly, the seriously ill or patients with organic brain disease (Seymour, 1985). It is suggested that as much as 7% of the population would not be able to use it (Kremer, 1981). Factors which may influence reliability and validity are learning, memory and perceptual judgement (Carlsson, 1983; Coll, 2004).
- *NRS*. There may be biases associated with this scale. Some patients may have a preference or an aversion to certain numbers, leading them to consistently choose or avoid those numbers.

Multidimensional measurements of clinical pain intensity

Multidimensional scales involve subscales, which represent different aspects of pain (see Figure 6.9). In an attempt to capture all aspects of pain, multidimensional scales are developing to support assessment of pain for those patients who cannot verbalise their pain experience.

The McGill Pain Questionnaire (MPQ) both long (LF-MPQ) and short (SF-MPQ) and the Non-verbal Pain Scale (NVPS) are described. The McGill Pain Questionnaires are the most widely utilised in both research and clinical practice for multidimensional measurement of pain.

The SF-MPQ was developed to provide a brief assessment. The LF-MPQ and SF-MPQ can be either interviewer administered or self-administered. The LF-MPQ takes 5–10 minutes to administer, and the SF-MPQ 2–5 minutes.

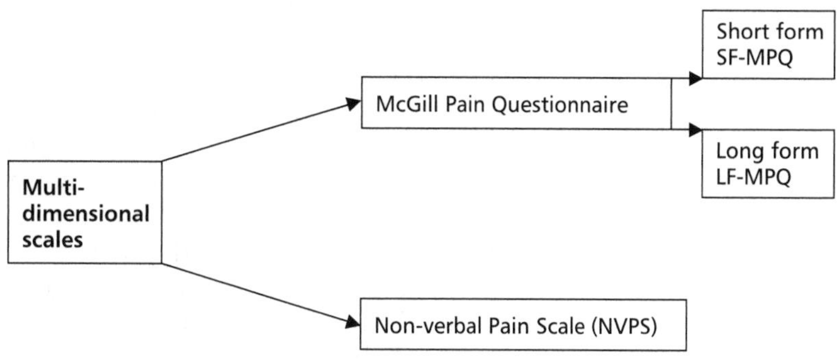

Figure 6.9 Multidimensional scales

Evidence base

The McGill Pain Questionnaire (MPQ) was developed in 1971 following much debate regarding language and meaning of pain (Melzack and Torgeson, 1971). Debate continues and conflicting views may be found with regard to factorial validity and transferability of the scales in the MPQ to other languages. The MPQ has now been translated into Spanish, Danish, Arabic, Chinese, French, German, Italian, Japanese, Norwegian, Polish and Slovak. In 1987, Melzack found the sensory, affective and total scores of the MPQ and SF-MPQ to be significantly correlated (Melzack, 1987). The MPQ has been more widely used in chronic pain than acute pain. It is suggested that acute pain involves less differentiation of sensory, affective and evaluative language dimensions (Reading, 1982).

The SF-MPQ compares well with the long form of the MPQ (Melzack, 1987; Dudgeon *et al.*, 1993). More recently, Grafton *et al.* (2005) studied 57 patients with osteoarthritis and suggested that it is a highly reliable measure of pain

The adapted Non-verbal Pain Scale (NVPS) described here is currently being tested by the University of Rochester Medical Centre.

Long-form McGill Pain Questionnaire (LF-MPQ)

The long McGill Pain Questionnaire (see Figure 6.10) comprises a top sheet to record necessary medical information, line drawings of the body to indicate the distribution of the pain, and word descriptors. The questionnaire consists primarily of three major classes of word descriptors – sensory, affective and evaluative – that are used by patients to specify subjective pain experiences. It contains an intensity scale and other items to determine the properties of the pain experience. The questionnaire was designed to provide quantitative measures of clinical pain that can be treated statistically. The three measures commonly used are: (1) the **p**ain **r**ating **i**ndex (**pri**) based on two types of numerical values that can be assigned to each word descriptor; (2) the number of words chosen; (3) the **p**resent **p**ain **i**ntensity (**ppi**) based on a 1–5 intensity scale, in which each number is associated with the following words: 1 = mild, 2 = discomforting, 3 = distressing, 4 = horrible and 5 = excruciating. The pri is based on values assigned to each pain word chosen, which are added up for a total score.

The MPQ groups pain-related words into three major classes and 16 subclasses. The classes are, firstly, words that describe the sensory qualities of the experience in terms of temporal, spatial, pressure, thermal and other properties; secondly, words that describe affective qualities in terms of tension, fear and autonomic properties that are part of the pain experience; and thirdly, evaluative words that describe the subjective overall intensity of the total pain experience.

Generally, the questionnaire requires 5–10 minutes to complete, but depending on patient profile, can take up to 20 minutes. The MPQ provides quantitative information that can be treated statistically. It is

McGILL PAIN QUESTIONNAIRE
RONALD MELZACK

Patient's Name ______________ Date ________ Time ______ am/pm

PRI: S ______ (1–10) A ______ (11–15) E ______ (16) M ______ (17–20) PRI(T) ______ (1–20) PPI ______

1 FLICKERING QUIVERING PULSING THROBBING BEATING POUNDING	11 TIRING EXHAUSTING
2 JUMPING FLASHING SHOOTING	12 SICKENING SUFFOCATING
3 PRICKING BORING DRILLING STABBING LANCINATING	13 FEARFUL FRIGHTFUL TERRIFYING
4 SHARP CUTTING LACERATING	14 PUNISHING GRUELLING CRUEL VICIOUS KILLING
5 PINCHING PRESSING GNAWING CRAMPING CRUSHING	15 WRETCHED BLINDING
6 TUGGING PULLING WRENCHING	16 ANNOYING TROUBLESOME MISERABLE INTENSE UNBEARABLE
7 HOT BURNING SCALDING SEARING	17 SPREADING RADIATING PENETRATING PIERCING
8 TINGLING ITCHY SMARTING STINGING	18 TIGHT NUMB DRAWING SQUEEZING TEARING
9 DULL SORE HURTING ACHING HEAVY	19 COOL COLD FREEZING
10 TENDER TAUT RASPING SPLITTING	20 NAGGING NAUSEATING AGONIZING DREADFUL TORTURING
	PPI 0 NO PAIN 1 MILD 2 DISCOMFORTING 3 DISTRESSING 4 HORRIBLE 5 EXCRUCIATING

BRIEF MOMENTARY TRANSIENT	RHYTHMIC PERIODIC INTERMITTENT	CONTINUOUS STEADY CONSTANT

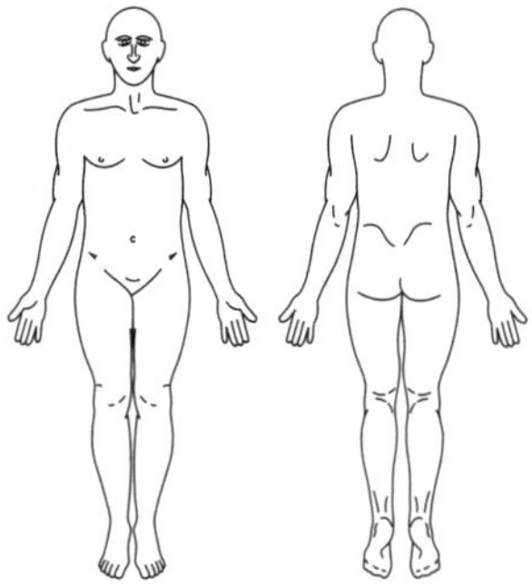

E = EXTERNAL
I = INTERNAL

COMMENTS:

Figure 6.10 Long-form McGill Pain Questionnaire (LF-MPQ). Reproduced with permission from Elsevier. First published in Pain Journal 3: 277–299, Melzack, © 1975 International Association for the Study of Pain.

sufficiently sensitive to detect differences among different methods to relieve pain. It also provides information about the relative effects of a given manipulation on the sensory, affective and evaluative dimensions of pain.

It is important for the interviewer to ensure that the patient understands the meaning of the words as some of the words may be beyond the patient's vocabulary. The length of time to administer the MPQ restricts its widespread use in ward situations where time is a precious commodity.

Short-form McGill Pain Questionnaire (SF-MPQ)

A short-form MPQ (SF-MPQ) has been developed (see Figure 6.11). The main component of the SF-MPQ consists of 15 descriptors (11 sensory and 4 affective), which are rated on an intensity scale as 0 = none, 1 = mild, 2 = moderate or 3 = severe. Three pain scores are derived from the sum of the intensity rank values of the words chosen for sensory, affective and total descriptors. The SF-MPQ also includes the present pain intensity (ppi) index of the standard MPQ and a Visual Analogue Scale.

This may be useful where qualitative information is important as well as pain intensity scores. It takes less time than the long form of the MPQ.

SHORT FORM McGILL PAIN QUESTIONNAIRE

PATIENT'S NAME:____________________ DATE:________

	NONE	MILD	MODERATE	SEVERE
THROBBING	0)___	1)___	2)___	3)___
SHOOTING	0)___	1)___	2)___	3)___
STABBING	0)___	1)___	2)___	3)___
SHARP	0)___	1)___	2)___	3)___
CRAMPING	0)___	1)___	2)___	3)___
GNAWING	0)___	1)___	2)___	3)___
HOT-BURNING	0)___	1)___	2)___	3)___
ACHING	0)___	1)___	2)___	3)___
HEAVY	0)___	1)___	2)___	3)___
TENDER	0)___	1)___	2)___	3)___
SPLITTING	0)___	1)___	2)___	3)___
TIRING-EXHAUSTING	0)___	1)___	2)___	3)___
SICKENING	0)___	1)___	2)___	3)___
FEARFUL	0)___	1)___	2)___	3)___
PUNISHING-CRUEL	0)___	1)___	2)___	3)___

NO PAIN |______________________________| WORST POSSIBLE PAIN

0	NO PAIN	___
1	MILD	___
2	DISCOMFORTING	___
3	DISTRESSING	___
4	HORRIBLE	___
5	EXCRUCIATING	___

Figure 6.11 Short-form McGill Pain Questionnaire(SF-MPQ). Reproduced with permission from Elsevier. First published in Pain Journal 30 (2): 191–197, Melzack, © 1987 International Association for the Study of Pain.

Adult Non-verbal Pain Scale (ANVPS)

Cognitively impaired patients present unique challenges to pain assessment. Scales which require verbal or numeric skills are not useful and alternative approaches must be used. The ANVPS, for example, takes account of multiple indicators of pain: posture, usual behaviours, self report, facial expression, mood and activities of daily living (see Figure 6.12).

Possible manifestations of pain are presented below. Remember, however, that observation is interpretative and dependent on the health professional assessing the pain behaviours.

Adult non-verbal pain scale University of Rochester Medical Center

Categories	0	1	2
Face	No particular expression or smile	Occasional grimace, tearing, frowning, wrinkled forehead	Frequent grimace, tearing, frowning, wrinkled forehead
Activity (movement)	Lying quietly, normal position	Seeking attention through movement or slow, cautious movement	Restless, excessive activity and/or withdrawal reflexes
Guarding	Lying quietly, no positioning of hands over areas of body.	Splinting areas of the body, tense	Rigid, stiff
Physiology (vital signs)	Stable vital signs	Change in any of the following: * SBP > 20 mm Hg * HR > 20/minute	Change in any of the following: * SBP > 30 mm Hg * HR > 25/minute
Respiratory	Baseline RR/SpO_2 Complaint with ventilator	RR > 10 above baseline or 5% ↓SpO_2 mile asynchrony with ventilator	RR > 20 above baseline or 10% ↓SpO_2 severe asynchrony with ventilator

Abbreviations: HR, heart rate; RR, respiratory rate; SBP, systolic blood pressure; SpO2, pulse oximetry. Instructions: Each of the 5 categories is scored from 0–2, which results in a total score between 0 and 10. Document total score by adding numbers from each of the 5 categories. Scores of 0–2 indicate no pain, 3–6 moderate pain, and 7–10 severe pain. Document assessment every 4 hours on nursing flow-sheet and complete assessment before and after intervention to maximize patient comfort. Sepsis, hypo-volemia, hypoxia need to be excluded before interventions.

Figure 6.12 Adult non-verbal pain scale. Reproduced with permission of the University of Rochester Medical Centre. First published in Dimensions in Critical Care Nursing, 2003.

Behavioural indicators:

- Verbal expression
- Aggression
- Agitation
- Crying
- Facial grimaces
- Restlessness
- Increased confusion
- Change in appetite
- Withdrawal
- Sleep disruption
- Moaning
- Fidgeting
- Guarding or rubbing of body parts

Wegman (2005) describes the adult non-verbal pain scale which is a 10-point scale with five categories that are scored on 0, 1 or 2 point system. This scale is an adaptation of the original NVPS scale (Odhner *et al.*, 2003). Further research was conducted on this revised scale in 2005 (Freeland, 2006). The research involved 111 observations, and internal reliability exceeds minimum expectations for newly developed scales at .79 (Coefficient alpha).

Staff nurse in an intensive-care unit

I find it quite difficult to be confident in my assessment of pain when most of my patients are unconscious and cannot communicate their pain. I have, however, become more self assured in my decisions after increasing my understanding of the physiology of pain on the advice of a more senior nurse. She said that once I understand the pain pathways and the body's physiological responses I would view communication of pain differently to my current approaches. She was right. I am beginning to realise that not all communication of pain is verbal or coherent but that by paying attention to all the non-verbal signs, being more aware of physiological signs such as tachycardia which could indicate pain, and by approaching the patient more holistically I can be more confident in my assessment of pain.

Key points Top tips

- Pain assessment is integral to overall pain management
- Pain assessment should be included as part of overall pain strategy
- Pain assessment approaches utilised should be based on audit of patient need
- Pain tools chosen should be appropriate to patient case mix
- Assessment of pain should occur initially and regularly thereafter
- Pain should be assessed as part of assessment of vital signs
- Pain should be assessed both at rest and during activity
- Pain relief from interventions should be assessed for adequacy

Pain persisting beyond usual course

Sue is a 42-year-old accountant who presented to her general practitioner with pain in her right side (see case study in Chapter 4). She is fit – running 45–60 minutes on the treadmill five days a week. She is slim and eats sensibly. She is studying part-time for a law degree and seems to be very busy with a full life. She has had the pain for some time and is now getting anxious. The general practitioner suspects gallstones and refers Sue to the local hospital. Three weeks later, Sue is reviewed by the general surgeon who elicits a full history and performs a physical examination. Agreeing with the general practitioner, he suspects gallstones and orders an ultrasound to confirm diagnosis. Sue is subsequently diagnosed with gallstones despite being an atypical profile. The ultrasound identifies three rather large stones in the gallbladder and one in the biliary tract. She is scheduled for a laparoscopic cholecystectomy the next month.

When admitting Sue to the ward, the nurse asks details about her pain, eliciting that the pain occurs randomly more likely in the afternoon than the morning. While the pain is generally in the right iliac fossa region Sue suffers some right shoulder pain at times. The pain has been coming and going for about 12 months. Sue describes it as a sharp biting kind of pain which is very acute. She also mentions a residual dull pain that comes and goes more often in the same region.

The nurse is satisfied that the pain is classic for gallstones and asks Sue if the three student nurses on the ward can ask her a few questions about the pain. Sue agrees, happy that a rather straightforward diagnosis is made which can be rectified by what the surgeon has described as a simple procedure.

Sue returns from her surgery which the general surgeon declares is a success. Sue, herself, is relieved to be back in the ward but is rather alarmed with the amount of pain she is suffering. She is on a PCA morphine pump and though a bit nervous of it, is utilising it satisfactorily. Her pain is rated four- to six-hourly on a 10 cm Visual Analogue Scale. After two days, her pump is removed and she is commenced on a low-dose nonsteroidal anti-inflammatory and discharged home the next day.

Sue's partner Michael is rather alarmed at the slow rate of Sue's recovery. Like Sue, he had expected her to be up and about within two days. Sue's pain persists over the next three weeks but she is reassured by her review with the surgeon at three weeks who tells her that everything is getting back to normal. Six weeks later, Sue still gets pain from time to time.

- What additional information would you have elicited from Sue's pain history?
- Was Sue's pain assessed appropriately after her surgery?
- If Sue's pain persists what course of action would you recommend her to take?

Rapid recap

1 What qualities should a pain assessment tool have?
2 What are the three main pain intensity tools used?
3 What can a pain audit contribute when deciding which pain assessment tool to use?

References

Acute Pain Management Guideline Panel (1992). *Acute pain management: operative or medical procedures and trauma: Clinical practice guideline.* Agency for Health Care Policy and Research, Public Health Service, U.S. Department of Health and Human Services, Washington DC.

American Pain Society (2000) *Pain assessment and treatment in the managed care environment. A position statement from the American Pain Society.* American Pain Society, Seattle.

Black A.M.S. (1991) Taking pains to take away pain. *BMJ*, **302**: 1165–1166.

Bowman J.M. (1994) Perception of surgical pain by nurses and patients. *Clinical Nursing Research*, **3**(1): 69–76.

Breivik E.K., Bjornsson G.A., Skovlund E. (2000) A comparison of pain rating scale by sampling from clincial trial data. *Clinical Journal of Pain*, **16**(1): 22–28.

Carlsson A.M. (1983) Assessment of chronic pain: I. Aspects of the reliability and validity of the Visual Analogue Scale. *Pain*, **16**: 87–101.

Choiniere M., Melzack R., Girard N., Rondeau J. and Paquin M.J. (1990) Comparisons between patient's and nurses' assessment of pain and medication efficacy in severe burns injuries. *Pain*, **40**: 143–152.

Coll A.M., Jamal A. and Mead D. (2004) Postoperative pain assessment tools in day surgery: a literature review. *Journal of Advanced Nursing*, **46**(2): 124–133.

Cork R.C., Isaac I., Elsharydah A., Saleemi S., Zavisca F., Alexander L., (2004) A Comparison of the Verbal Rating Scale and the Visual Analog Scale for pain assessment. *The Internet Journal of Anesthesiology*, **8**(1) www.ispub.com/ostia/index.php?xmlFilePath=journals/ija/vol8n1/vrs.xml.

Dudgeon D., Raubertas R.F. and Rosenthal S.N. (1993) The Short-Form McGill Pain Questionnaire in chronic cancer pain. *Journal of Pain and Symptom Management*, **8**(4): 191–195.

Field L. (1996) Are Nurses still underestimating patients' pain postoperatively? *British Journal of Advanced Nursing*, **5**(13): 778–784.

Francke A.L., Garssen B., Abu-Saad H.A. and Grypdonck M. (1996) Qualitative needs assessment prior to a continuing education program. *The Journal of Continuing Education in Nursing*, **27**(1): 34–41.

Freeland N., Odhner M., Wegman D., and Ingersoll G.L. (2006). Refinement of a nonverbal pain assessment scale for nonverbal, critically ill adults. Unpublished research report, University of Rochester Medical Center, Rochester, NY.

Grafton K.V., Foster N.E. and Wright C.C. (2005) Test-retest reliability of the Short-Form McGill Pain Questionnaire: assessment of intraclass correlation coefficients and limits of agreement in patients with osteoarthritis. *Clinical Journal of Pain,* **21**(1): 73–82.

Harrison A. (1993) Comparing nurses' and patients' pain evaluations: A study of hospitalised patients in Kuwait. *Social Science Medicine*, **36**(5): 683–692.

Hastings F. (1995) Introduction of the use of structured pain assessment for post-operative patients in Kenya: implementing change using a research based co-operative approach. *Journal of Clinical Nursing*, **4**: 169–176.

Huskisson E.C. (1974) Measurement of pain. *Lancet*, **9**: 1127–1131.

Idvall E., Hamrin E., Sjostrom B. and Unosson M. (2002) Patient and nurse assessment of quality of care in postoperative pain management. *Quality & Safety in Health Care*, **11**(4): 327–334.

Joint Commission on Accreditation of Healthcare Organisations (2000–2001) *Standards for ambulatory care accreditation policies, standards, intent statements by the Joint Commission on Accreditation of Healthcare Organizations.* Joint Commission on Accreditation of Healthcare Organisations.

Kremer E., Atkinson J.H. and Ignelzi R.J. (1981) Measurement of pain: patient preference does not compound pain measurement. *Pain*, **10**: 241–248.

McCaffrey M. (1983) *Nursing the patient in Pain,* 2nd edn. Harper and Row, London, p. 276.

McCaffrey, M., and Ferrell, B.R. (1994). Nurses' assessment of pain intensity and choice of analgesic dose. *Contemporary Nurse*, **3**(2): 68–74.

McDowell I. and Newell C. (1996) Measuring health: a guide to rating scales and questionnaires, 2nd edn. Oxford University Press, Oxford, pp. 341–351.

Melzack R. (1975) The McGill Pain Questionnaire: major properties and scoring methods. *Pain*, **1:** 277–299.

Melzack R. (1987) The short-form McGill Pain Questionnaire. *Pain*, **30**: 191–197.

Melzack R. and Katz J. (1994) Pain measurement in persons in pain. In: *Textbook of Pain,* 3rd edn. (eds. Melzack R. and Wall P.). London, Churchill Livingstone, p. 337.

Melzack R. and Torgeson W.S. (1971) On the language of pain. *Anaesthesiology*, **34**: 50–59.

Moore A., Edwards J., Barden J. and McQuay H. (2004). Measuring pain. In *Bandolier's Little Book of Pain.* Oxford University Press, Oxford, p. 7.

National Cancer Institute. (www.nci.nih.gov/cancertopics/pdq/supportivecare/pain/HealthProfessional/page2#Section_44). National Health and Medical Research Council, Australia Acute Pain Management Scientific Evidence of 1999 (www.nhmrc.gov.au).

Odhner M., Wegman D., Freeland N., Steinmetz A. and Ingersoll G.L. (2003). Assessing pain control in nonverbal critically ill adults. *Dimensions in Critical Care Nursing*, **22**: 260–267.

Ohnhaus E.E. and Adler R. (1975) Methodological problems in the measurement of pain: a comparison between the verbal rating scale and the visual analogue scale. *Pain*, **1**: 379–384.

Reading A.E. (1982) A comparison of the McGill Pain Questionnaire in chronic and acute pain. *Pain,* **13**, 185–192.

Royal College of Anaesthetists and The Pain Society, the British Chapter of the International Association for the Study of Pain (2003) *Pain Management Services – Good Practice.* The Royal College of Anaesthetists and The Pain Society, London, p. 4.

Royal College of Surgeons and Anaesthetists (1990) *Commission on the Provision of Surgical Services, Report on the Working Party on Pain after Surgery*. Royal College of Surgeons and Anaesthetists, London.

Scott J. and Huskisson E.C. (1976) Graphic representation of pain. *Pain*, **2**: 175–184.

Seymour R.A., Simpson J.M., Charlton J.E. and Phillips M.E. (1985) An evaluation of length and end-phrase of Visual Analogue Scales in dental pain. *Pain*, **21**: 177–185.

Sloman R., Rosen G., Rom M. and Shir Y. (2005) Nurses' assessment of pain in surgical patients. *Journal of Advanced Nursing*, **52**(2): 125–132.

Sriwatanakul K., Kelvie W., Lasagna L., Calimlin J.F., Weis O.F. and Mehta G. (1983) Studies with different types of visual analog scales for measurement of pain. *Clinical. Pharmacological Therapeutics,* Aug: 234–239.

Taylor H. (1997) Pain scoring as a formal pain assessment tool. *Nursing Standard*, **11**(35): 40–42.

Wegman D.A. (2005) Tool for pain assessment. *Critical Care Nurse*, **25**(1):14.

Zalon M.L. (1993) Nurse's assessment of postoperative patients' pain. *Pain*, **54**: 329–334.

7 Pain interventions

> **Learning outcomes**
>
> By the end of this chapter you should be able to:
>
> ★ Understand the types of pain interventions available and the benefits of combining approaches to pain management
>
> ★ Understand the main pharmacological approaches to pain management
>
> ★ Identify the location of modulation of pain on the pain pathway for various pain interventions.

Introduction

There are many interventions used to manage pain, from strong opioids to transcutaneous electrical nerve stimulation (TENS) machines to acupuncture. It is important for you as a health professional to be knowledgeable about these interventions, their actions and interactions. Clinical services often rely on the way they have managed pain for many years and are slow to introduce new methods of pain relief. However, the evidence for pain interventions is constantly changing and services should take the time to review and audit the levels and effectiveness of their pain intervention strategies. The choice of intervention to manage pain should be based on accurate, appropriate assessment of the patient's pain and knowledge of the physiology of pain. This chapter details the more common pain interventions highlighting where on the pain pathway they are effective. Different analgesic schemes to support maximisation of medication usage are described.

Pain interventions

Chapter 4 described the physiology of pain in detail and highlighted the importance of understanding where on the pain pathway different interventions modulate pain.

> ***Reflective activity***
>
> Consider the last pain intervention you performed. Was it administering an opioid to a postoperative patient? Consider where on the pain pathway this intervention modulated the patient's pain.

Health care professionals can treat pain more effectively and efficiently if they identify the type of pain and then select the most appropriate intervention. Thus, the pain assessment process is critical to successful interventions. Chapter 6 detailed the various types of pain assessment and in which clinical situations they are most effective. Patients may be suffering from more than one type of pain and, therefore, may need combination interventions to manage their pain experience. The choice of pain interventions, like any aspect of patient care, should be based on the best available evidence. As technology, skills and knowledge grow, nurses and health care professionals need to develop systems to ensure they are accessing, interpreting and utilising the best available evidence. Throughout this book reference has been made to evidence-based practice and pain resources available. These should be accessed regularly in order to ensure the chosen pain intervention is appropriate, up to date and evidence based. In particular, medications and their dosages change and new medicines come on the market. This chapter details medications, their use and side-effects in order to give you a better understanding of approaches to managing pain and their mechanisms. However, given the dynamic nature of medications and the individual responses of patients to interventions, you should always refer to your most up-to-date source of information before choosing or administering medications.

The extent of pain interventions available is broader than just medications, for example there is physiotherapy, cognitive behavioural therapy, TENs, relaxation etc. This means that health professionals need to engage in a systematic approach to assessment and monitoring of a patient's pain to ensure that the patient is receiving the most effective intervention or combination of interventions. Figure 7.1 details the pain assessment and monitoring cycle.

Table 7.1 will remind you of the various types and causes of pain.

Table 7.1 Types and causes of pain

	Cutaneous pain	Somatic pain	Visceral pain	Neuropathic pain
Cause	Produced by stimulation of the pain receptors in the skin, e.g. superficial burn.	Produced by stimulation of pain receptors in the deep structures, i.e. muscles, bones, joints, tendons, ligaments.	Produced by stimulation of pain receptors in the viscera, e.g. stomach, kidney, gallbladder, urinary bladder, intestines.	Radiating or specific, e.g. trigeminal neuralgia, limb amputation.
Description	Pin prick, stabbing, or sharp. Can be accurately localised due to the large number of receptors in the skin.	Unlike cutaneous pain, deep somatic pain is dull, intense and prolonged. It is usually associated with autonomic stimulation, e.g. sweating, vomiting and changes in heart rate.	Is poorly localised and is often referred or radiates to other sites.	Electric, tingling or shooting in nature. It may be continuous or paroxysmal in presentation.

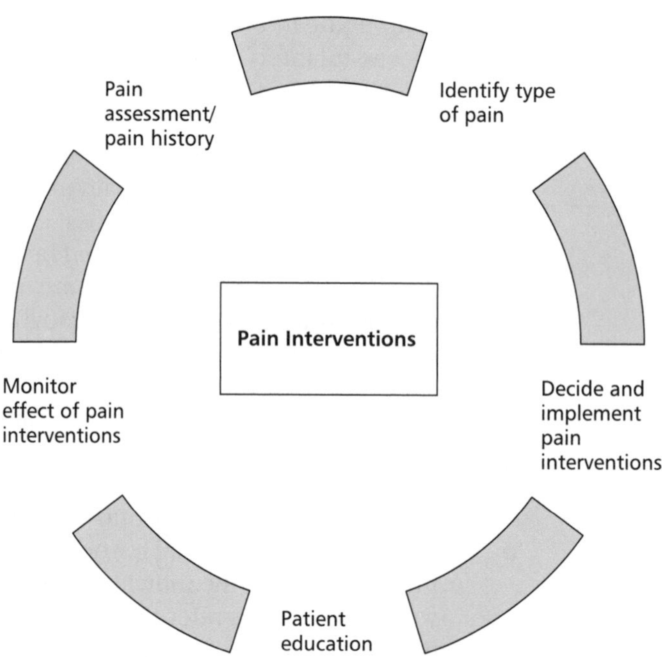

Figure 7.1 Assessment and monitoring of patients' pain and pain interventions

> ### Reflective activity
>
> Consider the last two pain interventions you performed. What type of pain did the patients have? How did they describe their pain? How did you assess the pain? Looking back on how you assessed the pain, would you do anything different?

Table 7.2 details the more common pain interventions and the part of the pain pathway at which these are effective. See Figure 4.1 page 48 to remind you of the pain pathways.

Medications for pain management

Medications are the mainstay of pain management. The three main classes of medication effective for pain management are opioids, nonsteriodal anti-inflammatories (NSAIDs) and anticonvulsants. Each is described below. Acetaminophen (paracetamol) is also described.

Table 7.2 Common pain interventions

Nervous system	Specific area	Aim of modulation	Interventions
CNS	Brain and spinal cord	The inhibition of the release of chemical transmitters at the various synapses within the dorsal horn of the spinal cord and brain as a result of the uptake of naturally occurring morphine-like substances by specialised receptors on relevant neurons. These receptors are known as mu (μ), delta (δ) and kappa (κ) receptors.	Opioid drugs will bind to these specialised receptors and reduce pain perception.
CNS	Brain	To inhibit prostaglandin synthesis.	Acetaminophen (paracetamol)
CNS	Spinal cord	To prevent transmission of pain signals through the dorsal horn in the spinal cord in order that they cannot travel to the brain (Gate Control Theory).	TENs Heat and cold
CNS	Spinal epidural space	To block or modulate pain signals in the spinal epidural space preventing their transmission to the brain.	Nerve blocks. Both epidural local anaesthetics and epidural opioids can produce analgesia.
PNS	Nerve fibre	To prevent the transmission of pain signals along the nerve cell. Nerve conduction depends on sodium ion channels in the axon.	Local anaesthetic agents such as lignocaine are absorbed across the membrane of the neurone and block the sodium channels. This means that the electrical impulse cannot be transmitted.
PNS	Nociceptor	To prevent transmission of the pain signal at the site of pain. Pain at the site is exacerbated by the presence of certain chemicals, such as prostaglandins or bradykinin.	NSAIDs act at the site of pain reducing the presence of prostaglandins.

Acetaminophen (paracetamol)

Paracetamol or acetaminophen acts by inhibition of prostaglandin synthesis (production of potent, hormone-like substances that mediate a wide range of physiological functions) in the CNS. It is an analgesic and antipyretic. It has no anti-inflammatory effects. Side-effects are minimal once taken in recommended doses. However, those with liver or renal impairment are advised to avoid it.

Opioids

Opiates originally came from the seed capsule of the opium poppy (*Papaver somniferum*). Opioids are derivatives of opium and include naturally occurring opium derivatives, partially synthetic derivatives of morphine and synthetic compounds (Irving and Wallace, 1997). Opium derivatives have had a mixed history over time, and are used in many formulations for perception-altering purposes. Opioids are potent analgesics. They have been both used and abused, challenging governments to develop regulations and legislation to support a balance for opioid use. Thus, while opioids form the cornerstone of the pharmacological armoury for the treatment of pain (Ferrante, 1996) and are often the drugs of choice in the first-line management of acute pain, opioids are controlled substances and subject to regulation. Common opioids in use are morphine, diamorphine, pethidine, methadone, hydromorphone, oxycodone, fentanyl and buprenorphine (McQuay, 1999).

In 1973, it was first discovered that opioids act by binding to specific sites in the CNS (Park and Fulton, 1991). Mu (μ), sigma (σ) and kappa (κ) opioid receptors are found throughout the nervous system and produce analgesia. When activated they reduce the excitability of nociceptors. The potency or intensity of the analgesic effect is dependent upon, firstly, access to the receptor and, secondly, binding affinity at the site (Ferrante, 1996).

Although opioid compounds are active in the PNS, it is in the CNS that they primarily produce analgesia by inhibiting nociceptive transmission. McQuay (1999) states that there is little difference between the various opioids in speed of onset and duration of effect. Faster onset and longer effect are achieved by changing the route of administration or formulation. The onset time by IV route is approximately two minutes and by IM route 20 minutes (the more lipophilic the drug the faster the onset). According to Collins *et al.* (1998), morphine reaches maximum concentration at different times depending on formulation:

- Immediate-release oral formulations – one hour
- Controlled-release oral formulations – three hours
- Once-daily formulations – nine hours.

Opioids produce a number of side-effects which require monitoring and management. Table 7.3 highlights the key side-effects, clinical assessment and management techniques required as detailed by Fine and Portenoy (2004).

The Royal College of Surgeons and Anaesthetists report (1990) recommends that in order to improve the efficacy of opioid administration, the dose and frequency should be adjusted in response to the needs of each patient. Patients should have an individualised treatment regimen. Efficacy and side-effects should be recorded regularly and treatment modified accordingly.

In 2001, the American Academy of Pain Medicine, the American Pain Society and the American Society of Addiction Medicine agreed a consensus document on definitions related to the use of opioids and the treatment of pain. The consensus document states that most specialists agree that patients treated with prolonged opioid therapy usually do develop physical dependence and sometimes develop tolerance but do not usually develop addictive disorders. The actual risk is, however,

Table 7.3 Opioids: key side-effects, clinical assessment and management techniques (Source: Fine and Portenoy, 2004)

Side effect	Description	Clinical assessment	Management
Constipation	Most common and persistent side-effect is bowel dysmotility leading to constipation.	Depends on time, course of its development and medical setting. Is the relationship with the drug clear? Other contributing factors such as inactivity and dehydration may be present. History taking and physical examination should be completed.	Tolerance to opioids develops very slowly and a large proportion of patients require laxative therapy while taking opioids. For some patients dietary modification is adequate. Fluid intake should be increased. Mobility should be encouraged.
Nausea and vomiting	May occur after taking an opioid; however, tolerance usually develops rapidly.	Assess for contributing factors such as constipation or other medications.	Administration of an anti-emetic at the time of nausea. Routine prophylactic administration of an anti-emetic agent is not typically indicated.
Somnolence and cognitive impairment	Somnolence (mental clouding) typically wanes over a period of days or weeks. Can range from mild to severe. Cognitive impairment can range from slight inattention to extreme confusion. Persistence is atypical.	Assess for contributing factors.	Address any contributing causes. If analgesia is adequate it may be possible to reduce dose. Fine and Portenoy (2004) suggest that if these are not effective there is a large body of clinical experience in the use of psychostimulants to treat opioid-induced cognitive impairment.
Pruritus	May occur with any opioid and may be caused by the opioid mediated release of histamine from mast cells.	Assess extent and duration of itch.	Pharmacological management with trial use of an antihistamine.
Respiratory depression	Rarely a problem when used according to accepted guidelines. Tolerance usually develops quickly, allowing escalation of the dose incrementally. Combining opioids with other medications such as hypnotics or benzodiazepines should be monitored closely.	Close monitoring of respiration and sedation scores.	Naloxone should be administered for symptomatic respiratory depression.

unknown and probably varies with genetic predisposition among other factors. They recommended the following definitions of **addiction**, **physical dependence** and **tolerance** and their use (see Keywords).

Chapter 10 provides more detail on the use of opioids and chronic non-malignant pain and Chapter 11 describes the use of opioids for cancer pain.

Keywords

Addiction
Addiction is a primary, chronic, neurobiologic disease, with genetic, psychosocial and environmental factors influencing its development and manifestations. It is characterised by behaviours that include one or more of the following: impaired control over drug use, compulsive use, continued use despite harm, and craving

Physical dependence
This is a state of adaptation that is manifested by a drug-class specific withdrawal syndrome that can be produced by abrupt cessation, rapid dose reduction, decreasing blood level of the drug, and/or administration of an antagonist

Tolerance
This is a state of adaptation in which exposure to a drug induces changes that result in a diminution of one or more of the drug's effects over time

Nonsteroidal anti-inflammatories (NSAIDs)

Nonsteroidal anti-inflammatory drugs (NSAIDs) are among the most widely used medications on both a prescription basis and over the counter (Abramson and Weaver, 2005). NSAIDs have anti-inflammatory, analgesic and antipyretic effects and inhibit thrombocyte aggregation. NSAIDs act by decreasing prostoglandin production by inhibiting the production of the enzyme cyclo-oxygenase.

A major limiting factor is the risk of gastrointestinal toxicity. Recent studies indicate that this risk has declined 67% since 1992 (Fries *et al.*, 2004). This is as a result of the use of lower doses of NSAIDs, use of gastroprotective agents such as proton pump inhibitors (PPIs), and the introduction of the selective cyclo-oxygenase-2 (COX-2) inhibitors.

Possible cardiovascular risks are being debated with regard to COX-2 inhibitors. The FDA advisory committee (USA) voted that all COX-2 inhibitors that have been approved for use in the USA significantly increase the risk of cardiovascular events (American College of Rheumatology, 2005). NSAIDs should be used with caution with asthma, impaired renal function and those on antiplatelet regimes including aspirin.

Systematic reviews have found no important differences in effect between different NSAIDs or doses, but have found differences in toxicity related to increased doses and possibly due to the nature of the NSAID itself (Gotzche, 2000).

Anticonvulsants

Anticonvulsants are a group of medicines commonly used for treating epilepsy, and they are also effective for treating pain. Nurmikko *et al.* (1998) state that anticonvulsant drugs have an established role in the treatment of chronic neuropathic pain, especially when patients complain of shooting sensations.

Reflective activity

Consider the profile of your patients (e.g. surgical, older person, renal etc.). What types of analgesics do you use in your clinical area? Take a sample of five patient medication charts. It is likely you use all of the above described medications. Discuss with a pharmacist and nurse specialist the use and actions of the analgesics you use regularly.

Routes of analgesia

It is possible to administer analgesia via many routes but some are more effective than others. Pharmokinetics describes the uptake, distribution and elimination of the drug. There is wide variation between individuals and, sometimes, within the same individual at different times. Patient characteristics which may influence analgesic pharmacokinetic variability include age (the elderly have a diminished volume of distribution), hepatic disease, renal disease, acid base balance, hypothermia, hypothyroidism and concurrent drug administration. Figure 7.2 details the main methods of administration of analgesia.

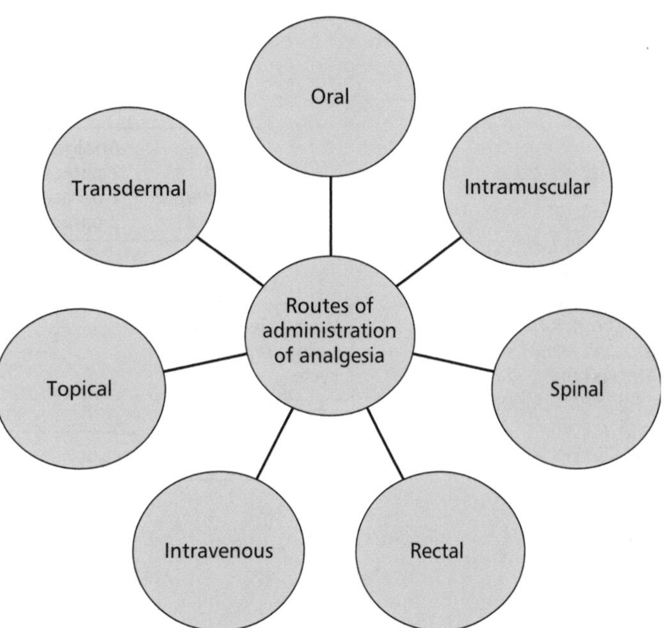

Figure 7.2 Main methods of administration of analgesia

Evidence base

'Epidural analgesia is highly effective for controlling acute pain after surgery or trauma to the chest, abdomen, pelvis or lower limbs. It can, however, cause serious, potentially life threatening complications and its safe, effective management requires a co-ordinated multidisciplinary approach.' This is the introduction to the document *Good practice in the management of continuous epidural analgesia in the hospital setting* produced by the Royal College of Anaesthetists, The Royal College of Nursing, The Association of Anaesthetists of Great Britain and Ireland, The British Pain Society and The European Society of Regional Anaesthesia and Pain Therapy (2004). Go to the British Pain Society website (www.britishpainsociety.org) to access this document. Review the recommendations for use of epidural analgesia.

Analgesic schemes

It is evident that there is often benefit from combining different analgesics as part of a regime for a patient. This is more effective if it is planned in the form of a patient protocol using analgesic schemes.

Moore *et al.* (2003) describe the three-pot system: paracetamol, paracetamol and opioid combination and NSAIDs. The authors state that the system is based on best evidence and uses cheapest available analgesics. Further research is underway. There are two systems, one for those who can take NSAIDs and one for those who cannot (see Figures 7.3 and 7.4).

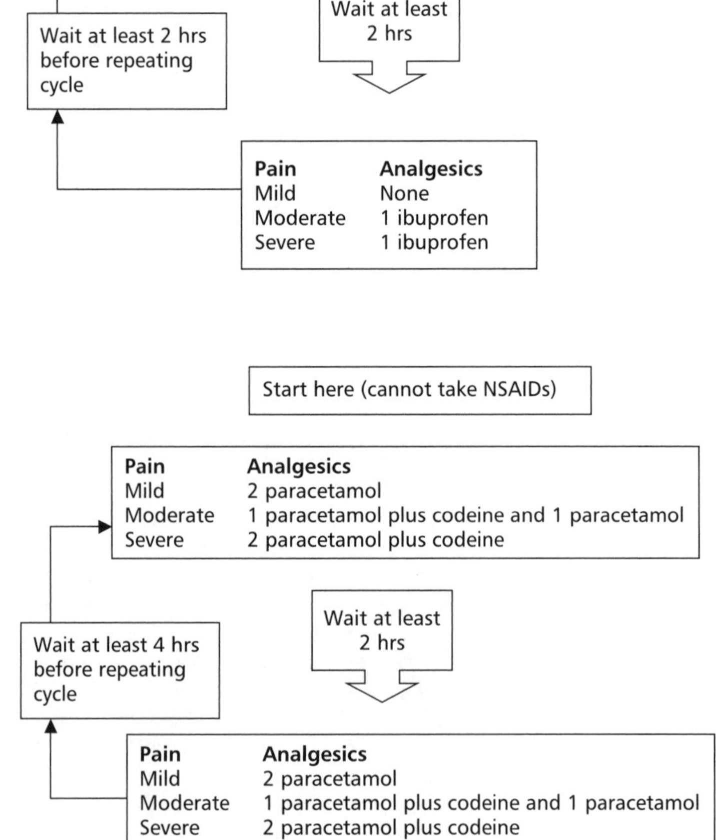

Figure 7.3 A simple scheme (three pot) for acute and chronic pain relief using paracetamol/opioid combination drugs for patients who can take NSAIDS (Moore et al. *2003, p. 432). Reproduced with permission from* Bandolier's Little Book of Pain: An Evidence Based Guide to Treatments *by Moore* et al.*, 2003 Oxford University Press.*

Figure 7.4 A simple scheme (three pot) for acute and chronic pain relief using paracetamol/opioid combination drugs for patients who cannot take NSAIDS (Moore et al. *2003, p. 433). Reproduced with permission from* Bandolier's Little Book of Pain: An Evidence Based Guide to Treatments *by Moore* et al.*, 2003 Oxford University Press.*

The WHO analgesic ladder was a major landmark in the management of pain (see Figure 7.5). It was first produced by the WHO in 1986. The WHO (2006) website states 'If a pain occurs, there should be a prompt oral administration of drugs in the following order: non-opioids (aspirin or paracetamol); then, as necessary, mild opioids (codeine); or the strong opioids such as morphine, until the patient is free of pain. To maintain freedom from pain, drugs should be given "by the clock", that is every 3–6 hours, rather than "on demand". This three-step approach of administering the right drug in the right dose at the right time is inexpensive and 80–90% effective.' Moore *et al.* (2003) suggest that while the WHO analgesic ladder can relieve pain for approximately 80% of patients, pain management must be optimal, which is not always the case in practice. They suggest using the ladder going upwards for chronic pain, starting with non-opioids and in reverse starting with strong opioid opioids +/– non-opioid for acute pain.

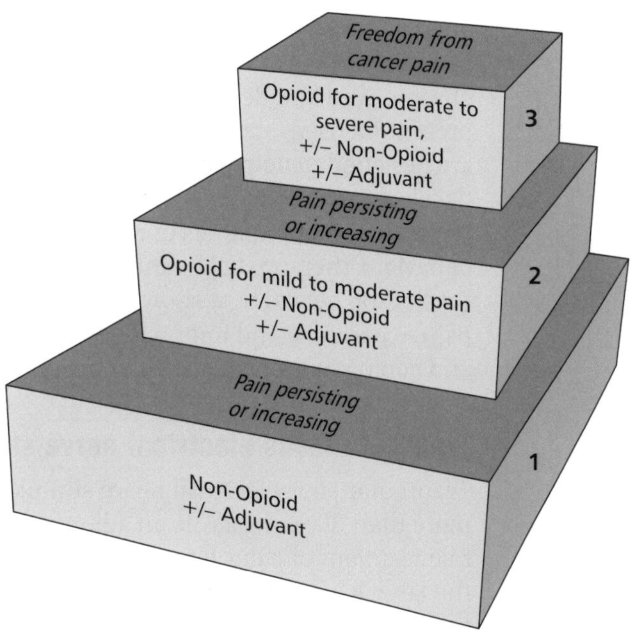

Figure 7.5 WHO's pain relief ladder. World Health Organization Analgesic Ladder (WHO, 1986)

Clinical Pharmacist

I work as a clinical pharmacist supporting five medical wards, one of which is an oncology unit. I audit medication charts weekly and order stocks for the ward areas. What concerns me most is the reactive prescribing for medications in general and specifically for pain. In order to address this, I have met with the clinical nurse manager and consultant and presented my findings. As a result, we are devising an analgesic protocol to try to make analgesic prescription and administration more consistent and planned. We will combine this with short education sessions and information material.

Non-pharmacological approaches

It is appropriate to consider and utilise non-pharmacological pain management options to support patients through their pain experience, particularly those patients with mild or persistent chronic pain. Reference is made here to cognitive behavioural therapy, TENs, heat and cold, and acupuncture.

Cognitive-behavioural therapy

Given that pain is a personal and unique experience for the individual, the emotive and contextual aspects of pain will influence the pain experience. For those with chronic pain extending over long periods of time it is logical to consider complementary approaches to support the individual to cope with both the psychological and functional facets of that pain. Turk (2003) suggests that cognitive-behavioural (CB) approaches should be viewed as important complements to more traditional, pharmacological, physical and surgical interventions for chronic pain and describes CB approaches as: 'characterised by being present focused, active, time-limited and structured. CB interventions are designed to help patients identify maladaptive patterns and acquire, develop and practice more adaptive ways of responding'. A systematic review and meta-analysis of randomised controlled trials of cognitive behaviour therapy (CBT) and behaviour therapy for chronic pain (excluding headaches) showed that CBT was effective in reducing the pain experience and improving positive behaviour expression, appraisal and coping in individuals with chronic pain (Morley *et al.,* 1999).

Transcutaneous electrical nerve stimulation (TENS)

Transcutaneous electrical nerve stimulation (TENS) was introduced more than 30 years ago as an adjunct to the pharmacological management of pain. It involves application of electrical stimulation to the large low-threshold fibres through the skin. It is based on the principles of the Gate Control Theory (see Chapter 4). The effectiveness of TENS remains under debate. In 1996, Carroll *et al.*, following systematic review, judged that of 15 out of 17 randomised controlled trials (RCTs) there was no benefit achieved with TENS compared to placebo for postoperative patients.

A Cochrane systematic review found limited and inconsistent evidence to support the use of TENS as an isolated intervention in the management of chronic lower back pain. Only two RCTs met the criteria for inclusion (Khadilkar *et al.* 2005). Moore *et al.* (2003), on review of the evidence for TENS, state that the clinical bottom line is that there is no conclusive evidence that TENS is effective for either postoperative or chronic pain.

Heat and cold

The effectiveness of heat and cold is described anecdotally. However, research in the form of well-designed trials is needed to assess the effectiveness of both for relieving pain. Where used, heat and cold should be applied with caution following assessment of the patient to ensure that there are no contraindications.

Heat stimulates the thermoreceptors in the skin and deeper tissues. Theoretically, this can help reduce pain by closing the gating system in the spinal cord (see Chapter 4 for details on Gate-Control Theory). Heat is used extensively for muscle spasm, menstrual pain and joint stiffness. It can be applied in many ways, for example hot baths, heating pads, hot water bottles or heat packs. Chandler *et al.* (2002) caution that use of heat therapy in hospitals is often limited due to safety issues with heating devices.

Cold will cause vasoconstriction and reduce swelling and should be applied using ice packs or compresses. Cold should not be applied directly to the skin. Atraksinen *et al.* (2004) describe a randomised, blinded controlled trial assessing whether cold gel reduced pain and disability in minor soft-tissue injuries (n = 74). The active cold gel with menthol and ethanol showed decreased pain at rest and movement compared with the placebo group.

Acupuncture

Acupuncture involves inserting fine needles into specific points in the surface of the body. The needles are often rotated to provide stimulus. Moore *et al.* (2003) state that while acupuncture is widely used, there is little evidence that it is effective. They highlight the difficulties with the quality of the studies particularly in relation to the correctness of the acupuncture procedure, appropriateness of control interventions and blinding of participants. They state, on review of available trials, that the clinical bottom line is that acupuncture for back pain is ineffective, that there is no convincing evidence for acupuncture for neck and back pain and that there is no evidence of it being more effective in arthritis. A strong case is made for high-quality, large long-term trials.

One more recent randomised controlled trial (Berman *et al.* 2004) concluded that acupuncture appeared to provide improvement in function and pain relief as an adjunctive therapy for osteoarthritis of the knee when compared with credible sham acupuncture and education control groups (570 patients over 26 weeks).

See Chapter 8 for further discussion of alternative and complementary therapies.

Key points Top tips

- There are many pain interventions available, from medications to TENs, acupuncture and cognitive behavioural therapy
- Knowledge of the physiology of pain is critical to deciding on the most appropriate pain intervention
- There is benefit in combining different analgesics as part of a regime for a patient
- Non-pharmacological approaches support pain management; however, there is limited evidence for effectiveness of some of these such as heat and cold

Patterns of analgesic use

Jennifer is a 50-year-old journalist who has had a hysterectomy. She is two days post surgery but is mobilising very slowly and appears to be in some pain. Margaret is the nurse on duty. She is an experienced surgical nurse and sits down with Jennifer to review her progress. Jennifer was on a PCA morphine pump for 24 hours, which, on review of her pain scores, had been providing adequate pain relief.

Margaret begins by asking Jennifer how her pain has been, what her current pain score on VAS is now and whether she is able to walk or take deep breaths. Jennifer's pain score is 3.5 at rest but 7 on mobilisation. Margaret realises that pain scores had only been taken at rest, not during movement, which explained why Jennifer's PCA pump was discontinued.

Margaret reviewed Jennifer's medication chart and is concerned when she sees that she is prescribed paracetamol, two different NSAIDs and morphine 10 mg intramuscularly (IM) all on a pre re nata (PRN) basis. It seems that she has been seen by three different doctors in the past 24 hours for her pain and each has prescribed a different medication. For a summary of what has been administered since discontinuation of the PCA pump see Table 7.4.

- What other information should Margaret seek before deciding on the next steps?
- Why is it so important to assess pain on movement as well as pain at rest for surgical patients?
- If you were to rewrite Jennifer's medication plan, what would you do?

Table 7.4 Medication Chart

Time	Medication
9 a.m.	PCA discontinued
12 midday	NSAID (no. 1) PR
6 p.m.	Paracetamol
11 p.m.	Morphine 10 mg IM
8 a.m.	NSAID (no. 2) PO
2 p.m.	Margaret is reviewing pain medications and deciding on next steps

Rapid recap

1 Name two side-effects of opioids.
2 What are the principles of the WHO analgesic ladder?
3 What is the medication of choice for chronic neuropathic pain?
4 What are the major effects of NSAIDs?
5 What are the limiting factors for use of NSAIDs?

References

Abramson S.B. and Weaver A.L. (2005) Current state of therapy for pain and inflammation. *Arthritis Research & Therapy*, **7**(suppl 4): S1–S6.

American Academy of Pain Medicine, the American Pain society and the American Society of Addiction Medicine (2001). Definitions related to the use of opioids and the treatment of pain. A consensus document from the American Academy of Pain Medicine, the American Pain Society, and the American Society of Addiction Medicine. Available at http://painmed.org/productpub/statements/.

American College of Rheumatology, The safety of COX-2 inhibitors: deliberations from February 16–18, 2005, FDA meeting. http://www.rheumatology.org/publications/hotline/0305NSAIDs.asp.

Atraksinen O.V., Kyrklund N., Latvala K., Kouri J.P., Gronblad M. and Kolari P. (2004) Cold gel reduced pain and disability in minor soft-tissue injury. *Journal of Bone and Joint Surgery*, **86**(5): 1101.

Berman B.M., Lao L., Langenberg P., Lin Lee W., Gilpin A.M.K. and Hochberg M.C. (2004) Effectiveness of acupuncture as adjunctive therapy in osteoarthritis of the knee. *Annals of Internal Medicine*, **141**(12): 901–910.

Carroll D., Tramer M., McQuay H. and Moore A. (1996) Randomisation is important in studies with pain outcomes: systematic review of transcutaneous electrical nerve stimulation in acute postoperative pain. *British Journal of Anaesthesia*, **77**: 798–803.

Chandler A., Preece J. and Lister S. (2002) Using heat therapy for pain management. *Nursing Standard*, **17**(9): 40–42.

Collins S.L., Faura C.C., Moore R.A. and McQuay H.J. (1998) Peak plasma concentrations after oral morphine – a systematic review. *Journal of Pain and Symptom Management*, **16**: 388–402.

Ferrante F.M. (1996) Principles of Opioid Pharmacotherapy: Practical Implications of Basic Mechanisms. *Journal of Pain and Symptom Management*, **11**(5): 265–273.

Fine P.G. and Portenoy R.K. (2004) *A Clinical Guide to Opioid Analgesia.* McGraw-Hill Inc, USA.

Fries J.F., Murtagh K.N., Bennerr M., Zatarain E., Lingala B. and Bruce B. (2004) The rise and decline of nonsteroidal anti-inflammatory drug-associated gastropathy in rheumatoid arthritis. *Arthritis Rheum*, **50**: 2433–2440.

Gotzche P.C. (2000) Non-steroidal anti-inflammatory drugs. *BMJ*, **320**: 1058–1061.

Irving GA and Wallace MS (1997) Opioid Pharmacology. In *Pain Management for the Practising Physician.* Churchill Livingstone, Edinburgh, pp.17–30.

Khadilkar A., Milne S., Brosseau L., Robinson V., Saginur M., Shea B. *et al.* (2005). Transcutaneous electrical nerve stimulation (TENS) for chronic low-back pain. *The*

Cochrane Database of Systematic Reviews. Issue 3. Art. No.: CD003008. DOI: 10.1002/14651858.pub2.

McQuay H. (1999) Opioids in pain management. *The Lancet*, **353**: 2229–2232.

Moore A., Edwards J., Barden J. and McQuay H. (2003) *Bandolier's Little Book of Pain*. Oxford University Press, Oxford.

Morley S., Eccleston C. and Williams A. (1999) Systematic review and meta-analysis of randomised controlled trials of cognitive behaviour therapy for chronic pain in adults, excluding headache. *Pain*, **80**: 1–13.

Nurmikko T.J., Nash T.P. and Wiles J.R. (1998) Recent advances: control of chronic pain. *BMJ*, **317**: 1438–1441.

Park G. and Fulton B. (1991) *The Management of Acute Pain.* Oxford Medical Publications, Oxford.

Royal College of Nursing, The Association of Anaesthetists of Great Britain and Ireland, The British Pain Society and The European Society of Regional Anaesthesia and Pain Therapy (2004) *Good practice in management of continuous epidural analgesia in the hospital setting*. Available at www.britishpainsociety.org/pub_pub.html.

Royal College of Surgeons and Anaesthetists (1990) *Commission on the Provision of Surgical Services, Report of the Working Party on Pain after Surgery*. Royal College of Surgeons and Anaesthetists, London.

Turk D.C. (2003) Cognitive-behavioural approach to the treatment of chronic pain patients. *Regional Anaesthesia and Pain Medicine*, **28**(6): 573–579.

World Health Organization (2006) Pain Ladder website. Available at: www.who.int/cancer/palliative/painladder/en/index.html.

8 The role of complementary and alternative therapies in pain management

Lynne Wigens

Learning outcomes

By the end of this chapter you should be able to:

- ★ Define and discuss a range of complementary and alternative medicine
- ★ Appreciate the influence and widespread use of complementary and alternative therapies in the field of pain care
- ★ Examine a range of evidence relating to complementary and alternative medicine
- ★ Discuss the practitioner–patient relationship and its impact on pain management.

Defining complementary alternative medicine (CAM)

Complementary and alternative medicine (CAM) has been defined as health care practices and products outside the realm of conventional medicine, which are yet to be validated using scientific methods (Eisenberg, 2002). No book on pain management could ignore the role of complementary and alternative therapies. Within this chapter a range of therapies are reviewed, with particular reference to the evidence base for practice. The ways that health care practitioners may integrate CAM is discussed, and it is concluded that there is a need for a strong practitioner–patient relationship, whether the care delivered is conventional or complementary/ alternative.

The term 'complementary medicine' tends to be used for therapies that have been widely integrated with conventional medicine, e.g. aromatherapy and massage combined with palliative care analgesics.

Alternative medicine is used as a collective term for treatments that are used in place of conventional medicine, e.g. accessing osteopathy rather than seeking conventional medical management of lower back pain. Traditional medicine refers to health practices, approaches, knowledge and beliefs incorporating plant, animal and

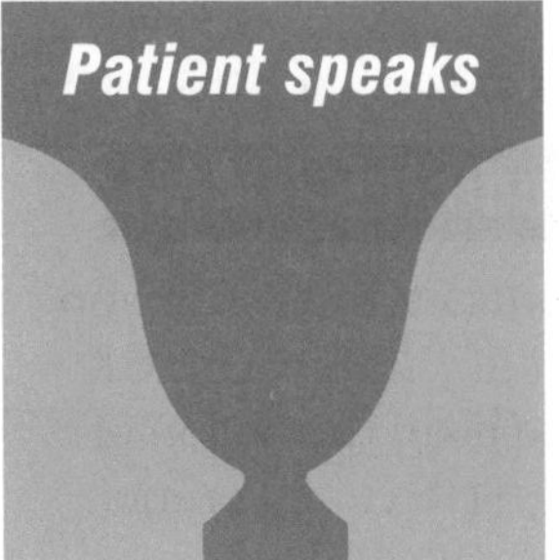

Patient speaks

I am receiving palliative care treatment for my cancer and I go to the hospice for day treatment, and as part of this I have 30-minute sessions of aromatherapy and massage. They use lavender and rose oils in a grapeseed oil base. As the treatment begins I start to feel more relaxed. Over time the aches and pains across my body seem to reduce. The massage is so relaxing, even though only the lightest touch and stroking is used. It seems to get the tension out from my neck and shoulders and I feel heavenly for quite a while afterwards.

mineral-based medicines, spiritual therapies, manual techniques and exercises, applied singularly or in combination to treat, diagnose and prevent illnesses or maintain wellbeing (World Health Organization (WHO), 2003).

Different complementary therapies have very different philosophies and practices, but most share a common view of health and healing, emphasising wellness that is perceived to stem from a balance between the mind, body and its environment. Complementary therapies concentrate on the whole person in a '**holistic**', individualised approach, often calling for the patient to actively change their lifestyle or behaviours. Complementary therapists believe that this self-healing is the basis of all healing. These factors may be major contributing factors to the increasing popularity of complementary therapies in the management of pain.

Keywords

Holistic care
This is concerned with the interrelationships of body, mind and spirit in an ever-changing environment (Dossey, 2000). It means that care has to focus on the whole person rather than on one specific problem or disease.

Underpinning concepts/beliefs about CAM therapies

- Illness is a disharmony or deviation from health, affecting the person as part of the larger environment/universal system
- Health is a balance of opposing forces, and treatment is about strengthening healing forces
- Holistic in nature, strengthening the wellbeing of the whole person
- Less high-technology interventions or diagnostics are used
- The patient should be active in their cure

Reflective activity

What experience have you had with CAM? Have you received complementary or alternative therapies yourself, or treated others?

Think about your current view of CAM and its potential use in pain management.

Use of complementary alternative medicine (CAM)

Complementary medicine has been used by patients for their pain and other health care needs for many years (Lewith *et al.*, 2002). The UK annual expenditure on CAM in 2004/05 is likely to be in the region of £4.5 billion (Smallwood, 2005, p. 22). Within the NHS confederation leading-edge report on the future of acute care (Black, 2005) the complementary and alternative medicine market is viewed as being undervalued. A successful approach to the future should include the non-NHS 'health economy' which is much bigger than some health care practitioners realise (Black, 2005). It is suggested that the current UK market for CAM could be in excess of £5 billion. Within one small market town in 2004 there were 40 CAM practitioners (double that of the locality's general practitioners (GPs), and this is almost completely funded from discretionary payments by individuals (Black, 2005).

Over to you

Take a look at at least two of these websites and identify what they indicate about the current status of CAM within the UK.

- The British Holistic Medical Association
  www.bhma-sec.dircon.co.uk
- Institute for Complementary Medicine
  www.icmedicine.co.uk
- Complementary Medical Association
  www.the-cma.org.uk
- The British Complementary Medicine Association
  www.bcma.co.uk

There is clearly a large proportion of the UK population choosing to access CAM and in many instances funding their own treatments. In Vallerand *et al.*'s (2005) study with 723 participants about their self-treatment choices they found that participants reported using the following pain treatments:

- 75% were taking non-opoid analgesics
- 11% were taking adjuvant analgesics
- 29% were taking herbal products and supplements
- 68% were using non-pharmacological modalities, e.g. osteopathy
- 28% had not informed their primary care practitioners of their self-treatment choices.

Reflective activity

Are you surprised by Vallerand *et al.*'s (2005) findings?

From your own experience as a giver and receiver of health care do you think similar findings would be found if the study was replicated in your locality?

It has been suggested that the rise in the take up of CAM is due to the failure of conventional medicine to respond to patients as individual human beings (Graham, 1999). Motivators that have been identified as leading to patients accessing CAM include:

- the need for chronic symptom relief
- perceived effectiveness
- safety (fewer side-effects) and non-invasiveness
- emphasis on the whole person 'high touch/ low tech'
- sense of patient control over the treatment process, and being 'heard'
- good therapeutic relationship and support
- accessibility
- dissatisfaction with conventional medicine (Smallwood, 2005).

There has been an increase in acceptance of Eastern and other healing practices and methods that reflect the interconnectedness between mind and body, and this has occurred at a time when there has been a growth in self-help and support programmes. The number of adults that use some form of complementary or alternative therapy is high, with many people obtaining their own therapies through health-food stores and the internet, as well as consulting therapists. In order to provide optimal and comprehensive care of patients with pain, health care professionals need to be aware of the patient's use of CAM. Caring is not fully realised without an understanding of the personal meaning in a patient's pain.

Any list of what is considered a CAM changes continually as some become integrated into conventional medicine and additional alternative therapies become more widely known. Table 8.1, therefore, can only give a brief description of some complementary and alternative therapies most commonly used to reduce pain and is not an exhaustive list.

CAM therapies can be classified into five main groups:

1. Alternative medical systems: Based on Eastern medical philosophies such as traditional Chinese medicine and Ayurveda (ancient Indian subcontinent medicine).
2. Mind–body interventions: These use the mind's capacity to affect bodily functions and problems, e.g. meditation.
3. Physiological treatments: These often use substances found in nature, such as herbs. An example of this could be dietary supplements.
4. Manipulation of the body therapies: These are based on the manipulation of one or more body parts, e.g. chiropractic.
5. Energy therapies: These involve the use of energy fields, e.g. Reiki.

Table 8.1 CAM therapies and treatments in common use

Acupuncture	Chinese medical treatment that involves inserting fine needles into the skin at specific points in the body. It seems to relieve pain by diverting or changing the painful sensations that are sent to the brain from damaged tissues and also by stimulating 'natural painkillers' (endorphins, encephalins and serotonin).
Alexander technique	The technique teaches people to prevent unwanted and harmful habits, such as muscle tension and poor posture, by improving an individual's body alignment.
Aromatherapy and massage	Plant oils are massaged into the skin, inhaled or used in the bath, which have a variety of properties. Examples of those that are used to alter pain perception include peppermint and lavender. Massage involves a manual technique in which a rhythmic movement using a variety of strokes, kneading or tapping is undertaken to move the muscles and soft tissue of the body. Massage reduces anxiety and stress levels and relieves muscular tension and fatigue.
Chiropractic	Chiropractors manipulate the joints to try to restore alignment, as problems in alignment are viewed as causing a range of problems in other organs. Chiropractic works towards the vertebrae in the spine being in the correct position, and if there are problems with the alignment of the vertebrae this is thought to cause a range of problems in other organs.
Dietary supplements	These supplements are often bought from chemists, health-food shops or in 'added nutritional foods'. One example is Omega 3 essential fatty acids which are naturally found in oily fish, and thought to be beneficial for people with inflammatory forms of arthritis
Healing	Healing links with a range of belief systems, which may be religious, spiritual, social or cultural, e.g. faith healing. The healer assesses an individual's 'energy field' and then tries to pass energy to the body by gentle touch or by sweeping their hands over the body. Distance healing tries to achieve this through thought, meditation or prayer.
Herbal medicine	Whole plant derived medicines that assist in mobilising the healing mechanisms within the body. Herbal medicine has been present throughout history. One example is Phytodolor which is used to reduce rheumatic pain
Hypnotherapy	The person allows the hypnotherapist to bring them into a daydream or trance-like state in which they can relax and drift away, making use of the unconscious mind.
Homeopathy	Problems are treated with low-dose preparations that induce similar symptoms. Homeopathy is based on the principle that 'like can be cured with like'. Homoeopathy usually also requires a change in lifestyle, which could include a change of diet, more relaxation or exercise, to complement the treatment.
Meditation	Generally involves eliciting a relaxation state, centred on breathing which allows the person to focus attention freely from one thought to the next.
Osteopathy	Osteopathy uses manipulation of the bones and other parts of the musculoskeletal system to diagnose and treat. Osteopaths believe that manipulation of the muscles and joints helps the body to combat illness and heal itself.
Reflexology	Reflexology is a treatment where varying degrees of pressure are applied to the reflex areas of the feet, and sometimes hands, to promote health and wellbeing. It is based on the belief that every part of the body is connected by 'pathways' which terminate in the soles of the feet, palms of the hands, ears, tongue and head.
Reiki	Reiki energy is perceived to flow from the practitioner who lightly touches the patient in certain positions with their hands. Hand positions are static, there is no manipulation of the tissues. and this is done to tap into healing energy (termed *ki*).
Relaxation	This includes techniques such as progressive muscle relaxation (to increase body awareness and decrease perception of pain), guided imagery (using the imagination to reframe the pain and increase a sense of control), biofeedback (learning to use relaxation to achieve a measurable end point) and distraction.
Shiatsu	The term 'Shiatsu' means 'finger pressure', and various parts of the practitioner's body (fingers, thumbs, palms, forearms, even feet and knees) are used to apply pressure to the patient's body. This can be targeted at general areas or specific points, and this is done in conjunction with stretches, joint rotations and joint manipulation to give a 'holistic' treatment that works on the internal energy of the patient.

The evidence base for CAM therapies with pain management

The evidence base for CAM therapies continues to be an area for debate. The knowledge claims have been particularly contested, as much of the past research into CAM has been with limited sample sizes and with flawed methodologies. The main criticisms of CAM are outlined here.

Critique of alternative therapies

- Focuses on the individual rather than on overall public health issues, so can be seen as individual responsibility-based and 'blaming'
- Encourages a cultural nostalgia for an imagined past society/wholeness
- Calls for changed consciousness and lifestyle that is difficult to enact
- Evidence base for many of the therapies is inconclusive
- Only accessible by higher-income population
- May stop patients accessing conventional treatments that could assist

There continues to be a questioning of CAM by some conventional health care practitioners. The findings from the following article within the evidence-base activity is discussed on the General Osteopathic Council's website www.osteopathy.org.uk.

Evidence base

Canter *et al.* (2005) found that the evidence does not demonstrate that spinal manipulation is an effective intervention for any condition. Given the possibility of adverse effects, this review did not suggest that spinal manipulation was a treatment to be recommended.

Take a look at this systematic review article and then look at the response that osteopaths made to this.

The General Osteopathic Council's response to this paper was to state that spinal manipulation was only one element of treatment, which also includes guidance on lifestyle, diet and exercise. They also state that chronic pain is rarely a single problem and that this is influenced by psychological and social factors and requires treatment that is tailored to individual needs. Another paper could also be looked at that suggests that there is a statistically significant reduction in lower back pain with osteopathic manipulation (Licciardone *et al.*, 2005).

Despite the difficulties in determining an agreed evidence base for CAM treatments, the WHO has suggested that the scientific evidence does presently support some CAM therapies. Scientific evidence from randomised clinical trials is strong for many uses of acupuncture, some herbal medicines and for some of the manual therapies (WHO, 2003). Further research is needed to ascertain the efficacy and safety of several other practices and medicinal plants (WHO, 2003). Acupuncture has been proven effective in relieving postoperative pain, nausea during pregnancy, nausea and vomiting resulting from chemotherapy, and dental pain, with extremely low side-effects. It can also alleviate anxiety, panic disorders and insomnia (WHO, 2003).

An example of the evidence associated with acupuncture is a randomised controlled trial on the effectiveness of acupuncture pain relief for patients with osteoarthritis of the knee, in comparison to sham acupuncture (Berman *et al.*, 2004). This study found that acupuncture seems to improve function and pain relief when compared to sham acupuncture or patient education control groups. While some scientific evidence, such as this, exists regarding CAM therapies, there continue to be difficulties with researching CAM that may not be assisted by using the same forms of research methodologies.

Keywords

Placebo

A placebo is a sham treatment without biological activity, which in many cases induces biological and/or psychological effects in people. There are thought to be two main reasons why this can occur: a) as a conditioned response, b) due to patient expectations. Endorphins can be released which mediate the placebo effect, mimicking the pain relief anticipated by the treatment

Key difficulties in developing clinical guidelines based on evidence are the **placebo** effect and minimising bias, and this has led to an emphasis on randomised controlled trials.

The effectiveness of a placebo pain reliever varies as a function of its believed effectiveness, e.g. a morphine placebo, will be believed to be more potent than an aspirin placebo. It is argued that, as many CAM approaches attempt to induce self-healing by changing the context and meaning of illness, some could view this as the placebo effect of the treatment, and this interacts with the non-placebo elements of the therapy in complex ways (Moerman, 2000). The placebo effect could even be reconceptualised as a legitimate part of treatment (Lewith *et al.*, 2002).

Randomised controlled trials try to 'bracket out' human factors such as the ability to self-heal, which is viewed as important in CAM. The point of CAM therapies are that they are individualised, and this makes them difficult to be properly judged through randomised controlled trials. It is argued that what is needed is 'real', long-term studies, which requires considerable funding, but there is a lack of incentive to fund research in CAM, as research funding routes for treatments are often from pharmaceutical companies.

It could be argued that researching CAM treatments for pain purely using the accepted 'gold standard' of randomised controlled trials is not the appropriate way to judge the efficacy of a CAM treatment. As these therapies are holistic they may be better researched from a naturalistic approach. The objective of naturalistic research is to understand and describe human experience, as expressed by those who participate in the experience.

GP/Complementary Therapist

My experience as a GP who is also a complementary therapist has led me to believe that complementary therapies can augment conventional medicine in ways that add considerable value. However, there seems to be a huge gap between what we as practitioners and patients say about the effectiveness of treatments, and what researchers tell us.

Keywords

The Quality Adjusted Life Year (QALY)

This has been created to determine the outcomes from treatments and other health-influencing activities by combining the quantity and quality of life. The basic idea of a QALY is that it takes one year of perfect health-life expectancy to be worth 1, but regards one year of less-than-perfect life expectancy as less than 1. QALYs can therefore provide an indication of the benefits gained from a variety of therapies in terms of quality of life as well as survival for the patient. Quality of life is an important component of pain management

The high levels of CAM usage suggest that many people hold the belief that the benefits of these therapies outweigh their costs. However, the majority of CAM remain to be evaluated in terms of cost benefits, apart from certain CAM therapies such as acupuncture and some manipulative therapies (Herman *et al.*, 2005). Within the UK cost effectiveness studies show that spinal manipulation and acupuncture can represent an additional cost to usual care, but that estimates of cost per **Quality Adjusted Life Year** (QALY) compare favourably to conventional treatments (Canter *et al.*, 2005).

Spinal manipulation is viewed as a cost-effective addition to 'best care' for back pain in general practice, judged by participant's average QALY (UK BEAM, 2004). Manipulation alone probably gives better value for money than manipulation followed by exercise (UK BEAM, 2004). This one example of a cost benefit study illustrates the complexity of the evidence-base movement for CAM therapies. Not only is there a call for studies that support efficacy, but there is also a requirement for cost-effectiveness to be determined if these treatments and therapies are to be integrated into NHS and health service practice.

Integrating CAM into conventional health care working

Some CAM practitioners have been seeking acceptance and integration into conventional health service working. There has been a drive for the professionalisation of CAM therapists that has involved promotion of the cause from a political, educational and clinical perspective through the following strategies:

- accreditation of educational qualifications and the profession
- alignment to science and evidence-based practice
- contained knowledge claims, differentiating the CAM therapy from other treatments

- boundary construction to ensure that others do not encroach on this area of practice.

For instance the General Osteopathic Council's website www.osteopathy.org.uk places on its front page the statement that the role of the General Osteopathic Council as a regulatory body was placed in statute in the Osteopaths Act of 1993. The other information mirrors the regulations expected of other conventional health care professions. There is a register of practitioners who are the only ones able to call themselves an osteopath. Courses to qualify as an osteopath are a four- to five-year honours degree with underpinning clinical training, and there is a requirement for continuous professional development (CPD) and protection of the public from poor clinical practice. The internet site also indicates that the uptake of this treatment is on the increase, with over 700 million osteopath consultations in the UK in 2005. As integration of CAM progresses within the NHS, and as CAM practitioners also seek professionalisation, there is a risk that barriers could be increased between CAM and patients. The practitioner–patient relationship is addressed in the next section of this chapter.

The Smallwood Report (2005), commissioned by the Prince of Wales, examined the 'Big five' CAM areas of osteopathy, chiropractic, acupuncture, homeopathy and herbal medicine, which are the areas most frequently referred to by doctors. The Department of Health recommends that only those therapies that are statutorily regulated or have robust self-regulation should be available through public funding. As well as looking at the available evidence regarding efficacy, there was also an examination of the potential cost effectiveness of these treatments. For instance back pain accounts for 200 million days lost from work each year at an estimated cost of £11 billion (Smallwood, 2005). The report looked at ways to integrate CAM into NHS treatment, so that it would be possible to increase accessibility by low-income families.

The Smallwood report (2005) found that the most effective CAM therapies (acupuncture for postoperative pain and nausea, and for lower back pain and migraine; manipulation therapies for acute and chronic lower back pain and arthritis) correspond to areas where there is an existing 'effectiveness gap' in NHS services. The typical effectiveness reported for both CAM and conventional practices is in the order of 70–80% (Lewith *et al.*, 2002). It was suggested that where CAM treatments were available this could reduce costs by reducing the number of medical consultations, prescribed medications and pain clinics (Smallwood, 2005 p.12).

At the moment there are a range of methods for the delivery of CAM within the UK. These include:

- private CAM practitioner
- cam service delivered by a GP or nurse
- on-site multidisciplinary team that incorporates CAM practitioners

- specialist CAM centres which are part of the NHS
- specialist CAM centres contracted by the NHS
- off-site CAM practitioners contracted by the NHS
- hospital-based services using CAM
- palliative care services providing CAM. (Adapted from Smallwood, 2005.)

Many nurses, midwives and other health professionals have integrated CAM into their practice or are aware of patients also accessing this independently. The Nursing and Midwifery Council (NMC) offer the following guidance: 'If a registrant is caring for a patient/client who wishes to continue their homeopathic or alternative therapies, then this decision must be respected. If administering the alternative treatments, the registrant must have undertaken an approved course and be deemed competent to offer this treatment. CAM should be discussed with the multidisciplinary team.' (NMC, 2006).

The NMC Code of Professional conduct: Standards for conduct, performance and ethics (2004) also states that the practitioner should ensure that the use of complementary or alternative therapies is safe and in the interests of patients and clients, and discussed with the interprofessional team as part of the therapeutic process. The patient must always have granted consent for CAM use.

Surveys indicate that nurses are mainly using a narrow range of therapies, e.g. aromatherapy and massage, reflexology, therapeutic touch, relaxation and visualisation, acupuncture, hypnotherapy, shiatsu, homeopathy and herbalism (Rankin Box, 1997).

Example of a text for a visualisation session for a patient with pain

- Sit comfortably and relax as much as possible
- Concentrate on your breathing, allow it to become slow, gentle and rhythmic
- Become aware of your pain and picture it as being in the shape of a circle
- Direct your breathing into this circle, allowing it to become deeper
- As you do this allow the circle to become larger and larger, and as the circle increases in size the pain begins to decrease
- Continue to increase the size of the circle and feel the pain decrease until it has gone away

Lewandowski *et al.* (2005) examined how verbal descriptors of pain changed with the use of guided imagery techniques. Participants in the treatment group who received guided imagery over a four-day consecutive period moved their description of pain away from 'pain is never ending' prominent in both the control group and the pre-treatment group towards a description of pain as 'changeable' (Lewandowski *et al.*, 2005).

One measure of the integration of CAM into NHS practice is in evidence in the development of competencies for practice for a range of complementary therapies.

Over to you

Take a look at the Skills for Health website and the range of therapies with competency frameworks already developed. www.skillsforhealth.org.uk/frameworks.

Find out what complementary therapies are used for pain care in your current practice area.

NHS Trusts should have local guidance for health care professionals who wish to undertake complementary therapies so that the suitability of this can be assessed. This integration of CAM into nursing could be seen as just another caring task for nurses or as nurses re-engaging with the caring component of the role. Whatever the viewpoint, nurses need to practice with an appropriate degree of critical self-appraisal, and to risk assess any pain intervention against the possible benefits.

Evidence base

Take a look at the following two articles:

Chandler A. and Lister S. (2002) Using heat therapy for pain management. *Nursing Standard* 17(9): 40–42.

This article looks at some of the safety issues in using heat therapy within a hospital setting.

Snyder M. and Wieland J. (2003) Complementary and alternative therapies: what is their place in the management of chronic pain? *Nursing Clinics of North America* 38(3): 495–508

This article looks at the therapies nurses might consider when planning care for patients with chronic pain, particularly those which can promote self-care, e.g. massage and imagery. They advocate for nurses to weigh the risks and benefits before suggesting a therapy to promote comfort, and to evaluate its effectiveness.

Complementary therapies are increasingly available in the NHS and are beginning to compete with conventional medicines for scarce resources

(Zollman and Vickers, 1999). Given the known association between low quality studies and positive outcomes, further high-quality research is needed covering the range of CAM approaches. Better treatment outcomes are likely to occur when the psychological contributors as well as the physiological factors involved in pain are addressed. The appeal of CAM depends on its philosophical assumptions as well as its practical effects, and its acceptance and growth in popularity means that practitioners working in the field of pain care need to understand these therapies and to integrate these where deemed appropriate.

Accessing alternative and complementory therapies

Jennie, a 41-year-old pharmacist living in London, started to suffer with lower back pain when she was expecting her third child. She was told that the loosening of the ligaments caused this, which is a common problem during pregnancy. Six months after she gave birth to her third son the situation had not improved, and she was finding it hard to get out of bed, walk or to get down the stairs. Her GP had referred her to a physiotherapist but the lower back pain continued. She was taking strong analgesics, prescribed by her doctor, and decided to attend an Alexander Technique class. Despite this, she continued to complain about her pain, and felt that the drugs she was taking only served to mask her symptoms rather than deal with an underlying problem. Her GP decided to refer her to a local homeopathic hospital. Her first appointment was for 45 minutes, where she was questioned about her lifestyle, diet and stress and given a tailor-made homeopathic treatment. The doctors who treated her were also conventionally trained. She then attended for follow-ups (lasting about 20 minutes) whilst taking two homeopathic pills twice a day 'to tighten the ligaments' until the pain eased. Over the course of the next few months her pain eased and she ceased treatment.

Although back pain is the most common reason patients use CAM, patients' knowledge about these therapies is limited (Sherman *et al.*, 2004).

Jennie paid for her Alexander Technique classes but received her homeopathic treatment through NHS funding. There is an expressed wish by some patients for the more established forms of alternative therapy to be more widely available on the NHS.

- What issues have been highlighted by the case study in relation to this?

The practitioner–patient relationship

Although both conventional medicine and complementary therapies emphasise the quality of the relationship between the practitioner and patient, the variability of the practitioner–patient relationship remains apparent. In fact some CAM practitioners use their therapy as a springboard for an attack on conventional approaches (Vickers, 1998). It is helpful, therefore, to look at the nurse–patient relationship as this will be a component of pain care management.

When Watson (1996) discusses a 'caring science' she includes art and humanities in this, acknowledging the connections between individuals, others, the community and the wider world. She particularly advocates the many ways of knowing combining clinical and empirical enquiry with other forms such as personal, intuitive and spiritual knowing. Watson first started to develop her 'Theory of Human Caring' during the 1970s, and was trying to make explicit the values, knowledge and practice of human caring which nurses bring to the health setting. This is particularly pertinent in the pain care field, as the management of pain is often not a measure of 'cure'.

An adapted version of Watson's (1996) 10 key caring processes are listed here.

1 Delivering practice within a humanistic, altruistic and loving context.
2 Being authentically present, instilling faith and hope.
3 Cultivating sensitivity to self and to others.
4 Developing and sustaining a helping-trusting relationship.
5 Being present and supportive of the expression of positive and negative feelings.
6 Using self creatively, and all ways of knowing, as part of the caring process.
7 Engaging in genuine teaching-learning experiences.
8 Creating a healing environment (physical/psychological/social) including dignity and respect.
9 Assisting with basic needs.
10 Attending to the spiritual dimensions of life and death.

Keywords

Therapeutic relationship

This requires the practitioner to respect and have genuine interest in the person, to show emotional warmth, tolerance and non-judgemental acceptance of the patient. It also calls for the practitioner to use 'self' in nursing interactions, whilst maintaining awareness of their limitations and adherence to ethical codes. The patient also plays a part in a therapeutic relationship by trusting and co-operating with the intervention and being motivated to understand the treatment/ care

Just from reading these 10 factors it becomes clear that Watson looks at nursing as at the intersection between the personal and the professional, seeing communication as central to a **therapeutic relationship**.

In a similar manner to complementary and alternative therapy practitioners, the therapeutic relationship moves away from a 'modern', technical view of nursing towards a focus on the uniqueness of each situation and the wholeness of the person, regardless of illness and/or pain. The nurses' own life experiences are seen as integral to their patient care. As Watson states:

> I emphasize that it is possible to read, study, learn about, even teach and research the caring theory; however, to truly 'get it', one has to personally experience it; thus the model is both an invitation and an opportunity to interact with the ideas, experiment with and grow within the philosophy, and living it out in one's personal/ professional life.
> (Watson, 1996 p. 161)

Reflective activity

Think about your worst experience of pain and how this affected your thoughts about pain and pain care management.

Then go on to think about a patient care episode where you were pleased with the pain care that was achieved. What were the factors about the pain care that made this a pleasant incident to reflect on?

The patient–practitioner relationship and the explanatory frameworks provided by CAM are perceived as important components of the therapeutic process (Cartwright and Torr, 2005). Strong therapeutic relationships impact on patient satisfaction, treatment concordance and compliance and treatment outcomes (Leach, 2005). CAM treatments are viewed as serving a variety of functions beyond the relief of symptoms such as pain; these include increased energy and relaxation, the facilitation of coping, enhancing self- and others' awareness (Cartwright and Torr, 2005).

Key points | Top tips

- Alternative and complementary therapies take a holistic, individualised approach to a patient, and believe that this self-healing is the basis of all healing
- CAM treatments are widely used within the UK, with over £4.5 billion spent on this annually
- CAM therapies can be classified into five main groups: alternative medical systems, mind–body interventions, physiological treatments, manipulation of the body therapies, and energy therapies
- The evidence base for CAM therapies continues to be an area for debate, although the scientific evidence from randomised clinical trials is strong for many uses of acupuncture, some herbal medicines and for some of the manual therapies
- CAM therapists are becoming more regulated and there is increasing professionalisation
- If a health care professional uses CAM within their practice they must have undertaken an approved course and be deemed competent to offer this treatment. CAM should be discussed with the patient and consent must be given, and the multidisciplinary team should be involved
- The patient–practitioner relationship is perceived as an important component of the therapeutic process, and has a part to play in pain care management.

Rapid recap

1 Outline the main differences between complementary medicine and alternative medicine.
2 List four underpinning concepts held by CAM practitioners.
3 What CAM treatments currently have the strongest empirical evidence base for their use in pain care?
4 What is a placebo effect?
5 What would a health care practitioner need to do if they wanted to integrate and deliver complementary therapies within their care setting?
6 Define a therapeutic practitioner–patient relationship.

References

Berman B., Lao L., Langenberg P., Lee W., Gilpin A. and Hochberg M. (2004) Effectiveness of acupuncture as adjunctive therapy in osteoarthritis of the knee. *Annals of Internal Medicine*, **141**: 901–910.

Black A. (2005) *The future of Acute Care*. A personal view commissioned by the NHS Confederation. NHS Confederation, London.

Canter P., Coon J. and Ernst E. (2005) Cost effectiveness of complementary treatments in the United Kingdom: systematic review. *British Medical Journal*, **331**: 880–881.

Cartwright T. and Torr R. (2005) Making sense of illness: the experiences of users of complementary medicine. *Journal of Health Psychology*, **10**(4): 559–572.

Dossey B (2000) *Holistic nursing: A handbook for practice,* 3rd edn. Aspen, New York.

Eisenberg D. (2002) Complementary and integrative medical therapies. *Current trends and future trends.* Harvard Medical School, Boston.

Graham H. (1999) *Complementary therapies in context. The psychology of healing*. Jessica Kingsley Publishers, London.

Herman P., Craig B. and Caspi O. (2005) Is complementary alternative medicine (CAM) cost-effective? A systematic review. *Biomed Central Complementary Alternative Medicine*, **5**: 11.

Leach M. (2005) Rapport: a key to treatment success. *Complementary therapies in Clinical Practice*, **11**(4): 262–265.

Lewandowski W., Good M. and Draucker C. (2005) Changes in the meaning of pain with the use of guided imagery. *Pain Management Nursing*, **6**(2): 58–67.

Lewith G., Jonas W. and Walach H. (eds) (2002) *Clinical Research in Complementary Therapies. Principles, Problems and Solutions*. Churchill Livingstone, Edinburgh.

Licciardone J., Brimhall A. and King L. (2005) Osteopathic manipulative treatment for low back pain: a systematic review and meta-analysis of randomized controlled trials. *Biomedical Central Musculoskeletal disorders*, **6**: 43.

Moerman D. (2000) Cultural variations in the placebo effect: Ulcers, anxiety and blood pressure. *Medical Anthropology Quarterly*, **14**: 15–72.

Nursing and Midwifery Council (2004) *Code of Professional conduct: Standards for conduct, performance and ethics.* NMC, London.

Nursing and Midwifery Council (2006) *A–Z Advice sheet. Complementary, Alternative therapies and Homeopathy.* NMC, London.

Rankin Box D. (1997) Therapies in Practice: a survey assessing nurses' use of complementary therapies. *Complementary Therapies in Nursing and Midwifery*, **3**: 92–99.

Sherman K., Cherkin D., Connelly M., Erro J., Savetsky J., Davis R., *et al.* (2004) Complementary and alternative medical therapies for chronic low back pain: What treatments are patients willing to try? *Biomedical Central Complementary Alternative Medicine*, **4**(1): 9.

Smallwood Report (2005) *The role of complementary and alternative medicine in the NHS.* An investigation into the potential contribution of mainstream complementary therapies to health care in the UK. Freshminds, London.

UK BEAM trial team (2004) United Kingdom back pain exercise and manipulation randomised trial: cost effectiveness of physical treatments for back pain in primary care. *British Medical Journal*, **329**(7479): 1381.

Vallerand A., Fouladbakhsh J., Templin T. (2005) Patients' choices for the self-treatment of pain. *Applied Nursing Research*, **18**(2): 90–96.

Vickers A. (ed)(1998) *Examining Complementary Medicine 'The Skeptical Holist'.* Stanley Thornes, Cheltenham.

Watson J (1996) Watson's theory of transpersonal caring. In *Blueprint for use of nursing models: Education, research, practice and administration*. Walker P. and Neuman B. (eds.) NLN Press, New York, pp. 141–184.

World Health Organization. (2003) *Traditional medicine*. Fact sheet no. 134. WHO, Geneva.

Zollman C. and Vickers A. (1999) ABC of complementary medicine. What is complementary medicine? *British Medical Journal*, **319**: 693–696.

9 Management of acute pain

Learning outcomes

By the end of this chapter you should be able to:

- ★ Describe various forms of acute pain
- ★ Detail methods of managing acute post-operative pain
- ★ Examine the importance of acute pain management.

Introduction

This chapter will help you to consider the broader context of acute pain. Methods of managing acute pain are discussed. Traditionally, acute pain is described as pain that subsides as healing takes place, i.e. it has a predictable end and it is of brief duration, usually less than six months. An example of acute pain could be postoperative pain that occurs following surgery. There are, however, many examples of acute pain – from pain due to trauma, pain due to disease processes such as pancreatitis, to chest pain (see Figure 9.1). Within this chapter surgical urgent care and medical acute-pain management will be discussed.

Good practice in acute-pain management

The Institute for Clinical Systems Improvement (ICSI) (2004) suggests that acute pain is not a diagnosis, it is a symptom. It usually

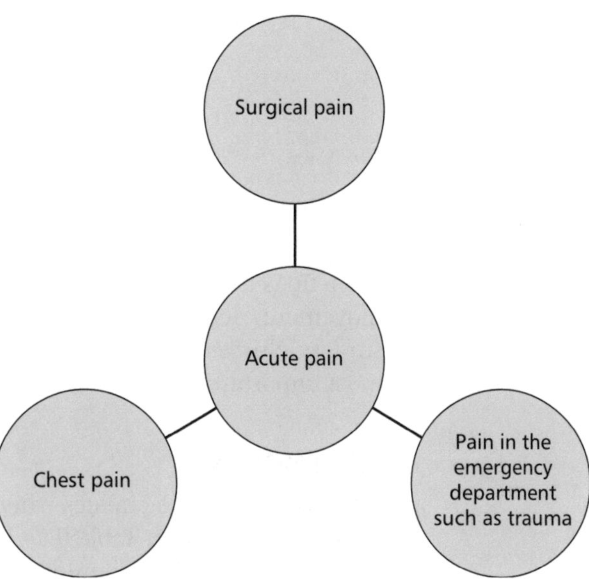

Figure 9.1 Common acute-pain presentations

occurs following surgery or an acute trauma. However, the cause is not always clear. ICSI recommends that a general history, pain history, clinical examination, diagnostic studies and specialty consultation should be conducted as appropriate.

Particular elements of acute pain assessment are outlined within Chapter 6. Figure 9.2 summarises the important issues for acute-pain assessment.

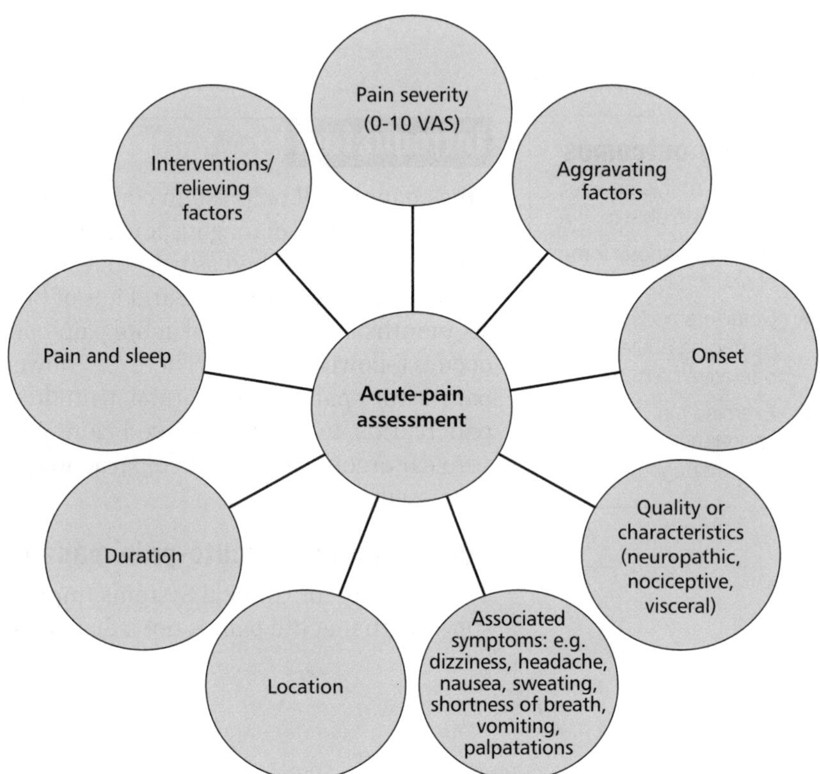

Figure 9.2 Assessment of acute pain

A top tip is to remember that pain assessment is dynamic, e.g. on rest, movement, deep breathing and coughing especially after trauma and surgery. Nurses nowadays decide and document which activity is the most important to assess in regards to pain.

Interventions

There are extensive choices when treating acute pain and examples of these are outlined in Table 9.1. The decisions in relation to acute-pain management choices should be based on sound decision making and the best available evidence.

Table 9.1 Modalities for treatment of acute pain

	Examples
Pharmacological preparations	Opioids NSAIDs Acetaminophen (paracetamol)
Operative procedures	Surgery
Physical modalities	Physiotherapy Manipulation Elevation Heat and cold TENs
Regional anaesthesia	Epidural infusions of local anaesthetics +/– opioids Nerve blocks +/– opioids
Complementary modalities	Acupuncture, relaxation, massage

Surgical pain

Acute pain is an expected outcome of any surgical procedure and the extent of surgery will not necessarily be a reliable indicator of the likely level of pain to be suffered. It is the most common form of acute pain. Postoperative pain studies demonstrate that patients suffer moderate to severe pain after their surgery (Apfelbaum *et al.*, 2003; Mac Lellan, 2004; Coll and Ameen, 2006). Dolan *et al.* (2002) conducted a review of published data considering three types of analgesic techniques and concluded that over the period 1973–1999 there has been a highly significant reduction ($p < .0001$) of the incidence of moderate to severe pain at rest of 1.9 (1.1–2.7%) per year. Table 9.2 summarises the incidence of overall moderate to severe and severe pain based on

Table 9.2 Incidence of overall moderate to severe and severe pain based on method of analgesic administration (Source: Dolan *et al.*, 2002)

Confidence intervals in brackets	Intramusclar (IM)	PCA	Epidural	Overall
Moderate to severe pain	67.2 (58.1–76.2)	35.8 (31.4–40.2)	20.9 (17.8–24)	29.7 (26.4–33)
Severe pain	29.1 (18.8–39.4)	10.4 (8.0–12.8)	7.8 (6.1–9.5)	10.9 (8.4–13.4)

method of analgesic administration using pooled data from 165 papers, 20 000 patients for the time period. Mean and 95% confidence interval are reported.

> **Over to you**
>
> Consider Table 9.2. What does it mean? Is intramuscular (IM) administered analgesia the least effective? Go to your library and get a full copy of the article: Dolan S.J., Cashman J.N. and Bland J.M. (2002). Effectiveness of acute postoperative pain management: I. Evidence from published data. *British Journal of Anaesthesia*. 89(3): 409–423. Three levels of evidence are identified for the papers used in the study. What does this mean?

Various physiological responses are associated with acute pain (Jurf and Nirschl, 1993). The stress response initiated by the autonomic nervous system causes increased respiratory rate, increased cardiac output, elevated blood pressure, increased skeletal muscle tone, vasospasm of peripheral vessels and smooth-muscle relaxation. Pain can cause emotions such as anxiety and fear, which also stimulate the autonomic nervous system. These physiological consequences of acute pain, which are present with post surgical pain, if allowed to reach a certain intensity, can lead to a number of complications.

Undertreated severe pain is associated with a number of harmful effects including decreased lung volumes, myocardial ischaemia, decreased gastric and bowel motility and anxiety (Macintyre and Ready, 2002). High pain scores have been associated with an increased incidence of nausea. The psychological effects of pain include both anxiety and fear.

The objectives of postoperative pain control should be to minimise discomfort, facilitate recovery and avoid treatment related side-effects. Management of surgical pain is complicated and challenging because of large variations in pain experience, analgesic requirements and the many techniques available to treat postoperative pain (Lynch *et al.*, 1997). The choice of the most appropriate method to manage pain will be governed by the nature of the surgery, the intensity and expected duration of the pain, the availability of medication and expertise, and patient factors such as illness, age, contraindications and psychological state. Patients vary greatly in their responses to surgery and procedures as well as their responses to pain and interventions and their personal preferences.

As surgery becomes less invasive and a high proportion of surgical procedures become day surgery cases, the forms of pain care interventions will need to maintain the same levels of effectiveness, whilst being appropriate for patient self-administration.

Pharmacological intervention is the mainstay in the management of acute-pain management, although non-pharmacological approaches provide good adjunctive therapy in many cases (Day, 1997). An integrated approach to pain management is recommended that includes:

- cognitive-behavioural interventions such as relaxation, distraction and imagery: these can be taught preoperatively and can reduce pain, anxiety and the amount of drugs needed for pain control
- systematic administration of nonsteroidal anti-inflammatory drugs (NSAIDs) or round-the-clock administration of opioids
- patient-controlled analgesia (PCA) which usually means self-medication with intravenous doses of an opioid; this can include other classes of drugs administered orally or by other routes
- epidural analgesia, usually an opioid and/or local anaesthetic injected intermittently or infused continuously
- intermittent or continuous local neural blockade (examples of the former include intercostal nerve blockade with local anaesthetic or cryoprobe; the latter includes infusion of local anaesthetic though an interpleural catheter)
- transcutaneous electrical nerve stimulation.

Pharmacological management of postoperative pain

The use of medications remains the mainstay of management of acute pain. It is evident, however, that patients continue to suffer from moderate to severe pain while in hospitals.

Pharmacological management of mild to moderate postoperative pain should begin (unless there is a contraindication) with paracetamol and/or an NSAID. Opiates remain the mainstay of systemic analgesia for the treatment of moderate to severe pain (Australian and New Zealand College of Anaesthetists and Faculty of Pain Medicine, 2005). The concurrent use of paracetamol, opioids and NSAIDs often provides more effective analgesia than either class alone, while reducing side-effects. Refer to chapter 7 for more detail on these medications, their use and side effects.

Studies support the concept that current prescribing patterns are not supporting comprehensive pain management.

Evidence base

Timeline

- **2003** Manias following prospective audit of 100 patients found that while almost all patients received some form of infusion, the use of 'as required' analgesics varied from one-third to over two-thirds of patients during the postoperative period.
- **2001** Schafheutle *et al.* surveyed nurses who stated that analgesic regimens were 'inadequate', 'inappropriate' or 'ineffective'. This included insufficient frequency of dosing or inadequate flexibility in the choice of analgesics.
- **1997** Boer *et al.* found that the prescribed daily dose of morphine was only received by 4.2% of patients.
- **1997** Mac Lellan reported that 97% of patients were prescribed more than one analgesic. Mean number of doses of analgesia administered daily varied from 1.4 to 3.2. Mean amount of analgesia administered varied from 4% to 41% of the maximum possible for the first five days post surgery.
- **1994** Oates reported that those patients with moderate and severe pain received only 36% of their prescribed analgesics.
- **1993** Juhl found that 91% of patients had analgesia prescribed pro re nata (PRN) and that only 4% of patients had analgesics prescribed for regular use. He found that on average patients received 70% of the maximally prescribed dose of analgesic during the first 24 hours and an average of 43% during the following day.
- **1992** Closs examined patterns of analgesic provision and found that the number of doses given peaked at two points during the 24-hour cycle. The highest number of doses were give between 8 a.m. and 12 noon and 8 p.m. and 12 midnight. Fewer doses were given at night between midnight and 4 a.m. In the study, pain was found to be the most common form of night-time sleep disturbance, with analgesics helping more patients to get back to sleep than any other intervention. Almost 50% of patients said that their pain was worse at night. Analgesic provision at night, therefore, did not appear to be explicitly related to need. Of those prescribed intermittent opioids (n = 79) they received 23 ± 2% of their theoretical maximum dose.

Pain in the accident and emergency department and emergency assessment unit

Pain is the single most common reason for presentation to emergency departments (Campbell *et al.* 2004). Cordell *et al.* (2002), reviewing charts over one week (n = 1665), found a prevalence of 52.2% of pain, identifying it as the chief complaint for visits to emergency departments (United States). A Canadian survey of 525 patients showed that abdominal, chest and musculoskeletal pain were the most common diagnoses and that more than two-thirds of patients had non-traumatic pain (Todd *et al.*, 2004). Patients in this survey had high levels of pain; however, only half the patients received any analgesic and these analgesics were administered two hours after presentation to the emergency department. Patients themselves, however, reported high levels of satisfaction and 88% of those untreated for pain did not request analgesics.

When approaching the management of pain in the emergency department it is important to remember that the basic principles of pain management as detailed in Chapter 7 apply. Campbell *et al.* (2004) demonstrate that by implementing a pain protocol in the emergency department a significant improvement in early pain management and patient satisfaction can be achieved. Regular documented pain assessment is of particular importance in the emergency department (see chapter 6) as the patient's pain level may alter very quickly, indicating a deteriorating condition. Cohen *et al.* (2004) suggest that improved pain management in trauma patients leads to not only increased comfort but has been shown to reduce morbidity and improve long-term outcomes. The authors' approach to the management of pain in trauma is outlined in Table 9.3.

Table 9.3 Modalities for treatment of trauma pain (Source: Cohen *et al.*, 2004)

	Examples
Pharmacological preparations	• Acetaminophen (paracetamol) • NSAIDs • Opioids • Ketamine (blocks NMDA receptors – see chapter 4) • Local anaesthetics • Tricyclic antidepressants (neuropathic pain) • Anticonvulsants (neuropathic pain) • Clonadine (analgesic and sedative properties) • Benzodiazepines (lacks analgesic properties but promotes sedation and muscle relaxation) • Entonox • Corticosteroids
Physical modalities	Physiotherapy Manipulation TENs Heat and cold Immobilisation
Regional anaesthesia	Regional blocks Epidural infusions
Complementary modalities	Acupuncture, TENs, hypnosis, psychological interventions

A top tip to bear in mind is: although the acute pain interventions listed in the table are used within urgent-care settings, nursing advice and patient care also impacts on the total pain experience of the patient, e.g. elevation of a limb that has been plastered following a fracture.

In addition to the usual effects and side effects of pain interventions, there are special considerations for many of the traditional approaches to pain management for the emergency department. These are detailed below (Dolan, 2000).

Morphine:
- is usually administered intravenously in the emergency department.
- causes sedation
- should not be given to shocked patients
- if used in coronary thrombosis may further slow pulse and lower blood pressure.

NSAIDs:
- are particularly effective in relieving pain with inflammation and thus are useful for musculoskeletal disorders and trauma to peripheral tissues.

Non-pharmacological management:
- information to reduce anxiety
- immobilisation and elevation
- warm and cold compresses
- distraction.

Entonox is a gaseous mixture of 50% oxygen and 50% nitrous oxide (Butcher, 2004). Common examples of its use are with soft tissue injury such as wounds, abscesses, burns, traumas to the abdomen, chest and limb fractures. Entonox is contraindicated in pneumothorax and certain head injuries where there is an altered state of consciousness.

The use of local anaesthesia can be particularly effective for pain in the emergency department (Edwards, 2000). Local infiltration into an area surrounding a wound site is ideal for the suturing and extensive cleaning of minor wounds and the drainage of superficial abscesses. Peripheral nerve blocks such as ring block will achieve anaesthesia of a digit. Intravenous regional anaesthesia (Bier's block) can be used for anaesthesia below the elbow, for example, for manipulation of a Colles fracture. NSAIDS are particularly effective in musculoskeletal conditions, and specifically in limb trauma involving major joints (knee etc.).

Chest pain

Chest pain is one the common acute-pain problems that patients present with to the health services. Research indicates that chest pain can account for 2–4% of all new attendances at emergency departments per year in the UK (Herren and Mackway-Jones, 2001). There are many different causes of chest pain, some of which are life threatening, requiring medical interventions (Tough, 2004) (see Table 9.4).

Table 9.4 Causes of chest pain

Cardiovascular	Myocardial infarction Unstable angina
Pulmonary	Pleurisy Pulmonary embolism Pneumothorax Pneumonia
Musculoskeletal	Costocondritis Trauma
Gastrointestinal	Reflux Gastric ulcers Gallstones Pancreatitis
Non-organic	Anxiety

Management of chest pain is complex and begins with a detailed assessment of the pain. The cause of the pain should be established without delay.

McAvoy (2000) and Efre (2004) refer to acronyms such as OLD CART to assist in this assessment. OLD CART is described in Table 9.5.

Table 9.5 OLD CART chest pain assessment

Onset	When did the pain start? Are you having the pain now?
Location	Where is the pain located?
Duration	How long have you been having this pain? Does it come and go or is it consistent?
Characteristics	What does it feel like? Pressure, tightness, heaviness? Describe how it feels.
Accompanying symptoms	What other signs and symptoms accompany the pain? Nausea? Sweating? Dizziness or light-headedness?
Radiation	Does the pain travel to any other part of your body– your left or right arm, neck, jaw, back?
Treatment	What makes the pain better or worse? If you've had this kind of pain before, what relieved it?

In addition to determining previous medical history, risk factors, medication history and social history the points described in Figure 9.3 should assist in establishing the cause of pain (Tough, 2004).

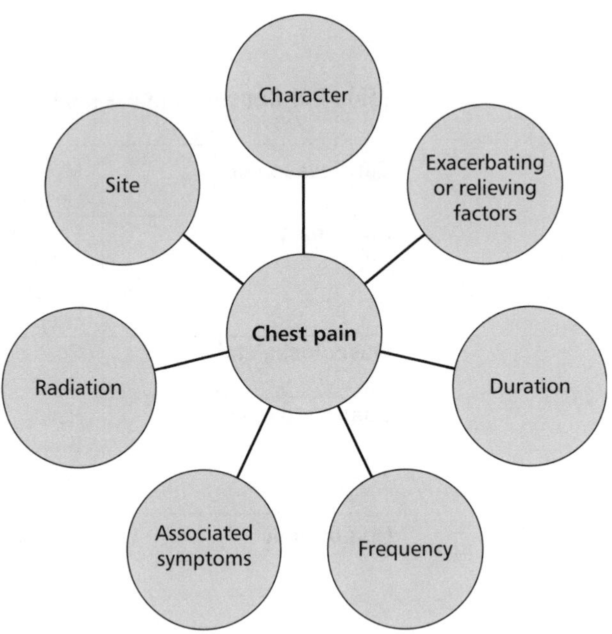

Figure 9.3 Chest pain assessment

Detail of further diagnostic tests and treatment for chest pain to relieve symptoms, limit myocardial damage and risk of cardiac event are beyond the scope of this book. Indeed, much immediate treatment is now protocol and guideline driven with the use of various chest pain assessment services such as chest pain assessment units, rapid access chest pain clinics as well as emergency departments and coronary care units (Aroney *et al.*, 2003; Fox, 2001). One of the medications of choice to relieve cardiovascular chest pain based on appropriate assessment is morphine administered intravenously. However, it should be noted that for **acute coronary syndrome** effective and early pain relief remains a clinical priority and no one agent offers the ideal solution to controlling the pain.

Keywords

Acute coronary syndrome
Describes a spectrum of illness from ischaemic heart disease to unstable angina to myocardial infarction

Nitrates have an important role and Opie and Gersh (2001) recommend that at onset of the angina the patient should rest in the sitting position and take nitroglycerin sublingually (0.3–0.6 mg) every five minutes until the pain is relieved. Castle (2003) suggests that the early use of opiates, betablockers and nitrates, as well as reassuring patients, have vital roles to play in providing effective analgesia for acute coronary syndrome.

However, the pain may not be cardiac in origin, for example the pain may be musculoskeletal in origin and if so an NSAID may the most appropriate medication.

Triage Nurse

I started working as a triage nurse in the accident and emergency department about two years ago. One of the most difficult pains to manage is chest pain because it can be anything from a heart attack to a strained muscle. In order to be confident in my triage decision, I always do a comprehensive pain assessment.

Good practice in acute-pain management should be part of a continuous cycle as outlined in Figure 9.4.

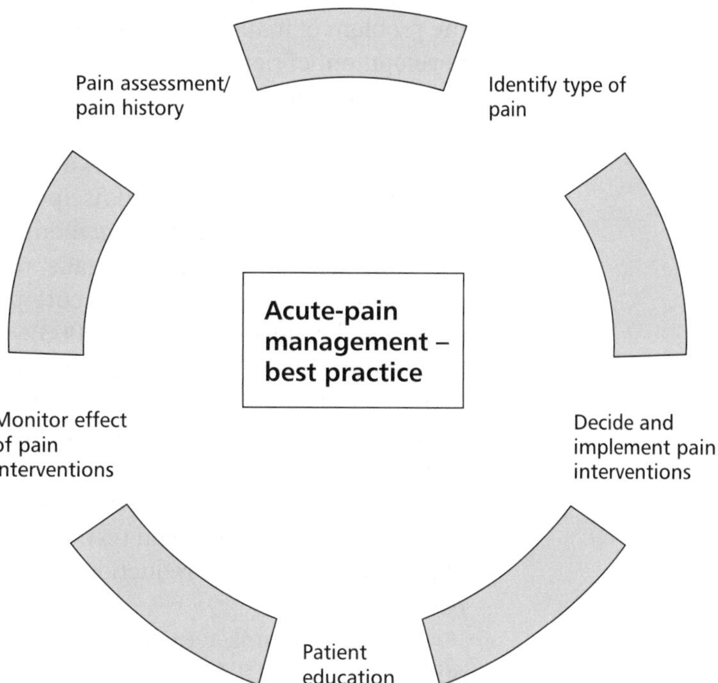

Figure 9.4 Good practice in acute-pain management

Reflective activity

Consider the last patient you managed with acute pain. How did you assess his/her pain? How were decisions regarding pain interventions for that acute pain made? Was the effect of the pain interventions monitored? For example, if the person was on an opioid did it relieve the pain? Could the patient mobilise? Did the patient have any side-effects, e.g. constipation?

Acute-pain services

Formalising services for acute pain has become a trend within the health service ever since Ready *et al.* in 1988 drew attention to the potential role of an acute-pain service by developing an anaesthesiology-based postoperative pain management service. They said: 'just as chronic pain management has become a special area of medical practice, treatment of acute pain deserves a similar commitment by practitioners with special expertise'.

The evidence as detailed in Chapter 3 suggests that the solution to the problem of inadequate postoperative pain relief lies not so much in development of new techniques but in the development of a formal organisation for better use of existing techniques (Rawal and Berggren, 1994).

Following systematic review of acute pain teams, McDonnell *et al.* (2003) describe them as multidisciplinary teams who assume day-to-day responsibility for the management of postoperative pain. Team members generally include specialist nurses, anaesthetists and pharmacists. The prevalence of acute-pain teams in the UK is high, as evidenced by McDonnell *et al.* (2003). Their survey highlights the fact that 84% of acute English hospitals performing inpatient surgery for adult patients have an acute pain team (McDonnell *et al.*, 2003). Surveys report that 42% of US hospitals (Warfield, 1995) have acute-pain management programmes and 53% of Canadian hospitals (Zimmermann and Stewart 1993). Many benefits are ascribed to acute-pain services and acute-pain teams, such as a more consistent standard of postoperative care, a reduction in pain scores and increased safety for patients.

Acute pain teams/acute pain services encompass the qualities outlined in Figure 9.5.

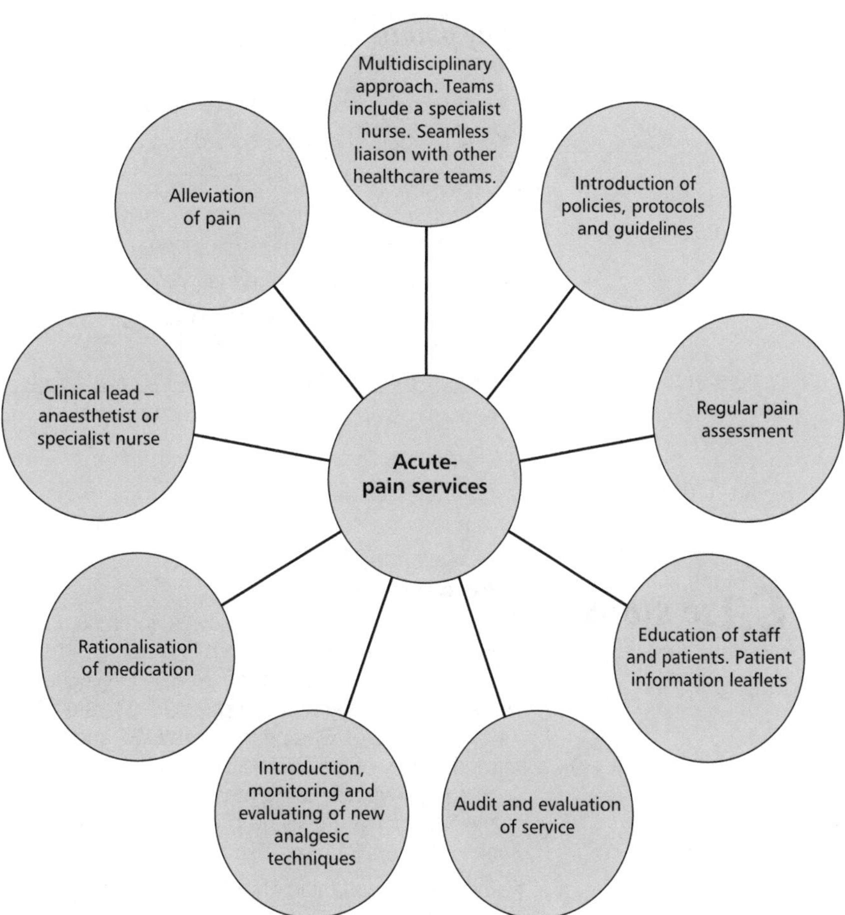

Figure 9.5 Acute-pain services

Impact of technology on acute-pain management

Technology has revolutionised modes of analgesic administration allowing for smaller, more regular amounts of analgesia to be administered in a safe and efficient manner. Patients have been enabled to take more control over pain relief. It is suggested that refinements in systemic opioid administration and epidural analgesia have by far the greatest impact on the quality of acute-pain care (Carr *et al.*, 2005). Patient-controlled analgesia (PCA) using traditional intravenous opioids, the newer concept of fentanyl hyrdrochloride patient-controlled transdermal system (PCTS) and epidural analgesia are reviewed in Chapter 3.

Key points Top tips

- The prevalence of acute pain is high
- Acute pain should be considered a symptom not a diagnosis
- Evidence-based approaches should be used to manage acute pain
- There are extensive choices for managing acute-pain, from pharmaceutical preparations to complementary modalities
- Medications remain the mainstay of management of acute severe pain
- Assessment and monitoring of the effect of the pain intervention is the key to good acute-pain management

Chest pain

Mark is a 45-year-old man who owns and runs a corner shop. He is married with three children all under the age of six. He is sitting at home watching TV one Saturday night and suddenly experiences a sharp pain in his chest and neck. His wife Sarah drives him to the local emergency department. On arrival, the nurse assesses his pain as 7 out of 10 on a VAS. She performs an ECG and takes bloods. She begins to take a detailed history of his pain as outlined in Table 9.6.

In addition to assessing Mark's pain the nurse begins a history, asking Mark about his medical history, family history of illness, any medications that he is on and any other risk factors for heart disease.

- Why is it important in Mark's case history to assess more than his pain?
- How do you think Mark's pain should be managed?
- How would you explain Mark's pain to him and his wife Sarah?

Table 9.6 Mark's OLD CART chest pain assessment

Onset	Pain is present on attending the emergency department. Mark's pain began suddenly two hours ago.
Location	The pain is in his chest and radiating up his neck.
Duration	The pain is constant and has been present for about two hours.
Characteristics	Mark describes the pain as 'pressure'
Accompanying symptoms	He is sweating slightly and feels somewhat nauseous. He thinks this may be due to feeling very anxious.
Radiation	The pain is radiating up his neck.
Treatment	Mark has never had this kind of pain before and is not on medication for his heart.

Rapid recap

1. Define acute pain.
2. Name and give examples of three modalities for reducing acute pain.
3. What special considerations are there with the use of morphine in the accident and emergency department?
4. When assessing chest pain what does the acronym OLDCART stand for?
5. What are the main qualities of an acute pain service?

References

Acute Pain Management Guideline Panel. (1992) *Acute Pain Management: Operative or Medical Procedures and Trauma. Clinical Practice Guideline*. Rockville, MD: AHCPR Pub. No. 92–0032. Agency for Health Care Policy and Research, Public Health Service, US Department of Health and Human Services.

Apfelbaum J.L., Chen C., Mehta S.S. and Gan T.J. (2003) Postoperative pain experience: results from a national study suggest postoperative pain continues to be undermanaged. *Anesthesia and Analgesia*, **97**: 534–540.

Aroney C.N., Dunlevie H.L. and Bett J.H.N. (2003) Use of an accelerated chest pain assessment protocol in patients at intermediate risk of adverse cardiac events. *Medical Journal of Australia*, **178**(8): 370–374.

Australian and New Zealand College of Anaesthetists and Faculty of Pain Medicine (2005) Acute pain management: scientific evidence. Available at www.anzca.edu.au/publications/acutepain.htm.

Boer C., Treebus A.N., Zuurmond W.W.A. and de Lange J.J. (1997) Compliance in administration of prescribed analgesics. *Anaesthesia*, **52**: 1177–1181.

Butcher D. (2004) Pharmacological techniques for managing acute pain in emergency departments. *Emergency Nurse*, **12**(1): 26–35.

Campbell P., Dennie M., Dougherty K., Iwaskiw O. and Rollo K. (2004) Implementation of an ED protocol for pain management at triage at a busy level 1 trauma centre. *Journal of Emergency Nursing*, **30**(5): 431–437.

Carr D.B., Reines D., Schaffer J., Polomano R.C. and Lande S. (2005) The impact of technology on the analgesic gap and quality of acute pain management. *Regional Anesthesia and Pain Medicine*, **30**(3): 286–291.

Castle N. (2003) Effective relief of acute coronary syndrome. *Emergency Nurse*, **10**(9): 15–19.

Closs S.J. (1992) Patients' night-time pain, analgesic provision and sleep after surgery. *International Journal of Nursing Studies*, **29**(4): 381–392.

Cohen S.P., Crhisto P.J. and Moroz L. (2004) Pain management in trauma patients. *American Journal Physical Medicine Rehabilitation*, **83**: 142–161.

Coll A.M. and Ameen J. (2006) Profiles of pain after day surgery: patients' experiences of three different operation types. *Journal of Advanced Nursing*, **53**(2): 178–187.

Cordell W.H., Keene K.K., Giles B.K., Jones J.B., Jones J.H. and Brizendine E.J. (2002) The high prevalence of pain in emergency care medical care. *American Journal of Emergency Medicine*, **20**(3): 165–169.

Day R. (1997) A pharmacological approach to acute pain. *Professional Nurse Supplement*, **13**(1): S9–S12.

Dolan B. (2000) Physiology for A&E Practice in *Accident and Emergency Theory into Practice.* Balliere Tindell, London.

Dolan S.J., Cashman J.N. and Bland J.M. (2002) Effectiveness of acute postoperative pain management: I. Evidence from published data. *British Journal of Anaesthesia*, **89**(3): 409–423.

Edwards B. (2000) Physiology for A&E Practice in *Accident and Emergency Theory into Practice.* Balliere Tindell, London.

Efre A.J. (2004) Gender bias in acute myocardial infarction. *Nurse Practitioner*, **29**(11): 42–55.

Fox K.F. (2001) Chest pain assessment services: the next steps. *Quarterly Journal of Medicine*, **94**: 717–718.

Herren K.R., and Mackway-Jones K. (2001) Emergency management of cardiac chest pain: a Review. *Emergency Medical Journal*, **18**: 6–10.

Institute for Clinical Systems Improvement (ICSI) (2004) Assessment and management of acute pain. ICSI, London.

Juhl I.U. (1993) Postoperative pain relief, from the patients' and the nurses' point of view. *Acta Anaesthesiology Scandinavia*, **37**: 404–409.

Jurf J.B. and Nirschl A.L. (1993). Acute postoperative pain management: A comprehensive review and update. *Critical Care Nursing Quarterly*, **16**(1): 8–25.

Lynch E.P., Lazor M.A., Gellis J.E., Orav J., Goldman L. and Marcantonio E.R. (1997) Patient experience of pain after elective noncardiac surgery. *Anaesthesia and Analgesia*, **85**: 117–23.

Manias E. (2003) Medication trends and documentation of pain following surgery. *Nursing and Health Sciences*, **5**: 85–94.

McAvoy J.A. (2000) Cardiac pain: discover. *Nursing*, **30**(3)34–40.

McDonnell A., Nicholl J. and Reid S.M. (2003) Acute pain teams in England: current provision and their role in postoperative pain management. *Journal of Clinical Nursing*, **12**: 387–393.

Macintyre P.E. and Ready L.B. (2002) *Acute Pain Management, A Practical Guide*, 2nd edn. W.B. Saunders, Elsevier Science, Philadelphia.

Mac Lellan K. (1997) A Chart Audit reviewing the prescription and administration trends of analgesia and the documentation of pain, after surgery. *Journal of Advanced Nursing*, **26**: 345–350.

Mac Lellan K. (2004) Postoperative pain: strategy for improving patient experiences *Journal of Advanced Nursing*, **46**(2): 179–185.

Oates J.D.L., Snowden S.L. and Jayson D.W.H. (1994) Failure of pain relief after surgery. *Anaesthesia*, **49**: 755–758.

Opie L.H. and Gersh B.J. (2001) *Drugs for the heart*, 5th edn. W.B. Saunders, Elsevier Science, Philadelphia.

Pain Management Guideline Panel (1992) Clinicians Quick Reference Guide to Postoperative Pain Management in Adults. *Journal of Pain and Symptom and Management,* **7**(4): 214–228.

Rawal N. and Berggren L. (1994) Organisation of acute pain services: a low cost model. *Pain*, **57**: 117–123.

Ready B.L., Oden R., Chadwick H.S., Benedetti C., Rooke G.A., Caplan R. *et al.*(1988) Development of an anaestiology-based postoperative pain management service. *Anaesthesiology*, **68**(1): 100–106.

Schafheutle E.I., Cantrill J.A. and Noyce P.R. (2001) Why is pain management suboptimal on surgical wards? *Journal of Advanced Nursing*, **33**(6): 728–737.

Todd K.H., Sloan E.P., Chen C., Eder S. and Wanstad K. (2004) Survey of pain etiology, management practices and patient satisfaction in two urban emergency departments. *Journal of the Canadian Association of Emergency Physicians,* **4**(4): 252–256.

Tough J. (2004) Assessment and treatment of chest pain. *Nursing Standard*, **18**(37): 45–53.

Warfield C.A. and Kahn C.H. (1995) Acute pain management programs in U.S. hospitals and experiences and attitudes among U.S. adults. *Anaesthesiology*, **83**: 1090–1094.

Zimmermann D.L. and Stewart J. (1993) Postoperative pain management and acute pain service activity in Canada. *Canadian Journal of Anaesthesia*, **40**(6): 568–575.

10 Management of chronic pain

Learning outcomes

By the end of this chapter you should be able to:

- ★ Describe various types of chronic pain
- ★ Detail methods of managing chronic pain
- ★ Detail special considerations for the role of opioids and chronic non-malignant pain
- ★ Examine the importance of chronic-pain care management.

Introduction

This chapter will help you to consider chronic-pain care management. The range of interventions for chronic-pain management will be detailed. Chronic pain tends to be considered as pain without apparent biological value that has persisted beyond the normal tissue healing time (usually taken to be three months). It is linked to maladaptive repsonses that have adverse psychological consequences, and often the cause of the pain cannot be identified. Figure 10.1 identifies some common conditions associated with chronic pain. Many other conditions are, however, associated with chronic pain such as cardiovascular disease, gastrointestinal conditions (e.g. ulcers, liver disease), endocrinological conditions (e.g. diabetes), cerebrovascular conditions (e.g. stroke, multiple sclerosis) (Sprangers *et al.*, 2000). Chapter 11 explores cancer pain management and palliative care.

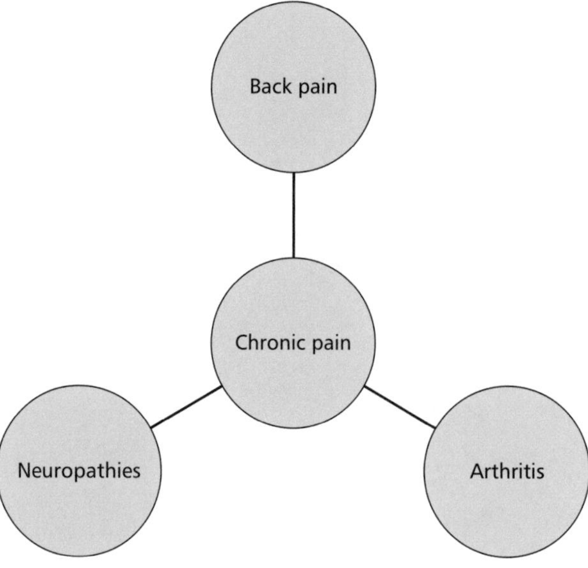

Figure 10.1 Common chronic-pain conditions

Prevalence and effect of chronic pain

Macfarlane (2005) reviewed the epidemiology of chronic pain over the past 50 years. He concluded that the burden of musculoskeletal pain and the prevalence of pain may have increased during the past half century. Early studies on the aetiology of chronic pain concentrated on mechanical injury factors while more recent studies have emphasised the even greater influences of individual psychological factors and the social environment, according to Macfarlane.

Evidence base

Prevalence of chronic pain

Numerous studies chronicle the prevalence of chronic pain. The following timeline identifies key large population studies from the 1990s to the present date.

Timeline

- **2005** Dobson reports from his research that approximately a fifth of adults in Europe have moderate to severe chronic pain and in many cases their symptoms are inadequately managed.
- **2005** Rustoen reports age differences in pain prevalence rates for age groups (younger, middle-aged and older) with prevalence rates of 19.2%, 27.5% and 31.2% respectively (n = 1912, Norwegian study).
- **2005** Veillette *et al.* identifies that between 18% and 29% of Canadians experience chronic pain.
- **2002** Papageorgious *et al.* conducted a seven-year study to document the natural course of chronic widespread pain in a general population (n = 1386). Prevalence at year one was 11% and 10% at year seven. The authors conclude that the proportion of subjects changing from chronic widespread pain to no pain was very low over a seven-year period and suggested that, once established, pain is likely to persist or recur.
- **2000** Palmer *et al.*, report on two prevalence surveys of back pain at an interval of 10 years. Over a 10-year interval the one-year prevalence of back pain, standarised for the age and sex distribution, rose from 36.4% to 49.1%.
- **1999** Elliot *et al.*, in a UK survey of 29 general practices (5036 patients, 72% response rate), report that 50.4% of patients in the community self-report chronic pain. Back pain and arthritis were the most common complaints.
- **1998** American Geriatrics Society (AGS) Panel find that 25–50% of those living in the community suffer significant pain problems
- **1995** Ferrell reports 62% of nursing-home residents have pain.

Chapter 2 identified some of the challenges of reviewing studies that measure prevalence of chronic pain due to variations in population sampled, methods used to collect data and criteria used to define chronic pain. Standard definitions for chronic pain are not available.

Chronic pain has a significant effect on the lives of those experiencing that pain. It also impacts on their friends and their families. Chronic pain affects patients' mood, social relationships and quality of life. Breivik (2004), quoted in a WHO media release, suggests that chronic pain is a disease in its own right.

Chronic pain in the workforce affects individuals who experience a variety of conditions resulting in increased financial burden to their employers and increased use of health care resources. Given the economic impact of chronic pain, it has been suggested that employers and managed care organisations should evaluate the potential benefits in productivity resulting from workplace initiatives such as ergonomic modifications, rest breaks or pain management programmes (Pizzi *et al.*, 2005).

Davidson and Jhangri (2005) report on the impact of chronic pain in haemodialysis patients concluding that chronic pain in these patients is associated with depression and insomnia and may predispose patients to consider withdrawal of dialysis. There is increasing evidence that psychological disorders such as depression (Tsai, 2005) often coexist with or are exacerbated by chronic pain.

A population-based survey of 1953 patients assessed whether chronic pain predicts future psychological distress (McBeth *et al.*, 2002). This was shown to be the case; however, the authors concluded that it is the interaction between chronic widespread pain and physical and psychological co-morbidities that predicts future distress. Unsurprisingly, with ongoing pain, increased pain intensity is associated with decreased quality of life (Laursen *et al.*, 2005).

Good practice in chronic-pain management

Traditionally, pain is treated as a symptom which is appropriate in patients with an acute injury or disease. However, patients are often left with persistent pain once acute injury or disease has subsided. With chronic pain a general history, pain history, clinical examination, diagnostic studies and specialty consult should be conducted as appropriate. Turk and McCarberg (2005) support the concept of an interdisciplinary treatment approach for chronic pain that focuses on self-management and functional restoration. Clinicians have extensive choices when treating chronic pain as outlined in Table 10.1 (Turk, 2002).

Table 10.1 Options for treating chronic pain

	Examples
Pharmacological preparations	Opioids Nonsteroidal anti-inflammatories (NSAIDs) Anticonvulsants Tricyclic antidepressants NMDA antagonists Topical preparations
Operative procedures	For example, surgery for osteoarthritic knee
Physical modalities	Ultrasound Transcutaneous electrical nerve stimulation (TENs) Diathermy Physiotherapy
Regional anaesthesia	For example, epidural infusions of local anaesthetics +/– opioids Nerve blocks +/– opioids Denervation
Neuroaugmentation modalities	Spinal column stimulators (SCSs) Implantable drug delivery systems (IDDSs)
Comprehensive pain rehabilitation programme	Interdisciplinary pain centres Functional restoration programmes
Complementary modalities	Acupuncture, cognitive behavioural therapy, guided imagery, relaxation

Reflective activity

Consider the last patient you managed with chronic pain. How did you assess his/her pain? How were decisions regarding pain interventions for that chronic pain made? Was the effect of the pain interventions monitored? For example, if the person was attending a pain clinic did he/she keep a pain diary? Was the extent of functional status monitored over time to see if, for example, the patient could mobilise better with a particular medication regime? Were any adverse effects experienced?

Management of chronic pain will involve the following:

- pain assessment
- a pain management plan
- progress evaluated at regular intervals
- monitoring of quality of life.

Pain assessment and ongoing monitoring of interventions for pain are critical. Pain assessment processes for chronic pain are described in Chapter 6. Figure 10.2 summarises the important issues for chronic-pain assessment.

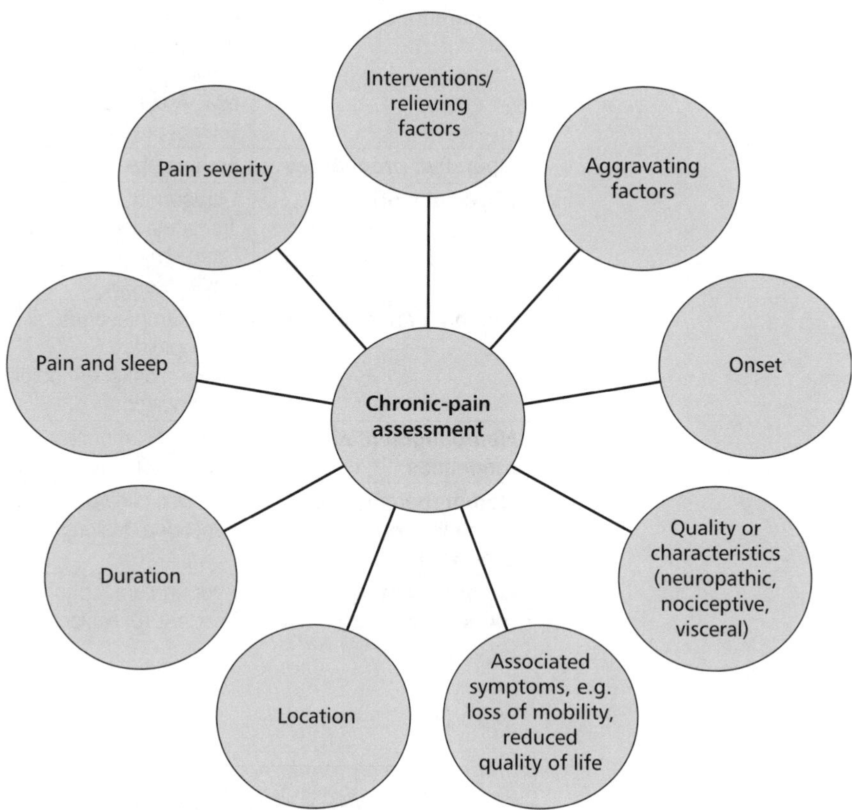

Figure 10.2 Chronic-pain assessment

Long-term use of pharmacological preparations for chronic pain

The long-term use of pharmacological preparations for pain management expose patients to more medication side-effects. Chapter 7 describes each of the medication classes in detail. Patients on long-term medications should be monitored regularly particularly for hepatic and renal effects. In addition, nonsteroidal anti-inflammatories (NSAIDs) have a high risk of gastric toxicity and caution should be utilised for long-term use. The long-term use of opioids in particular is the subject of much debate with special considerations for use in chronic non-malignant pain. These are described below.

Opioids in chronic pain

The goal of management of chronic non-cancer pain is to keep the patient functional, both physically and mentally, with improved quality of life. Relief of pain may be an essential factor in this and opioids are only one aspect of the overall rehabilitative strategy for the patient. The actions and side-effects of opioids are described in Chapter 7. There are, however, special considerations when a person is on long-term opioids with chronic non-malignant pain. Opioids are not effective in every patient with pain and randomised clinical trials (RCTs) indicate that no criteria have been identified that predict a good response to opioids in any particular condition (Kalso, 2005). Devulder *et al.* (2005) evaluated 11 studies of long-term treatment with opioids in patients with chronic non-malignant pain and subsequent quality of life (n = 2877). They suggest that long-term treatment with opioids can lead to significant improvement in functional outcomes including quality of life. However, the authors caution that there remains a need for future long-term rigorous research.

Kalso *et al.* (2003) provide recommendations for using opioids in chronic non-cancer pain. Their conclusions are:

- the management of pain should be directed by the underlying cause of pain
- opioid treatment should be considered for both continuous neuropathic and nociceptive pain if other reasonable therapies fail to provide adequate analgesia within a reasonable timeframe
- the aim of opioid treatment is to relieve pain and improve the patient's quality of life. Both of these should be assessed during a trial period
- the prescribing physician should be familiar with the patient's psychosocial status
- the use of sustained-release opioids administered at regular intervals is recommended
- treatment should be monitored
- a contract setting out the patient's rights and responsibilities may help emphasise the importance of patient involvement
- opioid treatment should not be considered a lifelong treatment.

Misconceptions regarding the use of opioids have made clinicians reluctant to prescribe these agents. Fear of side-effects such as addiction, misuse, tolerance and respiratory depression have contributed as barriers to the effective treatment of chronic pain. In 2001, the American Academy of Pain Medicine, the American Pain Society and the American Society of Addiction Medicine agreed a consensus document on the use of opioids and the treatment of pain and provided definitions of addiction, physical dependence and tolerance. The consensus document states that most specialists agree that patients treated with prolonged opioid therapy usually develop physical dependence and sometimes develop tolerance, but do not usually develop addictive disorders. The actual risk is, however, unknown and probably varies with genetic predisposition among other factors.

The American Academy of Pain Medicine and the American Pain Society in 1997 provided a consensus statement on the use of opioids for the treatment of chronic pain. They reiterate that pain is one of the most common reasons that people consult a physician but that, frequently, it is inadequately treated. They devised the following principles of good practice to guide the prescribing of opioids:

- **Evaluation of the patient**: pain history, assessment of impact of pain on the patient, a directed physical examination, a review of previous diagnostic studies, a review of previous interventions, a drug history and an assessment of coexisting conditions.
- **Treatment plan**: tailored to both the individual and the presenting problem. Consideration should be given to different treatment modalities. If a trial of opioids is selected, the physician should ensure that the patient is informed of the risks and benefits of opioid use and conditions under which they will be prescribed.
- **Consultation**: a consultation with a specialist or with a psychologist may be warranted.
- **Periodic review of treatment efficacy**: this should occur periodically to assess the functional status of the patient, continued analgesia, opioid side-effects, quality of life and indication of medication misuse. Periodic re-examination is warranted to assess the nature of the pain complaint and to ensure that opioid therapy is still indicated. Attention should be given to the possibility of a decrease in global function or quality of life as a result of opioid use.
- **Documentation**: this is essential for supporting the evaluation, the reason for opioid prescribing, the overall pain management treatment plan, any consultation received and periodic review of the status of the patient.

The British Pain Society (2005) together with the Royal College of Anaesthetists, the Royal College of General Practitioners and the Royal College of Psychiatrists prepared a consensus statement *Recommendations for the appropriate use of opioids for persistent non-cancer pain*.

Over to you

Go to the British Pain Society website (www.britishpainsociety.org) and download the recommendations for the appropriate use of opioids for persistent non-cancer pain. Are any of the recommendations in practice in your clinical area? How would you go about creating a local guideline to support best practice in the use of opioids for chronic pain?

Back pain

Back pain is one of the most common types of chronic pain reported. In 1999, Elliot *et al.*, in a UK survey of 29 general practices (5036 patients, 72% response rate) report that 50.4% of patients self-report chronic pain. Back pain and arthritis were the most common complaints. Palmer *et al.* (2000) report on two prevalence surveys of back pain at an interval of 10 years. Measurements included low back pain and low back pain which made it impossible to put on hosiery. Over a 10-year interval, the one-year prevalence of back pain, standarised for the age and sex distribution, rose by 12.7%.

Guzman *et al.* (2001) conducted a systematic review of 10 trials using multidisciplinary rehabilitation for chronic low back pain.
The authors suggest that there was strong evidence that intensive multidisciplinary biopsychosocial rehabilitation with functional restoration improves function when compared with inpatient or outpatient non-multidisciplinary treatments and moderate evidence that such rehabilitation reduces pain. Ospina and Harstall (2003) support this through analysis of the literature concluding that the evidence for the effectiveness of multidisciplinary pain programmes is strong for chronic low back pain.

The Swedish Council on Technology Assessment in Health Care (2000) following a review of the scientific literature (2000 studies) summarised that:

- back pain is common and not usually harmful – patients should stay active; however, it is important to identify rare cases where back pain has a specific cause
- consequences of back pain may be more problematic than the pain itself
- preventative measures are known but not practiced
- societal costs of back pain are three times higher than the total cost of all types of cancer
- more research is needed.

In addition the Swedish Council identify the following evidence in relation to medications for conservative treatments for *reducing* low back pain (see Table 10.2).

Table 10.2 Evidence base for conservative treatments for reducing low back pain (Source: Swedish Council, 2000)

Pain type	Treatment	Level of evidence
Acute and subacute low back pain *(up to 3 or 12 weeks)*	Muscle relaxants (e.g. benzodiazepines) and NSAIDs	Strong
Acute low back pain	Paracetamol	Moderate
Chronic low back pain	Muscle relaxants, NSAIDs	Limited
Acute low back pain	Anti-depressants	None

Beliefs and attitudes

The influence of attitudes and beliefs are increasingly accepted as an important role in the improvement of functioning with back pain. An Australian study evaluated the effectiveness of a population-based, state-wide public health intervention designed to alter beliefs about back pain, influence medical management and reduce disability and costs of compensation (Buchbinder *et al.*, 2001). The authors concluded that such a strategy improves population and general practitioner beliefs about back pain and seems to influence medical management and reduce disability and workers' compensation costs related to back pain.

Brief pain-management techniques

Hay *et al.* (2005), following a randomised clinical trial, suggest that brief pain management techniques delivered by appropriately trained clinicians offer an alternative to physiotherapy incorporating manual therapy and could provide a more efficient first-line approach for management of non-specific subacute low back pain in primary care. The brief techniques involve assessment of psychosocial risk factors with an emphasis on return to normal activity through functional goal setting, with educational strategies to overcome psychosocial barriers to recovery.

Transcutaneous electrical nerve stimulation (TENS)

Transcutaneous electrical nerve stimulation (TENS) was introduced more than 30 years ago as an adjunct to the pharmacological management of pain. However, despite its widespread use, the usefulness of TENS for chronic low back pain is still controversial. In a Cochrane systematic review, Khadilkar *et al.* conclude that there is limited and inconsistent evidence to support the use of TENS as an isolated intervention in the management of chronic lower back pain. Only two RCTs met the criteria for inclusion (Khadilkar *et al.*, 2005).

Injection therapy

Injections with anaesthetics and/or steroids is one of the treatment modalities used in patients with chronic low back pain. Nelemans *et al.* (1999) looked at the evidence in a Cochrane systematic review with 21 RCTs. The authors conclude that convincing evidence on the effects of injection therapies for low back pain is lacking and that there is a need for more well-designed explanatory trials in this field.

Behavioural treatment for chronic low back pain

Behavioural treatment is primarily focused on reducing disability through modification of environmental contingencies and cognitive processes. Ostelo *et al.* (2005), in a Cochrane systematic review of 21 studies, could not conclude from the review whether clinicians should refer patients with chronic low back pain to behavioural treatment programmes or to active conservative treatment.

> **Over to you**
>
> If your patient had chronic back pain and you were giving them an information session to support an improved quality of life, what sort of issues would you discuss with them?

Neuropathic pain

The IASP (1994) define neuropathic pain as pain initiated or caused by primary lesion or dysfunction of the nervous system. An example of neuropathic pain is post-herpetic neuralgia which is a serious complication of herpes zoster (shingles). Herpes zoster is an acute infection that occurs when the latent varicella zoster virus (VZV) is reactivated. Risk factors include immunodeficiency and age.

Abnormal sensory symptoms and signs are associated with neuropathic pain and are outlined in Table 10.3.

Anticonvulsants are a group of medicines commonly used for treating epilepsy but which are also effective for treating pain. Nurmikko *et al.* (1998) state that anticonvulsant drugs have an established role in the treatment of chronic neuropathic pain, especially when patients complain of shooting sensations.

Wiffen *et al.* (2005), following a Cochrane systematic review, conclude that although anticonvulsants are used widely in chronic-pain, surprisingly few trials show analgesic effectiveness (migraine and headache were excluded) (23 trials were included). The authors state that in chronic-pain syndromes other than trigeminal neuralgia, anticonvulsants should be withheld until other interventions have been tried. While gabapentin is increasingly being used for neuropathic pain,

Table 10.3 Abnormal sensory symptoms (Source: IASP, 2004)

Allodynia	Pain due to a stimulus which does not normally provoke pain.
Dysthesias	An unpleasant abnormal sensation, whether spontaneous or evoked.
Hyperalgesia	An increased response to a stimulus which is normally painful.
Heperpathia	A painful syndrome characterised by an abnormally painful reaction to a stimulus, especially a repetitive stimulus, as well as an increased threshold.
Paresthsias	An abnormal sensation, whether spontaneous or evoked.

the evidence would suggest that it is not superior to carbamazepine. In their synopsis, the authors state that neuropathic pain responds well to anticonvulsants and approximately two-thirds of patients who take either carbimazole or gabapentin can be expected to achieve good pain relief.

Arthritis

The term 'arthritis' is a generic term that refers to more than 100 conditions with osteoarthritis and rheumatoid arthritis (RA) being the most common (American Pain Society, 2002). These conditions can cause pain, stiffness and swelling of the joints. These diseases may also affect supporting structures such as muscles, bones, tendons and ligaments and have a systemic effect. Most forms of arthritis cause chronic pain which can range from mild to severe and can last days, months or years. Arthritis sufferers will also suffer acute pain which by its nature is temporary and diminishes over time. Rheumatoid arthritis affects approximately 1% of the US population with peak incidence between the ages of 40 and 60 (Romano, 2006). In patients with rheumatoid arthritis, pain is the most common reason for seeking medical care (Anderson, 2001).

Arthritis pain has many causes and may be due to inflammation of the synovial membrane, tendons, ligaments and muscle strain. A pain management plan for arthritis will need to be developed following a general history, pain history, clinical examination, diagnostic studies and specialty consultation as appropriate. An example of a specific pain scale developed for rheumatoid arthritis (RA) is RAPS (Rheumatoid Arthritis Pain Scale) (Anderson, 2001). This scale has four subscales:

- physiological – clinical manifestations of RA
- affective – moment by moment unpleasantness, distress and annoyance that closely co-vary with the intensity of the painful sensation
- sensory-discriminative – intensity, duration, location and quality of pain sensation
- cognitive – secondary stage of pain-related affect based on cognitive process.

The scale contains statements such as 'I have morning stiffness of one hour or more' and 'Pain interferes with my sleep' and the patient scores from 0 (always) to 6 (never) how he/she rates each question on the scale.

Management of arthritis pain will involve the patient and their health care team developing long-term plans to manage both episodes of acute pain and chronic pain over time, possibly a lifetime. Pain episodes due to inflammation are often unpredictable.

Like any chronic pain, arthritis will affect the patient's quality of life and patients and their families will need support to cope with a lifelong disease. In addition to management of direct pain, a holistic approach relevant to the patient's lifestyle will need to be developed. This will involve supporting the patient to maintain a healthy diet, develop good sleep patterns, exercise as appropriate, be informed of disease pattern and treatments, and ongoing monitoring of quality of life.

The American Pain Society (2002) in a set of clinical guidelines for treating arthritis pain recommend that:

- All treatment for arthritis should begin with a comprehensive assessment of pain and function.
- For mild to moderate pain, acetaminophen is the choice because of its mild adverse effects, over-the-counter availability and low cost.
- For moderate to severe pain from both osteoarthritis and RA, COX-2 NSAIDs are the medications of choice.
- Opioids are recommended for treating severe pain for which COX-2 drugs or non-specific NSAIDs do not provide substantial relief.
- Unless there are medical contraindications most individuals with arthritis including the obese and elderly should be referred for surgical treatment when drug therapy is ineffective and function is severely impaired to prevent minimal physical activity. It is advised that surgery be recommended before the onset of severe deformity and advanced muscular deterioration.
- An ideal weight is maintained.
- Referrals are made for physical and occupational therapy to evaluate and reduce impairments in range of motion, strength, flexibility and endurance.

Table 10.4 identifies some of the options for pain relief for arthritis suffers which will be part of an overall patient management plan. Methods of pain relief chosen will depend on the type of arthritis and the disease progression. Methods chosen should be based on sound pain assessment and adhere to good pain management practice for chronic pain. Further detail of diagnostic tests and treatment options are beyond the scope of this book.

Best practice in chronic-pain management should be part of a continuous cycle as outlined in Figure 10.3.

Table 10.4 Options for pain relief in arthritis

Short-term relief	*Medications*	Paracetamol (Zhang *et al.* 2004 on review of 10 trials suggest that paracetamol reduces osteoarthritis pain more than placebo but does not affect functioning or stiffness) NSAIDs
	Heat and cold	
	Joint protection	Splints and braces to allow joints to rest and protect them from injury
	TENs	
	Physiotherapy	
	Occupational therapy	
Long-term relief	*Medications*	– Biological response modifiers (new drugs for treatment of RA to reduce inflammation) – NSAIDs – Disease modifying anti-rheumatic drugs (DMARDs). – Corticosteroids – Opioids – Intra-articular injections
	Weight reduction	If necessary to reduce stress on weight-bearing joints
	Exercise	As appropriate
	Surgery	An example is knee replacement
	Complementary therapies	For example relaxation, meditation.
	Physical therapy	
	Occupational therapy	

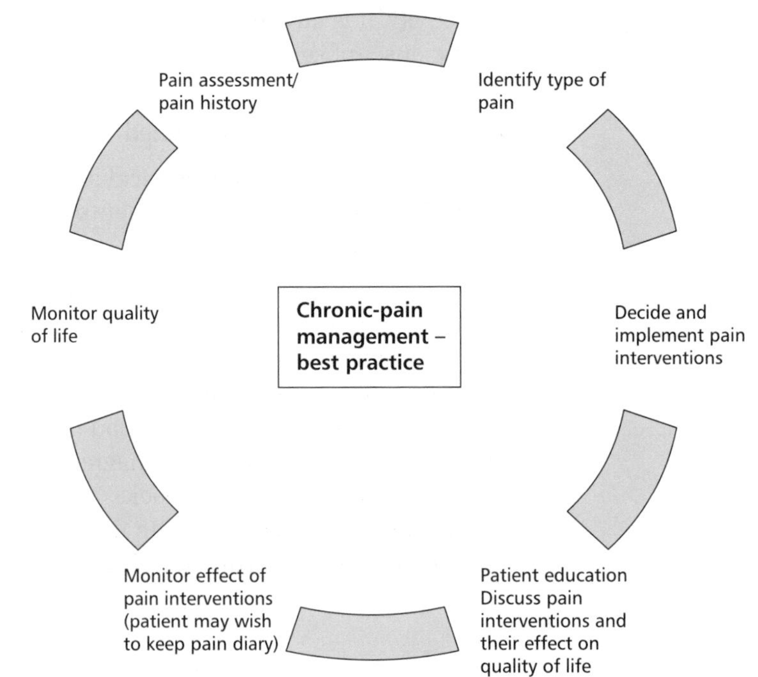

Figure 10.3 Best practice in chronic-pain management

Chronic-pain services

Many patients with chronic pain continue to have symptoms and may develop psychological distress, overall disability and increased dependency on family members and social services even though there are many advances in pain relieving techniques. Pain management programmes have been developed to enhance the patient's physical performance and help them cope more effectively with their pain (Nurmikko *et al.*, 1998).

The literature describes various methods to help patients cope with chronic pain. Van Korff (1998) describes an RCT in a primary care setting in the USA where an educational back pain self-management group intervention led by trained lay people reduced back pain worries and activity limitations and increased self-care confidence at six months. This was achieved in the absence of reducing pain intensity. An internet-delivered cognitive-behavioural intervention with telephone support shows some improved coping skills such as feeling of control over pain and ability to decrease pain in patients with chronic low back pain (Buhrman *et al.*, 2005).

Flor *et al.* (1992) performed a meta-analysis evaluating the efficacy of multidisciplinary treatments for chronic pain and suggested that patients treated in multidisciplinary pain clinics showed improvements in pain and functioning compared to conventional treatments. The analysis showed that patients treated in a multidisciplinary pain clinic are almost twice as likely to return to work than the untreated or unimodally treated patients.

Good practice in chronic-pain management suggests the provision of core services for chronic pain in all district general hospitals and most specialist hospitals (The Royal College of Anaesthetists and The Pain Society, 2003).

Veillette *et al.* (2005) report on a Canadian survey of the availability of hospital-based anaesthesia departments with chronic non-cancer pain services. The survey indicates that 73% of anaesthesia departments offer chronic non-cancer pain services with 26% providing some form of multidisciplinary assessment and treatment. However, 4500 patients were waiting for their first appointment to see a pain consultant, with 67% of these waiting for nine months or more.

Chapter 3 provides more detail on chronic-pain services but it should be borne in mind that there is limited published empirical work on the prevalence or effectiveness of chronic-pain services. It emerges, however, that chronic-pain services should include the elements detailed in Figure 10.4.

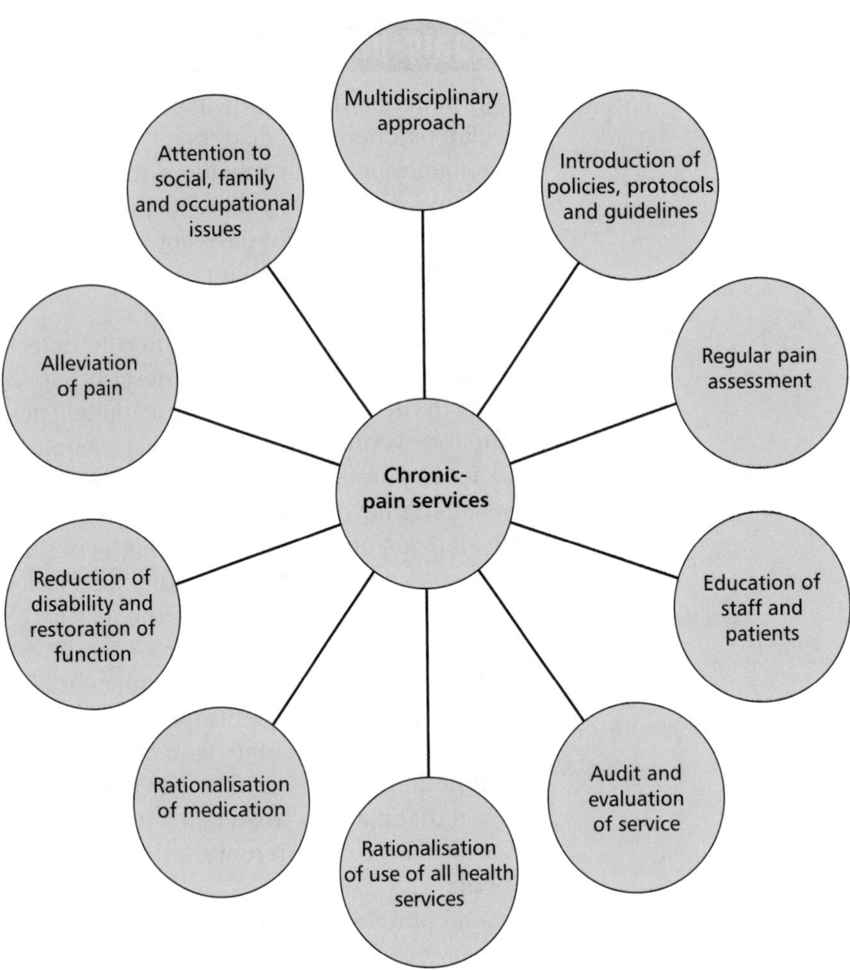

Figure 10.4 Chronic-pain services

Key points Top tips

- The prevalence of chronic pain is high
- Evidence-based approaches should be used to manage chronic pain
- There are extensive choices for managing chronic pain from pharmaceutical preparations to complementary modalities.
- Specific guidance applies to the use of opioids in chronic non-malignant pain
- Assessment and monitoring of the effect of the pain intervention is the key to good chronic-pain management

Chronic back pain

Catriona is a 30-year-old bank clerk. She has had chronic back pain for eight years following an accident at work where a roof collapsed on top of her. She was trapped under the roof and continues to get nightmares about being trapped under the roof. She attends her general practitioner every two months. At this stage she says she is very fed up as she feels that she no longer has the quality of life that her friends have. For example, when her friends start talking about going on holidays and ask her to come along she feels she is preventing them from going on any adventure or active holidays. Catriona has been on every medication from NSAIDs to morphine. She has tried physiotherapy, TENs and swimming. Her doctor thinks that she might benefit from attending a pain clinic in the local hospital.

- How has Catriona's pain affected her quality of life?
- What benefits would Catriona gain from attending the local pain clinic?
- What sort of pain assessment would help monitor Catriona's pain?

Rapid recap

1. Define chronic pain.
2. What are the main qualities of a chronic-pain service?
3. Name and give examples of three modalities for reducing chronic pain.
4. Identify four principles of good practice to guide the prescribing of opioids for chronic non-cancer pain.
5. How strong is the evidence for the use of TENS with low back pain?

References

American Academy of Pain Medicine, the American Pain Society and the American Society of Addiction Medicine (2001) *Definitions related to the use of opioids and the treatment of pain.* A consensus document from the American Academy of Pain Medicine, the American Pain Society, and the American Society of Addiction Medicine, www.painmed.org/.

American Academy of Pain Medicine and the American Pain society (1997) *The Use of Opioids for the Treatment of Chronic Pain.* A consensus statement from the American Academy of Pain Medicine and the American Pain society. Available at www.painmed.org/productpub/statements/

American Geriatrics Society (AGS) Panel on Chronic Pain in Older Persons (1998) The management of chronic pain in older persons: AGS Panel on Chronic Pain in Older Persons. *Journal of the American Geriatrics Society*, **46**: 635–651.

American Pain Society (2002) APS guideline for the management of pain in osteoarthritis, rheumatoid arthritis and juvenile chronic arthritis. American Pain Society, www.ampainsoc.org.

Anderson D.L. (2001) Development of an instrument to measure pain in rheumatoid arthritis: rheumatoid arthritis pain scale (RAPS). *Arthritis Care & Research,* **45**: 317–323.

Breivik (2004) World Health Organization supports global effort to relieve chronic pain. Geneva: WHO/70/2004.

British Pain Society (2005) Recommendations for the appropriate use of opioids for persistent non-cancer pain. A consensus statement prepared on behalf of the Pain Society, the Royal College of Anaesthetists, the Royal College of General Practitioners and the Royal College of Psychiatrists. www.britishpainsociety.org.

Buchbinder R., Jolley D. and Wyatt M. (2001) Population based intervention to change back pain beliefs and disability: three-part evaluation. *BMJ*, **322**: 1516–1520.

Buhrman M., Faltenhag S., Strom L., Andersson G. and Polly D.W. (2005) An internet-delivered cognitive-behavioural intervention with telephone support improved some coping skills in patients with chronic low back pain. *Journal of Bone and Joint Surgery*, **87**(5): 1169.

Davidson S.N. and Jhangri G.S. (2005) The impact of chronic pain on depression, sleep, and the desire to withdraw from dialysis in haemodialysis patients. *Journal of Pain and Symptom Management*, **30**(5): 465–473.

Devulder J., Richarz U. and Nataraja S.H. (2005) Impact of long-term use of opioids on quality of life in patients with chronic, non-malignant pain. *Current Medical Research and Opinions*, **21**(10): 1555–1568.

Dobson R. (2005) Chronic pain is poorly managed. *BMJ*, **331**: 476.

Elliot A.M., Smith B.H., Penny K.I., Cairns Smith W. and Chambers W.A.(1999) Epidemiology of chronic pain in the community. *Lancet*, **354**: 1248–1252.

Ferrell B.A. (1995) Pain evaluation and management in a nursing home. *Ann Intern Med*, **123**: 681–687.

Flor H., Fydrich T. and Turk D.C. (1992) Efficacy of multidisciplinary pain treatment centres: a meta-analytic review. *Pain*, **49**: 221–230.

Guzman J., Esmail R., Karjalainen K., Malmivaara A., Irvin E. and Bombardier C. (2001) Multidisciplinary rehabilitation for chronic low back pain: systematic review. *BMJ*, **322**: 1511–1516.

Hay E.M., Mullis R., Vohara K., Watson P., Sim J., Minns Lowe C. *et al.* (2005) Comparison of physical treatments versus a brief pain-management programme for back pain in primary care: a randomised clinical trial in physiotherapy practice. *The Lancet*, **365**(9476): 2024–2030.

IASP Task Force on Taxonomy (1994) Classification of chronic pain, 2nd edn (eds. Merskey H. and Bogduk N.). IASP Press, Seattle.

Kalso E. (2005) Opioids for persistent non-cancer pain. *BMJ*, **330**: 156–157.

Kalso E., Allen I., Dellemijn P.L.I., Faura C.C., Ilias W.K., Jenson T.S. *et al.* (2003) Recommendations for using opioids in chronic non-cancer pain. *Europena Journal of Pain*, **7**: 381–386.

Khadilkar A., Milne S., Brosseau L., Robinson V., Saginur M., Shea B. *et al.* (2005) Transcutaneous electrical nerve stimulation (TENS) for chronic low-back pain. *The Cochrane Database of Systematic Reviews.* Issue 3. Art No.: CD003008. DOI: 10.1002/14651858.pub2.

Laursen B.S., Bajaj P., Olesen A.S., Delmar C. and Arendt-Nielsen L. (2005) Health related quality of life and quantitative pain measurement in females with chronic non-malignant pain. *European Journal of Pain*, **9**: 267–275.

McBeth J., Macfarlane G.J. and Silman A.J. (2002) Does chronic pain predict future psychological distress? *Pain*, **96**: 239–245.

Macfarlane G.J. (2005) Looking back: developments in our understanding of the occurrence, aetiology and prognosis of chronic pain 1954–2004. *Rheumatology*, Suppl. **4**: iv23–iv26.

Nelemans P.J., de Bie R.A., de Vet H.C.W. and Sturmans F. (1999) Injection therapy for subacute and benign low-back pain. *The Cochrane Database of Systematic Reviews.* Issue 4. Art. No.: CD001824. DOI: 10.1002/14651858.CD001824.

Nurmikko T.J., Nash T.P. and Wiles J.R. (1998) Recent advances: control of chronic pain. *BMJ*, **317**: 1438–1441.

Ospina M. and Harstall C. (2003) Multidisciplinary pain programmes for chronic pain: Evidence from systematic reviews. Alberta Heritage Foundation for Medical Research – Health Technology Assessment. HTA 30 (Series A): 1–48.

Ostelo R.W.J.G., van Tulder M.W., Vlaeyen J.W.S., Linton S.J., Assendelft W.J.J. (2005) Behavioural treatment for chronic low-back pain. *The Cochrane Database of Systematic Reviews*, Issue 1. Art. No.: CD002014. DOI: 10.1002/14651858. CD002014.pub2.

Palmer K.T., Walsh K., Bendall H., Cooper C. and Coggon D. (2000) Back pain in Britain: Comparison of two prevalence surveys at an interval of 10 years. *BMJ*, **320**: 1577–1578.

Papangeorgious A.C., Silman A.J. and Macfarlane G.J. (2002) Chronic widespread pain in the population: a seven-year follow up study. *Annals of Rheumatology*, **61**: 1071–1074.

Pizzi L.T., Carter C.T., Howell J.B., Vallow S.M., Crawford A.G. and Frank E.D. (2005) Work loss, health care utilization and costs among US employees with chronic pain. *Disease Management and Health Outcomes*, **13**(3): 201–208.

Romano T. (2006) Rheumatologic Pain. In *Weiner's Pain Management A Practical Guide for Clinicians,* 7th edn.(eds. Boswell M.V. and Cole B.E.) American Academy of Pain Management. CRC Press, Taylor and Francis Group.

Royal College of Anaesthetists and The Pain Society, The British Chapter of the International Association for the Study of Pain (2003*) Pain Management Services – Good Practice*. Royal College of Anaesthetists and The Pain Society, London.

Rustoen T., Wahl A.K., Hanestad B.R., Lerdal A., Paul S. and Miaskowski C. (2005) Age and the experience of chronic pain. Differences in health and quality of life among younger, middle-aged and older adults. *Clinical Journal of Pain*, **21**: 513–523.

Sprangers M.A.G., de Regt E.B., Andries F., van Agt H.M.E., Bilјl R.V., de Boer J.B. *et al.* (2000) Which chronic conditions are associated with better or poorer quality of life? *Journal of Clinical Epidemiology*, **53**: 895–907.

Swedish Council on Technology Assessment in Health Care (2000) *Back pain, neck pain: an evidence based review*. Swedish Council on Technology Assessment in Health Care. www.sbu.se.

Tsai P.F. (2005) Predictors of Distress and Depression in Elders with Arthritic Pain. *Journal of Advanced Nursing*, **51**(2): 158–165.

Turk D.C. (2002) Clinical effectiveness and cost-effectiveness of treatments for patients with chronic pain. *The Clinical Journal of Pain*, **18**: 355–365.

Turk D.C. and McCarberg B. (2005) Non-pharmacological treatments for chronic pain. A disease management context. *Disease Management and Health Outcomes*, **13**(1): 19–30.

Van Korff M., Moore J.E., Lorig K. *et al*. (1998) Back pain self management groups led by lay people increased self care confidence and reduced activity limitations at 6 months. *Spine*, **23**: 2608–2615.

Veillette Y., Dion D., Altier N. and Choiniere M. (2005) The treatment of chronic pain in Quebec: a study of hospital-based services offered within anesthesia departments. *Canadian Journal of Anesthesia*, **52**(6): 600–606.

Wiffen P., Collins S., McQuay H., Carroll D., Jadad A. and Moore A. (2005) Anticonvulsant drugs for acute and chronic pain. *The Cochrane Database of Systematic Reviews.* Issue 3. Art. No.:CD001133. DOI:10.1002/14651858.CD001133. pub2.

Zhang W., Jones A. and Doherty M. (2004) Review: paracetamol reduces pain in osteoarthritis but is less effective than NSAIDs. *Evidence Based Nursing*, **63**: 901–907.

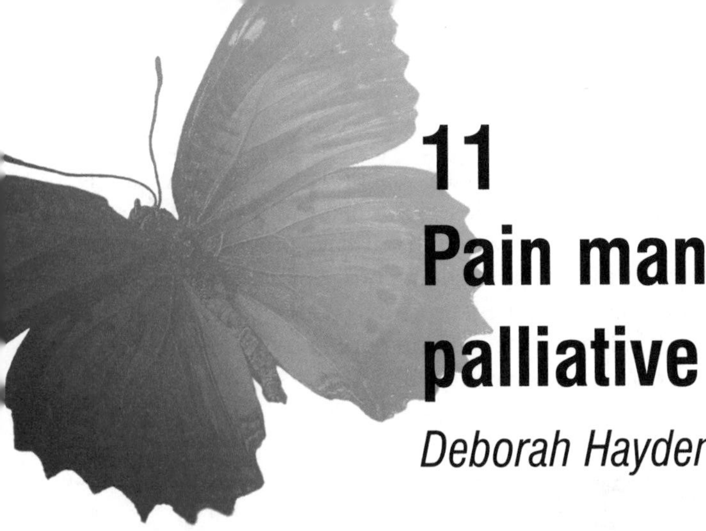

11 Pain management in palliative care

Deborah Hayden

Learning outcomes

By the end of this chapter you should be able to:

- ★ Appreciate the history of hospice and palliative care
- ★ Recognise the need for palliative care
- ★ Articulate the concept of palliative care with particular reference to total pain
- ★ Apply the principles of palliative care in order to manage pain in your own work area utilising a holistic and individual approach in order to contribute towards alleviating suffering
- ★ Perform pain assessment whilst mindful of the psychological, social and spiritual factors that will often impact the person's experience of pain
- ★ Refer to standard analgesic guidelines to direct safe and effective pharmacological interventions.

Introduction

> 'The right to die with dignity with as little pain and as comfortably as possible is as important as the right to life.'
>
> (Archbishop Desmond Tutu, 2005)

This chapter strives to enhance health care professionals' understanding of the meaning, assessment and management of pain in order to provide true holistic care to adults requiring palliative care. Understandably, people frequently fear the involvement of hospice or palliative care teams in their care. This is often due to their lack of knowledge of what palliative care entails. It is therefore imperative that all health care professionals understand the concept and philosophy of hospice and palliative care in order to alleviate unfounded fears and myths, and contribute positively to people's understanding of the benefits of modern palliative care involvement.

History of hospice care and palliative care

The meaning of the word hospice has changed over the centuries. Historically, hospices were institutions whose primary purpose was to provide nursing and spiritual care to the destitute and frail, with particular focus on the dying aspect of care. The shift to 'modern' palliative care is largely due to the work of Dame Cicely Saunders, who was the woman responsible for establishing the discipline and the culture of palliative care. During her lifetime she worked as a nurse, medical social worker, volunteer and eventually as a physician. Witnessing the unnecessary suffering of others, she strived to improve the care of dying patients.

In response to her distress, Saunders founded the first modern hospice, St. Christopher's Hospice in London, in 1967. By creating St. Christopher's Hospice as a 'place' to care for the dying, she modelled a health care system where personhood and dignity were preserved, pain was managed and family-centred care was provided. Hospice care is therefore a term that is often used to describe a place of care and a philosophy of care offered to people when the disease process is at an advanced stage. The term may be applied in a range of care settings. Saunder's clinical work has transformed society's perspective on the treatment of suffering, and led to the development and expansion of hospice and palliative care services worldwide.

Palliative care defined

In the 1960s Balfour Mount, a Canadian physician, coined the term palliative care. The word 'palliative' is derived from the Latin word '*pallium*', meaning a 'cloak'. Twycross (2003) identifies that within palliative care, symptoms such as pain are 'cloaked' with treatments whose primary aim is to promote comfort. The WHO (2002, p. 84) defines palliative care as follows: 'Palliative care is an approach that improves the quality of life of patients and their families facing the problems associated with life threatening illness, through the prevention and relief of suffering by means of early identification and impeccable assessment and treatment of pain and other problems, physical, psychosocial and spiritual.'

The WHO (2002) further elaborates on the definition by stating that palliative care affirms life and regards dying as a normal process. It intends neither to hasten nor postpone death, whilst aiming to provide relief from pain and other distressing symptoms. This is achieved by attending not only to the physical aspects of the person, such as managing pain, but also to the psychological, social and spiritual dimensions of the individual and their family. Therefore, palliative care extends far beyond merely providing symptom relief. Rather than waiting to relieve the suffering, the WHO (2002) advocates the *prevention* of suffering by means of early identification and impeccable assessment. Central to the philosophy of palliative care is the family. It offers a support system to help the family to cope during the person's illness and in their own bereavement.

Palliative care proudly encompasses end-of-life care. However, it is now widely acknowledged that a palliative care approach focuses on the active *living* rather than merely on the anticipated dying. The involvement of palliative care aims to improve the quality of life of people with life-threatening illnesses such as cancer, and may also positively influence the course of the illness. Consequently, palliative care 'is also applicable early in the course of a person's illness, in conjunction with other therapies that are intended to prolong life, such as chemotherapy or radiation therapy, and includes those investigations needed to better understand and manage distressing clinical complications' (WHO, 2002, p. 84).

Palliative care professionals 'share' the care of patients who are receiving therapies to modify the disease, as outlined in Figure 11.1. For this reason, this chapter focuses on alleviating pain not just at the end of life, but throughout the person's illness trajectory.

Finally, the philosophy of palliative care advocates the use of a team approach to address the needs of patients and their families. Interdisciplinary care is provided by a many and varied team each providing a function in reaction to the person's needs.

It is evident from the WHO's (2002) definition that palliative care is not confined to any specific disease or illness. However, approximately 95% of patients referred to specialist palliative care services have cancer. Payne *et al.* (2004) partly proportion this inequity of service to the historical developments in hospice care and key funding from cancer charities. The global report 'Suffering at the End of Life – The State of the World' (Help the Hospices, 2005) claims that there are currently six million cancer deaths and over 10 million new cases of cancer every year, and this is expected to rise to 15 million by 2020. It also reports that 100 million people worldwide need access to hospice and palliative care at the current time. For millions more, access to palliative care *will* become their core essential need.

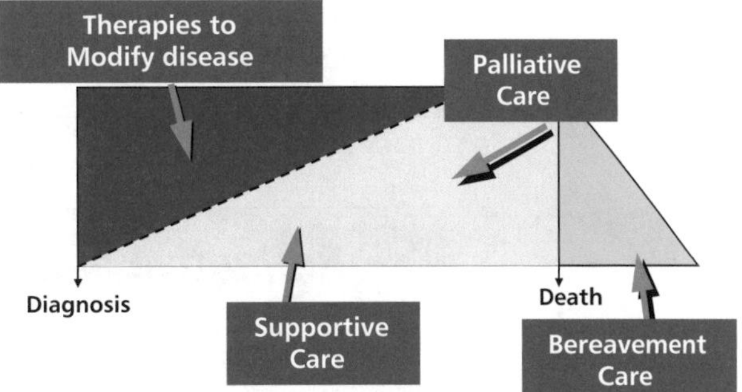

Figure 11.1 'Sharing' the care during the person's illness trajectory

Interdisciplinary approach to pain management in palliative care

The WHO (2002) states that palliative care uses a team approach to address the needs of patients and their families. Thereby, the philosophy of palliative care advocates an interdisciplinary approach to the practice of pain management. The terms 'interdisciplinary teamwork' and 'multidisciplinary teamwork' are used interchangeably. Both terms refer to individual members within a team, each with specific roles and skills. However, interdisciplinary work involves collaboratively intertwined work within a connected team, each member aware of the other's role, and all members sharing and striving towards providing the best care for the individual and their family. Effective continuous communication between the team members is therefore essential.

The National Cancer Institute (NCI) (2005) maintains that assessment involves both the clinician and the patient. However, true interdisciplinary teamwork necessitates the *whole* team conducting pain assessment. All assessment activities should be documented and notes should be accessible to the entire interdisciplinary members. This will enable everyone to understand and appreciate the person's experience (Fink and Gates, 2001) and consequently plan a comprehensive management strategy (Paz and Seymour, 2004).

Key points Top tips

Care within the palliative philosophy involves the following:

- Treating the person, not the disease.
- Individualised, holistic and person focused care by:
  - Attending not only to the physical, but to also the psychological, social and spiritual dimensions of each person
  - Appreciating that palliative care is appropriate throughout the person's illness trajectory
  - Interdisciplinary teamwork
  - Including the family

Reflective activity

Imagine that a person on your ward with an advanced disease is waiting for the palliative care team to visit them for the first time.

- How do you think they might be feeling and thinking?
- What might the family be feeling, or does it matter?

Evidence base

For further information and facts on palliative care, visit the following websites:

- The National Council for Palliative Care (2005) *Palliative Care Explained.* Available online at: www.ncpc.org.uk/palliative_care.html.
- World Health Organization (2004) *Palliative Care: The Solid Facts.* Available online at: www.euro.who.int/document/E82931.pdf.

The concept of 'total pain'

Dame Cicely Saunders transformed pain management for people with life-threatening illnesses. She sought to help dying people to meet the challenges that they face, but without pain. Hence, she identified the concept of *total pain*. She emphasised that effective, individualised pain management is promoted through attention not only to the physical, but to also the psychological, social and spiritual dimensions of distress, which are intertwined in the fabrics of holistic care (Figure 11.2). Saunders opened the door to current advances in pain management by demonstrating the safety and efficacy of opioid drug therapy such as morphine, and its impact on improving the quality of life for patients suffering from moderate to severe pain (Doyle, 2005).

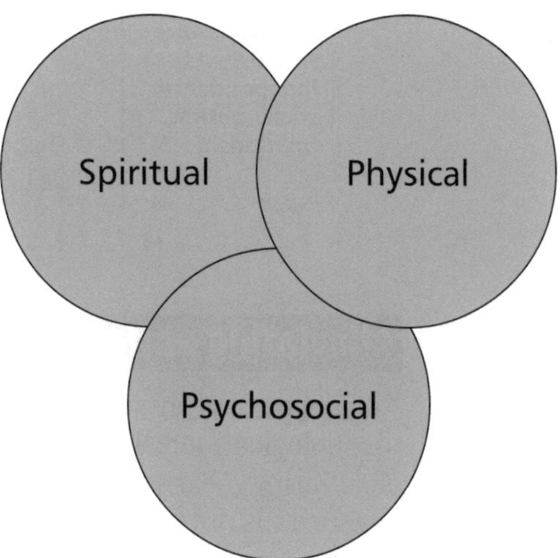

Figure 11.2 Intertwined holistic care as recognised by Dame Cicely Saunders (1918–2005)

The concept of total pain has been a pivotal tool in helping to explain the holistic nature of palliative care. It serves to remind all health care professionals that pain is a deeply personal experience that requires more than merely considering the physiological causes (Paz and Seymour, 2004). Attending to the person holistically requires attentive listening not only to the words but also to the message behind the words. This may enable us to begin to understand the person's experience of total pain (Figure 11.3).

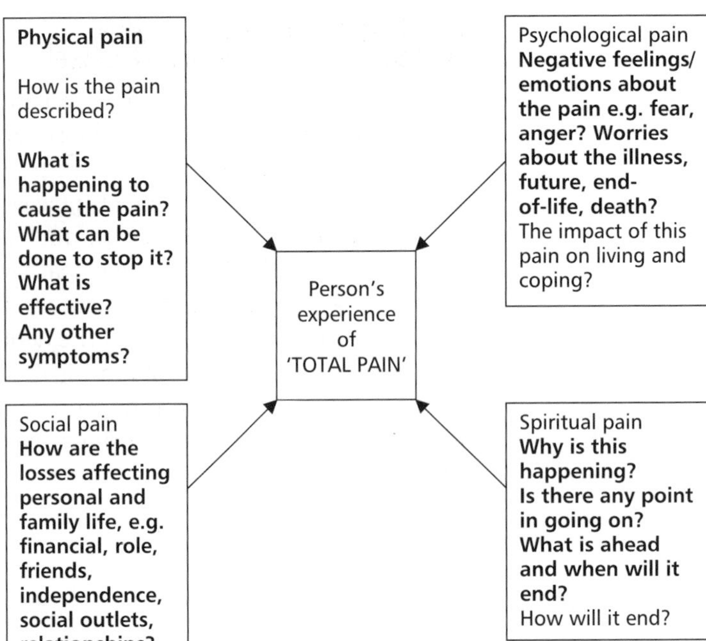

Figure 11.3 Concept of total pain: understanding the person's psychological, social and spiritual issues that impinge on their experience of pain

Alleviating suffering

The anguish of physical pain is often made more complex by the extra psychological, social or spiritual suffering. 'Helping' a person in this type of suffering means finding ways of enabling that person to endure and live with his or her experience. Besides the pharmacological interventions, this involves staying with the person in their suffering. Our willingness to support and empathise with the person may help them find meaning in their suffering. The seminal work of Victor Frankyl (1984) demonstrates that if people can find meaning in their suffering, then it ceases to be meaningless suffering. Although this may appear complex, often it is simply about just 'being there' for the person. Kearney (2000) reassures that rather than having all the answers, helping a person has a lot to do with 'who we are' as carers.

Reflective activity

Imagine that you are asked to explain the concept of 'total pain' to a nursing colleague. Despite your best efforts, the nurse fails to see beyond the physical sensation of pain.

Hints: To assist you in explaining the concept of total pain, consider the image of an iceberg. Imagine that the visible tip of the iceberg represents the physical aspect of pain. In order to care holistically for the person, it is necessary to look beyond the visible and physical, and to assess the deeper psychological, social and spiritual dimensions to the person's experience of pain.

What questions might you consider asking in order to assess what the person's pain experience means to them, hence gaining a holistic understanding of their pain?

Over to you

View the following website to support your answer and to introduce the process of holistic pain assessment.

- Cancer Pain Release. Available at: www.whocancerpain.wisc.edu/contents.html (www.whocancerpain.wisc.edu/eng/14_2/resources.html)

For more information on Dame Cicely Saunders and the concept of total pain, visit the following websites:

- Cicely Saunders Foundation Available at: www.cicelysaundersfoundation.org/ (The Foundation website has an audio interview of Dame Cicely by Professor Irene Higginson.)
- Obituary. Dame Cicely Saunders. 2005. Available at: http://bmj.bmjjournals.com/cgi/content/full/331/7509/DC1

Definition of pain within a palliative care context

Many palliative care professionals espouse the definition 'pain is whatever the patient says hurts' (Twycross and Wilcock, 2002) to capture the subjective, individual experience of pain. However, it is useful to consider a definition that encompasses the pain theories, which have evolved throughout the centuries. The International Association for the Study of Pain (IASP) defines pain as an unpleasant sensory and emotional experience associated with actual or potential tissue damage, or described in terms of such damage (Merskey and Bogduck, 1994).

This definition implies that the pain process is much more than a physiological mechanism that causes the person to experience an unpleasant sensation. It also implies that a person may have pain without a known cause. Therefore, the physiological mechanism of pain is *not* equivalent to pain. Most importantly, the IASP definition recognises that pain is an emotional experience.

This was not always the case. Up until the first half of the twentieth century, pain was viewed solely by the 'specifity theory of pain.' This mechanistic understanding of pain was merely based on the rigid and direct relationship between physical stimulus causing the pain and the sensation felt by the pain. The psychological, affective and social factors influencing pain were ignored. However, Paz and Seymour (2004) cite Leriche's, Beecher's and Bonica's pioneering research on pain in the post-war period, and Melzack and Wall's 'gate-control theory of pain' in the 1960s as greatly contributing to our present day comprehension of pain. Pain is now understood as 'a multidimensional and individual experience with physical, social, psychological, emotional and cultural components' (Paz and Seymour, 2004).

Incidence of pain in palliative care

Portney and Lasage (2001) report that pain is experienced by 70–90% of people with advanced disease. Ross (2004) reports that in the USA, pain ocurs in 25% of all patients at time of diagnosis, and two-thirds of patients receiving anti-cancer therapy. As the stage of the disease advances, the pain also increases, resulting in 75% of patients hospitalised with advanced cancer reporting unrelieved pain (Ross, 2004). Nonetheless, it is imperative to be positive in our interpretation; cancer and pain are not synonymous. Twycross (2003) emphasises the fact that approximately 25% of patients with advanced cancer do not have pain. However, it is worth noting that one-third of those who do suffer pain, one-third experience a single pain, one-third have two pains, and a further one-third have more than two pains (Grond *et al.*, 1996). It is also important to identify the cause, as cancer does not account for all pains. Treatments for the cancer, secondary effects of the cancer, and concurrent disorders must also be considered (Twycross, 2003).

It is also crucial to examine the incidence of non-malignant pain, which Regnard and Kindlen (2004) report is often underestimated. The authors surmise that approximately 60% of patients with cardiac disease, neurological disorders and AIDS suffer with troublesome pain. However, fewer patients with non-malignant conditions are being treated for pain compared to those with malignant pain (Regnard and Kindlen, 2004). Solano *et al.*'s (2005) review of the findings of 64 studies on symptoms experienced in palliative care echo this statement. The smallest and greatest percentage of pain experienced by patients with far advanced cancer, AIDS, heart disease, chronic obstructive pulmonary disease (COPD) and renal disease ranges from 34% to 96% (Solano *et al.*, 2005) as listed in Table 11.1.

Table 11.1 Prevalence of pain in cancer and other diseases (Source: Solano *et al.*, 2005)

Symptom	Cancer	AIDS	Heart disease	Renal disease	COPD
Pain	35–96%	63–80%	41–77%	34–77%	47–50%

Evidence base

For information on the global efforts to tackle pain management in palliative care, visit the following website:

- Help the Hospices (2005) *Suffering at the End of Life – The State of the World.* Available on line at: www.helpthehospices.org.uk/documents/state_of_the_world.pdf.

Classification of pain

Chapter 4 describes pain mechanisms and types of pain. In addition to the definitions described there the following are relevant for palliative care.

Breakthrough pain:
- pain that is more severe than the baseline pain
- common, transitory, exacerbation of pain that is present in patients whose pain is relatively stable and adequately controlled.

Incident pain:
- predictable pain
- occurs in approximately 30% of palliative care patients
- always caused by specific activities (example: someone who is pain free at rest but develops left leg pain on sudden movement).

End of dose failure pain
- occurs towards end of dosing interval of regular analgesic
- present in approximately 16% of palliative care patients
- indication that the regular analgesics require increasing.

Pain assessment in palliative care

The National Cancer Institute (2005) maintains that failure to assess pain is a critical factor leading to under-treatment. Palliative care prevents and relieves suffering by means of *early identification and impeccable assessment* and treatment of pain and other problems, physical, psychosocial and spiritual (WHO, 2002). Pain assessment is therefore pivotal to effective pain management within a palliative care context. In relation to palliative nursing, Fitzsimons and Ahmedzai (2004) concur that the purpose of assessment is to identify *individual* patients' needs or problems in order to set appropriate, achievable and effective goals. Utilising the most appropriate diagnostic and therapeutic considerations, pain assessment will contribute towards defining the cause and directing treatment (Fink and Gates, 2001).

McCaffrey (1983) proclaims that assessment of pain and its relief is no simple matter. More than two decades later, assessment remains problematic and inconsistent (Gordon *et al.*, 2005).

Fitzsimons and Ahmedzai (2004) identify certain fundamental concepts that underpin nursing assessment in palliative care in an attempt to surmount the difficulties with assessment. According to the authors, assessment should be dynamic, individualised, patient and family centred, holistic, therapeutic, sensitive and appropriate to the patient and their family's needs, comprehensive, contextual, and provide reliable and valid information. Furthermore, pain assessment should be evidence-based, and focus upon process and outcomes of care, as evidence of effectiveness of interventions, treatments or services in palliative care is now vital (Fitzsimons and Ahmedzai, 2004).Therefore, the use of an appropriate pain assessment tools is essential in order to objectively measure and capture the sensory and emotional aspects of the individual's pain. Chapter 6 reviews pain assessment tools in detail. As no one scale is suitable for all persons experiencing pain, health care professionals are advised to choose a tool that appropriately meets the needs and capabilities of each person, whilst conscious of the fact that people with advanced disease may tire easily. It is also imperative to facilitate the patient's own story through the use of effective communication skills such as open questions and active listening.

The National Cancer Institute (2005) assert that assessment should occur at regular intervals after initiation of treatment; at each new report of pain; and at a suitable interval after pharmacological or non-pharmacological intervention, e.g., 15–30 minutes after parenteral drug therapy and one hour after oral administration. Impeccable assessment involves assessing the person's description, physical causes and non-physical causes, whilst considering the psychosocial and spiritual aspects of pain. Table 11.2 illustrates the key points to assessing pain within a palliative care context.

Table 11.2 Key points to assessing pain within a palliative care context

Assess Description Quality of the pain: **attentive listening to the individual's descriptive words provides valuable clues to its aetiology/mechanism** Location: **may be more than one pain** Temporal features: **including duration and onset** Severity/intensity: **e.g. numeric/visual analogue scales. Ask about breakthrough and incident pain** Aggravating factors: **ask the individual to identify factors that makes the pain worse** Interventions/Relieving factors: **ask the individual to identify factors that ease the pain, including the effects of analgesia** Associated symptoms: **e.g. dizziness, nausea, sweating, vomiting, shortness of breath**
Assess Physical Cause Disease: **including malignant +/– non-malignant disease** Treatment: **e.g. chemotherapy** Debility: **effects of disease on independence, mobility etc.** Concurrent disorders: **e.g. osteoarthritis**
Assess Mechanism **1. Nocioceptive** **(a) Somatic** **(b) Visceral** **2. Neuropathic**
Assess Psychological, Social and Spiritual Aspects *Impact on the person's life* *Meaning of pain to the person* **Their experience of suffering**
To aid impeccable assessment by. . . A**nticipating pain and early identification** B**elieving the person's experience and rating of pain** C**lassifying pain** D**efining the cause and** D**irecting treatment** E**valuating treatment** F**orwarding (redirecting) treatment**

Student nurse

'It definitely takes time to assess pain properly. I never knew there was so much to it! I used to ask the patient had they got pain, that was it. Rating the pain using the numerical scale is useful, but it's not enough. Now I try to listen to the patient and also to what the family have to say. With the help of the other nurses, I try to work out the type of pain, document how the pain is affecting the person and then we work on what makes it better. But you're never finished. Pain assessment is ongoing, a real challenge, but it's worth it when you see the patients more comfortable.'

Pain management guidelines

According to two WHO publications, *Palliative Care: The Solid Facts* (2004b) and *Better Palliative Care for Older People* (2004c), many Europeans die in unnecessary pain and discomfort because health systems lack the skills and services to provide care towards the end of life. There is strong evidence to suggest that palliative care, through the early identification and treatment of pain and other health problems, can make a dramatic difference in the quality of life of the dying and those who care for them. In 1986, the WHO published guidelines on pain management titled *Cancer Pain Relief*. The guidelines indicate that the appropriate use of simple therapies can effectively relieve pain in the majority of patients.

The guidelines recommend that health care professionals use a three-step analgesic ladder developed for cancer pain relief. The successful implementation of this analgesic ladder depends on the availability of drugs that are safe and effective in relieving chronic severe pain, such as morphine or other opioids (Joranson *et al.*, 2004).

The WHO (1996) advocate that analgesics should be administered in the following way:

- 'by the ladder' (in standard doses at regular intervals in stepwise fashion)
- 'by the mouth' (the oral route is the preferred route for administration when possible)
- 'by the clock' (to maintain freedom from pain, drugs should be given regularly, rather than waiting for the individual to request pain relief)
- 'for the individual' (the analgesic ladder is a framework of principles rather than a rigid protocol)
- 'attention to detail' (attention to each individual's unique experience of pain is required when directing treatment).

The WHO (2005) website states: 'If a pain occurs, there should be a prompt oral administration of drugs in the following order: non-opioids (aspirin or paracetamol); then, as necessary, mild opioids (codeine); or the strong opioids such as morphine, until the patient is free of pain. To maintain freedom from pain, drugs should be given "by the clock", that is every three to six hours, rather than "on demand". This three-step approach of administering the right drug in the right dose at the right time is inexpensive and 80–90% effective'. See Figure 7.5 on page 109 for WHO's Analgesic Ladder.

The analgesic ladder provides a safe, consistent and standard method of pain control (Hanks *et al.*, 2001). However, since its introduction in 1986 there have been major developments in the field of palliative

Keywords

Adjuvant analgesics
Drugs that have a primary indication other than pain but are used to enhance analgesia in specific circumstances. They are mainly for neuropathic pain, also used for bony pain

medicine. Thus, some of the recommendations have been modified. The Expert Working Group of the Research Network of the European Association for Palliative Care (EAPC) revised and updated guidelines for the use of opioids (Hanks *et al.*, 2001). The recommendations recognise that pain relief should be provided to all seriously ill and dying patients, not only cancer patients. Additionally, the middle step of the ladder using mild opioids is often skipped in seriously ill and dying patients as their pain is so severe that strong opioids are needed. Furthermore, a range of **adjuvant analgesics** can also be used to treat neuropathic pain and other specific pain conditions at all stages of the ladder (Hanks *et al.*, 2001).

Morphine

The opioid of first choice for moderate to severe cancer pain is morphine, as it remains the most researched and most widely used opioid (Hanks *et al.*, 2001). In the UK, diamorphine is the preferred injectable opioid when patients are unable to take oral morphine. However, there are alternatives for when morphine or diamorphine are unsuitable (e.g. hydromorphone, oxycodone, fentanyl, methadone and buprenorphine). It is important to address the various misconceptions, the cognitive effects and the limitations to using morphine as discussed in Chapter 7.

The safe and appropriate use of morphine

Morphine is a safe drug when used properly. The Europen Association for Palliaitive Care guidelines for the use of opioids state that ideally, two types of morphine formulation are required: normal release (for dose titration) and modified release (for maintenance treatment). The simplest method of dose titration is with a dose of normal release morphine given every four hours and the same dose for breakthrough pain. This rescue dose may be given as often as required (up to hourly) and the total daily dose of morphine should be reviewed daily. One-sixth of the daily 24-hour dose is regarded as an appropriate rescue dose. The regular dose can then be adjusted to take into account the total amount of rescue morphine (Hanks *et al.*, 2001). Alternatively, modified release morphine may be started at 20–30 mg twice daily. Normal release morphine tablets (e.g. sevredol) or solution (e.g. oramorph) are provided for breakthrough use. The dose of the modified release morphine should be increased every two to three days until there is adequate relief throughout each 12-hour period, taking pre re nata (PRN) use into account (i.e. the rescue doses for the breakthrough pain). However, caution must be exercised with the elderly population due to the likelihood of reduced clearance of opioids.

Clinical Caseload . . .

John is prescribed a normal release morphine (oromorph) 5 mg four-hourly for cancer pain, which he took six times yesterday. The staff nurse realises that John also took oramorph 5 mg four times for breakthrough pain within the same 24 hour period. She therefore suggests to the physician that John's normal release morphine will need to be increased immediately, in order to manage his pain effectively. The physician works out John's new appropriate and safe dose of oramorph as follows:

5 mg x 6 doses oramorph = 30 mg oramorph in 24 hours for baseline pain

5 mg x 4 doses oramorph = 20 mg oramorph in 24 hours for breakthrough pain

30 mg + 20 mg = 50 mg oramorph total in 24 hours

$1/6^{th}$ of 50 mg oramorph = 50 divided by 6 = 8.33 mg oramorph (rounded to 10 mg for convenience)

New appropriate and safe dose of oramorph = 10 mg 4 hourly and 10 mg as required

Evidence base

Visit the following WHO website to see the relevant 2004 reports, which aim to ensure that all individuals and families have the opportunity to be appropriately supported towards the end of their lives and not to die in unnecessary pain.

- World Health Organization Website (2004d) *People die in unnecessary pain*. Available at: www.kcl.ac.uk/depsta/palliative/research/who.html.

Continuous subcutaneous infusion (CSCI)

A continuous subcutaneous infusion (CSCI) is an effective method of drug administration that is particularly suited to palliative care when the oral route is inappropriate (Dickman *et al.*, 2005). British practitioners commonly refer to a CSCI as a 'syringe driver' (Graham and Clark, 2005). It is a lightweight, portable, battery-operated infusion pump, that delivers drugs over a specified period of time (usually 24 hours).

There are two types of syringe driver manufactured by SIMS Graseby that are widely used in palliative care:

- MS16A with an *hourly* rate (mm/h) syringe driver and a *blue* front panel

- MS26 with a *daily* rate (mm/24h) syringe driver and a *green* front panel.

The majority of centres in the UK use the MS26 because setting the rate is simpler and perhaps safer. However, the MS16A is more flexible, particularly when larger volumes of drugs are required. It is safer if only one or other type is used in a given locality in order to minimise the likelihood of errors (Carlisle *et al.*, 1996). Confusion between the two, in relation to the setting, has led to fatal errors (Dickman *et al.*, 2005). Staff training is therefore essential to highlight the differences (Carlisle *et al.*, 1996).

The use of a CSCI is often incorrectly seen as 'the last resort' and wrongly associated with imminent death. Rather, a CSCI is an effective method of relieving certain symptoms by injection, for example intractable nausea and vomiting (Dickman *et al.*, 2005). Other indications for using a CSCI include dysphagia, intestinal obstruction, severe weakness, unconsciousness, poor absorption of oral drugs (rare), and patient preference (e.g. large amounts of tablets).

As drugs are delivered continuously over the specified period, the CSCI maintains constant plasma levels of the drugs. A great benefit is that more than one medication can be mixed in the CSCI, thereby allowing management of multiple symptoms with a combination of drugs. Most of all, the CSCI avoids the need for repeated injections, thus reducing patient discomfort and requirement for repeated injections. Before setting up a syringe driver, it is important to explain to the patient and the family the rationale for its use, and how it works.

Knowledge of drug compatibility is essential when using a CSCI. The prescription should be checked to determine whether the drug combination, and the solution that the drug is diluted in, is physically compatible (refer to medication information leaflet). As a general rule, drugs with similar pH are more likely to be compatible than those with widely differing pH. As most drug solutions are acidic, alkaline drugs such as ketorolac, diclofenac, phenobarbitol and dexamethasone often cause compatibility problems when used in a combination with other drugs. It is therefore recommended to administer these drugs in a separate infusion. Dexamethasone should always be added last to an already dilute combination of drugs in order to reduce the risk of incompatibility.

Dickman *et al.* (2005) report that a greater number of drugs are now being administered by a CSCI. Usually a maximum of three drugs are mixed in the one syringe, although some centres combine up to four drugs. Table 11.3 lists the drugs that are suitable for delivery by a CSCI. However, it is important to note that although these drugs have product licences, the majority of the drugs are unlicensed for administration via a CSCI (Dickman *et al.*, 2005).

Until recently, the recommended diluent for CSCI was water for injection because it was thought that there was less chance of precipitation. However, Dickman *et al.* (2005) recommend that NaCL should be used for dilution as the majority of drugs commonly used in palliative care have an osmolarity, the same or less than NaCL. There are two exceptions to this general rule. Water for injection must be used as a diluent for solutions containing cyclizine (as cyclizine causes crystal formation in the presence of chloride ions), and for solutions of high concentrations of diamorphine (>40 mg/ml). If in any doubt, the prescribing physician or pharmacist should be contacted.

It is also imperative to note the equal analgesic dose of subcutaneous opioids compared to oral opioids. For example, subcutaneous morphine is twice as potent as oral morphine, therefore morphine sulphate 30 mg orally in 24 hours is equivalent to 15 mg of morphine sulphate subcutaneously over 24 hours.

Table 11.3 Drugs suitable for delivery by a CSCI

Alfentanil	Haloperidol	Octreotide
Clonazepam	Hydromorphone	Ondanestron
Cyclizine	Hyoscine butylbromide	Oxycodone
*Dexamethasone	Hyoscine	*Phenobarbitol
Diamorphine	Hydrobromide	Promethazine
*Diclofenac	Ketamine	Ranitidine
Dihydrocodine	*Ketorolac	Sufentanil
Dimenhydrinate	Levomepromazine	Tramadol
Fentanyl	Methadone	
Glycoprronium	Metoclopramide	
	Midazolam	
	Morphine	

* Indicates drugs to be administered in a separate infusion

Evidence base

For further information on the safe and appropriate use of CSCI, and drug compatibilities, refer to:

- Dickman A., Schneider, J., Varga J. (eds.) (2005) *The Syringe Driver: Continuous subcutaneous infusions in palliative care,* 2nd edn. Oxford University Press, Oxford. Alternatively, visit www.palliative drugs.com, a website that provides essential, comprehensive and independent information for health professionals about the use of drugs in palliative care. It highlights drugs given for unlicensed indications or by unlicensed routes and the administration of multiple drugs by continuous subcutaneous infusion.

See Table 11.4 for the key points of the analgesic ladder

Table 11.4 Key points of the analgesic ladder

Step	Class	Drug example	Additional drugs
STEP 1	Non-opioid	Paracetamol Aspirin NSAIDs (nonsteroidal anti-inflammatory drugs)	+/– adjuvant drugs
If pain persists or increases, go to step 2			
STEP 2	Mild opioid for mild to moderate pain (Codeine)	Solpadeine Solpadol Tramadol	+/– adjuvant drugs +/– non-opioid
If pain persists or increases, go to step 3			
STEP 3	Strong opioid for moderate to severe pain	Morphine Hydromorphone Buphenorphine Oxycodone Methadone Fentanyl	+/– adjuvant drugs +/– non-opioid

A palliative care approach to pain management

Jane is a 42-year-old accountant receiving chemotherapy for malignant breast cancer and local bone metastasis. She is graduating with a law degree next week and just wants the pain in her ribcage sorted now so she can plan her graduation party with her fiancé James. She is taking modified 12-hourly release morphine sulphate tablets 30 mg twice daily and wants something for breakthrough pain. However, you note that she is not prescribed normal release morphine. When you report her pain to the physician, he tells her that the palliative care team are coming to visit her this morning. Shocked and horrified, she admits to you that she has no idea why they are visiting or what they plan to offer. She incorrectly presumes that her disease is advancing and that she is going to die very shortly.

You are asked to:

1 Explain the role of the palliative care team to Jane.
2 Discuss how their input may positively influence the course of Jane's illness.
3 What do you do for her pain whilst waiting for the palliative care team to visit?

continued

Hints:

- To assist you in explaining the concept of palliative care, find out what palliative care means to Jane and her family (James). Explore why she is shocked and horrified, including any previous experience of hospice/palliative care involvement.
- Offer Jane accurate information in relation to the benefits of shared supportive/palliative care, in order to empower her.
- Refer to the analgesic ladder and the EAPC recommendations for guiding Jane's pain management, in particular to opioid titration.

Key points Top tips

- People die in unnecessary pain and discomfort because health systems lack the skills and services to provide care towards the end of life
- There is strong evidence to suggest that palliative care, through the early identification and treatment of pain and other health problems, can make a dramatic difference in the quality of life of the dying and those who care for them
- Pain management is fundamental in creating the conditions for a person with advanced disease to address their personal healing
- Failure to identify, assess and treat pain will result in mismanagement of the other elements of a person's total suffering

Rapid recap

1. Outline the philosophy of a palliative care approach.
2. What is the purpose of pain assessment within a palliative care context?
3. Following the analgesic ladder guidelines, how should analgesics be administered?

References

Archbishop Desmond Tutu (2005) State of the World Report – Launch. BBC World Service Broadcast. Available online at: www.helpthehospices.org.uk/news/index.asp?submenu=5&newsid=171.

Cancer Pain Release. Available at: www.whocancerpain.wisc.edu/contents.html.

Carlisle D., Upton D. and Cousins D. (1996) Infusion Confusion. *Nursing Times*, **92**: 48–49.

Dickman A., Schneider, J. and Varga J. (eds.) (2005) *The Syringe Driver: Continuous subcutaneous infusions in palliative care*. 2nd edn. Oxford University Press, Oxford.

Doyle, D. (2005) Tribute to Dame Cicely Saunders. *IAHPC News On-line* (Hospice & Palliative Care News & Information), **6**(8).

Fink R. and Gate R. (2001) Pain Assessment. In: *Textbook of Palliative Nursing* (eds. Rolling Ferrell, B. and Coyle, N.) Oxford University Press, Oxford.

Fitzsimons D. and Ahmedzai S.H. (2004) Approaches to assessment in palliative care. In: *Palliative Care Nursing: Principles and Evidence for Practice* (eds. Payne S., Seymour J. and Ingleton C.) Open University Press, Berkshire.

Frankyl V. (1984) *Man's Search for Meaning.* New York, Washington Square Press.

Gordon D.B., Dahl J.L., Miaskowski C., McCarbera B., Todd K.H., Paice J.A. *et al.* (2005) American Pain Society recommendations for Improving the Quality of Acute and Cancer Pain Management. *Archives of Internal Medicine*, **65**: 1574–1580.

Graham F. and Clark D. (2005) The syringe driver in palliative care; the inventor, the history and the implications. *Journal of Pain & Symptom Management*, **29**(1): 32–40.

Grond S. *et al.* (1996) Assessment of cancer pain: a prospective evaluation in 2266 cancer patients referred to a pain service. *Pain*, **64**: 107–114.

Hanks G.W., De Conno F., Cherney N., Hanna M., Kalso E., McQuay H.J. *et al.* (2001) Morphine and alternative opioids in cancer pain: the EAPC recommendations. *British Journal of Cancer*, **84**(5): 587–593.

Help the Hospices (2005) 'Suffering at the End of Life – The State of the World'. Available at: www.helpthehospices.org.uk/documents/state_of_the_world.pdf.

Joranson D., Ryan K. and Jorenby R. (2004) Availability of Opioid Analgesics in Romania, Europe, and the World (2001 data). University of Wisconsin Pain and Policy Studies Group/WHO Collaboration Center for Policy and Communication in Cancer Care. Madison, Wisconsin, USA.

Kearney, M. (2000) *A Place of Healing.* Oxford, Oxford University Press.

McCaffrey M. (1983) *Nursing the Patient in Pain*, 2nd edn. Harper and Row, London, p. 276.

Merskey H. and Bogduck N. (1994) Classification of Chronic Pain: Description of Chronic Pain Syndromes and Definition of Pain Terms. Report by the International Association for the Study of Pain Task Force on Taxonomy, 2nd edn. IASP Press, Seattle, WA.

National Cancer Institute (2005) Available at: www.nci.nih.gov/cancertopics/pdq/supportivecare/pain/HealthProfessional/page2#Section_44.

Payne S., Seymour J. and Ingleton C. (eds.) (2004) *Palliative Care Nursing: Principles and Evidence for Practice.* Open University Press, Berkshire.

Paz S.and Seymour J. (2004). Pain: Theories, evaluation and management. In: Payne S., Seymour J. and Ingleton C. (eds.) *Palliative Care Nursing: Principles and Evidence for Practice*. Open University Press, Berkshire.

Portney R.K. and Lesage P. (2001) Management of cancer pain. The Pain Series. Available at: www.thelancet.com/journal/vol357/issss1.

Regnard C. and Kindlen M. (2004) What is pain? In: *Helping the Patient with Advanced Disease* (ed. Regnard C.). Radcliffe Medical Press, Oxford.

Ross E. (2004) *Pain Management*. Hanley & Belfus, Philadelphia.

Solano J.P., Games B. and Higginson I.J. (2005) A comparison of symptom prevalence in far advanced cancer, AIDS, heart disease, chronic obstructive pulmonary disease (COPD) and renal disease. *Journal of Pain and Symptom Management*, **31**(1): 58–69. Also available at: www.worldday.org/documents/state_of_the_world.pdf (page 13).

The National Council for Palliative Care (2005) *Palliative care explained.* Available at: www.ncpc.org.uk/palliative_care.html.

Twycross R. (2003) *Introducing Palliative Care*, 4th edn. Radcliffe Medical Press, Oxford.

Twycross R.G. and Wilcock A. (2002) *Symptom Management in Advanced Cancer*, 3rd edn. Radcliffe Medical Press, Oxford.

Twycross R.G., Wilcock A., Charlesworth S. and Dickman A. (2002) *Palliative care formulary,* 2nd edn. Radcliffe Medical Press, Oxford.

World Health Organization (1986) *Cancer Pain Relief*. WHO, Geneva.

World Health Organization (1996) *Cancer Pain Relief: with a Guide to Opiod Availability*, 2nd edn. WHO, Geneva.

World Health Organization (2002) *National cancer control programmes: policies and managerial guidelines,* 2nd edition. WHO, Geneva. Available at: www.who.int/cancer/en/

World Health Organization (2004a) *Global Day Against Pain*. WHO, Geneva. Available at: www.who.int/mediacentre/news/releases/2004/pr70/en/index.html.

World Health Organization (2004b) *Palliative Care: The Solid Facts*. WHO, Geneva. Available at: www.euro.who.int/document/E82931.pdf.

World Health Organization (2004c) *Better Palliative Care for Older People*. WHO Regional Office for Europe. Available at: www.euro.who.int/document/E82933.pdf.

World Health Organization (2004d) *People die in unnecessary pain*. Available at: www.kcl.ac.uk/depsta/palliative/research/who.html.

World Health Organization (2005) Pain Ladder Website. Available at: www.who.int/cancer/palliative/painladder/en/index.html.

12 Conclusion – Nurses, health care professionals and organisational roles

Learning outcomes

By the end of this chapter you should be able to:

★ Understand the role of nurses and health professionals in pain management

★ Describe the importance of organisational commitment to pain management

★ Describe the benefits of a multidisciplinary approach to pain.

Introduction

This chapter will highlight the role of nurses and health professionals in pain management. It will draw on all other chapters and act as a concluding chapter to the book. It will detail the need for a consistent approach to pain management, the role of professional judgement and the need for education and continuing professional development in pain management for all health professionals. The chapter will support the concept that patients/clients get a better service from a multidisciplinary approach to care. The most important message emerging from this book is the *critical role of evidence-based practice*.

Pain as an important issue for society

Pain has become a world public health issue. Pain is widely prevalent and it is evident that both acute and chronic pain are often poorly managed. The reasons for this vary from cultural to attitude of health professionals and patients, education of staff and lack of multidisciplinary team working. Patients do appear to be generally satisfied with their pain management (Tasso and Behar-Horenstein, 2004). However, as has been seen in the various chapters throughout this book, patients both in hospitals and communities continue to suffer moderate to high levels of pain. Decreased lung volumes, myocardial ischaemia, decreased gastric and bowel motility and anxiety are all harmful side effects associated with under-treated severe pain (Macintyre and Ready, 2002). Pain and in particular chronic and cancer pain affects both quality of life and functional status. There is thus an economic and social burden associated with pain. Pain management has over time become a priority for health care policy makers and providers. Indeed organisations such as the World Health Organization, the International Association for the Study of Pain and the British Pain Society have taken lead roles in promoting best practice in pain management.

Pain as an important issue for individuals

Pain is a personal and unique experience for the individual. While much is known about the physiology of pain, the emotive and contextual aspects of pain continue to give rise to debate. It is interesting that even with increasing knowledge of the physiological theories such as the Gate Control Theory, knowledge of pain physiology could be considered still in its infancy. It is likely that with increased technology such as magnetic resonance imaging (MRI) scanning and increasingly sophisticated research our understanding of pain will increase at a fast pace. Research into genetics and highly developed medications and administration devices will continue to contribute to improving the patient's pain experience.

The cause of an individual's pain will relate highly to how that pain is experienced by any individual, i.e. the extent of pain will relate to the level of nociception involved. Even with greater understandings of the physiology of pain the context of that pain will continue to shape the experience and subsequent management of that pain. Patients' knowledge of pain and analgesia, their expectations of pain, past experiences of pain, fear of addiction, anxiety, culture, age, lack of information, the influence of public and organisational policy and health professionals responsible for care all form part of the pain experience. Worldwide mobility has raised the profile of culture, race and ethnicity in health care in general and in pain management specifically. It emerges from Chapter 5 that in order to enhance communication with patients and improve their pain management, health care professionals should:

- be sensitive to individual needs of patient and their family
- utilise a comprehensive pain history and assessment appropriate to classification of pain
- pay constant attention to communications
- embrace the underlying philosophy of pain management that 'pain is what the patient says it is'.

Reflective activity

Think back to when you looked after your first patient in pain. How did you empathise with the patient? How did you assess their pain? Have you developed more sophisticated methods of assessing pain over time?

Research and evidence-based practice

Pain management, like any aspect of patient care, should be based on the best available evidence. The management of pain is the subject of ongoing research and debate. As such evidence changes rapidly all health professionals should continuously update and review developments. Good evidence is likely to come from good systematic reviews of sound clinical trails. This means that health professionals must be able to access, understand and interpret research in order to provide evidence-based practice.

It is evident throughout this book that ongoing research is necessary in a number of areas. In particular the use of multimodal pain interventions and their evidence base needs continued ongoing research as new information, medications and therapeutic interventions emerge. New technologies continue to develop which will support the development of analgesic management.

Nurses and health care professionals need to be able to lead, initiate and understand research and evidence-based practice. Education and ongoing professional development are key to this as not only does the evidence change but methods used to design and review research studies continuously evolve over time. In the past, one good well-designed randomised controlled trial (RCT) was considered very strong evidence for practice. Now it is evident that even stronger evidence can come from systematic reviews and meta-analysis of research studies. Additionally search tools have become more sophisticated and powerful and there is increasing access to research from all countries regardless of language.

Over to you

Having read through each of the chapters in the book what areas of pain management do you think should be prioritised for research? What are the gaps in our knowledge with regard to pain?

Barriers to effective pain management

Numerous barriers to effective pain management are detailed throughout this book. It is important that as health professionals we seek solutions to these barriers and become proactive in our outlook and approaches to pain management. Table 12.1 summarises some of these barriers as detailed by Carr (2002).

Table 12.1 Barriers to effective pain management (Source: Carr, 2002)

Prevalence and incidence of pain	• Little has changed over 25 years. • Problem is likely to increase as population grows older
Patients	• Often reluctant to take analgesia (have concerns about its potential harm, constipation and not being in control) • Widespread public education is needed to change lack of public knowledge regarding pain in order to shift pain culture and empower patients to participate in decisions about their pain treatment
Professional knowledge	• Deficits in knowledge and lack of regular assessment often blamed for poor management of pain • Multiple demands compete for nurses' time and pain is not viewed as a priority
Organisational and hospital management priorities	• May impact on nurses' ability to deliver effective pain management.
Perceived harmlessness of pain	• Deleterious effects of pain such as immobility, deep vein thrombosis, depression and anxiety are frequently not seen as consequences of omitting to assess pain and administer appropriate analgesics.

The identification of these barriers is the first step to improving pain management. There is sufficient well-documented pain information available to any service or individual professional who wishes to review their own service area and begin the process of improving approaches to pain management. The literature and evidence available provides as many solutions as barriers.

Reflective activity

Did you complete the 'over to you' exercise in Chapter 2, page 18? If yes consider the results, if not this is a reminder so that you can complete the exercise.

Consider your patient profile. Do you audit your pain prevalence?

If not complete this simple quick task:

- What would you estimate is the prevalence of pain in your clinical area?
- Take a simple numeric rating scale and do a point prevalence for 10 patients (this will take about five minutes)

Are the pain levels what you expected? How do they compare to national and international statistics?

Having completed the exercise are you satisfied that the levels of pain on your clinical area are in line with best practice? What do you think are the barriers that limit effective pain management in your organisation?

Multidisciplinary teams

Responsibility for pain management lies with all of the health care team: nurse, doctor, anaesthetist, physiotherapist, pharmacist, the patient and others as appropriate. Chapter 2 describes the various teams (acute, chronic, palliative care) and the evidence to support their effectiveness. It is evident through the various research studies presented in this book that patients benefit from care from teams.

> **Over to you**
>
> Consider the evidence for multidisciplinary team management for pain in this book. What do you think are the key benefits for patients?

The key desirable characteritsics within these teams are outlined in Figure 12.1.

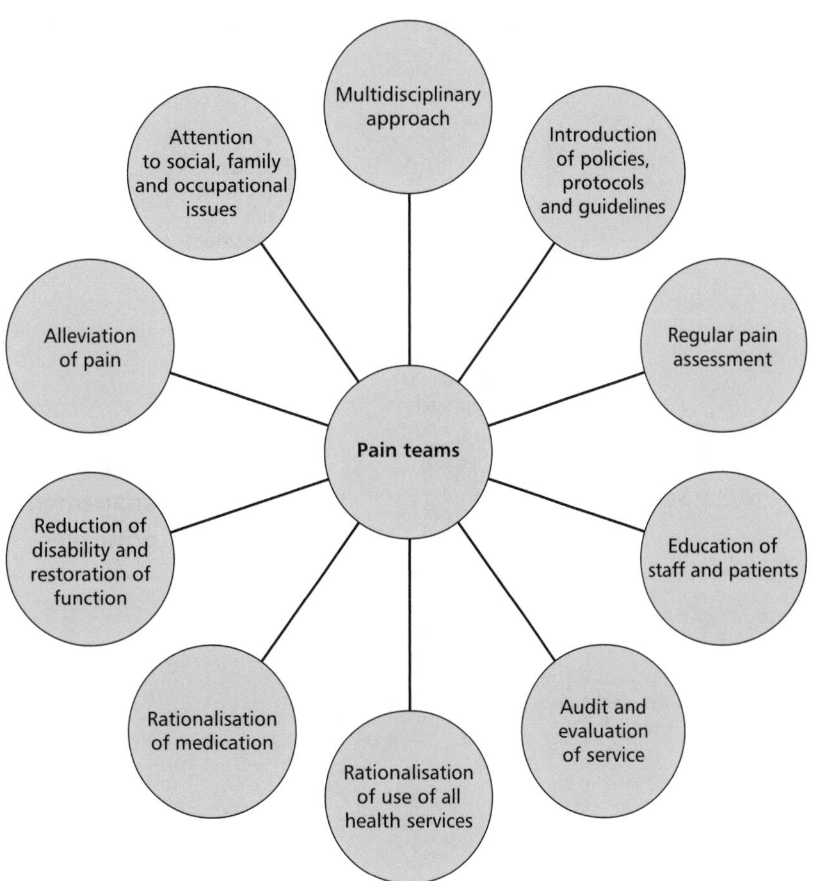

Figure 12.1 Key desirable characteristics of a pain team

In order to manage pain effectively, health professionals should have a firm understanding of the physiology of pain including the concept that each individual perceives his/her pain uniquely. This provides the basis for management and modulation of pain. The options for modulation of pain at each stage of the pain process and pain pathway should be understood. The principles of pain assessment and the need for ongoing monitoring of pain are part of the key knowledge base for health care professionals to be able to manage pain effectively. A basic knowledge base is needed for all health professionals to embrace their role supported by organisational policies and guidelines. Additionally health professionals need to be able to interact with each other effectively and efficiently. This means developing relationships between primary, secondary and tertiary care. It is of little benefit to the patient if a sophisticated pain management plan is developed in the hospital but is not transferred to and supported by the health care professionals in the community. The role of complementary and alternative therapies in a mixed-method approach to holistic pain care management should also be appreciated. This is discussed in Chapter 8.

Drawing together the various experts provides the patient with the most comprehensive pain plan. In addition modern medicine may have brought new understanding and improved technology, but even without

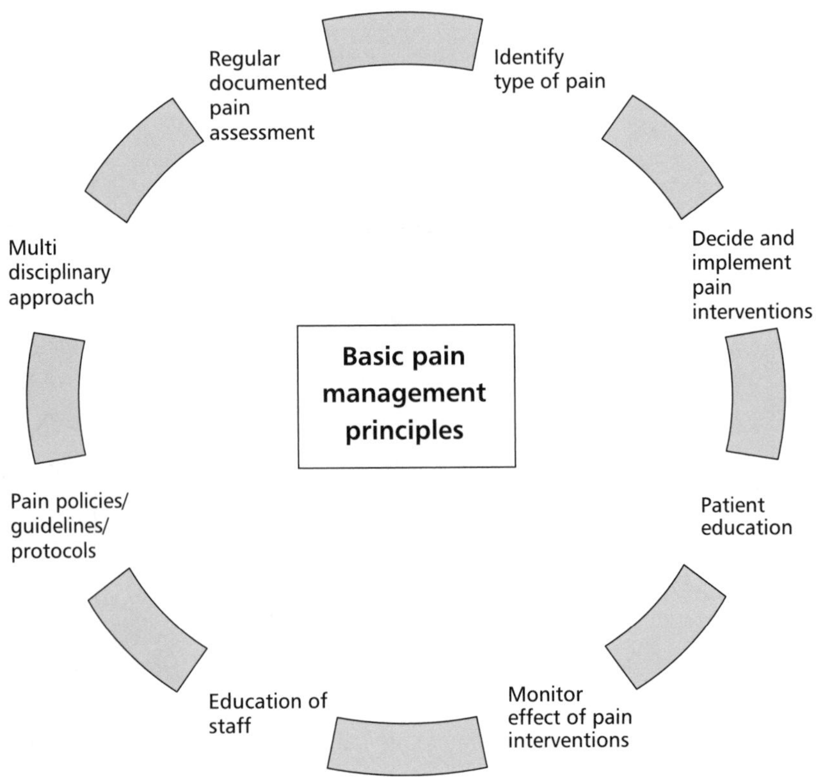

Figure 12.2 Basic pain management principles

new techniques pain management can be improved through an understanding and application of basic pain management principles. Again this evidence is presented throughout the book and is detailed in Figure 12.2.

Nurse's role

The nurse's role as part of the multidisciplinary team is of particular importance in pain management, given that they provide care on a 24 hour basis. Increasingly, nurses have taken on more specialist and advanced practice roles in pain management. They are seen as the lead in some pain teams (Mackintosh and Bowles, 1997). Titles such as pain resource nurses (Holley *et al.*, 2005), nurse specialists and pain nurse consultants have all emerged. Nurses are seen are key members of the multidisciplinary team in managing pain (Clinical Standards Advisory Group (CSAG, 2000).

The nurses' role as detailed in Chapter 6 is very important in pain assessment. It is increasingly evident that appropriate, regular pain assessment is key to pain management. The nurse interprets pain, administers and evaluates pain management procedures, provides information to patients and works as a member of the multidisciplinary team. Certain skills and knowledge are needed in order that the nurse can embrace effectively this role in pain management. Ongoing strategic in-service education is necessary to keep nurses updated. Maximising the nurses' role and utilising basic pain management principles have been shown to decrease patients' pain scores (Bardiau *et al.*, 2003; Mac Lellan, 2004).

Table 12.2 details facets of the nurse's role in pain management. These facets relate to the key areas of functioning necessary for the nurse to support evidence-based care and a holistic approach to pain management. The knowledge and skills required by nurses to manage pain are outlined. Use of the table by matching knowledge and skill to role facet provides guidelines on how nurses can perform an effective role in pain management by applying basic pain management principles.

The Pain Society (2002) produced recommendations for nursing practice in pain management. Nursing competencies for a career pathway in pain management from novice to intermediate leading to higher-level practice are outlined. Seven standards are outlined:

1 Providing effective health care.
2 Improving quality and health outcomes.
3 Evaluation and research.
4 Leading and developing practice.
5 Innovation and changing practice.
6 Developing self and others.
7 Working across professional and organisational boundaries.

Table 12.2 The nurse's role in pain management (Source: Adapted from Mac Lellan, 2000)

Role facet	Knowledge	Skills
Information giving to patients – Methods of pain relief – Assessment of pain – The roles and functions of the health care team in pain management – Role of the patient and family	Pain relief methods Pain assessment methods	● Effective communication skills
Assessment of pain – Verbal assessment – Non-verbal assessment	Pain assessment tools Pain physiology Pain theories	● Ability to use assessment tools reliably ● Ability to interpret non-verbal cues of pain and undertake holistic assessment of patient
Development of therapeutic programmes	Pain management processes Quality of life issues Supports to improve functional status	● Ability to complete assessment of patient and develop holistic pain management plans
Administration and monitoring of effect of analgesia – Opioids – NSAIDs – Anti-convulsants – Paracetamol – Other	Analgesic medications (action, time of effect, side-effects)	● Ability to administer by many routes ● Ability to use technology, e.g. administration pumps ● Ability to integrate theory with practice
Documentation of pain	Best practice in documentation	● Ability to write clearly and concisely
Team work	Team dynamics	● Effective communication skills
Complementary approaches to pain management	Other approaches to pain relief, e.g. relaxation, cold, heat, distraction	● Competency in alternative approaches to pain management
Holistic approach to patient care	Pain management Integrated approach to care Health promotion	● Ability to empower and support patient to improve their health and wellbeing ● Ability to manage patient as a service user and as a member of a wider community
Evidence-based practice	Clinical audit Sources of evidence	● Ability to use results of clinical audit to evaluate pain management service ● Ability to access best evidence and integrate it into practice ● Ability to integrate theory with practice

Reflective activity

Consider your patient caseload. How many suffer moderate to severe levels of pain? What is your role in their pain management? Do you have the knowledge to be effective in your role?

Knowledge of health care staff

A basic knowledge base is needed for all health professionals to embrace their role in pain management. It can be seen by the extent of information provided on pain definitions, pain physiology, pain assessment and pain management techniques that health professionals require ongoing continuing professional development as well as a sound foundation in undergraduate education in pain management. The literature, however, indicates that health care professionals' knowledge and attitudes are not always adequate to ensure a strong evidence-based culture of pain management (Hamilton and Edgar, 1992; Clarke *et al.*, 1996; Furstenberg *et al.*, 1998; McCaffrey, 2002; Jastrzab *et al.*, 2003; Horbury, 2005). Jastrzab *et al.* (2003) found the best knowledge scores for nurses were in the 'nursing assessment and management' section. An interesting small-scale survey (sample 101, response rate 81%) (Coulling, 2005) highlighted misconceptions and inadequate knowledge of both doctors and nurses. What was interesting to note was that nurses were more knowledgeable in assessment (similar to Jastrzab *et al.*, 2003) and analgesic delivery systems and doctors were more knowledgeable in pharmacology. It would seem that traditional roles in pain management continue to exist which may not be supporting holistic patient care.

There is a need to recognise new ways of learning and working to improve delivery of care. It is important to note that education in pain management improves knowledge, as evidenced by both Jones *et al.* (2004) and Innis *et al.* (2004). This is particularly important given the increased blurring of traditional role boundaries when working within a team. One example is the expanded role of nurses in prescribing established in the UK, USA and Australia and just emerging in Ireland.

Service providers, educators and policy makers

It is evident that individual health care professionals and indeed health care teams can improve their knowledge base and subsequently improve practice. However, this enduring health issue requires both service providers and policy makers to take the issue seriously and propose and implement measures to improve the patients' experience. There are staff and resource implications, but economic justification can be found in the reduced morbidity, faster convalescence and improved satisfaction in patients who receive adequate relief from pain.

Organisational managers, to assure that best practice in pain management is being carried out, should support quality assurance procedures. Throughout this book numerous ways of improving pain management have been detailed, from education for staff, information for patients, use of evidence-based guidelines and the utilistation of all the skills available in interprofessional teams.

Education and training of many health care professionals, including nursing staff, may not be providing the skills and competencies necessary to provide a modern health service. Education needs to ensure that enough emphasis on contemporary methods of pain assessment and management is contained within pre- and post-registration curricula.

Pain management cannot be effective if its implementation is based on inadequate knowledge and erroneous beliefs. Brunier (1995) showed that nurses with a university education scored significantly higher in a knowledge and attitude survey. She also demonstrated that nurses who had attended educational sessions on pain management within the preceding year scored significantly higher than those who did not.

Undergraduate courses need to highlight the importance of pain management and treat pain management as a holistic module. Postgraduate courses should include a pain module, while advanced clinical practice courses should include pain management as a specialty. Collaboration between educationalists, organisational managers and clinicians is necessary to ensure such education is available and that practice goals can be met. Such collaboration can and should be supported by health policy at national and international level – see Figure 12.3.

Figure 12.3 Collaboration to support best practice in pain management

Patient benefits

All health systems exist to improve the health of their nation. Each national health system is influenced by international and national governmental policy. Investment in particular areas of health care are often at the cost benefit of other care areas and as such governments must make choices. These choices are ideally based on evidence for best outcomes for patients and the population utilising sophisticated cost-benefit processes. This is complex given the difficulties in health economics and measurement of quality of life. How do you choose one area over the other? The dynamics of this choice are often multifaceted and you should not underestimate the influence of strong evidence based on scientific rigour. You will find these dynamics evident at all levels of society and the health care system. They exist at a macro level (pain as a public health issue), meso level (organisational responses to pain) and a micro level (how the individual experiences his/her pain).

Reflective activity

Consider your role in pain management. Is it as a staff nurse caring for patients, a clinical nurse manager with ward responsibility, or other? Reflect on your level of influence on how a person experiences their pain. Is it at macro, meso or micro level? Are there other ways you could influence pain management?

The evidence in this book and the tools and processes you have encountered to support you to continually update your knowledge on pain should give you a clear and unambiguous 'armoury' for building up a case for resources, time, education etc. to improve pain management for your patients. It is important to manage and treat an individual's pain directly but it is as important to ensure that best practice in pain management is performed in your organisation. You as an individual as well as being part of a team have a responsibility to your patient caseload to utilise your knowledge to improve their experiences. In this way you are an important part of the process for improving the health of the nation. You may ask yourself why should you be proactive? Why is it not someone else's responsibility? As a qualified (or soon to be qualified) professional you have the knowledge and duty to improve your patients' pain experiences in the best way you can.

Put simply, what will an improved pain service mean for the individual patient who could be your mother, your sister, your partner or even you? Figure 12.4 details the benefits to individual patients when pain management is improved.

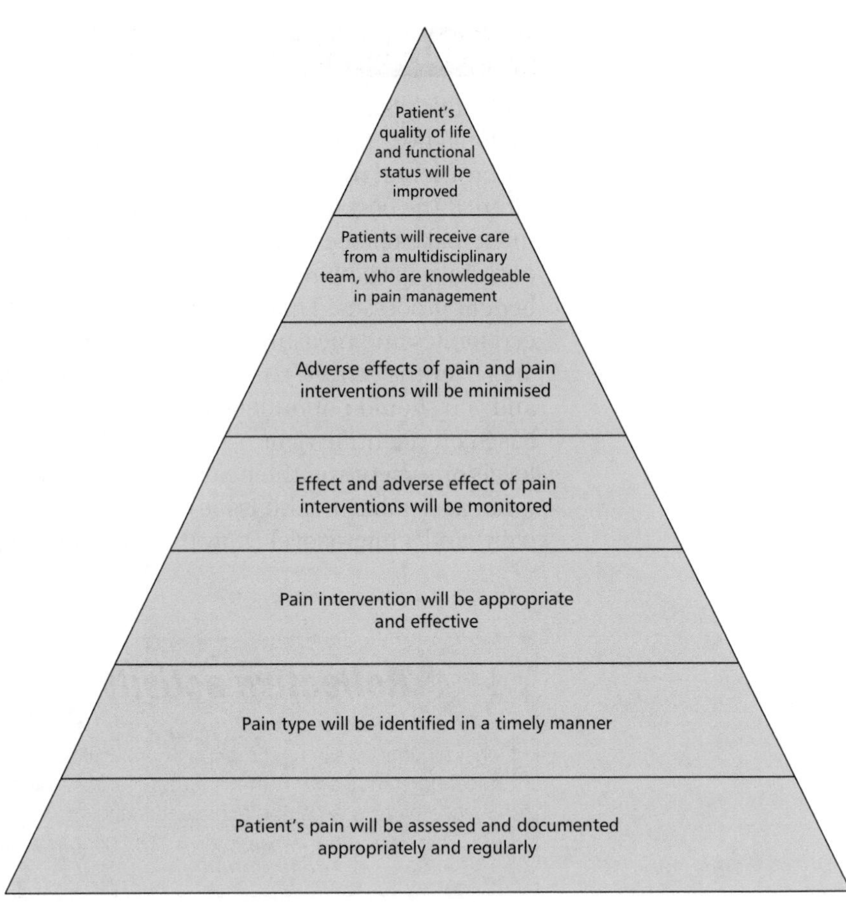

Figure 12.4 Patient benefits from improving pain management

Key points Top tips

- The economic and social cost of pain is high
- The prevalence of pain is high in both the hospital and the community
- Multidisciplinary pain teams support high-quality responsive patient care
- Clinical audit of pain supports high-quality pain services
- Evidence-based approaches should be used to manage pain
- Further research in pain management is needed

A multidisciplinary appraoch to pain management

Anne has just qualified as a nurse and begins work on a care of the older person unit. She is allocated a senior nurse as a preceptor who will provide her with orientation and be available for any queries she might have. One of the patients allocated to her has limited mobility and an extensive leg ulcer on her right ankle. The leg ulcer is causing quite a bit of pain and Anne thinks that this may be one of the reasons why her mobility is so poor. The lady also has arthritis. The patient is prescribed paracetamol and an NSAID pre re nata (PRN) for pain. Anne speaks to her preceptor who tells her that the lady has had the leg ulcer for six months and is being seen regularly by the tissue viability nurse who has prescribed specific dressings for the ulcer. In fact the tissue viability nurse is now considering referring the patient to a Consultant Physician specialising in vascular problems. Anne is asked to accompany the patient for an afternoon appointment at the pain clinic for review of her arthritis pain. Anne considered that when she qualified she had a lot of new knowledge and was ready to manage a group of patients. It is beginning to dawn on her that many patients have complex histories and require the expertise of a number of professionals to support good-quality care. She also realises that she is going to have to continually develop her own knowledge in order to develop expertise in the area of clinical specialty that she is working. She reviews the hospital in-service propectus.

- How will the patient benefit from the expertise of more than one health professional?
- What areas of continuing professional development should Anne engage in?
- How can Anne's preceptor help her develop the expertise she needs to work in the care of older people?

Rapid recap

1. Why is pain management important?
2. What are the main qualities of a pain service?
3. Name and give examples of three areas of knowledge that nurses should have in order to care for patients in pain.

References

Bardiau F.M., Taviaux N.F., Albert A., Boogaerts J.G. and Stadler M. (2003) An intervention study to enhance postoperative pain management. *Anesthesia and Analgesia*, **96**: 179–185.

Brunier G. (1995) What do nurses know and believe about patients with pain? Results of a hospital survey. *Journal of Pain and Symptom Management*, **10**(6): 436–445.

Carr E.C.J. (2002) Removing barriers to optimize the delivery of pain management. *Journal of Clinical Nursing*, **11**: 703–704.

Clarke E.B., French B., Bilodeau M.L., Capasso V.C., Edwards A. and Empoliti J. (1996) Pain Management Knowledge, Attitudes and Clinical Practice: The Impact of

Nurses' Characteristics and Education. *Journal of Pain and Symptom Management*, **11**(1): 18–31.

Clinical Standards Advisory Group (2000) *Services for Patients with Pain*. Department of Health, London.

Coulling S. (2005) Nurses' and doctors' knowledge of pain after surgery. *Nursing Standard,* **19**(34): 41–49.

Furstenberg C.T., Ahles T.A., Whedon M.B., Pierce K.L., Dolan M., Roberts L. *et al*. (1998) Knowledge and attitudes of health care providers toward cancer pain management. A comparison of physicians, nurses and pharmacists in the state of New Hampshire. *Journal of Pain and Symptom Management*, **15**: 335–349.

Hamilton J. and Edgar L. (1992) A survey examining nurses' knowledge of pain control. *Journal of Pain and Symptom Management*, **7**(1): 18–26.

Holley S., McMillan S.C., Hagan S.J., Palacios P. and Rosenberg D. (2005) Training pain resource nurses: Changes in their knowledge and attitudes. *Oncology Nursing Forum*, **32**(4): 843–8.

Horbury C., Henderson A. and Bromley B. (2005) Influences of patient behaviour on clinical nurses' pain assessment: Implications for continuing education. *The Journal of Continuing Education in Nursing*, **36**(1): 18–24.

Innis J., Bikaunieks N., Petryshen P., Zellermeyer V. and Ciccarelli L. (2004) Patient satisfaction and pain management: an educational approach. *Journal of Nursing Care Quality*, **19**(4): 322–327.

Jastrzab G., Fairbrother G., Kerr S. and McInerney M. (2003) Profiling the 'pain-aware' nurse: acute care nurses' attitudes and knowledge concerning adult pain management. *Australian Journal of Advanced Nursing*, **21**(2): 27–32.

Jones K.R., Fink R., Petter G., Hutt E., Vojir C.P., Scott J. *et al*. (2004) Improving nursing home staff knowledge and attitudes about pain. *The Gerontologist*, **44**(4): 469–478.

McCaffrey M. and Robinson E.S. (2002) Your patient is in pain here's how you respond. *Nursing*, **32**(10): 36–45.

Macintyre P.E. and Ready L.B. (2002) *Acute Pain Management, A Practical Guide*, 2nd edn. Saunders Elsevier Science, Philadelphia.

Mackintosh B.A. and Bowles S. (1997) Evaluation of a nurse-led acute pain service. Can clinical nurse specialists make a difference? *Journal of Advanced Nursing*, **25**: 30–37.

Mac Lellan (2000) An Evaluation of Pain Management Post Surgery. Unpublished PhD thesis. University of Dublin, Trinity College, Ireland.

Mac Lellan (2004) Postoperative pain: strategy for improving patient experiences. *Journal of Advanced Nursing*, **46**(2): 179–185.

Pain Society, The British Chapter of the International Association for the Study of Pain (2002) *Recommendations for Nursing Practice in Pain Management.* The Pain Society, London.

Tasso K. and Behar-Horenstein L.S. (2004) Patients' perceptions of pain management and use of coping strategies. *Hospital Topics*, **82**(4): 10–19.

Appendix: Rapid recap answers

Chapter One

1 What are main dimensions of pain?

1 The main pain dimensions are: sensory, emotional and intensity dimensions.

2 What is the main message for health care professionals coming from the more common definitions of pain?

2 The main message from the more common definitions of pain is that pain is always subjective.

3 Which parts of the nervous system are concerned with the transmission of pain?

3 Both the central and peripheral nervous system are concerned with the transmission of pain.

4 List five desirable characteristics of a pain care service.

4 A pain service should comprise a multidisciplinary team, it should have a policy of continuous quality improvement and education and empowerment of other health care staff, it should provide diagnosis, treatments and interventions as appropriate.

Chapter Two

1 How do you define prevalence of pain?

1 Prevalence of pain is defined as the proportion of individuals in a population who have pain at a specific instant.

2 How would you describe the economic burden of pain?

2 The economic burden of pain can be described in terms of direct costs (such as pain management medications), indirect costs (lost earnings due to a patient being unable to work) and intangible costs (reduced quality of life).

3 What are the sources of research evidence?

3 Sources of research evidence for pain management include evidence-based journals, the Cochrane database and databases such as Medline and CINAHL.

Chapter Three

1 Name two new technologies that have emerged in relation to analgesic administration in the last 30 years.

1 Two new technologies that have emerged in relation to the administration of analgesia in the last 30 years are: patient-controlled analgesia and patient-controlled transdermal analgesia.

2 What are the main elements of a pain service?

2 The main qualities of a pain service include the introduction of policies, protocols and guidelines, education of staff and patients, audit and evaluation, regular pain assessment, introducing and monitoring new analagesic techniques.

3 What new roles in pain management are emerging for nurses?

3 New roles for nurses in pain management include: pain nurse consultants, pain nurse specialists, pain resource nurses.

Chapter Four

1 What are the main ascending pain pathways?

1 The main ascending pain pathways are the neospinothalamic tract (fast ascending fibres) and paleospinothalamic tract (slow ascending fibres).

2 **How do the various chemicals at the site of pain work?**

2 Chemicals at the site of pain are thought to excite nociceptors and thus increase the pain sensation.

3 **What is the Gate Control Theory of Pain?**

3 The Gate Control Theory of Pain proposes that a neural mechanism in the dorsal horns of the spinal cord acts like a gate and can increase or decrease the flow of nerve impulses from the peripheral fibres to the central nervous system.

Chapter Five

1 **Name three factors which form the context of patients' pain.**

1 Three factors that form the context of patients' pain are the meaning of the pain, culture and anxiety.

2 **Define what is meant by culture.**

2 Culture can be defined as the beliefs, customs and behaviours of a group of individuals due to ethnicity, religion, origin or current residence.

3 **Name two organisations who view pain as a public health issue.**

3 The World Health Organization and International Association for the Study of Pain are two organisations which view pain as a public health issue.

Chapter Six

1 **What qualities should a pain assessment tool have?**

1 The qualities that a pain assessment tool should have are: validity, reliability and ease of use.

2 **What are the three main pain intensity tools used?**

2 The three main pain intensity tools used are the Visual Analogue Scale, Verbal Rating Scale and Numeric Rating Scale.

3 **What can a pain audit contribute when deciding which pain assessment tool to use?**

3 When deciding which pain assessment tools to use a pain audit will provide patterns and baseline of pain for clinical area.

Chapter Seven

1 **Name two side-effects of opioids.**

1 Two side-effects of opioids are constipation and respiratory depression.

2 **What are the principles of the WHO analgesic ladder?**

2 The principles of the WHO analgesic ladder are that if a pain occurs, there should be prompt oral administration of drugs in the following order: non-opioids (aspirin or paracetamol); then, as necessary, mild opioids (codeine); or the strong opioids such as morphine, until the patient is free of pain. To maintain freedom from pain, drugs should be given 'by the clock', that is every 3–6 hours, rather than 'on demand'.

3 **What is the medication of choice for chronic neuropathic pain?**

3 Anticonvulsants are the class of medication of choice for chronic neuropathic pain.

4 **What are the major effects of NSAIDs?**

4 NSAIDs have anti-inflammatory, analgesic and antipyretic effects and inhibit thrombocyte aggregation.

5 **What are the limiting factors for use of NSAIDs?**

5 A major limiting factor is the risk of gastrointestinal toxicity. Additionally there are possible cardiovascular risks and NSAIDs should be used with caution with asthma, impaired renal function and those on anti-platelet regimes including aspirin.

Chapter Eight

1 **Outline the main differences between complementary medicine and alternative medicine.**

1 Complementary medicine therapies tend to be more widely accepted and are therefore used in an integrated way with conventional medicine. On the other hand, alternative medicine tends to be used as a collective term for treatments that are used in place of conventional medicine.

2 **List four underpinning concepts held by CAM practitioners.**

2 Illness is a disharmony or deviation from health, affecting the person as part of the larger

environment/universal system; health is a balance of opposing forces, and treatment is about strengthening healing forces. Holistic in nature, strengthening the wellbeing of the whole person. Less high-technology interventions or diagnostics are used. The patient should be active in their cure.

3 What CAM treatments currently have the strongest empirical evidence base for their use in pain care?

3 Acupuncture, some herbal medicines and manual therapies (osteopathy, chiropractic).

4 What is a placebo effect?

4 The placebo effect occurs when a sham treatment without any known biological activity induces biological and/or psychological effects in people, in line with a therapeutic treatment. There are thought to be two main reasons why this can occur either as a conditioned response or due to patient expectations.

5 What would a health care practitioner need to do if they wanted to integrate and deliver complementary therapies within their care setting?

5 If administering complementary or alternative treatments, a health care practitioner must have undertaken an approved course and be deemed competent to offer this treatment. CAM should be discussed with the multidisciplinary team, and the patient must always have granted consent for CAM use. The health care practitioner should ensure that their practice is in line with national guidance from their professional body and their NHS Trusts' local guidance. They may have to have their competency assessed formally using a skills framework.

6 Define a therapeutic practitioner–patient relationship.

6 A therapeutic practitioner–patient relationship requires the practitioner to respect and have genuine interest in the patient and also to show emotional warmth, tolerance and a non-judgemental acceptance. It requires the practitioner to use 'self' in their interactions, whilst maintaining awareness of their limitations and adherence to ethical codes. The patient also plays a part in a therapeutic relationship by trusting and co-operating with the intervention and being motivated to understand the treatment/care.

Chapter Nine

1 Define acute pain.

1 Traditionally, acute pain is described as pain that subsides as healing takes place, i.e. it has a predictable end and it is of brief duration, usually less than six months.

2 Name and give examples of three modalities for reducing acute pain.

2 Table 1 below details three modalities for reducing acute pain.

3 What special considerations are there with the use of morphine in the accident and emergency department?

3 Special considerations with the use of morphine in the emergency department include that it:

a. is usually administered intravenously in the emergency department
b. causes sedation
c. should not be given to shocked patients
d. should not be used in pancreatitis
e. if used in coronary thrombosis it may further slow pulse and lower blood pressure.

4 When assessing chest pain what does the acronym OLDCART stand for?

4 When assessing chest pain the acronym OLDCART stands for:

Onset
Location
Duration
Characteristics
Accompanying symptoms
Radiation
Treatment

Table 1 Modalities for reducing pain

	Examples
Pharmacological preparations	Opioids NSAIDs Paracetamol
Physical modalities	Physiotherapy Manipulation TENs
Complementary modalities	Acupuncture Relaxation

5 What are the main qualities of an acute pain service?

5 Acute pain services consist of a multidisciplinary team including specialist nurses, anaesthetists and pharmacists who support seamless liaison with other health care teams. Their role is to introduce policies, protocols, guidelines and regular pain assessment. It is part of their remit to introduce, monitor and evaluate new pain-relieving techniques as well as ongoing audit of service provided. Additionally, acute pain services provide education of staff and patients.

Chapter Ten

1 Define chronic pain.

1 Chronic pain tends to be considered as pain without apparent biological value that has persisted beyond the normal tissue healing time (usually taken to be three months).

2 What are the main qualities of a chronic-pain service?

2 The main qualities of a chronic-pain service include the introduction of policies, protocols and guidelines, education of staff and patients, audit and evaluation, regular pain assessment, introducing and monitoring new analgesic techniques.

3 Name and give examples of three modalities for reducing chronic pain.

3 Table 2 below details three modalities for reducing chronic pain.

Table 2 Modalities for reducing chronic pain

	Examples
Pharmacological preparations	Opioids NSAIDs Anticonvulsants Tricyclic antidepressants NMDA antagonists Topical preparations
Physical modalities	Ultrasound TENs Diathermy
Comprehensive pain rehabilitation programme	Interdisciplinary pain centres Functional restoration programmes

4 Identify four principles of good practice to guide the prescribing of opioids for chronic non-cancer pain.

4 Four principles of good practice to guide the prescribing of opioids for chronic non-cancer pain include: *evaluation of patient* to include pain history, assessment of impact of pain on the patient, a directed physical examination, a review of previous diagnostic studies, a review of previous interventions, a drug history and an assessment of coexisting conditions. *Treatment plan* which is tailored to both the individual and the presenting problem. Consideration should be given to different treatment modalities. *Periodic review of treatment efficacy* to occur periodically to assess the functional status of the patient, continued analgesia, opioid side-effects, quality of life and indication of medication misuse. Periodic re-examination is warranted to assess the nature of the pain complaint and to ensure that opioid therapy is still indicated. *Documentation* to support the evaluation, the reason for opioid prescribing, the overall pain management treatment plan, any consultation received and periodic review of the status of the patient.

5 How strong is the evidence for the use of TENS with low back pain?

5 In relation to low back pain there is limited and inconsistent evidence to support the use of TENS as an isolated intervention in the management of chronic lower back pain.

Chapter Eleven

1 Outline the philosophy of a palliative care approach.

1 A palliative care approach focuses on an individualised approach to treating the person, not the disease. It includes care of the family as well as the person. It aims to improve the individual's quality of life by preventing and relieving suffering by means of early identification and impeccable assessment and treatment of pain and other symptoms associated with life-threatening illness. In addition, palliative care offers the following:

It provides relief from pain and other distressing symptoms.

It affirms life and regards dying as a normal process.

It intends neither to hasten nor postpone death.

It integrates the psychological, social and spiritual aspects of patient care.

It offers a support system to help patients live as actively as possible until death.

It offers a support system to help the family cope during the patient's illness and in their own bereavement.

It uses a team approach to address the needs of patients and their families, including bereavement counselling, if indicated.

It will enhance quality of life, and may also positively influence the course of illness.

It is applicable early in the course of illness, in conjunction with other therapies that are intended to prolong life, such as chemotherapy or radiation therapy, and includes those investigations needed to better understand and manage distressing clinical complications (WHO, 2002).

2 What is the purpose of pain assessment within a palliative care context?

2 The purpose of assessment within a palliative care context is to identify *individual* patients' needs or problems in order to set appropriate, achievable and effective goals.

Utilising the most appropriate diagnostic and therapeutic considerations, pain assessment will contribute towards defining the cause and directing treatment.

3 Following the analgesic ladder guidelines, how should analgesics be administered?

3 Following the analgesic ladder guidelines, the WHO (1996) advocates that analgesics should be administered in the following way:

'By the ladder' (in standard doses at regular intervals in stepwise fashion.) If a pain occurs, there should be a prompt oral administration of drugs in the following order: non-opioids (aspirin or paracetamol); then, as necessary, mild opioids (codeine); or the strong opioids such as morphine, until the patient is free of pain.

'By the mouth' (the oral route is the preferred route for administration when possible) 'By the clock' (to maintain freedom from pain, drugs should be given regularly, rather than waiting for the individual to request pain relief).

'For the individual' (the analgesic ladder is a framework of principles rather than a rigid protocol).

'Attention to detail' (attention to each individual's unique experience of pain is required when directing treatment).

Chapter Twelve

1 Why is pain management important?

1 Pain management is important because of the adverse effects and social and economic burden of pain.

2 What are the main qualities of a pain service?

2 The main qualities of a pain service include the introduction of policies, protocols and guidelines, education of staff and patients, audit and evaluation, regular pain assessment, introducing and monitoring new analgesic techniques.

3 Name and give examples of three areas of knowledge that nurses should have in order to care for patients in pain.

3 Table 3 details three areas of knowledge that nurses should have in order to care for patients in pain.

Table 3 Areas of knowledge

Role facet	Knowledge
Assessment of pain – Verbal assessment – Non-verbal assessment	Pain assessment tools Pain physiology Pain theories
Administration and monitoring of effect of analgesia – Opioids – NSAIDs – Anti-convulsants – Paracetamol – Other	Analgesic medications (action, time of effect, side-effects)
Evidence-based practice	Clinical audit Sources of evidence

Index

Page reference in italics indicate figures or tables